THIS
BOOK

Belongs to

THE
ILLUSTRATED
FAMILY
BIBLE

THE BUILDING OF KING SOLOMON'S TEMPLE

THE
ILLUSTRATED
FAMILY
BIBLE

Consultant Editor

DR CLAUDE-BERNARD COSTECALDE

✥

Illustrated by

PETER DENNIS

DORLING KINDERSLEY
London • New York • Stuttgart

BOOK HOUSE   11·4·00 $36·00

A DORLING KINDERSLEY BOOK

Project Editor Linda Esposito
Art Editors Carole Oliver, Mark Regardsoe
Editor Joanna Buck
Design Assistant Robin Hunter
Editorial Assistant Rebecca Smith
Senior Art Editor Jacquie Gulliver
Managing Editor Anna Kruger
Managing Art Editor Peter Bailey
Production Josie Alabaster
DTP Designer Nicola Studdart
Picture Research Rachel Leach, Sharon Southren

HISTORICAL CONSULTANTS

Dr Rupert Chapman,
Palestinian Exploration Fund, London

Dr Jonathan Tubb,
Western Asiatic Department, British Museum, London

RELIGIOUS CONSULTANTS

OLD TESTAMENT
Rev Robin Duckworth,
Director of Studies, Ushaw College, Durham

Mary J Evans,
London Bible College

Jenny Nemko,
Jewish writer and
broadcaster for the BBC

NEW TESTAMENT
Rev Robin Duckworth,
Director of Studies,
Ushaw College, Durham

Rev Stephen Motyer,
London Bible College

SPECIAL PHOTOGRAPHY
Barnabas and Annabel Kindersley

First published in Great Britain in 1997 by
Dorling Kindersley Ltd, 9 Henrietta Street, London WC2E 8PS.

Reprinted 1997
Copyright © 1997 Dorling Kindersley Limited, London.
A CIP catalogue record for this book is available from the
British Library ISBN 0 7513 5490 2

Visit us on the World Wide Web at: http://www.dk.com

Colour reproduction by Bright Arts, Hong Kong
Printed and bound by Partenaires, France

Scripture taken from THE HOLY BIBLE,
NEW INTERNATIONAL VERSION. Copyright © 1973, 1978, 1984
by International Bible Society. Used by permission of
Hodder & Stoughton Ltd. All rights reserved.

CONTENTS

NEW TESTAMENT

HOW TO USE THIS BOOK

This book tells Bible stories through selected passages of original texts and full-colour narrative illustrations. There are also a number of special features aimed at enhancing the family's enjoyment of these stories and giving a deeper understanding of the context in which they were written.

Original texts from the Bible's New International Version, which is transdenominational

Chapter number

Verse number

Book of the Bible

Important words and phrases fundamental to understanding the story are italicized in the text and explained in side panels. Chapter and verse numbers cross-refer to the relevant word or phrase in the Bible text

Selected Bible texts are linked by short narrative paragraphs

JESUS' LAST DAYS

MATTHEW 25

THE MASTER'S FORTUNE

25 "THE KINGDOM OF HEAVEN will be like...¹⁴"a man going on a journey, who called his servants and entrusted his property to them. ¹⁵To one *he gave five talents of money*, to another two talents, and to another one talent, each according to his ability. Then he went on his journey. ¹⁶The man who had received the five talents went at once and put his money to work and gained five more. ¹⁷So also, the one with the two talents gained two more. ¹⁸But the man who had received the one talent went off, dug a hole in the ground and hid his master's money."

When the master returned, he wanted to know what his servants had done with the talents he had left them. He was equally pleased with the two men who had doubled his investment. He said the same to both.

²¹"'Well done... You have been faithful with a few things; I will put you in charge of many things. Come and share your master's happiness!'

The servant digs a large hole to bury his talent

✦
CHAPTER 25 VERSE 15
"He gave five talents of money"
The word "talent" derives from this story. It means aptitude. The

THE MASTER'S FORTUNE / THE SHEEP AND THE GOATS

MATTHEW 25

THE SHEEP AND THE GOATS

25 "WHEN³¹ THE SON OF MAN comes in his glory, and all the angels with him, he will sit on his throne in heavenly glory. ³²All the nations will be gathered before him, and he will separate the people one from another as a shepherd separates the sheep from the goats. ³³He will put *the sheep on his right and the goats on his left*.

³⁴"Then the King will say to those on his right, 'Come, you who are blessed by my Father; take your inheritance, the kingdom prepared for you since the creation of the world. ³⁵For I was hungry and you gave me something to eat, I was thirsty and you gave me something to drink, I was a stranger and you invited me in, ³⁶I needed clothes and you clothed me, I was sick and you looked after me, I was in prison and you came to visit me...' ⁴⁰"Whatever you did for one of *the least of these brothers of mine*, you did for me.'

⁴¹"Then he will say to those on his left, 'Depart from me, you who are cursed, into the eternal fire prepared for the devil and his angels... ⁴⁵Whatever you did not do for one of the least of these, you did not do for me.' ⁴⁶"Then they will go away to eternal punishment, but the righteous to eternal life."

✦
CHAPTER 25 VERSE 33
"The sheep on his right and the goats on his left"
In the Bible, "sheep" represent God's people. Middle-Eastern shepherds tended mixed flocks of sheep and goats. At first sight, it was not easy to distinguish one from the other. As in many cultures, right and left symbolize good and bad.

Goat

The shepherd separates the sheep from the goats: sheep on the right and goats on the left

Sheep

✦
CHAPTER 25 VERSE 40
"The least of these brothers of mine"
Jesus calls on those who follow him to do all they can to help the poor, the humble, and the deprived. Whatever people do to alleviate the suffering of those less fortunate, they do for God.

UNDERSTANDING THE STORY

One day, God will judge the whole world, Jews and non-Jews alike. Those who have served the needs of others for Jesus' sake will be rewarded in abundance. These fortunate people will enjoy a never-ending life in God's presence. But those who fail God's judgement will be eternally damned.

SHEPHERDESS
The practice of keeping mixed flocks continues in Israel. This girl is tending sheep and goats in the Judean hills.

²⁴"Then the man who had received the one talent came. 'Master,' he ... are a hard man... ²⁵So I was afraid and went out ... the ground. See, here is what belongs to you.' ... ,'*You wicked, lazy servant!* So you knew that I ... where I have not sown and gather where I have ... attered seed? ²⁷Well then, you should have put my ... on deposit with the bankers, so that when I ... ed I would have received it back with interest. ... Take the talent from him and give it to the one ... has the ten talents. ²⁹For everyone who has will ... be given more, and he will have an abundance. ... Whoever does not have, even what he has will be taken from him... ³⁰Throw that worthless servant outside, into the darkness...'"

The master praises the two who put their talents to work

The one who buried his talent finds that his master is furious

UNDERSTANDING THE STORY
... success is not the amount that people achieve, it is ... abilities to the full. The servants knew that one day ... unt to their master. The two who use their abilities ... heir master are rewarded; the other loses everything.

Artwork and annotations tell the story in a simple way for younger readers

Understanding the story is made easy with a short passage at the end of each story explaining the meaning and significance of the Bible text

Photographs of places and artefacts, together with maps, set the stories in their historical, cultural, and geographical context

The side panels include additional factual information

THE BOOKS OF THE BIBLE

The Bible contains the sacred texts of the Jews and Christians. Its name derives from "biblia", the Greek for "books", because the Bible is made up of a number of books. The theme holding all these books together is the story of the relationship, or covenants, that God establishes with his people. Both the Jews and Christians believe the Bible to be a book of covenants. Traditionally, the Christian Bible is divided into two sections called "testaments", an old translation of the Hebrew word for "covenant". The first section, the Old Testament, tells the story of God's chosen people, the Israelites, their dealings with God, and their expectation of the promised saviour, the Messiah. The second section, the New Testament, deals with the life of that Messiah – who Christians believe to be Jesus – his teachings, and the beginnings of Christianity.

CODEX SINAITICUS
This is part of a 4th-century codex, the oldest complete version of the New Testament. It was found near Mt Sinai.

DEAD SEA SCROLL
Some pottery jars found in caves near the Dead Sea contained an almost complete version of the Old Testament dating from *c.* 50 BC.

The Old Testament
The name "Old Testament" was given to the first part of the Bible by the early Christians. It is made up of 39 books, which were written over a span of nearly ten centuries. The first five books of the Bible may have been written as early as 1400 BC; the latest, Ezra and Nehemiah, date from *c.* 450 BC. The Old Testament texts were originally written in Hebrew. But some passages from the Books of Daniel, Ezra, and Jeremiah were written in Aramaic, a Persian dialect of Assyrian.

The Hebrew Bible
The Old Testament was originally grouped into three sections: the Torah or Law (the first five books), the Prophets (the following eight), and the Writings (the next eleven). Altogether, they make up 24 books instead of 39, because some books were grouped into single books (see pages 16–17).

Around AD 90, a council of Jewish rabbis from Palestine officially recognized, or "canonized", this grouping, and so it came to be known as the Palestinian Canon. The Palestinian Canon is also known as the Scriptures, or the Hebrew Bible. This is the sacred book of the Jews.

The Christian Bible
The Old Testament in most Christian Bibles follows a different order from that of the Hebrew Bible. The books are grouped according to the Septuagint, or Greek Canon. This was compiled by a group of Greek-speaking Jewish scholars during the 2nd century BC. It has four sections: the Pentateuch, the Historical Books, Poetry and Wisdom, and Prophets.

The New Testament
The second section of the Bible, the New Testament, is made up of 27 books. All the books were written by the early followers of Jesus Christ and deal with his life and teachings. They were written in Greek, the common language of the time, over a period of about fifty years. They begin with the Book of James (*c.* AD 45) and end with 3 John (*c.* AD 97).

THE APOCRYPHA
The Apocrypha, from the Greek word meaning "keep secret", is a collection of books written in Greek between the Old and New Testament times. These books were not included in the Hebrew Bible, which contains only those written originally in Hebrew or Aramaic. The Apocrypha is rarely included in modern Christian Bibles, although the Roman Catholic Church retains certain books, which are known as the Deuterocanonicals, the Greek for "second canon".

1 Esdras · 2 Esdras · Tobit · Judith · Additions to Esther · Wisdom of Solomon · Ecclesiasticus · Baruch · Letter of Jeremiah · The Song of the Three Children · Susanna · Bel and the Dragon · Prayer of Manasseh · 1 Maccabees · 2 Maccabees

PENTATEUCH

Genesis · Exodus · Leviticus · Numbers · Deuteronomy

HISTORICAL BOOKS

Joshua · Judges · Ruth · 1 Samuel · 2 Samuel · 1 Kings · 2 Kings · 1 Chronicles · 2 Chronicles · Ezra · Nehemiah · Esther

POETRY AND WISDOM

Job · Psalms · Proverbs · Ecclesiastes · Song of Songs

PROPHETS

Isaiah · Jeremiah · Lamentations · Ezekiel · Daniel · Hosea · Joel · Amos · Obadiah · Jonah · Micah · Nahum · Habakkuk · Zephaniah · Haggai · Zechariah · Malachi

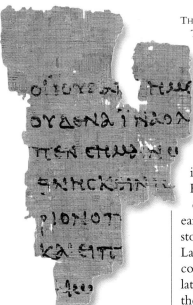

Authors of the Bible

The books of the Bible were written over a period covering nearly sixteen centuries. Not all of the authors can be identified. Many of the books do not mention an author – among these are the first fourteen books. Some of the books record events that occurred a long time before they were written – an example of this is the Book of Ruth.

Other books may have had several authors, as well as editors who revised the texts. There are scholars who believe the Book of Isaiah to be one of these.

Israelite tradition and the early Church attributed a number of books to famous Bible characters. For example, the first five books of the Bible are attributed to Moses, even though it is obvious that some of the passages could not have been written by him, such as the account of his death (Deuteronomy 34: 5–8).

THE GOSPEL OF JOHN
The New Testament was originally written in Greek. This fragment (c. AD 125) from John 18 is the oldest yet discovered.

History of the texts

There are no original manuscripts of Bible texts in existence today. However, many ancient copies have survived. Some early texts were written on stone (like the tablets of the Law). Much later, texts were copied on leather, and, even later, on papyri scrolls. From the 2nd century AD, copies were put together into papyri codices (sewn together like books). The most ancient complete Hebrew text of the Old Testament is the Leningrad codex in the St Petersburg library, which dates from AD 1008. From the beginning of the 2nd century until the end of the Middle Ages, the Bible was also copied on parchment.

THE BOOK OF KELLS (C. 800)
This illuminated manuscript of the four Gospels was produced by monks at an Irish monastery.

THE ROLE OF ARCHEOLOGY

Over the course of centuries, the Bible has been the subject of exhaustive studies. Since the nineteenth century, archeologists have applied more scientific methods to their discoveries. This has enabled accurate dating. In the last fifty years, evidence has been unearthed that verifies much of the cultural, geographical, and political information given in the biblical texts.

BABYLONIAN CLAY TABLET (605 BC)
Fragment of a chronicle recording Judah's defeat by Nebuchadnezzar in 597 BC.

THE GUTENBERG BIBLE (1455)
The first book ever printed was a Latin version of the Bible. It was the work of the German inventor of moveable type, Johannes Gutenberg.

Chapters and verses

Originally, the Bible was not divided into chapters and verses. Between the 6th–7th centuries AD, verse divisions were introduced into the Hebrew Bible. In the early 13th century, Stephen Langton, later Archbishop of Canterbury, divided the Bible into chapters. In 1555, Robert Estienne, a French Protestant, published a Bible divided into chapters, with verse numbers in the margin. Ten years later, Théodore de Bèze inserted verse numbers into the text.

The Family Bible

The books of the Bible were not arranged chronologically. The authors considered themselves to be agents of God, and their main purpose was to convey his message.

The Family Bible presents selected texts chronologically whenever possible in order to place the Bible within a historical framework. Special features, such as this, and the explanatory notes that accompany the Bible passages are provided to help bring understanding to the texts.

GOSPELS   ACTS   EPISTLES

THE BOOKS OF THE BIBLE
For many centuries, all Christian Bibles followed the Greek Canon. However, today most Protestant Bibles do not include the Apocrypha.

THE COVENANTS OF THE BIBLE

The Bible is a book of covenants, or agreements, made between God and his people. Each one contains promises and demands that both parties agree to keep. All of the Bible covenants are sealed with a sign that serves to remind the people of their part in the agreement. They also usually contain a symbolic element. The Old Testament contains God's covenants with individuals and with the Israelites, and the New Testament contains the last covenant, established between God and all those who have faith in Jesus.

God intended his first covenant with humanity to be permanent. However, the presence of evil in the world causes humankind to break their part of the agreement, leading to their separation from God. In the Old Testament, the original covenant is renewed several times as people continue to break faith with God. Each time, God shows mercy and gives a new start to humankind.

THE TREE OF KNOWLEDGE
This 15th-century painting depicts the forbidden fruit.

1. Adam and Eve (Genesis 2–3)

The first Bible covenant is between God and Adam and Eve. God gives them the garden of Eden, a perfect place on earth. He places the Tree of Life in the garden, which acts as a reminder of their covenant and symbolizes their immortality. In return, Adam and Eve must look after God's creation and obey God's instruction not to eat from the Tree of Knowledge of Good and Evil. However, evil enters the world in the form of a serpent and tempts Eve to eat the forbidden fruit. Adam and Eve are banished from Eden. They become mortals and are cut off from God.

2. Noah and the ark (Genesis 9)

God renews his covenant with humankind through Noah. He sends a flood to destroy the world, which is corrupt and full of violence, but rescues Noah and his family, who are righteous. After the flood, they are instructed to multiply on earth. They are forbidden to kill each other and may not eat anything that "has its lifeblood in it" (Genesis 9: 4). God promises never to destroy the world again by a flood. As a sign of his covenant, God sets a rainbow in the sky.

NOAH AND THE ARK
15th-century stained-glass window

CANAAN, THE PROMISED LAND
This fertile valley in Israel was part of the land that God promised to Abraham.

3. Abraham and the Promised Land (Genesis 15–18)

Noah's descendants increase in numbers but do not keep their promise. So God establishes a new covenant with Abraham, who is righteous. God promises him that he will be the father of a great nation, and that his descendants will inherit the land of Canaan. In return, God requires Abraham and his people to remain faithful to him (Genesis 18: 19). As a sign of their covenant, the males in Abraham's household are required to be circumcised. This covenant establishes Abraham's descendants, the Israelites, as God's chosen people.

4. Moses and the Law (Exodus 19–20)

The Israelites lose faith in God when they suffer slavery in Egypt. God brings them out of Egypt, but stipulates new terms for the covenant. Through the prophet Moses, he gives the Israelites the Ten Commandments and detailed moral and ritual laws. God promises to protect his people from their enemies if they remain faithful to these laws.

The Israelites must seal their promise by consecrating their firstborn sons to God (Exodus 34: 19). This recalls the time when God saved their firstborn males during the plagues in Egypt. Moses is also instructed to build a portable shrine, called the Tabernacle. This holy place symbolizes God's presence.

THE ARK OF THE COVENANT
Moses' Laws were kept in a sacred chest, called the Ark, inside the Tabernacle (Exodus 37: 1–9). This stone carving of the Ark comes from Capernaum, Israel.

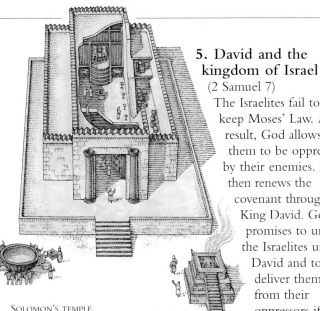

SOLOMON'S TEMPLE
The Temple's layout was similar to that of the Tabernacle. It contained a courtyard and an outer and inner sanctuary.

5. David and the kingdom of Israel
(2 Samuel 7)

The Israelites fail to keep Moses' Law. As a result, God allows them to be oppressed by their enemies. He then renews the covenant through King David. God promises to unite the Israelites under David and to deliver them from their oppressors if they remain faithful to the covenant laws. He also promises David that his descendants will inherit an everlasting dynasty. God seals his promise to David by giving him instructions to build a temple, which is to replace the Tabernacle. It will be built by David's son Solomon. Solomon's Temple is a symbol of God's permanent presence among his people and is a reminder of the renewed covenant.

The Prophets: the promise of a new covenant

When the Israelites continue to disobey the covenant laws, God sends prophets to them who bring messages of warning and hope. They foretell the Israelites' exile from the Promised Land, but also speak of a new covenant that God will establish with his people.

The promise of this new covenant is brought to the Israelites by the prophet Jeremiah. He explains that there will be a spiritual transformation in peoples' hearts, and that God will forgive the people for their sins (Jeremiah 31: 31).

The prophets Jeremiah, Isaiah, Malachi, and Micah also prophesy the arrival of a saviour. This saviour, or Messiah, will establish the new covenant between God and his people.

THE PROPHET ISAIAH
The prophet Isaiah predicted that the future Messiah would be born from the house of David (Isaiah 11). This detail of Isaiah is from a painting by Pietro Rugino (c. 1445–1523).

6. Jesus Christ and the new covenant
(The New Testament)

Jesus is sent by God to be the mediator in the final covenant with humankind. He is the saviour announced by the prophets in the Old Testament scriptures. He calls on people to repent of their sins and change their ways so that they may return to God and attain eternal life.

Christ's death and resurrection are signs of the new covenant. Before his death, Jesus offers his disciples a cup of wine and says "This is my blood of the new covenant, which is poured out for many for the forgiveness of sins" (Matthew 26: 28).

The apostles are witnesses to Jesus' death and resurrection and ask all those who believe in Christ to be baptized. Baptism is a symbol of cleansing and rebirth. It is also a sign of the new covenant, which is offered to the whole of humankind.

COMMUNION CHALICE
This Roman silver chalice (6th century AD) is believed to have been used in Communion services. The top border of the cup is inscribed in Greek and reads "Holy is God, Holy the Mighty One, Holy the Immortal One, Have mercy upon us".

THE CROSS
This Roman mosaic (4th–7th century) from Carthage has the sign of the cross. The cross serves as a reminder of Jesus' death and has come to symbolize faith in Christ.

THE LAST SUPPER
Simon Uschakow's 17th-century painting depicts Jesus' last meal with his disciples. Christians partake in the sharing of bread and wine in remembrance of Christ. This practice is known as Communion or the Eucharist.

LANDS OF THE BIBLE

LANDS OF

	1	2	3	4

ITALY
- Rome
- Puteoli

A

SICILY
- Rhegium
- Syracuse

MALTA

B

BULGARIA

BLACK SEA

- Philippi
- Amphipolis
- Thessalonica
- Berea

GREECE

- Troas
- Adramyttium
- Pergamum
- Thyatira
- Smyrna
- Sardis
- Philadelphia
- Antioch in Pisidia
- Corinth
- Athens
- Ephesus
- Laodicea
- Iconium
- Lystra
- Perga
- De

PATMOS

CRETE

CYPRUS

- Paphos

MEDITERRANEAN SEA

- Pithom
- Succoth

EGYPT

THE HOLY LAND

	i	ii	iii

- Zarephath
- Mt Hermon ▲

a

- Tyre
- Caesarea Philippi

MEDITERRANEAN SEA

- Hazor

- Capernaum
- Cana
- *SEA OF GALILEE*

b

- Mt Carmel ▲
- Mt Tabor ▲
- Nazareth
- Shunem
- Endor
- Megiddo
- Jezreel
- Caesarea
- Beth-Shean
- Mt Gilboa ▲

River Jordan

River Jabbok

c

- Samaria
- Shechem
- Succoth
- Joppa
- Shiloh
- Adam
- Ramah (Arimathea)
- Rabbah
- Lydda

- Bethel
- Ai
- Gilgal
- Michmash
- Jericho
- Gibeon
- Gibeah
- Ekron
- Timnah
- Emmaus
- Ashdod
- Beth Shemesh
- Bethphage
- Bethany
- Mt Nebo ▲
- Gath
- Jerusalem
- Ashkelon
- Bethlehem

d

DEAD SEA

- Lachish
- Mamre
- Hebron

- Carmel
- Masada

e

- Beersheba

River Nile

KEY

- ● Town or city
- ▲ Mountain
- ☐ The Fertile Crescent

SCALE

0	1 inch	23 miles
0	25mm	37km

SCALE

0	1 inch	150 miles
0	25mm	240km

	1	2	3	4

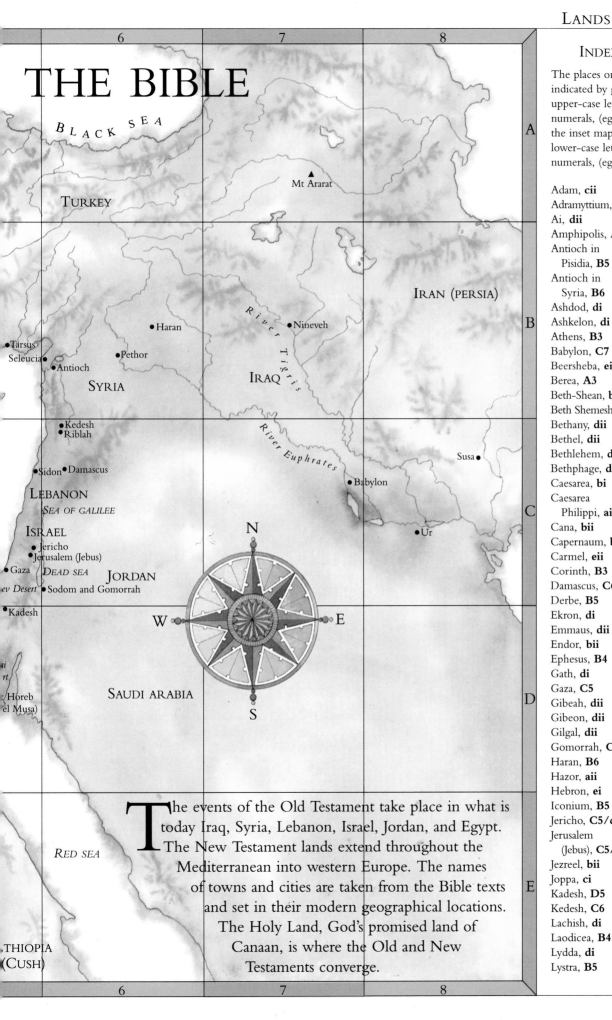

THE BIBLE

BLACK SEA

TURKEY

Mt Ararat

Haran

Tarsus

Seleucia

Antioch

Pethor

SYRIA

IRAN (PERSIA)

River Tigris

Nineveh

IRAQ

Kedesh

Riblah

River Euphrates

Sidon

Damascus

Susa

LEBANON

SEA OF GALILEE

Babylon

ISRAEL

Jericho

Jerusalem (Jebus)

Gaza

DEAD SEA

JORDAN

Ur

ev Desert

Sodom and Gomorrah

Kadesh

N

W   E

S

SAUDI ARABIA

/Horeb
el Musa)

RED SEA

THIOPIA
(CUSH)

The events of the Old Testament take place in what is today Iraq, Syria, Lebanon, Israel, Jordan, and Egypt. The New Testament lands extend throughout the Mediterranean into western Europe. The names of towns and cities are taken from the Bible texts and set in their modern geographical locations. The Holy Land, God's promised land of Canaan, is where the Old and New Testaments converge.

INDEX OF PLACES

The places on the large map are indicated by grid references with upper-case letters and Arabic numerals, (eg B2). Places on the inset map are shown with lower-case letters and Roman numerals, (eg bii).

THE OLD TESTAMENT

"LOVE THE LORD YOUR GOD
with all your heart and with all your
soul and with all your strength.
These commandments that I give you
today are to be upon your hearts.
Impress them on your children."

DEUTERONOMY 6: 5–7

THE OLD TESTAMENT

TORAH SCROLL
15th-century
parchment scroll
from Germany

The Old Testament is a collection of writings about the Israelite people (the Hebrews) and their special relationship with God. It describes the main events in their history, from their origins to life in exile and their return to the Promised Land, Canaan. Most of the Old Testament events take place in an area of land east of the Mediterranean, known as the "Fertile Crescent". This area extended from southern Mesopotamia, around to Canaan, and down to northern Egypt.

The Old Testament is the sacred book of the Jewish people. It is also the first half of the Christian Bible. All Christian communities accept the Hebrew texts as authoritative, as the Christian faith grew out of Judaism. To Christians, Jesus Christ is the Messiah prophesied in the Old Testament scriptures.

THE STRUCTURE

The original Hebrew Old Testament texts were grouped into three sections: the Law (Torah), the Prophets (Naviim), and the Writings (Kethubim). The modern Jewish Bible is organized in the same way and is sometimes referred to as the "Tanak". This is an acronym based on the first letters of these Hebrew words (TNK). The content of the Christian Old Testament is the same, but it is arranged differently (see page 8).

The Law

Both Jews and Christians refer to the "Law of Moses", after the first great leader, Moses, who gave the Law to the Israelites. The books of the Law are called the "Torah", which means "instruction". They contain all the teachings that the people of Israel had to learn and observe. The Law also includes historical accounts of the Israelites up until their entry into the Promised Land.

THE LAW (TORAH)
The books of the Law are also known as the "Pentateuch", which is Greek for "five books". These contain laws, narratives, family trees, sermons, and poetry.

THE PROPHETS
This section comprises eight books. The minor prophets are Hosea, Joel, Amos, Obadiah, Jonah, Micah, Nahum, Habakkuk, Zephaniah, Haggai, Zechariah, and Malachi.

THE WRITINGS
This group contains eleven books. The first three are books of poetry and wisdom, the next five are official records (read at important festivals), and the last three are historical and prophetic.

The Prophets

This section contains the historical books, which were written by the Israelite prophets. They describe events from the conquest of Canaan to the end of the Israelite monarchy and chronicle the Israelites' constant struggle to keep the Laws of Moses. The Prophets were mediators between God and the Israelites. They explained the meanings of events and warned the Israelites of the dangers of disobeying God. The prophets predicted many future events and announced the coming of a Messiah, who would lead his people back to God.

The Writings

This collection comprises books of wisdom, poetry, prophecy, and history, which are not arranged chronologically. The Writings express the Israelites' relationship with God in times both of faithfulness and disobedience. They also offer words of wisdom and advice, which the Israelites meditated on as part of their worship. The Book of Psalms, a compilation of 150 hymns and prayers, is the longest book in the Bible. Parts of the book were used by the Israelites in their daily services.

ELIJAH IS TAKEN UP TO HEAVEN
This 13th-century Italian fresco depicts the prophet Elijah being carried to heaven on a chariot (2 Kings 2). Elijah ministered during the reigns of Kings Ahab and Ahaziah. He condemned the Israelites' pagan worship at that time.

KING DAVID ENTHRONED
The Israelite king David is pictured in this ivory carving from France. David wrote many of the psalms contained in the Bible. These were set to music and used in worship.

ISRAELITE WORSHIP

Early Israelite worship involved the offering of sacrifices to God. The Patriarchs (the Israelite forefathers) made offerings on altars built out of stone to commemorate wherever God appeared to them (Genesis 28: 18–22).

Under the leadership of Moses, Israelite worship became much more complex. Services took place in the Tabernacle, a portable shrine, also known as the Tent of Meeting. The Tabernacle contained the Ark of the Covenant, which was a chest containing the Law of Moses and the stone tablets inscribed with the Ten Commandments. Sacrifices were no longer carried out by the people, but by the Levite priests on specially built altars in the Tabernacle. The Levites were the only people allowed to set up the Tabernacle.

About 500 years later, when Israel became a united kingdom, the Tabernacle was replaced by Solomon's Temple. Daily services and sacrifices all took place in the Temple.

ISRAELITE WORSHIP IN MOSES' TIME
This 19th-century engraving depicts a Levite priest sacrificing a bull at the ceremonial altar.

THE HEBREW TEXT

Much of the significance of the original Hebrew texts has been lost in translation. The symbolism of words, expressions, names, and even stories, cannot be fully appreciated without understanding the traditions and culture of the Old Testament writers.

The importance of names

The Hebrew names given to people and places are much more than just "labels". They were chosen to express something about a person or an event. For example, "Isaac" means "laughter". He received this name because his parents laughed in disbelief when God told them they would have a son at such an old age (Genesis 18). Some names indicate the future role of a person, such as "Joshua", which means "The Lord is Saviour". Moses named the place where many Israelites died because of their greed "Kibbroth Hattaavah", which means "graves of gluttony".

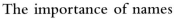

JEWISH SCRIBE
This professional scribe is copying the original Hebrew texts by hand onto a Torah scroll. Sections from the scroll are read during Jewish services.

Old Testament symbols

Many people, events, and objects in the Old Testament have a symbolic significance. For example, Noah represents all that is good and righteous in the world, and the Flood symbolizes God's wrath and judgement. The burning bush on Mount Sinai also signifies God's presence, and emphasizes his power. God uses fire to guide his people (Exodus 13: 21).

The Book of Exodus is full of symbolism. The Tabernacle represents a "meeting-place" between God and man, and the Ark of the Covenant symbolizes the constant presence of God, because it contains the Laws.

Old Testament numbers

Some numbers are meant to be taken literally, such as the detailed dimensions given for the construction of the Tabernacle. However, many numbers have a purely symbolic function. "Seven" represents perfection, and "four" and "ten" are symbols of completion. "Six" is often associated with humankind, "twelve" refers to God's will, and "forty" is always used to indicate a long period of time.

Some of the ages of the Patriarchs, such as Noah who lived to be 950 (Genesis 9: 29), are also intended to be symbolic, rather than literal.

PRAYER BOX
Phylacteries are leather boxes containing Hebrew texts taken from the Pentateuch. This phylactery was found in the Qumran Caves.

JEWISH FESTIVALS

THE FESTIVAL OF PURIM

The Sabbath
Jewish people rest on the seventh day, the Sabbath. This is a Saturday in the Jewish calendar. It commemorates God's day of rest after the six days of Creation.

The Festival of the Passover
This falls on 14th Nisan (March–April) and recalls when God sent a plague to kill every firstborn Egyptian, which "passed over" Israelite homes (Exodus 12). The Passover is also known as the "Festival of Unleavened Bread". This refers to the unleavened bread prepared by the Israelites in their hurried departure from Egypt. Today Jewish people share a special meal to celebrate Passover.

Shavuot (Feast of Weeks)
Shavuot is a festival to celebrate the wheat harvest. It falls on 6th Sivan (May–June).

Rosh Hashanah (Head of Year)
In the Bible, this festival is called the "Day of Sounding the Shophar (trumpet)". It is a time when Jewish people reflect on the past year. It falls on 1st Tishri (September–October).

Yom Kippur (Day of Atonement)
This is a day of fasting and prayer. In biblical times, a scapegoat was sent into the wilderness as a sacrifice (10th Tishri).

Succoth (Feast of Booths)
People camp in huts or tents to remember the Israelites' time in the desert (15th–21st Tishri).

Hanukkah (Feast of Lights)
This celebration begins on 25th Kislev (December) and recalls Judas Maccabeus re-dedicating the Temple (1 Maccabees 4: 36).

Purim
Purim falls on 14th/15th Adar (February–March) and recalls when Queen Esther of Persia saved the Jews from death (Esther 9).

DATING THE OLD TESTAMENT

Archeologists and biblical scholars have used a variety of sources and methods to try to date the events of the Old Testament periods. The Bible itself provides a detailed chronology of Israelite history and gives insights into ancient ways of life, which archeologists can then try to establish as typical of a certain historical period. Documents and artefacts from other ancient Middle-Eastern civilizations also provide information relevant to biblical events. Modern studies of population movements and settlement patterns add further weight to this evidence, making it possible to set the Bible in its historical context.

OBELISK OF SHALMANESER
This panel carving depicts Shalmaneser III of Assyria receiving tribute money from the Israelite King Jehu. It is part of a black limestone obelisk (*c.* 825 BC) and is the only existing representation of an Israelite king.

THE BIBLE CHRONOLOGY
The dates contained within this chronology are all approximate, as archeologists disagree over the dating of many key events in the Bible, particularly the Exodus. This timeline gives the earlier of two possible dates for the Exodus, which differ by a period of 200 years (see pages 64–65).

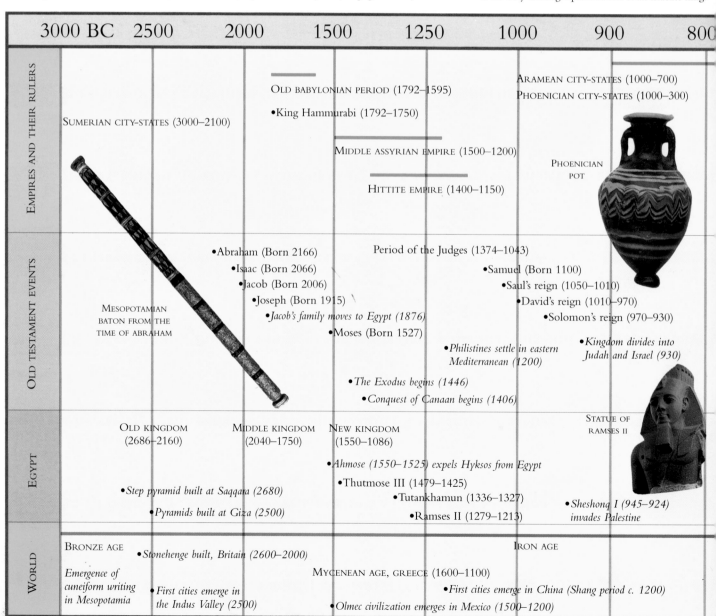

	3000 BC	2500	2000	1500	1250	1000	900	800
EMPIRES AND THEIR RULERS	SUMERIAN CITY-STATES (3000–2100)		OLD BABYLONIAN PERIOD (1792–1595) • King Hammurabi (1792–1750)	MIDDLE ASSYRIAN EMPIRE (1500–1200) HITTITE EMPIRE (1400–1150)		ARAMEAN CITY-STATES (1000–700) PHOENICIAN CITY-STATES (1000–300)	PHOENICIAN POT	
OLD TESTAMENT EVENTS	MESOPOTAMIAN BATON FROM THE TIME OF ABRAHAM	•Abraham (Born 2166) •Isaac (Born 2066) •Jacob (Born 2006) •Joseph (Born 1915) •*Jacob's family moves to Egypt (1876)* •Moses (Born 1527)		Period of the Judges (1374–1043) •*The Exodus begins (1446)* •*Conquest of Canaan begins (1406)*	•*Philistines settle in eastern Mediterranean (1200)*	•Samuel (Born 1100) •Saul's reign (1050–1010) •David's reign (1010–970) •Solomon's reign (970–930) •*Kingdom divides into Judah and Israel (930)*		
EGYPT	OLD KINGDOM (2686–2160) •*Step pyramid built at Saqqara (2680)* •*Pyramids built at Giza (2500)*	MIDDLE KINGDOM (2040–1750)	NEW KINGDOM (1550–1086) •*Ahmose (1550–1525) expels Hyksos from Egypt* •*Thutmose III (1479–1425)* •*Tutankhamun (1336–1327)* •*Ramses II (1279–1213)*		STATUE OF RAMSES II •*Sheshonq I (945–924) invades Palestine*		
WORLD	BRONZE AGE Emergence of cuneiform writing in Mesopotamia	•*Stonehenge built, Britain (2600–2000)* •*First cities emerge in the Indus Valley (2500)*	MYCENEAN AGE, GREECE (1600–1100) •*Olmec civilization emerges in Mexico (1500–1200)*		IRON AGE •*First cities emerge in China (Shang period c. 1200)*		

Establishing a chronology

There is much uncertainty about the chronology of events in the early history of the Israelite people. However, recent archeological discoveries of Middle-Eastern records dating from the 1st and 2nd centuries BC have made it possible to establish a widely accepted system of dating for the kings of Judah and Israel. Clay tablets discovered in Nineveh and other Assyrian cities have provided information about the death of King Ahab of Israel. These tablets list the dates and battles of Assyrian rulers from the period 892–748 BC and set Ahab's death at 853 BC.

Another important source of information came from a Babylonian chronicle discovered in the 1950s. The chronicle records the deportation of people from Judah to Babylon (c. 598 BC) and agrees with the date given by the Hebrew texts, "the seventh year" of Nebuchadnezzar's reign (Jeremiah 52: 28).

There is very little archeological evidence of Bible events before the Israelite Kings. However, a chronology of Israel's early history can be built up by using the dates recorded in the Bible and then working backwards from established Bible events.

SIR WILLIAM FLINDERS PETRIE
The British archeologist Sir William Flinders Petrie carried out excavations in Palestine in 1890. He compared Palestinian artefacts with similar Egyptian objects that had been dated, and so established a chronology for ancient Palestine. This technique is known as cross-dating.

EXCAVATIONS OF BETH-SHEAN
This important biblical city is modern day "Tell el-Husn".

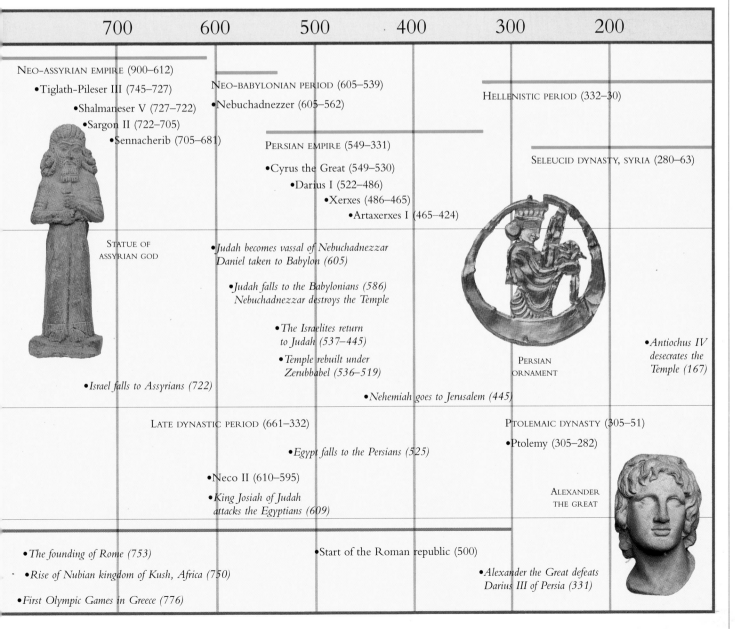

	700	600	500	400	300	200

NEO-ASSYRIAN EMPIRE (900–612)
•Tiglath-Pileser III (745–727)
•Shalmaneser V (727–722)
•Sargon II (722–705)
•Sennacherib (705–681)

NEO-BABYLONIAN PERIOD (605–539)
•Nebuchadnezzer (605–562)

HELLENISTIC PERIOD (332–30)

PERSIAN EMPIRE (549–331)
•Cyrus the Great (549–530)
•Darius I (522–486)
•Xerxes (486–465)
•Artaxerxes I (465–424)

SELEUCID DYNASTY, SYRIA (280–63)

STATUE OF ASSYRIAN GOD

•Judah becomes vassal of Nebuchadnezzar
Daniel taken to Babylon (605)

•Judah falls to the Babylonians (586)
Nebuchadnezzar destroys the Temple

•The Israelites return to Judah (537–445)
•Temple rebuilt under Zerubbabel (536–519)

•Israel falls to Assyrians (722)

•Nehemiah goes to Jerusalem (445)

PERSIAN ORNAMENT

•Antiochus IV desecrates the Temple (167)

LATE DYNASTIC PERIOD (661–332)

PTOLEMAIC DYNASTY (305–51)
•Ptolemy (305–282)

•Egypt falls to the Persians (525)

•Neco II (610–595)

•King Josiah of Judah attacks the Egyptians (609)

ALEXANDER THE GREAT

•The founding of Rome (753)

•Start of the Roman republic (500)

•Rise of Nubian kingdom of Kush, Africa (750)

•Alexander the Great defeats Darius III of Persia (331)

•First Olympic Games in Greece (776)

IN THE BEGINNING

The first book of the Bible is Genesis. It takes its name from the first word of the original Hebrew text, "bereshith", which means "In the beginning". "Genesis" is the Greek translation of the Hebrew word. This book describes the creation of the world, the fall of humankind, and the early history of the nation of Israel. It also establishes important themes that recur throughout the Bible, such as sin, redemption, wrath, and mercy. It provides clues for understanding the rest of the Hebrew texts.

READING FROM THE TORAH SCROLL
This Jewish boy is celebrating his Bar Mitzvah. At thirteen, Jewish boys are recognized as adults and read from the Torah scroll at the synagogue for the first time.

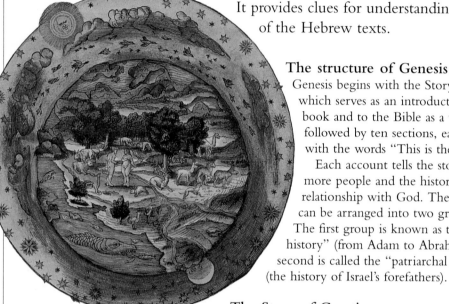

THE CREATION
Illustration from the Lutheran Bible depicting Adam and Eve (c. 1530)

The structure of Genesis

Genesis begins with the Story of Creation, which serves as an introduction to the book and to the Bible as a whole. This is followed by ten sections, each beginning with the words "This is the account of ". Each account tells the story of one or more people and the history of their relationship with God. The ten sections can be arranged into two groups of five. The first group is known as the "primeval history" (from Adam to Abraham). The second is called the "patriarchal history" (the history of Israel's forefathers).

The Story of Creation

The accounts of the Creation are contained within two chapters of the Book of Genesis. Some biblical scholars maintain that they derive from two different traditions. Genesis 1 gives an overview of the beginnings of the universe, describing the creation of the heavens and earth, which took place over a period of six days; Genesis 2 focuses more on the creation of humankind and its place within the universe.

The purpose of Genesis

Genesis was initially written to teach the Israelites about their origins, their faith, and their responsibilities as God's chosen people. Its content was arranged in clearly defined sections to help the readers or listeners to remember God's instructions. The text contains repetitions and patterns of words and phrases that also reinforce God's message.

Ancient Middle-Eastern myths

Parts of Genesis bear a resemblance to other creation literature from the ancient Middle East. The most common elements are the concepts of the separation of the earth from the sky, and the creation of man from the earth. A Babylonian poem known as "The Akrakhasis" is closest to the Biblical account. The poem describes how man is ordained to toil the earth (Genesis 3) and is then destroyed by a great flood (Genesis 7–9).

The Garden of Eden is often depicted as a lush green oasis.

The Garden of Eden

Adam and Eve lived in the Garden of Eden, which has come to represent paradise on earth. When the Hebrew text was translated into Greek, the word used for garden was "paradeisos". This then became "paradise" in the English version.

The God of Genesis

There are many words for God in the Bible. In Genesis, God is referred to by at least six different Hebrew names, all of which emphasize a different aspect of his nature. The most important of these is Yahweh (Exodus 3: 14), which means "I am who I am". This name is so sacred to Jewish people that they avoid using it and say "Adonai" instead, which means "Lord". God is sometimes simply referred to as "El", which expresses God's might.

YAHWEH
This sacred name is written between the two hands on this 19th-century Moroccan papercut. God's name is spelled with the four Hebrew letters YHWH. This is referred to as the "Tetragrammaton".

How does God appear?

In the Bible, only a few people meet with God in person, and on these occasions he is concealed by a bright radiance. God often manifests himself through various forms of nature, such as thunder, lightning, and smoke. Moses warns the Israelites not to look directly at God because they might perish (Exodus 19: 21).

God also appears to his people through visions and dreams. The prophet Isaiah received a vision of God enthroned (Isaiah 6: 1), and Jacob saw God at the top of a high stairway in a dream (Genesis 28: 15).

NAMES OF GOD

El Elyon
means MOST HIGH
from GENESIS (14: 18-20)

✛

Shapat
means JUDGE
from GENESIS (18: 25)

✛

El Olam
means THE ETERNAL GOD
from GENESIS (21: 33)

✛

Yahweh-Jireh
means THE LORD WILL PROVIDE
from GENESIS (22: 14)

✛

El Elohe-Yisra'el
means GOD, THE GOD OF ISRAEL
from GENESIS (33: 20)

✛

El Shaddai
means GOD ALMIGHTY
from GENESIS (49: 25)

THE RAINBOW
This is a symbol of God's mercy and glory (Genesis 9; Ezekiel 1: 28).

LIGHTNING, A SYMBOL OF GOD'S POWER

Authorship of Genesis

The Book of Genesis makes no reference to its author. However, Jewish and Christian traditions accredit the first five books of the Bible to Moses. The early material would have been handed down in written or oral form, and then collected and recorded by Moses.

To make sense of the Genesis texts, they should be seen in the context of the time they were written, which was after the Israelites had received Moses' Law. The Hebrew readers could recognize any references to these laws because they were familiar with them. The laws contained detailed instructions for worship, sacrifices, and civil and moral obligations.

Sacrifices

The Israelites offered animals or other possessions as sacrifices in order to obtain God's forgiveness for their sins. The first offerings mentioned in the Bible are made by Cain and Abel. God accepts Abel's sacrifice of his finest firstborn lambs, but rejects Cain's gift of "fruit from the soil" (Genesis 4: 3).

The Book of Leviticus contains detailed requirements for ritual sacrifices. Cain displeased God because he did not offer the best of his crop (23: 10).

NOAH AND THE ARK
This tiled window depicts Noah offering sacrifices when his family safely reached dry land.

Clean and unclean

God asked Noah to take seven of every clean and two of every unclean animal onto the ark (Genesis 7: 2). Unclean animals include those with cloven hooves that do not chew the cud, fish without fins and scales, birds of prey, winged insects, and some "crawling animals" (Leviticus 11).

Genealogies

Genesis contains many lists of names. One of these traces the descendants of Noah's sons, Ham, Japheth, and Shem (Genesis 10). The people descended from Shem became known as the Semites. Ham's descendants are associated with the Hamitic and Canaanite people, whereas Japheth's are identified with the people of Asia Minor, Greece, and the Mediterranean islands.

GENESIS 1–2

THE STORY OF CREATION

CHAPTER 1 VERSE 2
"Formless and empty"
God calls the world into existence in an ordered, symmetrical way. These two words provide a structure for the six days of creation. The first three days (forming) correspond to the last three days (filling).

CHAPTER 1 VERSES 3, 10
"And God said... And God saw that it was good"
God is presented as a person. He commands the universe into being. These key expressions give shape to the whole story of the creation. The first introduces each act of creation, and the second emphasizes the perfection of God's work.

CHAPTER 1 VERSE 5
"And there was evening, and there was morning"
The Israelites calculated the day from sunset to sunset, which is why evening is mentioned before morning. The seventh day is the beginning of human history, and so it has no morning or evening.

1 IN[1] THE BEGINNING God created the heavens and the earth. [2]Now the earth was *formless and empty*, darkness was over the surface of the deep, and the Spirit of God was hovering over the waters. [3]*And God said*, "Let there be light," and there was light. [4]God saw that the light was good, and he separated the light from the darkness. [5]God called the light "day", and the darkness he called "night". *And there was evening, and there was morning* – the first day.

[6]And God said, "Let there be an expanse between the waters to separate water from water."... [7]And it was so. [8]God called the expanse "sky". And there was evening, and there was morning – the second day.

[9]And God said, "Let the water under the sky be gathered to one place, and let dry ground appear."... [10]God called the dry ground "land", and the gathered waters he called "seas". *And God saw that it was good.* [11]Then God said, "Let the land produce vegetation... according to their various kinds." And it was so... [12]And God saw that it was good. [13]And there was evening, and there was morning – the third day.

[14]And God said, "Let there be lights in the expanse of the sky to separate the day from the night, and *let them serve as signs to mark seasons and days and years...*" And it was so. [16]God made two great lights – the greater light to govern the day and the lesser light to govern the night. He also made the stars... [18]And God saw that it was good. [19]And there was evening, and there was morning – the fourth day.

In the beginning, the earth was formless, empty, and dark

God creates the sky

Dry ground appears and divides the water

God makes the sun, the moon, and the stars to separate day from night

God creates light and separates it from darkness

²⁰And God said, "Let the water teem with living creatures, and let birds fly above the earth"... ²¹And God saw that it was good. ²²God blessed them and said, "Be fruitful and increase in number..." ²³And there was evening, and there was morning – the fifth day.

²⁴And God said, "Let the land produce living creatures according to their kinds: livestock, creatures that move along the ground, and wild animals, each according to its kind." And it was so. ²⁵And God saw that it was good. ²⁶Then God said, "Let us make man in our image, in our likeness, and let them rule over... all the earth..." ²⁷So *God created man in his own image*, in the image of God he created him; male and female he created them. ²⁸God blessed them and said to them, "Be fruitful and increase in number; fill the earth and subdue it. Rule... every living creature..." ²⁹Then God said, "I give you every seed-bearing plant... and every tree that has fruit with seed in it. They will be yours for food..." And it was so. ³¹God saw all that he had made, and it was very good. And there was evening, and there was morning – the sixth day.

2 ¹Thus the heavens and the earth were completed in all their vast array. ²By the seventh day God had finished the work he had been doing; so on the seventh day he rested from all his work. ³And *God blessed the seventh day* and made it holy, because on it he rested from all the work of creating that he had done.

UNDERSTANDING THE STORY

Genesis 1 tells the first account of the creation. It celebrates the unity and perfection of the universe and emphasizes God's grandeur and power. The repetition of key phrases forms a pattern, and reflects the orderly way in which God created the world. The story of creation takes place over seven days, and "seven" has come to represent perfection and completion.

CHAPTER 1 VERSE 14
"Let them serve as signs to mark seasons and days and years"
The lights appear on the fourth day, which is the mid-point in the seven days. These lights are the sun, moon, and stars. Ancient religious calendars were based on solar and lunar cycles, which set the time for feast days and festivals.

ASTRONOMERS
This 15th-century engraving depicts Arabian astronomers calculating the position of the moon and stars.

CHAPTER 1 VERSE 27
"God created man in his own image"
Humankind (man and woman) reflects God in a spiritual, rather than a physical sense. God grants people the ability to rule, create, and make moral choices.

CHAPTER 2 VERSE 3
"God blessed the seventh day"
God's creation set a pattern for people's lives: six days of work, then a day of rest (the Sabbath).

The land teems with animals of every kind

God creates mankind, male and female

Every type of plant grows

GENESIS 2

IN THE GARDEN OF EDEN

CHAPTER 2 VERSE 4
*"God made the earth
and the heavens"*
In the first creation story, the
word order is reversed: "God
created the heavens and the earth"
(Genesis 1: 1). Genesis 1 describes
the creation of the universe as a
whole; this account focuses on
the creation of humanity.

CHAPTER 2 VERSE 7
"The breath of life"
Only human life is given the breath
of God, which distinguishes it from
animal life. The Hebrew word for
"breath" can also mean "spirit".
The Spirit of God enables people
to think, experience emotions, and
have an awareness of their creator.

CHAPTER 2 VERSE 8
"A garden in the east, in Eden"
The east symbolized life and light
to ancient Middle-Eastern cultures.
Eden is the Hebrew word for
"delight". It was a place of pleasure.

2 WHEN[4] THE LORD *God made the earth and the heavens* – [5]and no plant of the field had yet sprung up, for the LORD God had not sent rain... [6]but streams came up from the earth and watered the whole surface of the ground – [7]the LORD God formed the man from the dust of the ground and breathed into his nostrils *the breath of life*, and the man became a living being.

[8]Now the LORD God had planted *a garden in the east, in Eden*; and there he put the man he had formed. [9]And the LORD God made all kinds of trees to grow out of the ground – trees that were pleasing to the eye and good for food. In the middle of the garden were the tree of life and the tree of the knowledge of good and evil.

[10]A river watering the garden flowed from Eden; from there it was separated into four headwaters. [11]The name of the first is *the Pishon...* [13]the second river is *the Gihon...*[14]the third river is *the Tigris...* And the fourth river is *the Euphrates*. [15]The LORD God took the man and put him in the Garden of Eden to work it and take care of it. [16]And the LORD God commanded the man, "You are free to eat from any tree in the garden; [17]but you must not eat from the tree of the knowledge of good and evil, for when you eat of it you will surely die."

[18]The LORD God said, "It is *not good for the man to be alone...*"

[19]Now the LORD God had formed out of the ground all the beasts of the field and all the birds of the air. He brought them to the man to see what he would name them;

God creates man from
the dust of the ground

God plants a garden
in Eden and fills it
with birds and beasts

Man gives every living
creature a name

and whatever the man called each living creature, that was its name. [20]So the man gave names to all the livestock, the birds of the air and all the beasts of the field.

But for Adam no suitable helper was found. [21]So the LORD God caused the man to fall into a deep sleep; and while he was sleeping, he took one of the man's ribs and closed up the place with flesh. [22]Then *the LORD God made a woman from the rib* he had taken out of the man, and he brought her to the man.

[23]The man said, "This is now bone of my bones and flesh of my flesh; she shall be called 'woman', for she was taken out of man."

[24]For this reason a man will leave his father and mother and be united to his wife, and they will become one flesh. [25]The man and his wife were both naked, and they felt no shame.

UNDERSTANDING THE STORY

Genesis 2 gives the second account of the Creation story, which emphasizes God's love and concern for humanity. Here God does not create by command, but by tender actions. He makes a covenant with humankind: man and woman may live in the "Garden of Paradise" as long as they remain obedient to their creator.

In the middle of the garden are the tree of life and the tree of knowledge

Man may eat from any tree, except from the tree of knowledge

While man is asleep, God takes a rib from him and creates woman

CHAPTER 2 VERSES 11–14
"The Pishon… the Gihon… the Tigris… the Euphrates"
Only the Tigris and the Euphrates are well-known today. They flow through the fertile area that used to be called Mesopotamia (modern-day Iraq). The two other rivers are hard to identify. Some scholars think that the Gihon is a small river or canal in the Euphrates Valley.

THE TIGRIS AND EUPHRATES
The delta of the Tigris and Euphrates is very swampy. Marsh Arabs have lived here for centuries.

CHAPTER 2 VERSE 18
"Not good for the man to be alone"
This phrase contrasts with Genesis 1, where everything is described as "good". It highlights the importance of God's next act of creation.

CHAPTER 2 VERSE 22
"The LORD God made a woman from the rib"
Man is incomplete and lonely without a partner, and so God creates woman. The rib is taken from near Adam's heart – a symbol of love, and from under his arm – a symbol of protection. This imagery conveys the biblical ideal of marriage.

THE TREE OF LIFE AND THE TREE OF KNOWLEDGE
The Tree of Life symbolizes the gift of eternal life, which God offers to humanity. Man and woman may eat freely from this tree. The Tree of Knowledge of Good and Evil represents moral choice. Eating its fruit leads to independence from God, and so it is forbidden.

GENESIS 3

ADAM AND EVE

Some ancient Middle-Eastern cultures associated serpents with wisdom and divination. In the Bible, the snake is often depicted as a symbol of evil. Later tradition has linked the serpent with the devil. The Hebrew word for serpent, "nahash", is similar to the word "nashah", meaning "deceive". This use of wordplay emphasizes the snake's role as tempter.

INCENSE BURNER
Canaanite pottery adorned with snakes (*c.* 1000 BC)

❖
CHAPTER 3 VERSE 6
"The fruit of the tree was good"
Although the fruit is not named, it is often depicted as an apple. This tradition probably dates from the 5th century, when the Bible was translated into Latin. The Latin word for evil, "malum", also means apple.

ADAM
AND EVE
French plaque depicting the forbidden fruit as apples (*c.* 1570)

❖
CHAPTER 3 VERSE 19
"Dust you are and to dust you will return"
Adam will no longer experience eternal life, because he ate from the "tree of knowledge". Man was created out of the dust (Genesis 2: 7), and God will return him to the same state. God's words establish the physical cycle of life and death.

3 **N**OW[1] THE SERPENT was more crafty than any of the wild animals the LORD God had made. He said to the woman, "Did God really say, 'You must not eat from any tree in the garden'?"

[2]The woman said to *the serpent*, "We may eat fruit from the trees in the garden, [3]but God did say, 'You must not eat fruit from the tree that is in the middle of the garden... or you will die.' "

[4]"You will not surely die," the serpent said to the woman. [5]"For God knows that when you eat of it your eyes will be opened, and you will be like God, knowing good and evil."

[6]When the woman saw that *the fruit of the tree was good* for food and pleasing to the eye, and also desirable for gaining wisdom, she took some and ate it. She also gave some to her husband, who was with her, and he ate it. [7]Then the eyes of both of them were opened, and they realised that they were naked; so they sewed fig leaves together and made coverings for themselves.

[8]Then the man and his wife heard the sound of the LORD God as he was walking in the garden in the cool of the day, and they hid from the LORD God among the trees of the garden.

God asked them if they had eaten from the tree of knowledge – because they were embarrassed by their nakedness – and Adam said that Eve had given him the fruit to eat. Eve told God that she had been deceived by the serpent.

God cursed the serpent and condemned it to a life crawling on its belly and eating dust from the ground. He punished Eve by greatly increasing the pains of childbearing.

[17]To Adam he said, "Because you listened to your wife and ate from the tree about which I commanded you, 'You must not eat of it,' cursed is the ground because of you; through painful toil you will eat of it all the days of your life. [18]It will produce thorns and thistles for you, and you will eat the plants of the field. [19]By the sweat of your brow you will eat your food until you return to the ground, since from it you were taken; for *dust you are and to dust you will return.*"

[20]*Adam named his wife Eve*, because she would become the mother of all the living.

[21]The LORD God made garments of skin for Adam and his wife... [22]And the LORD God said, "The man has now become like one of us, knowing good and evil. He must not be allowed to reach out his hand and take also from the tree of life and eat, and live for ever." [23]So the LORD God banished him from the Garden of Eden to work the ground from which he had been taken. [24]After he drove the man out, he placed on the east side of the Garden of Eden *cherubim and a flaming sword* flashing back and forth to guard the way to the tree of life.

Tree of knowledge

The serpent tempts Eve to eat from the tree

Eve gives some of the forbidden fruit to Adam. God punishes humankind when he discovers Adam and Eve have sinned

God banishes Adam and Eve from the Garden of Eden

CHAPTER 3 VERSE 20
"Adam named his wife Eve"
"Eve" is Hebrew for "living". It is significant that Adam gives woman this name just after God talks to him about death. Adam knows that God will continue to bless humanity even though they have both sinned. The Hebrew word for "man" is "Adam". Its similarity to "adamah", meaning "ground", serves as a reminder of how God created man.

CHAPTER 3 VERSE 24
"Cherubim and a flaming sword"
Cherubim are often depicted as angelic beings who act as divine guardians. Sculptures of cherubim decorated Solomon's Temple. These representations may have been modelled on ancient Middle-Eastern carvings of winged lions and bulls with human heads.

WINGED CREATURE (1300 BC)
Found in Megiddo, Palestine

UNDERSTANDING THE STORY

The innocence and tranquility of Eden are destroyed by Adam and Eve's sin. By eating from the Tree of Knowledge, they challenge God's will. God punishes them for this by taking away his gift of eternal life and expelling them from the garden. Their sin leads to humanity's separation from God.

GENESIS 4
CAIN AND ABEL

❖
CHAPTER 4 VERSE 1
"With the help of the LORD I have brought forth a man"
Eve acknowledges that God is the creator of all things. Her son's name reinforces this. "Cain" means "to acquire" in Hebrew.

❖
CHAPTER 4 VERSE 2
"She gave birth to his brother Abel"
The Hebrew word "Abel" means "a breath". It suggests something that fades away to nothing, signalling Abel's fate.

❖
CHAPTER 4 VERSE 5
"On Cain and his offering he did not look with favour"
Although the Bible does not explain why God rejects Cain's offering, it is understood when seen in the context of Israelite sacrificial laws. The Scriptures state that firstborn animals should be offered to God (Exodus 13: 2), and the first fruits of a crop dedicated at harvest time (Leviticus 23: 10). Abel carefully selects the offering he makes to God, but Cain does not.

CAIN AND ABEL
This Italian fresco is one of a series of paintings that tell the story of Adam and Eve and Cain and Abel. This scene depicts Cain and Abel presenting their offerings to God.

❖
CHAPTER 4 VERSE 7
"If you do what is right"
God's words imply that Cain knew his offering was not acceptable. Only perfect gifts can be dedicated to God (Leviticus 22: 20–22).

4 ADAM[1] LAY WITH HIS WIFE EVE, and she became pregnant and gave birth to Cain. She said, *"With the help of the LORD I have brought forth a man."* [2]Later *she gave birth to his brother Abel.*

Adam and Eve have two sons, named Cain and Abel

Abel keeps flocks, and gives his firstborn sheep to God

Cain works the soil and offers some of his crops to God

Now Abel kept flocks, and Cain worked the soil. [3]In the course of time Cain brought some of the fruits of the soil as an offering to the LORD. [4]But Abel brought fat portions from some of the firstborn of his flock. The LORD looked with favour on Abel and his offering, [5]but *on Cain and his offering he did not look with favour.* So Cain was very angry, and his face was downcast.

[6]Then the LORD said to Cain, "Why are you angry? Why is your face downcast? [7]*If you do what is right*, will you not be accepted? But if you do not do what is right, *sin is crouching at your door; it desires to have you, but you must master it."*

[8]Now Cain said to his brother Abel, "Let's go out to the field." And while they were in the field, Cain attacked his brother Abel and killed him.

[9]Then the LORD said to Cain, "Where is your brother Abel?"

"I don't know," he replied, "Am I my brother's keeper?"

[10]The LORD said, "What have you done? Listen! Your brother's blood cries out to me from the ground.

God prefers Abel's offering

Cain kills his brother in a fit of jealousy

God condemns Cain to a life
of restless wandering

¹¹Now you are under
a curse and driven from
the ground, which opened
its mouth to receive your
brother's blood from your
hand. ¹²When you work
the ground, it will no longer
yield its crops for you. You
will be a restless wanderer
on the earth."

¹³Cain said to the LORD,
"My punishment is more than
I can bear. ¹⁴Today you are driving me from the land, and I will be
hidden from your presence; I will be a restless wanderer on the earth,
and whoever finds me will kill me."

¹⁵But the LORD said to him, "Not so; if anyone kills Cain, *he will
suffer vengeance seven times over.*" Then the LORD *put a mark on Cain* so
that no-one who found him would kill him. ¹⁶So Cain went out from
the LORD's presence and lived in *the land of Nod*, east of Eden.

²⁵Adam lay with his wife again, and she gave birth to a son and named
him Seth, saying, "God has granted me another child in place of Abel,
since Cain killed him." ²⁶Seth also had a son, and he named him Enosh.

UNDERSTANDING THE STORY

Cain's jealousy destroys all family bonds of affection and leads to a wicked
act. His sin is greater than that of Adam and Eve. Not only is he unrepentant,
but he also protests against his punishment. God sends Cain further away
from the "Garden of Eden" to live with the constant reminder of his sin.

God puts a mark on Cain to
protect him from his enemies

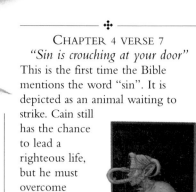

CHAPTER 4 VERSE 7
"Sin is crouching at your door"
This is the first time the Bible
mentions the word "sin". It is
depicted as an animal waiting to
strike. Cain still
has the chance
to lead a
righteous life,
but he must
overcome
his envious
thoughts.

ENVY
Envy is depicted
as a demon in
this 14th-century
fresco by Giotto.

CHAPTER 4 VERSE 15
*"He will suffer vengeance seven
times over"*
Despite Cain's lack of remorse, God
offers to look after him. God's
mercy is greater than his wrath.
The number seven signifies God's
absolute and perfect protection.

CHAPTER 4 VERSE 15
"Put a mark on Cain"
The Bible does not specify how
God marked Cain. The mark is a
symbol of God's protection and a
reminder of Cain's sin. It has often
been depicted as a tattoo.

CHAPTER 4 VERSE 16
"The land of Nod"
The Hebrew word "Nod" means
"wandering". Cain is condemned
to wander in a barren land where
he cannot grow crops. This
punishment is worse than
Adam's. God sentenced
Adam to work a land
choked with thorns
and thistles.

GENESIS 6–7
NOAH BUILDS THE ARK

CHAPTER 6 VERSE 11
*"The earth was corrupt
in God's sight"*
In God's eyes the earth was dying.
He had entrusted his creation to
humankind, but people were leading
wicked lives and contaminating
everything around them. By
contrast, Noah was blameless
because he led a righteous life,
respecting God and his creation.
In Hebrew, his name means
"comfort". Noah was to bring
comfort to the cursed earth.

6 NOAH[9] WAS A RIGHTEOUS MAN, blameless among the people of his time, and he walked with God. [10]Noah had three sons: Shem, Ham and Japheth.

[11]Now *the earth was corrupt in God's sight* and was full of violence... [13]So God said to Noah, "I am going to put an end to all people, for the earth is filled with violence because of them. I am surely going to destroy both them and the earth. [14]So *make yourself an ark* of cypress wood; make rooms in it and coat it with pitch inside and out. [15]This is how you are to build it: The ark is to be 450 feet long, 75 feet wide and 45 feet high. [16]Make a roof for it and finish the ark to within 18 inches of the top. Put a door in the side of the ark and make lower, middle and upper decks... [21]You are to take every kind of food that is to be eaten and store it away..."

[22]Noah did everything just as God commanded him.

The earth has become an evil place.
Only Noah leads a righteous life

God tells Noah he will send
a flood to destroy all life

God will save Noah and
his family and every
species of animal

Shem

Japheth

Ham

Noah

God gives Noah detailed
instructions for building the ark

7 ¹The LORD then said to Noah, "Go into the ark, you and your whole family, because I have found you righteous in this generation. ²Take with you seven of every kind of clean animal, a male and its mate, and two of every kind of unclean animal, a male and its mate, ³and also seven of every kind of bird, male and female, to keep their various kinds alive throughout the earth. ⁴Seven days from now I will send rain on the earth for *forty days and forty nights*, and I will wipe from the face of the earth every living creature I have made."

⁵And Noah did all that the LORD commanded him...

¹¹In the six hundredth year of Noah's life, on the seventeenth day of the second month – on that day all the springs of the great deep burst forth, and the floodgates of the heavens were opened...

¹³On that very day Noah and his sons, Shem, Ham and Japheth, together with his wife and the wives of his three sons, entered the ark. ¹⁴They had with them every wild animal according to its kind... and every bird according to its kind, everything with wings.

¹⁵Pairs of all creatures that have the breath of life in them came to Noah and entered the ark. ¹⁶The animals going in were male and female of every living thing, as God had commanded Noah.
Then the LORD shut him in.

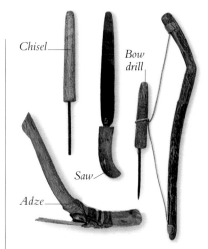

BOAT-BUILDING TOOLS
Middle-Eastern workmen used tools like these 3,000-year-old Egyptian examples. An adze was used for hacking and planing, and a bow drill bored holes for pegging wood.

Chisel

Bow drill

Saw

Adze

✢

CHAPTER 6 VERSE 14
"Make yourself an ark"
Ark is the Hebrew word for "box" or "container". In the Bible, it is also used to describe the basket of baby Moses. Noah's ark, like Moses' basket, represents God's protection and salvation.

THE GREAT FLOOD
There are stories of a great flood in many cultures all over the world. Among them, "The Gilgamesh Epic" from ancient Mesopotamia also features an ark and animals. The pagan gods in this story caused a flood because they were being kept awake by the terrible noise that people were making.

✢

CHAPTER 7 VERSE 4
"Forty days and forty nights"
In the Bible, the number forty is associated with most of God's mighty acts. Here, the flood is seen as a story of salvation leading to a new era rather than an act of destruction.

✢

CHAPTER 7 VERSE 16
"Then the LORD shut him in"
God is symbolically separating the righteous from the wicked.

A male and female of every animal are gathered together

The women collect food to store in the ark

Every kind of bird flocks to the ark

Cypress trees provide wood for the ark

Noah's wife calls the animals

GENESIS 7–9

THE FLOOD AND THE RAINBOW

✠

CHAPTER 8 VERSE 1
"He sent a wind over the earth, and the waters receded"
The "wind" calls to mind the "Spirit" of God, who "was hovering over the waters" in the Creation story. God said in the beginning, "Let the water under the sky be gathered... let dry ground appear".

✠

JESUS AND THE FLOOD
Jesus told his disciples that the end of the world would happen just as unexpectedly as the flood: "For in the days before the flood, people... knew nothing about what would happen until the flood came and took them all away. That is how it will be..." (Matthew 24: 38–9).

7

8

FOR [17] FORTY DAYS the flood kept coming on the earth... [18]The waters rose and increased greatly on the earth, and the ark floated on the surface of the water... [23]Every living thing on the face of the earth was wiped out... Only Noah was left, and those with him in the ark.

[24]The waters flooded the earth for a hundred and fifty days.

[1]But God remembered Noah and all the wild animals and the livestock that were with him in the ark, and *he sent a wind over the earth, and the waters receded*. [2]Now the springs of the deep and the floodgates of the heavens had been closed, and the rain had stopped falling from the sky. [3]The water receded steadily from the earth. At the end of the hundred and fifty days the water had gone down, [4]and on the seventeenth day of the seventh month *the ark came to rest on the mountains of Ararat...*

[6]After forty days Noah opened the window he had made in the ark [7]and sent out a raven, and it kept flying back and forth... [8]Then he sent out a dove... [9]But the dove could find no place to set its feet because there was water over all the surface of the earth; so it returned to Noah in the ark... [10]He waited seven more days and again sent out the dove from the ark. [11]When the dove returned to him in the evening, there in its beak was *a freshly plucked olive leaf!* Then Noah knew that the water had receded from the earth. [12]He waited seven more days and sent the dove out again, but this time it did not return to him.

[13]By the first day of the first month of Noah's six hundred and first year, the water had dried up from the earth... [14]By the twenty-seventh day of the second month the earth was completely dry.

[15]Then God said to Noah, [16]"Come out of the ark..."

It rains incessantly for forty days and nights. But Noah, his family, and all the animals are safe inside the ark

The water covers the entire earth, and every living thing drowns in the flood

The ark lands on the mountains of Ararat

A rainbow appears as a sign of God's covenant with Noah

The animals leave the ark

The dove returns to Noah with an olive leaf in its beak

¹⁸So Noah came out, together with his sons and his wife and his sons' wives. ¹⁹All the animals and all the creatures that move along the ground and all the birds... came out of the ark, one kind after another.

²⁰Then Noah built an altar to the LORD and, taking some of all the clean animals and clean birds, he sacrificed burnt offerings on it. ²¹The LORD smelled the pleasing aroma and said in his heart: "Never again will I curse the ground because of man, even though every inclination of his heart is evil from childhood. And never again will I destroy all living creatures... ²²As long as the earth endures, seedtime and harvest, cold and heat, summer and winter, day and night will never cease."

9   ¹Then God blessed Noah and his sons, saying to them, "Be fruitful and increase in number and fill the earth... ⁹I now establish my covenant with you and with your descendants after you ¹⁰and with every living creature...

¹²And God said, "This is the sign of the covenant I am making between me and you and every living creature with you, a covenant for all generations to come: ¹³I have set *my rainbow in the clouds*, and it will be the sign of the covenant between me and the earth."

Noah gives thanks to God by sacrificing some of the animals

UNDERSTANDING THE STORY

The Creation story describes the first beginning when God brought order out of chaos. The flood takes the world back to chaos but also makes a new start possible. Seas and dry land find their place again; animals and humans spread out and receive God's blessing in a new creation.

CHAPTER 8 VERSE 4
"The ark came to rest on the mountains of Ararat"
This story does not specify Mount Ararat, it refers to the mountains of a region known as Ararat since the 6th century BC. This later became Armenia, and its highest mount was then called Ararat.

CHAPTER 8 VERSE 11
"A freshly plucked olive leaf!"
The plucked olive leaf signals that God has created a new world. The modern symbol of peace – a dove carrying an olive branch – has its origins in this story.

OLIVE BRANCH

CHAPTER 9 VERSE 13
"My rainbow in the clouds"
The Bible's word for rainbow is also the word for "war-bow". An instrument of war has now become a symbol of peace. Set in the clouds, the rainbow becomes a visual seal of God's commitment never again to destroy all living creatures.

GENESIS 9–11
THE TOWER OF BABEL

CHAPTER 9 VERSE 25
"Cursed be Canaan!"
Noah's curse will come to fruition. The Canaanites (descended from Noah's son Ham) will be known for moral decadence. Their enemies the Israelites (descendants of Shem) will one day dominate them. By contrast, Shem's descendants, the Semites, are blessed.

CHAPTER 9 VERSE 29
"Noah lived 950 years"
Noah is the last of ten people mentioned in the Old Testament said to have lived to a remarkably old age. Methuselah died at the age of 969, and his name has become proverbial for longevity.

CHAPTER 10 VERSE 8
"Nimrod... a mighty warrior"
Ham's descendant was an ideal ruler. He was a hunter, warrior, and builder. Nimrod is Hebrew for "we shall rebel". Instead of following God's path, Nimrod sought to further his own ambitions.

CHAPTER 10 VERSE 10
"The first centres of his kingdom"
Nimrod's kingdom stretched over a large area. The tower of Babel was built in the plain of Shinar, probably at Babylon, and Jewish tradition regards Nimrod as the architect.

AREA OF NIMROD'S KINGDOM

9 THE[18] SONS OF NOAH who came out of the ark were Shem, Ham and Japheth. (Ham was the father of Canaan.) [19]These were the three sons of Noah, and from them came the people who were scattered over the earth.

Despite God's salvation, humanity is still inclined towards sinfulness. Noah, blameless before the flood, gets drunk and sleeps uncovered. His son Ham sees his nakedness, which was forbidden, and so dishonours him.

[24]When Noah awoke from his wine and found out what his youngest son had done to him, [25]he said,
"*Cursed be Canaan!* The lowest of slaves will he be to his brothers."

Noah curses Ham's descendants but blesses Shem and Japheth and their descendants.

[29]Altogether, *Noah lived 950 years*, and then he died.

Nimrod supervises the building of a city

One of Ham's descendants, Nimrod, becomes very powerful.

10 [8]*Nimrod... grew to be a mighty warrior* on the earth. [9]He was a mighty hunter before the LORD... [10]*The first centres of his kingdom* were Babylon, Erech, Akkad and Calneh, in Shinar. [11]From that land he went to Assyria, where he built Nineveh...

11 [1]Now the whole world had one language and a common speech. [2]As men moved eastward, they found a plain in Shinar and settled there.

³They said to each other, "Come, let's make bricks and bake them thoroughly." They used brick instead of stone, and bitumen for mortar. ⁴Then they said, "*Come, let us build ourselves a city, with a tower* that reaches to the heavens, so that we may make a name for ourselves and not be scattered over the face of the whole earth."

⁵But the LORD came down to see the city and the tower that the men were building. ⁶The LORD said, "If as one people speaking the same language they have begun to do this, then nothing they plan to do will be impossible for them. ⁷Come, let us go down and confuse their language so they will not understand each other."

And suddenly the people of the town found that they could not understand a word of whatever anyone else was saying.

⁸So the LORD scattered them from there over all the earth, and they stopped building the city. ⁹That is why *it was called Babel* – because there the LORD confused the language of the whole world. From there the LORD scattered them over the face of the whole earth.

The people build a tower that reaches to the heavens

God confuses the people's language so that they can no longer understand each other

Everyone loses interest in the tower and they begin to leave

Mud bricks dry in the sun

UNDERSTANDING THE STORY

The message in this story is that "pride comes before a fall". The people of Babel want to be like God. The tower they build is for their own glory, and their vanity leads to their downfall. What they fear the most finally happens to them: confusion and separation.

❖

CHAPTER 11 VERSE 4
"Come, let us build ourselves a city, with a tower"
The tower of Babel was probably a Babylonian temple, known as a ziggurat. These multi-storied towers were sometimes 100m (300ft) high. They were square at the base and had a high stairway leading to a small shrine at the top. Some ziggurats had names, such as "The House of the Link Between Heaven and Earth".

ZIGGURAT
Ruins of ziggurats have been found at Babylon and Ur (modern-day Iraq).

❖

CHAPTER 11 VERSE 9
"It was called Babel"
To the Babylonians, "Babel" meant "Gate of heaven", but in Hebrew "babel" sounded like the word "confusion". The arrogant builders could no longer communicate and were condemned to babble.

BUILDING WITH BRICKS
In Israel, stone and mortar were the usual building materials, but these were not available in ancient Mesopotamia. The builders of the tower used mud bricks, which are still made in the Middle East today.

MAKING MUD BRICKS

ABRAHAM AND THE CHOSEN PEOPLE

The story of the Israelites begins with the story of Abraham, about two thousand years before the birth of Jesus. Ever since God had made a covenant with Noah, the people had become faithless and lapsed into worshipping other gods. So God called on a man named Abram to leave his country and set out for a new land.

God promised Abram a country especially set aside for him and his descendants. Even though Abram was childless and very old, God also promised, "I will make you into a great nation" (Genesis 11: 2). This was God's covenant, and to signify this, God changed Abram's name, which means "the father is exalted", to Abraham, meaning "father of multitudes". Abraham was to become the forefather of the Israelites.

ABRAHAM AND ISAAC
This medieval panel from an English church shows Abraham preparing to sacrifice his son Isaac. This sacrifice was a test of Abraham's obedience to God, and Isaac was not harmed.

THE STANDARD OF UR (C. 2600 BC)
The Standard of Ur was recovered from the royal graves at Ur. It is a double-sided mosaic of shell and lapis lazuli. This detail shows a man playing the lyre at a victory banquet.

Mesopotamia – the land of Abraham's birth

Abraham was born in Ur, capital of the ancient kingdom of Sumer in southern Mesopotamia. The city of Ur is now identified with the ancient site of Ur on the River Euphrates, near Basra in modern Iraq.

Mesopotamia, Greek for "land between the two rivers", was the area between the Tigris and Euphrates rivers. The Sumerians settled in southern Mesopotamia c. 3300 BC. It was an exceptionally fertile land, and a prosperous agricultural economy developed. Farming villages around the rivers gradually grew into cities such as Ur and Babylon, inhabited by thousands of people. Trade flourished with countries as far away as India, and a rich civilization emerged.

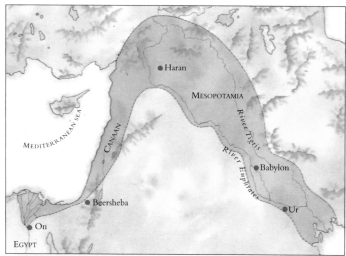

FROM UR TO EGYPT
Ur lay in the Fertile Crescent, an area stretching from southern Mesopotamia around to northern Egypt. Abraham's family settled in Haran. When Abraham left for Canaan, he eventually stayed at Beersheba. His great grandson, Joseph, lived in Egypt, where he married the daughter of On's chief priest.

Mesopotamian culture

Mesopotamia saw the rise of one of the earliest civilizations. The wheel, units of weights and measures, and writing all originated in Mesopotamia. Sumerian scribes later developed this writing into cuneiform ("wedge-shaped") script. They used wedge-shaped styli to engrave wet clay tablets, which were then baked. Archeologists have unearthed thousands of these clay tablets. They record such things as the annals of kings, literature, religious writings, dictionaries, and works of science.

CUNEIFORM WRITING
The text on this terracotta vase tells of a border dispute between cities.

The gods of Sumer

The Sumerians worshipped hundreds of gods, and each city was under the protection of its own deity. One of the most popular was the moon god Sin, whose centre of worship was Ur. The cult of Sin extended all over Mesopotamia and spread into Canaan and as far as Egypt.

Abraham reaches Haran

In c. 2000 BC, wave upon wave of invading tribes descended on Ur, eventually conquering the city. Terah, Abraham's father, may have set out for Canaan with his family to escape these attacks. They probably followed one of the trade routes skirting the desert. However, when they reached Haran in northern Mesopotamia, they settled there. Haran was a cult centre for moon worship, and it is suggested that Terah might have dealt in religious figurines.

Canaan – the Promised Land

God made a covenant with Abraham, promising a new country for him and his descendants. So Abraham left Haran and went to Canaan. The name refers both to the land of Canaan and to the descendants of Noah's grandson, Canaan.

"Canaan" possibly means "land of purple". Phoenicia, a region along Canaan's northern coast, has the same meaning in Greek. This was because Canaan was a major producer of purple dye, a luxury product that was highly prized by royalty. Canaan's coastal ports and its position between Egypt and Asia made it a nation of traders, and the name "Canaanite" came to mean "merchant".

Canaanite culture

Archeological findings at sites such as Ugarit (Ras Shamra on Syria's Mediterranean coast), Megiddo, and Jerusalem reveal that Canaan had a highly refined civilization in Abraham's time. Its greatest legacy was a system of writing that forms the basis of our modern alphabet. Canaan was divided into walled city-states, each ruled by a king. These kingdoms often fought against each other. Canaan's most ancient city was Jericho, which was first inhabited in about 8000 BC. Outside the walled cities were scattered villages and nomadic herdsmen, such as Abraham. His people lived in tents, because they had to keep moving in search of new grazing land for their flocks.

IVORY PLAQUE FROM MEGIDDO
This decorative plaque is a rare depiction of Canaanite courtly life. The king is shown riding victorious in his chariot and sitting on his throne at a celebratory feast.

THE PATRIARCHS

The origin of the Israelites is traced back to Adam through certain men called Patriarchs. The ten Patriarchs from Adam to Noah are known as the antediluvian Patriarchs, because they precede the Flood. Those after Noah are known as the postdiluvian Patriarchs. However, the term Patriarch refers more specifically to Abraham and his descendants Isaac, Jacob, and Joseph.

The family of Abraham

Abraham's descendants would eventually multiply into the twelve tribes of Israel through Isaac, his son by Sarah.

Abraham's eldest son was Ishmael, by Hagar, Sarah's Egyptian maid. Ishmael was also the forefather of twelve tribes (Genesis 17: 20), known collectively as the Ishmaelites.

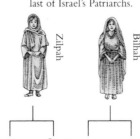

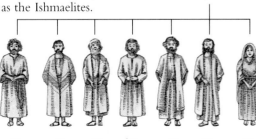

ABRAHAM
God made a covenant with Abraham, who is considered the first Patriarch because the nation of Israel descended from him.

ISAAC
God fulfilled his covenant by blessing the aged Abraham and Sarah with a son, Isaac, who became the next Patriarch.

JACOB
Although Esau was Isaac's elder son, God chose to renew his covenant with Jacob, Esau's younger brother.

JOSEPH
Through Jacob's son Joseph, the Israelites prospered and grew in Egypt. Joseph was the last of Israel's Patriarchs.

Family tree figures labelled: Sarah, ABRAHAM, Hagar; ISAAC, Rebekah, Laban, Ishmael; Esau, JACOB, Leah, Rachel, Zilpah, Bilhah; Reuben, Simeon, Levi, Judah, Issachar, Zebulun, Dinah, JOSEPH, Benjamin, Gad, Asher, Dan, Naphtali.

The Patriarchs in Egypt

Egypt's abundant economy made it a place of refuge during times of famine.

Abraham lived there during the Middle Kingdom (2040–1750 BC), a time when Egypt was experiencing its second great cultural age.

Joseph and his family settled in Egypt during the Second Intermediate period (1750–1650 BC), which saw a decline of royal authority and the rise to power of foreign rulers, the Hyksos. These Pharaohs adopted the customs and the culture of Egypt.

OSIRIS MUMMY
This corn-stuffed "mummy" is modelled on Osiris, a fertility god and ruler of the dead. During the Middle Kingdom, the cult of Osiris grew rapidly in popularity.

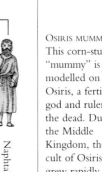

GENESIS 11–12

ABRAM AND GOD'S CALL

❖

CHAPTER 11 VERSE 31
"They set out from Ur"

In 1922, the probable site of Ur was discovered in present-day Iraq. The excavated ruins and artefacts reveal a highly sophisticated culture. The city flourished from 3000 to 1900 BC, when it was attacked and destroyed.

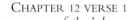

UR TREASURES
These items of adornment, made from gold, lapis lazuli, and carnelian, were discovered in Ur's royal burial pits.

11 ᵀ ERAH[31] TOOK HIS SON ABRAM, his grandson Lot son of Haran, and his daughter-in-law Sarai... and together *they set out from Ur* of the Chaldeans to go to Canaan. But when they came to Haran, they settled there. ³²Terah lived 205 years, and he died in Haran.

12 ¹The LORD had said to Abram, "*Leave your country, your people and your father's household* and go to the land I will show you. ²*I will* make you into a great nation and I will bless you; I will make your name great, and you will be a blessing. ³I will bless those who bless you, and whoever curses you I will curse; and all peoples on earth will be blessed through you."

Abram answers God's call and leads his people into Canaan

❖

CHAPTER 12 VERSE 1
"Leave your... father's household"

The book of Joshua records that "Terah lived beyond the Euphrates and worshipped other gods" (24: 2). Ur was an important centre of worship of the Mesopotamian moon god Sin. When Abram crossed the Euphrates into Canaan, he turned his back on the gods of his father and placed his trust in God.

MESOPOTAMIAN BOUNDARY STONE
This stone shows gods invoked to protect the land. The god Sin is centre top.

⁴So Abram left, as the LORD had told him... Abram was seventy-five years old when he set out from Haran. ⁵He took his wife Sarai, his nephew Lot, all the possessions they had accumulated and the people they had acquired in Haran, and they set out for the land of Canaan, and they arrived there.

⁶Abram travelled through the land as far as the site of *the great tree of Moreh* at Shechem. At that time the Canaanites were in the land. ⁷The LORD appeared to Abram and said, "To your offspring I will give this land." So he built an altar there to the LORD, who had appeared to him.

⁸From there he went on towards the hills east of Bethel and pitched his tent, with Bethel on the west and Ai on the east. There he built an altar to the LORD and called on the name of the LORD. ⁹Then Abram set out and continued towards the Negev.

¹⁰Now there was a famine in the land, and Abram went down to Egypt to live there for a while because the famine was severe.

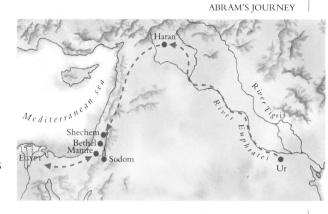

ABRAM'S JOURNEY

¹¹As he was about to enter Egypt, he said to his wife Sarai, "I know what a beautiful woman you are. ¹²When the Egyptians see you, they will say, 'This is his wife.' Then they will kill me but will let you live. ¹³Say you are my sister, so that I will be treated well for your sake and my life will be spared because of you."

¹⁴When Abram came to Egypt, the Egyptians saw that she was a very beautiful woman. ¹⁵And when Pharaoh's officials saw her, they praised her to Pharaoh, and she was taken into his palace. ¹⁶He treated Abram well for her sake, and Abram acquired sheep and cattle... donkeys, menservants and maidservants, and camels.

¹⁷But the LORD inflicted serious diseases on Pharaoh and his household because of Abram's wife Sarai. ¹⁸So Pharaoh summoned Abram, "What have you done to me?" he said. "Why didn't you tell me she was your wife? ¹⁹Why did you say, '*She is my sister*,' so that I took her to be my wife? Now then, here is your wife. *Take her and go!*"

Abram builds an altar to God under the great tree of Moreh

Abram's people packed their possessions and travelled back to Canaan. They lived together peacefully until the grazing land became scarce. Then Abram and his nephew Lot agreed to part company. Lot took his people and settled at Sodom.

When they arrive in Egypt, Abram tells Sarai to say she is his sister

Sarai

Lot

Pharaoh takes Sarai as his wife and makes Abram a wealthy man

God sends a plague on Pharaoh's household

Pharaoh discovers that he is being punished because Sarai is Abram's wife. He tells Abram to take everything and leave Egypt

Abram's people pack up their belongings and go

CHAPTER 12 VERSE 2
"I will"
The word "will" is repeated seven times in God's promise to Abram. The number signifies the perfection of God's choice. Through Abram, God will renew his covenant with humankind.

CHAPTER 12 VERSE 6
"The great tree of Moreh"
It is likely that this tree was an oak, which could grow to a height of 300m (1,000ft). In Bible times, oak forests were a feature of Palestine's landscape. Canaanites worshipped Baal and other fertility gods under great oaks. In the "Promised Land" of his descendants, Abram builds an altar to God.

CHAPTER 12 VERSE 19
"She is my sister"
Abram did not lie to the pharaoh. Abram's wife was also his half-sister (Genesis 20: 12). If the pharaoh had known Sarai was married to Abram, he would have killed Abram before taking her into his harem.

CHAPTER 12 VERSE 19
"Take her and go!"
The pattern of Abram's refuge in Egypt and subsequent expulsion will be repeated generations later. His descendants, the Israelites, enter Egypt to escape a famine during the time of Joseph and then leave with Moses during the Exodus.

UNDERSTANDING THE STORY
God's original blessing on humanity, which was renewed through Noah, now passes to Abram. He trusts completely in God's promise, despite the obstacles he faces. The self-reliant people of Babel failed to achieve greatness. By relying on God, Abram will succeed. He will become the "father of Israel".

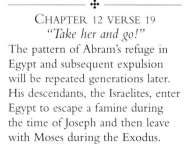

GENESIS 15–16

THE PROMISE OF A SON

15

T HE[1] WORD OF THE LORD came to Abram *in a vision*: "Do not be afraid, Abram. I am your shield, your very great reward." [2]But Abram said, "O Sovereign LORD, what can you give me since I remain childless and the one who will inherit my estate is Eliezer of Damascus?" [3]And Abram said, "You have given me no children; so *a servant in my household will be my heir.*"

[4]Then the word of the LORD came to him: "This man will not be your heir, but a son coming from your own body will be your heir." [5]He took him outside and said, "Look up at the heavens and count the stars – if indeed you can count them." Then he said to him, "So shall your offspring be."

Hagar, Sarai's Egyptian servant

Sarai wants to build a family through Hagar

Abram agrees to take Hagar as his wife

God says Abram's descendants will be as countless as the stars

[6]*Abram believed the LORD,* and he credited it to him as righteousness...
[13]Then the LORD said to him, "Know for certain that your descendants will be strangers in a country not their own, and they will be enslaved and ill-treated four hundred years. [14]But I will punish the nation they serve as slaves, and afterwards they will come out with great possessions. [15]You, however, will go to your fathers in peace and be buried at a good old age..."

16 [1]Now Sarai, Abram's wife, had borne him no children. But she had an Egyptian maidservant named Hagar; [2]so she said to Abram, "The LORD has *kept me from having children.* Go, sleep with my maidservant; perhaps *I can build a family through her.*"

Abram agreed to what Sarai said. [3]So after Abram had been living in Canaan ten years, Sarai his wife took her Egyptian maidservant Hagar and gave her to her husband to be his wife. [4]He slept with Hagar, and she conceived.

CHAPTER 15 VERSE 1
"In a vision"
A vision is a supernatural revelation. It differs from a dream in that the person is awake rather than asleep.

CHAPTER 15 VERSE 3
"A servant... will be my heir"
In ancient Middle-Eastern cultures, a wealthy, childless man could adopt one of his male servants to be his heir. This practice is recorded in texts written on clay tablets dating from 2500 to 1500 BC, uncovered at Nuzi on the Tigris River, near Kirkuk in modern Iraq.

THE NUZI TABLETS
About 20,000 tablets were found at Nuzi, an ancient city of Mesopotamia. The tablets disclose a sophisticated culture and include detailed records of public and private contracts, such as hire-purchase agreements.

CHAPTER 15 VERSE 6
"Abram believed the LORD"
This is the first specific mention of faith in the Bible. Abram relies on God to fulfil his promise to him.

CHAPTER 16 VERSE 2
"Kept me from having children"
Sarai does not share Abram's trust. She blames God for her barrenness.

CHAPTER 16 VERSE 2
"I can build a family through her"
Sarai's proposal was an ancient custom, confirmed by the Nuzi texts and the Code of Hammurabi. The chief wife had authority over children born to a slave-wife.

When she knew she was pregnant, she began to despise her mistress. [5]Then Sarai said to Abram, "You are responsible for the wrong I am suffering. I put my servant in your arms, and now that she knows she is pregnant, she despises me. May the LORD judge between you and me."

[6]"Your servant is in your hands," Abram said. "Do with her whatever you think best." Then Sarai ill-treated Hagar; so she fled from her.

[7]The angel of the LORD found Hagar near a spring in the desert; it was the spring that is beside *the road to Shur*. [8]And he said, "Hagar, servant of Sarai, where have you come from, and where are you going?"

"I'm running away from my mistress Sarai," she answered.

[9]Then the angel of the LORD told her, "Go back to your mistress and submit to her." [10]The angel added, "*I will so increase your descendants* that they will be too numerous to count."

THE CODE OF HAMMURABI
Here, King Hammurabi of Babylon (1792–1750 BC) receives his Code from the Babylonian god of justice. The Code is a complex system of law and is inscribed on the lower part of the stele. It is governed by the principle that the strong should not injure the weak.

✛

CHAPTER 16 VERSE 7
"The road to Shur"
The exact location of Shur is not known. The name means "wall" and refers to the forts on Egypt's eastern border. Hagar is fleeing to Egypt, her country of birth.

✛

CHAPTER 16 VERSE 10
"I will so increase your descendants"
Hagar's son Ishmael had twelve sons. They became tribal rulers of a nomadic people, known as the Ishmaelites.

✛

CHAPTER 16 VERSE 15
"Abram gave the name Ishmael to the son"
Ishmael means "God hears". Abram acknowledges the words that the angel spoke to Hagar: "The LORD has heard of your misery" (16: 11).

Sarai complains to Abram about Hagar's conceit

Hagar flees from Sarai's ill-treatment

An angel tells Hagar to return. He says she will have a son called Ishmael

Hagar rests at a spring in the desert

[11]The angel of the LORD also said to her: "You are now with child and you will have a son. You shall name him Ishmael, for the LORD has heard of your misery..."

[13]She gave this name to the LORD who spoke to her: "You are the God who sees me," for she said, "I have now seen the One who sees me." [14]That is why the well was called Beer Lahai Roi; it is still there, between Kadesh and Bered.

[15]So Hagar bore Abram a son, and *Abram gave the name Ishmael to the son* she had borne. [16]Abram was eighty-six years old.

UNDERSTANDING THE STORY

Unlike Abram, who waits patiently for God to fulfil his promise, Sarai's doubt leads to impatience. Abram is content to rely on God, but Sarai decides to take matters into her own hands. The resulting disruption and strife indicate that Sarai's scheme is not God's will and that Ishmael is not Abram's promised son.

DESCENDANTS OF ISHMAEL
Moslem Arabs claim to be descendants of Abram, through his son Ishmael.

GENESIS 17–18

ABRAHAM AND GOD'S COVENANT

CHAPTER 17 VERSE 2
"My covenant"
In Abram's time, relations between rulers and their subject peoples were governed by treaties. Abram and his descendants are subject to God's authority. It is God's covenant, because he initiates and establishes the terms of their agreement.

CHAPTER 17 VERSE 5
"Your name will be Abraham"
Abram (exalted father) becomes Abraham (father of a multitude of nations). The change of name is a confirmation of Abraham's role. He will be the forefather of all who have faith in God.

CHAPTER 17 VERSE 10
"Every male among you shall be circumcised"
God orders the removal of each male's foreskin. This is to serve as a physical reminder of commitment to God's covenant.

Abraham rushes out to greet three strangers and offers them a meal

MODERN-DAY NOMADS
Bedouins live a similar life to Abraham and his people. A portable home is essential because they have to move from place to place in search of suitable grazing land for their herds. Bedouin tents are made from tough goat's-hair cloth, which can withstand extremes of temperature and torrential rains.

BEDOUINS MAKING BREAD IN JORDAN

17 WHEN[1] ABRAM WAS ninety-nine years old, the LORD appeared to him and said, "I am God Almighty; walk before me and be blameless. [2]I will confirm *my covenant* between me and you and will greatly increase your numbers."

[3]Abram fell face down, and God said to him, [4]"As for me, this is my covenant with you: You will be the father of many nations. [5]No longer will you be called Abram; *your name will be Abraham*, for I have made you a father of many nations."

And God made a promise to Abraham to give him and his descendants the land of Canaan and to be their everlasting Lord. God then told Abraham what he must do to fulfil his part of the agreement:

Abraham hears God's voice and falls to the ground

Abraham does not know that he is talking to the Lord and two angels

[10]*Every male among you shall be circumcised.* [11]You are to undergo circumcision, and it will be the sign of the covenant between me and you. [12]For the generations to come every male among you who is eight days old must be circumcised, including those born in your household or bought with money from a foreigner – those who are not your offspring... [13]My covenant in your flesh is to be an everlasting covenant. [14]Any uncircumcised male, who has not been circumcised in the flesh... will be cut off from his people; he has broken my covenant."

[15]God also said to Abraham, "As for Sarai your wife, you are no longer to call her Sarai; her name will be Sarah. [16]I will bless her and will surely give you a son by her... she will be the mother of nations; kings of peoples will come from her."

[17]Abraham fell face down; *he laughed* and said... "Will a son be born to a man a hundred years old? Will Sarah bear a child at the age of ninety?... [18]If only Ishmael might live under your blessing!"

[19]Then God said, "Yes, but your wife Sarah will bear you a son,

and you will call him Isaac. I will establish my covenant with him as an everlasting covenant for his descendants after him. ²⁰And as for Ishmael, I have heard you: I will surely bless him... ²¹But my covenant I will establish with Isaac..." ²²When he had finished speaking with Abraham, God went up from him. ²³On that very day Abraham took his son Ishmael and... every male in his household, and circumcised them as God told him. ²⁴Abraham was ninety-nine years old when he was circumcised, ²⁵and his son *Ishmael was thirteen...*

18   ¹The LORD appeared to Abraham near the great trees of Mamre while he was sitting at the entrance to his tent in the heat of the day. ²Abraham looked up and saw three men... He hurried... to meet them and bowed low... ³He said, "If I have found favour in your eyes, my Lord, do not pass your servant by... ⁵Let me get you something to eat."

Abraham and Sarah killed their best calf and prepared a meal with bread, curds, and milk. God again told Abraham that his wife would have a son. Sarah overheard their conversation from the entrance of the tent.

¹²Sarah laughed to herself as she thought, "After I am worn out and my master is old, will I now have this pleasure?" ¹³Then the LORD said to Abraham, "Why did Sarah laugh..? ¹⁴Is anything too hard for the LORD?..." ¹⁵Sarah was afraid, so she lied and said, "I did not laugh."

UNDERSTANDING THE STORY

God's original promise to Abram is confirmed in a formal agreement. The new covenant includes obligations on both sides. Both Abram and Sarai are given new names to signify their status as forebears of God's chosen people. Ishmael will be blessed, but Isaac will inherit God's covenant.

CHAPTER 17 VERSE 17
"He laughed"
The Hebrew verb is a pun on the name "Isaac", which means "he laughs". Isaac's birth will change his parents' laughter of disbelief into laughter of delight.

CEREMONY OF CIRCUMCISION
Before circumcision, Turkish boys traditionally ride on a white horse.

CHAPTER 17 VERSE 25
"Ishmael was thirteen"
In some Middle-Eastern cultures, boys are circumcised at puberty, symbolizing the passage from child to man. Moslem Arabs are circumcised at thirteen, like Ishmael, from whom they are traditionally descended.

Sarah hears the Lord say that she will soon bear Abraham a son

Abraham shows his visitors great hospitality

Sarah laughs at the idea of becoming a mother at the age of ninety

GENESIS 18–19

THE DESTRUCTION OF SODOM

CHAPTER 18 VERSE 25
"Far be it from you"
The covenant between God and Abraham opens the way to a more intimate relationship. Abraham uses this friendship to plead for Sodom.

Sodom is known for its wickedness

Abraham pleads with the Lord to spare the righteous in Sodom

Two angels leave for Sodom. They will tell the Lord what they find there

SODOM AND GOMORRAH
These cities were probably located on the south-eastern shore of the Dead Sea. This dry, sulphurous area was once fertile and well-populated, and archeologists have discovered ruins of five cities from the period.

THE DEAD SEA
A view facing east across the sea towards the traditional site of Sodom

DEAD SEA SALT
The Dead Sea lies below sea level at the lowest point on earth. No outlet and high evaporation have produced a salt content four times higher than other seas, which means nothing can live in it. The salt forms crystal structures, which can be seen in the water and along the shore.

18 W**HEN**[16] THE MEN got up to leave, they looked down towards Sodom, and Abraham walked along with them to see them on their way... [20]Then the L**ORD** said, "The outcry against Sodom and Gomorrah is so great and their sin so grievous [21]that I will go down and see if what they have done is as bad as the outcry..."

[22]The men turned away and went towards Sodom, but Abraham remained standing before the L**ORD**. [23]Then Abraham approached him and said: "Will you sweep away the righteous with the wicked? [24]What if there are fifty righteous people in the city?... [25]*Far be it from you* to do such a thing... Will not the Judge of all the earth do right?"

[26]The L**ORD** said, "If I find fifty righteous people in the city of Sodom, I will spare the whole place for their sake."

Abraham pleaded and bargained with the Lord until the number was down to ten.

19 [1]The two angels arrived at Sodom in the evening, and Lot was sitting in the gateway of the city. When he saw them, he got up to meet them and bowed down with his face to the ground. [2]"My lords," he said, "please turn aside to your servant's house. You can wash your feet and spend the night and then go on your way early in the morning."

Lot took his guests home and prepared a meal for them. Later that evening, every man in the city came to his house.

The angels arrive at Sodom in the evening. Lot is at the city gates

Lot greets the strangers and invites them to stay with him

The Sodomites told Lot to hand over his guests for their pleasure. Lot tried to reason with them, but they threatened Lot and tried to break down the door.

¹⁰But the men inside reached out and pulled Lot back into the house and shut the door. ¹¹Then they struck the men who were at the door of the house, young and old, with blindness.

The two angels told Lot that the city would be destroyed because of the wickedness of the Sodomites. They urged Lot and his family to flee to the mountains, warning them that they must not look back at Sodom.

²⁴Then the LORD rained down burning sulphur on Sodom and Gomorrah... ²⁶But Lot's wife looked back, and *she became a pillar of salt.*
²⁷Early the next morning Abraham... ²⁸looked down towards Sodom and Gomorrah... and he saw dense smoke rising from the land, like smoke from a furnace. ²⁹So when God destroyed the cities of the plain, he remembered Abraham, and *he brought Lot out of the catastrophe.*

UNDERSTANDING THE STORY

The destruction of Sodom and the rescue of Lot demonstrate the justice of God's judgement. God punishes the evil and saves the righteous. The fate of Lot's wife will serve as a reminder to Abraham and his descendants that it is foolish to disobey the word of God.

That night the men of Sodom gather outside Lot's home, demanding that he hand over his guests to them

Lot goes outside to plead with the angry crowd

CHAPTER 19 VERSE 26
"She became a pillar of salt"
Lot's wife ignored the angel's command and looked back at the city. Her disobedience meant that she perished with the Sodomites.

LOT'S WIFE
This salt rock formation on Mount Sodom is known as "Lot's wife".

Lot's wife looks back and turns into a pillar of salt

Burning sulphur rains down on Sodom

Lot and his family run for their lives

The angels pull Lot back inside the house, then strike the crowd with blindness

The angels tell Lot to take his family and flee from the town, warning that they must not look back

CHAPTER 19 VERSE 29
"He brought Lot out of the catastrophe"
Lot did not know that the two men who walked into Sodom were divine beings. He risked his own life to protect complete strangers. Lot's actions brought him salvation.

MIDDLE-EASTERN HOSPITALITY
In ancient times, it was the practice to offer visitors hospitality. The nomadic desert tribes viewed this as a necessity, because a traveller's life might depend upon a hospitable reception. The Bedouin people continue this custom today, greeting visitors with the words: "You are among your family".

GENESIS 21–22

ABRAHAM'S TEST

Abraham and Sarah hold a feast to celebrate Isaac's weaning

CHAPTER 21
VERSE 8
"On the day Isaac was weaned"
In Abraham's time, infant mortality was common. It was customary to celebrate the dangerous passage from infancy to childhood when the child was two or three years old.

CHAPTER 21 VERSE 9
"Mocking"
The Bible does not explain how Ishmael mocked Isaac, but the New Testament has interpreted Ishmael's actions as persecution: "The son born in the ordinary way persecuted the son born by the power of the Spirit" (Galatians 4: 29).

WATERSKIN
Waterskins like the one that Ishmael took into the desert are still used today. These Egyptian women are preparing goatskins to be used to carry water.

CHAPTER 22 VERSE 2
"Your only son"
Isaac was the only son of promise. In the New Testament, Abraham's willingness to sacrifice Isaac can be compared to God's willingness to sacrifice his only Son (John 3: 16).

21 NOW[1] THE LORD WAS GRACIOUS to Sarah as he had said... ²Sarah became pregnant and bore a son to Abraham in his old age, at the very time God had promised him. ³Abraham gave the name Isaac to the son Sarah bore him. ⁴When his son Isaac was eight days old, Abraham circumcised him, as God commanded him. ⁵Abraham was a hundred years old when his son Isaac was born to him...

⁸*On the day Isaac was weaned* Abraham held a great feast. ⁹But Sarah saw that the son whom Hagar... had borne to Abraham was *mocking,* ¹⁰and she said to Abraham, "Get rid of that slave woman and her son for [he] will never share in the inheritance with my son Isaac."

Abraham loved Ishmael and did not want to send him away. But God told him to listen to Sarah and promised to protect Hagar and Ishmael. So Abraham gave them food and a waterskin, and they wandered in the desert. When the water ran out and they were close to death, God saved them by providing a well. Ishmael lived in the desert and married an Egyptian.

Abraham sends Ishmael away because he mocked Isaac

In the desert, Hagar and Ishmael run out of water. God saves them by providing a well

22 ¹Some time later God tested Abraham. He said to him... ²"Take your son, *your only son,* Isaac, whom you love, and go to *the region of Moriah.* Sacrifice him there as a burnt offering on one of the mountains I will tell you about."

God tells Abraham he must offer Isaac as a sacrifice

The servants wait at the bottom

Isaac takes the wood for the burnt offering

Abraham and Isaac climb the mountain together

Abraham, Isaac, and two servants travel to Mount Moriah

Early the next morning, Abraham left with his son Isaac and two servants. He took with him a knife and wood for the burnt offering.

⁵He said to his servants, "Stay here with the donkey while I and the boy go over there. We will worship and then *we will come back to you."*...
⁹When they reached the place God had told him about, Abraham built an altar there and arranged the wood on it. He bound his son Isaac and laid him on the altar, on top of the wood. ¹⁰Then he reached out his hand and took the knife to slay his son. ¹¹But the angel of the LORD called out to him from heaven, "Abraham! Abraham!...¹²Do not lay a hand on the boy," he said. "Do not do anything to him. Now I know that you fear God, because you have not withheld from me your son, your only son."

An angel stops Abraham from killing Isaac

Abraham binds Isaac and lays him on the altar

A ram caught in a thicket is offered as a sacrifice in place of Isaac

¹³Abraham looked up and there in a thicket he saw a ram caught by its horns. He went over and took the ram and sacrificed it as a burnt offering instead of his son. ¹⁴So Abraham called that place The LORD Will Provide. And to this day it is said, "On the mountain of the LORD it will be provided."...
¹⁹Then Abraham returned to his servants, and they set off together for Beersheba. And *Abraham stayed in Beersheba.*

UNDERSTANDING THE STORY

Abraham's faith and hope support him during the agonizing journey to Moriah. As the story unveils, it becomes clear that God does not want Abraham to kill Isaac, but he puts his commitment to the ultimate test. Abraham's willingness to sacrifice the son that he loves is proof that he places God above everything.

CHAPTER 22 VERSE 2
"The region of Moriah"
"Moriah" is Hebrew for "the Lord will provide". The name of the place where Isaac was to die gives a clue to God's real intention. If Abraham puts his faith in God, then God will provide an answer to the dilemma. Mount Moriah is traditionally identified as the hill in Jerusalem where Solomon built the Temple.

DOME OF THE ROCK
In the 7th century AD, the Moslems conquered Jerusalem and built a mosque where the Temple once stood.

CHAPTER 22 VERSE 5
"We will come back to you"
Abraham obeys God's call to sacrifice Isaac. Yet he also believes God's promise that, through Isaac, he will be the "father of many nations". He does not question this contradiction. His faith leads him to believe God will return Isaac to him.

CHAPTER 22 VERSE 19
"Abraham stayed in Beersheba"
The town was founded on the spot where Abraham dug a well. Beersheba means "well of seven". Abraham gave seven lambs to the local king in order to settle a dispute over the ownership of the well (Genesis 21: 30).

BEERSHEBA
Aerial view of the ancient city

GENESIS 24–25

ISAAC AND REBEKAH

24

A BRAHAM[1] WAS NOW OLD... and the LORD had blessed him in every way. [2]He said to the chief servant in his household, the one in charge of all that he had, *"Put your hand under my thigh.* [3]I want you to swear by the LORD, the God of heaven and the God of earth, that you will not get a wife for my son from the daughters of the Canaanites, among whom I am living, [4]but will go to my country and my own relatives and get a wife for my son Isaac...

[6]"Make sure that you do not take my son back there... [7]The LORD... will send his angel before you so that you can get a wife for my son from there..." [9]So the servant put his hand under the thigh of his master and swore an oath to him concerning this matter.

CHAPTER 24 VERSE 2
"Put your hand under my thigh"
The loins were considered the source of procreative power. To swear an oath in this way made it solemn and binding. The custom was particularly appropriate in this case, because the oath will fulfil God's promise to Abraham that his line would descend through Isaac.

CHAPTER 24 VERSE 10
"All kinds of good things"
In Abraham's time, a dowry was a gift that the bridegroom gave to the bride's father as compensation for losing his daughter. It was not a payment, but it showed how much she was valued. The bride also received a dowry, from her father. This remained her property, and so she entered the marriage with independent means.

DOWRY BAG
This Afghan dowry bag is hung on the camel that takes a bride to her new home.

THE CAMEL
Domesticated since *c.* 2500 BC, the camel is uniquely suited to desert life. Its three separate stomachs can hold a total of 70 litres (15 gallons) of water, and fat is stored in its hump for use when food is scarce.

CAMEL CARAVAN IN THE SAHARA
Each rider leads a line of camels, which are tied one behind another.

Abraham sends his trusted servant back to Mesopotamia to find a wife for his son Isaac

The servant waits at a well outside a town and asks God to help him find a suitable bride

The camels are loaded with gifts from Abraham

Rebekah is the answer to his prayer

[10]Then the servant took ten of his master's camels and left, taking with him *all kinds of good things* from his master. *He set out for Aram Naharaim* and made his way to the town of Nahor. [11]He made the camels kneel down near the well outside the town; it was towards evening, the time the women go out to draw water.

[12]Then he prayed, "O LORD, God of my master Abraham, give me success today... [13]See, I am standing beside this spring, and the daughters of the townspeople are coming to draw water. [14]May it be that when I say to a girl, 'Please let down your jar that I may have a drink,' and she says, 'Drink, and I'll water your camels too' – let her be the one you have chosen for your servant Isaac..."

¹⁵Before he had finished praying, Rebekah came out with her jar on her shoulder. She was the daughter of Bethuel son of Milcah, who was the wife of Abraham's brother Nahor. ¹⁶The girl was very beautiful.

Rebekah gave the servant and the camels some water, and so the servant's prayer was answered. He gave Rebekah and Bethuel's household the precious gifts Abraham had sent and told them the purpose of his journey. Rebekah agreed to go with him to marry Isaac and left the next day with her maids.

25 Isaac²⁰ was forty years old when he married Rebekah... ²¹Isaac prayed to the LORD on behalf of his wife, because she was barren. The LORD answered his prayer, and his wife Rebekah became pregnant. ²²The babies jostled each other within her, and she said, "Why is this happening to me?" So she went to enquire of the LORD.

²³The LORD said to her, "Two nations are in your womb, and two peoples from within you will be separated; one people will be stronger than the other, and *the older will serve the younger.*"

²⁴When the time came for her to give birth, there were twin boys in her womb. ²⁵The first to come out was red, and his whole body was like a hairy garment; so they named him Esau. ²⁶After this, his brother came out, with his hand grasping Esau's heel; so he was named Jacob. Isaac was sixty years old when Rebekah gave birth to them.

Isaac's prayer for children is answered when Rebekah has twin boys

The first born has red hair and is named Esau

The second born is named Jacob. He is Rebekah's favourite

²⁷The boys grew up, and Esau became a skilful hunter, a man of the open country, while Jacob was a quiet man, staying among the tents. ²⁸Isaac, who had a taste for wild game, loved Esau, but Rebekah loved Jacob.

UNDERSTANDING THE STORY

When Abraham sends his servant to find a wife for Isaac, he trusts in God to control the outcome. The servant relies on God to help him, and he meets Rebekah, who is the perfect choice in every way. Rebekah is willing to leave everything to marry a stranger in a distant land. These are all acts of faith.

CHAPTER 24 VERSE 10
"He set out for Aram Naharaim" "Aram Naharaim" means "Aram of the two rivers". It was situated between the Euphrates and Tigris rivers in northern Mesopotamia.

CARRYING CONTAINERS
These women live in a remote village in Iran. Like Rebekah, they carry things on their heads or shoulders. This makes a load easier to manage.

CHAPTER 25 VERSE 23
"The older will serve the younger" The hostility between Jacob and Esau began in the womb. Usually, a younger brother would serve the eldest son, who would also inherit a double share of the father's estate.

ESAU AND JACOB
"Esau" means "red and shaggy", which describes his appearance. The name "Jacob" means "supplanter".

THE DEATH OF ABRAHAM
Sarah lived to be 127 but died before Isaac married. Abraham had six more children with his concubine Keturah. He was 175 when he died, and he was buried beside Sarah in a cave he had bought as a family tomb (Genesis 25: 1–10).

CAVE OF ABRAHAM
A traditional site of the cave is in Hebron, beneath the Mosque of Abraham, a Moslem shrine.

GENESIS 25–27

JACOB AND ESAU

25 **O**NCE[29] WHEN JACOB was cooking... Esau came in from the open country, famished. [30]He said to Jacob, "Quick, let me have some of that red stew!.. (That is why *he was also called Edom*.) [31]Jacob replied, "First *sell me your birthright*."...

[32]"I am about to die," Esau said. "What good is the birthright to me?"

[33]But Jacob said, "Swear to me first." So he swore an oath, selling his birthright to Jacob. [34]Then Jacob gave Esau some bread and some lentil stew... *So Esau despised his birthright*...

27 When[1] Isaac was old and his eyes were so weak that he could no longer see, he called for Esau his older son and said to him...

[2]"I am now an old man and don't know the day of my death. [3]Now then, get your weapons – your quiver and bow – and go out in the open country to hunt some wild game for me. [4]Prepare me the kind of tasty food I like and bring it to me to eat, so that I may give you *my blessing before I die.*"

Rebekah overheard what Isaac had said and, while Esau was away, prepared a meal with two goats that Jacob brought her. Jacob put on his brother's best clothes and Rebekah covered his hands with the goatskins. When he went to his father with the food, Jacob asked him which son he was.

[19]"I am Esau your firstborn. I have done as you told me. Please sit up and eat some of my game so that you may give me your blessing."

CHAPTER 25 VERSE 30
"He was also called Edom"
"Edom" is the Hebrew word for "red". This name recalls the description of Esau at his birth: "The first to come out was red" (Genesis 25: 25). God told Rebekah that two nations would be born from her sons. The tribe descended from Esau was called the Edomites.

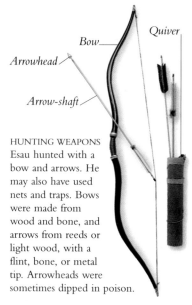

Bow

Quiver

Arrowhead

Arrow-shaft

HUNTING WEAPONS
Esau hunted with a bow and arrows. He may also have used nets and traps. Bows were made from wood and bone, and arrows from reeds or light wood, with a flint, bone, or metal tip. Arrowheads were sometimes dipped in poison.

CHAPTER 25 VERSE 31
"Sell me your birthright"
It was customary for the eldest son to inherit most of the family's estate on the death of his father. Although a twin, Esau was considered the elder son because he was born first.

CHAPTER 25 VERSE 34
"So Esau despised his birthright"
As Isaac's eldest son, Esau would also inherit the covenant God made with Abraham. By rejecting his birthright for a bowl of stew, he showed that he did not value God's covenant. He was no longer worthy of his inheritance.

Esau is famished. He agrees to give his birthright to Jacob in return for some stew

Isaac is old and his eyes are weak. He asks Esau, his favourite son, to prepare a special meal so that he may give him his blessing

Rebekah overhears her husband's conversation with Esau. She favours Jacob and wants Isaac to bless him

²⁰Isaac asked his son, "How did you find it so quickly, my son?"

"The LORD your God gave me success," he replied.

²¹Then Isaac said to Jacob, "Come near so I can touch you, my son, to know whether you really are my son Esau or not."

²²Jacob went close to his father Isaac, who touched him and said, "The voice is the voice of Jacob, but the hands are the hands of Esau… ²⁶Come here, my son, and kiss me."

²⁷So he went to him and kissed him. When Isaac caught the smell of his clothes, he blessed him and said,

"Ah, the smell of my son is like the smell of a field that the LORD has blessed. ²⁸May God give you of heaven's dew and of earth's richness – an abundance of grain and new wine. ²⁹May nations serve you and peoples bow down to you. Be lord over your brothers… May those who curse you be cursed and those who bless you be blessed."

As soon as Jacob left his father, Esau returned. Isaac trembled violently when he realised he had blessed Jacob instead of the son he loved. Esau wept aloud and vowed to kill his brother after his father's death. Rebekah told Jacob to flee at once to her brother Laban, who lived in Haran.

UNDERSTANDING THE STORY

When Isaac blesses Jacob he fulfils God's promise to Rebekah that her younger son would rule over the elder. Although Jacob obtains his father's blessing in a deceitful way, it is still valid. Rebekah suffers for her role in the deception, because her favourite son is forced to leave his home.

CHAPTER 27 VERSE 4
"My blessing before I die"
In the ancient Middle East, blessings were legally binding. They were usually given to confirm inheritance rights, either before a long journey or when someone was dying. Clay writing tablets discovered at Nuzi give an account of a son's legal battle over his inheritance. He won because there were witnesses to his father's blessing.

DOMESTIC POTTERY
The Hebrews used clay pots for cooking, storing, and serving food. Water and olive oil were stored in giant clay jars. This Canaanite pottery dates from the same period (2000–1700 BC).

REBEKAH
The Hebrew text highlights Rebekah's role in the story. There is a play on words that links the name Rebekah with birthright (bekorah) and blessing (berakah).

Esau vows to kill Jacob

Rebekah prepares the meal for Jacob

Esau goes out to hunt wild game for his father

Jacob disguises himself as Esau by covering his hands with goatskin and wearing Esau's clothes

Isaac believes he is touching Esau and gives his blessing

When Esau returns, Isaac realises what he has done and trembles with rage

GENESIS 28–29

JACOB'S FLIGHT

CHAPTER 28 VERSE 18
"Set it up as a pillar"
The Canaanites used to worship sacred stones, which were symbols of their gods. Jacob set up the stone pillar to mark the site of his vision of God, not as an object of worship. When God made his covenant with Moses, the Israelites were forbidden to worship statues or idols (Leviticus 26: 1).

CHAPTER 28 VERSE 19
"He called that place Bethel"
The Hebrew word "Bethel" means "House of God". Jacob returned to Bethel much later and built an altar there, just as his grandfather Abraham had done (Genesis 12: 7).

Jacob is on his way to Haran and stops for the night. Using a stone for a pillow, he lies down to sleep

28 JACOB[10] LEFT BEERSHEBA and set out for Haran. [11]When he reached a certain place, he stopped for the night because the sun had set. Taking one of the stones there, he put it under his head and lay down to sleep.

[12]He had a dream in which he saw a stairway resting on the earth, with its top reaching to heaven, and the angels of God were ascending and descending on it. [13]There above it stood the LORD, and he said: "I am the LORD, the God of your father Abraham and the God of Isaac. I will give you and your descendants the land on which you are lying. [14]Your descendants will be like the dust of the earth, and you will spread out to the west and to the east, to the north and to the south. All peoples on earth will be blessed through you and your offspring. [15]I am with you and will

Jacob dreams of a stairway to heaven, lined with angels

God speaks from high above. He repeats to Jacob the promise he first made to Abraham watch over you wherever you go, and I will bring you back to this land. I will not leave you until I have done what I have promised you."

¹⁶When Jacob awoke from his sleep, he thought, "Surely the LORD is in this place, and I was not aware of it." ¹⁷He was afraid and said, "How awesome is this place! This is none other than the house of God; this is the gate of heaven."

¹⁸Early the next morning Jacob took the stone he had placed under his head and *set it up as a pillar* and poured oil on top of it. ¹⁹*He called that place Bethel*, though the city used to be called Luz.

²⁰Then *Jacob made a vow*, saying, "If God will be with me and will watch over me on this journey I am taking and will give me food to eat and clothes to wear ²¹so that I return safely to my father's house, then the LORD will be my God ²²and this stone that I have set up as a pillar will be God's house, and of all that you give me *I will give you a tenth*."

Jacob continued his journey and arrived at a well in Haran. While he was asking shepherds if they knew his uncle, Laban's daughter Rachel arrived to water her father's sheep. On seeing her, Jacob rolled the stone away from the well and kissed her. He explained that he was related to Laban.

29   ¹³As soon as Laban heard the news about Jacob, his sister's son, he hurried to meet him. He embraced him and kissed him and brought him to his home, and there Jacob told him all these things.

UNDERSTANDING THE STORY

While Jacob is dreaming, God appears to him for the first time. God tells Jacob that he will inherit the covenant made with his forefathers, Abraham and Isaac. Jacob does not proclaim his faith in God immediately, but promises to serve God if he returns home safely to his father.

JACOB'S LADDER
In his dream, Jacob sees a stairway leading to heaven. The description of his vision resembles a ziggurat. These Mesopotamian temples had steps leading to an altar at the top. The partially reconstructed ziggurat pictured above was built at Ur, *c.* 2100 BC.

❖

CHAPTER 28 VERSE 20–22
"Jacob made a vow... I will give you a tenth"
This is the longest vow in the Old Testament. Jacob asks God to protect him, and in return he will recognize God as his own Lord and master. He also promises to give God a tenth of his possessions. It was customary at this time for people to pay a tenth of their income to their king.

Laban hears of his nephew's arrival and hurries to meet him

Jacob journeys to Haran and stops at a well. His cousin Rachel arrives there to water her sheep

When Jacob wakes up, he anoints the stone he had used as a pillow. He names the place Bethel

Jacob kisses Rachel

JACOB AND LABAN'S DAUGHTERS

CHAPTER 29 VERSE 16
"The older was Leah... the younger was Rachel"
The name Leah means "cow", and Rachel means "ewe". These names were popular with herdspeople because they symbolized prosperity.

LABAN'S DECEPTION
Men often celebrated separately from women during Middle-Eastern weddings, and a lot of wine was drunk during the feasting. Jacob was probably intoxicated when Laban brought him the bride, who traditionally wore a veil to shield her face from the groom. To help carry through his deception, Laban used the night's darkness. This recalls how Jacob had deceived his father by taking advantage of Isaac's blindness.

FACE VEIL
In the Middle East today, veils are usually worn as a sign of modesty. Styles vary from region to region. This Bedouin woman's veil is decorated with tassels and coins.

CHAPTER 29 VERSE 26
"It is not our custom here"
There is no evidence to validate this custom. Moses' Law later forbids a man to marry his wife's sister while his wife is still living.

CHAPTER 29 VERSE 27
"Another seven years of work"
A man was entitled to a dowry for a daughter. Jacob worked for Laban because he had no wealth to pay for Rachel. Laban tricked Jacob into another seven years' work.

---

29 N̄ow[16] LABAN HAD TWO DAUGHTERS; the name of *the older was Leah*, and the name of *the younger was Rachel*. [17]Leah had weak eyes, but Rachel was lovely in form, and beautiful. [18]Jacob was in love with Rachel and said, "I'll work for you seven years in return for your younger daughter Rachel."...

[20]So Jacob served seven years... [21]Then Jacob said to Laban, "Give me my wife. My time is completed, and I want to lie with her."

[22]So Laban brought together all the people of the place and gave a feast. [23]But when evening came, he took his daughter Leah and gave her to Jacob, and Jacob lay with her. [24]And Laban gave his servant girl Zilpah to his daughter as her maidservant.

Jacob falls in love with Rachel, one of Laban's two daughters

Leah

Rachel

Jacob

Laban agrees to let Jacob marry Rachel in return for seven years' work

[25]When morning came, there was Leah! So Jacob said to Laban, "What is this you have done to me? I served you for Rachel, didn't I? Why have you deceived me?"

[26]Laban replied, "*It is not our custom here* to give the younger daughter in marriage before the older one. [27]Finish this daughter's bridal week; then we will give you the younger one also, in return for *another seven years of work.*"

[28]And Jacob did so. He finished the week with Leah, and then Laban gave him his daughter Rachel to be his wife. [29]Laban gave his servant girl Bilhah to his daughter Rachel as her maidservant. [30]Jacob lay with Rachel also, and he loved Rachel more than Leah...

On the wedding night, Laban brings Leah to Jacob, who thinks she is Rachel

In the morning, Jacob is shocked to find Leah

[31]When the LORD saw that Leah was not loved, he opened her womb, but Rachel was barren. [32]Leah became pregnant and gave birth to a son. She named him Reuben, for she said, "It is because the LORD has seen my misery. Surely my husband will love me now."

Leah gave Jacob three more sons: Simeon, Levi, and Judah. But Rachel remained barren. Even though Rachel was loved by Jacob, she became very jealous of her sister.

30 When[1] Rachel saw that she was not bearing Jacob any children... [4]*she gave him her servant Bilhah as a wife*. Jacob slept with her, and she became pregnant and bore him a son. [6]Then Rachel said, "God has vindicated me... and given me a son." Because of this she named him Dan. [7][Bilhah] bore Jacob a second son. [8]Then Rachel said, "I have had *a great struggle with my sister*, and I have won." So she named him Naphtali.

When Leah bore no more children, she gave Jacob her own servant Zilpah as a wife, who had two sons. Then Leah bore another two sons and a daughter.

[22]Then God remembered Rachel; he listened to her and opened her womb. [23]She became pregnant and gave birth to a son...

Rachel and Leah compete for Jacob's affections

Jacob has a large family

Leah has six sons and a daughter

Rachel finally gives birth to Joseph

Reuben · Simeon · Levi · Judah · Dinah · Zebulun · Issachar · Naphtali · Gad · Jacob · Dan · Asher

After twenty years working for Laban, Jacob decides to return to Canaan, the land of his birth

Rachel's servant Bilhah gives Jacob two sons

Leah's servant Zilpah also has two sons

[25]*After Rachel gave birth* to Joseph, Jacob said to Laban, "Send me on my way so that I can go back to my own homeland. [26]Give me my wives and children, for whom I have served you..."

Laban offered to pay Jacob in livestock if he stayed. Laban did his best to cheat Jacob, but whatever he did made no difference. Jacob's herd grew and grew.

[43]In this way [Jacob] grew exceedingly prosperous and *came to own large flocks*, and maidservants and menservants, and camels and donkeys.

UNDERSTANDING THE STORY

Jacob, who deceived his brother out of his birthright, is in turn deceived by his uncle. Laban tricks Jacob into twenty years' service, yet Jacob comes out of the situation very well. Through God's blessing he becomes wealthy and fathers twelve sons, who will be the forefathers of the twelve tribes of Israel.

CHAPTER 30 VERSE 4
"She gave him her servant Bilhah as a wife"
Rachel resorted to the same solution as Sarah to deal with her infertility. By giving her servant to her husband, Rachel would be the legal mother of any children.

CHAPTER 30 VERSE 8
"A great struggle with my sister"
Laban's deception caused great unhappiness to both his daughters. Leah was desperate for Jacob's love, and Rachel was jealous of Leah's fertility. Their conflict is reflected in the names that they gave their children, such as Reuben, which means "see, a son", and Naphtali, which means "my struggle".

CHAPTER 30 VERSE 25
"After Rachel gave birth"
Once Jacob had a son by the wife he loved, he was ready to return to the Promised Land. But God's covenant will not be inherited by one son alone. Ironically, it is Leah's son Judah who will be the forefather of the royal line of David.

CHAPTER 30 VERSE 43
"Came to own large flocks"
In the semi-nomadic times of the Patriarchs, a man's wealth was measured by the size of his herds. Sheep and goats provided meat, milk, cheese, and yoghurt, and their wool was made into cloth.

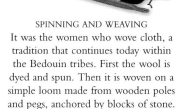

SPINNING AND WEAVING
It was the women who wove cloth, a tradition that continues today within the Bedouin tribes. First the wool is dyed and spun. Then it is woven on a simple loom made from wooden poles and pegs, anchored by blocks of stone.

GENESIS 31–35

JACOB RETURNS TO CANAAN

MESOPOTAMIAN GODS
This stele depicts the goddess of water being worshipped by other deities.

31 THEN[3] THE LORD SAID TO JACOB, "Go back to the land of your fathers and to your relatives, and I will be with you."

[4]So Jacob sent word to Rachel and Leah to come out to the fields where his flocks were. [5]He said to them... [6]"You know that I've worked for your father with all my strength, [7]yet your father has cheated me by changing my wages ten times. However, God has not allowed him to harm me..."

[14]Then Rachel and Leah replied... [16]"Do whatever God has told you."

[17]Then Jacob put his children and his wives on camels, [18]and he drove all his livestock ahead of him, along with all the goods he had accumulated in Paddan Aram, to go to his father Isaac in the land of Canaan.

[19]When Laban had gone to shear his sheep, Rachel stole her father's *household gods*... [21]So [Jacob] fled with all he had.

God tells Jacob to return to Canaan. So, Jacob takes his family and all his possessions and leaves Laban's household

Jacob is afraid as he waits for Esau and asks God for his protection

A man appears and wrestles with Jacob

The man touches Jacob's hip and dislocates it

WASHING IN THE JABBOK
These women are washing clothes at a point where the river is shallow enough to wade across.

Laban pursued Jacob, and when he caught up with him there was a furious argument. But God spoke to Laban in a dream and warned him not to harm Jacob, so the dispute was settled peacefully, and Laban returned home.

32 Jacob[3] sent messengers ahead of him to his brother Esau in the land of Seir... [6]When the messengers returned to Jacob, they said, "We went to your brother Esau, and now he is coming to meet you, and four hundred men are with him." [7]In great fear and distress... [9]Jacob prayed... [11]"Save me, I pray, from the hand of my brother Esau, for I am afraid that he will come and attack me, and also the mothers with their children..."

¹³From what he had with him he selected a gift for his brother Esau: ¹⁴two hundred female goats and twenty male goats, two hundred ewes and twenty rams, ¹⁵thirty female camels [and cows, bulls, and donkeys].

²²That night Jacob got up and took his two wives, his two maidservants and his eleven sons and crossed *the ford of the Jabbok*. ²³After he had sent them across the stream, he sent over all his possessions. ²⁴So Jacob was left alone, and *a man wrestled with him* till daybreak. ²⁵When the man saw that he could not overpower him, he *touched the socket of Jacob's hip* so that his hip was wrenched as he wrestled with the man. ²⁶Then the man said, "Let me go, for it is daybreak." But Jacob replied, "I will not let you go unless you bless me."

The man blessed him and, when he had gone, Jacob prepared to meet Esau. To Jacob's relief and delight, Esau greeted him warmly. Esau accepted Jacob's gifts and returned to Seir. Jacob discarded the household gods and went on to Bethel. There Jacob built an altar, and God spoke to him.

Jacob is delighted when he realises that Esau has forgiven him

Jacob

Esau

35   ¹⁰God said... "Your name is Jacob, but you will no longer be called Jacob; *your name will be Israel*... ¹²The land I gave to Abraham and Isaac I also give to you, and I will give this land to your descendants after you."...

¹⁶Then they moved on from Bethel... Rachel began to give birth and had great difficulty... ¹⁸As she breathed her last – for she was dying – she named her son *Ben-Oni*. But his father named him *Benjamin*.

²⁷Jacob came home to his father Isaac in Mamre... ²⁸Isaac lived a hundred and eighty years. ²⁹Then he breathed his last and died and was gathered to his people... And his sons Esau and Jacob buried him.

UNDERSTANDING THE STORY

When God made his original promise to Jacob at Bethel, Jacob did not immediately acknowledge God as his Lord. Unlike Abraham and Isaac, Jacob has to struggle with his faith. But experience shows Jacob that God is always with him. When Jacob returns to Bethel, he accepts God unconditionally.

❖

CHAPTER 32 VERSE 24
"A man wrestled with him"
Alone and afraid, Jacob encounters a mysterious man. The wrestling match is the culmination of a lifetime's struggle for Jacob, both with his family and his faith. The man is a manifestation of God, who said he would always be with Jacob. He appears in Jacob's darkest hour.

WRESTLING MATCH (GREEK COIN)
The biblical authors use a popular ancient sport to represent Jacob's struggle.

❖

CHAPTER 32 VERSE 25
"Touched the socket of Jacob's hip"
The Bible text (32: 31–32) says that Jacob limped thereafter. The limp was a constant reminder to Jacob that, despite all his efforts, he was ultimately dependent on God.

❖

CHAPTER 35 VERSE 10
"Your name will be Israel"
The name means "he strives with God". After a long struggle, Jacob finally acknowledges God as the source of his blessing. Jacob, "the usurper", is a changed man. God gives him a new name and renews with "Israel" the covenant he made with Abraham and Isaac.

❖

CHAPTER 35 VERSE 18
"Ben-Oni... Benjamin"
Rachel died giving birth to Jacob's twelfth son. Her name for him, "Ben-Oni", means "son of my trouble". Jacob renamed him "Ben-Jamin", which means "son of my right hand". The name can also be translated as "son of the south". This is because the Hebrews based direction on facing east, which meant that south was on the right. Benjamin was the only one of Jacob's sons to be born in the south.

GENESIS 37, 39

JOSEPH AND HIS BROTHERS

CHAPTER 37 VERSE 34
"Jacob... put on sackcloth"
Sackcloth is a coarse material
made from goat or camel hair. The
Israelites wore it as a sign of prayer,
repentance, or mourning. When a
person died, it was usual for the
bereaved to stay home and fast for
a few days. They also rubbed ash or
dirt on their faces and into their hair.

37 JOSEPH[2], A YOUNG MAN OF SEVENTEEN, was tending the flocks with his brothers... and he brought their father a bad report about them. [3]Now Israel [Jacob] loved Joseph more than any of his other sons, because he had been born to him in his old age; and he made a richly ornamented robe for him. [4]When his brothers saw that their father loved him more than any of them, they hated him.

Joseph had two dreams. In the first dream, he and his brothers were binding sheaves of corn when his brothers' sheaves bowed down to his sheaf. In the second dream, the sun and moon and eleven stars all bowed down to Joseph. On hearing this, the brothers thought he intended to rule over them and hated him even more. One day, Jacob told Joseph to go to find his brothers, who were working in the fields, and see if all was well.

Jacob

Joseph is Jacob's favourite son and he gives him a beautiful coat

Joseph

The brothers dip Joseph's coat in goat's blood

Joseph

Joseph visits his brothers out in the fields. They hate him so much that they decide to kill him

Reuben does not want to kill him, so they strip Joseph and throw him down a cistern

Jacob sees Joseph's blood-stained coat and grieves for his favourite son

JOSEPH'S ROBE
The Greek translation describes Joseph's coat as multi-coloured. Here it is more accurately described as "richly ornamented" (37: 3), as it was probably made from cloth woven with coloured threads. Embroidered clothing was highly valued in Egypt and Mesopotamia at this time.

ANCIENT EMBROIDERY
Early Coptic fabric from Upper Egypt

[19]"Here comes that dreamer!" they said to each other... [20]"Let's kill him and throw him into one of these cisterns and say that a ferocious animal devoured him..."
[21]When Reuben heard this, he tried to rescue him from their hands... [22]"Don't shed any blood. Throw him into this cistern... but don't lay a hand on him."...
[23]So when Joseph came to his brothers, they stripped him of his robe... and threw him into the cistern... [25]As they sat down to eat their meal, they looked up and saw a caravan of Ishmaelites...

²⁸His brothers pulled Joseph up out of the cistern and sold him for twenty shekels of silver to the Ishmaelites, who took him to Egypt...

³¹Then they got Joseph's robe, slaughtered a goat and dipped the robe in the blood. ³²They took the ornamented robe back to their father... ³³He recognised it and said, "It is my son's robe! Some ferocious animal has devoured him. Joseph has surely been torn to pieces." ³⁴Then *Jacob tore his clothes, put on sackcloth* and mourned for his son many days...

39   ¹Now Joseph had been *taken down to Egypt.* Potiphar, an Egyptian who was one of Pharaoh's officials, the captain of the guard, bought him from the Ishmaelites who had taken him there.

²The LORD was with Joseph and he prospered... ³When his master saw that the LORD... gave him success in everything he did, ⁴Joseph found favour in his eyes and became his attendant...

CARAVAN OF ISHMAELITES
The Ishmaelites were descendants of Ishmael, Abraham's eldest son. They were divided into 12 tribes, and they lived in the deserts of northern Arabia. "Ishmaelite" was also a general term used to describe all Arabian merchants.

EGYPTIAN MARKETS
This merchant is selling handwoven rugs and carpets at a bazaar in Giza. In Egypt, outdoor markets are an integral part of town centres.

Joseph's brothers sell him to some passing traders

The traders take Joseph to Egypt, where they sell him to Potiphar, one of Pharaoh's officials

⁶Now Joseph was well-built and handsome, ⁷and after a while his master's wife took notice of Joseph... ¹²She caught him by his cloak and said, "Come to bed with me!" But he left his cloak in her hand and ran out of the house.

Potiphar's wife kept the cloak and told her husband that Joseph had made advances towards her. Potiphar was furious and imprisoned Joseph.

Joseph runs out of the house, leaving his cloak in her hand

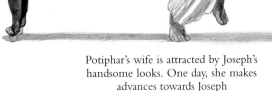

Potiphar's wife tells her husband that Joseph tried to seduce her, and so Potiphar has him imprisoned

Potiphar's wife is attracted by Joseph's handsome looks. One day, she makes advances towards Joseph

CHAPTER 39 VERSE 1
"Taken down to Egypt"
Although Joseph was taken to Egypt to be sold, slave trading was not common practice. Arabian merchants mostly brought spices and aromatic resins. The Egyptians needed large quantities of these goods for the manufacturing of perfumes and medicines and for mummification. Egypt's main exports were gold, linen, papyrus, fish, and grain.

UNDERSTANDING THE STORY

Jacob's favouritism and Joseph's dreams are too much for the brothers to bear, and they decide to kill Joseph. However, God has other plans for Joseph. His life is spared, and he manages to prosper in Egypt despite his circumstances. God is with Joseph, as he was with Abraham, Isaac, and Jacob before him.

GENESIS 39–41

PHARAOH'S DREAMS

CHAPTER 40 VERSE 22
"He hanged the chief baker"
In Hebrew, "to hang" either meant "to impale" or to display a corpse in public. It is unclear which is meant in this case. In Egypt, some corpses were impaled after being beheaded. Egyptians believed that beheading people prevented their souls from entering the afterlife.

The prison warder favours Joseph and puts him in charge of the prisoners

DREAMS
In the ancient Middle East, people believed that dreams had specific meanings that could determine the future if properly interpreted. In Egypt, the pharaoh's dreams were considered particularly important, because he was worshipped as the earthly form of the sun god Horus. Egyptians believed that Egypt's fate depended on the fate of the pharaoh.

PHARAOH'S DREAM
This illustration from The Golden Haggadah, a Jewish medieval manuscript, depicts the cattle and corn of the pharaoh's dream.

THE SEVEN COWS
The setting for the pharaoh's dream would have been a familiar sight to Egyptians, because cattle immersed themselves in the Nile for protection against insects and the heat. One of the Egyptian goddesses, Hathor, was often depicted as a cow emerging from the Nile. She was believed to be the source of Egypt's fertility.

39 WHILE[20] JOSEPH WAS THERE IN THE PRISON, [21]the LORD was with him; he showed him kindness and granted him favour in the eyes of the prison warder. [22]So the warder put Joseph in charge of all those held in the prison, and he was made responsible for all that was done there...

Two of Pharaoh's officials are put into Joseph's care

One night, the cupbearer and baker have strange dreams

Joseph interprets their dreams

40 Some[1] time later, the cupbearer and the baker of the king of Egypt offended their master... [2]Pharaoh was angry with his two officials... [3]and put them in custody in the house of the captain of the guard... [4]The captain of the guard assigned them to Joseph, and he attended them.

One night, the two officials had prophetic dreams, and Joseph interpreted them. Joseph told them that the cupbearer would return to serve Pharaoh within three days and that the baker would die within three days. Joseph asked the cupbearer to mention his name to Pharaoh when Pharaoh frees him.

[20]Now the third day was Pharaoh's birthday, and he gave a feast for all his officials... [21]He restored the chief cupbearer to his position, so that he once again put the cup into Pharaoh's hand, [22]but *he hanged the chief baker*, just as Joseph had said to them in his interpretation. [23]The chief cupbearer, however, did not remember Joseph...

Three days later, Pharaoh has a feast for his birthday

Joseph's predictions come true

The baker is hanged

Pharaoh reinstates the cupbearer

Two years later, Pharaoh had disturbing dreams. In the first dream, he saw seven fat and healthy cows coming out of the River Nile to feed. These were followed by seven thin cows, who ate up the seven fat cows. In his second dream, seven plump ears of corn were growing on a single stalk. Then, seven thin and shrivelled ears of corn sprouted and swallowed up the seven healthy ears.

41 ⁸In the morning his mind was troubled, so he sent for all *the magicians and wise men of Egypt*... But no-one could interpret [the dreams] for him... ⁹Then the chief cupbearer [was] reminded [of Joseph]. ¹⁴So Pharaoh sent for Joseph... *When he had shaved* and changed his clothes, he came before Pharaoh. ¹⁵Pharaoh said to Joseph... "I have heard it said of you that when you hear a dream you can interpret it."

Pharaoh has two strange dreams that no-one can interpret

Pharaoh's dreams foretell seven years of plenty, followed by seven years of famine

Joseph is brought before Pharaoh to explain the dreams. Pharaoh makes Joseph his highest official

¹⁶"I cannot do it," Joseph replied to Pharaoh, "but God will give Pharaoh the answer he desires... ²⁸God has shown Pharaoh what he is about to do... ²⁹Seven years of great abundance are coming throughout the land of Egypt, ³⁰but *seven years of famine* will follow them..."

Joseph told Pharaoh to store up grain so that there would be enough to last Egypt in the famine. Pharaoh was so impressed that he made Joseph his chief minister.

UNDERSTANDING THE STORY

Joseph's predictions about the cupbearer and baker come true. However, Joseph has to wait patiently for the significance of his own dreams to be revealed. God continues to be with him and, after thirteen years of slavery and imprisonment in Egypt, Joseph is appointed to the pharaoh's highest office.

CHAPTER 41 VERSE 8
"The magicians and wise men of Egypt"
Egyptians believed in magic. They wore amulets and recited spells to ward off evil. Magic was also used to treat illness and to help prevent the dangers of childbirth. It was common practice for people to consult sorcerers and dream interpreters.

CHAPTER 41 VERSE 14
"When he had shaved"
Most Israelite men wore full beards. This was later a requirement under Moses' Law: "Do not cut the hair at the sides of your head, or clip off the edges of your beard (Leviticus 19: 27). Egyptian men, however, were clean-shaven. Priests shaved their heads completely, which was necessary to ensure their cleanliness.

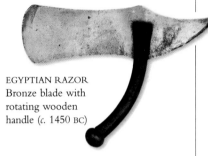

EGYPTIAN RAZOR
Bronze blade with rotating wooden handle (*c.* 1450 BC)

CHAPTER 41 VERSE 30
"Seven years of famine"
Ancient sources record severe famines in Egypt at this time. The Nile was vital to life in Egypt. The river's annual floodwaters brought the fertile soils needed for farming. If the water was too low, or flooded too high, the result was disastrous for agriculture.

THE NILE IN FLOOD
Detail from a painting by Charles Theodore Frere (1814–88)

GENESIS 41–46

JOSEPH'S FAMILY IN EGYPT

41

PHARAOH[42] TOOK his *signet ring* from his finger and put it on Joseph's finger. He dressed him in *robes of fine linen* and put a *gold chain* around his neck... ⁴⁵Pharaoh gave Joseph the name *Zaphenath-Paneah* and gave him Asenath daughter of Potiphera, priest of On, to be his wife... ⁴⁶Joseph was thirty years old when he entered the service of Pharaoh... ⁵⁰Before the years of famine came, two sons were born to Joseph... ⁵¹Joseph named his first-born *Manasseh* and... ⁵²the second he named *Ephraim*.

Pharaoh gives Joseph his ring, fine clothes, and a gold chain

Joseph marries Asenath, and she gives birth to two sons

For the next seven years, Joseph stored up grain. Then the famine began, and people from distant countries came to Egypt to buy Joseph's grain. His brothers also came, but they did not recognise him. Joseph wanted to know if his brothers had changed. He tested them by hiding a silver cup in Benjamin's bag. When the brothers started for home, Joseph sent his steward after them to search their bags. The steward found the cup and took them back to Joseph. Judah pleaded with Joseph not to enslave Benjamin and offered to stay in his place.

CHAPTER 41 VERSE 42
"Signet ring... robes of fine linen... gold chain"

The pharaoh appointed Joseph to the position of vizier, the pharaoh's chief minister. He was responsible for the administration of the land. It was customary in Egypt for the vizier to be given the king's ring, which signified the royal seal of authority, and fine garments, which befitted his high status. The gold chain is believed to represent control over the food supply.

SIGNET RING

The underside of this ancient Egyptian ring is carved in the shape of a scarab beetle. The scarab symbolized the sun god Khepri.

CHAPTER 41 VERSE 45
"Zaphenath-Paneah"

Joseph's new Egyptian name serves as a reminder of how he rose to power. It means "revealer of secrets".

During the famine, people come to Egypt to buy the grain Joseph has stored

Joseph's brothers also come to Egypt, but they do not recognise Joseph

CHAPTER 41 VERSES 51–52
"Manasseh... Ephraim"

In Hebrew, "Manasseh" means "to forget". The birth of Joseph's first son helped him to forget the bitter experience of his earlier years. Joseph called his second son "Ephraim", which means "fruitful". Ephraim's descendants were to become one of the largest of Israel's twelve tribes.

45

¹Then Joseph could no longer control himself [and]... ⁴said to his brothers, "Come close to me." When they had done so, he said, "I am your brother Joseph, the one you sold into Egypt! ⁵And now, do not be distressed and do not be angry with yourselves for selling me here, because it was to save lives that God sent me ahead of you.

⁶For two years now there has been famine in the land, and for the next five years there will not be ploughing and reaping. ⁷But God sent me ahead of you to preserve for you a remnant on earth and to save your lives by a great deliverance.

Joseph decides to test his brothers to see if they have changed

Before his brothers return home, Joseph hides a silver cup in Benjamin's bag

Judah pleads with Joseph not to enslave Benjamin and offers to take his place

Joseph forgives his brothers and tells them who he is. He asks them to bring his whole family to Egypt

When the missing cup is discovered, the brothers are brought back to face Joseph

POTIPHERA, PRIEST OF ON
Potiphera lived in the city of On, which is 10km (6 miles) north-east of modern-day Cairo. On was the centre of worship for the sun god Ra, and the priest of On was one of the most influential men in Egypt. The city was renamed "Heliopolis" by the Greeks, which means "City of the Sun".

SUN GOD RA
This limestone relief depicts the Egyptian sun god Ra as a falcon with the disc of the sun on its head. It dates from *c.* 1200 BC.

9"Now hurry back to my father and say to him... 'Joseph says: God has made me Lord of all Egypt. Come down to me; don't delay. 10You shall live *in the region of Goshen* and be near me – you, your children and grandchildren, your flocks and herds, and all you have. 11I will provide for you there...' "

46 ¹So Israel [Jacob] set out with all that was his, and when he reached Beersheba, he offered sacrifices to the God of his father Isaac. ²And God spoke to Israel [Jacob] in a vision at night and said... ³"I am God, the God of your father," he said. "Do not be afraid to go down to Egypt, for I will make you into a great nation there. ⁴I will go down to Egypt with you, and I will surely bring you back again. And Joseph's own hand will close your eyes."

BENJAMIN
Jacob's youngest son was particularly loved by his father. Jacob believed that Benjamin was the only surviving child of his favourite wife Rachel. Joseph remembered how his brothers had treated him and could not forgive them until he was sure that they had changed.

CHAPTER 45 VERSE 10
"In the region of Goshen"
The region of Goshen was situated in the north-eastern part of the Nile Delta. Goshen was a fertile area and is described as "the best part of the land" (Genesis 47: 11). In the Bible, it is also referred to as the "Land of Rameses".

Jacob and his family settled in Goshen and looked after Pharaoh's herds. Joseph made peace with his brothers. He was a powerful ruler in Egypt all his life and died at the age of a hundred and ten.

Joseph's family sets out for Egypt. On the way, they stop at Beersheba, where Jacob offers sacrifices to God

Jacob sees God in a vision. God tells Jacob that he will be the father of a great nation

GOSHEN
This small village is believed to be in the region that was once called Goshen.

UNDERSTANDING THE STORY

Joseph realizes that his brothers' evil act saved his family from the famine and that his rise to power was part of God's plan. With his family reunited in Egypt, Joseph finally understands the significance of his dreams. The eleven stars and sheaves of corn represent his brothers, who now serve under him.

FROM SLAVERY TO FREEDOM

Once settled in Egypt, Jacob's family grew over generations into the tribes of Israel. They lived peaceably among the Egyptians until the start of the New Kingdom. At this time, the Egyptians felt threatened by the Israelites' increasing numbers and enslaved them. This was foretold in God's covenant with Abraham: "Your descendants will be strangers in a country not their own, and will be enslaved and mistreated for four hundred years." (Genesis 15: 13). When this period had elapsed, God chose Moses to free his people from Egyptian oppression and lead them back to Canaan, the land he had promised his forefathers.

THE RIVER NILE
The Nile was the life-blood of Egypt. Its annual floods brought fertility to the land, and most Egyptians were farmers.

THE NEW KINGDOM OF EGYPT

In about 1570 BC, a Theban prince overthrew the Hyksos (Asian) rulers of Egypt and became Ahmose I, founder of the 18th dynasty of pharaohs. This was the start of the New Kingdom (1550–1086 BC). This period is also known as the Empire, because Egypt expanded its territories and became the dominant power in the Ancient World.

Memphis, in northern Egypt, became the political capital. Thebes, the old capital in the south, remained the religious centre. Egypt enjoyed economic prosperity, and the pharaohs embarked on massive building projects. Ramses II was the most prolific of all. The south's dry climate has preserved some of his monumental structures, such as Luxor Temple and the rock-cut statues at Abu Simbel.

LUXOR TEMPLE (THEBES)

The power of the pharaoh

The Egyptians believed that their king was a living god and that through him they could achieve eternal life. The pharaoh had absolute power. He was head of the army and controlled the religious life in Egypt through an elite priesthood. He ruled the country with the help of a "vizier", or chief official, who ran a complex civil service, employing thousands of scribes.

Prisoners and slaves

Slavery was uncommon in Egypt until the 18th dynasty, when Egypt embarked on a policy of expansion and made slaves of foreign prisoners of war. The Israelites were one of many non-Egyptian peoples who had settled in the fertile Nile Delta during the period of Hyksos control. Egypt's expulsion of the Hyksos marked a new era of nationalism. Foreign settlers were set to harsh labour on the pharaohs' grand building projects.

POWER OVER FOREIGNERS
Bound prisoners, painted under the foot of an Egyptian mummy case

Worship and idolatry

The Egyptians worshipped countless gods who, they believed, ruled their lives. Most people worshipped at household shrines and wore amulets to ward off bad luck. The most important god was the sun god Ra, giver of life. Many gods took animal forms, such as Bastet, a cat goddess that helped ripen crops. The Nile was said to be the sweat of Sobek, a crocodile god.

BASTET

DATING THE EXODUS	1900BC	1800	1700	1600	1500	1400	1300	1200

Two dates are given for the Exodus. According to 1 Kings 6: 1, Solomon began building the Temple 480 years after the Israelites left Egypt. As the Temple was begun in 966 BC, this dates the Exodus to 1446 BC, the "early" date.

Some scholars claim that the pharaoh at the time of the Exodus was Ramses II, of the 19th dynasty. This would give the "later" date of about 1275 BC.

The Family Bible uses the earlier system of dating.

NEW KINGDOM

1876 BC (12th dynasty)   1446BC
EARLY DATE
ENTRY INTO EGYPT   EXODUS

THUTMOSE III 1479–1425 (18th dynasty)

1705 BC (14th dynasty)   1275BC
LATER DATE
ENTRY INTO EGYPT   EXODUS

RAMSES II 1279–1213 (19th dynasty)

THE EXODUS

When God told Moses that he had chosen him to lead the Israelites out of Egypt, Moses felt unable to take on such an enormous task. But his faith in God gave him the courage to challenge the might of the pharaoh.

The ten plagues

The pharaoh was not willing to release his Israelite slaves. The Egyptians had a deep belief in magic, and so Moses turned his staff into a snake to convince the pharaoh of God's power. God then sent nine devastating plagues, which also failed to change the pharaoh's mind. But, after the sudden deaths of all first-born Egyptian males, he finally relented and gave Moses permission for the Israelites to leave Egypt.

DESERT ENCAMPMENT, painting by David Roberts (1796–1864)

Life in the desert

Desert conditions are harsh. The high temperatures of the day drop to below freezing at night, and food and water are scarce. The Israelites were vast in number. Only God's miraculous intervention could ensure their survival during the three-month journey from Egypt to Mount Sinai.

ANIMAL SKIN
An ancient method of carrying water

The Law

Surrounded by idolatry in Egypt, the Israelites were constantly tempted to follow false gods. They were also about to enter a land whose inhabitants worshipped pagan gods. This is why the Israelites received God's Law in the desert at Mount Sinai, before they entered Canaan. God gave his Law to the Israelites through Moses. The words God spoke covered all aspects of social, moral, and spiritual life, and they are contained in The Book of the Covenant (Exodus 20: 22–23: 33). This was later extended to include Deuteronomy (31: 9, 26). God's Law is summarized in the Ten Commandments.

THE TABERNACLE

This was a portable shrine and became the focus of religious life. When the Israelites set up camp, the Tabernacle was placed in an enclosed court.

The outer court

Sacrifices were prepared in the outer court and offered on the altar. Priests washed in a bronze basin before performing the sacrifice.

The sanctuaries

The Tabernacle was divided into an inner and outer sanctuary by a veil. The inner sanctuary (the Holy of Holies) housed the Ark of the Covenant, which held the stone tablets inscribed with the Ten Commandments.

Priests of the Tabernacle

Aaron, Moses' brother, was the first High Priest. He and his sons were responsible for worship. Aaron was a Levite, and he was forefather of the Israelite priesthood.

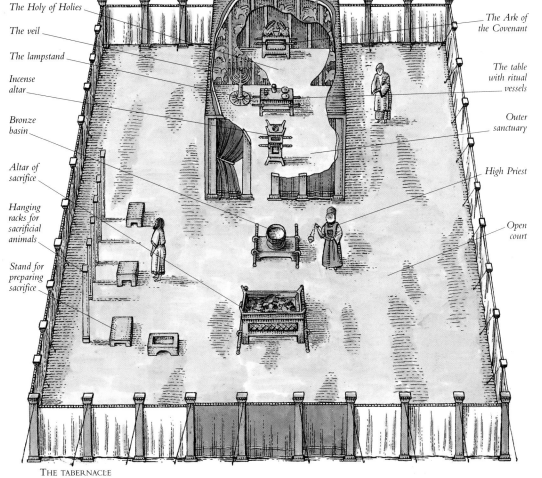

The Holy of Holies

The veil

The lampstand

Incense altar

Bronze basin

Altar of sacrifice

Hanging racks for sacrificial animals

Stand for preparing sacrifice

The Ark of the Covenant

The table with ritual vessels

Outer sanctuary

High Priest

Open court

THE TABERNACLE

EXODUS 1–2

MOSES AND THE ISRAELITES

✤

CHAPTER 1 VERSE 7
"The Israelites... multiplied greatly"
Moses was born nearly 300 years after Joseph's death and, during this time, the Israelites grew into a large nation. God's earlier promise to Abraham is fulfilled (Genesis 17: 2).

✤

CHAPTER 1 VERSE 8
"A new king"
This king was possibly Ahmose 1 (*c.* 1550–1525 BC), who expelled all foreign rulers from Egypt and founded the New Kingdom. Only one Egyptian source mentions the Israelites as a settled people, and this is the Merenptah stele, pictured below.

VICTORY STELE
This dates from the reign of Merenptah (*c.* 1213–1203 BC), who was the son and successor of Ramses II.

✤

CHAPTER 1 VERSE 11
"Pithom and Rameses"
These store cities were situated in the Nile Delta region. "Rameses" is often attributed to Ramses II (*c.* 1279–1213 BC), who is renowned for his massive building projects. However, it was probably built earlier, as Ramses often claimed credit for building cities he only rebuilt.

ANCIENT EGYPTIAN CITY
This ruined city was once used to store agricultural and military supplies and is a possible site of Rameses or Pithom.

1 NOW⁶ JOSEPH AND ALL HIS BROTHERS and all that generation died, ⁷but *the Israelites were fruitful and multiplied greatly* and became exceedingly numerous.

⁸Then *a new king*, who did not know about Joseph, came to power in Egypt. ⁹"Look," he said to his people... "¹⁰We must deal shrewdly with them or they will become even more numerous and, if war breaks out, will join our enemies, fight against us and leave the country."

¹¹So they put slave masters over them to oppress them with forced labour, and they built *Pithom and Rameses* as store cities for Pharaoh. ¹²But the more they were oppressed, the more they multiplied and spread; so the Egyptians came to dread the Israelites ¹³and worked them ruthlessly.

Pharaoh puts slave masters over the Israelites, who have grown into a large people

Finally, Pharaoh orders all the Israelite baby boys to be drowned

The baby's sister watches from a distance to see what will happen to him

A Levite woman puts her son into a papyrus basket and hides him in the reeds along the Nile

Pharaoh told the Hebrew midwives to kill all boys born to the Israelites. But the midwives feared God and would not do it. When Pharaoh questioned them, the midwives said that the Hebrew women were strong and gave birth before they arrived. God rewarded the midwives and gave them their own families.

One day, Pharaoh's daughter goes to bathe in the Nile

²²Then Pharaoh gave this order to all his people: "Every boy that is born you must throw into the Nile, but let every girl live."

2 Now[1] a man of the house of Levi married a Levite woman, [2]and she became pregnant and gave birth to a son. When she saw that he was a fine child, she hid him for three months. [3]But when she could hide him no longer, she got *a papyrus basket* for him and coated it with tar and pitch. Then she placed the child in it and put it among the reeds... of the Nile. [4]His sister stood at a distance to see what would happen to him.

[5]Then Pharaoh's daughter went down to the Nile to bathe, and her attendants were walking along the river bank. She saw the basket among the reeds and sent her slave girl to get it. [6]She opened it and saw the baby. He was crying, and she felt sorry for him. "This is one of the Hebrew babies," she said.

[7]Then his sister asked Pharaoh's daughter, "Shall I go and get one of the Hebrew women to nurse the baby for you?"

[8]"Yes, go" she answered. And the girl went and got the baby's mother. [9]Pharaoh's daughter said to her, "Take this baby and nurse him for me, and I will pay you." So the woman took the baby and nursed him.

[10]When the child grew older, she took him to Pharaoh's daughter and *he became her son. She named him Moses*, saying, "I drew him out of the water."

UNDERSTANDING THE STORY

The pharaoh feels threatened by the growing number of Israelites, but all his efforts to destroy them are thwarted. Moses, who will eventually lead the Israelites out of their misery, is rescued by the pharaoh's own daughter and is brought up under her protection.

Pharaoh's daughter sees the basket in the reeds and sends her slave to fetch it

The slave finds Moses in the basket

Pharaoh's daughter sends for a wet-nurse

Moses' sister brings their mother

When he is older, Pharaoh's daughter adopts Moses as her own son

CHAPTER 2 VERSE 3
"A papyrus basket"
The Hebrew word for "basket" is also used to describe Noah's "ark". The ark rescues Noah from the flood and brings about a new era for humanity. The basket offers protection to Moses, who will deliver the Israelites from slavery.

PAPYRUS IN LATE SEASON

CHAPTER 2 VERSE 10
"He became her son"
It was not uncommon at this time in Egypt for foreign boys to be raised in the royal palace and trained for service in the army or the Temple.

CHAPTER 2 VERSE 10
"She named him Moses"
In Hebrew, Moses means "drawn out". In Egyptian, it means "born of". This name occasionally linked pharaohs with Egyptian gods, such as Thutmose, which means "son of Thoth". Thoth was god of wisdom.

EXODUS 2–3

THE BURNING BUSH

CHAPTER 2 VERSE 11
"After Moses had grown up"
Moses was brought up in the royal harem, where he would have learned to read and write Egyptian hieroglyphs and received military training. The main pastime of courtiers was hunting. Desert animals were herded into special enclosures and then used as quarry. Nobles hunted wildfowl on the banks of the Nile using throwsticks, which were similar to boomerangs.

❖

CHAPTER 2 VERSE 15
"Moses... went to live in Midian"
Midian is a region in the Arabian desert near the Gulf of Aqaba. It is possibly named after Abraham and Keturah's son Midian (Genesis 25: 1–6). His descendants, the Midianites, were a nomadic tribe that frequently fought against the Israelites after the Exodus.

HOREB, MOUNTAIN OF GOD
Horeb is the Hebrew word for "desert" or "desolation". Mount Horeb is also referred to as Mount Sinai. Its exact location is uncertain, but the most widely accepted site is Jebel Musa, pictured above. This is a 2,286m (7,500ft) granite mountain in the Sinai Peninsula.

❖

CHAPTER 3 VERSE 2
"Flames of fire"
God's presence is often symbolized by fire, which serves as a reminder of his power and holiness. Fire is also used to express divine judgement (Isaiah 66: 15–16).

2 ONE[11] DAY, *after Moses had grown up*, he went out to where his own people were and watched them at their hard labour. He saw an Egyptian beating a Hebrew, one of his own people. [12]Glancing this way and that and seeing no-one, he killed the Egyptian and hid him in the sand. [13]The next day he went out and saw two Hebrews fighting. He asked the one in the wrong, "Why are you hitting your fellow Hebrew?"

[14]The man said, "Who made you ruler and judge over us? Are you thinking of killing me as you killed the Egyptian?" Then Moses was afraid and thought, "What I did must have become known."

[15]When Pharaoh heard of this, he tried to kill Moses, but *Moses fled from Pharaoh and went to live in Midian.*

When Moses is an adult he sees an Egyptian beating an Israelite

Moses kills the Egyptian and buries him in the sand

Moses befriended Jethro, a Midianite priest, and married his daughter Zipporah. Moses lived in Midian for many years. During that time, Pharaoh died and a new king came to the throne. Yet the Israelites remained in slavery.

3 Now[1] Moses was tending the flock of Jethro his father-in-law... and he led the flock to the far side of the desert and came to Horeb, the mountain of God. [2]There the angel of the LORD appeared to him in *flames of fire* from within a bush. Moses saw that though the bush was on fire it did not burn up. [3]So Moses thought, "I will go over and see this strange sight – why the bush does not burn up."

Moses flees to Midian, where he lives with a priest named Jethro

He marries one of Jethro's daughters

One day, Moses takes Jethro's flock to the far side of the desert

⁴When the LORD saw that he had gone over to look, God called to him from within the bush... ⁵"Do not come any closer... *Take off your sandals*, for the place where you are standing is holy ground." ⁶Then he said, "I am the God of your father, the God of Abraham, the God of Isaac and the God of Jacob... ⁷I have indeed seen the misery of my people in Egypt... ⁸So I have come down to rescue them... and to bring them up out of that land into a good and spacious land, a land flowing with milk and honey."

God told Moses that he was sending him back to Pharaoh to free the Israelites from their slavery in Egypt. Moses did not feel worthy of this role.

¹²And God said, "I will be with you. And this will be a sign to you that it is I who have sent you: When you have brought the people out of Egypt, you will worship God on this mountain."

¹³Moses said to God, "Suppose [the Israelites] ask me, 'What is his name?' Then what shall I tell them?"

MOSES ON THE MOUNTAIN OF GOD
This detail from a mosaic in San Vitale Church, Ravenna, depicts Moses walking on holy ground.

CHAPTER 3 VERSE 5
"Take off your sandals"
God asks Moses to remove his sandals as a sign of respect for a holy place. It was customary to perform religious ceremonies barefoot in the ancient Middle East. This was to ensure that the sanctuaries were kept free from dirt.

Moses comes to Mount Horeb, where God calls out to him

God speaks to Moses from within a burning bush

Moses removes his sandals as a sign of respect

God tells Moses that he must lead the Israelites out of Egypt to the Promised Land

¹⁴God said to Moses, "*I AM WHO I AM*. This is what you are to say to the Israelites: 'I AM has sent me to you... The LORD, the God of your fathers... has sent me to you.' ¹⁵This is my name for ever, the name by which I am to be remembered from generation to generation..."

UNDERSTANDING THE STORY

The Israelites' suffering is the central theme of these passages. Despite his upbringing in the Egyptian court, Moses is concerned for his own people and kills the Egyptian slave driver. God shows that he has not forgotten his chosen people by summoning Moses to lead the Israelites into the Promised Land.

CHAPTER 3 VERSE 14
"I AM WHO I AM"
The Bible uses several names to refer to God. Each one describes a different aspect of his nature, such as "Shapat", which is Hebrew for "Judge", or "El Elyon", which means "Almighty". The phrase "I am who I am" is the Hebrew word "Yawheh". The Jewish people consider this to be God's most sacred name and do not pronounce it.

EXODUS 4–5
MOSES RETURNS TO EGYPT

M OSES[1] ANSWERED, "What if they do not believe me... and say, 'The LORD did not appear to you'?" [2]Then the LORD said to him, "What is that in your hand?"

"*A staff*," he replied.

[3]The LORD said, "Throw it on the ground."

Moses threw it on the ground and it became a snake, and he ran from it. [4]Then the LORD said to him, "Reach out your hand and take it by the tail." So Moses reached out and took hold of the snake and it turned back into a staff in his hand. [5]"This," said the LORD, "is so that they may believe that the LORD, the God of their fathers... has appeared to you."...

[10]Moses said to the LORD, "O Lord, I have never been eloquent... [13]please, send someone else to do it."

[14]Then the LORD's anger burned against Moses and he said, "What about your brother, *Aaron the Levite?* I know he can speak well..."

God told Moses that Aaron would speak to the people for him, and that Moses should perform miraculous signs with his staff. Then Moses went to see Jethro, his father-in-law, and asked to go back to Egypt. Jethro agreed, and Moses left with his family. God instructed Aaron to meet Moses in the desert. Aaron obeyed, and Moses told him everything that God had said.

CHAPTER 4 VERSE 2
"A staff"

Moses' staff is his shepherd's crook. In the Bible it is referred to as the "staff of God" (Exodus 4: 20). The ancient Egyptians believed that magical sticks could protect them from evil spirits, but Moses' staff was a symbol of God's authority.

Magical symbols

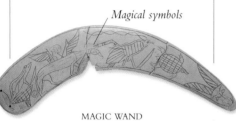

MAGIC WAND
This Egyptian wand is made from a hippo tusk. It was used to mark out areas of protection in people's homes.

CHAPTER 4 VERSE 14
"Aaron the Levite?"

Aaron was three years older than Moses (Exodus 7: 7). His role as Moses' spokesman anticipates his role as Israel's first High Priest. Aaron will be responsible for the spiritual leadership of the Israelites.

Moses is reluctant to accept his role, and so Aaron speaks to the leaders for him

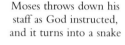

Moses throws down his staff as God instructed, and it turns into a snake

God tells Moses to perform miraculous signs with his staff so that the Israelites will believe he is sent from God

Aaron

The Israelite elders

The elders see the miracles and believe that God will deliver them from slavery

[29]Moses and Aaron brought together all the elders of the Israelites, [30]and Aaron told them everything the LORD had said to Moses. He also performed the signs before the people, [31]and they believed. And when they heard that the LORD was concerned about them... they bowed down and worshipped.

5   [1]Afterwards Moses and Aaron went to Pharaoh and said, "This is what the LORD... says: 'Let my people go...' " [2]Pharaoh said, "Who is the LORD, that I should obey him and let Israel go?..."

[6]That same day Pharaoh gave this order to the slave drivers... [7]"You are no longer to supply the people with *straw for making bricks*; let them go and gather their own straw.

⁸But require them to make the same number of bricks as before..." ¹⁵Then the Israelite foremen went and appealed to Pharaoh: "Why have you treated your servants this way?..."

¹⁷Pharaoh said, "Lazy, that's what you are – Lazy! That is why you keep saying, 'Let us go and sacrifice to the LORD.' ¹⁸Now get to work..." ¹⁹The Israelite foremen realised they were in trouble... ²⁰They found Moses and Aaron waiting to meet them, ²¹and they said, "May the LORD look upon you and judge you! You have... put a sword in their hand to kill us."

²²Moses returned to the LORD and said, "O LORD, why have you brought trouble upon this people?..."

God reassured Moses that he would free the Israelites from slavery and fulfil his promise to give them the land of Canaan. But when Moses went back and reported this to his people, they would not listen because of the hardship they were suffering.

Moses and Aaron go to Pharaoh and ask him to free the Israelites

Pharaoh refuses to let the Israelites go

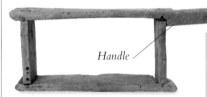

CHAPTER 5 VERSE 7
"Straw for making bricks"
Most Egyptian buildings were made out of bricks, although sandstone, granite, and marble were also used. Labourers moulded the bricks out of a mixture of mud, sand, and straw, then left them to dry in the sun.

Handle

WOODEN BRICK MOULD

THE ISRAELITE ELDERS
The Hebrew word for "elders" also means "bearded ones". During this period, the Israelite elders were usually senior members of their clans, who became leaders because of their wisdom and experience.

The Israelites have to gather straw to make the bricks

The same day, Pharaoh orders his slave drivers to make the Israelites work even harder

The Israelite foremen blame Aaron and Moses for the harsh treatment they are receiving

UNDERSTANDING THE STORY

Moses is unwilling to take on the role that God has planned for him. However, God's miraculous signs and Aaron's appointment as his spokesman persuade him. The Israelites' initial belief in Moses turns to anger when, instead of receiving their freedom, they suffer even greater oppression under the Egyptians.

EXODUS 7–10

THE STAFF AND THE PLAGUES

7 THE[8] LORD SAID TO MOSES AND AARON, [9]"When Pharaoh says to you, 'Perform a miracle,' then say to Aaron, 'Take your staff and throw it down before Pharaoh,' and *it will become a snake.*"

[10]So Moses and Aaron went to Pharaoh... Aaron threw his staff down in front of Pharaoh and his officials, and it became a snake.

Moses and Aaron ask Pharaoh to let the Israelites go

Pharaoh refuses and summons his magicians

The magicians copy Aaron

Aaron throws down his staff

Aaron's staff turns into a snake

The magicians' snakes are swallowed up

Moses

[11]Pharaoh then summoned the wise men and sorcerers, and the Egyptian magicians also did the same things by their secret arts: [12]Each one threw down his staff and it became a snake. But Aaron's staff swallowed up their staffs. [13]Yet Pharaoh's heart became hard and he would not listen to them, just as the LORD had said...

[14]Then the LORD said to Moses, "Pharaoh's heart is unyielding; he refuses to let the people go... [19]Tell Aaron, 'Take your staff and stretch out your hand over the waters of Egypt'... and they will turn to blood..." [20]Moses and Aaron did just as the LORD had commanded... and all the *water was changed into blood...*

God's first plague on Egypt turns the waters of the Nile into blood, and all the fish die

8 [25]Seven days passed after the LORD struck the Nile... [6]Aaron stretched out his hand [and] frogs came up and covered the land... [15]Pharaoh hardened his heart and would not listen to Moses... [17]When Aaron stretched out his hand with the staff and struck the dust of the ground, gnats came upon men and animals... [19]But Pharaoh's heart was hard and he would not listen...

Seven days later, there is a plague of frogs

A plague of gnats follows the plague of frogs

After the gnats, there is a plague of flies

²⁰The LORD said to Moses... "Confront Pharaoh as he goes to the water and say to him... ²¹'I will send swarms of flies... ²²But on that day I will deal differently with the land of Goshen, where my people live; no swarms of flies will be there... ²³I will make a distinction between my people and your people.' "... ²⁴Dense swarms of flies poured into Pharaoh's palace and into the houses of his officials, and throughout Egypt.

But Pharaoh still refused to let the Israelites go. And so a terrible plague killed all the livestock in Egypt. Then God sent a dust over the whole land, and festering boils broke out on men and animals. He sent thunder and hail, which struck men and animals. An east wind blew across the land and locusts covered the ground. But the land of Goshen was spared each time.

God's sixth plague inflicts boils on man and beast

10 ²¹Then the LORD said to Moses, "Stretch out your hand towards the sky so that darkness will spread over Egypt..." ²²So Moses stretched out his hand towards the sky, and total *darkness covered all Egypt* for three days... ²³Yet all the Israelites had light in the places where they lived.

²⁴Then Pharaoh summoned Moses and said, "Go, worship the LORD. Even your women and children may go with you; only leave your flocks and herds behind." ²⁵But Moses said, "You must allow us to have sacrifices and burnt offerings to present to the LORD our God..."

The storms are followed by a plague of locusts

²⁷But the LORD hardened Pharaoh's heart, and he was not willing to let them go. ²⁸Pharaoh said to Moses, "Get out of my sight!"

UNDERSTANDING THE STORY

God's first plague strikes at the heart of Egyptian life, and plague follows plague as the pharaoh stubbornly refuses to release the Israelites from bondage. The timing of the plagues and the fact that Goshen is spared are both evidence of divine intervention. God challenges and defeats the religious system in Egypt.

THE EGYPTIAN GODS

An ancient text lists more than seven hundred Egyptian deities. All the forces of nature were represented by a different god or goddess. Throughout Egypt, awesome temples were erected to worship these gods, and a vast priesthood performed sacred rituals in their honour. The plagues demonstrated that the gods of Egypt were powerless to resist God's will.

The fifth plague kills all the livestock

MIRACULOUS PLAGUES OR NATURAL DISASTERS?

Egypt's plagues could all be considered natural disasters. The Nile was occasionally polluted with red sediments from the Ethiopian highlands during a high flood. Freak seasonal weather, sandstorms that obliterated the light, and various epidemics were not uncommon in Egypt. The miraculous nature of these events was the divine control behind them.

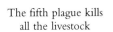

Next comes hail and thunder

✤

CHAPTER 10 VERSE 22
"Darkness covered all Egypt"
The sun god Ra was Egypt's chief deity. The Egyptians worshipped the sun in many forms. The rising, midday, and setting sun were each personified by a separate deity. To be cut off from the source of all life would have terrified the Egyptians.

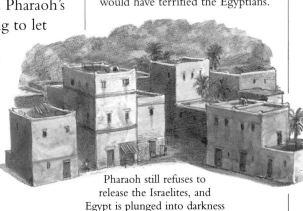

Pharaoh still refuses to release the Israelites, and Egypt is plunged into darkness

EXODUS 11–12

PASSOVER AND THE LAST PLAGUE

✣

CHAPTER 11 VERSE 1
"I will bring one more plague"
A different Hebrew word is used to name this plague, because this was God's final judgement on the Egyptians and the most devastating manifestation of his power.

✣

CHAPTER 12 VERSE 2
"This month is to be... the first month of your year"
This passage establishes the religious calendar of ancient Israel. New Year will be celebrated in remembrance of Israel's deliverance from Egypt. The religious year coincided with the old Hebrew agricultural calendar, which began in spring. The first month (March/April) was Abib, a Canaanite name meaning "ripening grain". It was later called Nisan.

✣

CHAPTER 12 VERSE 8
"Bitter herbs, and bread made without yeast"
The taste of bitter herbs was intended to remind the Israelites of the bitterness of their slavery. The unleavened bread was symbolic of the haste with which the people had to leave Egypt. There was not enough time for the bread to rise.

COS LETTUCE

ENDIVE   *CHICORY*

BITTER HERBS
The original bitter herbs were probably sour-tasting salad vegetables, such as sorrel, dandelions, chicory, and lettuces. Today, horseradish is often chosen to represent the bitter herbs.

11   Now[1] THE LORD said to Moses, *"I will bring one more plague* on Pharaoh and on Egypt. After that, he will let you go from here, and when he does, he will drive you out
12   completely... *²"This month is to be for you the first month, the first month of your year.* ³Tell the whole community of Israel that on the tenth day of this month each man is to take a lamb for his family... ⁵The animals you choose must be year-old males without defect... ⁶Take care of them until the fourteenth day of the month, when all the people of the community of Israel must slaughter them at twilight. ⁷Then they are to take some of the blood and put it on the sides and tops of the door-frames of the houses where they eat the lambs.

The Israelites mark their doors with the blood of lambs, so that death will "pass over" their homes

⁸"That same night they are to eat the meat roasted over the fire, along with *bitter herbs, and bread made without yeast...* ¹¹This is how you are to eat it: with *your cloak tucked into your belt,* your sandals on your feet and your staff in your hand. Eat it in haste; it is the LORD's Passover.

Staff in hand

Bread made without yeast

God tells the Israelites what they must eat for their last meal in Egypt and how they must eat it

Cloak tucked into belt

Sandals on feet

Bitter herbs

Lamb, slaughtered and roasted

¹²"On that same night I will pass through Egypt and strike down every firstborn – both men and animals – and *I will bring judgment on all the gods of Egypt.* I am the LORD. ¹³The blood will be a sign for you on the houses where you are; and when I see the blood, I will pass over you.

No destructive plague will touch you when I strike Egypt.

[14]"This is a day you are to commemorate; for the generations to come you shall celebrate it as a festival to the LORD..."

[21]Then Moses summoned all the elders of Israel and said to them... [24]"Obey these instructions as a lasting ordinance for you and your descendants. [25]When you enter the land that the LORD will give you as he promised, observe this ceremony. [26]And when your children ask you, 'What does this ceremony mean to you?' [27]then tell them, 'It is the Passover sacrifice to the LORD, who passed over the houses of the Israelites in Egypt and spared our homes when he struck down the Egyptians.' " Then the people bowed down and worshipped. [28]The Israelites did just what the LORD commanded Moses and Aaron.

[29]At midnight the LORD struck down all the firstborn in Egypt, from the firstborn of Pharaoh, who sat on the throne, to the firstborn of the prisoner, who was in the dungeon, and the firstborn of all the livestock as well. [30]Pharaoh and all his officials and all the Egyptians got up during the night, and there was loud wailing in Egypt, for · there was not a house without someone dead.

The last plague brings death to the firstborn of every Egyptian family

The firstborn of the animals also die

[31]During the night Pharaoh summoned Moses and Aaron and said, "Up! Leave my people, you and the Israelites! Go, worship the LORD as you have requested. [32]Take your flocks and herds, as you have said, and go. And also bless me."

UNDERSTANDING THE STORY

The Egyptians can no longer doubt the supreme power of God. The pharaoh's court magicians have been defeated, and there is nothing in nature that can be compared to this devastating event. God's final act of judgement breaks the will of the pharaoh. He releases the Israelites and humbly asks for God's blessing.

This festival is called Passover because the Lord "passed over" the homes of the Israelites, sparing them the Egyptians' fate. The Passover meal is eaten in remembrance of the Israelites' last night in Egypt and does not begin until after dark.

COMMEMORATING THE PASSOVER
Jewish families continue to observe the traditions of the Passover meal. Before the food is eaten, the youngest child asks, "How is this night different from others?" The oldest family member then recounts the story of the Passover.

❖

CHAPTER 12 VERSE 11
"Your cloak tucked into your belt"
By doing this, they were ready to leave at a moment's notice. Men often tucked their robes into their belts while they worked, so that their legs were free from hindrance.

❖

CHAPTER 12 VERSE 12
"I will bring judgment on all the gods of Egypt"
Egyptians believed that many gods lived on earth as animals, and Egyptian gods were often depicted in animal-form. The death of the first-born animals demonstrated that the Egyptian gods were powerless to protect their worshippers.

GOD OF THE FLOOD
The ram-headed god Khnum was worshipped as guardian of the Nile flood.

EXODUS 12–14
THE EXODUS

12 THE[33] EGYPTIANS URGED THE PEOPLE to hurry and leave the country. "For otherwise," they said, "we will all die!" [34]So the people took their dough before the yeast was added, and carried it on their shoulders in kneading troughs wrapped in clothing...

[37]The Israelites journeyed from Rameses to Succoth. There were about *six hundred thousand men* on foot, besides women and children... [38]as well as large droves of livestock, both flocks and herds....

[40]Now the length of time the Israelite people lived in Egypt was 430 years. [41]At the end of the 430 years, to the very day, all the LORD's divisions left Egypt.

13 When[17] Pharaoh let the people go, God did not lead them on the road through the Philistine country, though that was shorter. For God said, "If they face war, they might change their minds and return to Egypt." [18]So God led the people around by the desert road towards the Red Sea... [19]Moses took *the bones of Joseph* with him...

[20]After leaving Succoth they camped at Etham on the edge of the desert. [21]By day the LORD went ahead of them in *a pillar of cloud* to guide them on their way and by night in *a pillar of fire* to give them light, so that they could travel by day or night.

After the Israelites had fled, Pharaoh changed his mind about letting them go. He pursued the Israelites with his army until he caught up with them as they camped by the sea near Pi Hahiroth. When the Israelites saw the Egyptian army, they were terrified.

Thousands of Israelites and their livestock flee Egypt and trek across the desert towards the Red Sea

The Israelites are pursued by the Egyptian army

God guides Moses and his people from within a pillar of cloud

In a rush to leave, many carry unrisen dough in kneading troughs

14 ¹⁵Then the LORD said to Moses... ¹⁶"Raise your staff and stretch out your hand over the sea to divide the water so that the Israelites can go through the sea on dry ground..." ¹⁹The pillar of cloud also moved from in front and stood behind them, ²⁰coming between the armies of Egypt and Israel.

So Moses obeyed. That night he raised his staff over the sea and the waters divided. The Israelites went across, with a wall of water on their right and left. The Egyptians followed them into the sea, but the Lord threw them into confusion and caused the wheels to fall off their chariots.

²⁷Moses stretched out his hand over the sea, and at daybreak the sea went back to its place... ²⁸The water flowed back and covered the chariots and horsemen – the entire army of Pharaoh that had followed the Israelites into the sea. Not one of them survived.

THE RED SEA
This sea gets its name because its waters are periodically turned reddish-brown by dying algae. The sea stretches 2,100km (1,300 miles) from the Suez Canal to the Gulf of Aden, separating Africa and Arabia.

When Moses raises his staff, the waters of the Red Sea divide, and the Israelites cross over

When the Egyptian army tries to follow, Moses raises his staff a second time

The sea crashes down on the Egyptians, and they all perish

UNDERSTANDING THE STORY

The Israelites are given dramatic proof that God is the architect of their deliverance from slavery. The Exodus is the beginning of God's plan for his people. Through the leadership of his servant Moses, God brings the Israelites safely out of Egypt to begin their journey to the Promised Land.

❖

CHAPTER 13 VERSE 21
"A pillar of cloud... a pillar of fire"
Cloud and fire are symbols of God's immediate presence. These pillars are a visible demonstration to the Israelites that God is there to lead and protect them on their journey.

EXODUS 16–17

MANNA FROM HEAVEN

16

O^{N¹} THE FIFTEENTH DAY of the second month after they had come out of Egypt [the Israelites came to the *Desert of Sin*]. ²In the desert the whole community grumbled against Moses and Aaron. ³The Israelites said to them, "If only we had died by the LORD's hand in Egypt. There we sat round pots of meat and ate all the food we wanted, but you have brought us out into this desert to starve this entire assembly to death."

⁴Then the LORD said to Moses, "I will rain down bread from heaven for you."... ¹³*That evening quail came* and covered the camp, and in the morning there was a layer of dew around the camp. ¹⁴When the dew was gone, thin flakes like frost on the ground appeared on the desert floor. ¹⁵When the Israelites saw it, they said to each other, "What is it?"...

Moses said to them, "It is the bread the LORD has given you to eat. ¹⁶This is what the LORD has commanded: 'Each one is to gather as much as he needs... ²⁶Six days you are to gather it, but on *the seventh day, the Sabbath*, there will not be any." ²⁷Nevertheless, some of the people went out on the seventh day to gather it, but they found none...

God sends a flock of quail to the Israelites, who are starving in the desert

The next morning, the ground is covered with white flakes

God tells the Israelites to collect as much of this food as they need

They call the food "manna"

³¹*The people of Israel called the bread manna.* It was white like coriander seed and tasted like wafers made with honey... ³⁵The Israelites ate manna for forty years, until... they reached the borders of Canaan.

17

¹The whole Israelite community set out from the Desert of Sin, travelling from place to place as the LORD commanded. They camped at Rephidim, but there was no water for the people to drink.

CHAPTER 16 VERSE 1
"The Desert of Sin"
The Desert of Sin was a district in the Sinai Peninsula. In Bible times, the peninsula was divided into five regions: the deserts of Sin, Shur, Sinai, Paran, and Zin. Although barren and desolate, these deserts have been inhabited by Bedouin tribes for thousands of years. The Sinai Peninsula lies between Egypt and Israel and is bounded by the Mediterranean Sea in the north and the Red Sea in the south.

CHAPTER 16 VERSE 13
"That evening quail came"
Quail cross the Sinai Peninsula on migrations between Europe and Africa. These small birds can fly quickly for a short period of time. When travelling long distances, they stretch out their wings and use the wind to help them. It is possible that the wind dropped, and the quail landed because of exhaustion.

THE COMMON QUAIL
Quail are small, brown-speckled game birds belonging to the same family as the pheasant.

CHAPTER 16 VERSE 26
"The seventh day, the Sabbath"
This is the first time that the Bible uses the word "Sabbath", which is Hebrew for "rest". God did not provide food on the seventh day, because it was to be set aside for worship and rest. The principle of the Sabbath day is based on God's creation of the world (Genesis 2: 3).

The Israelites complained bitterly to Moses that they would die of thirst in the desert. Moses asked God for his help.

⁵The LORD answered Moses... "Take with you some of the elders of Israel and take in your hand the staff with which you struck the Nile, and go. ⁶I will stand there before you by the rock at Horeb. Strike the rock, and water will come out of it for the people to drink." So Moses did this in the sight of the elders of Israel. ⁷And he called the place *Massah and Meribah* because the Israelites quarrelled and because they tested the LORD saying, "Is the LORD among us or not?" ⁸*The Amalekites* came and attacked the Israelites at Rephidim. ⁹Moses said to Joshua, "Choose some of our men and go out to fight [them]... I will stand on top of the hill with the staff of God in my hands."... ¹¹As long as Moses held up his hands, the Israelites were winning... ¹²When Moses' hands grew tired, they took a stone and put it under him and he sat on it. Aaron and Hur held his hands up... so that his hands remained steady till sunset. ¹³So Joshua overcame the Amalekite army with the sword.

The Israelites complain that they have no water

Moses strikes the rock with his staff, and water gushes out

The Amalekites attack the Israelites, and Moses holds up the staff of God until the enemy is defeated

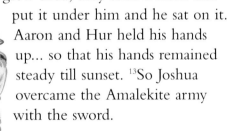

Aaron and Hur help Moses

After these events, Moses chose several wise men to act as judges over the people. The Israelites travelled on to the Desert of Sinai, and they camped in front of the mountain of God.

UNDERSTANDING THE STORY

The Israelites begin to lose faith in God when they are faced with hunger and thirst in the desert. However, God demonstrates concern for his people when he miraculously provides them with food and water, and he brings them success in battle. Despite God's actions, the Israelites continue to doubt him.

CHAPTER 16 VERSE 31
"The people... called the bread manna"
"Manna" is a Hebrew expression meaning "What is it?" Scientists are unable to formally identify the source of this food substance. Some suggest that it is the sweet liquid produced by insects living on the Tamarisk Bush in the Sinai Peninsula. Others believe it is a sticky resin secreted by a number of desert plants.

HAMMADA SHRUB
This plant grows in southern Sinai. It produces a sweet, white substance, which Bedouins use today as a sweetner.

CHAPTER 17 VERSE 7
"Massah and Meribah"
Moses named this place "Massah", which means "testing", and "Meribah", which means "striving". These Hebrew names serve to remind the Israelites of their struggle for faith in God.

CHAPTER 17 VERSE 8
"The Amalekites"
This semi–nomadic people were descended from Esau's grandson Amalek (Genesis 36: 12). At the time of Moses, the Amalekites lived mainly in the Arabian and Sinai Peninsulas and claimed the territory as their own. They were the first people to attack the Israelites and remained their enemies throughout the Old Testament.

JOSHUA
Joshua was from the tribe of Ephraim. He was the Israelites' military leader, and he was also Moses' assistant. Joshua accompanied Moses when Moses talked with God outside the camp (Exodus 33: 11). Joshua's original name was Hoshea. Moses renamed him "Joshua" (Numbers 13: 16). "Jesus" was a variation of the Hebrew name "Joshua".

EXODUS 19–20, 23

THE TEN COMMANDMENTS

19

O N[16] THE MORNING of the third day there was thunder and lightning, with a thick cloud over the mountain, and a very loud trumpet blast. Everyone in the camp trembled. [17]Then Moses led the people out of the camp to meet with God, and they stood at the foot of the mountain. [18]Mount Sinai was covered with smoke, because the LORD descended on it in fire. The smoke billowed up from it like smoke from a furnace, the whole mountain trembled violently, [19]and the sound of the trumpet grew louder and louder. Then Moses spoke and the voice of God answered him...

20

[1]And God spoke *all these words*: [2]"*I am the LORD your God*, who brought you out of Egypt, out of the land of slavery.

[3]"You shall have *no other gods before me.*

[4]"*You shall not make for yourself an idol* in the form of anything in heaven above or on the earth beneath or in the waters below...

[7]"You shall not misuse the name of the LORD your God...

[8]"Remember the Sabbath day by keeping it holy...

[12]"Honour your father and your mother...

[13]"You shall not murder.

[14]"You shall not commit adultery.

[15]"You shall not steal.

[16]"You shall not give false testimony against your neighbour.

[17]"You shall not covet... anything that belongs to your neighbour."

Many other laws, with detailed penalties, were given to the people of Israel: laws regarding slaves, personal injuries, property damage, social responsibility, justice and mercy, and festivals. Then God sealed his covenant saying:

CHAPTER 20 VERSE 1
"All these words"

In the ancient Middle East, the stipulations in a treaty between a king and his vassals were known as "words". The ten "words" that God spoke to Moses are what God demands from the Israelites. They lay down the principles of Israel's relationship with God and others. These "ten commandments" form the basis of Israel's Covenant Law.

Moses leads the people out of the camp to meet with God

CHAPTER 20 VERSE 2
"I am the LORD your God"

God's speech to Moses and the Israelites follows the same pattern as ancient royal treaties. First there is an introduction, which identifies the king. This is followed by a historical preamble (reminding the subjects of the king's gracious acts). Then the terms of the treaty are laid down, and these must be obeyed. In the Covenant Law, God is the king and the Israelites are his subject people.

The people stand at the foot of the mountain. God descends as fire, and the mountain is covered with smoke and trembles violently

YOU SHALL HAVE
NO OTHER GODS
BEFORE ME

YOU SHALL NOT
MAKE FOR
YOURSELF AN IDOL

YOU SHALL NOT
MISUSE THE NAME OF
THE LORD YOUR GOD

REMEMBER THE
SABBATH DAY BY
KEEPING IT HOLY

HONOUR YOUR
FATHER AND
YOUR MOTHER

23 ²²"If you... do all that I say, I will be an enemy to your enemies and will oppose those who oppose you... ²⁴"Do not bow down before their gods or worship them or follow their practices... ²⁵"Worship the LORD your God... ²⁷I will send my terror ahead of you and throw into confusion every nation you encounter... ²⁸I will send the hornet ahead of you to drive the Hivites, Canaanites and Hittites out of your way. ²⁹But I will not drive them out in a single year, because the land would become desolate and the wild animals too numerous for you. ³⁰Little by little I will drive them out before you, until you have increased enough to take possession of the land. ³¹"I will establish your borders from the Red Sea to the Sea of the Philistines, and from the desert to the River. I will hand over to you the people who live in the land and you will drive them out before you. ³²Do not make a covenant with them or with their gods. ³³Do not let them live in your land, or they will cause you to sin against me, because the worship of their gods will certainly be a snare to you."

Moses speaks, and the voice of God answers. God gives the Israelites ten commandments

UNDERSTANDING THE STORY

In the beginning, God created order out of chaos with ten commands (Genesis 1). In the same way, God creates order in Israel with ten commandments. The Covenant Law is Israel's constitution. It sets down what is right and wrong, and what pleases and displeases the Creator.

❖

CHAPTER 20 VERSE 3
"No other gods before me"
The Israelites are to worship only God. The first commandment is the essential principle on which the covenant agreement is founded.

❖

CHAPTER 20 VERSE 4
"You shall not make... an idol"
Unlike contemporary tribes and nations, the Israelites are forbidden to make images of their God. The divine nature of God cannot be defined by a visual representation.

❖

CHAPTER 23 VERSE 22
"If you... do all that I say"
The assurances of these promises are very close to the protection clauses found in ancient Middle-Eastern treaties. In return for their full obedience, God will reward the Israelites and ensure their security.

JESUS AND THE COMMANDMENTS
The commandments deal firstly with how people should relate to God and, secondly, to each other. A teacher of the Law once asked Jesus, "Of all the commandments, which is the most important?" Jesus replied, "The most important one is... 'Love the Lord your God with all your heart and with all your soul and with all your mind and with all your strength'. The second one is... 'Love your neighbour as yourself'. There is no greater commandment than these." (Mark 12: 29–31). In this way, Jesus summed up the essence of the Ten Commandments.

YOU SHALL
NOT MURDER

YOU SHALL
NOT COMMIT
ADULTERY

YOU SHALL
NOT STEAL

YOU SHALL NOT GIVE
FALSE TESTIMONY AGAINST
YOUR NEIGHBOUR

YOU SHALL NOT COVET...
ANYTHING THAT BELONGS
TO YOUR NEIGHBOUR

EXODUS 24–25, 32–40

THE GOLDEN CALF

CHAPTER 24 VERSE 12
"The tablets of stone"
The Covenant Law was inscribed on two tablets. This followed the ancient Middle-Eastern tradition of drafting two copies of a treaty; one was kept by the king and the other by his vassal. It is likely that Moses' tablets contained two identical copies of the Ten Commandments. These were placed in the Ark, as testimony to God's covenant with his people.

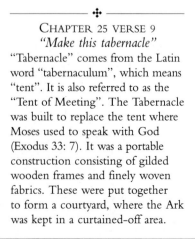

Moses goes to the mountain of God, where he receives the Covenant Law

CHAPTER 24 VERSE 18
"Forty days and forty nights"
The number "forty" is used symbolically in the Bible and means "a lot". It is associated with nearly all the new beginnings in the Bible, such as the Flood (Genesis 7: 12), the exploration of Canaan (Numbers 13: 25), and the period between Jesus' resurrection and ascension (Acts 1: 3).

CHAPTER 25 VERSE 9
"Make this tabernacle"
"Tabernacle" comes from the Latin word "tabernaculum", which means "tent". It is also referred to as the "Tent of Meeting". The Tabernacle was built to replace the tent where Moses used to speak with God (Exodus 33: 7). It was a portable construction consisting of gilded wooden frames and finely woven fabrics. These were put together to form a courtyard, where the Ark was kept in a curtained-off area.

24 THE[12] LORD SAID TO MOSES, "Come up to me on the mountain and stay here, and I will give you *the tablets of stone*, with the law and commands I have written for their instruction."...

¹⁵When Moses went up on the mountain, the cloud covered it... ¹⁸Then Moses entered the cloud as he went on up the mountain. And he stayed on the mountain *forty days and forty nights.*

25 ¹The LORD said to Moses, ²"Tell the Israelites to bring me an offering. You are to receive the offering for me from each man whose heart prompts him to give... ⁸Then have them make a sanctuary for me, and I will dwell among them. ⁹*Make this tabernacle* and all its furnishing exactly like the pattern I will show you..."

Moses is away for forty days, and the Israelites fear he will not return

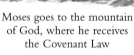

Aaron collects gold ear-rings, which he casts into a golden idol

The people persuade Aaron to make an image of God in the form of a golden calf

32 ¹When the people saw that Moses was so long in coming down from the mountain, they gathered round Aaron and said, "Come, make us gods who will go before us. As for this fellow Moses who brought us up out of Egypt, we don't know what has happened to him."

²Aaron answered them, "Take off the gold ear-rings that your wives, your sons and your daughters are wearing, and bring them to me."... ⁴He took what they handed him and made it into *an idol cast in the shape of a calf*, fashioning it with a tool. Then they said, "These are your gods, O Israel, who brought you up out of Egypt."

⁵When Aaron saw this, he built an altar in front of the calf and announced, "Tomorrow there will be a festival to the LORD." ⁶So the next day the people rose early and sacrificed burnt offerings and presented fellowship offerings. Afterwards they sat down to eat and drink and got up to indulge in revelry...

¹⁹When Moses approached the camp and saw the calf and the dancing, his anger burned and he threw the tablets out of his hands, breaking them to pieces at the foot of the mountain... ³⁵And the LORD struck the people with a plague because of what they did with the calf Aaron had made...

When Moses returns, he smashes the tablets in anger

The Israelites sacrifice burnt offerings and indulge in revelry

Moses went up Mount Sinai again with two new stone tablets and wrote down the Ten Commandments. The Israelites made the tabernacle according to God's instructions.

40   ¹Then the LORD said to Moses: ²"Set up the tabernacle, the Tent of Meeting, on the *first day of the first month*. ³Place the *ark of the Testimony* in it and shield the ark with the curtain... ¹³Then dress Aaron in the sacred garments, anoint him and consecrate him so that he may serve me as priest. ¹⁴Bring his sons... [and] ¹⁵anoint them as you anointed their father... Their anointing will be to a priesthood that will continue for all generations to come...

³⁴Then the cloud covered the Tent of Meeting, and the glory of the LORD filled the tabernacle... ³⁶In all the travels of the Israelites, whenever the cloud lifted from above the tabernacle, they would set out... ³⁸So the cloud of the LORD was over the tabernacle by day, and fire was in the cloud by night, in the sight of all the house of Israel during all their travels.

Moses returns to the mountain, and God renews the Covenant Law with him

UNDERSTANDING THE STORY

The Israelites' acceptance of the Covenant Law is short-lived: even before Moses returns from the mountain of God, they break one of the commandments. Despite their disobedience, God renews the covenant with his chosen people. The Tabernacle is constructed to provide them with a place of worship.

CHAPTER 32 VERSE 4
"An idol... in the shape of a calf"
Ancient pagan civilizations often depicted their gods as bulls, which were symbols of power and virility. The golden calf is believed to have been modelled on the Apis Bull, the Egyptian god of fertility. Israel's worship of idols violated the second commandment (Exodus 20: 4).

EGYPTIAN GOD APIS
This limestone stela (*c.* 500 BC) shows Apis, who was worshipped in the form of a living bull.

CHAPTER 40 VERSE 2
"First day of the first month"
This date is significant because it falls exactly one year after Israel's deliverance from Egypt (Exodus 12: 2–6).

CHAPTER 40 VERSE 3
"Ark of the Testimony"
"Ark" comes from the Latin word "arca", meaning chest. The Ark was a rectangular box made out of acacia wood and gold and was constructed to house the stone tablets of the Law. The Israelites carried the Ark by placing poles through gold rings attached to its sides.

ARK OF THE COVENANT
This illustration from the Nuremberg Bible depicts the construction of the Ark.

FROM SINAI TO CANAAN

After receiving God's law on Mount Sinai, the Israelites were now ready to enter the Promised Land. Canaan was a rich country with large cedar forests and fertile valleys. A group of twelve men who went to spy out the country described Canaan as a "land of milk and honey". However, the Israelites were afraid of the people living there and refused to enter Canaan. As a result of their disobedience to God, they wandered homeless in the desert for forty years.

FORTY YEARS IN THE DESERT

God determined that those who rejected Canaan would never live to see it. The Israelites remained in the desert until a whole new generation had emerged. During this time, they used a place called Kadesh as their base camp. After Aaron's death on Mount Hor (Numbers 33: 37–38), they went north to the Plains of Moab, travelling east of the River Jordan.

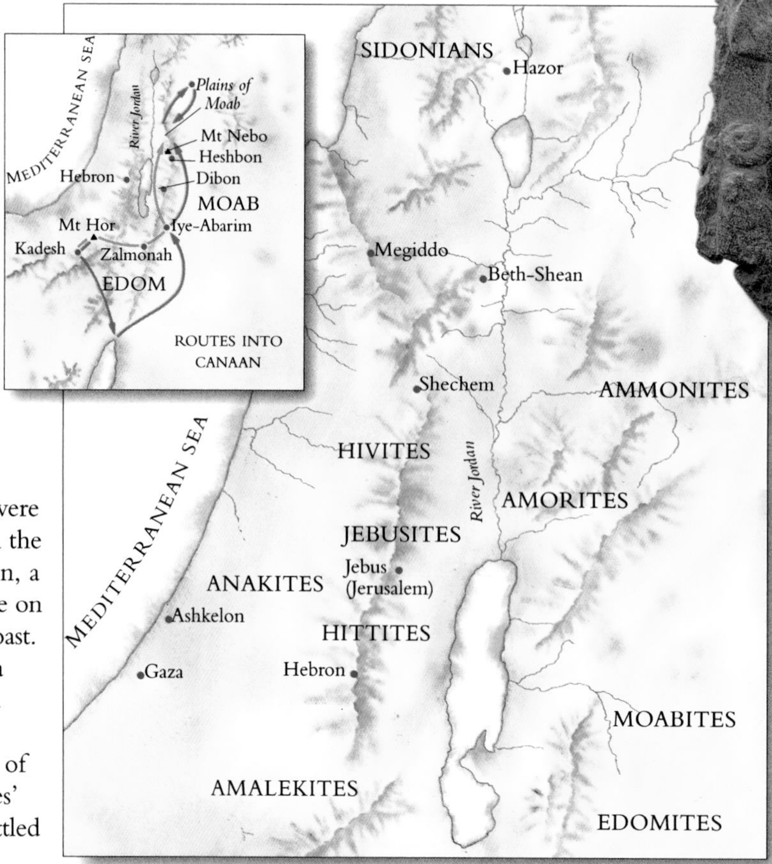

THE ISRAELITES'
ROUTE INTO CANAAN
Two different routes may be traced from the Bible texts. The green route is taken from Numbers 20–21, and the blue route follows the places mentioned in Numbers 33.

People of Canaan

Canaan was inhabited by many different tribes.

The **Sidonians** were Phoenicians from the city-state of Sidon, a commercial centre on the north-west coast.

The **Hittites**, a people from Asia Minor, had once ruled over much of Canaan. In Moses' time, they had settled around Hebron.

HITTITE PRISONER
Tile from the temple of Ramses III, Egypt

Jebusites were the original inhabitants of Jebus, which would later become Jerusalem.

The **Anakites** were a race of giants. They settled in and around Philistine cities such as Gaza and Ashkelon.

The **Hivites** lived around the mountains of Lebanon. No reference to this group of people exists outside the Bible.

ROUTES INTO CANAAN

Map labels: MEDITERRANEAN SEA, River Jordan, Plains of Moab, Mt Nebo, Heshbon, Dibon, MOAB, Hebron, Mt Hor, Iye-Abarim, Kadesh, Zalmonah, EDOM

THE TRIBAL AREAS OF CANAAN AND TRANSJORDAN

Map labels: SIDONIANS, Hazor, MEDITERRANEAN SEA, Megiddo, Beth-Shean, Shechem, AMMONITES, HIVITES, River Jordan, AMORITES, JEBUSITES, Jebus (Jerusalem), ANAKITES, Ashkelon, HITTITES, Gaza, Hebron, MOABITES, AMALEKITES, EDOMITES

Transjordan tribes

Apart from the Canaanites, the Israelites also came across tribes that had settled in the Transjordan (east of the river). These peoples were originally related to the Israelites.

The **Midianites** were the descendants of Midian, son of Abraham by his concubine Keturah. They were desert dwellers, who inhabited the area east of Moab and Edom. **Moabites** descended from Moab, Lot's son by his elder daughter.

MOABITE RELIEF
(*c.* 1000 BC)

The **Ammonites** were descendants of Ben-Ammi, who was Lot's son by his younger daughter.

The **Edomites** descended from Jacob's twin brother, Esau. Edom was another name for Esau. Their territory extended south of Moab. In later years, they migrated to the south of Jerusalem to an area that became Idumea.

The **Amalekites** descended from Amalek, Esau's grandson. These people were the first to attack the Israelites.

JOSHUA DEFEATS THE AMORITE KINGS
19th-century engraving by Shnorr Von Carolsfeld

The **Amorites** had an extensive kingdom that gradually formed into city-states throughout Syria and Palestine. A large settlement east of the River Jordan was destroyed by the Israelites prior to their entry into the Promised Land. Amorite was often used as a generic term to describe all Canaanite tribes.

KING DAVID KILLS AN AMALEKITE
David slew the Amalekite who confessed to killing King Saul.

TWELVE TRIBES OF ISRAEL

The twelve tribes that settled in the Promised Land claimed their descent and territories from Jacob's blessing (Genesis 49).

In the ancient Middle East, the last words of a father were considered his will. Usually, the eldest son received a double portion of his father's estate. But Jacob assigned lands and roles to his descendants, not according to tradition but according to God's revelation to him. Later, the tribes became associated with certain emblems, some of which derived from the blessing.

The Levites

Levi was not assigned any territory because of his part in the slaughter at Shechem (Genesis 34), and his descendants were not considered to be one of the twelve tribes. However, the Levites were faithful to God when the other Israelites worshipped the Golden Calf, and so God gave them the responsibility of the priesthood. They were allocated 48 cities, where they led the Israelites in worship.

Reuben did not inherit his "double share" as the eldest, because he dishonoured his father by sleeping with Jacob's concubine Bilhah. The tribe of Reuben settled on the eastern side of the Dead Sea.

Simeon, together with Levi, had killed all the males of Shechem, because their sister, Dinah, was raped by the son of the city's ruler. Jacob condemned this slaughter and did not apportion any land to Simeon or Levi. The tribe of Simeon was scattered within the territory of Judah.

Judah became the most important tribe. Jacob called Judah "a lion's cub". The tribe settled in the southern hill country. King David was descended from Judah. In Revelation, Jesus (who was of David's line) is called "The lion of the tribe of Judah" (5: 5).

Zebulun "will live by the seashore". Jacob's words imply that this tribe originally settled along the coast.

THE TRIBES OF ISRAEL AND THEIR TERRITORIES

Issachar is described as "a rawboned donkey" who will "submit to forced labour". The tribe of Issachar was allotted lands between the mountains of Gilboa and Tabor. This fertile region was often occupied by the Canaanites.

Dan "will be a serpent by the roadside". This tribe, although very small, was made up of brave and fearless men. They conquered the Canaanite city of Laish and renamed it Dan.

Gad "will be attacked by a band of raiders, but he will attack them at their heel". The tribe of Gad was located north of the Dead Sea in the forests of Gilead. The Moabites and the Ammonites, on the southern and eastern borders, were constantly at war with them.

Asher "will provide delicacies fit for a king". This tribe settled in the rich farmland of the north, close to the Mediterranean Sea.

Naphtali "is a doe set free that bears beautiful fawns". This tribe settled in the famous cedar forests close to Lebanon.

Ephraim and Manasseh inherited the double share of their father Joseph, Jacob's favourite son. Jacob adopted the two as his own. The tribe of Ephraim settled in the south-central hill country and became the most powerful tribe in the Northern Kingdom during the divided monarchy (930–722 BC).

Manasseh was the elder brother, but Jacob gave his blessing to Ephraim first. The tribe of Manasseh held the largest territory, which was situated on both sides of the Jordan.

Benjamin "is a ravenous wolf; in the morning he devours the prey, in the evening he divides the plunder". The tribe of Benjamin was renowned for the savagery of its exploits (Judges 19). The Benjamites settled north of Jerusalem. Saul, who hunted down David like a wolf, was from the tribe of Benjamin.

NUMBERS 10–12
ISRAEL COMPLAINS

This name means "burning". The fire that symbolized God's presence among the Israelites becomes an instrument of divine judgement.

CHAPTER 11 VERSE 4
"The rabble"
The Hebrew word conveys the idea of a mixed people. They were non-Israelites who left Egypt during the Exodus and followed the Israelites to the Promised Land. These people were often the source of complaints within the camp. The Israelites incurred God's anger because they allowed themselves to be influenced by them.

In the desert, the people start moaning about their hardship

CHAPTER 11 VERSE 6
"This manna!"
Manna was the Israelites' "daily bread", a gift from God and a sign of his providence. Manna was a sweet, seedlike substance that appeared like dew on every day except the Sabbath. Manna tasted like honey. It could either be boiled or ground up with a mortar and baked into cakes.

CHAPTER 11 VERSE 31
"A wind... drove quail"
In Bible times, millions of quail crossed this area of desert during migration. For much of the distance, the quail glided on wind currents.

10 SO[33] THEY SET OUT from the mountain of the LORD and travelled for three days. The ark of the covenant of the LORD went before them during those three days to find them a place to rest...

11 ¹Now the people complained about their hardships in the hearing of the LORD, and when he heard them his anger was aroused. Then fire from the LORD burned among them and consumed some of the outskirts of the camp. ²When the people cried out to Moses, he prayed to the LORD and the fire died down. ³So that place was called *Taberah*, because fire from the LORD had burned among them.

⁴*The rabble* with them began to crave other food, and again the Israelites started wailing and said, "If only we had meat to eat! ⁵We remember the fish we ate in Egypt at no cost – also the cucumbers, melons, leeks, onions and garlic. ⁶But now we have lost our appetite; we never see anything but *this manna!*"...

¹⁰Moses heard the people of every family wailing, each at the entrance to his tent. The LORD became exceedingly angry... ³¹Now *a wind went out from the LORD and drove quail* in from the sea.

God is angered by the complaints and sets fire to the outskirts of the camp

When the people grumble about eating manna every day, God sends thousands of quail

It brought them down all around the camp... as far as a day's walk in any direction. ³²All that day and night and all the next day the people went out and gathered quail. No-one gathered less than *ten homers*. Then they spread them out all around the camp. ³³But while the meat was still between their teeth and before it could be consumed, the anger of the LORD burned against the people, and he struck them with a severe plague.

³⁴Therefore the place was named *Kibroth Hattaavah*, because there they buried the people who had craved other food.

³⁵From Kibroth Hattaavah the people travelled to Hazeroth and stayed there.

12 ¹Miriam and Aaron began to talk against Moses because of his Cushite wife... ²"Has the LORD spoken only through Moses?" they asked. "Hasn't he also spoken through us?" And the LORD heard this...

⁵Then the LORD came down in a pillar of cloud; he stood at the entrance to the Tent and summoned Aaron and Miriam. When both of them stepped forward, ⁶he said, "Listen to my words:

"When a prophet of the LORD is among you, I reveal myself to him in visions... ⁷But this is not true of my servant Moses... ⁸With him I speak face to face, clearly and not in riddles... Why then were you not afraid to speak against my servant Moses?"... ¹⁰When the cloud lifted from above the Tent, there stood Miriam – leprous, like snow...

¹³So Moses cried out to the LORD, "O God, please heal her!"

¹⁴The LORD replied... "Confine her outside the camp for seven days; after that she can be brought back." ¹⁵So Miriam was confined outside the camp... and the people did not move on till she was brought back.

UNDERSTANDING THE STORY

On their journey to the Promised Land, God has guided and protected his people and provided for their needs. By rejecting his gift of manna and questioning his choice of leader, the Israelites are showing contempt for their God.

CHAPTER 11 VERSE 32
"Ten homers"
A homer was a "donkey load". The enormous amount of quail that each person amassed was a testimony to the Israelites' greed.

LADEN DONKEY

CHAPTER 11 VERSE 34
"Kibroth Hattaavah"
The Hebrew name means "graves of gluttony". The place marked the graves of those who had rejected the manna and craved other food.

MIRIAM
Miriam was the sister of Moses and Aaron. She had helped rescue the baby Moses from death. Miriam was a prophetess (Exodus 15: 20). Both Miriam and Aaron had become jealous of Moses' authority. It was this, not Moses' foreign wife, that was at the root of their discontent.

God descends as a cloud

The people who eat the quail are struck dead by a plague

Miriam and Aaron challenge Moses' leadership

When the cloud lifts, Miriam is afflicted with leprosy

Moses asks God to cure Miriam

NUMBERS 13–14
ISRAEL REJECTS CANAAN

❖

CHAPTER 13 VERSE 21
"[Kadesh]... from the Desert of Zin as far as Rehob"
After their long journey from Egypt, the Israelites were now poised to enter the Promised Land. They were camped at Kadesh, an oasis in the desert bordering southern Canaan. Rehob was 400km (250 miles) to the north.

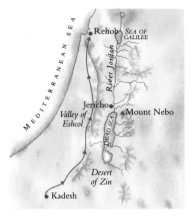

THE EXPLORATION OF CANAAN
The exploration of Canaan took the twelve men from the south of the land to its northernmost limits.

❖

CHAPTER 13 VERSE 22
"[They] came to Hebron"
Hebron is Palestine's highest town, lying 927m (3,040ft) above sea level in the Judean hills. Abraham, Isaac, and Jacob were all buried at Hebron. At the time of the Patriarchs, Hebron was just a trading place for shepherds and herdsmen. Four centuries later, the explorers saw a large, fortified town, which was the royal city of the Anakites.

❖

CHAPTER 13 VERSE 23
"The Valley of Eshcol"
"Eshcol" is Hebrew for "cluster". The valley was given this name because it was where the explorers picked the grapes. These were so large that one branch yielded just a single cluster. The size of the grapes they brought back to Moses represented the goodness of the land that God was giving to the Israelites.

13 T HE[1] LORD SAID TO MOSES, [2]"Send some men to explore the land of Canaan, which I am giving to the Israelites. From each ancestral tribe send one of its leaders."...

[17]When Moses sent them to explore Canaan, he said, [18]"See what the land is like and whether the people who live there are strong or weak, few or many. [19]What kind of land do they live in?... [20]Do your best to bring back some of the fruit of the land."... [21]So they [left *Kadesh*] and explored the land *from the Desert of Zin as far as Rehob*... [22]and *came to Hebron*... [23]When they reached *the Valley of Eshcol*, they cut off a branch bearing a single cluster of grapes. Two of them carried it on a pole between them, along with *some pomegranates* and figs... [25]At the end of forty days they returned from exploring the land...

[27]They gave Moses this account: "We went into the land to which you sent us, and it does flow with milk and honey! Here is its fruit. [28]But the people who live there are powerful, and the cities are fortified and very large. We even saw *the descendants of Anak* there... [31]We can't attack those people; they are stronger than we are..." [32]And they spread among the Israelites a bad report about the land they had explored...

14 [2]All the Israelites grumbled against Moses and Aaron... [4]And they said to each other, "We should choose a leader and go back to Egypt."...

Moses waits forty days for the twelve men to return from Canaan

Aaron

The explorers bring back fruit from Canaan

Ten of the explorers feel that the Israelites are too weak to conquer the Canaanites

Caleb and Joshua try to persuade the Israelites to trust in God

⁶Joshua [from Ephraim's tribe] and Caleb [from Judah's tribe], who were among those who had explored the land, tore their clothes ⁷and said... "The land we passed through and explored is exceedingly good. ⁸If the LORD is pleased with us, he will lead us into that land..."

¹⁰Then the glory of the LORD appeared ¹¹[and] said to Moses, "How long will these people treat me with contempt?... ³⁰Not one of you will enter the land I swore with uplifted hand to make your home, except Caleb son of Jephunneh and Joshua son of Nun. ³¹As for your children... I will bring them in to enjoy the land you have rejected. ³²But you – your bodies will fall in this desert. ³³Your children will be shepherds here for forty years, suffering for your unfaithfulness..."

³⁶So the men... ³⁷responsible for spreading the bad report about the land were struck down and died of a plague before the LORD. ³⁹When Moses reported this to all the Israelites, they mourned bitterly. ⁴⁰Early the next morning they went up towards the high hill country. "We have sinned," they said. "We will go up to the place the LORD promised."

Moses told them not to go, but they ignored him. As God was not with them, the Israelites were beaten by the Canaanites and forced to wander in the wilderness.

CHAPTER 13 VERSE 23
"Some pomegranates"
This fruit was plentiful throughout Canaan. Pomegranates were eaten or made into wine. Their skins, which are high in tannin, were used for tanning leather. The pomegranate became a symbol of Canaan's fruitfulness. It was a decorative motif on the walls of Solomon's Temple and the High Priest's robes.

POMEGRANATE FRUIT
Pomegranates still grow in Israel. They are often stored to be eaten in winter.

God speaks to Moses. The Lord is angry that the Israelites have rejected the Promised Land

The Israelites realise that they have sinned and try to enter Canaan

They are defeated by the tribes living there

Joshua Caleb

The ten men who gave a bad report about the Promised Land are struck dead; only Caleb and Joshua are spared

UNDERSTANDING THE STORY
The Israelites' sin is to doubt the word of God. His punishment is to deny the Israelites the land he had promised them. But God has not abandoned his chosen people. He renews his covenant with the next generation. They will inherit the land that their parents rejected.

CHAPTER 13 VERSE 28
"The descendants of Anak"
The Anakites were a race of giants that lived in Canaan, and they frightened the Israelite explorers. Caleb later defeated the Anakites and took their land for the tribe of Judah. A few surviving Anakites sought refuge with the Philistines.

DAVID SLAYS GOLIATH, BY TITIAN
The Philistines' champion, Goliath, was probably an Anakite.

NUMBERS 22–24
BALAAM

22 THE[1] ISRAELITES TRAVELLED to the plains of Moab and camped along the Jordan across from Jericho. [2]Now Balak son of Zippor saw all that Israel had done to *the Amorites*, [3]and Moab was terrified because there were so many people... [4]So Balak son of Zippor, who was king of Moab at the time, [5]sent messengers to summon *Balaam son of Beor*, who was at *Pethor, near the River*, in his native land. Balak said: "A people has come out of Eygpt... [6]Now come and put a curse on [them], because they are too powerful for me... For I know that those you bless are blessed, and those you curse are cursed." [7]The elders of Moab and Midian left, taking with them the fee for divination. When they came to Balaam, they told him what Balak had said.

Balak, king of Moab, is afraid of the Israelites

He sends messengers to ask Balaam to put a curse on them

Balaam asked the men to stay, while he waited for God's instructions. That night, God told Balaam he must not curse the Israelites as they were blessed. So Balaam did not go with the men. Balak sent more envoys to Balaam and tried to tempt him with handsome rewards. Again Balaam waited for God's answer.

[20]God came to Balaam and said, "Since these men have come to summon you, go with them, but do only what I tell you."... [22]But *God was very angry* when he went, and the angel of the LORD stood in the road to oppose him. Balaam was riding on his donkey... [23]When the donkey saw the angel... in the road with a drawn sword in his hand, she turned off the road into a field. Balaam beat her to get her back on the road.

Balaam rides to meet Balak

The donkey sees an angel barring their path and swerves off the road

Balaam cannot see the angel and beats his donkey

CHAPTER 22 VERSE 2
"The Amorites"
This tribe lived to the north of Moab. "Amorite" is a Semitic word for "the west". They were called this because they had settled in the land west of Mesopotamia. The Israelites had totally destroyed them when the Amorite king refused the Israelites permission to travel through his land.

THE LANDS OF MOAB
The Israelites were camped east of the River Jordan, just north of the Dead Sea. They planned to invade Canaan from there, but they had no intention of attacking the Moabites.

CHAPTER 22 VERSE 5
"Balaam son of Beor"
Balaam worshipped God, but he was also well-known for practising divination. According to Moses' Law, occult practices were strictly forbidden (Deuteronomy 18: 10–12).

SHEEP'S LIVER
In ancient times, diviners predicted the future using instruments such as this clay mould of a sheep's liver.

The angel reappeared, and the donkey pressed herself close to a wall, crushing Balaam's foot. When the angel blocked her path, she lay down under Balaam, afraid to go on. Both times Balaam beat her. Then God let the donkey speak.

[28]"What have I done to you to make you beat me these three times?" [29]Balaam answered the donkey, "You have made a fool of me! *If I had a sword* in my hand, I would kill you right now." [30]The donkey said to Balaam, "Am I not your own donkey, which you have always ridden, to this day? Have I been in the habit of doing this to you?"... [31]Then the LORD opened Balaam's eyes, and he saw the angel of the LORD standing in the road with his sword drawn. So he bowed low...

[35]The angel of the LORD said to Balaam, "Go with the men, but speak only what I tell you."... [41]The next morning Balak took Balaam up to Bamoth Baal, and from there he saw part of the people.

23 [1]Balaam said, "Build me seven altars here, and prepare seven bulls and seven rams for me." [2]Balak did as Balaam said.

The word of God came upon Balaam, and he uttered seven oracles. The first four blessed Israel, and Balak grew very angry as he listened to Balaam speak. In his fourth oracle, Balaam told of the promise of a king.

Balaam meets the king of Moab, and they go up to Bamoth Baal, where they can see the Israelites

Instead of cursing the Israelites, Balaam blesses them

The Israelites' camp

Balak and the Moabites are furious with Balaam

Balak builds seven altars

24 [17]"*A sceptre will rise out of Israel.* He will crush the foreheads of Moab... [18]But Israel will grow strong... [19]and destroy the survivors of the city."

Balak listened to Balaam's last three oracles, which predicted the destruction of Israel's enemies. He refused to pay Balaam his money and returned home in anger.

UNDERSTANDING THE STORY

This story illustrates God's commitment to fulfil his covenant promise. Balaam is famous for his powerful curses, but he cannot contradict God's will. Instead of putting a curse on the Israelites, Balaam blesses them. God puts words into Balaam's mouth as easily as he puts words into the mouth of Balaam's donkey.

CHAPTER 22 VERSE 5
"Pethor, near the River"
"The River" is the Euphrates. Pethor was in northern Mesopotamia and is traditionally believed to be modern-day Tell Ahmar in Syria.

POTTERY
This vase (*c.* 2000 BC) was found at Tell Ahmar.

CHAPTER 22 VERSE 22
"God was very angry"
God told Balaam not to go with Balak's envoys. A true worshipper would have carried out God's will, but Balaam was tempted by the money. He was wrong to question God a second time to try to gain his approval. Balaam's masters were God and money. Both the Old and the New Testaments teach that it is impossible to serve both.

CHAPTER 22 VERSE 29
"If I had a sword"
The fact that the angel does have a sword serves to contrast the donkey's faithfulness with Balaam's lack of faith. The donkey sees the danger in their path and suffers to serve his master. Balaam is blinded by greed.

CHAPTER 24 VERSE 17
"A sceptre will rise out of Israel"
This was the last of Balaam's four prophetic poems that affirmed God's covenant with Abraham. The oracle anticipates King David, who destroyed the Moabites a few centuries later (2 Samuel 8: 2).

DEUTERONOMY 31–34, JOSHUA 1–3

THE CROSSING OF THE JORDAN

CHAPTER 31 VERSE 2
"A hundred and twenty years old"
According to the Jewish tradition, Moses was forty years old when he left Egypt for Midian. Forty years later, when he was eighty (Exodus 7: 7), he challenged the pharaoh and led the Israelites out of Egypt. Moses spent the last forty years of his life in the desert, which was God's punishment on the Israelites for rejecting the Promised Land.

CHAPTER 31 VERSE 2
"You shall not cross the Jordan"
After many years in the desert, Moses disobeyed God's instructions. God told him to speak to a rock to make water gush out, but Moses struck the rock with his staff instead. God told him, "Because you did not trust me enough to honour me as holy in the sight of the Israelites, you will not bring this community into the land I give them" (Numbers 20: 12).

MOUNT NEBO
This monument marks the place where Moses viewed the Promised Land.

JOSHUA
Joshua was one of the twelve men chosen to explore Canaan forty years earlier. Only he and Caleb had brought back good reports, and God rewarded their faith. They were allowed to enter Canaan, while the rest of the Exodus generation was condemned to die in the desert. As Moses' successor, Joshua will bring Israel's salvation to completion. The name "Joshua" means "The Lord is Saviour".

31 M OSES[1] WENT OUT and spoke these words to all Israel: "[2]I am now *a hundred and twenty years old* and I am no longer able to lead you. The LORD has said to me, '*You shall not cross the Jordan.*' [3]The LORD your God himself will cross over ahead of you. He will destroy these nations before you, and you will take possession of their land. Joshua also will cross over ahead of you..."

Moses wrote down all God's laws. This "Book of the Law" was placed next to the ark of the covenant. Then Moses blessed the Israelites, tribe by tribe.

34 [1]Then Moses climbed Mount Nebo... There the LORD showed him the whole land... [4]Then the LORD said to him, "This is the land I promised on oath to Abraham, Isaac and Jacob... I have let you see it with your eyes, but you will not cross over into it." [5]And Moses the servant of the LORD died there in Moab, as the LORD had said. [6]He buried him in Moab... but to this day no-one knows where his grave is.

Before Moses dies, he climbs to the top of Mount Nebo. There, God shows him the whole of the Promised Land

1 [1]After the death of Moses... the LORD said to Joshua... [2]"Moses my servant is dead. Now then, you and all these people, get ready to cross the Jordan River into the land I am about to give them – to the Israelites... [7]Be strong and very courageous. Be careful to obey all the law my servant Moses gave you... [8]Do not let this Book of the Law depart from your mouth; meditate on it day and night..."

2 [1]Then Joshua son of Nun secretly sent two spies from Shittim. "Go, look over the land," he said, "especially Jericho." So they went and entered the house of a prostitute named Rahab and stayed there.

Joshua sends two spies to Jericho. When the king of Jericho tries to capture the spies, a prostitute helps them to escape

When the king of Jericho heard that the men were in his town, he asked Rahab to bring them to him. Instead, she hid them on the roof of her house. She knew that God was with the Israelites and that they would take the land.

[She said] [11]For *the LORD your God is God in heaven above and on the earth below...* [12]Please swear to me by the LORD... [13]that you will save [my family] from death."... [14]"If you don't tell what we are doing, we will treat you kindly and faithfully when the LORD gives us the land." [15]So she let them down by a rope through the window, for the house she lived in was part of the city wall... [17]The men said to her, "This oath you made us swear will not be binding on us [18]unless, when we enter the land, you have tied *this scarlet cord* in the window..."

The men left and returned to Joshua with the good news that everybody in that land was afraid of the Israelites. The next day, they prepared to cross the Jordan.

Priests carry the ark and lead the people into the Promised Land

When they reach the River Jordan, the water stops flowing

3   [6]Joshua said to the priests, "*Take up the ark of the covenant* and pass on ahead of the people." So they took it up and went ahead of them... [15]Now *the Jordan is in flood all during harvest.* Yet as soon as the priests who carried the ark reached the Jordan and their feet touched the water's edge, [16]the water from upstream stopped flowing. It piled up in a heap a great distance away, at a town called Adam in the vicinity of Zarethan, while the water flowing down to the Sea of the Arabah (the Salt Sea) was completely cut off. So the people crossed over opposite Jericho... [17]until the whole nation had completed the crossing on dry ground.

UNDERSTANDING THE STORY

The miraculous crossing of the Jordan is reminiscent of the parting of the Red Sea, when Moses led the Israelites out of Egypt. Now Israel has a new leader in Joshua, and the years of wandering in the desert are at an end. God is with his people as they finally enter the land that he promised to the Patriarchs.

❖

CHAPTER 2 VERSE 11
"The LORD... is God in heaven above and on the earth below"
In the New Testament, Rahab is remembered as a model of faith. When she confesses that God is her Lord, she is accepted as one of his covenant people. She leaves behind her life of prostitution and begins a new life as a wife and mother. The Gospel of Matthew lists Rahab as an ancestor of Jesus (1: 5).

❖

CHAPTER 2 VERSE 18
"This scarlet cord"
The scarlet cord recalls the blood of the lambs that the Israelites daubed on their doors on the night before the Exodus. The blood distinguished the Israelites from the doomed Egyptians. The scarlet cord will distinguish Rahab's family and save them from the Canaanites' fate.

❖

CHAPTER 3 VERSE 6
"Take up the ark of the covenant"
The Ark was the Tabernacle's most sacred furnishing and symbolized God's throne. It was carried ahead of the people to show that God himself was taking Israel into the land of his covenant promise.

❖

CHAPTER 3 VERSE 15
"The Jordan is in flood all during harvest"
The grain harvest took place in April and May. For most of the year the Jordan could be forded easily, but during the harvest the river was in flood because of snow melting on Mount Hermon and spring rains. By holding back the river, God demonstrated his presence and brought honour to Joshua, the Israelites' new leader.

RIVER JORDAN IN FLOOD

JOSHUA 5–6

THE FALL OF JERICHO

Known as the "City of Palms", Old Testament Jericho stood in a lush oasis. Excavations of the site reveal a mound of ancient cities, built and destroyed, one above another. The most recent carbon testing links the destruction of a heavily walled city to the time of Joshua (*c.* 1400 BC).

ANCIENT JERICHO
Ruins at Tell es-Sultan show settlements dating between *c.* 9600 and 1400 BC. Jericho's walls were first built in *c.* 8000, making it the world's oldest walled city.

CHAPTER 5 VERSE 2
"Flint knives"
At this time, most weapons were made from bronze. Now that the Israelites are ready to take Canaan, the entire male population is rededicated to God with knives of flint. In the Bible, this material is associated with strength and determination of purpose.

CHAPTER 6 VERSE 4
"Trumpets of rams' horns"
The national trumpet of Israel is called a "shophar". The instrument produces a loud, strident noise that was used both as a summons to battle and a call to worship.

SHOPHAR
The "shophar" is still sounded during some Jewish prayer services.

5 AT[2] THAT TIME THE LORD said to Joshua, "Make *flint knives* and circumcise the Israelites again." [3]So Joshua made flint knives and circumcised the Israelites at Gibeath Haaraloth. [4]Now this is why he did so: All those who came out of Egypt – all the men of military age – died in the desert on the way after leaving Egypt. [5]All the people that came out had been circumcised, but all the people born in the desert during the journey from Eygpt had not... [8]And after the whole nation had been circumcised, they remained where they were in camp until they were healed...

6 [1]Now Jericho was tightly shut up because of the Israelites. No-one came out and no-one came in.

God gives Joshua precise instructions for the defeat of Jericho

The walled city is shut up tight because of the Israelites

On the seventh day, the priests march around the city blowing their trumpets. They do this seven times

The ark is carried around the city every day for six days

Seven priests march in front of the ark

[2]Then the LORD said to Joshua, "See, I have delivered Jericho into your hands, along with its king and its fighting men. [3]March around the city once with all the armed men. Do this for six days. [4]Make seven priests carry *trumpets of rams' horns* in front of the ark. On the seventh day, march around the city seven times, with the priests blowing the trumpets. [5]When you hear them sound a long blast on the trumpets, make all the people give a loud shout; then the wall of the city will collapse and the people will go up, every man straight in."

Joshua did exactly what he was told and, on the seventh day, after the seventh time around, the trumpets sounded.

[20]The people shouted, and at the sound of the trumpet, when the people gave a loud shout, the wall collapsed; so every man charged straight in, and they took the city. [21]They *devoted the city to the LORD* and destroyed with the sword every living thing in it – men and women, young and old, cattle, sheep and donkeys...

[24]Then they burned the whole city and everything in it, but they put the silver and gold and the articles of bronze and iron into the treasury of the LORD's house.

CHAPTER 6 VERSE 21
"Devoted the city to the LORD"
The Israelites honoured God as the architect of their victory by offering all the spoils of war to him. Those things that were devoted to the Lord were sacred and denied to all others. The city and everything in it was sacrificed to the Lord. Metals and other objects that could not be destroyed by fire were placed in the Lord's treasury.

The walls collapse and the city burns

With a loud shout, the Israelites storm the city

The Israelites destroy every living thing

CANAANITE GOLD
This star pendant dates from the 16th century BC.

Gold, silver, and other metals are put into the Lord's treasury

[25]But Joshua spared Rahab the prostitute, with her family and all who belonged to her, because she hid the men Joshua had sent as spies to Jericho – and she lives among the Israelites to this day.

[26]At that time Joshua pronounced this solemn oath: "*Cursed before the LORD* is the man who undertakes to rebuild this city, Jericho: At the cost of his firstborn son will he lay its foundations; at the cost of his youngest will he set up its gates." [27]So the LORD was with Joshua, and his fame spread throughout the land.

UNDERSTANDING THE STORY

Joshua leads the Israelites, but God is always in command. The battle is a success because Joshua obeys God's instructions. Jericho is the "first fruit" of Canaan, and the entire city is offered as a sacrifice to the Lord. Rahab the Canaanite is spared, demonstrating that God accepts those who turn to him.

THE SEVEN-DAY SIEGE
The number seven symbolized perfection and completion. It recurs throughout the story of the siege, highlighting the sacred significance of Israel's victory: the triumphant entry of God's people into the Promised Land.

CHAPTER 6 VERSE 26
"Cursed before the LORD"
Hiel of Bethel rebuilt a walled city at Jericho in the 9th century BC. This act cost Hiel both his eldest and youngest son and so fulfilled Joshua's curse (1 Kings 16: 34).

JOSHUA 7–8

THE BATTLE OF AI

❖
CHAPTER 7 VERSE 1
"Achan"
In the Bible, Achan is also referred to as "Achar" (1 Chronicles 2: 7), which means "trouble". Achan violated God's command not to plunder Jericho (Joshua 6: 17) and so brought trouble upon the Israelites. The Israelites had devoted Jericho to God (Joshua 6: 21), and so its spoils of war were called "devoted things".

❖
CHAPTER 8 VERSE 2
"You may carry off their plunder"
Moses' Law stipulated that plunder had to be purified. Everything had to be washed and metals put through fire beforehand. Soldiers were to wash their clothes on the seventh day after the battle (Numbers 31: 22–30). The Law also gave instructions as to how the spoils should be divided.

WARFARE AND WEAPONRY
The Israelites were poorly trained, and their weapons and equipment were inferior to those of their enemies. Consequently, they had to rely on tactical methods to win their battles. The Israelites were generally unarmoured, but effective use of long-range weapons, such as the sling, helped them to avoid close combat.

SPEAR-HEAD
This bronze weapon was discovered in a grave at Tell es-Sa'idiyeh, Jordan. It dates to the time of Joshua.

❖
CHAPTER 8 VERSE 18
"The javelin that is in your hand"
The Hebrew word for "javelin" is "kidon". Although the Israelites did use javelins in battle, a document from the caves at Qumran describes the "kidon" as a sword, one-and-a-half cubits long (about 67.5cm/27in).

7 THE[1] ISRAELITES acted unfaithfully in regard to the devoted things; *Achan* son of Carmi... of the tribe of Judah, took some of them. So the LORD's anger burned against Israel. ²Now Joshua sent men from Jericho to Ai, which is near Beth Aven to the east of Bethel, and told them, "Go up and spy out the region."

The Israelites stone Achan and his family to death for stealing some of God's treasures

The men returned and decided that they could take the city of Ai with only a few thousand men. However, their attack failed. God told Joshua that this was because one of the Israelites had violated God's command. When Joshua confronted the people, Achan confessed to plundering Jericho, and he and his family were stoned to death.

8 ¹Then the LORD said to Joshua, "Do not be afraid... Take the whole army with you, and go up and attack Ai. For I have delivered into your hands the king of Ai, his people, his city and his land. ²You shall do to Ai and its king as you did to Jericho and its king, except that *you may carry off their plunder* and livestock for yourselves. Set an ambush behind the city."

³So Joshua and the whole army moved out to attack Ai. He chose thirty thousand of his best fighting men and sent them out at night ⁴with these orders: "Listen carefully. You are to set an ambush behind the city. Don't go very far from it. All of you be on the alert. ⁵I and all those with me will advance on the city, and when the men come out against us, as they did before, we will flee from them. ⁶They will pursue us until we have lured them away from the city, for they will say, 'They are running away from us as they did before.' So when we flee from them, ⁷you are to rise up from ambush and take the city. The LORD your God will give it into your hand... See to it; you have my orders."

Joshua follows God's instructions and lures the king of Ai and his army away from the city

Once the ambush was set, Joshua and his men advanced on Ai. The king led his army out of the city to challenge them. When the Israelites fled, Ai's army pursued them.

Joshua holds out his javelin to signal the ambushers to attack

[18]Then the LORD said to Joshua, "Hold out towards Ai *the javelin that is in your hand...*" [19]As soon as he did this, the men in the ambush rose quickly from their position and rushed forward. They entered the city and captured it and quickly set it on fire... [21]When Joshua and all Israel saw that the ambush had taken the city and that smoke was going up from the city, they turned round and attacked the men of Ai. [22]The men of the ambush also came out of the city against them, so that they were caught in the middle, with Israelites on both sides. Israel cut them down, leaving them neither survivors nor fugitives... [24]The Israelites returned to Ai and killed [everyone] in it...

[28]So Joshua burned Ai and made it a permanent heap of ruins... [29]He hung the king of Ai on a tree and left him there until evening. At sunset, Joshua ordered them to *take his body from the tree* and throw it down at the entrance of the city gate.

UNDERSTANDING THE STORY

One man's disobedience leads to the punishment of the entire Israelite nation, just as Adam's original sin affected all of humanity. The death of Achan and his family serves as a warning to others that God requires total devotion from his people and that he cannot be deceived.

CHAPTER 8 VERSE 29
"Take his body from the tree"
Joshua acted in accordance with Moses' Law. A law breaker could be hung from a tree, or impaled, as a public reminder of his crime, but his body had to be taken down and buried before nightfall (Deuteronomy 21: 22–23).

THE CITY OF AI
"Ai" is Hebrew for "ruin", which serves as a reminder of the city's total destruction. It is traditionally identified as Et-Tell. However, recent excavations of the ancient city there show that it was destroyed about 1,000 years before the time of Joshua. It could not have been a large, prosperous city at the time of the conquest. Ai may have been a smaller settlement built on the remains of the older city.

ET-TELL
These ancient ruins are located 25km (15 miles) from the city of Jericho.

The Israelite ambushers capture Ai and then attack Ai's army from the rear

Ai is set on fire

The Israelites return to the city and kill everyone they can find

As soon as they see the city burning, the Israelites turn on Ai's army

Not one person survives the Israelites' slaughter

ISRAEL IN THE PROMISED LAND

After they entered Canaan, the Israelites were still not a unified nation. For about three centuries (*c.* 1380–1050 BC), they had no central administration or king (Judges 17: 6).

The twelve tribes were scattered in Canaan, with enemy territory in between. Living among the Canaanites, the Israelites soon became attracted to the Canaanite religion. In response to this, a strong Israelite leader periodically emerged to provide moral and military leadership. These leaders were called "Judges". Each story in the Book of Judges follows the same pattern: the Israelites are sinful, God punishes them by raising enemies against them, the Israelites turn to God, and God sends a Judge to save them. And then the whole cycle begins again.

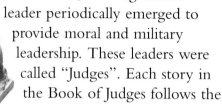

CANAANITE CRAFTSMANSHIP
This box carved from a single piece of ivory (*c.* 13th–12th century BC) is a testament to the Canaanites' reputation for fine craftsmanship.

SAMSON SLAYS THE PHILISTINES
A 12th-century Italian relief features the Israelite Judge and hero Samson slaying the Philistines with a donkey's jaw-bone.

Israel's enemies

When the Israelites entered the Promised Land, nine and a half of their tribes occupied the area between the River Jordan and the Mediterranean; the rest lived on the other side of the Jordan. In the north, the tribes were separated by the Canaanite city-states of Megiddo, Dothan, and Beth-Shean. The Canaanite territory north of the Dead Sea extending westwards to the Mediterranean separated the Israelite tribes of the south. The Israelites also had to contend with the Midianites, Ammonites, Amalekites, and Moabites in the east, as well as the Philistines in the west.

The Judges

The Judges were primarily military leaders. In a time of crisis, they would raise an army from volunteers. Judges also took on the role of magistrates. They resolved disputes, either at a central location or at certain towns they visited regularly.

Not all Judges were the same. Many were weak and could not enforce the law for long. Some are only briefly mentioned, and these are known as the "minor" Judges. Some Judges, such as Samuel, were more influential and emerged as religious leaders.

GIDEON'S VICTORY OVER THE MIDIANITES AND THE AMALEKITES
When the Midianites and the Amalekites invaded from the east, Gideon rallied an army against them. This 17th-century engraving shows Gideon and a band of three hundred men using trumpets and torches to terrify the enemy camp.

THE JUDGES OF ISRAEL

OTHNIEL (1374–1334 BC) saved the Israelites from the armies of western Mesopotamia.

EHUD (1316–1236 BC) delivered the Israelites from the Moabites, the Ammonites, and the Amalekites.

SHAMGAR (dates not known) was a Judge during the early rule of Deborah. He killed six hundred Philistines with an ox goad.

DEBORAH (1216–1176 BC) was a woman Judge and prophetess. With Barak, she defeated the Canaanites.

GIDEON (1169–1129 BC) caused havoc among the Midianites.

TOLA (1126–1103 BC), from the tribe of Issachar, was a minor Judge.

JAIR (1103–1081 BC), a wealthy man, was probably from the tribe of Manasseh. He was a minor Judge.

JEPHTHAH (*c.* 1100 BC), from Gilead, ravaged many of the Ammonites' cities.

IBZAN (1100–1093 BC), from Bethlehem, was a minor Judge.

ELON (1093–1083 BC) was also a minor Judge. He was from the tribe of Zebulun.

ABDON (1083–1077 BC), from the tribe of Ephraim, was a minor Judge .

SAMSON (1103–1083 BC) systematically attacked the Philistines. He was betrayed by Delilah, who told the Philistines the secret of Samson's strength – his hair.

ELI (ruled for 40 years) was the priest at the Tabernacle at Shiloh. He became Samuel's guardian.

SAMUEL (1050–1043 BC) was the last Judge and a prophet. When he was a boy, Samuel heard God's call at the Temple at Shiloh. He prophesied for Israel for forty years (1050–1010).

Samuel brought the nation of Israel together spiritually and politically. Under him, the Philistine invasions came to an end. Samuel's sons were rejected as Judges. The people asked Samuel for a king, and God instructed him to anoint Saul.

The dates give the ruling periods of the Judges. They are all approximate.

Canaanite worship

The Canaanites were successful farmers. They attributed the fertility of their land to the union of their nature gods, particularly that of Baal, the weather god, and his consort Ashtoreth, goddess of love and war. Each year, the Canaanite kings re-enacted the fertility ritual with temple prostitutes to ensure a good harvest. Farmers did likewise at local shrines.

Israel's unfaithfulness

Many Israelites found pagan worship difficult to resist. Some began to adopt Canaanite gods alongside the God of Israel. Many people gave up worshipping their God altogether in favour of the pagan gods of Canaan, who appeared to have more control over agriculture.

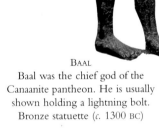

BAAL
Baal was the chief god of the Canaanite pantheon. He is usually shown holding a lightning bolt. Bronze statuette (c. 1300 BC)

THE TABERNACLE AND THE TRIBES OF ISRAEL (17TH-CENTURY ENGRAVING)

Israelite religious festivals

To combat the corruption within Israelite religious practice, the Judges held annual religious festivals. These served to maintain and reinforce the separate identity of the Israelites. Prayers and sacrifices were offered and the Law reaffirmed. The Israelites renewed their promises to God and to each other.

These festivals were probably held at Shiloh, where the Tabernacle was set up. Shiloh was the main centre of worship for Israel during the time of the Judges.

The tribal life of Israel

Originally, the Patriarchs ruled their own households. During Israel's time in Egypt, a system of tribal elders developed. Later, Moses organized a hierarchy of elders with judicial powers over groups of ten, fifty, one hundred, and a thousand people.

By the time the Israelites reached Canaan, these elders headed large family clans and carried out much day-to-day administration. When the elders could not settle disputes, they consulted the Judges.

THE PROPHET SAMUEL
Samuel was the last Judge. His sole concern was the welfare of the Israelite nation. He united the tribes and introduced the monarchy.

THE PHILISTINES

Israel's greatest enemies, the Philistines, are thought to have come from Crete. They settled on the coastal strip between Egypt and Joppa, and the Egyptians called them "Peleset". In Hebrew, they were called "Pelishtim". "Palestine" derives from the Greek name given to descendants of the Philistines.

Philistines organized themselves around five city states: Ashdod, Ashkelon, Ekron, Gath, and Gaza. Each of these cities, with the surrounding villages, was ruled by a "lord". Together, the five lords formed a ruling council. This gave the Philistines an advantage over the dispersed Israelites, who had no central leadership. The Philistines also held a monopoly over iron and ironworking, which gave them the advantage of superior weaponry.

COFFIN LID
The Philistines decorated their clay coffins with faces.

PHILISTINE POT
The markings on Philistine pottery show Mycenaean influence from across the Mediterranean.

JUDGES 2–5

DEBORAH AND SISERA

ASHTORETH
This Canaanite figurine represents
the goddess Ashtoreth (*c.* 1300 BC).

❖

CHAPTER 2 VERSE 16
"The LORD raised up judges"
The Judges ruled Israel from Joshua's
death until the time of the kings
(*c.* 1374–1043 BC). There were more
than twelve Judges. Most were
military leaders, but some also acted
as legal advisors. They were chosen
by God to deliver the Israelites from
their oppressors and to try to keep
the people faithful to his laws.

DEBORAH
Deborah was the fourth Judge of
Israel and one of the few women in
the Bible to rule over the Israelites.
She was a "judge" in the modern
sense of the word, as well as being
a military leader and prophetess. Her
victory song "The Song of Deborah"
is one of the earliest examples of
Hebrew poetry and records the
battle with Sisera in detail (Judges 5).

2 THE[7] PEOPLE SERVED the LORD throughout the lifetime of Joshua and of the elders who outlived him... [10]After that whole generation had been gathered to their fathers, another generation grew up, who knew neither the LORD nor what he had done for Israel. [11]Then the Israelites did evil in the eyes of the LORD... [13]They forsook him and

The Israelites abandon
God and worship idols

served *Baal and the Ashtoreths.* [14]In his anger against Israel the LORD handed them over to raiders who plundered them. He sold them to their enemies all around... [15]They were in great distress.

[16]Then *the LORD raised up judges*, who saved them out of the

hands of these raiders. [17]Yet they would not listen to their judges...
[19]They refused to give up their evil practices and stubborn ways...

4 [2]So the LORD sold them into the hands of *Jabin, a king of Canaan, who reigned in Hazor.* The commander of his army was Sisera... [3]Because he had nine hundred iron chariots and had cruelly oppressed the Israelites for twenty years, they cried to the LORD for help.

[4]Deborah, a prophetess, the wife of Lappidoth, was leading Israel at that time. [5]She held court under the Palm of Deborah... and the Israelites came to her to have their disputes decided. [6]She sent for Barak... from Kedesh in Nephtali and said to him, "The LORD, the God of Israel, commands you: 'Go, take with you ten thousand men... and lead the way to Mount Tabor. [7]I will lure Sisera... with his chariots and his troops to the Kishon River and give him into your hands.' "

Deborah, a judge,
instructs Barak to lead
the Israelites against
Sisera and the
Canaanites

Barak would not go into battle without Deborah. She warned Barak that he would receive no honour in battle because God would hand Sisera over to a woman. Barak and Deborah summoned 10,000 men to Kedesh and then marched to Mount Tabor. Heber the Kenite was camping near Kedesh. His tribe told Sisera the news, and Sisera led his army to the River Kishon.

The Israelites attack Sisera's army from Mount Tabor

God sends a storm, which floods the area

Sisera's chariots cannot move in the mud, and his army is defeated

Sisera escapes on foot and flees to Jael, who is camped nearby

¹⁴Then Deborah said to Barak, "Go!"... ¹⁵At Barak's advance, *the LORD routed Sisera* and all his chariots and army by the sword... ¹⁷Sisera, however, fled on foot to the tent of Jael, the wife of Heber the Kenite. ¹⁸Jael... said to him, "Come, my lord, come right in. Don't be afraid." So he entered her tent, and she put a covering over him... ²⁰"Stand in the doorway of the tent," he told her. "If someone comes by and asks you, 'Is anyone here?' say 'No.' " ²¹But Jael... picked up a tent peg and a hammer and went quietly to him while he lay fast asleep, exhausted. She drove the peg through his temple into the ground and he died...

²⁴And the hand of the Israelites grew stronger and stronger against Jabin, the Canaanite king, ²⁴until they destroyed him...

5   ³¹Then the land had peace for forty years.

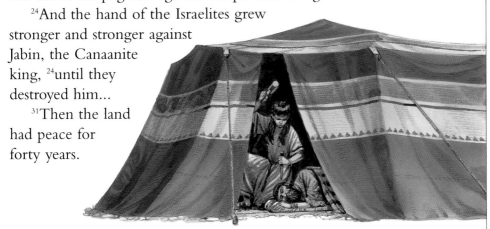

Sisera asks Jael to stand guard while he rests

When Sisera falls asleep, Jael drives a tent peg through his temple

UNDERSTANDING THE STORY

The Israelites' rejection of God leads them to suffering at the hands of their enemies. God rescues them from their oppressors by influencing people and events. Deborah and Jael play an important role in the Israelites' deliverance, and their courage and strength contrast with the weakness of Barak and Sisera.

✢

CHAPTER 4 VERSE 2
"Jabin... who reigned in Hazor"
The name "Jabin" was possibly a royal title, as the Bible mentions another Jabin who ruled in Hazor (Joshua 11: 1–11). Hazor was one of the largest and most prosperous cities in Canaan. It was strategically placed on the main trade route from Egypt to Mesopotamia.

CANAANITE STELE
This object of worship was discovered in the temple at Hazor (*c.* 1400 BC).

HEBER THE KENITE AND JAEL
Heber and Jael belonged to the semi-nomadic tribe of Kenites, who were metalworkers. Their tribe's name derives from the Hebrew word for "smith". The Kenites maintained periods of friendly relations with both the Israelites and the Canaanites.

✢

CHAPTER 4 VERSE 15
"The LORD routed Sisera"
Deborah's victory song tells how God sent a storm, which flooded the area and devastated Sisera's army (Judges 5: 20–2). Barak's name serves as a reminder of God's intervention. It means "lightning". The Israelite army was unaffected by the flood because they were on high ground.

THE AREA OF DEBORAH'S CAMPAIGN

JUDGES 6–7

GIDEON AND THE MIDIANITES

CHAPTER 6 VERSE 1
"The hands of the Midianites"
These were a nomadic people from north-west Arabia. They were descended from Midian, the son of Abraham and his concubine Keturah. Abraham sent Midian away with the rest of his concubines' children because they were a threat to Isaac's inheritance (Genesis 25: 6). The Midianites were not always the Israelites' enemy (Exodus 2: 21).

CHAPTER 6 VERSE 5
"The men and their camels"
Camels were domesticated as early as *c.* 2500 BC. This is the first time that the Bible mentions camels being used in warfare. They were particularly useful for long-range attacks in the difficult desert terrain.

CAMELS IN WARFARE
This relief from Ashurbanipal's palace, Nineveh, depicts Arab raiders on camels in battle against the Assyrians (*c.* 650 BC).

CHAPTER 6 VERSE 12
"The LORD is with you"
Gideon's calling is similar to that of Moses (Exodus 3). Like Moses, Gideon feels unfit for the task ahead and asks for a sign from God.

CHAPTER 6 VERSE 25
"The Asherah pole"
This represented Asherah, the Canaanite fertility goddess, who was associated with sacred trees. The Asherah pole was carved out of wood. It was possibly a tree trunk with its branches cut off.

6 AGAIN[1] THE ISRAELITES did evil in the eyes of the LORD, and for seven years he gave them into *the hands of the Midianites*. [2]Because the power of Midian was so oppressive, the Israelites prepared shelters for themselves in mountain clefts, caves and strongholds... [3]The Midianites, Amalekites and other eastern peoples... [5]came up with their livestock and their tents like swarms of locusts. It was impossible to count *the men and their camels*; they invaded the land to ravage it.

[6]Midian so impoverished the Israelites that they cried out to the LORD for help...

[11]The angel of the LORD came and sat down under the oak in Ophrah that belonged to Joash the Abiezrite, where his son Gideon was threshing wheat in a winepress to keep it from the Midianites. [12]When the angel of the LORD appeared to Gideon, he said, "*The LORD is with you*, mighty warrior... [14]Go in the strength you have and save Israel out of Midian's hand..."

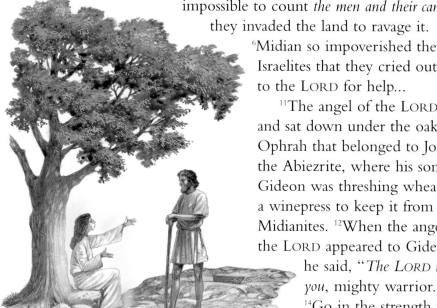

An angel appears and tells Gideon that God has chosen him to save the Israelites

Gideon asked the angel why God had chosen him, since he belonged to the weakest Israelite clan. He also wanted proof of God's will. He made an offering of meat and unleavened bread, and God caused them to burst into flames. So Gideon accepted his task and built an altar.

[25]That same night the LORD said to him... "Tear down your father's altar to Baal and cut down *the Asherah pole* beside it. [26]Then build *a proper kind of altar* to the LORD your God on the top of this height."

Gideon cuts down the Asherah pole as God commanded

Gideon tears down his father's altar to Baal

Gideon did this at night, because he was afraid how his people would react. When they discovered what he had done, they wanted to kill him. But his father intervened and he was spared. After Gideon received two more signs from God, he assembled an army. From thousands of men, only three hundred were chosen to attack the Midianite camp. This would prove that God's power alone brings victory.

7 [16][That night, Gideon divided] the three hundred men into three companies, he placed trumpets and empty jars in the hands of all of them, with torches inside... [20]The three companies blew the trumpets and smashed the jars. Grasping the torches in their left hands and holding in their right hands the trumpets they were to blow, they shouted, "A sword for the LORD and for Gideon!" [21]While each man held his position... all the Midianites ran, crying out as they fled.

Gideon assembles three hundred men outside the Midianite camp at night

Every Israelite soldier has a trumpet, a jar, and a torch

The soldiers blow the trumpets and smash the jars

The Midianites panic and start to kill each other in the confusion

The rest of the Midianites flee, and victory falls to the Israelites

[22]When the *three hundred trumpets sounded*, the LORD caused the men throughout the camp to turn on each other with their swords.

The Midianite army was utterly defeated and the survivors fled to safety. The Israelites asked Gideon if he would be their leader. He refused and told them that only God would rule over them. They lived in peace for forty years. However, when Gideon died, the Israelites returned to worshipping idols.

UNDERSTANDING THE STORY

God chooses unlikely servants to carry out his will. Gideon is the son of a struggling farmer who has abandoned God. Yet he proves himself to be worthy of the role by risking his own life to destroy his father's pagan altar. Under God's guidance and protection, Gideon leads his people to victory.

ANCIENT ALTARS
The Hebrew word for altar means "a place of sacrifice or slaughter". Although the Israelites used altars mostly for sacrificial offerings, some were built as memorials of sacred events. Gideon's father built an altar to a pagan god and so broke God's first commandment (Exodus 20: 3).

CANAANITE ALTAR
This oval altar (*c.* 2500–1850 BC) was uncovered at Megiddo.

❖

CHAPTER 6 VERSE 26
"A proper kind of altar"
God gave the Israelites specific instructions for building an altar. It should have no steps leading up to it, and it should be constructed from uncut stone. This would ensure that the altar remained pure: "You will defile it if you use a tool on it" (Exodus 20: 25–26).

STONEMASON AT WORK
The Israelites were skilled stoneworkers. Stonemasons constructed many public buildings from carefully cut stone blocks.

❖

CHAPTER 7 VERSE 22
"Three hundred trumpets sounded"
The sound of the trumpets, together with the shouting and smashing of jars, created the impression that a huge army had surrounded the Midianite camp.

JUDGES 11

JEPHTHAH'S DAUGHTER

11

JEPHTHAH[1] THE GILEADITE was a mighty warrior. His father was *Gilead*; his mother was a prostitute. [2]Gilead's wife also bore him sons, and when they were grown up, they drove Jephthah away... [3]So Jephthah fled from his brothers and settled in *the land of Tob*, where *a group of adventurers* gathered around him and followed him.

Jephthah is outlawed by his brothers

[4]Some time later, when *the Ammonites* made war on Israel, [5]the elders of Gilead went to get Jephthah from the land of Tob.

They asked him to lead a counterattack against the Ammonites. Jephthah agreed, on the condition that he would remain their leader if the Israelites won the battle. Jephthah then sent messengers to try to reason with the Ammonite king, who claimed the Israelites had taken his land. But the King paid no attention.

The Israelite elders ask Jephthah to lead an attack on the Ammonites

Jephthah agrees to go to battle if he is made the tribal leader

Jephthah leads a band of outlaws

[29]Then the Spirit of the LORD came upon Jephthah. He crossed Gilead and Manasseh, passed through Mizpah of Gilead, and from there he advanced against the Ammonites.

[30]And *Jephthah made a vow* to the LORD: "If you give the Ammonites into my hands, [31]whatever comes out of the door of my house to meet me when I return in triumph from the Ammonites will be the LORD's, and *I will sacrifice it as a burnt offering.*"

CHAPTER 11 VERSE 1
"Gilead"
Gilead was a grandson of Manasseh (Joseph's elder son) and founded the tribal family of Gileadites (Joshua 17: 1). This tribe lived in Gilead, which was a densely forested, mountainous region east of the River Jordan. It stretched from the southern end of the Sea of Galilee to the northern end of the Dead Sea.

CHAPTER 11 VERSE 3
"The land of Tob"
This district was situated east of the Jordan, just north of Gilead. It was inhabited by Arameans, known to be allied to the Ammonites.

CHAPTER 11 VERSE 3
"A group of adventurers"
The Hebrew word for "adventurer" also means "fugitive". The wooded hills in that region were renowned as a refuge for outlaws such as Jephthah, who survived by carrying out raids on the surrounding areas.

CHAPTER 11 VERSE 4
"The Ammonites"
The Ammonites were a nomadic tribe, whose territory bordered southern Gilead. They were descended from Ben-Ammi, one of Lot's sons. After the death of his wife, Lot had two sons by his daughters (Genesis 19: 30–38).

LOT AND HIS DAUGHTERS
Jan Massy's painting (1563) depicts Lot's daughters plying Lot with drink.

³²Then Jephthah went over to fight the Ammonites, and the LORD gave them into his hands. ³³He devastated twenty towns...

³⁴When Jephthah returned to his home in Mizpah, who should come out to meet him but his daughter, *dancing to the sound of tambourines!* She was an only child... ³⁵When he saw her, he tore his clothes and cried, "Oh! My daughter! You have made me miserable and wretched, because I have made a vow to the LORD I cannot break."

³⁶"My father," she replied, "you have given your word to the LORD. Do to me just as you promised, now that the LORD has avenged you of your enemies... ³⁷But grant me this one request," she said. "Give me two months to roam the hills and weep with my friends, because *I will never marry.*"

³⁸"You may go," he said... ³⁹After the two months, she returned to her father and he did to her as he had vowed... From this comes the Israelite custom ⁴⁰that each year the young women of Israel go out for four days to commemorate the daughter of Jephthah the Gileadite.

Jephthah vows to sacrifice the first thing he sees on his return if he defeats the Ammonites

He destroys twenty Ammonite towns

His daughter tells Jephthah he must fulfil his vow

She weeps because she will never marry

Jephthah's daughter runs out to meet him, rejoicing in his victory

Jephthah tears his clothes in grief when he sees her

UNDERSTANDING THE STORY

Jephthah's exile turns him into a mighty warrior. When he is asked to lead the Israelites into battle, he shrewdly secures his position as their Judge. This is in contrast to his subsequent rash behaviour, when he foolishly tries to bargain with God. He achieves success in battle, but at the expense of his only daughter.

✛
CHAPTER 11 VERSE 30
"Jephthah made a vow"
Jephthah is one of several key figures in the Bible to make a promise to God, such as Jacob (Genesis 28: 20) and David (Psalm 132: 2–5). Vows were usually made in return for God's blessing or as a form of thanks for his help. Moses' Law stated that all vows were binding (Numbers 30: 2). Jephthah acted foolishly by taking an oath without considering the consequences.

✛
CHAPTER 11 VERSE 31
"I will sacrifice it as a burnt offering"
Israelite Law specifically forbade human sacrifice (Leviticus 18: 21). It also required all offerings to be made at the Tabernacle (Deuteronomy 12: 5), but a priest would not have sacrificed Jephthah's daughter.

✛
CHAPTER 11 VERSE 34
"Dancing to the sound of tambourines!"
These celebrations were common in ancient Middle-Eastern countries. Women usually came out of the town to greet victorious armies returning from battle. They would play timbrels and sing praises.

PHOENICIAN POTTERY
This 10th-century figurine depicts a Phoenician god playing the timbrel.

✛
CHAPTER 11 VERSE 37
"I will never marry"
Some have questioned if Jephthah sacrificed his daughter "as a burnt offering" or dedicated her to a life of celibacy serving God. However, the text clearly says that he fulfilled his vow to God (v. 39).

JUDGES 13–14

SAMSON AND THE LION

13 AGAIN[1] THE ISRAELITES did evil in the eyes of the LORD, so the LORD delivered them *into the hands of the Philistines* for forty years. [2]A certain man of Zorah, named Manoah, from the clan of the Danites, had a wife who was sterile and remained childless. [3]The angel of the LORD appeared to her and said... "You are going to conceive and have a son... [5]No razor may be used on his head, because *the boy is to be a Nazirite*, set apart to God from birth, and he will begin the deliverance of Israel from the hands of the Philistines...

When Manoah's wife told him this news, Manoah was confused and prayed for the angel to reappear. The angel did so, but in the guise of an ordinary man. The man told Manoah to make a burnt offering to the Lord. Manoah asked the man his name, but the angel refused to tell it.

An angel brings a message

As the angel promised, Manoah and his wife have a son, Samson, who will deliver Israel from the Philistines

Manoah and his wife fall down in awe

Philistine woman

Samson falls in love with a Philistine woman and decides to marry her

BAAL, GOD OF NATURE
Assyrian granite stele from a palace in Jordan

✛

CHAPTER 13 VERSE 1
"Into the hands of the Philistines"
The Bible often gives a reason for Israel's troubles. The Philistine oppression was God's punishment on the Israelites for worshipping Philistine gods, such as Dagon, Ashtoreth, and Baal.

Ashdod
Timnah
Zorah
Ekron
Lehi
Ashkelon
Gath
Gaza
DEAD SEA

▮ *Philistines*

THE PHILISTINE SETTLEMENTS
The Philistines came from the north-eastern Mediterranean. In c. 1200 BC they invaded the coastal plain of Judah and established five cities: Gaza, Gath, Ekron, Ashkelon, and Ashdod. During this period, the Philistines were fierce enemies of Israel. Samson was the first Israelite leader to attack them successfully. Philistines were also known as the Peleset – hence the name "Palestine".

[19]And the LORD did an amazing thing while Manoah and his wife watched: [20]As the flame blazed up from the altar towards heaven, the angel of the LORD ascended in the flame. Seeing this, Manoah and his wife fell with their faces to the ground...

[24]The woman gave birth to a boy and named him Samson. He grew and the LORD blessed him, [25]and the Spirit of the LORD began to stir him...

14 [1]Samson went down to Timnah and saw there a young Philistine woman. [2]When he returned, he said to his father and mother,

"*I have seen a Philistine woman* in Timnah; now get her for me as my wife." ³His father and mother replied, "Isn't there an acceptable woman among your relatives or among all our people?... "

But Samson said to his father, "Get her for me. She's the right one for me." ⁴(His parents did not know that this was from the LORD, who was seeking an occasion to confront the Philistines...) ⁵Samson went down to Timnah together with his father and mother. As they approached the vineyards of Timnah, suddenly a young lion came roaring towards him. ⁶The Spirit of the LORD came upon him in power so that he tore the lion apart with his bare hands as he might have torn a young goat. But he told neither his father nor his mother what he had done. ⁷Then he went down and talked with the woman, and he liked her.

On his way to meet his future wife, Samson is attacked by a lion

Samson talks with his bride-to-be

Bride

God gives Samson the strength to tear apart the lion

Some weeks later, Samson finds a swarm of bees has nested in the lion's carcass

NAZIRITE
Egyptian wall tile from the Palace of Ramses III in Yahudya, *c.* 1150 BC

CHAPTER 13 VERSE 5
"The boy is to be a Nazirite"
In Israel, a person consecrated to God for a special purpose was called a Nazirite. Nazirites never cut their hair, which was thought to be the source of life, and they were forbidden alcohol so that the Spirit of God alone could determine their actions. They were supposed to avoid contact with dead bodies, so as to remain pure and ready for God to work through them.

CHAPTER 14 VERSE 2
"I have seen a Philistine woman"
The Israelites were forbidden to intermarry, because they thought foreigners might encourage them to worship pagan gods (Deuteronomy 7: 3–4).

Samson eats some honey, even though he is forbidden to touch a dead body

HEAD OF THE FAMILY
In Bible times, authority rested with the father. This often included the choice of wife for his sons. Samson's father went reluctantly to talk to the Philistine woman because he knew his son was breaking God's Law. However, Manoah did not know that God intended that the wedding should provoke the Philistines.

⁸Some time later, when he went back to marry her, he turned aside to look at the lion's carcass. In it was a swarm of bees and some honey, ⁹which he scooped out with his hands and ate as he went along. When he rejoined his parents, he gave them some, and they too ate it. But he did not tell them that he had taken the honey from the lion's carcass.

JUDGES 14–15

SAMSON AND THE PHILISTINES

CHAPTER 14 VERSE 10
"Samson made a feast there"
In the ancient Middle East, wedding feasts lasted seven days. The groom had a group of companions, one of whom was the equivalent of today's "best man". During such feasts much wine was drunk – Samson would have broken his vows as a Nazirite by drinking alcohol.

SYRIAN WEDDING
In some areas of the Middle East, it is still the tradition for men to celebrate separately from women. The festivities may last several days.

CHAPTER 14 VERSE 12
"Let me tell you a riddle"
Riddles were a common form of entertainment during feasts. But Samson's riddle was intended to humiliate the Philistines. He believed no one would find the answer, because even his parents knew nothing of his encounter with the lion. He confidently expected to gain a prize of great value from each companion.

CHAPTER 14 VERSE 19
"The Spirit of the LORD came upon him"
The "Spirit of the Lord" is also mentioned in connection with other rulers of Israel, such as Gideon and Jephthah. They were given power to deliver the people from their enemies. God's purpose for Samson was to humble the Philistines, whose rulers sought to dominate the Israelites.

14 N OW[10] HIS FATHER went down to see the woman. And *Samson made a feast there*, as was customary for bridegrooms. [11]When he appeared, he was given thirty companions.

[12]*"Let me tell you a riddle,"* Samson said to them. "If you can give me the answer within the seven days of the feast, I will give you thirty linen garments and thirty sets of clothes. [13]If you can't tell me the answer, you must give me thirty linen garments and thirty sets of clothes."

"Tell us your riddle," they said. "Let's hear it."

[14]He replied, "Out of the eater, something to eat; out of the strong, something sweet."

The companions were baffled and threatened Samson's bride with death unless she found out the answer. Samson finally gave in to her entreaties, but he realised his wife had betrayed him when, on the seventh day, the companions announced the solution to the riddle:

[18]"What is sweeter than honey? What is stronger than a lion?"...
[19]Then *the Spirit of the LORD came upon him.*

Samson attacked thirty Philistines at Ashkelon and gave their clothes to the thirty wedding companions as promised. Later, Samson went to visit his wife. Her father told him that he had given her in marriage to Samson's friend.

At his wedding, Samson poses a riddle to the guests

The guests demand the answer from Samson's wife, and she betrays him

Samson gets revenge on the Philistines by setting fire to their corn

Samson's companions are puzzled

Samson attaches burning torches to foxes' tails

15 Samson said: [3]"This time I have a right to get even with the Philistines; I will really harm them." [4]So he went out and caught three hundred foxes and tied them tail to tail in pairs.

He then fastened a torch to every pair of tails, ⁵lit the torches and let the foxes loose in the standing corn of the Philistines. He burned up the shocks and standing corn, together with the vineyards and olive groves.

⁶When the Philistines asked, "Who did this?" they were told, "Samson, the Timnite's son-in-law, because his wife was given to his friend."

So *the Philistines went up and burned her and her father to death.* ⁷Samson said to them, "Since you've acted like this, I won't stop until I get my revenge on you." ⁸He attacked them viciously and slaughtered many of them.

Samson escaped, but the Philistines wanted to take him prisoner. They followed him to Judah, and set up camp near Lehi. Three thousand men of Judah, fearing the Philistines' anger, tied up Samson and handed him over to them.

¹⁴The Spirit of the LORD came upon him... The ropes on his arms became like charred flax, and the bindings dropped from his hands. ¹⁵Finding a fresh jaw-bone of a donkey, he grabbed it and struck down a thousand men... ¹⁸Because he was very thirsty, he cried out to the LORD,

CHAPTER 15 VERSE 6
"The Philistines... burned her and her father to death"
The Philistines' cruelty to their own people would explain the Israelites' great fear of this race. The main cause of hostility between these two peoples was that they both wanted to occupy the same land.

PHILISTINE WARRIOR
Wall relief, mortuary temple of Ramses III
(*c.* 1150 BC)

CHAPTER 15 VERSE 19
"And water came out of it"
Samson's prayer is answered in a miraculous manner. His experience is similar to that of the Israelites in the desert, who witnessed many miracles during the Exodus. God shows mercy to his chosen leader, just as he had shown mercy to his chosen people.

Samson flees to the desert, where God provides him with water

The Philistines burn Samson's bride and her father to death

The Philistines take Samson prisoner, but he bursts free from his bindings and attacks them with a jaw-bone

JUDEAN DESERT
Lehi was on the edge of the Judean Desert, where water was often scarce.

LEHI
The name "Lehi" means "jaw-bone". The place received its name after the events told in this story. Samson's weapon was an added insult to the Philistines as a donkey was considered a lowly animal.

DONKEY'S JAW-BONE

"You have given your servant this great victory. Must I now die of thirst and fall into the hands of the uncircumcised?" ¹⁹Then God opened up the hollow place in Lehi, *and water came out of it.*

JUDGES 16
SAMSON AND DELILAH

CHAPTER 16 VERSE 4
"Whose name was Delilah"
The name Delilah means "flirt"
and has become associated with
treachery. Delilah also means
"dainty". In contrast, Samson
means "sun-one", alluding
to his strength and vitality.

CHAPTER 16 VERSE 5
"The rulers of the Philistines"
Philistia was a confederation of five
prosperous cities, each governed by
a prince. These princes are called
"rulers" in the Book of Judges.

CHAPTER 16 VERSE 5
"Eleven hundred shekels of silver"
The Philistines (a word that meant
"tyrants" in Hebrew) paid a
fortune to capture Samson – about
275 times the price of a slave.

SILVER SHEKEL

CHAPTER 16 VERSE 20
"The Lord had left him"
The real source of Samson's
strength was God. The seven braids
of Samson's hair symbolized God's
presence. Samson had allowed a
foreign woman to rob him of the
sign of his consecration to God.

CHAPTER 16 VERSE 21
*"The Philistines... gouged out his
eyes and took him down to Gaza"*
Weak and humiliated, Samson was
led to to the city of Gaza, a place
where he had once displayed great
strength. Samson had escaped the
Philistines by lifting the doors of
the city gate on his shoulders.

16 SOME[4] TIME LATER, [Samson] fell in love with a woman in the Valley of Sorek *whose name was Delilah.* [5]*The rulers of the Philistines* went to her and said, "See if you can lure him into showing you the secret of his great strength and how we can overpower him... Each one of us will give you *eleven hundred shekels of silver.*

[6]So Delilah said to Samson, "Tell me the secret of your great strength and how you can be tied up and subdued."

Samson teased her with lies, and the Philistines tried to catch him three times without success. But Delilah continued to nag him, day after day.

[17]So he told her everything. "No razor has ever been used on my head," he said, "because I have been a Nazirite set apart to God since birth. If my head were shaved, my strength would leave me, and I would become as weak as any other man."

[18]When Delilah saw that he had told her everything, she sent word to the rulers of the Philistines... So the rulers of the Philistines returned with the silver in their hands. [19]Having put him to sleep on her lap,

Delilah betrays Samson by
telling the Philistines the
secret of his strength

While he is sleeping,
Samson's hair is cut off

she called a man to shave off the seven braids of his hair, and so began to subdue him. And his strength left him.

[20]Then she called, "Samson, the Philistines are upon you!"

He awoke from his sleep and thought, "I'll go out as before and shake myself free." But he did not know that *the LORD had left him.*

[21]Then *the Philistines seized him, gouged out his eyes and took him down to Gaza.* Binding him with bronze shackles, they set him to grinding in the prison. [22]But the hair on his head began to grow again after it had been shaved.

²³Now the rulers of the Philistines assembled to offer *a great sacrifice to Dagon* their god and to celebrate, saying, "Our god has delivered Samson, our enemy, into our hands."... ²⁵While they were in high spirits, they shouted, "Bring out Samson to entertain us." So they called Samson out of the prison, and he performed for them.

The temple was full, and about three thousand people had crowded onto the roof. Samson asked to be led to the pillars that supported the temple. There, he prayed to God for his strength to return one more time.

²⁸"*Let me with one blow get revenge on the Philistines* for my two eyes." ²⁹Then Samson reached towards the two central pillars on which the temple stood. Bracing himself against them... ³⁰Samson said, "Let me die with the Philistines!" Then he pushed with all his might, and down came the temple on the rulers and all the people in it. Thus he killed many more when he died than while he lived.

³¹Then his brothers and his father's whole family... buried him between Zorah and Eshtaol in the tomb of Manoah his father.

When Samson is humiliated before the Philistines, God gives him the strength to pull down their temple

Samson is blind and in chains

Supporting pillar

UNDERSTANDING THE STORY

This story shows how God uses Samson's weaknesses to bring about Israel's deliverance. By breaking his Nazirite obligations and pursuing foreign women, Samson symbolizes the Israelites, who abandon God's law to worship idols. Yet, like the people he leads, he knows where to turn in times of need, and God shows him mercy.

PHILISTINE TEMPLES
Only one Philistine temple has been excavated from the time of Samson. The pillars in this temple were made from wood. These pillars supported a flat roof, which had a covered area where people could assemble. This wooden structure could not have supported the weight of 3,000 people.

PHILISTINE TEMPLE
These temple ruins were excavated at Tel Quasile, a Philistine town destroyed by King David in the 10th century BC.

CHAPTER 16 VERSE 28
"Let me with one blow get revenge on the Philistines"
Samson's final plea is to be allowed to take revenge for the loss of his sight. All his life, Samson fought the Philistines for personal reasons. However, the Bible states that, whatever his motives, Samson was an instrument of God.

RUTH 1–2
NAOMI AND RUTH

1 IN[1] THE DAYS when the judges ruled, there was a famine in the land, and a man from *Bethlehem in Judah*, together with his wife and two sons, went to live for a while *in the country of Moab*. [2]The man's name was Elimelech, his wife's name Naomi, and the names of his two sons were Mahlon and Kilion...

[3]Now Elimelech, Naomi's husband, died, and she was left with her two sons. [4]They married Moabite women, one named Orpah and the other Ruth. After they had lived there about ten years, [5]both Mahlon and Kilion also died, and Naomi was left without her two sons and her husband.

Then, Naomi heard that God had provided food for the Israelites, and so she decided to return to Bethlehem. She blessed both of her daughters-in-law and told them that they should return to live with their families. Naomi hoped that they would both be able to find new husbands among their own people. She knew that they would have a very uncertain future with her. Eventually, Orpah did what Naomi asked and returned to her family. Naomi pleaded with Ruth to do the same.

[16]But Ruth replied... "Where you go I will go, and where you stay I will stay. Your people will be my people and your God my God..."
[22]So Naomi returned from Moab accompanied by Ruth the Moabitess, her daughter-in-law, arriving in Bethlehem as the barley harvest was beginning.

When Naomi's husband and two sons die, she decides to leave Moab

---

❖

CHAPTER 1 VERSE 1
"Bethlehem in Judah"
The name of this village, situated a few miles south of Jerusalem, means "House of Bread". At the beginning of this story, Bethlehem is a place without food. But, by the end, Bethlehem deserves its name.

❖

CHAPTER 1 VERSE 1
"In the country of Moab"
The Moabites were related to the Israelites through Lot, Abraham's nephew, and occupied parts of what is now central Jordan, on the eastern side of the Dead Sea. They never forgot how the Israelites invaded their towns after the Exodus, but there were periods of friendly relations, such as this one.

BURYING THE DEAD
Most burials were either in caves or in shallow pit graves. The poor were usually buried along with simple pottery vessels, such as the "dipper" jug. The burial chambers of the wealthy contained more ornate items. During this period, people believed that they would go on to live in "Sheol", a place of peace and quiet.

"DIPPER" JUG
A small jug used to take liquid out of large containers

Naomi's daughter-in-law Ruth wants to go with her

In Bethlehem, Ruth makes a living by picking up the gleanings of the harvest

2 ¹Now Naomi had a relative on her husband's side from the clan of Elimelech, a man of standing, whose name was Boaz.

²And Ruth the Moabitess said to Naomi, "*Let me go to the fields* and pick up the leftover grain behind anyone in whose eyes I find favour."

Naomi said to her, "Go ahead, my daughter." ³So she went out and began to glean in the fields behind the harvesters. As it turned out, she found herself working in a field belonging to Boaz...

⁴Just then Boaz arrived from Bethlehem and greeted the harvesters, "The LORD be with you!"

"The LORD bless you!" they called back.

⁵Boaz asked the foreman of his harvesters, "Whose young woman is that?" ⁶The foreman replied, "She is the *Moabitess* who came back from Moab with Naomi..."

⁸So Boaz said to Ruth, "My daughter, listen to me. Don't go and glean in another field... ⁹Watch the field where the men are harvesting, and follow along after the girls. I have told the men not to touch you. And whenever you are thirsty, go and get a drink from the water jars the men have filled... ¹²May you be richly rewarded by the LORD, the God of Israel, under whose wings you have come to take refuge."...

²³So Ruth stayed close to the servant girls of Boaz to glean *until the barley and wheat harvests were finished.*

Ruth catches the attention of Boaz

Boaz rides around his fields, inspecting his harvest

The women bind the barley into sheaves

CHAPTER 2 VERSE 2
"Let me go to the fields"
In Israel, landowners were supposed to obey this law: "When you reap the harvest of your land, do not reap to the very edges of your field or gather the gleanings of your harvest. Leave them for the poor, the alien, the fatherless, and the widow". In the dark days of the Judges, there were still generous and honest people like Boaz. But there were less honourable men among the harvesters, and Boaz offered Ruth protection from them.

WOMEN HARVESTING
The practice of leaving the edges of fields unharvested still continues in the Middle East.

CHAPTER 2 VERSE 6
"Moabitess"
Ruth is a foreigner from a people generally despised by Israelites. But, because of her faith in the God of Israel and her kindness to her mother-in-law, she becomes a good example to the Israelites. At the time of the Judges, many of her adopted people were worshipping other gods and living immorally.

CHAPTER 2 VERSE 23
"Until the barley and wheat harvests were finished"
Barley and wheat were harvested in April and May respectively. Men cut the crops with sickles, and women bound them into sheaves. Stalks of grain were left behind.

WHEATSHEAF AND SICKLE

RUTH 3–4

RUTH AND BOAZ

3 ONE[1] DAY NAOMI her mother-in-law said to her, "My daughter, should I not try to find a home for you, where you will be well provided for? [2]Is not Boaz, with whose servant girls you have been, a kinsman of ours? *Tonight he will be winnowing barley on the threshing-floor.* [3]Wash and perfume yourself, and put on your best clothes. Then go down to the threshing-floor, but don't let him know you are there until he has finished eating and drinking. [4]When he lies down, note the place where he is lying. Then go and uncover his feet and lie down. He will tell you what to do."

Naomi wants Ruth to look her best for Boaz

Ruth washes and perfumes herself

[5]"I will do whatever you say," Ruth answered. [6]So she went down to the threshing-floor and did everything her mother-in-law told her to do.

[7]When Boaz had finished eating and drinking and was in good spirits, he went over to lie down at the far end of the grain pile. Ruth approached quietly, uncovered his feet and lay down. [8]In the middle of the night something startled the man, and he turned and discovered a woman lying at his feet.

[9]"Who are you?" he asked.

He wakes to find Ruth lying at his feet

Ruth asks Boaz for his protection

Boaz sleeps by the newly harvested grain to protect it from thieves

"I am your servant Ruth," she said. "*Spread the corner of your garment over me, since you are a kinsman-redeemer.*"

[10]"The LORD bless you, my daughter," he replied. "This kindness is greater than that which you showed earlier: You have not run after the younger men, whether rich or poor... [11]I will do for you all you ask. All my fellow townsmen know that you are a woman of noble character. [12]Although it is true that I am near of kin, there is a kinsman-redeemer nearer than I... [13]If he wants to redeem, good; let him redeem. But if he is not willing, as surely as the LORD lives I will do it..."

Naomi was very pleased to hear what Boaz had said to Ruth.

4 ¹Meanwhile *Boaz went up to the town gate* and sat there. When the kinsman-redeemer he had mentioned came along, Boaz said, "Come over here, my friend, and sit down..." ²Boaz took ten of the elders of the town and said, "Sit here," and they did so.

When the kinsman-redeemer heard that, if he bought Naomi's piece of land which belonged to her husband and sons, he also had to acquire the dead man's widow, he refused to redeem it.

⁸So the kinsman-redeemer said to Boaz, "Buy it yourself." And *he removed his sandal.*

When the kinsman-redeemer hears that if he buys Naomi's piece of land he also has to acquire Ruth, he refuses to redeem it

Boaz buys the right to marry Ruth

Boaz takes the sandal to seal the agreement

The town elders witness the transaction

⁹Boaz announced to the elders and all the people, "Today you are witnesses that I have bought from Naomi all the property of Elimelech, Kilion and Mahlon. ¹⁰I have also acquired Ruth the Moabitess, Mahlon's widow, as my wife, in order to maintain the name of the dead with his property, so that his name will not disappear from among his family or from the town records..."

¹³So Boaz took Ruth and she became his wife... and she gave birth to a son...

¹⁶Then Naomi took the child, laid him in her lap and cared for him. ¹⁷The women living there said, "Naomi has a son." And they named him *Obed. He was the father of Jesse, the father of David.*

Ruth's son Obed gives Naomi a new purpose in life

UNDERSTANDING THE STORY

Ruth, a foreigner, leads a righteous life at a time when many Israelites have abandoned God. The selfless love of Ruth and Boaz brings Naomi from emptiness to fulfilment. Their child is to be the grandfather of David, Israel's first king, and he will demonstrate selfless love in his fight to bring Israel from turmoil to peace.

✣

CHAPTER 4 VERSE 1
"Boaz went up to the town gate"
In the Middle East, the town gate was the place where people made business deals and legal transactions, as witnesses were easily available.

CITY GATE
This reconstruction shows the gates of Laish, a Canaanite city (northern Israel).

✣

CHAPTER 4 VERSE 8
"He removed his sandal"
The sandal was a sign of possession. In ancient Israel, to legalize the transfer of property, one party gave his sandal to the other.

SANDAL
This dates from the Roman period and was found at Masada.

✣

CHAPTER 4 VERSE 17
"Obed... father of David"
Ruth the foreigner, becomes great-grandmother of the famous King David. The New Testament shows that this line ends with Jesus.

NAMES IN THE BOOK OF RUTH
Many names in the Bible have hidden meanings. In Hebrew, Naomi means "pleasant". However, she calls herself Mara (bitter) when she loses her husband. The names of Naomi's sons, Mahlon (illness) and Kilion (weakling) appear to herald their early deaths. Orpah (nape) suggests the neck of one who turns away, as she did from Naomi. Ruth (friendship or comfort) describes her relationship with Naomi. Boaz (in him is strength) gives protection and stability to Ruth and Naomi. The birth of Obed (servant of the Lord) brings fulfilment to the family.

1 SAMUEL 1–3

THE CALL OF SAMUEL

CHAPTER 1 VERSE 1
"A Zuphite from the hill country of Ephraim"
Elkanah was a Levite, a tribe that had no land of its own. Instead, the Levites were allotted towns within the territories of the other tribes. Ramathaim was one of these towns. It was situated in Ephraim about 10km (6 miles) north of Jerusalem.

CHAPTER 1 VERSE 3
"Shiloh"
After Joshua led the Israelites into Canaan, he brought the Ark of the Covenant to Shiloh and set up the first permanent Tabernacle there. Joshua was an Ephraimite, and the town was in his tribal land. Shiloh was the main religious centre during the period of the Judges.

CHAPTER 1 VERSE 9
"Eli the priest"
As High Priest at Shiloh, Eli was regarded as a leader, or judge, of his people. He was a deeply pious man, but his two sons behaved wickedly (1 Samuel 2: 12–25). Eli was unable to control them.

Eli the High Priest sees Hannah weeping. She is praying for a child

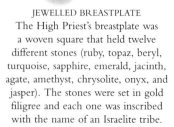

JEWELLED BREASTPLATE
The High Priest's breastplate was a woven square that held twelve different stones (ruby, topaz, beryl, turquoise, sapphire, emerald, jacinth, agate, amethyst, chrysolite, onyx, and jasper). The stones were set in gold filigree and each one was inscribed with the name of an Israelite tribe.

THERE[1] WAS A CERTAIN MAN from Ramathaim, *a Zuphite from the hill country of Ephraim,* whose name was Elkanah... [2]He had two wives; one was called Hannah and the other Peninnah. Peninnah had children, but Hannah had none. [3]Year after year this man went up from his town to worship and sacrifice to the LORD Almighty at *Shiloh,* where... the two sons of Eli were priests of the LORD...

[9]Once when they had finished eating and drinking in Shiloh, Hannah stood up. Now *Eli the priest* was sitting on a chair by the doorpost of the LORD's temple. [10]In bitterness of soul Hannah wept much and prayed to the LORD. [11]And she made a vow, saying, "O LORD Almighty, if you will only look upon your servant's misery and remember me, and not forget your servant but give her a son, then I will give him to the LORD for all the days of his life, and no razor will ever be used on his head."...

[20]So in the course of time Hannah conceived and gave birth to a son. She named him Samuel, saying, "Because I asked the LORD for him."...

[24]After he was weaned, she took the boy with her, young as he was, along with a three-year-old bull, an *ephah of flour* and a skin of wine, and brought him to the house of the LORD at Shiloh... [26]and she said to [Eli]... [27]"I prayed for this child, and the LORD has granted me what I asked of him. [28]So now I give him to the LORD..."

Hannah's prayers are answered, and she bears a son called Samuel

She brings offerings to God

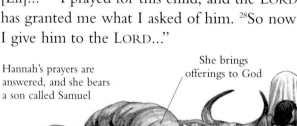

Eli

Hannah vows that Samuel will serve God, and takes him to the temple to be brought up as a priest

Some years later, a prophet came to Shiloh. He told Eli that calamity would strike his house and that his two wicked sons would die.

3 ²One night... ³*The lamp of God* had not yet gone out, and Samuel was lying down in the temple of the LORD, where the ark of God was. ⁴Then the LORD called Samuel. Samuel answered, "Here I am." ⁵And he ran to Eli... But Eli said, "I did not call; go back and lie down."

CHAPTER 1 VERSE 24
"Ephah of flour"
An ephah was a unit equal to one-tenth of a homer, which was the standard unit for dry measurements. A homer was equivalent to a normal donkey load. Hannah's gift of wine and flour was in accordance with Moses' Law, but she brought much greater quantities than were required.

CHAPTER 3 VERSE 3
"The lamp of God"
This seven-branched lampstand was made from gold and decorated with almond buds and blossoms. The almond was the first tree to bloom in the spring and was symbolic of God's constancy. The lamp was kept burning throughout the night.

Samuel is asleep in the temple when he hears God's voice

God says that Eli will be punished for his sons' wicked behaviour

BYZANTINE MEDALLION
8th-century gold medallion, embossed with the seven-branched "menorah"

This happened two more times, and Eli realised that it was God calling Samuel. He told Samuel to answer God.

¹⁰The LORD came and stood there, calling... "Samuel! Samuel!" Then Samuel said, "Speak, for your servant is listening." ¹¹And the LORD said to Samuel... "¹²I will carry out against Eli everything I spoke against his family... ¹³His sons made themselves contemptible, and he failed to restrain them..."

¹⁵Samuel... was afraid to tell Eli the vision, ¹⁶but Eli called him and said... "¹⁷Do not hide it from me..." ¹⁸So Samuel told him everything...

¹⁹The LORD was with Samuel as he grew up... ²⁰And all Israel *from Dan to Beersheba* recognised that Samuel was attested as *a prophet of the LORD*.

UNDERSTANDING THE STORY

Hannah's situation recalls the stories of Sarah, Rebecca, and the mother of Samson, because God intervenes to end the misery of barrenness. In all four cases, a child is born who has a special relationship with God and who fulfils a special purpose. Samuel is to be God's prophet.

CHAPTER 3 VERSE 20
"From Dan to Beersheba"
This expression was used to describe the boundaries of the Promised Land. Dan was in the north and Beersheba in the south.

CHAPTER 3 VERSE 20
"A prophet of the LORD"
Samuel was the last Judge and the first great prophet to be named after Moses. Prophets were chosen by God and came from many different sections of society, from farmers to priests. Their main role was to proclaim God's word in order to guide the people towards righteousness. Samuel prepared for his vocation from early childhood.

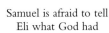

Samuel is afraid to tell Eli what God had said, but Eli insists on knowing everything

1 SAMUEL 4–6
THE PHILISTINES AND THE ARK

CHAPTER 4 VERSE 3
"Let us bring the ark of the LORD's covenant"
The Israelites regarded the Ark as a symbol of God's presence. The elders remembered how it had brought Israel victory at Jericho (Joshua 6) and believed it would do the same against the Philistines. Although a small nation, the Philistines were a fierce opponent. They had a permanent, well-trained army, whereas the Israelite army was made up of farmers and labourers.

PHILISTINE SOLDIERS
Detail of relief from Rameses III's temple at Thebes showing Philistine soldiers with swords and round shields

CHAPTER 4 VERSE 18
"Eli… died"
Eli served as Israel's High Priest for forty years and died at the age of 98. He was judged harshly by God because he did not curb his sons' greed and selfishness. They violated the rituals of sacrifices and seduced the women serving at the sanctuary. The death of his sons had been foretold by a prophet, who predicted the ruin of Eli's family (1 Samuel 2: 31–36).

CHAPTER 5 VERSE 2
"Carried [the ark of God] into Dagon's temple"
In Middle-Eastern cultures at this time, it was customary for a victorious nation to transfer captured idols into its own temples. This symbolized the belief that its gods were superior to those of the defeated nation. The Philistines treated the Ark as a captured idol.

4 NOW[1] THE ISRAELITES went out to fight against the Philistines… [2]The Philistines deployed their forces to meet Israel, and as the battle spread, Israel was defeated by the Philistines, who killed about four thousand of them on the battlefield. [3]When the soldiers returned to camp, the elders of Israel asked, "Why did the LORD bring defeat upon us today before the Philistines? *Let us bring the ark of the LORD's covenant* from Shiloh, so that it may go with us and save us from the hand of our enemies."…

[5]When the ark of the LORD's covenant came into the camp, all Israel raised such a great shout that the ground shook. [6]Hearing the uproar, the Philistines… [7]were afraid. "A god has come into the camp," they said. "We're in trouble!… [8]Who will deliver us from the hand of these mighty gods? They are the Gods who struck the Egyptians with all kinds of plagues in the desert… [9]Be strong, Philistines!.. Be men, and fight!"

The Philistines launched a fierce attack against the Israelites and captured the ark of God. The Israelites suffered heavy losses, and both of Eli's sons were killed. The rest fled to their tents. A messenger ran back to Shiloh to tell Eli the news.

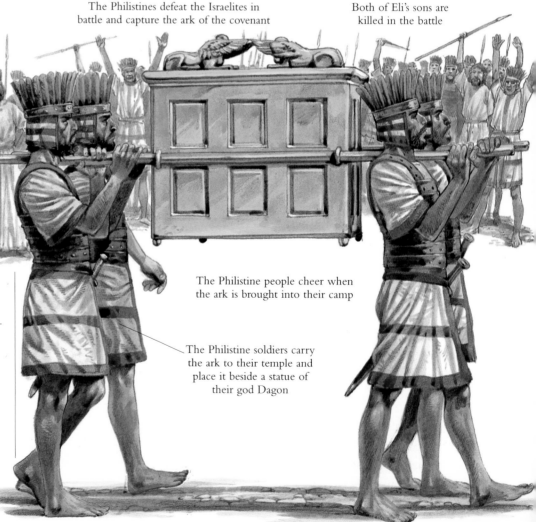

The Philistines defeat the Israelites in battle and capture the ark of the covenant

Both of Eli's sons are killed in the battle

The Philistine people cheer when the ark is brought into their camp

The Philistine soldiers carry the ark to their temple and place it beside a statue of their god Dagon

5 ¹⁸*Eli fell backwards off his chair... His neck was broken and he died...* ¹The Philistines... ²carried [the ark of God] into Dagon's temple* and set it beside Dagon. ³When the people of Ashdod rose early the next day, there was Dagon, fallen on his face on the ground before the ark of the LORD!.. ⁴His head and hands had been broken off and were lying on the threshold... ⁶The LORD's hand was heavy upon the people of Ashdod and its vicinity; he brought devastation upon them and afflicted them with tumours.

The ark was taken to other Philistine cities. Everywhere it went it brought plagues and death. After seven months, the Philistine priests and diviners told their people to send the ark away on a cart pulled by two untrained cows, and to make gold models of the rats and tumours that were destroying their country.

A messenger tells Eli the bad news

Eli falls back off his chair and breaks his neck

The ark

That night, the statue of Dagon falls to the floor

Dagon's hands and head break off

Terrible plagues afflict the people, and so they send the ark to other Philistine cities

❖

"CHAPTER 6 VERSE 11
"The gold rats and the models of the tumours"
The people were instructed to make models of the rats, which were the most likely cause of the plague, and tumours, which were the symptoms. The models were made out of gold to compensate Israel for taking the Ark. The Philistines believed that these models had magical powers, and thought that if they sent them away, the disease would go too.

❖

CHAPTER 6 VERSE 12
"Beth Shemesh"
Beth Shemesh was a town on the other side of the Philistine border. It was situated in land allotted to the tribe of Judah, but the town belonged to the Levites (Joshua 21: 16). The fact that the two untrained cows pulled the Ark directly to an Israelite town confirmed that God was the cause of the Philistines' suffering.

6 ¹¹They placed the ark of the LORD on the cart and along with it the chest containing *the gold rats and the models of the tumours*. ¹²Then the cows went straight up towards *Beth Shemesh*... ¹³The people of Beth Shemesh... rejoiced at the sight... [and] ¹⁵offered burnt offerings.

The ark was then taken to Kiriath Jearim, where it remained for twenty years. Samuel became the next judge and leader of the Israelites.

UNDERSTANDING THE STORY

The Ark of the Covenant represents God's presence and power. By losing the Ark, the Israelites learn that they cannot manipulate God. The Philistines' belief in the superiority of their gods is short-lived. God demonstrates that the destiny of both nations is under his control.

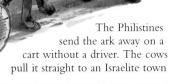

The Philistines send the ark away on a cart without a driver. The cows pull it straight to an Israelite town

ISRAEL RULED BY KINGS

The people of Israel had become dissatisfied with their leadership, which had passed from the prophet Samuel to his sons. At this time, they were also suffering renewed attacks from their old enemies the Philistines (c. 1100 BC). In an attempt to unite their tribal groups against the Philistines, the Israelite elders started making demands for a king. Despite Samuel's warnings of taxation and conscription, the people of Israel decided to become one nation under Saul, the first king of Israel. The kingdom reached its peak during the time of King Solomon, when it became a large trading empire.

IVORY TRADE
Ivory came from Africa and India. It was a large part of Solomon's trade.

THE FIRST KINGS

Samuel played an important role in the institution of the monarchy. He helped to select the first two kings: Saul (c. 1050–1010 BC) and David (c. 1010–970 BC), who each reigned for a period of about forty years. David chose his son Solomon to be the third king of Israel. He also reigned for forty years (c. 970–930).

CINNAMON

ANOINTING OILS
The Old Testament gives detailed instructions for making the special anointing oil (Exodus 30: 22–33). The ingredients were liquid myrrh, cinnamon (pictured above), fragrant cane, and cassia. These were to be mixed together with purified olive oil.

The anointing of kings

The Israelites used to anoint their priests, which involved rubbing a sacred oil onto the priests' skin. This act symbolized their consecration to God for religious office. From the time of Samuel, the Israelites also anointed their kings. This practice indicated that the kings were not chosen by the people, but by God.

The anointing also signified a king's allegiance to God and his dedication to the people of Israel. The king of Israel became known as the "Messiah", which is Hebrew for "the anointed one". The Greek word for "messiah" is "christos", from which the English word "Christ" is derived.

DAVID'S ANOINTMENT
This 3rd-century wall-painting shows the prophet Samuel anointing David.

SAUL'S REIGN

Saul belonged to the tribe of Benjamin, which was the smallest of the twelve tribes of Israel. The Benjamites occupied the land between Ephraim in the north and Judah in the south. Saul was therefore a good choice of king for a united Israel as he would appeal to both northern and southern tribes.

Saul the soldier

Saul was an excellent military leader. From the different tribes of Israel he formed a single army that, despite having inferior weapons, fought successfully against the Ammonites and the Philistines. However, Saul's victories are given only a brief mention in the Bible. Instead, Saul is heavily criticized for his disobedience to God (1 Samuel 13, 15). God rejected Saul, which caused him to become increasingly suspicious and jealous, particularly of David, who served him in his palace. Saul wasted much time persecuting David, and consequently the nation of Israel suffered. In the final years of his reign, Saul saw David as a threat to his power.

SAUL AND THE AMMONITES
This ancient engraving depicts the Ammonites suffering heavy losses at Jabesh-Gilead (1 Samuel 11). It was Saul's first battle after he became king.

DAVID'S REIGN

Following Saul's death, David was anointed king by his fellow tribesmen of Judah. However, he inherited a divided kingdom. One of Saul's sons, Ish-Bosheth, was made king over the northern tribes of Israel by Saul's army commander, Abner. This caused a war. Ish-Bosheth was finally killed, and David was anointed king by the northern tribes.

David's military achievements

David was a brave soldier and a skilled general. He subdued neighbouring nations from all sides. He defeated the Ammonites, Moabites, and Edomites in the east, the Philistines in the west, and the Syrians (Arameans) in the north. The decline of Egypt and the weakening power of other major civilizations allowed David to make successful alliances to secure his borders from the Nile to the Euphrates.

David captures Jerusalem

David captured the ancient city of Jerusalem from the Jebusites and made it the religious and political centre of his kingdom. It was an ideal location, being centrally placed between the northern and southern tribes of Israel. The old Israelite capital was in Hebron, which was much further south. Jerusalem was also conveniently situated on a high plateau and was heavily fortified. David installed the Ark of the Covenant (containing the Laws of Moses) in his new capital.

THE CITY OF JERUSALEM
Detail from a Jewish wedding contract, Padua, Italy (1732)

Opposition to David

David transformed the Israelites' tribal society into a centralized state. He also raised taxes to pay for his military campaigns and building projects. This caused much hostility amongst the Israelite tribes that did not feel the benefits of his reforms. A revolt was led by Sheba, a Benjamite, who wanted to split up the kingdom and destroy the monarchy. However, David defeated the rebels at Abel Beth Maacah.

David's reign was also overshadowed by troubles inside his family. One of David's sons, Absalom, tried to take the throne for himself, and David was forced to flee from Jerusalem. These internal problems underline the instability of the monarchy at this time.

SHEBA'S REVOLT
This painting by Matthaus Merian (1593–1650) depicts David's forces besieging Abel Beth Maacah and decapitating Sheba.

SOLOMON'S REIGN

David appointed his son Solomon to succeed him. His reign was a peaceful one, and he expanded his kingdom by signing treaties with other nations. However, Solomon tended to be dictatorial, and the people thought of him as an oppressive ruler. Solomon brought great wealth and prestige to his kingdom. He was also renowned for his wisdom and learning. Many of Solomon's writings are contained in the Bible. These are a collection of proverbs, love poems, and psalms.

Solomon's trade

Solomon initiated a system of trade agreements with neighbouring countries. Some trade was carried out overland using camel caravans, but most trade was conducted by sea. He built a large fleet of ships with the help of King Hiram of Tyre. Solomon's trading brought him into contact with the Queen of Sheba (1 Kings 10: 1–13).

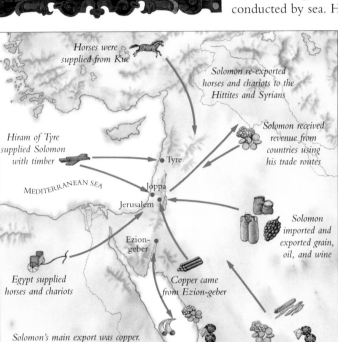

Horses were supplied from Kue

Solomon re-exported horses and chariots to the Hittites and Syrians

Hiram of Tyre supplied Solomon with timber

Solomon received revenue from countries using his trade routes

MEDITERRANEAN SEA

Tyre

Joppa

Jerusalem

Solomon imported and exported grain, oil, and wine

Ezion-geber

Egypt supplied horses and chariots

Copper came from Ezion-geber

Solomon's main export was copper. He traded this for monkeys, parrots, precious stones, sandalwood, gold, and ivory from Africa and Arabia.

Gold, perfumes, and precious stones came from Sheba

SOLOMON'S TRADE ROUTES
Solomon built up a large fleet of ships at Ezion-geber, from where he traded with Arabia and north-east Africa. He also had a fleet in the Mediterranean.

Solomon the builder

There were no wars during Solomon's reign, which enabled him to undertake major building projects. His palace, a series of five structures, took thirteen years to construct. He built store cities and fortresses to protect his kingdom, such as Hazor, Megiddo, and Gezer. Solomon used foreign slaves to work on these projects. He also conscripted the Israelites to collect building materials for him from Lebanon.

The Temple of Jerusalem

The most important of Solomon's building projects was the Temple. Nothing remains today of this magnificent building, but the Book of Kings describes it in great detail (1 Kings 6). It was divided into three main sections: the Most Holy Place, the Holy Place, and the outer courtyards. Its layout was similar to the Tabernacle (the Israelites' portable shrine). Solomon was assisted by Houram-Abi, a gifted artisan from Tyre. The Bible describes him as the second "Oholiab", who helped to construct the Tabernacle.

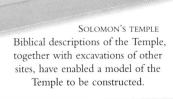

Main hall lined with cedar (The Holy Place)

The Most Holy Place

Bronze columns

SOLOMON'S TEMPLE
Biblical descriptions of the Temple, together with excavations of other sites, have enabled a model of the Temple to be constructed.

1 SAMUEL 8–10
ISRAEL ASKS FOR A KING

CHAPTER 8 VERSE 7

*"They have rejected me
as their king"*

The covenant that God made with Israel through his servant Moses was formulated in the same way that ancient Middle-Eastern treaties were made between kings and their subjects. God was Israel's king. Moses and Joshua ruled over Israel but their authority came from God. Under the Judges, the leadership had become more regional.

PSUSENNES I
(*c.* 1039–991 BC)
At the time that the Israelites asked for a king, Psusennes 1 was king of Egypt. The pharaoh had absolute power. He led the army, controlled the legal system, and set the amount of taxes to be paid.

CHAPTER 9 VERSE 1

"A Benjamite"

Benjamin was the youngest of Jacob's twelve sons and Joseph's only full brother. In Samuel's day, Benjamin was the smallest of Israel's tribes. It had been virtually wiped out by the rest of Israel when the Benjamites had failed to punish a brutal rape. The six hundred men who survived were given wives from other tribes (Judges 19–21).

THE CUP FROM BENJAMIN'S SACK
This 13th-century painting by Giotto depicts the retrieval of the silver cup Joseph hid to test his brothers.

8 WHEN[1] SAMUEL GREW OLD, he appointed his sons as judges for Israel... ³But his sons did not walk in his ways. They turned aside after dishonest gain and accepted bribes and perverted justice. ⁴So all the elders of Israel gathered together and came to Samuel at Ramah. ⁵They said to him, "You are old, and your sons do not walk in your ways; now appoint a king to lead us, such as all the other nations have."

⁶But... this displeased Samuel; so he prayed to the LORD. ⁷And the LORD told him: "Listen to all that the people are saying to you; it is not you they have rejected, but *they have rejected me as their king.*"

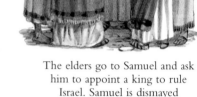

The elders go to Samuel and ask him to appoint a king to rule Israel. Samuel is dismayed

Samuel told the elders that a king would make their lives much harsher, but they would not listen to him.

²¹When Samuel heard all that the people said, he repeated it before the LORD. ²²The LORD answered, "Listen to them and give them a king."...

9 ¹There was *a Benjamite,* a man of standing, whose name was Kish... ²He had a son named Saul, an impressive young man without equal among the Israelites – a head taller than any of the others.

God tells Samuel to give Israel a king

³Now the donkeys belonging to Saul's father Kish were lost, and Kish said to his son Saul, "Take one of the servants with you and go and look for the donkeys."

Saul searched in several districts but did not find the donkeys. As he was about to return home, his servant told him about the prophet Samuel, who might be able to help them. They asked for directions and, as they reached the prophet's town, Samuel was walking towards them.

Samuel

Saul is searching for his father's donkeys. He hopes that the prophet Samuel can tell him where to find them

Saul's servant

¹⁵Now the day before Saul came, the L<small>ORD</small> had revealed this to Samuel: ¹⁶"About this time tomorrow I will send you a man from the land of Benjamin. Anoint him leader over my people Israel; he will deliver my people from the hand of the Philistines... ¹⁷When Samuel caught sight of Saul, the L<small>ORD</small> said to him, "This is the man I spoke to you about; he will govern my people."

¹⁸Saul approached Samuel in the gate-way and asked, "Would you please tell me where the seer's house is?"

¹⁹"I am the seer", Samuel replied... ²⁷"Stay here awhile, so that I may give you a message from God."

10   ¹Then Samuel took a flask of oil and poured it on Saul's head and kissed him, saying, "Has not the L<small>ORD</small> *anointed* you *leader over his inheritance*?... "

¹⁷Samuel summoned the people of Israel... ¹⁸and said to them... ¹⁹"Present yourselves before the L<small>ORD</small> by your tribes and clans." ²⁰When Samuel brought all the tribes of Israel near, the tribe of Benjamin was chosen... ²¹Finally Saul son of Kish was chosen. But... he was not to be found... ²²And the L<small>ORD</small> said... "He has hidden himself among the baggage."

²³They ran and brought him out, and... he was a head taller than any of the others. ²⁴Samuel said... "Do you see the man the L<small>ORD</small> has chosen? There is no-one like him among all the people."

Then the people shouted, "Long live the king!"

God tells Samuel that he has chosen Saul to lead the Israelites

Saul

Samuel tells Saul what God has decided and then anoints him with oil

Samuel summons together the tribes of Israel

Saul is overwhelmed and hides among some baggage

Samuel presents Saul to the Israelites, who are delighted to see that their new king is so tall

UNDERSTANDING THE STORY

Israel's demand for a king amounts to a rejection of God's leadership. Nevertheless, God grants this request and provides the Israelites with a national leader who will unite the tribes and deliver them from their enemies.

❖

C<small>HAPTER</small> 10 <small>VERSE</small> 1
"Anointed"
Anointing people and objects with oil consecrated them to God. Jacob anointed the stone at Bethel (Genesis 35: 14), and Aaron was anointed as Israel's first High Priest (Exodus 30: 30). Saul's anointment meant that he was ordained by God to rule Israel. The kings of Israel were known as the "Lord's anointed".

❖

C<small>HAPTER</small> 10 <small>VERSE</small> 1
"Leader over his inheritance"
Samuel uses the word "leader" rather than "king". The implication is that only God can be king of Israel. The Israelites – and the land that they live in – belong to God. Israel's monarchy will not be the same as other nations. Saul will rule as God's earthly representative.

1 SAMUEL 13–14

SAUL AND JONATHAN

CHAPTER 13 VERSE 5
"They... camped at Michmash"
Michmash was strategically placed on a major east–west pass. By occupying it, the Philistine army effectively drove a wedge between Israelite settlements. The Philistines had established a strong presence in the hill country of central Israel, controlling the area through garrison outposts. They gathered in strength to fight Saul, because Saul had attacked their outpost at Gibeah, killing the Philistine governor.

13 THE[5] PHILISTINES ASSEMBLED to fight Israel, with three thousand chariots, six thousand charioteers, and soldiers as numerous as the sand on the seashore. *They went up and camped at Michmash,* east of Beth Aven. [6]When the men of Israel saw that their situation was critical and that their army was hard pressed, they hid in caves and thickets, among the rocks, and in pits and cisterns...

[7]Saul remained at Gilgal, and all the troops with him were quaking with fear. [8]He waited for seven days, the time set by Samuel; but Samuel did not come to Gilgal, and Saul's men began to scatter. [9]So he said, "Bring me the burnt offering and the fellowship offerings." And Saul offered up the burnt offering. [10]Just as he finished making the offering, Samuel arrived, and Saul went out to greet him.

[11]"What have you done?" asked Samuel.

Saul replied, "When I saw that the men were scattering, and that you did not come at the set time, and that the Philistines were assembling at Michmash, [12]I thought, 'Now the Philistines will come down against me at Gilgal, and I have not sought the LORD's favour.' So I felt compelled to offer the burnt offering."

[13]"You acted foolishly," Samuel said. "*You have not kept the command the LORD your God gave you;* if you had, he would have established your kingdom over Israel for all time.

The Philistines gather a massive army to fight the Israelites

SAUL'S EARLY BATTLES
Saul began his reign successfully, bringing unity to the scattered tribes of Israel. His first victory was against the Ammonites, who were besieging Jabesh Gilead and threatening to mutilate its inhabitants. Saul then turned his attention to the Philistine presence.

The Israelite army is frightened by the might of the Philistines, and soldiers begin to desert

Instead of waiting for Samuel to arrive, Saul offers sacrifices to God for the impending battle

Samuel denounces Saul for disobeying God's command to wait

¹⁴But now your kingdom will not endure; the LORD has sought out a man after his own heart and appointed him leader of his people...”

¹⁶Saul and his son Jonathan and the men with them were staying in *Gibeah of Benjamin*, while the Philistines camped at Michmash... ¹⁹*Not a blacksmith could be found* in the whole land of Israel, because the Philistines had said, “Otherwise the Hebrews will make swords or spears!”... ²²So on the day of the battle not a soldier... had a sword or spear in his hand; only Saul and his son Jonathan had them.

Saul's son Jonathan and his armour-bearer attack the Philistines

At the same time, God sends an earthquake

Jonathan's armour-bearer

Jonathan

These events throw the whole Philistine army into a panic

Saul and his army join the battle, and the Philistines are defeated

²³A detachment of Philistines had gone out to the pass at Michmash. 14 ⁶Jonathan said to his young armour-bearer, “Come, let's go over to the outpost of those uncircumcised fellows. Perhaps the LORD will act on our behalf. Nothing can hinder the LORD from saving, whether by many or by few.”...

¹³Jonathan climbed up, using his hands and feet, with his armour-bearer right behind him. The Philistines fell before Jonathan, and his armour-bearer followed and killed behind him. ¹⁴In that first attack [they] killed some twenty men... ¹⁵Then panic struck the whole [Philistine] army [when] *the ground shook*. It was a panic sent by God...

²⁰Saul and all his men assembled and went to the battle. They found the Philistines in total confusion, striking each other with their swords... ²²When all the Israelites who had hidden... heard that the Philistines were on the run, they joined the battle in hot pursuit. ²³So the LORD rescued Israel that day.

UNDERSTANDING THE STORY

Saul's actions are understandable, considering his dwindling forces and the size of the Philistine army. However, his disobedience shows a lack of faith. By contrast, Jonathan's actions show his trust in God's power to deliver, whatever the odds.

❖

CHAPTER 13 VERSE 13
“You have not kept the command the LORD your God gave you”
Saul was Israel's king, but he was still under Samuel's authority, because God spoke and acted through his prophets. By disobeying Samuel, Saul had disobeyed the word of God. Furthermore, the Law of Moses decreed that only a priest could offer sacrifices.

❖

CHAPTER 13 VERSE 16
“Gibeah of Benjamin”
Gibeah was Saul's home town and Israel's capital city during his reign. Gibeah has been identified as Tell el-Ful, where the remains of a building dating from the 11th century BC have been uncovered. These ruins are believed to be Saul's “palace”. Excavations show a rectangular structure measuring 52 x 35m (170 x 115ft) of two storeys or more. Double stone walls and a tower at each corner suggest a fortress rather than a palace.

GIBEAH (TELL EL-FUL)

❖

CHAPTER 13 VERSE 19
“Not a blacksmith could be found”
In Saul's time, the Israelites still depended on the Philistines for iron tools. The Philistines controlled the availability of iron weapons through a monopoly on iron technology.

❖

CHAPTER 14 VERSE 15
“The ground shook”
Earthquakes were not uncommon in the region. However, in the Bible these events are always associated with God's power and intervention.

1 SAMUEL 15–16
DAVID IS CHOSEN TO BE KING

15 SAMUEL[1] SAID TO SAUL... ²"This is what the LORD Almighty says: '*I will punish the Amalekites* for what they did to Israel when they waylaid them as they came up from Egypt. ³Now go, attack the Amalekites and *totally destroy everything* that belongs to them. Do not spare them...' "

⁷Then Saul attacked the Amalekites... ⁸He took Agag king of the Amalekites alive, and all his people he totally destroyed with the sword [but spared] ⁹the best of the sheep and cattle...

God tells Saul to destroy the Amalekites, but he spares King Agag and the best sheep and cattle

¹⁰Then the word of the LORD came to Samuel: ¹¹"I am grieved that I have made Saul king, because he has turned away from me and has not carried out my instructions"...

¹²Early in the morning Samuel got up and went to meet Saul, but he was told, "Saul has gone to Carmel. There he has set up a monument in his own honour and has turned and gone on down to Gilgal."

Saul tries to stop Samuel leaving and tears his robe

Samuel tells Saul that God has rejected him

¹³When Samuel reached him, Saul said... "I have carried out the LORD's instructions." ¹⁴But Samuel said, "What then is this bleating of sheep in my ears?... ²⁶You have rejected the word of the LORD, and the LORD has rejected you as king over Israel!" ²⁷As Samuel turned to leave, Saul caught hold of the hem of his robe, and it tore. ²⁸Samuel said to him, "The LORD has torn the kingdom of Israel from you today and has given it to one of your neighbours – to one better than you. ²⁹He who is the Glory of Israel does not lie or change his mind; for he is not a man..." ³³And Samuel put Agag to death before the LORD at Gilgal... ³⁵Until the day Samuel died, he did not go to see Saul again, though Samuel mourned for him. And the LORD was grieved that he had made Saul king over Israel.

CHAPTER 15 VERSE 2
"I will punish the Amalekites"
The Amalekites launched an attack on the weary Israelites shortly after the Exodus. After Joshua's victory, God told Moses, "I will completely blot out the memory of Amalek from under heaven" (Exodus 17: 14). A few centuries after this, the Amalekites were defeated by Gideon, but they continued to pose a threat to the Israelites.

DESCENDANTS OF ESAU
The Amalekites descended from Amalek, the grandson of Esau. This detail from a 12th-century mosaic depicts Esau hunting.

CHAPTER 15 VERSE 3
"Totally destroy everything"
This command recalls the fate of Jericho, when the Israelites destroyed the city and killed every living thing in it (Joshua 6: 21). Like Jericho, the Amalekites were to be sacrificed to God. By obeying God's instructions the Israelites would effectively eliminate the threat of further raids on their settlements.

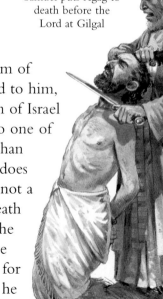

Samuel puts Agag to death before the Lord at Gilgal

16 ¹The LORD said to Samuel, "How long will you mourn for Saul, since I have rejected him as king over Israel? *Fill your horn with oil* and be on your way; I am sending you to *Jesse of Bethlehem*. I have chosen one of his sons to be king."...

⁴Samuel did what the LORD said. When he arrived at Bethlehem... ⁵he consecrated Jesse and his sons... ⁶Samuel saw Eliab and thought, "Surely the LORD's anointed stands here before the LORD."

⁷But the LORD said to Samuel, "Do not consider his appearance or his height, for I have rejected him. The LORD does not look at the things man looks at. Man looks at the outward appearance, but the LORD looks at the heart."...

¹⁰Jesse made seven of his sons pass before Samuel, but Samuel said to him, "The LORD has not chosen these." ¹¹So he asked Jesse, "Are these all the sons you have?"

God sends Samuel to Jesse of Bethlehem to anoint one of his sons as the future king

Seven sons pass before Samuel but none are chosen

Samuel asks Jesse if he has other sons

Jesse sends for his youngest son, David, and Samuel anoints him as God's chosen king

Jesse

David tends Jesse's sheep

"There is still the youngest," Jesse answered, "but *he is tending the sheep.*" Samuel... ¹²had him brought in. He was ruddy, with a fine appearance and handsome features.

Then the LORD said, "Rise and anoint him; he is the one."

¹³So Samuel took the horn of oil and anointed him in the presence of his brothers, and from that day on the Spirit of the LORD came upon David in power. Samuel then went to Ramah.

UNDERSTANDING THE STORY

God rejects Saul and chooses David to succeed him. Saul's disobedience means that a hostile tribe remains a danger to the Israelites, and his vanity sets them a bad example. A humble shepherd-boy seems an unlikely candidate for Israel's next king. But God has chosen a leader who will guide and protect his people.

CHAPTER 16 VERSE 1
"Fill your horn with oil"
This was not ordinary olive oil, it was a sacred anointing oil containing spices such as cinnamon and myrrh. God gave Moses a precise recipe for the oil and forbade its use for any other purpose (Exodus 30: 22–33).

ANCIENT HORN
Ivory and gold, 14th-century BC

CHAPTER 16 VERSE 1
"Jesse of Bethlehem"
In the Book of Ruth, Jesse is introduced as the grandson of Ruth and Boaz (Ruth 4: 17). Like his grandparents, Jesse lived in Bethlehem, a town in the hill country of Judah. In the 8th century BC, the prophet Micah predicted that the Messiah would come from Bethlehem.

CHAPTER 16 VERSE 11
"He is tending the sheep"
David's job was humble but carried great responsibility. A shepherd knew each animal in his flock. He found them food, kept them from straying, and protected them from wild animals. The "good shepherd" became the ideal model for Israel's kingship. Jesus once said about himself, "I am the good shepherd. The good shepherd lays down his life for the sheep" (John 10: 11).

David asks King Saul
for permission to
fight Goliath

1 SAMUEL 17
DAVID AND GOLIATH

17 **N**OW[1] THE
PHILISTINES
gathered their forces
for war and assembled at Socoh in Judah...
[2]Saul and the Israelites assembled and camped in *the
Valley of Elah* and drew up their battle line to meet the
Philistines. [3]The Philistines occupied one hill and the Israelites
another, with the valley between them.

[4]*A champion named Goliath*, who was from Gath, came out of the
Philistine camp. He was over nine feet tall. [5]He had a bronze helmet on
his head and wore a coat of scale armour of bronze... [8]Goliath stood and
shouted to the ranks of Israel... "Choose a man and have him come down
to me. [9]If he is able to fight and kill me, we will become your subjects..."
[11]Saul and all the Israelites were dismayed and terrified...

*Goliath shouted his challenge every morning and evening for forty days.
One morning, David, a shepherd boy from Bethlehem, arrived at the camp
with food for his brothers. David saw Goliath and asked the Israelites about him.
Then he went to Saul and persuaded the king to let him fight the giant.*

[37]Saul said to David, "Go, and the LORD be with you." [38]Then Saul
dressed David in his own tunic. He put *a coat of armour* on him and a
bronze helmet on his head... [39]"I cannot go in these," he said to Saul,
"because I am not used to them." So he took them off. [40]Then he...
chose five smooth stones from the stream, put them in the pouch of his
shepherd's bag and, with *his sling in his hand*, approached the Philistine...
[42][Goliath] looked David over and saw that he was only a boy, ruddy
and handsome, and he despised him. [43]He said to David, "Am I a dog,
that you come at me with sticks?" And the Philistine cursed David by
his gods. [David said] [45]"I come against you in the name of the LORD...
[47]the battle is the LORD's, and he will give all of you into our hands."...

Every day for forty days, the
Philistines' champion Goliath
challenges the Israelites to a fight

✛

CHAPTER 17 VERSE 2
"The Valley of Elah"
The name Elah means "terebinth",
a tall, spreading tree that is common
in the warm, dry hills of Palestine.
Turpentine is made from its sap.
Terebinth trees probably grew above
this valley, which ran east to west
between Judah and Philistia. The
Philistines often marched through
the valley to attack the Israelites.

[48]David ran quickly towards the battle line to meet him. [49]Reaching into his bag and taking out a stone, he slung it and struck the Philistine on the forehead. The stone sank into his forehead, and he fell face down on the ground... [51]David ran and stood over him. He took hold of the Philistine's sword and drew it from the scabbard. After he killed him, he cut off his head with the sword. When the Philistines saw that their hero was dead, they turned and ran. [52]Then the men of Israel and Judah surged forward with a shout and pursued the Philistines.

David refuses to wear armour, and his only weapon is a sling

David's stone pierces the giant's forehead, and Goliath falls to the ground

David cuts off Goliath's head

When the Philistines see their champion is dead, they flee

UNDERSTANDING THE STORY

Saul is no longer fit to be king. His fear of Goliath shows a lack of faith and leadership. The Israelites find a new leader in David, who takes up the challenge in God's name. David's courage might appear to be no match for the heavily armed and armoured giant, but he has absolute trust in God. His victory is a clear demonstration to the Israelites that God rewards those who keep faith in him.

CHAPTER 17 VERSE 4
"A champion named Goliath"
In ancient times, issues of war were sometimes settled by single combat. The opposing sides would each select a champion to represent them. This practice avoided heavy losses of soldiers. The outcome of the fight was accepted as the will of the gods.

CHAPTER 17 VERSE 38
"A coat of armour"
This is the first time that the Bible mentions the use of body armour by the Israelites. The earliest evidence of armour comes from Egyptian wall carvings, *c.* 3000 BC. Bronze was usually worn by royalty. The coats were made by lacing together metal plates.

IRON-AGE SWORD
Iron weapons were superior to bronze and gradually replaced them. The Philistines were skilled ironworkers.

CHAPTER 17 VERSE 40
"His sling in his hand"
Shepherds carried slings to protect their flocks from wild animals. The sling was also a common weapon of war in the ancient Middle East, and many armies had units of slingmen. The sling consisted of a broad pad with a cord attached on each side. A slinger put a stone on the pad, took the two cords in one hand, and then whirled the sling in the air – letting go of one cord to launch the missile.

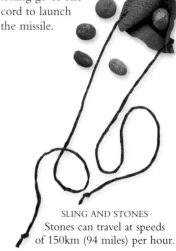

SLING AND STONES
Stones can travel at speeds of 150km (94 miles) per hour.

1 SAMUEL 18–23
SAUL TURNS AGAINST DAVID

CHAPTER 18 VERSE 4
"Jonathan took off [his robe]..."
This gesture of allegiance was a physical sign of their covenant. Friendship was not normally sealed by a covenant, which was a solemn undertaking. However, David was God's anointed, and Jonathan was Saul's heir. The covenant was Jonathan's initiative, making it clear that he accepted God's choice of David as the next king and that there was no rivalry between them.

DAVID RETURNS IN TRIUMPH
Israelite women greeted their victorious menfolk with songs of praise. In this painting by S G Battista, David is exhibiting the head of Goliath (Uffizi Gallery, Florence).

CHAPTER 18 VERSE 20
"Michal was in love with David"
Michal was Saul's younger daughter. Saul had promised Merab, his elder daughter, to the man who defeated Goliath. But Saul broke his oath and gave Merab to another man.

CHAPTER 18 VERSE 25
"No other price"
Despite reneging on his earlier promise, Saul still demanded a dowry from David for his younger daughter. This customary gift to the father of the bride was usually given in the form of goods. A bridegroom who had no real means might be asked to provide a service in lieu of payment. An example is Jacob, who gave Laban seven years' work for Rachel.

18 JONATHAN[3] MADE a covenant with David because he loved him as himself. [4]*Jonathan took off [his robe]* and gave it to David... [5]Whatever Saul sent him to do, David did it so successfully that Saul gave him a high rank in the army... [6]When the men were returning home after David had killed the Philistine, the women came out from all the towns of Israel to meet King Saul... [7]As they danced, they sang: "Saul has slain his thousands, and David his tens of thousands." [8]Saul was very angry; this refrain galled him... [9]And from that time on Saul kept a jealous eye on David... [20]Now Saul's daughter *Michal was in love with David*... [21]So Saul said... [25]"The king wants *no other price* for the bride than a hundred Philistine foreskins..." Saul's plan was to have David fall by the hands of the Philistines. [However] [27]David and his men went out and killed two hundred Philistines...

19 [1]Saul told his son Jonathan and all the attendants to kill David. [But] [4]Jonathan spoke well of David [and so Saul] [6]took this oath: "As surely as the LORD lives, David will not be put to death."... [9]But an evil spirit from the LORD came upon Saul as he was sitting in his house with his spear in his hand. While *David was playing the harp,* [10]Saul tried to pin him to the wall with his spear, but David eluded him as Saul drove the spear into the wall. That night David made good his escape.

Saul's son Jonathan and David become firm friends
Jonathan
Saul
Saul makes David an army commander
David

David plays the harp to soothe Saul's tormented mind

Saul's jealousy of David explodes in anger, and he throws a spear at David

Saul is possessed by an evil spirit

Saul sends soldiers to kill David

David's wife Michal helps him escape

She puts a dummy into David's bed

Saul is angry with Michal

CHAPTER 19 VERSE 9
"David was playing the harp"
David was a skilled harpist. When the spirit of God left Saul, he was often tormented by dark moods, and David's playing soothed him (1 Samuel 16: 23). The harp is the first instrument mentioned in the Bible (Genesis 4: 21), and it was used to play both secular and religious music. In the Bible, the word "harp" can also describe a lyre. There were several different styles of instruments, which could have between three and twelve strings.

JEWISH HARP
This instrument was made by stretching animal skin over a round soundbox. It is called a "nebel", which means "skin bottle".

¹¹Saul sent men to David's house to watch it and to kill him in the morning... Michal, David's wife, warned him [and] ¹²let David down through a window, and he fled and escaped. ¹³Then Michal took an idol and laid it on the bed, covering it with a garment and putting some goat's hair at the head. [Michal pretended that David was ill]. ¹⁶When the men entered, there was the idol in the bed.

¹⁷Saul said to Michal, "Why did you deceive me like this and send my enemy away so that he escaped?"...

¹⁹[Then] word came to Saul: "David is in Naioth at Ramah"... ²³So Saul went to *Naioth at Ramah*. But the Spirit of God came even upon him, and he walked along prophesying until he came to Naioth. ²⁴*He stripped off his robes and also prophesied in Samuel's presence...*

20   ¹Then David [fled] to Jonathan... ³⁰Saul's anger flared up at Jonathan and he said... ³¹"As long as the son of Jesse lives on this earth, neither you nor your kingdom will be established. Now send and bring him to me, for he must die!"... ³³Then Jonathan knew that his father intended to kill David.

David went into hiding and travelled from place to place, living in caves with his men. Saul continued to pursue him.

23   ¹⁵While David was at Horesh in the Desert of Ziph... ¹⁶Jonathan went to David [and said], ¹⁷"Don't be afraid... You shall be king over Israel, and I will be second to you. Even my father Saul knows this."

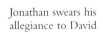

Jonathan swears his allegiance to David

CHAPTER 19 VERSE 23
"Naioth at Ramah"
The word "Naioth" means "dwelling camps" and probably refers to a place in the vicinity of Ramah where a group of prophets lived. Ramah was the prophet Samuel's home town. It was in the tribal land of Ephraim, a short distance north-east of Jerusalem. In the New Testament, Ramah was called Arimathea.

CHAPTER 19 VERSE 24
"He stripped off his robes and also prophesied in Samuel's presence"
In the presence of God's prophet, Saul was powerless. His robes were symbolic of his kingship, and Saul was compelled to strip himself of all authority. To "prophesy" did not always mean to utter the word of God. The term could also describe a mad ranting (1 Kings 18: 29).

UNDERSTANDING THE STORY

The result of God's rejection of Saul is tragically apparent. His behaviour becomes increasingly disturbed and deceitful, and even his children disobey him in favour of David. Whereas Jonathan accepts that David is God's choice as Saul's successor, Saul does his utmost to defy God's will.

1 SAMUEL 25
DAVID AND ABIGAIL

CHAPTER 25 VERSE 1
"The Desert of Maon"
Maon means "refuge". The hills and caves in this area of the Judean Desert provided abundant hiding places for David, who King Saul was pursuing and trying to kill.

EIN GEDI, ISRAEL
The caves where David sought refuge are now part of a desert nature reserve.

CARMEL
The name of this Judean town means "garden". It was situated near Hebron, in a region of pastureland bordering the Desert of Maon. Saul erected a monument in his own honour at Carmel – a foolish act that precipitated his downfall (1 Samuel 15).

25 ᵀHEN¹ DAVID MOVED down into *the Desert of Maon*. ²A certain man in Maon, who had property there at Carmel, was very wealthy... ³His name was *Nabal* and his wife's name was Abigail. She was an intelligent and beautiful woman, but her husband, *a Calebite*, was surly and mean in his dealings.

⁴While David was in the desert, he heard that Nabal was shearing sheep. ⁵So he sent ten young men and said to them, "Go up to Nabal at Carmel and greet him in my name. ⁶Say to him... ⁷I hear that it is sheep-shearing time. When your shepherds were with us, we did not ill-treat them, and the whole time they were at Carmel nothing of theirs was missing... ⁸Therefore be favourable towards my young men, since we come at a festive time. Please give your servants and your son David whatever you can find for them.' "...

¹⁰Nabal answered David's servants, "Who is this David?... ¹¹Why should I take my bread and water, and the meat I have slaughtered for my shearers, and give it to men coming from who knows where?"

¹²David's men turned round and went back [and] reported every word. ¹³David said to his men, "Put on your swords!"...

At sheep-shearing time, David sends some of his men to Nabal to ask for provisions

The men go back and tell David everything Nabal said

Nabal is a wealthy farmer

David is furious and decides to kill Nabal and all the men of Nabal's household

David's men remind Nabal that they protected his herds, but Nabal sends them away empty-handed

About four hundred men went up with David, while two hundred stayed with the supplies.

¹⁴One of the servants told Nabal's wife Abigail: "David sent messengers from the desert to give our master his greetings, but he hurled insults at them... ¹⁵Yet these men were very good to us... ¹⁶Night and day they were a wall around us all the time we were herding our sheep near them..."

Abigail said nothing to Nabal, but she acted immediately. She loaded large amounts of food and wine onto donkeys and set off with her servants to try to find David.

²⁰As she came riding her donkey into a mountain ravine, there were David and his men descending towards her, and she met them... ²³When Abigail saw David... ²⁴she fell at his feet and said: "My Lord, let the blame be on me alone... ²⁸Please forgive your servant's offence, for the LORD will certainly make a lasting dynasty for my master, because he fights *the LORD's battles*. Let no wrongdoing be found in you as long as you live..."

³⁵Then David accepted from her hand what she had brought to him and said, "Go home in peace..." ³⁶When Abigail went to Nabal, he was in the house holding a banquet like that of a king. He was in high spirits and very drunk. So she told him nothing until daybreak. ³⁷Then in the morning, when Nabal was sober, his wife told him all these things, and his heart failed him and he became like a stone. ³⁸About ten days later, the LORD struck Nabal and he died.

³⁹When David heard that Nabal was dead, he said, "Praise be to the LORD, who has upheld my cause against Nabal for treating me with contempt..." Then David sent word to Abigail, asking her to become his wife... ⁴³David had also married Ahinoam of Jezreel, and they both were his wives. ⁴⁴But Saul had given his daughter Michal, David's wife, to Paltiel son of Laish, who was from Gallim.

✣

CHAPTER 25 VERSE 3
"Nabal... a Calebite"
Nabal means "foolish". He was a descendant of Caleb, the hero who entered the Promised Land with Joshua. Caleb settled in Hebron, and his descendants spread out to surrounding towns, such as Maon.

DAVID THE FUGITIVE
David's many followers amounted to a private army. His men included a priest named Abiathar and the prophet Gad. So David already had the basic elements of government. This group and their families relied on the support of local people, who repaid David for protecting them with gifts of food and goods.

✣

CHAPTER 25 VERSE 28
The LORD's battles"
As the "Lord's anointed," David organized raids on the Philistines, crediting God for his victories. But David also respected Saul's kingship and never attacked Israelite troops.

A servant tells Abigail that Nabal has insulted David and that her household is facing disaster

Abigail loads donkeys with provisions. As she is riding through a ravine, she meets David on his way to kill Nabal

David accepts Abigail's gift and realises that she has stopped him acting rashly

UNDERSTANDING THE STORY

Nabal's foolishness is in sharp contrast to Abigail's wisdom. Her quick action saves her household from disaster and prevents David from making the same mistake as Saul: using his power for personal vengeance. The behaviour and characters of Nabal and Saul are very similar, and Nabal's sudden death foreshadows Saul's own fate.

1 SAMUEL 28–31
SAUL AND THE WITCH OF ENDOR

CHAPTER 28 VERSE 3
"Israel had mourned for him"
Samuel was the last Judge of Israel, and the Israelites acknowledged him as a great leader. The whole nation mourned him, as they had mourned Abraham and Moses and other great figures of the past.

Saul visits a witch to discover his fate

The witch conjures up Samuel's ghost

CHAPTER 28 VERSE 3
"The mediums and spiritists"
The Law of Moses strictly forbade necromancy: "Let no-one be found among you who practises divination or sorcery, interprets omens, engages in witchcraft, or casts spells, or who is a medium or spiritist or who consults the dead" (Deuteronomy 18: 10–11). The penalty for breaking this law was death by stoning.

CHAPTER 28 VERSE 6
"Urim"
A High Priest's jewelled breastpiece concealed a pouch. This lay next to his heart and contained sacred lots called the Urim (Curses) and the Thummim (Perfections). The High Priest used them to determine the will of God. It is not known how these lots were cast. They may have been thrown or ceremonially drawn, but they could only give a "yes" or "no" answer to a single question.

28 NOW[3] SAMUEL WAS DEAD, and all *Israel had mourned for him* and buried him in his own town of Ramah. Saul had expelled *the mediums and spiritists* from the land. [4]The Philistines assembled and came and set up camp at Shunem, while Saul gathered all the Israelites and set up camp at Gilboa. [5]When Saul saw the Philistine army, he was afraid; terror filled his heart. [6]He enquired of the LORD, but the LORD did not answer him by dreams or *Urim* or prophets. [7]Saul then said to his attendants, "Find me a woman who is a medium, so that I may go and inquire of her."

"There is one in Endor," they said.

[8]So Saul disguised himself, putting on other clothes, and at night he and two men went to the woman. "Consult a spirit for me," he said, "and bring up for me the one I name."

[9]But the woman said to him, "Surely you know what Saul has done. He has cut off the mediums and spiritists from the land. Why have you set a trap for my life to bring about my death?"

[10]Saul swore to her by the LORD, "As surely as the LORD lives, you will not be punished for this." [11]Then the woman asked, "Whom shall I bring up for you?" "Bring up Samuel," he said.

[12]When the woman saw Samuel, she cried out at the top of her voice and said to Saul, "Why have you deceived me? You are Saul!"

[13]The king said to her, "Don't be afraid. What do you see?"

The woman said, "I see a spirit coming up out of the ground."

[14]"What does he look like?" he asked.

"An old man wearing a robe is coming up," she said. Then Saul knew it was Samuel...

Samuel tells Saul that the Philistines will defeat Israel

Saul hears that he will die in the battle

The Philistine army launches a massive attack on the Israelites at Gilboa

Saul's sons are killed

Jonathan

¹⁵Samuel said to Saul, "Why have you disturbed me...?"

"I am in great distress," Saul said...

¹⁶Samuel said, "Why do you consult me, now that the LORD has turned away from you and become your enemy? ¹⁷The LORD has done what he predicted through me. The LORD has torn the kingdom out of your hands and given it to one of your neighbours – to David... ¹⁹The LORD will hand over both Israel and you to the Philistines, and tomorrow you and your sons will be with me. The LORD will also hand over the army of Israel to the Philistines."

The next day, the Philistines attacked the Israelites and defeated them. Jonathan and his brothers were killed, and Saul was badly wounded.

31 ⁴Saul said to his armour-bearer, "Draw your sword and run me through, or these uncircumcised fellows will come and run me through and abuse me." But the armour-bearer was terrified and would not do it; so Saul took his own sword and fell on it. ⁵When the armour-bearer saw that Saul was dead, he too fell on his sword and died with him. ⁶So Saul and his three sons and his armour-bearer and all his men died.

UNDERSTANDING THE STORY

Saul needs military advice, but God's rejection and Samuel's death have left him in total isolation. In desperation, he turns to a practice he had outlawed himself. Saul's reign ends in defeat and tragedy, and his hopes for a dynasty die with him.

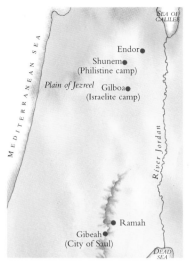

SAUL'S LAST BATTLE
Battles with the Philistines normally took place in the hill country of the south, but this time the Philistines attacked Israel in the north, along the plain of Jezreel. Fighting on flat ground was a tactical advantage to the Philistines, as they relied heavily on chariots.

CHAPTER 28 VERSE 7
"There is one in Endor"
Endor (modern En-ed) was allotted to the tribe of Manasseh. However, the Israelites never captured Endor. It was inhabited by Canaanites, and this explains why a witch could be found in that town.

DAVID IN PHILISTIA
David realized that the only way he could avoid confrontation with Saul was to leave Israel. He went to Philistia and became a mercenary for the King of Gath, who was easily convinced that David was an enemy of Israel. David pretended to make raids on the Israelites, when in fact his raids were directed against tribes that were Israel's enemies.

Many men die in the fierce fighting

Saul is badly wounded

Rather than fall into the hands of the Philistines, Saul commits suicide

Saul's armour-bearer also commits suicide

As Samuel predicted, the Israelite army is defeated by the Philistines

2 SAMUEL 2–5

DAVID, KING OF ISRAEL

❖

CHAPTER 2 VERSE 1
"To Hebron"

Hebron was a good choice for David's return to Israel. It was strategically well-situated – high in the hills of Judah, David's native land – and the people of Hebron had helped David during his years as an outlaw. At Hebron, Abraham had bought the cave of Machpelah from the Hittites as a family burial place.

HEBRON
The modern town of Haram el-Khalil now stands over Abraham's traditional burial place. The name means "sacred land of the friend", because Abraham was "the friend of God".

❖

CHAPTER 2 VERSE 8
"Abner son of Ner"

Abner was Saul's nephew, and he supported Ish-Bosheth as Saul's successor. The two later quarrelled, and Abner changed sides. But Joab, David's army leader, did not trust Abner's motives and murdered him.

JOAB MURDERS ABNER
Altar detail, enamel on copper, *c.* 1181

2 IN[1] THE COURSE OF TIME, David enquired of the LORD. "Shall I go up to one of the towns of Judah?" he asked.

The LORD said, "Go up."

David asked, "Where shall I go?"

"*To Hebron*," the LORD answered.

[2]So David went up there with his two wives... [3]David also took the men who were with him, each with his family, and they settled in Hebron and its towns. [4]Then the men of Judah came to Hebron and there they anointed David king over the house of Judah...

[8]Meanwhile, *Abner son of Ner*, the commander of Saul's army, had taken Ish-Bosheth son of Saul and... [9]made him king over... all Israel... [10]The house of Judah, however, followed David.

After Saul's death, there is civil war. Saul's son Ish-Bosheth rules in the north, and David rules in the south

A long civil war followed. But opposition to David crumbled when both Abner and Ish-Bosheth were murdered. David publicly condemned these killings.

5 [1]All the tribes of Israel came to David at Hebron and said, "We are your own flesh and blood. [2]In the past, while Saul was king over us, you were the one who led Israel on their military campaigns. And the LORD said to you, 'You shall shepherd my people Israel, and you shall become their ruler.' "

When Abner and Ish-Bosheth are murdered, the northern tribes make peace with David

At Hebron, the tribal elders anoint David king over Israel

³When all the elders of Israel had come to King David at Hebron, the king made a compact with them at Hebron before the LORD, and they anointed David king over Israel...

⁶The king and his men marched to Jerusalem to attack the Jebusites, who lived there. The Jebusites said to David, "You will not get in here; even the blind and the lame can ward you off". They thought, "David cannot get in here." ⁷Nevertheless, David captured *the fortress of Zion*, the City of David.

⁸On that day, David said, "Anyone who conquers the Jebusites will have to use the water shaft to reach those 'lame and blind' who are David's enemies." That is why they say, "The 'blind and lame' will not enter the palace."

Joab is the leader of David's army

David wants to make Jerusalem the capital of his kingdom, but it is heavily fortified

David gains access through a water shaft and conquers the city

⁹David then took up residence in the fortress and called it the City of David. He built up the area around it, from the supporting terraces inward. ¹⁰And he became more and more powerful, because the LORD God Almighty was with him.

¹¹Now Hiram King of Tyre sent messengers to David, along with cedar logs and carpenters and stonemasons, and they built a palace for David. ¹²And David knew that the LORD had established him as king over Israel and had exalted his kingdom for the sake of his people Israel.

¹³After he left Hebron, *David took more concubines and wives in Jerusalem*, and more sons and daughters were born to him.

UNDERSTANDING THE STORY

Although the murders of Abner and Ish-Bosheth occur without David's knowledge, their deaths effectively clear the way for him to become king. David lays the foundations for a new dynasty. The conquest of Jerusalem is his first step in establishing a lasting political and religious capital of Israel.

CHAPTER 5 VERSE 7
"The fortress of Zion"

This is the first mention of the word Zion, and it refers to the fortified city at the time of David's conquest. The use of the word expanded over time to include Solomon's Temple Mount, Jerusalem as a religious capital, the land of Judah, and, finally, the entire Israelite nation.

THE CONQUEST OF JERUSALEM

The city that David made his own was neutral territory between the northern and southern tribes. It was an ancient Canaanite city called Jebus. Its location on a high plateau surrounded by deep ravines had foiled several Israelite attempts to conquer the city. For this reason the Jebusites boasted that "even the blind and lame" could defend the city. David had gained access through a water shaft that brought water into the city from the Gihon spring, located on the valley floor.

CHAPTER 5 VERSE 13
"David took more concubines and wives in Jerusalem"

David's negotiations with Abner included the return of Michal, David's first wife, whom Saul had given to another man. As Saul's daughter, Michal strengthened David's claim to the throne. David took two more wives, Abigail and Ahinoam, during his exile. A king's wives reflected his status. However, God had expressly forbidden a king of Israel to have many wives "or his heart will be led astray" (Deuteronomy 17: 17).

DAVID AND ABIGAIL
This 19th-century engraving by Schnorr von Carolsfeld depicts Abigail pleading with David not to kill Nabal.

2 SAMUEL 6–8

THE ARK ENTERS JERUSALEM

CHAPTER 6 VERSE 12
"Brought up the ark of God"
David acknowledged that God was the true king of Israel. The Ark represented his earthly throne and contained his Ten Commandments, which formed the basis of Israel's Law. By bringing the Ark to Jerusalem, David was making the city the religious centre of Israel.

The entire Israelite nation follows the ark into Jerusalem

CHAPTER 6 VERSE 23
"Michal... had no children"
In Israel, childlessness was viewed as a punishment from God. It is not known whether Michal's barrenness was a physical condition or the result of David's rejection. The mention in the text is significant because it meant that Saul's dynasty ended. A son of David and Michal would have been Saul's grandson and therefore have held a strong claim to the throne.

THE TEMPLE SITE
David set up the Tabernacle on Mount Moriah, 40m (130ft) above the city, and brought the Ark there. This became the site of the Temple of Solomon, who extended Jerusalem's walls to enclose the area.

DAVID'S CITY
These ruins show part of a supporting wall dating from the time of David.

6 **S**O[12] DAVID WENT DOWN and *brought up the ark of God...* to the City of David with rejoicing... [14]David, wearing a linen ephod, danced before the LORD with all his might, [15]while he and the entire house of Israel brought up the ark of the LORD with shouts and the sound of trumpets...

[17]They brought the ark of the LORD and set it in its place inside the tent that David had pitched for it, and David sacrificed burnt offerings and fellowship offerings before the LORD... [19]Then he gave a loaf of bread, a cake of dates and a cake of raisins to each person in the whole crowd of Israelites, both men and women. And all the people went to their homes.

Cheering crowds accompany the ark to the sound of trumpets

[20]When David returned home to bless his household, Michal daughter of Saul came out to meet him and said, "How the king of Israel has distinguished himself today, disrobing in the sight of the slave girls of his servants as any vulgar fellow would."

[21]David said to Michal, "It was before the LORD, who chose me rather than your father or anyone from his house when he appointed me ruler over the LORD's people Israel – I will celebrate before the LORD. [22]I will become even more undignified than this, and I will be humiliated in my own eyes. But by these slave girls you spoke of, I will be held in honour." [23]And *Michal daughter of Saul had no children* to the day of her death.

7 ¹After the king was settled in his palace... ²he said to Nathan the prophet, "Here I am, living in a palace of cedar, while the ark of God remains in a tent."... ⁴That night *the word of the LORD came to Nathan*, saying:

⁵"Go and tell my servant David, 'This is what the LORD says:... ⁹I will make your name great... ¹²I will raise up your offspring to succeed you, who will come from your own body, and I will establish his kingdom. ¹³He is the one who will build a house for my Name... ¹⁶Your house and your kingdom shall endure for ever before me; your throne shall be established for ever.' "

To celebrate the occasion, David hands out gifts to every person in Israel

David's wife Michal watches the procession

Michal angers David when she accuses him of undignified behaviour

David dances before the ark of God

8 ¹In the course of time, David defeated the Philistines... ²David also defeated the Moabites... ¹³And David became famous after he returned from striking down eighteen thousand Edomites... ¹⁴and all the Edomites became subject to David. *The LORD gave David victory* wherever he went.

UNDERSTANDING THE STORY

Under David, the kingdom of Israel enters a golden age of expansion and prosperity. God's people are united and, for the first time, occupy the whole of the Promised Land. God's promises to Abraham and Moses are now fulfilled. Unlike Saul, David relies on God and worships him with all his heart. Through David, God renews his covenant with Israel.

CHAPTER 7 VERSE 4
"The word... came to Nathan"
Nathan was Samuel's successor and the most important prophet at David's royal court. God's promise to David that his "kingdom shall endure for ever" is considered to be one of the most important passages in the Old Testament. It established the Jewish belief that their Messiah would come from the line of David.

NATHAN AND DAVID
This panel from a 14th-century church in France depicts Nathan rebuking David for his adultery with Bathsheba.

CHAPTER 8 VERSE 14
"The LORD gave David victory"
David united the tribes, conquered the remaining Canaanite towns, and secured his borders. Israel became a major military power. The Philistines, Israel's most formidable enemy, were beaten back to a small coastal strip.

DAVID'S KINGDOM
Israel controlled most of the land between Egypt and the Euphrates.

2 SAMUEL 11–12
DAVID AND BATHSHEBA

David sees a beautiful woman bathing and asks who she is

11 I[N] THE SPRING, at the time *when kings go off to war, David sent Joab* out with the king's men and the whole Israelite army. They destroyed the Ammonites and besieged Rabbah. But David remained in Jerusalem. [2]One evening David got up from his bed and walked around on the roof of the palace. From the roof he saw a woman bathing. The woman was very beautiful, [3]and David sent someone to find out about her. The man said, "Isn't this Bathsheba, the daughter of Eliam and the wife of *Uriah the Hittite?*"

David sent for Bathsheba and they slept together. When Bathsheba became pregnant, David called Uriah back from the battlefront and instructed him to go home to his wife. But Uriah slept at the entrance of David's palace instead of going home.

Bathsheba is the wife of a soldier named Uriah, who is fighting with the Israelite army

David sends for Bathsheba and they commit adultery

CHAPTER 11 VERSE 1
"When kings go off to war"
In the ancient Middle East, military campaigns usually took place in springtime, just after the April/May grain harvests. This was a logical time, because the winter rains had ceased and it was before the intensive harvests of the summer.

PERFUMED OILS
After bathing, women rubbed perfumed oil into their skins. Oil was essential in a hot climate. Perfume was an expensive luxury and was kept in special containers.

PERFUME POT
9th–10th century BC

[10]When David was told, "Uriah did not go home," he asked him, "Haven't you just come from a distance? *Why didn't you go home?*"

[11]Uriah said to David, "The ark and Israel and Judah are staying in tents, and my master Joab and my lord's men are camped in the open fields. How could I go to my house to eat and drink and lie with my wife...?

[14]In the morning David wrote a letter to Joab and sent it with Uriah. [15]In it he wrote, "Put Uriah in the front line where the fighting is fiercest. Then withdraw from him so that he will be struck down and die."

[16]So while Joab had the city under siege, he put Uriah at a place where he knew the strongest defenders were. [17]When the men of the city came out and fought against Joab, some of the men in David's army fell; moreover, Uriah the Hittite was dead...

Bathsheba becomes pregnant, and David is afraid that Uriah will realise that the child is not his

David writes to his army chief, Joab, and tells him to put Uriah in the frontline of battle

Joab obeys, and Uriah is killed by the Ammonites

CHAPTER 11 VERSE 1
"David sent Joab"
Joab was the commander of David's army. He earned his position with his skill and valour during the conquest of Jerusalem. Joab was fiercely loyal to David. But he could also be ruthless and calculating, which made him many enemies. He often acted in his own interests, and even David had difficulty controlling him at times.

AMMAN, JORDAN
Rabbah was the capital city of the Ammonites and is now the site of modern Amman, capital of Jordan.

²⁶When Uriah's wife heard that her husband was dead, she mourned for him. ²⁷After the time of mourning was over, David had her brought to his house, and she became his wife and bore him a son. But the thing David had done displeased the LORD.

A prophet called Nathan was sent by God to David. Nathan told David a story about a rich man who had a visitor. Rather than killing one of his own animals to provide a meal for his guest, the rich man stole a poor man's only lamb. David was outraged by the story and said that the rich man deserved to die. Nathan said that David had behaved just like the rich man in the story. God condemned his treatment of Uriah and would punish him for his immoral behaviour.

David marries Bathsheba

12 ¹³Then David said to Nathan, "I have sinned against the LORD." Nathan replied, "The LORD has taken away your sin. *You are not going to die.* ¹⁴But because by doing this you have made the enemies of the LORD show utter contempt, the son born to you will die."...
¹⁸On the seventh day the child died...
²⁴Then David comforted his wife Bathsheba, and he went to her and lay with her. She gave birth to a son, and they named him Solomon.

UNDERSTANDING THE STORY
During a period of security when David is not needed at war, he covets another man's wife. He behaves deceitfully and commits adultery and murder. His genuine repentance leads to forgiveness, but the consequences of his sins will bring repercussions on his dynasty.

God punishes David for his immoral behaviour, and their child dies

CHAPTER 11 VERSE 3
"Uriah the Hittite"
Uriah was a Hittite who embraced the Israelite faith. His name means "My Light is the Lord", and he was one of David's best soldiers. The first book of Chronicles refers to him as a "mighty man" (11: 41).

CHAPTER 11 VERSE 10
"Why didn't you go home?"
David wanted to deceive Uriah by making him believe that Bathsheba's child was his. This is why he asked him to go home. Soldiers on active service took an oath to abstain from sexual relations. Uriah's exemplary behaviour led to his death.

CHAPTER 12 VERSE 13
"You are not going to die"
According to the Law of Moses, the penalty for adultery was death (Deuteronomy 22: 22).

2 SAMUEL 13–18

DAVID AND ABSALOM

CHAPTER 13 VERSE 2
"Amnon became frustrated"
Amnon was David's eldest son. His mother was Ahinoam, who David married when he was an outlaw. Amnon's love for Tamar could not lead to marriage, because this was forbidden. The Law of Moses stated that, "if a man marries his sister, the daughter of either his father or his mother, and they have sexual relations, it is a disgrace... He has dishonoured his sister and will be held responsible" (Leviticus 20: 17).

THE RAPE OF TAMAR
Jan Steen's painting depicts Amnon sending Tamar away after brutally raping her. Oil on oak panel (*c.* 1665).

CHAPTER 13 VERSE 37
"Talmai... the king of Geshur"
Geshur was a small Aramean city kingdom, situated north-east of the Sea of Galilee. Talmai was Absalom's grandfather. In the days when David was King of Judah, he had married Talmai's daughter Maacah to seal a political alliance with Geshur. This had given David a strong ally at the northern border of Israel when he was fighting Saul's son Ish-Bosheth, who was ruling the northern tribes of Israel.

CHAPTER 14 VERSE 24
"He must not see my face"
David's failure to punish Amnon led to Absalom's action. David did not punish Absalom either, but he refused to see him. This fuelled Absalom's resentment.

13 I N[1] THE COURSE OF TIME, Amnon son of David fell in love with Tamar, the beautiful sister of Absalom son of David. [2]*Amnon became frustrated* to the point of illness on account of his sister Tamar... [6]So [he] lay down and pretended to be ill. When the king came to see him, Amnon said to him, "I would like my sister Tamar to come and make some special bread in my sight, so that I may eat from her hand."

David sent Tamar to Amnon, who raped her and then sent her away in disgrace. David was furious when he found out, but did nothing to punish Amnon. Absalom plotted to avenge his sister and ordered his men to murder Amnon while he was drunk.

When Amnon rapes Absalom's sister, Absalom plans revenge

Absalom's servants kill Amnon while he is drunk

[37]Absalom fled and went to *Talmai son of Ammihud, the king of Geshur* [and] [38]stayed there for three years. [39]And the spirit of the king longed to go to Absalom, for he was consoled concerning Amnon's death...

14 [23]Then Joab [David's army commander] went to Geshur and brought Absalom back to Jerusalem. [24]But the king said, "He must go to his own house; *he must not see my face.*"...

[25]In all Israel there was not a man so highly praised for his handsome appearance as Absalom. From the top of his head to the sole of his foot there was no blemish in him.

Absalom courts popularity with the people and plots against his father

Many Israelites change their allegiance to Absalom. Finally, he declares himself king

²⁶Whenever he cut [his hair] its weight was two hundred shekels...
²⁸Absalom lived for two years in Jerusalem without seeing the king's face.

Many Israelites were becoming discontented with David's administration. Absalom made himself popular with these people and began to conspire against his father. He gathered many followers and proclaimed himself king. David fled from Jerusalem. One of David's advisors feigned desertion and gave bad advice to Absalom regarding battle tactics.

David's army defeats Absalom's army in a fierce battle

Joab

While fleeing from David's army, Absalom gets caught in the branches of a tree

Joab, David's army commander, sees Absalom hanging from the tree and kills him

18   ⁶The battle took place in the forest of Ephraim. ⁷There the army of Israel was defeated by *David's men*, and the casualties that day were great... ⁹Now Absalom happened to meet David's men. He was riding his mule, and as the mule went under the thick branches of *a large oak*, Absalom's head got caught in the tree. He was left hanging in mid-air, while the mule he was riding kept on going...

¹⁴Joab... took three javelins in his hand and plunged them into Absalom's heart while Absalom was still alive in the oak tree...

¹⁶Then Joab sounded the trumpet, and the troops stopped pursuing Israel, for Joab halted them. ¹⁷They took Absalom, threw him into a big pit in the forest and piled up a large heap of rocks over him.

UNDERSTANDING THE STORY

David's weakness in letting his sons' crimes go unpunished leads to their downfall. Their deaths fulfil Nathan's prophecy: "The Lord says: 'Out of your own household I am going to bring calamity on you'" (2 Samuel 12: 11). David is now suffering for his adultery with Bathsheba and Uriah's murder.

CHAPTER 18 VERSE 7
"David's men"
During his years as an exile in Philistia, David recruited a band of Philistine mercenaries who joined his band of soldiers. When David returned to Israel after Saul's death, these mercenaries maintained their allegiance to David and formed his personal bodyguard. So, the core of David's army was an elite fighting force with many years of military experience.

HOLLOW HEAD
At the beginning of the Bronze Age, javelins were made by strapping spearheads onto wooden shafts with leather thongs. In David's time, advances in technology meant that the metal could be cast with a hollow socket to take the shaft.

CHAPTER 18 VERSE 9
"A large oak"
The battle took place in Gilead, east of the River Jordan. This area, as with many in biblical Palestine, was covered in dense oak forests. There were more than twenty varieties of oak, some growing to heights of above 300m (1,000ft). The wood was used for shipbuilding.

ANCIENT OAK TREES, ISRAEL

1 KINGS 1
SOLOMON IS ANOINTED

CHAPTER 1 VERSE 3
"A Shunammite"
Abishag came from Shunem, a northern town in the Jezreel valley. Today, the town is called Solem. It is near Jesus' home town, Nazareth.

CHAPTER 1 VERSE 5
"Adonijah"
Adonijah was David's fourth son. He was born in Hebron while David was still fighting Ish-Bosheth for the throne of Israel. As the king's oldest surviving son, he would normally have expected to succeed him to the throne.

CHAPTER 1 VERSE 12
"Save your own life and the life of your son Solomon"
In the ancient Middle East, it was common practice for a usurper to eliminate his rivals. Bathsheba's life was also at risk because a queen mother played an important and influential role in the royal court.

CHAPTER 1 VERSE 13
"Solomon… shall be king after me"
The Bible says that when Solomon was born, "The Lord loved him" (2 Samuel 12: 24). Although David's promise to Bathsheba is not recorded in the Bible text, Adonijah's actions imply that he was aware that Solomon was David's chosen heir.

BATHSHEBA BATHING
This tapestry detail from the Davanzati Palace in Florence illustrates the story of David and Bathsheba's adultery.

1 **W**HEN[1] KING DAVID was old and well advanced in years, he could not keep warm even when they put covers over him. [2]So his servants said to him, "Let us look for a young virgin to attend the king and take care of him. She can lie beside him so that our lord the king may keep warm."

[3]Then they searched throughout Israel for a beautiful girl and found Abishag, *a Shunammite*, and brought her to the king. [4]The girl was very beautiful; she took care of the king and waited on him, but the king had no intimate relations with her.

When David is old, his son Adonijah declares himself king

Nathan the prophet

Abishag

Nathan tells David that many of his officials are supporting Adonijah

Bathsheba

Bathsheba reminds David that he promised that her son Solomon would be king

David says that he will keep his promise and gives orders for Solomon to be anointed

[5]Now *Adonijah…* put himself forward and said, "I will be king."… [6](His father [never asked] "Why do you behave as you do?"…) [7]Adonijah conferred with Joab… and with Abiathar the priest, and they gave him their support…. [9]He invited [his supporters and] all his brothers, the king's sons [to a thanksgiving sacrifice]… [10]But he did not invite Solomon.

[11]Then Nathan asked Bathsheba, Solomon's mother, "Have you not heard that Adonijah, the son of Haggith, has become king without our Lord David's knowing it? [12]Now then, let me advise you how you can *save your own life and the life of your son Solomon.* [13]Go in to King David and say to him, 'My lord the king, did you not swear to me your servant: "Surely *Solomon your son shall be king after me*, and he will sit on my throne"? Why then has Adonijah become king?' "

Bathsheba went to see the king and told him everything. Nathan then came before David and confirmed Bathsheba's report.

[29]The king then took an oath... [30]"I will surely carry out today what I swore to you by the LORD, the God of Israel: Solomon your son shall be king after me, and he will sit on my throne in my place." [Then] [32]David said, "Call in Zadok the priest, Nathan the prophet and Benaiah...

Benaiah, commander of the palace guard

Nathan

Zadok the priest

Zadok anoints Solomon as the next king of Israel

Palace guard

[38]So Zadok the priest, Nathan the prophet, Benaiah son of Johoiada, *the Kerethites and the Pelethites* went down and put Solomon on King David's mule and escorted him to *Gihon*. [39]Zadok the priest took the horn of oil from the sacred tent and anointed Solomon. Then they sounded the trumpet and all the people shouted, "Long live King Solomon!"... [50]But Adonijah, in fear of Solomon, went and took hold of *the horns of the altar*.

Solomon pardoned Adonijah, and soon after David died. But when Adonijah asked Solomon if he could marry Abishag, Solomon interpreted the request as a bid for the throne and ordered his execution. Solomon also dealt harshly with Adonijah's supporters. Abiathar the priest was exiled, and Joab lost his life.

UNDERSTANDING OF THE STORY

In his old age, David continues to suffer for the sins of his youth. Adonijah follows Absolom's example and challenges his father's kingship, and David's household is plunged into further strife. Either through weakness or infirmity, David fails to act assertively. The initiative is taken by Nathan and Bathsheba.

ZADOK, NATHAN, AND BENAIAH
These men were David's closest allies and advisors. Zadok the priest was a descendant of Aaron and succeeded Abiathar as High Priest of Israel. Nathan was the main prophet at David's court. The fact that he supported Solomon indicates that Solomon was God's choice as David's heir. Benaiah was the chief of David's foreign bodyguards.

❖

CHAPTER 1 VERSE 38
"The Kerethites and the Pelethites"
These were Philistine mercenaries. David recruited them during his years as an outlaw. They remained fiercely loyal to David and became his palace guard.

❖

CHAPTER 1 VERSE 38
"Gihon"
This spring outside the eastern wall of Jerusalem was the city's main source of water. It became a tradition for a new king to drink from the waters of the Gihon during his coronation.

THE GIHON SPRING
The people of Jerusalem still collect water from this natural source.

❖

CHAPTER 1 VERSE 50
"The horns of the altar"
Israelite altars had square, flat tops with curved projections at each corner. By holding these "horns" a person could claim sanctuary.

1 KINGS 3
SOLOMON'S WISDOM

3

SOLOMON[1] MADE AN ALLIANCE with *Pharaoh king of Egypt* and married his daughter. He brought her to the City of David until he finished building his palace and the temple of the LORD, and the wall around Jerusalem...

⁴*The king went to Gibeon* to offer sacrifices, for that was the most important high place, and Solomon offered a thousand burnt offerings on that altar. ⁵At Gibeon the LORD appeared to Solomon during the night in a dream, and God said, "Ask for whatever you want me to give you."

⁶Solomon answered... ⁷"O LORD my God, you have made your servant king in place of my father David. But I am only a little child and do not know how to carry out my duties... ⁹So give your servant a discerning heart to govern your people and to distinguish between right and wrong..."

¹⁰The LORD was pleased that Solomon had asked for this. ¹¹So God said to him... ¹²"I will do what you have asked. I will give you a wise and discerning heart... ¹³Moreover, I will give you what you have not asked for – both riches and honour... ¹⁴And if you walk in my ways and obey my statutes and commands as David your father did, I will give you a long life." ¹⁵Then Solomon awoke – and he realised it had been a dream...

CHAPTER 3 VERSE 1
"Pharaoh king of Egypt"

This pharaoh was probably Saamun (*c.* 1069–959 BC). Egypt's power in the Middle East had declined over the previous two centuries, and its empire had vanished. By this time, the pharaoh's foreign policy was to maintain peace with neighbouring lands through alliances. These were often sealed by a political marriage.

CITY OF DAVID
These excavations in Jerusalem are in the area known as the City of David. This was the extent of Jerusalem at the time of King David, before Solomon built the Temple and royal palace complex. Work on the Temple began in 960 BC.

CHAPTER 3 VERSE 4
"The king went to Gibeon"

The second Book of Chronicles says that Solomon went to Gibeon because the Tabernacle was there: "The bronze altar that Bezalel... had made was in Gibeon in front of the tabernacle of the LORD" (1: 5). The Ark was already in Jerusalem awaiting the Temple's completion.

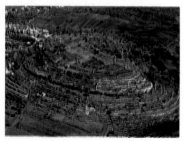

GIBEON (EL-JIB, ISRAEL)
This is an aerial view of the ancient site of Gibeon, which lies about 10km (6 miles) north-west of Jerusalem.

King Solomon is asked to settle a dispute between two prostitutes, who both claim to be the mother of a baby

God has given Solomon the gift of wisdom

One woman says that the other stole her son the night her own baby died

The other prostitute accuses her of lying. She claims that she is mother of the living baby

¹⁶Now *two prostitutes came to the king* and stood before him. ¹⁷One of them said, "My lord, this woman and I live in the same house. I had a baby while she was there with me. ¹⁸The third day after my child was born, this woman also had a baby... ¹⁹During the night this woman's son died because she lay on him. ²⁰So she got up in the middle of the night and took my son from my side while I your servant was asleep. She put him by her breast and put her dead son by my breast..." ²²The other woman said, "No! The living one is my son; the dead one is yours."...

²⁴Then the king said, "Bring me a sword."... ²⁵He then gave an order: "Cut the living child in two and give *half to one and half to the other*."

²⁶The woman whose son was alive... said to the king, "Please, my lord, give her the living baby! Don't kill him!" But the other said, "Neither I nor you shall have him. Cut him in two!"

²⁷Then the king gave his ruling: "Give the living baby to the first woman. Do not kill him; she is his mother."

²⁸When all Israel heard the verdict... they held the king in awe, because they saw that he had wisdom from God to administer justice.

UNDERSTANDING THE STORY

Solomon acknowledges his inexperience and demonstrates his desire to be a good king by asking God for the ability to serve his people with righteousness. His wisdom in solving this difficult dispute gains the respect of his subjects.

CHAPTER 3 VERSE 16
"Two prostitutes came to the king"
Although prostitution was against Moses' Law, the profession seems to have been tolerated in Israel as these women plied their trade in public places. They drew attention to themselves by their appearance. Women who wore seductive clothes or excessive jewellery and make-up were often branded as prostitutes.

EYE MAKE-UP
This spatula and alabaster kohl dish were used to apply kohl (eye paint). Hebrew women wore eye make-up, but the practice was viewed with disdain.

CHAPTER 3 VERSE 25
"Half to one and half to the other"
When ownership of a disputed property could not be determined, the judge would divide it evenly between the opposing parties. Solomon applied an accepted legal tradition to an unusual case.

Solomon gives orders for the baby to be cut in two

One prostitute would prefer to see the baby cut in half than let the other woman have him

The other prostitute would rather give up her claim than see the baby killed

The king declares that she is the mother and orders the child to be returned to her

1 KINGS 5–8
SOLOMON'S TEMPLE

CHAPTER 5 VERSE 1
"Hiram king of Tyre"
Hiram ruled over Tyre from *c.* 978 until 944 BC. Located north of Palestine, it was an important Phoenician seaport. Under Hiram, Tyre began to colonize areas on the Mediterranean coast, and it became the centre of a large trading empire.

KING HIRAM OF TYRE
Detail from his sarcophagus

CHAPTER 5 VERSE 3
"David... could not build a temple"
King David had wanted to build the Temple himself and had drawn up detailed plans for its construction. However, God said that David could not carry out the task because he was a warrior and had spilled blood. Instead, it would be built by David's son. So David passed on his plans to Solomon (1 Chronicles 28: 1–19).

CHAPTER 5 VERSE 17
"Removed from the quarry"
Stonecutters inserted wooden wedges into slits in the stone. The wood was soaked until it expanded, causing the stone to crack.

CHAPTER 8 VERSE 10
"The cloud filled the temple"
This symbolized God's presence and approval. The same event occurred when Moses set up the Tabernacle for the first time (Exodus 40: 34–35). The Temple was built to supersede the Tabernacle, and its design was very similar. They were both divided into three sections: a courtyard, a sanctuary, and an inner sanctuary.

5 **W**HEN[1] HIRAM KING OF TYRE heard that Solomon had been anointed king to succeed his father David, he sent his envoys to Solomon, because he had always been on friendly terms with David. [2]Solomon sent back this message to Hiram:

[3]"You know that because of the wars waged against my father *David from all sides, he could not build a temple* for the Name of the LORD... [4]But now the LORD my God has given me rest on every side, and there is no adversary or disaster. [5]I intend, therefore, to build a temple for the Name of the LORD my God... [6]So give orders that cedars of Lebanon be cut for me. My men will work with yours, and I will pay you for your men whatever wages you set."

Hiram was pleased when he heard the message and agreed to supply everything that Solomon requested. In return, Solomon provided Hiram's royal household with wheat and olive oil, year after year.

[15]Solomon had seventy thousand carriers and eighty thousand stonecutters in the hills, [16]as well as thirty-three hundred foremen who supervised the project and directed the workmen. [17]At the king's command they *removed from the quarry* large blocks of quality stone to provide a foundation... for the temple. [18]The craftsmen of Solomon and Hiram and the men of Gebal cut and prepared the timber and stone for the building of the temple...

6 [2]The temple that King Solomon built for the LORD was sixty cubits long, twenty wide and thirty high...

[14]So Solomon built the temple and completed it... [19]He prepared the inner sanctuary within the temple to set the ark of the covenant of the LORD there... [21]Solomon covered the inside of the temple with pure gold... [29]On the walls all round the temple, in both the inner and outer rooms, he carved cherubim, palm trees and open flowers... [38]The temple was finished in all its details according to its specifications. He had spent seven years building it...

8 [6]The priests then brought the ark of the LORD's covenant to its place in the inner sanctuary of the temple... [10]When the priests withdrew from the Holy Place, *the cloud filled the temple* of the LORD.

Solomon stood before the altar of the temple and said a prayer of dedication to God. Then he blessed all the people of Israel, and together they offered sacrifices.

UNDERSTANDING THE STORY

Solomon builds the Temple to provide a permanent dwelling place for God amongst his people. Its design and dedication recall the Tabernacle, which it is to replace. The Temple takes seven years to construct, symbolizing the perfection of its construction and the excellence of its workmanship.

The king of Tyre gives Solomon materials and men

Skilled workers carve cherubim, palm leaves, and flowers on the stone blocks

Men transport blocks of stone for the temple's foundation

Craftsmen cut and prepare the timber

Solomon oversees the work. He builds the temple according to David's plans

When everything is complete, Solomon places the ark inside the inner sanctuary and dedicates the temple to God

1 KINGS 4, 10

THE QUEEN OF SHEBA

CHAPTER 4 VERSE 20
"The people of Judah and Israel"
Although Solomon was king over both Judah and Israel, he administered them separately. He divided Israel into twelve districts and appointed governors to collect taxes from them. His own tribe, Judah, was exempt from tax. Solomon's kingdom stretched from the River Euphrates in the north to Egypt in the south. Its borders were the same as the borders God had promised Abraham (Genesis 15: 18).

4 T HE[20] PEOPLE OF JUDAH *and Israel* were as numerous as the sand on the seashore; they ate, they drank and they were happy. [21]And Solomon ruled over all the kingdoms from the River to the land of the Philistines, as far as the border of Egypt. These countries brought tribute and were Solomon's subjects all his life...

Solomon's fame spreads throughout many nations. The queen of Sheba hears about his wisdom

She travels to Jerusalem to see him. Her camels are laden with gifts

Queen of Sheba

The queen brings spices, gold, and precious stones

Camel caravan

CHAPTER 4 VERSE 32
"Three thousand proverbs"
The proverbs and sayings attributed to Solomon are contained in the Book of Proverbs. These were written down during his reign and are divided into three sections. They are poems of wisdom, which give advice on how to lead a good and moral life according to God's will. Many are based on ancient proverbs from Mesopotamia and Egypt.

SOLOMON AS A TEACHER
14th-century illustration for the Book of Proverbs

[29]God gave Solomon wisdom and very great insight [and] understanding... [30]Solomon's wisdom was greater than the wisdom of all the men of the East... [31]His fame spread to all the surrounding nations. [32]He spoke *three thousand proverbs* and his songs numbered a thousand and five. [33]He described plant life, from the cedar of Lebanon to the hyssop that grows out of walls. He also taught about animals and birds, reptiles and fish. [34]Men of all nations came to listen to Solomon's wisdom, sent by all the kings of the world...

10 [1]When *the queen of Sheba* heard about the fame of Solomon and his relation to the name of the LORD, she came to test him with hard questions. [2]Arriving at Jerusalem with a very great caravan – with camels carrying spices, large quantities of gold, and precious stones – she came to Solomon and talked with him about all that she had on her mind. [3]Solomon answered all her questions; nothing was too hard for the king... [4]When the queen of Sheba saw all the wisdom of Solomon and the palace he had built, [5]the food on his table, the seating of his officials, the attending servants in their robes, his cupbearers, and the burnt offerings he made at the temple of the LORD, she was overwhelmed.

⁶She said to the king, "The report I heard in my own country about your achievements and your wisdom is true. ⁷But I did not believe these things until I came and saw with my own eyes. Indeed, not even half was told me; in wisdom and wealth you have far exceeded the report I heard. ⁸How happy your men must be! How happy your officials, who continually stand before you and hear your wisdom! ⁹Praise be to the LORD your God, who has delighted in you and placed you on the throne of Israel. Because of the LORD's eternal love for Israel, he has made you king, to maintain justice and righteousness."

¹⁰*And she gave the king 120 talents of gold*, large quantities of spices, and precious stones. Never again were so many spices brought in as those the queen of Sheba gave to King Solomon...

¹³King Solomon gave the queen of Sheba all she desired and asked for, besides what he had given her out of his royal bounty. Then she left and returned with her retinue to her own country.

UNDERSTANDING THE STORY

Solomon's fame has spread to such an extent that the queen of a distant land hears about him. She visits Solomon at a time when his wealth and wisdom are at their greatest. Solomon's words and the magnificence of his court greatly impress her, and she recognizes that he has been blessed by God.

❖

CHAPTER 10 VERSE 1
"The queen of Sheba"
Sheba was located in south-west Arabia, modern-day Yemen. This kingdom traded luxury goods, such as jewels, frankincense, and gold. It transported them overland from India and Africa to the cities of Damascus and Gaza, where they were sold.

THE LADY FROM SHEBA
This stone head, from Solomon's time, is a woman of Sheba. Her name is written on her forehead in Sabean script.

❖

CHAPTER 10 VERSE 10
"And she gave the king... gold"
The Queen of Sheba's gifts were probably part of a trade agreement. Solomon controlled the trade routes north of the Arabian Peninsula, and the queen needed to negotiate rights of passage through his kingdom.

Solomon shows the queen around his palace, and she is very impressed

Solomon's official

Attendant

She asks Solomon many difficult questions, and he answers them all wisely

The queen is overwhelmed by Solomon's wisdom

The queen of Sheba gives Solomon many gifts before she returns to her own country

1 KINGS 10–11
SOLOMON'S WIVES

CHAPTER 10 VERSE 14
"Solomon received... 666 talents"
666 talents is about 25 tonnes. Solomon broke Moses' Law by amassing such extreme wealth (Deuteronomy 17: 17). The number 666 may have a symbolic significance. It is the sign of the "beast", or the "devil" (Revelation 13: 18). It is also associated with "imperfection", because six falls short of seven, and seven symbolized perfection.

CHAPTER 10 VERSE 26
"Solomon['s] chariots and horses"
Again Solomon disobeyed the Law, which forbade kings to acquire large numbers of horses for personal use (Deuteronomy 17: 16).

SOLOMON'S STABLES
These ancient ruins were discovered at Megiddo, which used to be one of Solomon's chariot cities.

CHAPTER 11 VERSE 3
"He had seven hundred wives"
Solomon sealed many trade agreements with foreign kings by marrying into their royal families. Diplomatic marriages were common in the ancient Middle East.

10 THE[14] WEIGHT OF THE GOLD that *Solomon received yearly was 666 talents,* [15]not including the revenue from merchants and traders and from all the Arabian kings and the governors of the land... [22]The king had a fleet of trading ships at sea along with the ships of [King] Hiram. Once every three years it returned carrying gold, silver and ivory... [26]*Solomon accumulated chariots and horses...* which he kept in the chariot cities and also with him in Jerusalem. [27][He] made silver as common in Jerusalem as stones, and cedar as plentiful as sycamore-fig trees...

11 [1]King Solomon, however, loved many foreign women besides Pharaoh's daughter – Moabites, Ammonites, Edomites, Sidonians and Hittites. [2]They were from nations about which the LORD had told the Israelites, "You must not intermarry with them, because they will surely turn your hearts after their gods." Nevertheless, Solomon held fast to them in love. [3]*He had seven hundred wives* of royal birth and three hundred concubines, and his wives led him astray. [4]As Solomon grew old, his wives turned his heart after other gods, and his heart was not fully devoted to the LORD his God, as the heart of David his father had been... [7]On a hill east of Jerusalem, Solomon built a high place for Chemosh the detestable god of Moab, and for Molech the detestable god of the Ammonites. [8]He did the same for all his foreign wives, who... offered sacrifices to their gods.

King Solomon has hundreds of wives from many different nations

Solomon stores up great wealth

As Solomon grows old, his wives persuade him to worship other gods

152

⁹The LORD became angry with Solomon because his heart had turned away from the LORD, the God of Israel... ¹¹So the LORD said to Solomon, "Since this is your attitude and you have not kept my covenant and my decrees, which I commanded you, I will most certainly tear the kingdom away from you and give it to one of your subordinates. ¹²Nevertheless, for the sake of David your father, I will not do it during your lifetime. I will tear it out of the hand of your son..."

Many men rose up against Solomon, but none could overthrow him. One day, Jeroboam, an official in Solomon's court, was told by the prophet Ahijah that he would rule over part of Solomon's kingdom.

³⁰Ahijah took hold of [his own] new cloak... and tore it into twelve pieces. ³¹Then he said to Jeroboam, "Take ten pieces for yourself, for this is what the LORD, the God of Israel, says: 'See, I am going to tear the kingdom out of Solomon's hand and give you ten tribes... ³⁶I will give one tribe to his son...'"

⁴⁰Solomon tried to kill Jeroboam, but Jeroboam fled to Egypt, *to Shishak the king*, and stayed there until Solomon's death... ⁴²Solomon reigned in Jerusalem over all Israel for forty years. ⁴³Then he rested with his fathers and was buried in the city of David his father.

Solomon builds altars for his wives

His wives offer sacrifices to foreign gods

God is angry and warns Solomon that a subordinate will take the kingdom from his son

Jeroboam is told that he will rule over the ten tribes of Israel

UNDERSTANDING THE STORY
Solomon, who built the Temple for God, now builds altars to foreign deities. He disregards God's covenant laws and abuses the gifts he has been given. Solomon's disobedience leads to the division of Israel. His son will rule only part of Solomon's inheritance.

MERCHANT SHIPS
Solomon built up a large network of maritime trade. He constructed a major port at Ezion-geber, in the Gulf of Aqaba, where a joint Israelite and Phoenician fleet was based. The 8th-century BC Assyrian relief pictured above depicts Phoenician ships transporting logs along the Syrian coast.

AHIJAH'S PROPHECY
The ten pieces of Ahijah's cloak represent the ten tribes that will make up the northern kingdom of Israel. The text says that just "one tribe" (11: 36) will be given to Solomon's son. This refers to the tribes of Judah and Benjamin, which together will form the southern kingdom. It may be that Judah and Benjamin were so closely identified at this time that only one tribe is mentioned in the text.

CHAPTER 11 VERSE 40
"To Shishak the king"
Shishak is the first pharaoh to be mentioned by name in the Bible. He was known as Sheshonq I, and he founded Egypt's twenty-second dynasty (*c.* 945–715 BC). After Solomon's death, Shishak invaded the southern kingdom of Judah and captured many fortified cities (1 Kings 14: 25).

KING SHISHAK
Silver miniature of his coffin (930 BC)

Ahijah tears his cloak into twelve pieces and gives ten of them to Jeroboam

THE KINGDOM DIVIDED

King Solomon's son Rehoboam ignored the tensions that existed between the ten northern and two southern tribes of Israel. His stubbornness and rivalry with Jeroboam, an ex-official in Solomon's court, led to the rebellion of the northern tribes, and two kingdoms were set up (*c.* 930 BC). The northern kingdom was called "Israel" and was ruled over by Jeroboam; the southern, "Judah", came under Rehoboam's control. Israel was ruled by a succession of kings until it was conquered by the Assyrians (*c.* 722 BC). Judah's kings, the descendants of King David, ruled in Jerusalem until the Babylonians invaded and exiled the southern tribes to Babylon (*c.* 586 BC).

REHOBOAM, KING OF JUDAH
Detail from a 12th-century painted ceiling, Church of St Martin, Switzerland

The Books of Kings

The period of the kings spans about 400 years, and most of this is recorded in two books – 1 and 2 Kings. These give an account of the death of David (*c.* 970 BC), the main events in Solomon's reign, and the histories of Israel and Judah.

The author of Kings, possibly an exile in Babylon, describes the reigns of the various kings according to their attitude towards the worship of God. He does not give an account of their political reigns. Many kings are judged against Jeroboam, who encouraged the worship of pagan gods: "He did evil in the eyes of the LORD, walking in the ways of Jeroboam" (1 Kings 15: 34). King David was used as a model of righteousness: "His heart was not fully devoted to the LORD... as the heart of David his forefather had been" (1 Kings 15: 3).

The Chronicles

The history of the kings of Judah is also found in 1 and 2 Chronicles. These books are often attributed to the scribe Ezra. They were written for the Jews who had returned to Judah after their exile in Babylon. The author's main aim was to convince the Jews that they were still God's chosen people.

The Books of Chronicles contain selective information about the kings of Judah, presenting them in a positive light. They mention very little about the kings of Israel, who are described as unfaithful to God. The author emphasizes the religious revivals led by the godly kings of Judah and highlights Jerusalem's role as the Holy city.

EZRA READING THE LAW
Wall-painting (*c.* AD 245) from the Dura Europas, one of the earliest known synagogues, located in Iraq

The first kings of Judah and Israel

Jeroboam had rebelled against King Solomon and fled to Egypt. After Solomon's death, he returned to Israel and, backed by the elders of the northern tribes, challenged Rehoboam's claim to the throne. He asked Rehoboam to abolish the forced labour and high taxes that Solomon had imposed. When Rehoboam refused, the ten northern tribes appointed Jeroboam as their king, and the kingdom split into two.

JEROBOAM SACRIFICES AT A PAGAN ALTAR
This 13th-century window shows Jeroboam sacrificing at his altar. A prophet foretells the destruction of all pagan altars (1 Kings 13: 1–3).

Dating the kings

The Bible texts give detailed information about the length of the reign of each king. However, it is difficult to date these reigns because Judah and Israel used different ways of calculating a king's first year. Many kings ruled jointly or reigned for part of the time of another king, which causes additional problems when giving dates.

LIST OF KINGS (SHOWN RIGHT)
★These reigns overlap with the preceding king's reign.

KINGS OF JUDAH

King	Reign
Rehoboam	930–913
Abijah	913–910
Asa	910–869
★Jehoshaphat	872–848
Jehoram	848–841
Ahaziah	841–841
Athaliah (Queen)	841–835
Joash	835–796
Amaziah	796–767
Uzziah (Azariah)	792–740
★Jotham	750–735
Ahaz	735–715
Hezekiah	715–686
★Manasseh	697–642
Amon	642–640
Josiah	640–609
Jehoahaz	609–609
Jehoiakim	609–598
Jehoiachin	598–597
Zedekiah	597–586

The fall of Israel

The succession of kings in the northern kingdom was often the result of internal feuds and murders. Despite Israel's advantage over Judah in location, with its good trade routes and thriving economy, Israel failed to establish a stable kingdom. In the 8th century BC, the Assyrian empire (under Tiglath-Pileser III) gradually took control in the ancient Middle East, and Israel was forced to pay tribute. Shalmanaser V and Sargon II finally destroyed Samaria, Israel's capital, in about 722 BC and took its inhabitants into captivity.

According to the Bible, the fall of Israel was the direct consequence of its people's disregard for God's covenant. Led by Jeroboam and other faithless kings, the Israelites abandoned God and worshipped pagan idols.

THE ASSYRIAN ARMY
This Assyrian wall-relief from Sennacherib's palace, Nineveh, depicts an Assyrian attack on the city of Lachish in Judah (2 Kings 18).

The fall of Judah

Judah managed to resist foreign invasions for a further 130 years, until the Babylonians came to power and made Judah a vassal state. King Nebuchadnezzar launched several attacks on Jerusalem, Judah's capital, and deported some of its people. The city finally fell in 586 BC, when the Babylonians destroyed the Temple, looted its treasures, and took the remaining people into captivity.

The Book of Chronicles describes the fall of Judah as divine punishment. Despite the prophets' warnings against disobedience to God, the people of Judah continued to disregard the covenant laws and so suffered God's wrath (2 Chronicles 36: 17).

KINGS OF ISRAEL	
King	Reign
Jeroboam	930–909
Nadab	909–908
Baasha	908–886
Elah	886–885
Zimri	885–885
Tibni	885–880
★Omri	885–874
Ahab	874–853
Ahaziah	853–852
Joram	852–841
Jehu	841–814
Jehoahaz	814–798
Jehoash	798–782
★Jeroboam II	793–753
Zechariah	753–753
Shallum	753–752
Menahem	752–742
Pekahiah	742–740
★Pekah	752–732
Hoshea	732–722

THE SACK OF JERUSALEM
This 19th-century engraving by Schnorr von Carolsfeld depicts the Babylonians destroying Jerusalem and deporting its people.

The exiles of Israel and Judah

After the Assyrian deportations in the northern kingdom, Assyria repopulated the Israelite cities with non-Israelite inhabitants. Many of the dispersed Israelites did not return to their native land, and those that had remained lost their identity, intermarried, and lived according to the customs of the occupying people.

After the Babylonian exile, the land of Judah was left depopulated and destroyed. Some exiles returned to their homeland about seventy years after the first captives had been taken away, and others followed later. But the majority dispersed throughout the Persian empire. They kept their national identity and worshipped together in synagogues. One of their prophets, Daniel, became an important ruler in Babylon.

It was from these days that the exiled people from Judah became known as "Jews" (a word deriving from "Judah"). Away from Jerusalem, and without proper Israelite leadership, the Jews meditated upon their history, their mistakes, and God's laws. This led to a religious revival, which gave birth to what is called "Judaism". Mesopotamia became the second most important centre of Judaism outside Palestine. By the end of their captivity, the Jews spoke in Aramaic (the language of the ancient Middle East) instead of Hebrew.

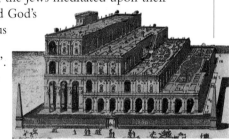
HANGING GARDENS OF BABYLON
The people of Judah were exiled to Babylon. This engraving (c. AD 1700) shows King Nebuchadnezzar's famous terraced gardens in Babylon.

The return to the Promised Land

The Persian king Cyrus II conquered the Babylonian empire in about 539 BC. He extended the borders further by taking control of Egypt and the area that is modern-day Turkey.

Cyrus reversed the policy of the Babylonians by allowing most of the tribes and nations under Persian control to return to their homelands. Some Jews went back to Judah, and those who remained were allowed to practise their Jewish customs. Cyrus helped the Jews to rebuild the Temple in Jerusalem and returned much of the plunder that had been captured by Nebuchadnezzar. The Book of Isaiah describes Cyrus as God's "anointed", and saviour of the Jews (Isaiah 45:1).

TOMB OF CYRUS
King Cyrus II was buried in this magnificent tomb at Pasargadae, Persia, in 529 BC.

1 KINGS 12–13
THE KINGDOM DIVIDES

REHOBOAM[1] WENT TO SHECHEM, for all the Israelites had gone there to make him king. [2]When Jeroboam son of Nebat heard this (he was still in Egypt, where he had fled from King Solomon), he returned from Egypt. [3]So they sent for Jeroboam, and he and the whole assembly of Israel went to Rehoboam and said to him: [4]*"Your father put a heavy yoke on us*, but now lighten the harsh labour and the heavy yoke he put on us, and we will serve you."...

[6]Then King Rehoboam consulted the elders who had served his father Solomon during his lifetime. "How would you advise me to answer these people?" he asked. [7]They replied, "If today you will be a servant to these people and serve them and give them a favourable answer, they will always be your servants." [8]But Rehoboam rejected the advice the elders gave him and consulted the young men who had grown up with him... [14]He followed the advice of the young men and said, "My father made your yoke heavy; I will make it even heavier..."

CHAPTER 12 VERSE 4
"Your father put a heavy yoke on us"

Since David's reign, Israel (the name given to the northern tribes) and Judah had been governed separately. Conditions for Israel had gradually worsened under Solomon's administration. Whereas Judah was exempt from taxes, Israel was heavily taxed and penalized by the compulsory conscription of labour and military service. The northern tribes hoped to change this situation.

SOLOMON'S MINES
Solomon became very rich through trade. However, his wealth was not enough to fund his massive building projects. This is why the people suffered the burden of taxation and forced labour. Many worked in the king's stone mines.

REHOBOAM AND JEROBOAM
Rehoboam was Solomon's son by Naama, an Ammonite princess. He, and all the kings of Judah after him, were David's descendants. Jeroboam had been an official at Solomon's court. Ahijah the prophet had predicted that Jeroboam would rule ten Israelite tribes, and that Solomon's son would only inherit two.

CHAPTER 12 VERSE 28
"Here are your gods"
By law, all Israelites had to go to Jerusalem to worship. Jeroboam hoped to prevent this by providing idols. He uses the same words as Aaron, who made a golden calf for the people after God had brought them out of Egypt (Exodus 32: 4–5).

Solomon's son Rehoboam meets the elders from the northern tribes of Israel

Jeroboam speaks for the elders

The people want Rehoboam to make life easier for them

Rehoboam says that he will make life even harder than it was under Solomon

Rehoboam takes advice from his young friends

The northern tribes make Jeroboam their king

[16]When all Israel saw that the king refused to listen to them, [they] [20]made [Jeroboam] king over all Israel. Only the tribe of Judah remained loyal to the house of David... [26]Jeroboam thought to himself, "The kingdom [will now] [27]offer sacrifices at the temple of the LORD in Jerusalem, they will again give their allegiance to... Rehoboam king of Judah..."

[So Jeroboam] [28]made two golden calves. He said to the people... *"Here are your gods*, O Israel, who brought you up out of Egypt." [29]One he set up in Bethel, and the other in Dan. [30]And this thing became a sin...

13 ¹By the word of the LORD a man of God came from Judah to Bethel, as Jeroboam was standing by the altar to make an offering. ²He cried out against the altar by the word of the LORD: "O altar, altar! This is what the LORD says: '*A son named Josiah* will be born to the house of David. On you he will sacrifice the priests of the high places who now make offerings here, and human bones will be burned on you.' "... ⁴When King Jeroboam heard what the man of God cried out against the altar at Bethel, he stretched out his hand from the altar and said, "Seize him!" But the hand he stretched out towards the man shrivelled up, so that he could not pull it back. ⁵Also, the altar was split apart... ⁶Then the king said to the man of God, "Intercede with the LORD your God and pray for me that my hand may be restored." So the man of God interceded with the LORD, and the king's hand was restored and became as it was before...

³³Even after this, Jeroboam did not change his evil ways... ³⁴This was the sin of the house of Jeroboam that led to its downfall.

The people of Judah also set up idols everywhere. Warfare continued between Rehoboam and Jeroboam until Rehoboam died. Abijah his son succeeded him.

Jeroboam makes two golden calves and sets one up at Bethel

Jeroboam is afraid that his people will go to Jerusalem to worship

A man of God denounces Jeroboam for building a pagan altar

He tries to seize the man of God, but his hand shrivels up

The altar is split apart

Jeroboam asks the man of God to pray for him, and God restores his hand

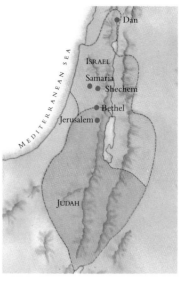

THE DIVIDED KINGDOM
The kingdom was split into Israel (the ten northern tribes) and Judah (the southern tribes of Judah and Benjamin). Jerusalem remained the capital of Judah, while Israel set up a new capital, first at Shechem, then at Tirzah, and finally at Samaria.

CHAPTER 13 VERSE 2
"A son named Josiah"
This prophecy was realized three centuries later, when Josiah became king of Judah. Josiah was a reforming king, who "walked in the ways of his father David". He tried to lead the people back to God and destroyed all the pagan altars. At Bethel, he burned the bones of its pagan priests on the altar to defile it (2 Kings 23: 16).

KING JOSIAH
In this 17th-century engraving, Josiah listens to a reading from the Book of the Law as pagan priests are burned to death.

UNDERSTANDING THE STORY

Solomon's son brings disaster to David's kingdom. Rehoboam is not a king who serves the best interests of his people, and his arrogance precipitates the kingdom's division. The northern tribes choose Jeroboam as their king, as Ahijah the prophet had predicted. But instead of placing his trust in God's word, Jeroboam makes pagan idols because he is afraid he will lose his new kingdom.

1 KINGS 16–17
KING AHAB AND ELIJAH

⁜

CHAPTER 16 VERSE 31
"Married Jezebel"

Ahab's marriage sealed a political alliance with the king of Sidon, a Phoenician city-state along the coast of present-day Lebanon. This gave Ahab an ally on the northwestern boundaries of his kingdom.

⁜

CHAPTER 16 VERSE 32
"The temple of Baal"

The "Baal" of Ahab's reign was the Phoenician god Melqart. Ahab was greatly influenced by Jezebel and began to worship her god. Jezebel sought to establish Baal-worship as the religion of Israel. She killed God's prophets (1 Kings 18: 4) and replaced them with Sidon's prophets of Baal.

⁜

CHAPTER 16 VERSE 32
"Samaria"

Ahab built the temple of Baal in the heart of the northern kingdom. Samaria was established as Israel's capital by King Omri, Ahab's father. Ahab completed and embellished the city. The remains of his palace show a white stone building inlaid with ivory (1 Kings 22: 39).

THE RAVEN
A raven was the first bird that Noah released from the ark. God uses this natural scavenger as an instrument of divine grace. He sustains Elijah in a miraculous way, recalling how he sustained the Israelites with manna during their years of wandering in the desert.

16 AHAB[30] SON OF OMRI did more evil in the eyes of the LORD than any of those before him. [31]He not only considered it trivial to commit the sins of Jeroboam son of Nebat, but he also *married Jezebel* daughter of Ethbaal king of the Sidonians, and began to serve Baal and worship him. [32]He set up an altar for Baal in *the temple of Baal* that he built in *Samaria...*

Jezebel

King Ahab marries Jezebel, daughter of the king of Sidon

Elijah

Ahab

God's prophet Elijah denounces King Ahab

Jezebel persuades Ahab to abandon God and worship Baal

Ahab builds a temple to Baal in Samaria, the capital city of the northern kingdom

Elijah says that God will punish Ahab for his idolatry by stopping the rain

17 [1]Now Elijah the Tishbite, from Tishbe in Gilead, said to Ahab, "As the LORD, the God of Israel, lives, whom I serve, there will be *neither dew nor rain* in the next few years except at my word."

[2]Then the word of the LORD came to Elijah: [3]"Leave here, turn eastward and hide in the Kerith Ravine, east of the Jordan. [4]You will drink from the brook, and I have ordered the ravens to feed you there."

[5]So he did what the LORD had told him... [6]The ravens brought him bread and meat in the morning and bread and meat in the evening, and he drank from the brook.

[7]Some time later the brook dried up because there had been no rain in the land. [8]Then the word of the LORD came to him: [9]"*Go at once to Zarephath of Sidon* and stay there. I have commanded a widow in that place to supply you with food." [10]So he went to Zarephath. When he came to the town gate, a widow was there gathering sticks.

Elijah asked her for bread and water. She said her family was starving and that all she had was a little oil and flour. Elijah told her to bake him a cake, because God would ensure that the oil and flour lasted until the rain came.

God tells Elijah to hide in a ravine on the east side of the River Jordan

The ravens bring him bread and meat every morning and evening

Elijah drinks from a brook

When the brook dries up, God sends Elijah to Sidon

¹⁵She went away and did as Elijah had told her. So there was food every day for Elijah and for the woman and her family... ¹⁷Some time later the son of the woman who owned the house became ill. He grew worse and worse, and finally stopped breathing. ¹⁸She said to Elijah, "What do you have against me, man of God?..." ¹⁹"Give me your son," Elijah replied. He took him from her arms, carried him to the upper room where he was staying, and laid him on his bed... ²¹Then he cried to the LORD, "O LORD my God, let this boy's life return to him!"

²²The LORD heard Elijah's cry, and the boy's life returned to him, and he lived... ²⁴Then the woman said to Elijah, "Now I know that you are a man of God and that the word of the LORD from your mouth is the truth."

Elijah stays with a widow and her son

One day, the son becomes ill. He grows steadily worse and eventually dies

The family lives in Sidon, the native land of Baal worship

The widow blames Elijah for her son's death

Each day, God replenishes their supply of oil and flour

Elijah prays to God and the boy recovers

The woman now believes in the power of God

UNDERSTANDING THE STORY

Under the influence of Jezebel, King Ahab brings the religious life of the northern kingdom to an unprecedented low. By withholding rain, God shows the powerlessness of his opponents. While Israelites suffer for their faithlessness, a Sidonian is rewarded for her trust and declares her belief in Israel's God.

CHAPTER 17 VERSE 1
"Neither dew"
Dew was an important source of water in Israel, especially in areas of minimal rainfall. Moisture from the Mediterranean cooled during the night and fell as dew on the ground. Dew accounted for up to a quarter of the water supply in some places.

CHAPTER 17 VERSE 1
"Nor rain"
This was a demonstration of God's supremacy. Baal was a weather god, whose emblem was a lightning flash. He was worshipped as the bringer of rain to water the crops. A drought meant that Israel faced famine.

CHAPTER 17 VERSE 9
"Go at once to... Sidon"
God sent Elijah to Jezebel's native land. By providing for his prophet in Baal's homeland, God proved the impotence of this pagan deity.

THE PROPHET ELIJAH
During Ahab's reign (874–53 BC) idolatry was widely practised. God's people were being led astray by their king's bad example. Elijah was God's champion. He dedicated his life to opposing Baal-worship. His message was total commitment to God and his commandments.

HOME COOKING
The widow probably cooked in a clay oven similar to this reconstruction. Ovens were fuelled by grasses or animal dung.

1 KINGS 18

THE PROPHETS OF BAAL

CHAPTER 18 VERSE 1
"In the third year"
The northern kingdom had suffered three years without rain. This was God's punishment on the Israelites for worshipping Baal.

CHAPTER 18 VERSE 18
"You have... followed the Baals"
There were many local gods called "Baal". The word means "master" or "possessor". Each locality gave their god a surname. Ahab worshipped Baal–Melqart, the god of Sidon, his wife's native land. Baal's consort was Asherah, a fertility goddess.

18 IN[1] THE THIRD YEAR, the word of the LORD came to Elijah: "Go and present yourself to Ahab, and I will send rain on the land."... ¹⁷When [Ahab] saw Elijah, he said to him, "Is that you, you troubler of Israel?" ¹⁸"I have not made trouble for Israel," Elijah replied. "But you and your father's family have. *You have* abandoned the LORD's commands and have *followed the Baals.* ¹⁹"Now summon the people from all over Israel to meet me on *Mount Carmel.* And bring the four hundred and fifty prophets of Baal and the four hundred prophets of Asherah, *who eat at Jezebel's table."* ²⁰So Ahab sent word throughout all Israel and assembled the prophets on Mount Carmel. ²¹Elijah went before the people and said, "How long will you waver between two opinions? If the LORD is God, follow him; but if Baal is God, follow him."

Elijah challenges the prophets of Baal to a contest

The prophets appeal to their god to light the altar

Elijah taunts the Baal prophets

King Ahab watches to see who will win the contest

The Baal prophets slash themselves in a frenzy

CHAPTER 18 VERSE 19
"Mount Carmel"
The Carmel is a mountain range extending 21km (13 miles) west from the hill country of Samaria to the Mediterranean coast. Mount Carmel overlooks the sea near modern Haifa. The Canaanites built sanctuaries on the mountain to the weather god Baal, which is why Elijah chose this place to challenge Baal's authority.

The Israelites gather at Mount Carmel

MOUNT CARMEL
The mountain rises sharply to 143m (470ft) above sea level.

But the people said nothing.

So Elijah challenged the prophets of Baal and told them to sacrifice a bull and ask their god to set fire to it. They did so, shouting to Baal without success.

²⁶And they danced around the altar they had made. ²⁷At noon Elijah began to taunt them. "Shout louder!" he said. "Surely he is a god!...

Maybe he is sleeping and must be awakened." ²⁸So they shouted louder and slashed themselves with swords and spears, as was their custom, until their blood flowed... ²⁹But there was no response...

³⁰Then Elijah said to all the people, "Come here to me." They came to him, and he repaired the altar of the LORD, which was in ruins. ³¹Elijah took twelve stones, one for each of the tribes descended from Jacob... ³²With the stones he built an altar in the name of the LORD, and he dug a trench round it... ³³Then he said to them, "Fill four large jars with water and pour it on the offering and on the wood."

CHAPTER 18 VERSE 19
"Who eat at Jezebel's table"
This position of honour indicates that the prophets of Baal were court counsellors, and that Baal-worship had become the state religion.

They did this three times and Elijah prayed to God.

The sky turns black, and there is torrential rain

Elijah builds an altar to God and digs a trench around it

In answer to Elijah's prayer, God sets fire to the altar

JEZEBEL AT THE WINDOW
This carved ivory plaque is believed to show Jezebel looking out of the window of her palace at Jezreel.

Elijah orders the execution of the Baal prophets

King Ahab rides back to Jezreel

Water is poured over the altar and into the trench

Elijah runs back to Jezreel ahead of King Ahab

³⁸Then the fire of the LORD fell and burned up the sacrifice, the wood, the stones and the soil, and also licked up the water in the trench. ³⁹When all the people saw this, they fell prostrate and cried, "The LORD – he is God! The LORD – he is God!"

⁴⁰Then Elijah commanded them, "Seize the prophets of Baal. Don't let anyone get away!" They seized them, and Elijah had them brought down to the Kishon valley and slaughtered there...

⁴⁵Meanwhile, the sky grew black with clouds, the wind rose, a heavy rain came on and Ahab rode off to Jezreel. ⁴⁶The power of the LORD came upon Elijah and, tucking his cloak into his belt, he ran ahead of Ahab all the way to *Jezreel*.

UNDERSTANDING THE STORY

Elijah challenges the prophets of Baal to a contest between God and Baal. God's prophet deliberately gives his opponents every advantage. But despite this, they are defeated, and all Israel witnesses a demonstration of God's power.

CHAPTER 18 VERSE 46
"Jezreel"
Ahab built a royal palace at Jezreel, and Jezebel made this her permanent home. The town lay at the foot of Mount Gilboa, about 40km (25 miles) from Mount Carmel.

1 KINGS 21
NABOTH'S VINEYARD

❖
CHAPTER 21 VERSE 1
"The vineyard was in Jezreel"
Jezreel was a city located about 38km (24 miles) north of Samaria. King Ahab had a residence in Jezreel, as well as his official palace in Samaria.

❖
CHAPTER 21 VERSE 1
"King of Samaria"
Samaria was the new capital of the northern kingdom of Israel. Ahab's father, Omri, moved it from Tirzah to Samaria in about 880 BC (1 Kings 16: 24). Samaria was built on a hill overlooking the main north–south route across Palestine. Its name means "lookout".

❖
CHAPTER 21 VERSE 3
"The LORD forbid"
Naboth's ancestors were allotted this land after the conquest of Canaan. Moses' Law forbade the Israelites to sell any of their ancestral land (Leviticus 25: 23–28).

Naboth owns a vineyard near King Ahab's palace

Ahab asks Naboth to sell him his vineyard, but Naboth refuses

Naboth

21 SOME[1] TIME LATER there was an incident involving a vineyard belonging to Naboth the Jezreelite. *The vineyard was in Jezreel*, close to the palace of Ahab *king of Samaria*. ²Ahab said to Naboth, "Let me have your vineyard to use for a vegetable garden, since it is close to my palace. In exchange I will give you a better vineyard or, if you prefer, I will pay you whatever it is worth."

³But Naboth replied, "*The LORD forbid* that I should give you the inheritance of my fathers." ⁴So Ahab went home, sullen and angry... He lay on his bed sulking and refused to eat...

⁷Jezebel his wife said, "Is this how you act as king over Israel? Get up and eat! Cheer up. I'll get you the vineyard of Naboth the Jezreelite."

Ahab sulks on his bed and refuses to eat

Jezebel thinks of a way to get Naboth's vineyard

She writes to the Israelite elders in Ahab's name

She conspires to have Naboth accused of blasphemy, knowing that this will lead to his death

⁸So she wrote letters in Ahab's name, placed his seal on them, and sent them to the elders and nobles who lived in Naboth's city with him... ¹¹So the elders and nobles who lived in Naboth's city did as Jezebel directed in the letters she had written to them. ¹²*They proclaimed a fast* and seated Naboth in a prominent place among the people. ¹³Then two scoundrels came and sat opposite him and *brought charges against Naboth* before the people, saying, "Naboth has cursed both God and the king." So they took him outside the city and stoned him to death... ¹⁶When Ahab heard that Naboth was dead, he got up and went down to take possession of Naboth's vineyard.

¹⁷Then the word of the LORD came to Elijah the Tishbite: ¹⁸"Go down to meet Ahab... He is now in Naboth's vineyard, where he has gone to take possession of it.

CHAPTER 21 VERSE 12
"They proclaimed a fast"
Israelites often fasted when a serious crime was committed, hoping this would prevent God from punishing the whole nation. Jezebel ordered a fast day so that people would think someone had broken the Law. She knew the Israelites would be afraid of the consequences and would want to rid themselves of the guilty person.

AHAB'S SEAL
Bronze ring inscribed
"Ahab King of Israel"

CHAPTER 21 VERSE 13
"Brought charges against Naboth"
According to Moses' Law, a person could not be put to death just on the evidence of one witness (Numbers 35: 30). Jezebel made sure her plan would succeed by instructing two men to testify against Naboth.

CHAPTER 21 VERSE 23
"Dogs will devour Jezebel"
This prediction was fulfilled ten years after Ahab's death when Jehu, a military commander, seized power from Jezebel. Under Jehu's orders, she was pushed out of a palace window and her body was torn apart by dogs (2 Kings 9: 30–35).

The Israelites stone Naboth to death

Ahab goes to the vineyard, where he meets Elijah

Elijah curses Ahab and Jezebel and prophesies the downfall of Ahab's kingdom

¹⁹"Say to him, 'This is what the LORD says: Have you not murdered a man and seized his property?... ²¹I am going to bring disaster on you. I will consume your descendants [and] ²³*dogs will devour Jezebel* by the wall of Jezreel...' " ²⁷When Ahab heard these words, he tore his clothes, put on sackcloth and fasted... ²⁸Then the word of the LORD came to Elijah... ²⁹"Because [Ahab] has humbled himself I will not bring this disaster in his day, but I will bring it on his house in the days of his son."

UNDERSTANDING THE STORY

By allowing Jezebel to act unlawfully, King Ahab is equally responsible for Naboth's murder. However, Ahab shows some remorse for his sin, and so God deals more leniently with him than with Jezebel. Ahab's dynasty will come to an untimely end, but not until a generation later, when his son is king.

THE DEATH OF JEZEBEL
19th-century engraving, Gustave Doré

ELIJAH IS TAKEN UP TO HEAVEN

2 KINGS 2

ELISHA

Elisha was Elijah's disciple and successor. His name is Hebrew for "God is salvation". It recalls Joshua's name, which means "The Lord is salvation". Elisha is often associated with Joshua, who also acted as God's servant and leader of the people after his master's death (Joshua 1: 1–6).

CHAPTER 2 VERSES 2, 4, 6
"I will not leave you"
Elisha's words to Elijah parallel the disciple Peter's words to Jesus, before Jesus is taken up to heaven (John 21: 15–17). Three times Peter declares his love for Jesus, just as Elisha declares three times that he will not leave his master. Elisha is to continue Elijah's work.

CHAPTER 2 VERSE 3
"The company of the prophets"
Many Israelites remained faithful to God at this time (1 Kings 19: 18). Among them were the prophets, who lived in religious communities in certain towns and villages. They called for repentance, gave guidance to the people, and preached God's message. Only a few prophets directly spoke the word of God.

CHAPTER 2 VERSE 8
"The water divided"
This event recalls the parting of the Red Sea: "Then Moses stretched out his hand over the sea [and] the waters were divided" (Exodus 14: 21).

RIVER JORDAN, ISRAEL
The river runs in a north–south direction over 323km (200 miles).

2 WHEN[1] THE LORD was about to take Elijah up to heaven in a whirlwind, Elijah and Elisha were on their way from Gilgal. [2]Elijah said to Elisha, "Stay here; the LORD has sent me to Bethel." But Elisha said, "As surely as the LORD lives and as you live, *I will not leave you.*" So they went down to Bethel.

A group of prophets follow Elijah and Elisha, who travel to the River Jordan

Elijah strikes the water with his cloak

The river divides, and Elijah and Elisha cross over on dry ground

Before Elijah is taken up, he asks Elisha if he has a final request

Elisha wants to inherit Elijah's ministry

[3]*The company of the prophets* at Bethel came out to Elisha and asked, "Do you know that the LORD is going to take your master from you today?"

"Yes, I know," Elisha replied, "but do not speak of it."

[4]Then Elijah said to him, "Stay here, Elisha; the LORD has sent me to Jericho." And he replied, "As surely as the LORD lives and as you live, *I will not leave you.*" So they went to Jericho.

[5]The company of the prophets at Jericho went up to Elisha and asked him, "Do you know that the LORD is going to take your master from you today?"

Elijah

A chariot and
horses of fire
suddenly appear

"Yes, I know," he replied, "but do not speak of it."
⁶Then Elijah said to him, "Stay here; the LORD has sent me to
the Jordan." And he replied, "As surely as the LORD lives... *I will
not leave you.*"... ⁷Fifty men of the company of
the prophets went and stood at a distance,
facing the place where Elijah and Elisha
had stopped at the Jordan. ⁸Elijah took
his cloak, rolled it up and struck
the water with it. *The water
divided* to the right and to
the left, and the two of
them crossed over
on dry ground.

⁹When they had crossed,
Elijah said to Elisha, "Tell
me, what can I do for you
before I am taken from you?"
"*Let me inherit a double portion* of
your spirit," Elisha replied.
¹⁰"You have asked a difficult
thing," Elijah said, "yet if you
see me when I am taken from
you, it will be yours –
otherwise not."
¹¹As they were walking
along and talking together,
suddenly a chariot of fire and
horses of fire appeared and
separated the two of them, and
Elijah went up to heaven in a
whirlwind. ¹²Elisha saw this and
cried out, "*My father! My father!
The chariots and horsemen of Israel!*"
And Elisha saw him no more.
Then he took hold of his own
clothes and tore them apart.

Elijah is taken up to heaven
in a whirlwind, and Elisha
tears his clothes in grief

CHAPTER 2 VERSE 9
"Let me inherit a double portion"
In ancient Middle-Eastern law, the
oldest son inherited twice as much
as any other family member. By
asking for the traditional share of a
firstborn son, Elisha was making a
formal request to be Elijah's spiritual
heir. He was not asking for twice
Elijah's spiritual power.

CHAPTER 2 VERSE 12
"My father! My father!"
Elisha's words to his master confirm
his new role as Elijah's successor.

CHAPTER 2 VERSE 12
"Chariots and horsemen of Israel!"
Elisha compares his master to the
army of Israel. His words describe
Elijah as the protector and defender
of Israelite faith. Elijah is taken up
to heaven in a tornado, a symbol of
God's strength and power.

WHIRLWINDS
Whirlwinds start inside thunderclouds,
when warm air spins at high speeds.

UNDERSTANDING THE STORY

Elijah's ministry has come to an end. Elisha assumes responsibility for renewing
the people's faith in God, just as Joshua does at the end of Moses' life. Elijah
and Elisha travel to places associated with the Israelites' entry into Canaan.
Their journey symbolizes the promise of a new beginning.

ELISHA HEALS NAAMAN

CHAPTER 5 VERSE 1
"The king of Aram"

Aram (Syria) was a group of small city states, of which Damascus was the dominant power. Naaman served in the army of Ben-Hadad II (860–43 BC), the king of Damascus. Aram and Israel were often at war with each other, although at this time they were both part of an alliance formed to oppose the threat of Assyrian expansion.

ARAMEAN ART
This column base was found in the ruins of a palace at Samal, an Aramean city-kingdom that is now Sinjali in modern Turkey. The winged sphinx was a recurring motif in art throughout the ancient Middle East.

CHAPTER 5 VERSE 3
"Cure him of his leprosy"

Leprosy is a chronic bacterial infection that attacks nerves, especially in the face and limbs, and leads to skin damage. In Bible times, people were unable to distinguish between this disease and a variety of less serious ailments, such as eczema. For this reason, leprosy described a range of skin ailments.

ELISHA
As Elijah's anointed successor, Elisha continued to demonstrate God's power and presence at a critical time in Israel's religious history. Elisha's ministry lasted about fifty years (*c.* 855–798 BC) and spanned the reigns of four kings: Jehoram, Jehu, Jehoahaz, and Jehoash. Elisha was more sociable than Elijah and preferred to live in the city.

2 ELISHA[13] PICKED UP THE CLOAK that had fallen from Elijah and went back and stood on the bank of the Jordan. [14]Then he took the cloak that had fallen from him and struck the water with it. "Where now is the LORD, the God of Elijah?" he asked. When he struck the water, it divided to the right and to the left, and he crossed over.

[15]The company of the prophets from Jericho, who were watching, said, "The spirit of Elijah is resting on Elisha." And they went to meet him and bowed to the ground before him.

Elisha continued to perform miracles in the same way that his master, Elijah, had done. He became well-known throughout Israel as a man of God.

After Elijah is taken up to heaven, Elisha picks up Elijah's cloak and strikes the water

The water divides

5 [1]Now Naaman was commander of the army of *the king of Aram*. He was a great man in the sight of his master and highly regarded, because through him the LORD had given victory to Aram. He was a valiant soldier, but he had leprosy.

[2]Now bands from Aram had gone out and had taken captive a young girl from Israel, and she served Naaman's wife. [3]She said to her mistress, "If only my master would see the prophet who is in Samaria! He would *cure him of his leprosy*."... [9]So Naaman went with his horses and chariots and stopped at the door of Elisha's house. [10]Elisha sent a messenger to say to him "Go, wash yourself seven times in the Jordan, and your flesh will be restored and you will be cleansed."

Naaman goes to Elisha's house to ask him to cure his leprosy

Elisha's servant tells Naaman to wash seven times in the River Jordan

Naaman's servants persuade him to obey Elisha's instructions

Naaman is angry that Elisha would not see him

¹¹But Naaman went away angry and said, "I thought that he would surely come out to me and stand and call on the name of the LORD his God, wave his hand over the spot and cure me of my leprosy. ¹²Are not Abana and Pharpar, *the rivers of Damascus*, better than any of the waters of Israel?…"

¹³Naaman's servants went to him and said, "My father, if the prophet had told you to do some great thing, would you not have done it?…"

¹⁴So he went down and dipped himself in the Jordan seven times… and his flesh was restored and became clean like that of a young boy.

¹⁵Then Naaman and all his attendants went back to the man of God. He stood before him and said… ¹⁷"Please let me, your servant, be given *as much earth as a pair of mules can carry*, for your servant will never again make burnt offerings and sacrifices to any other god but the LORD."

When Naaman comes out of the river, his leprosy is gone

He tells Elisha that he will worship only God

Naaman asks for as much earth as a pair of mules can carry

The earth is transported to Damascus, so that Naaman can worship the God of Israel on Israelite soil

UNDERSTANDING THE STORY

Elisha inherits his master's spiritual powers and continues Elijah's mission to reestablish God's covenant with Israel. Naaman's miraculous healing shows that God's care extends to other nations. Whereas Israel has abandoned God to worship foreign deities, a foreigner renounces his gods and worships the Lord.

CHAPTER 5 VERSE 12
"The rivers of Damascus"
The Abana (the modern-day Barada River) flowed through the centre of Damascus, and the Pharpar passed just south of the city. These twin rivers made Damascus and its environs a lush and fertile area.

BARADA RIVER, DAMASCUS

CHAPTER 5 VERSE 17
"As much earth as a pair of mules can carry"
In the ancient Middle East, people believed that gods could only be worshipped in the lands they ruled. Naaman asked for Israelite soil in order to consecrate a place in Aram where he could worship God.

ELISHA'S MIRACLES
Elisha performed twice as many miracles as Elijah, and they affected every level of society. Elisha acted as a court advisor, and his actions and advice brought Israel success in battle. The purpose of his political involvement was to bring Israel's monarchy back to God. Many of Elisha's miracles demonstrate God's concern for ordinary people.

THE WIDOW'S OIL
This illustration from a 15th-century Spanish Bible depicts one of Elisha's miracles. He multiplied a widow's supply of oil so that she could sell it to pay her debts.

JONAH 1–4
JONAH AND NINEVEH

CHAPTER 1 VERSE 1
"Jonah son of Amittai"
Jonah was a prophet who lived in the northern kingdom during the reign of Jeroboam II (c. 793–53 BC). The prophet lived in Gath Hepher, a short distance north-east of Jesus' home town, Nazareth.

CHAPTER 1 VERSE 3
"Jonah ran away from the LORD"
Jonah did not want to give the people of Nineveh warning of God's judgement. The Ninevites were enemies of the Israelites, and Jonah wanted God to destroy them.

God instructs Jonah to warn the Ninevites about their wickedness, but Jonah runs away to sea

1 THE[1] WORD OF THE LORD came to *Jonah son of Amittai*: [2]"Go to the great city of Nineveh and preach against it, because its wickedness has come up before me."

[3]But *Jonah ran away from the LORD* and *headed for Tarshish*. He went down to Joppa, where he found a ship bound for that port...

[4]Then the LORD sent a great wind on the sea, and such a violent storm arose that the ship threatened to break up. [5]All the sailors were afraid and each cried out to his own god. And they threw the cargo into the sea to lighten the ship. But Jonah had gone below deck, where he lay down and fell into a deep sleep. [6]The captain went to him and said: "How can you sleep? Get up and call on your god!..."

[7]Then the sailors said to each other, "Come, let us cast lots to find out who is responsible for this calamity." They cast lots and the lot fell on Jonah.

The sailors asked Jonah many questions, and he told them that he was a Hebrew running away from God. By now the sea was very rough, and the sailors were terrified. So Jonah told them to throw him overboard.

Jonah

God sends a violent storm, and the terrified sailors throw Jonah into the sea

CHAPTER 1 VERSE 3
"Headed for Tarshish"
Ships sailing to Tarshish brought back cargoes of precious metals. This city is identified with Tartessus in south-west Spain, where there was a Phoenician mining colony.

NINEVEH
Nineveh is first mentioned in the Book of Genesis as a city built by Nimrod, architect of the Tower of Babel. The city was located on the east side of the River Tigris in northern Mesopotamia. In Jonah's time, Nineveh was a royal city of Assyrian kings, and in 705 BC it was made capital of the entire empire.

Jonah expects to drown, but a great fish swallows him. He is in its belly for three days and three nights

¹⁵Then they took Jonah and threw him overboard, and the raging sea grew calm. ¹⁶At this the men greatly feared the LORD... ¹⁷But the LORD provided a great fish to swallow Jonah, and Jonah was inside the fish *three days and three nights.*

2 ¹From inside the fish Jonah prayed to the LORD his God... ¹⁰And the LORD commanded the fish, and it vomited Jonah onto dry land.

3 ¹Then the word of the LORD came to Jonah a second time. [This time] ³Jonah obeyed... ⁵The Ninevites believed God. They declared a fast, and all of them, from the greatest to the least, put on sackcloth... ¹⁰When God saw [them turn] from their evil ways, he had compassion and did not bring upon them the destruction he had threatened.

Jonah had run away because he had feared that this might happen. He was angry because he wanted God to destroy Israel's enemy. He went to sit on a hill overlooking the city, and God provided a vine for shade. Jonah was happy about the vine. But when God made the vine wither, Jonah became angry.

4 ⁹God said to Jonah, "Do you have a right to be angry about the vine?... ¹⁰You have been concerned about this vine, though you did not tend it or make it grow... ¹¹But Nineveh has more than a hundred and twenty thousand people... Should I not be concerned about that great city?"

CHAPTER 1 VERSE 17
"Three days and three nights"
There was an ancient pagan belief that the soul took three days and nights to reach the afterlife. Jonah was in the fish for a period that should have made death a certainty.

WHALE
There are a number of reliable accounts of people who have survived being swallowed by whales. Their survival is attributed to the fact that whales need to surface frequently for air.

Jonah is happy when God provides a vine to shade him from the sun, but he is angry when the vine withers

The Ninevites repent, and God spares the city. This makes Jonah angry

UNDERSTANDING THE STORY

Jonah begs for God's forgiveness, yet he cannot accept that God should extend his mercy to Gentiles. Jonah's concern for the vine highlights his lack of compassion for the Ninevites. He cares more for a plant than a city full of people.

Jonah prays to God to save him, and the fish vomits him onto the shore

2 CHRONICLES 28
KING AHAZ

AHAZ[1] WAS TWENTY YEARS OLD when he became king... [2]He walked in the ways of the kings of Israel and also *made cast idols* for worshipping the Baals. [3]He burned sacrifices in the *valley of Ben Hinnom* and sacrificed his sons in the fire, following the detestable ways of the nations that the LORD had driven out before the Israelites... [5]Therefore the LORD his God handed him over to the king of Aram. The Arameans defeated him and took many of his people as prisoners and brought them to Damascus.

He was also given into the hands of the king of Israel, who inflicted heavy casualties on him... [8]The Israelites took captive from their kinsmen two hundred thousand wives, sons and daughters. They also took a great deal of plunder, which they carried back to Samaria. [9]But a prophet of the LORD named Oded was there, and he went out to meet the army when it returned to Samaria. He said to them, "Because the LORD, the God of your fathers, was angry with Judah, he gave them into your hand. But you have slaughtered them in a rage that reaches to heaven...

CHAPTER 28 VERSE 2
"Made cast idols"
Metalsmiths in the ancient Middle East were highly skilled. Metal was heated to melting point and cast in moulds. The first alloy was invented in *c.* 3500 BC, by mixing copper and tin to form bronze. This rust-proof alloy revolutionized metalwork.

BRONZE ASTARTE
Figurine and mould of the Canaanite fertility goddess, 13th century BC

AHAZ, KING OF JUDAH
Ahaz ruled from 735–715 BC. His name appears in a list of vassals of the Assyrian king Tiglath-Pileser III.

King Ahaz abandons God and sacrifices his children to pagan deities

Israel attacks and plunders Judah

The Israelites take many captives

Israelite soldier

Prisoner from Judah

The prophet Oded denounces Israel

¹¹Now listen to me! Send back your fellow countrymen that you have taken as prisoners, for the LORD's fierce anger rests on you."

The elders of Israel ordered the soldiers to obey the prophet, and the prisoners were given back their belongings and allowed to return to Judah.

¹⁶At that time King Ahaz sent to the king of Assyria for help. ¹⁷The Edomites had again come and attacked Judah and carried away prisoners, ¹⁸while the Philistines had raided towns in the foothills... ²⁰Tiglath-Pileser king of Assyria came to him, but gave him trouble instead of help...

²²In his time of trouble King Ahaz... ²³offered sacrifices to the gods of Damascus, who had defeated him; for he thought, "Since [these gods] have helped them, I will sacrifice to them so that they will help me."

TIGLATH-PILESER III (745–27 BC)
Wall relief from his palace at Nimrud

THE ASSYRIANS
The Assyrians had dominated the Middle East since 911 BC, although for many years the empire had suffered from internal strife. Tiglath-Pileser's aggressive campaigns brought the empire to new heights. Aram and Israel wanted Judah to join their alliance against Assyria and attacked Judah when it refused.

King Ahaz closes the temple

The temple is stripped of its treasures

Judah becomes a vassal state of Assyria

But they were his downfall and the downfall of all Israel.
²⁴Ahaz gathered together the furnishings from the temple of God and *took them away*. He shut the doors of the LORD's temple and set up altars at every street corner in Jerusalem...
²⁷Ahaz rested with his fathers and was buried in the city of Jerusalem, but he was not placed in the tombs of the kings of Israel.

UNDERSTANDING THE STORY
King Ahaz abandons God and worships pagan deities. The result is disastrous for Judah. The closing of the Temple symbolizes the king's alienation from God. The fact that Ahaz is not buried with the kings of Judah indicates that the people have judged him an unworthy ruler. This offers some hope for their future.

❖

CHAPTER 28 VERSE 3
"Valley of Ben Hinnom"
This was a valley in Jerusalem where altars called "high places" were built, and children were sacrificed in a fire pit to the Canaanite god Molech. The area was later used as a rubbish dump, where fire burned constantly. In the New Testament, the valley was known as Gehenna and was associated with hell.

❖

CHAPTER 28 VERSE 24
"Took them away"
Ahaz became a vassal of Assyria and was forced to pay tribute to the Assyrian king. Part of the Temple treasures were offered as tribute.

2 KINGS 17

THE FALL OF ISRAEL

KING HOSHEA
Hoshea was the twentieth and last king of Israel. His predecessor, King Pekah, had formed an alliance with Aram and fought against King Tiglath-Pileser III of Assyria. As a result, Israel lost part of its territory. Hoshea assassinated Pekah in 732 BC, and Tiglath-Pileser rewarded Hoshea by making him his vassal king over what remained of Israel.

✛

CHAPTER 17 VERSE 3
"Shalmaneser king of Assyria"
Shalmaneser V succeeded Tiglath-Pileser and ruled from 727–722 BC.

17 I N[1] THE TWELFTH YEAR of Ahaz king of Judah, Hoshea son of Elah became king of Israel in Samaria, and he reigned for nine years... [3]*Shalmaneser king of Assyria* came up to attack Hoshea, who had been Shalmaneser's vassal and had paid him tribute. [4]But the king of Assyria discovered that Hoshea was a traitor, for he had sent envoys to So king of Egypt, and he no longer paid tribute to the king of Assyria, as he had done year by year. Therefore Shalmaneser seized him and put him in prison. [5]The king of Assyria invaded the entire land, marched against Samaria and *laid siege to it for three years*. [6]In the ninth year of Hoshea, the king of Assyria captured Samaria and *deported the Israelites* to Assyria. He settled them in Halah, in Gozan on the Habor River and in the towns of the Medes.

Israelite captives

King Hoshea refuses to pay tribute to Assyria, and so the Assyrians invade Israel

The Assyrians lay siege to the city of Samaria for three years

Samaria falls, and the Israelites are deported

✛

CHAPTER 17 VERSE 5
"Laid siege to it for three years"
The royal city of Samaria was strongly fortified and situated on the top of a hill, which is why it took so long to capture. The siege lasted from 724–21 BC. By the time the city fell, Sargon II had succeeded Shalmaneser as king of Assyria.

WINGED SPIRIT
This protective spirit is part of a wall relief from Sargon II's palace at Khorsabad in modern Iraq. He carries a pine cone and bucket, from which he draws holy water.

[7]All this took place because the Israelites had sinned against the LORD their God, who had brought them out of Egypt... [9]The Israelites secretly did things against the LORD their God that were not right... [16]They bowed down to all the starry hosts, and they worshipped Baal. [17]They sacrificed their sons and daughters in the fire. They practised divination and sorcery and sold themselves to do evil in the eyes of the LORD... [18]So the LORD was very angry with Israel and removed them from his presence. Only the tribe of Judah was left, [19]and even Judah did not keep the commands of the LORD their God...

[24]The king of Assyria brought people from Babylon, Cuthah, Avva, Hamath and Sepharvaim and settled them in the towns of Samaria to replace the Israelites...

²⁵When they first lived there, they did not worship the LORD; so he sent lions among them and they killed some of the people. ²⁶It was reported to the king of Assyria: "The people you deported and resettled in the towns of Samaria do not know what the god of that country requires. He has sent lions among them, which are killing them off...

²⁷Then the king of Assyria gave this order: "Make one of the priests you took captive from Samaria go back to live there and teach the people what the god of the land requires." ²⁸So one of the priests who had been exiled from Samaria came to live in Bethel and taught them how to worship the LORD. ²⁹Nevertheless, each national group made its own gods [and] set them up in the shrines *the people of Samaria* had made at the high places. ³⁰The men from Babylon made Succoth Benoth, the men from Cuthah made Nergal, and the men from Hamath made Ashima; ³¹the Avvites made Nibhaz and Tartak, and the Sepharvites burned their children in the fire as sacrifices to Adrammelech and Anammelech...

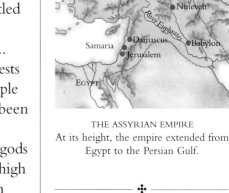

THE ASSYRIAN EMPIRE
At its height, the empire extended from Egypt to the Persian Gulf.

✛

CHAPTER 17 VERSE 6
"Deported the Israelites"
Assyria's policy of deportation was an effort to prevent rebellion in newly conquered lands. Sargon II's annals record that 27,290 Israelites were resettled in towns throughout the expanding Assyrian empire.

The various people who replace the Israelites worship their own gods

Lions kill many of the people

The king of Assyria realises that the "god of the land" is angry

Israelite priest

The Assyrians bring people from all over their empire to live in Israel

An exiled Israelite priest comes back to teach the people how to worship God

Pagan priest

³⁵They worshipped the LORD, but they also served their own Gods in accordance with the customs of the nations from which they had been brought... ⁴¹To this day their children and grandchildren continue to do as their fathers did.

UNDERSTANDING THE STORY

Generations of kings ignored God's prophets and failed to keep his covenant laws. Israel's exile from the Promised Land is the consequence of their actions. Only the southern kingdom of Judah is now left to represent God's people.

✛

CHAPTER 17 VERSE 29
"The people of Samaria"
This was the mixed population of the northern kingdom. Israelites who remained were joined by Babylonians, Arameans, and others who the conquering Assyrians had deported from their homelands. These people came to be known as Samaritans. They later rejected pagan beliefs and embraced the Israelite faith, maintaining a strict observance of the Law of Moses.

2 KINGS 18–20
JERUSALEM SURVIVES A SIEGE

CHAPTER 18 VERSE 1
"Hezekiah son of Ahaz"
Unlike his father, Hezekiah was a godly king, initiating many religious reforms. He reopened the Temple and destroyed pagan altars. When the northern kingdom fell to Assyria in 722 BC, Hezekiah invited the remaining Israelites to Jerusalem for the Passover. When he died, he was buried "in the upper tombs of the sons of David", a place of honour.

CHAPTER 18 VERSE 8
"He defeated the Philistines"
The Philistines had conquered parts of Judah during Ahaz's reign. King Sennacherib recalls in his annals that he forced Hezekiah to deliver the Philistine king of Ekron, who was being held prisoner in Jerusalem.

SENNACHERIB
Sennacherib came to the throne in 705 BC, when his father, Sargon II, was killed in battle. Sargon's death prompted rebellions throughout the Assyrian empire. Hezekiah joined a revolt that included Sidon, Egypt, and two Philistine cities. In 701 BC, Sennacherib launched a military campaign to crush these revolts.

SENNACHERIB IN HIS CHARIOT
This wall-relief is from the king's palace at Nineveh. Sennacherib abandoned the new capital built by his father at "Fort Sargon" (modern Khorsabad in Iraq). Ancient Nineveh remained the capital until Assyria's fall.

18 IN[1] THE THIRD YEAR of Hoshea son of Elah king of Israel, *Hezekiah son of Ahaz* king of Judah began to reign... [5]Hezekiah trusted in the LORD, the God of Israel... [7]And the LORD was with him; he was successful in whatever he undertook. He rebelled against the king of Assyria and did not serve him. [8]From watchtower to fortified city, *he defeated the Philistines*, as far as Gaza and its territory...

[13]In the fourteenth year of King Hezekiah's reign, Sennacherib king of Assyria attacked all the fortified cities of Judah and captured them.

The Assyrian army attacks and captures all the fortified cities in Judah

When Jerusalem is attacked, King Hezekiah asks God's prophet, Isaiah, for help

Then the Assyrian king laid siege to the city of Jerusalem. His commanders taunted the Israelite officials, saying that God could not save them from the Assyrian army. When Hezekiah heard this, he was afraid and sent some of his officials to see the prophet Isaiah.

19 [6]Isaiah said to them, "Tell your master, 'This is what the LORD says: Do not be afraid of what you have heard – those words with which the underlings of the king of Assyria have blasphemed me. [7]Listen! I am going to put such a spirit in him that when he hears a certain report, he will return to his own country, and there I will have him cut down with the sword... [32]*He will not enter this city* or *shoot an arrow* here... [34]I will defend this city and save it, for my sake and for the sake of David my servant.'"

In the morning, many of the soldiers are dead

During the night, the angel of the Lord enters the Assyrian camp

³⁵That night the angel of the LORD went out and put to death a hundred and eighty-five thousand men in the Assyrian camp. When the people got up the next morning – there were all the dead bodies! ³⁶So *Sennacherib king of Assyria broke camp and withdrew.* He returned to Nineveh and stayed there. ³⁷One day, while he was worshipping in the temple of his god Nisroch, his sons... cut him down with the sword.

20 ¹In those days Hezekiah became ill and was at the point of death. The prophet Isaiah son of Amoz went to him and said, "This is what the LORD says: Put your house in order, because you are going to die; you will not recover."

²Hezekiah turned his face to the wall and prayed to the LORD,

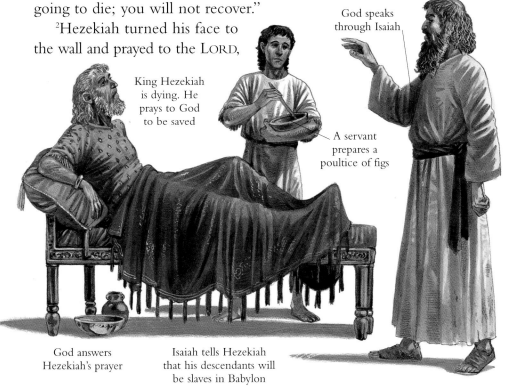

God speaks through Isaiah

King Hezekiah is dying. He prays to God to be saved

A servant prepares a poultice of figs

God answers Hezekiah's prayer

Isaiah tells Hezekiah that his descendants will be slaves in Babylon

³"Remember, O LORD, how I have walked before you faithfully and with wholehearted devotion and have done what is good in your eyes."

⁴Before Isaiah had left the middle court, the word of the LORD came to him: ⁵"Go back and tell Hezekiah... I have heard your prayer and seen your tears; I will heal you..." ⁷Then Isaiah said, "Prepare a poultice of figs." They did so and applied it to the boil, and he recovered... ¹⁶Then Isaiah said to Hezekiah... ¹⁷"The time will surely come when everything in your palace, and all that your fathers have stored up until this day, will be carried off to Babylon..."

¹⁹"The word of the LORD you have spoken is good," Hezekiah replied. For he thought, "Will there not be peace and security in my lifetime?"

UNDERSTANDING THE STORY

Judah faces the same fate as the northern kingdom of Israel. Jerusalem is under siege from the Assyrian army, but unlike Samaria, the city is not conquered. The Assyrians are God's instrument of judgement. Jerusalem is saved because Hezekiah follows the covenant laws and restores true worship.

CHAPTER 19 VERSE 32
"He will not enter this city"
Hezekiah prepared for the inevitable siege by fortifying Jerusalem's walls and digging a tunnel to bring water from the Gihon spring into the city.

THE POOL OF SILOAM
Hezekiah constructed this reservoir to hold the water channelled into the city.

CHAPTER 19 VERSE 32
"Shoot an arrow"
God's words meant that the siege would not end in a full assault on the city. Usually, in the final stages of a siege, the Assyrians mounted battering rams while archers provided covering fire.

CHAPTER 19 VERSE 36
"Sennacherib... withdrew"
The Greek historian Herodotus attributed the withdrawal to mice gnawing through the bowstrings of the Assyrians. Other scholars have suggested that the army was struck by a plague carried by rats. A prism commemorating King Sennacherib's successful campaign suggests that the siege ended because Hezekiah agreed to pay tribute to the Assyrian king.

THE PRISM OF SENNACHERIB
This plaque reports that Sennacherib captured 46 fortified cities and that he made Hezekiah a "prisoner in Jerusalem like a bird in a cage".

2 CHRONICLES 34–35
KING JOSIAH

CHAPTER 34 VERSE 5
"Burned the bones"
Josiah burned the bones of priests who had sacrificed on pagan altars. This had been prophesied three centuries before, during the reign of Jeroboam, the first king of Israel (1 Kings 13: 2).

King Josiah

KING JOSIAH
Grandson of the ungodly King Manasseh, Josiah came to the throne in 640 BC following the assassination of his father, Amon. Like King Hezekiah, Josiah initiated many religious reforms. Under his administration, Judah enjoyed a period of expansion. The Book of Kings described Josiah as Judah's most outstanding monarch (2 Kings 23: 25).

KING MANASSEH
This 15th-century book illustration depicts Manasseh held captive in an Assyrian prison.

CHAPTER 34 VERSE 14
"The Book of the... LORD"
There is debate among scholars whether this book was the entire Pentateuch or just the Book of Deuteronomy. It is probable that Manasseh and Amon, who both worshipped pagan gods, tried to destroy all Judah's sacred texts.

34 JOSIAH[1] WAS EIGHT YEARS OLD when he became king... ³In the eighth year of his reign, while he was still young, he began to seek the God of his father David. In his twelfth year he began to purge Judah and Jerusalem of high places... ⁴Under his direction the altars of the Baals were torn down... These he broke to pieces and scattered over the graves of those who had sacrificed to them. ⁵He *burned the bones* of the priests on their altars... ⁸[Then he began] to repair the temple of the LORD his God... ¹¹[He] gave money to the carpenters and builders to purchase dressed stone, and timber for joists and beams for the buildings that the kings of Judah had allowed to fall into ruin... ¹²The Levites... ¹³had charge of the labourers and supervised all the workers from job to job...

Josiah destroys all Judah's pagan altars

¹⁴While they were bringing out the money that had been taken into the temple of the LORD, Hilkiah the priest found *the Book of the Law of the LORD* that had been given through Moses. [He] ¹⁶took the book to the king... ¹⁹When the king heard the words of the Law, he tore his robes. ²⁰He gave these orders to Hilkiah... ²¹"Go and enquire of the LORD for me... about what is written in this book that has been found..." ²²Hilkiah and those the king had sent with him went to speak to the prophetess Huldah... She lived in Jerusalem, *in the Second District*. ²³She said to them... ²⁴"This is what the LORD says: I am going to bring disaster on this place and its people – all the curses written in the book... ²⁵Because they have forsaken me and burned incense to other gods... ²⁶Tell the king of Judah... ²⁷'Because your heart was responsive and you humbled yourself before God... ²⁸your eyes will not see all the disaster I am going to bring on this place and on those who live here.' "

During temple repairs, the high priest finds the Book of the Law

The king wants to know the meaning of God's Law

The king's officials visit a prophetess

The prophetess says that Judah will be punished for its wickedness

So they took her answer back to the king.

[30][The king] went up to the temple of the LORD [with] all the people from the least to the greatest. He read in their hearing all the words of the Book of the Covenant, which had been found in the temple of the LORD. [31]*The king stood by his pillar* and renewed the covenant [to] follow the LORD and keep his commands... with all his heart and all his soul...

The king gathers together all the people at the temple

Josiah reads from the Book of the Law and then renews the covenant with God

35   [1]Josiah celebrated the Passover to the LORD in Jerusalem [and it] [18]had not been observed like this in Israel since the days of the prophet Samuel...

[20]When Josiah had set the temple in order, Neco king of Egypt went up to fight at Carchemish on the Euphrates, and Josiah marched out to meet him in battle. [21]But Neco sent messengers to him, saying, "What quarrel is there between you and me, O king of Judah? *It is not you I am attacking* at this time, but the house with which I am at war."

Josiah attacked the Egyptian forces. He was seriously wounded in battle and taken back to Jerusalem, where he died. All Judah and Jerusalem mourned him.

UNDERSTANDING THE STORY

Josiah seeks to redress the damage imposed on Judah by the ungodly ways of his father and grandfather. The discovery of the lost book of God's Law becomes the focus for his religious reformation, but his reforms will not endure. Huldah prophesies that Judah is ultimately headed for the same fate as Israel.

✛

CHAPTER 34 VERSE 22
"In the Second District"
Huldah was married to the Temple wardrobe keeper. She lived in a newly developed area between the first and the second walls, in the north-western part of the city. The second wall, the "Broad Wall", was probably built by King Hezekiah when Judah was under attack by Assyria. The wall was later rebuilt by Manasseh (2 Chronicles 33: 14).

THE SECOND WALL
This section of the "Broad Wall" was excavated in the Temple area in 1970–74.

✛

CHAPTER 34 VERSE 31
"The king stood by his pillar"
King Solomon erected two decorated pillars in the portico of the Temple. He named one pillar "Jakin" (he establishes) and the other "Boaz" (in him is strength). The king of Judah traditionally stood by one of the pillars at his anointing and when the people gathered at the Temple for royal speeches or other state occasions.

✛

CHAPTER 35 VERSE 21
"It is not you I am attacking"
Pharaoh Neco ruled Egypt from 610–595 BC. He joined forces with Assyria to oppose the growing power of Babylon. During Josiah's reign, the Assyrian empire was in decline. The Babylonians had conquered Nineveh in 612 BC – one of a series of defeats they had inflicted on the Assyrians. The weakness of Assyria had allowed Judah to expand. Fear of an Assyrian revival was probably the reason why Josiah attacked Neco.

2 CHRONICLES 36, 2 KINGS 25, 2 CHRONICLES 36
THE FALL OF JERUSALEM

THE BABYLONIAN EMPIRE
Chaldean king Nebopolassar defeated Assyria in 612 BC. The new Babylonian empire reached its height in *c.* 600 BC under his son, Nebuchadnezzar, and contained most of Assyria's territories.

✢

CHAPTER 36 VERSE 16
"[They] scoffed at his prophets"
These prophets include Isaiah, Amos, Hosea, and Micah. They all wrote prophetic books warning the kings of the 8th century BC about the consequences of their ungodly ways. Despite the lessons to be learned from the fall of the northern kingdom in 722 BC and Josiah's religious reformation, the last kings of Judah reverted to pagan worship.

KING NEBUCHADNEZZAR
Nebuchadnezzar (605–562 BC) was a cruel but able ruler. He defeated Egypt and formed an alliance with Media. These were his two main opponents. The prophet Jeremiah viewed him as an instrument of God's wrath and advised Judah's kings to submit to his rule rather than face destruction.

NEBUCHADNEZZAR AND JEREMIAH
From a 10th-century Spanish Bible

36 THE[15] LORD, THE GOD OF THEIR FATHERS, sent word to them through his messengers again and again, because he had pity on his people and on his dwelling-place. [16]But they mocked God's messengers, despised his words and *scoffed at his prophets* until the wrath of the LORD was aroused against his people and there was no remedy. He brought up against them [Nebuchadnezzar] the king [of Babylon] **25** [1][who] marched against Jerusalem with his whole army. He encamped outside the city and built siege works all around it. [2]The city was kept under siege until... [3]famine in the city had become so severe that there was no food for the people to eat. [4]Then the city wall was broken through, and the whole army fled at night through the gate between the two walls near the king's garden, though the Babylonians were surrounding the city.

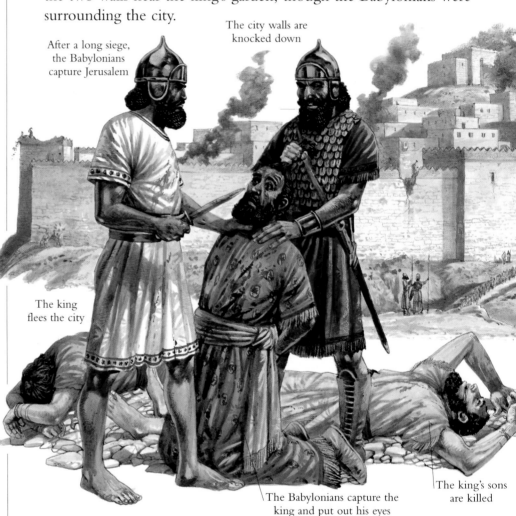

After a long siege, the Babylonians capture Jerusalem

The city walls are knocked down

The king flees the city

The Babylonians capture the king and put out his eyes

The king's sons are killed

They fled towards the Arabah, [5]but the Babylonian army pursued *the king* and overtook him in the plains of Jericho. All his soldiers were separated from him and scattered, [6]and he was captured. He was taken to the king of Babylon at Riblah... [7]They killed [his sons]. Then they put out his eyes, bound him with bronze shackles and took him to Babylon...

[8]Nebuzaradan commander of the imperial guard, an official of the king of Babylon, came to Jerusalem. [9]He set fire to the temple of the LORD, the royal palace and all the houses of Jerusalem. Every important building he burned down. [10]The whole Babylonian army, under the commander of the imperial guard, broke down the walls around Jerusalem. [11]Nebuzaradan the commander of the guard carried into exile the people who remained in the city, along with the rest of the populace and those who had gone over to the king of Babylon. [12]But the commander left behind some of the poorest people of the land to work the vineyards and fields.

The Babylonian army looted the temple and took away everything of value. They even broke up its massive pillars and took the bronze back to Babylon.

The temple is stripped of it treasures, and the city is looted

The Babylonians burn down the temple, the royal palace, and all the buildings in the city

Those in the city are taken captive

The people are taken into exile in Babylon

A few of the poorest people are left behind to work the land

[21]So Judah went into captivity, away from her land...

36   [21]The land *enjoyed its sabbath rests*; all the time of its desolation it rested, until the seventy years were completed in fulfilment of the word of the LORD spoken by Jeremiah.

UNDERSTANDING THE STORY

The exile of Judah and the destruction of Jerusalem and its Temple are God's judgement upon a rebellious people. Yet, through his prophet Jeremiah, God offers hope for the future. Judah's exile from the Promised Land will not be permanent. After seventy years, God will bring his people back from Babylon.

CHAPTER 25 VERSE 5
"The king"
The kings that followed Josiah became vassals of Egypt and then Babylon. This king was Zedekiah, placed on the throne of Judah by Nebuchadnezzar in 597 BC following a rebellion by Zedekiah's nephew, King Jehoiachin. Zedekiah later entered an anti-Babylonian alliance with Edom, Moab, Ammon, Tyre, and Sidon. Nebuchadnezzar retaliated by attacking Judah and laying siege to Jerusalem.

CHAPTER 36 VERSE 21
"Enjoyed its sabbath rests"
This expression, taken from Moses' Law (Leviticus 26), describes Israel's fate should the people ignore God and his commands: "The land will be deserted by them and will enjoy its sabbaths while it lies desolate without them. They will pay for their sins because they rejected my laws and abhorred my decrees."

THE PROPHET JEREMIAH AND THE LAST KINGS OF JUDAH
Jeremiah was a priest and prophet. He prophesied under the last five kings of Judah over a period of forty years – from 626 BC until the fall of Jerusalem (586 BC). Jeremiah supported Josiah in his attempt to reform and renew the religion of Judah, but he faced opposition, persecution, and imprisonment under Josiah's successors. Jeremiah predicted the ruin and deportations of these kings, as well as Jerusalem's fall and the length of Judah's exile in Babylon.

DANIEL 1–2
DANIEL IN BABYLON

CHAPTER 1 VERSE 4
"Qualified to serve"
Nebuchadnezzar chose from among Judah's leading families their most gifted young men to become court officials. This policy effectively eliminated the threat of a potential ruler who might lead a Jewish revolt.

GATEWAY TO BABYLON
The magnificent city of Babylon was built by Nimrod on the River Euphrates, (Genesis 10: 10). Nebuchadnezzar made Babylon the capital of his empire, building the massive Ishtar Gate, shown in the reconstruction above. Decorated with glazed bricks, it was the processional gateway into the city.

1 NEBUCHADNEZZAR[1]... [3]ordered Ashpenaz, chief of his court officials, to bring in some of the Israelites from the royal family and the nobility... [4]*qualified to serve* in the king's palace...

[6]Among these were some from Judah: Daniel, Hananiah, Mishael and Azariah. [7]The chief official gave them new names: to Daniel, the name Belteshazzar; to Hananiah, Shadrach; to Mishael, Meshach; and to Azariah, Abednego...

[17]To these four young men God gave knowledge and understanding of all kinds of literature and learning. And Daniel could understand visions and dreams of all kinds...

2 [1]In the second year of his reign, Nebuchadnezzar had dreams; his mind was troubled and he could not sleep. [2]So the king summoned the magicians, enchanters, sorcerers and astrologers to tell him what he had dreamed... [4]Then the astrologers *answered the king in Aramaic,* "O king, live for ever! Tell your servants the dream, and we will interpret it." [5]The king replied to the astrologers, "This is what I have firmly decided: If you do not tell me what my dream was and interpret it, I will have you cut into pieces and your houses turned into piles of rubble. [6]But if you tell me the dream and explain it, you will receive from me gifts and rewards and great honour..."

[10]The astrologers answered the king, "There is not a man on earth who can do what the king asks!"... [12]This made the king so angry [that he] ordered the execution of all the wise men of Babylon... [13]and men were sent to look for Daniel and his friends to put them to death...

Chief official

King Nebuchadnezzar's chief official presents some men from the Jewish nobility to serve at court

The king

The Jews are given new names

Nebuchadnezzar has a strange dream that troubles him

He asks his wise men what his dream was about and how to interpret it

The wise men find it an impossible task, and the king orders their execution

NEW NAMES
The Hebrew names of Daniel and the other Jews each contained the word "God". A different Babylonian god forms a part of each of their new names. The renaming and specialist training of these young men was an attempt to alienate them from their Jewish heritage.

Daniel sees the dream in a vision

¹⁹During the night the mystery was revealed to Daniel in a vision... ²⁴Then Daniel went to Arioch, whom the king had appointed to execute the wise men of Babylon, and said to him, "Do not execute the wise men... Take me to the king, and I will interpret his dream for him."...

²⁶The king asked Daniel... "Are you able to tell me what I saw in my dream and interpret it?" ²⁷Daniel replied, "No wise man [or magician] can explain to the king the mystery he has asked about, ²⁸but there is a God in heaven who reveals mysteries... ³¹You looked, O king, and there before you stood a large statue... ³²The head of the statue was made of pure gold, its chest and arms of silver, its belly and thighs of bronze, ³³its legs of iron, its feet partly of iron and partly of baked clay... ³⁴A rock was cut out... It struck the statue on its feet of iron and clay and smashed them. ³⁵Then the iron, the clay, the bronze, the silver and the gold were broken to pieces... But the rock that struck the statue became a huge mountain and filled the whole earth...

A statue of gold, silver, bronze, and iron is split apart by a rock

³⁷"You, O King... ³⁸are that head of gold. ³⁹After you, another kingdom will rise, inferior to yours. Next, a third kingdom, one of bronze, will rule over the whole earth. ⁴⁰Finally, there will

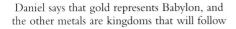

Daniel tells the king his dream and offers to interpret it

be a fourth kingdom, strong as iron... ⁴⁴In the time of those kings, the God of heaven will set up a kingdom that will never be destroyed..." ⁴⁶Then king Nebuchadnezzar fell prostrate before Daniel and paid him honour and ordered that an offering and incense be presented to him... ⁴⁸He made him ruler over the entire province of Babylon and placed him in charge of all his wise men. ⁴⁹Moreover, at Daniel's request the king appointed Shadrach, Meshach and Abednego administrators over the province of Babylon, while Daniel himself remained at the royal court.

The king is amazed

Daniel says that gold represents Babylon, and the other metals are kingdoms that will follow

UNDERSTANDING THE STORY

Daniel in Babylon recalls Joseph in Egypt. Both lived in exile under foreign rulers, and both remained faithful to the God of Israel. Like Joseph, Daniel interprets the king's dreams and rises to a high position in a foreign land. Neither sought greatness, but brought glory to God in the eyes of Gentile rulers.

✥

CHAPTER 2 VERSE 4
"Answered... in Aramaic"
Aramaic, a language close to Hebrew, originated in Aram (Syria). It became the diplomatic language of the Assyrians after they conquered Aram. By Nebuchadnezzar's time, Aramaic was the common language of the Babylonian empire.

TOMBSTONE OF KING UZZIAH
These words are in Aramaic and read: "Hither were brought the bones of Uzziah king of Judah. Not to be opened".

NEBUCHADNEZZAR'S DREAM
The four kingdoms represented by the statue have traditionally been identified as Babylon (gold), Persia (silver), Greece (bronze), and Rome (iron). The increasing endurance of these empires is symbolized by the increasing strength of the metals. The rock that grew into a mountain represents the kingdom of God, which will last forever.

DANIEL 3

NEBUCHADNEZZAR'S FURNACE

"A blazing furnace"
Huge furnaces fired the bricks used by Babylonian builders. The temperature was raised by the use of bellows. In the Bible, fire and the furnace are associated both with divine judgement (Psalm 21: 9) and salvation (Isaiah 43: 2).

MUD BRICK KILN
This kiln was built around the bricks, then covered with mud and fired.

NEBUCHADNEZZAR'S BUILDINGS
Nebuchadnezzar was renowned for his ambitious building projects, which included a massive irrigation system and elaborate temples to his gods. When his wife grew homesick for the hills of her native land, Nebuchadnezzar chose the plains of Babylon to erect his famous "hanging gardens", one of the seven wonders of the ancient world.

Three Jews are thrown into a furnace because they refuse to worship an idol

Nebuchadnezzar is amazed to see the three men walking around in the flames

The king sees a fourth man and knows that God has sent an angel to rescue his servants

3 KING[1] NEBUCHADNEZZAR made an image of gold, ninety feet high and nine feet wide, and set it up on the plain of Dura... [2]He then summoned [all the officials] to come to the dedication of the image he had set up... [8]At this time some astrologers came forward and denounced the Jews. They said to King Nebuchadnezzar... [12]"There are some Jews whom you have set over the affairs of the province of Babylon – Shadrach, Meshach and Abednego – [who] neither serve your gods nor worship the image of gold you have set up." [13]Furious with rage, Nebuchadnezzar summoned Shadrach, Meshach and Abednego [and said to them] [15]"If you do not worship it, you will be thrown immediately into *a blazing furnace...*"

[16][They replied] "O Nebuchadnezzar... [17]if we are thrown into the blazing furnace, the God we serve is able to save us from it..."

[19]Then Nebuchadnezzar... ordered the furnace to be heated seven times hotter than usual... [21]So these men, wearing their robes, trousers, turbans and other clothes, were bound and thrown into the blazing furnace... [24]Then King Nebuchadnezzar leaped to his feet in amazement...

[25]"Look! I see four men walking around in the fire, unbound and unharmed, and the fourth looks like a son of the gods." [26]Nebuchadnezzar [shouted] "Servants of the Most High God, come out! Come here!"... [28]Then Nebuchadnezzar said, "Praise be to [your God], who has sent his angel and rescued his servants!"

An angel appears in the flames

DANIEL 5

THE WRITING ON THE WALL

5 KING[1] BELSHAZZAR gave a great banquet for a thousand of his nobles and drank wine with them... [2]He gave orders to bring in the gold and silver goblets that Nebuchadnezzar his father had taken from the temple in Jerusalem, so that the king and his nobles, his wives and his concubines might drink from them... [4]As they drank the wine, they praised the gods of gold and silver, of bronze, iron, wood and stone.

[5]Suddenly the fingers of a human hand appeared and wrote on *the plaster of the wall*, near the lampstand in the royal palace.

King Belshazzar was terrified. Not one of his wise men could read the inscription. Eventually, they sent for Daniel, who told the king that the writing had appeared because they had used sacred goblets from Jerusalem's temple to praise pagan idols. Daniel told Belshazzar what the writing signified.

[25]"This is the inscription that was written: *MENE, MENE, TEKEL, PARSIN.* [26]This is what these words mean: Mene: God has numbered the days of your reign and brought it to an end. [27]Tekel: You have been weighed on the scales and found wanting. [28]Peres: Your kingdom is divided and given to the Medes and Persians"... [30]That very night *Belshazzar, king of the Babylonians, was slain*, [31]and Darius the Mede took over the kingdom, at the age of sixty-two.

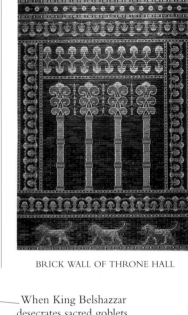

CHAPTER 5 VERSE 5
"The plaster of the wall"
Excavations of the Babylonian palace site revealed a throne hall that was built during the reign of King Nebuchadnezzar. One wall is decorated with blue glazed bricks, and the other walls are white plaster.

BRICK WALL OF THRONE HALL

When King Belshazzar desecrates sacred goblets, mysterious writing appears on the wall

KING BELSHAZZAR
Once derided as a fictional character, Belshazzar has now been identified as the son of Babylon's last king, Nabonidus (556–39 BC). Belshazzar acted as regent in Babylon, while his father spent the final years of his life in Arabia. Belshazzar was Nebuchadnezzar's descendant, as the word "father" often means "ancestor" in the Old Testament.

Only Daniel can interpret the words

He tells the king that his kingdom is about to fall

UNDERSTANDING THE STORIES

God shows that he has not abandoned his people in exile. He guides and protects those who remain true to their faith, and he judges and punishes those who oppose him. The power of Babylon is no challenge to God's authority.

CHAPTER 5 VERSE 30
"Belshazzar... was slain"
Greek historians Herodotus and Xenophon reported that, in 539 BC, the Persians took Babylon in a surprise attack while the King and his nobles were feasting.

DANIEL 6
DANIEL IN THE LIONS' DEN

CHAPTER 6 VERSE 10
"Towards Jerusalem"
When Solomon built the Temple, part of his "Prayer of Dedication" was a special plea for God's people if ever in exile: "If they turn back to you with all their heart and soul in the land of their captivity where they were taken, and pray towards the land that you gave their fathers, towards the city you have chosen and towards the temple that I have built for your Name... hear their prayer and their pleas and uphold their cause" (2 Chronicles 6: 38–39).

THE KING OF THE BEASTS
An Asian species of lion, now extinct, once inhabited many parts of the ancient Middle East. Lion hunting was a favourite sport of the upper classes, especially along the marshy banks of the Tigris and Euphrates rivers. In the royal cities, lions were kept in captivity and bred.

THE LION OF BABYLON
The lion was regarded as a symbol of kingship and power. It was adopted as a motif by the Babylonians. This detail is from a reconstruction of the gateway into Babylon.

6 IT[1] PLEASED DARIUS to appoint 120 satraps to rule throughout the kingdom, [2]with three administrators over them, one of whom was Daniel... [3]Now Daniel so distinguished himself among the administrators and the satraps by his exceptional qualities that the king planned to set him over the whole kingdom. [4]At this, the administrators and the satraps tried to find grounds for charges against Daniel in his conduct of government affairs, but they were unable to do so... [5]Finally these men said, "We will never find any basis for charges against this man Daniel unless it has something to do with the law of his God." [6]So the administrators and the satraps went as a group to the king and said: "O king Darius... the king should issue an edict and enforce the decree that anyone who prays to any god or man during the next thirty days, except to you, O king, shall be thrown into the lions' den..." [9]So King Darius put the decree in writing.

[10]Now when Daniel learned that the decree had been published, he went home to his upstairs room where the windows opened *towards Jerusalem*. Three times a day he got down on his knees and prayed, giving thanks to his God, just as he had done before. [11]Then these men went as a group and found Daniel praying and asking God for help. [12]So they went to the king and spoke to him about his royal decree...

King Darius' officials trick him into sentencing Daniel to death

Daniel breaks an edict that forbids him to pray to God

God prevents the lions from harming Daniel

Daniel is thrown into a den of lions

¹⁴When the king heard this, he was greatly distressed; he was determined to rescue Daniel and made every effort until sundown to save him. ¹⁵Then the men went as a group to the king and said to him, "Remember, O king, that according to the law of the Medes and Persians no decree or edict that the king issues can be changed." ¹⁶So the king gave the order, and they brought Daniel and threw him into the lions' den...

¹⁷A stone was brought and placed over the mouth of the den, and the king sealed it with his own signet ring and with the rings of his nobles, so that Daniel's situation might not be changed...

¹⁹At the first light of dawn, the king got up and hurried to the lions' den... ²⁰He called to Daniel in an anguished voice, "Daniel, servant of the living God, has your God, whom you serve continually, been able to rescue you from the lions?"

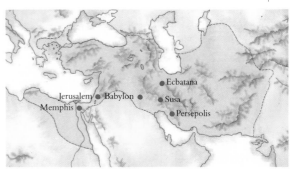

SATRAPS
The Persians developed an efficient system to administer the empire's many provinces. This was based on a network of local governors (satraps).

The next morning, King Darius hurries to the lions' den

Daniel says that God sent an angel to shut the lions' mouths

The king is overjoyed to see Daniel alive

The officials who tricked the king are fed to the lions

²¹Daniel [replied] ²²"My God sent his angel, and he shut the mouths of the lions..."

²³The king was overjoyed and... [at his] ²⁴command, the men who had falsely accused Daniel were brought in and thrown into the lions' den, along with their wives and children.

King Darius issued a decree in honour of the living God of Daniel, asking his people to fear and revere him.

²⁸So Daniel prospered during *the reign of Darius* and the reign of Cyrus the Persian.

CHAPTER 6 VERSE 28
"The reign of Darius"
Daniel was about eighty years old at this time. He died not long after Cyrus began his long reign. So "King Darius" could not be Darius I, who ruled 28 years after Cyrus' death. Some scholars believe that Darius was the throne name of Cyrus in Babylon. Others suggest that Darius was a famous general called Guburu. Cyrus appointed Guburu governor of Persia's largest province, which included Babylonia, Syria, Phoenicia, and Palestine.

UNDERSTANDING THE STORY

Daniel's rise to power does not compromise his integrity. He humbly acknowledges that God is the source of all his blessings. Rather than abandon his faith – even for a short period – Daniel is prepared to lose his position and face death. His faith never waivers, knowing he can rely on God to save him.

PERSIAN ARCHITECTURE
These steps led to the king's reception hall at the palace in Persepolis. The ruins give some idea of its former splendour.

EZRA 1–6

THE TEMPLE IS REBUILT

CHAPTER 1 VERSE 1
"In the first year of Cyrus"
Cyrus ruled Persia from 558–30 BC and was the founder of the greatest empire that the ancient world had yet seen, which began with the conquest of Media in 549 BC. This was the first year of Cyrus' reign in Babylon, which fell in 539.

KING CYRUS
6th-century BC
marble head

CHAPTER 1 VERSE 1
"The word... spoken by Jeremiah"
These words were in a letter that the prophet Jeremiah sent from Jerusalem to the exiles. The first exiles were taken to Babylon by Nebuchadnezzar in 605 BC. Jeremiah wrote: "This is what the LORD says: 'When seventy years are completed for Babylon, I will come to you and fulfil my gracious promise to bring you back to this place' " (Jeremiah 29: 10).

1 IN¹ THE FIRST YEAR *of Cyrus* king of Persia, in order to fulfil *the word of the LORD spoken by Jeremiah*, the LORD moved the heart of Cyrus king of Persia to make a proclamation throughout his realm and to put it in writing. ² "The LORD, the God of heaven, has given me all the kingdoms of the earth and he has appointed me to build a temple for him at Jerusalem in Judah. ³ Anyone of his people among you – may his God be with him, and let him go up to Jerusalem in Judah and build the temple of the LORD..."

⁵ Then the family heads of Judah and Benjamin, and the priests and Levites – everyone whose heart God had moved – prepared to go up and build the house of the LORD in Jerusalem. ⁶ All their neighbours assisted them with articles of silver and gold, with goods and livestock, and with valuable gifts, in addition to all the freewill offerings. ⁷ Moreover, King Cyrus brought out the *articles belonging to the temple* of the LORD, which Nebuchadnezzar had carried away from Jerusalem...

3 ¹ When [the Israelites] had *settled in their towns*, the people assembled as one man in Jerusalem... ² Jeshua son of Jozadak and his fellow priests and Zerubbabel son of Shealtiel and his associates began to build the altar of the God of Israel...

King Cyrus proclaims that the Jews can rebuild the temple in Jerusalem

News of the proclamation spreads, and many Jews prepare to leave for Jerusalem

Treasures belonging to the temple are loaded onto carts

Neighbours give the returning exiles gifts of livestock and other goods

When the temple foundations are laid, the people celebrate and give thanks to God

CHAPTER 1 VERSE 7
"Articles belonging to the temple"
Nebuchadnezzar destroyed the Temple in 586 BC and took its treasures to Babylon, but there is no record of what happened to the Ark. Before this time, Jeremiah had prophesied that the Ark would disappear (Jeremiah 3: 16–17).

CHAPTER 3 VERSE 1
"Settled in their towns"
The return from exile that began in 537 BC continued in several stages for more than a hundred years. More than 42,000 people left Babylon during the first return. But the Jews who remained in exile were far more numerous than those who went back to the land of Judah.

ZERUBBABEL
Zerubbabel, whose name means "offspring of Babylon", was born in captivity. He was a direct descendant of King David and the grandson of Jehoiachin, who Nebuchadnezzar took captive in 605 BC and replaced with a puppet king. Zerubbabel was appointed governor of Judah by Cyrus and became the Jews' spiritual and political leader. He led them from exile in Babylon, as Moses had brought the Israelites out of Egypt.

¹⁰When the builders laid the foundation of the temple of the LORD, the priests in their vestments and with trumpets, and the Levites... with cymbals, took their places to praise the LORD... ¹¹And all the people gave a great shout of praise to the LORD... ¹²But many of the older priests... who had seen the former temple, wept aloud...

4 ⁴Then the peoples around them set out to discourage the people of Judah and make them afraid to go on building. ⁵They hired counsellors to work against them and frustrate their plans during the entire reign of Cyrus king of Persia and down to the reign of Darius king of Persia.

King Darius issued a decree ordering the enemies of the Jews to let the rebuilding take place. All the necessary funds were provided by the royal treasury.

6 ¹⁴So the elders of the Jews continued to build and prosper under the preaching of Haggai the prophet and Zechariah, a descendant of Iddo... ¹⁵The temple was completed on the third day of the month Adar, in the sixth year of the reign of King Darius.

¹⁶Then the people of Israel – the priests, the Levites and the rest of the exiles – celebrated the dedication of the house of God with joy.

UNDERSTANDING THE STORY
The return of the exiles from Babylon recalls the Exodus. Their return is a new beginning in the Promised Land. The Jewish people have had time to consider their mistakes of the past, and they are now given the chance to rebuild their relationship with God. The restoration of a place of worship is very important.

THE CYRUS CYLINDER
This clay cylinder, inscribed with cuneiform writing, commemorates Cyrus' policy of repatriation. Jews were among many peoples taken captive by the Babylonians. Cyrus allowed these nations to return to their homelands, claiming that their gods had appointed him. This gained loyalty from subject nations, and enabled Cyrus to establish an effective system of administration.

ESTHER 1–2

ESTHER AND MORDECAI

CHAPTER 1 VERSE 5
"The king gave a banquet"
Xerxes was celebrating because he had successfully suppressed revolts in Babylonia and Egypt. During the festivities, Xerxes showed off the empire's wealth and power to his vassals.

GOLDEN HORN
An individually crafted gold drinking vessel from the period

CHAPTER 1 VERSE 10
"Seven eunuchs"
Male servants who served in the king's harem were castrated. Eunuchs gained positions of trust and influence in the royal court.

CHAPTER 2 VERSE 5
"The citadel of Susa"
Susa, unbearably hot in summer, was the winter capital of the Persian kings. The citadel was a fortified acropolis at the centre of the city. King Darius I built a magnificent palace there.

THE PALACE GUARD
The glazed-brick walls of Susa's palace were Babylonian in style. This is one of the 10,000-strong palace guard, known as "the immortals". When a guard died, he was immediately replaced.

1 THIS[1] IS WHAT HAPPENED during the time of Xerxes, the Xerxes who ruled over 127 provinces stretching from India to Cush... [3]In the third year of his reign... [5]*the king gave a banquet*, lasting seven days, in the enclosed garden of the king's palace, for all the people from the least to the greatest, who were in the citadel of Susa... [7]Wine was served in goblets of gold, each one different from the other... [9]Queen Vashti also gave a banquet for the women in the royal palace of King Xerxes.

King Xerxes asks Queen Vashti to attend a banquet, but she refuses to come

At the banquet are vassal kings from all over Xerxes' empire

The king is furious and decides to find a new queen

[10]On the seventh day, when King Xerxes was in high spirits from wine, he commanded the *seven eunuchs* who served him... [11]to bring before him Queen Vashti... [12]But when the attendants delivered the king's command, Queen Vashti refused to come. Then the king became furious and burned with anger.

Xerxes was advised by his wise men to depose Vashti and take another queen. The king proclaimed an order to bring the most beautiful girls in Persia to the palace. One of them would become his queen.

2 [5]Now there was in *the citadel of Susa* a Jew of the tribe of Benjamin, named Mordecai son of Jair, the son of Shimei, the son of Kish, [6]who had been carried into exile from Jerusalem by Nebuchadnezzar king of Babylon...

Esther receives beauty treatments

King Xerxes chooses Esther to be his queen

Hegai is in charge of the harem

Esther is one of many beautiful young women who are brought to the palace

CHAPTER 2 VERSE 8
"Under the care of Hegai"
This name appears in ancient records as an official of King Xerxes.

CHAPTER 2 VERSE 9
"Beauty treatments"
To make themselves more attractive, women bathed in aromatic oils, removed body hair, and lightened their skins. They used a variety of cosmetics. Kohl (copper carbonate) and galena (lead sulphide) shadowed the eyes, mulberry juice gave a blush to the cheeks, iron oxide reddened the lips, and crushed henna stained finger and toe-nails.

ARMLET
Rich women wore exquisite gold jewellery. This armlet is decorated with horned griffins, which was a popular motif in Persian art.

⁷Mordecai had a cousin named Hadassah, whom he had brought up because she had neither father nor mother. This girl, who was also known as Esther, was lovely in form and features...

⁸Many girls were brought to the citadel of Susa and put *under the care of Hegai*. Esther also was taken to the king's palace and entrusted to Hegai, who had charge of the harem. ⁹The girl pleased him and won his favour. Immediately he provided her with *beauty treatments* and special foods... ¹⁵And Esther won the favour of everyone who saw her...

¹⁷Now the king was attracted to Esther more than to any of the other women, and she won his favour... So he set a royal crown on her head and made her queen instead of Vashti. ¹⁸And the king gave a great banquet, Esther's banquet...

¹⁹Mordecai was sitting *at the king's gate*. ²⁰But Esther had kept secret her family background and nationality just as Mordecai had told her to do, for she continued to follow Mordecai's instructions as she had done when he was bringing her up.

²¹During the time Mordecai was sitting at the king's gate, Bigthana and Teresh, two of the king's officers who guarded the doorway, became angry and conspired to assassinate King Xerxes. But Mordecai found out about the plot and told Queen Esther, who in turn reported it to the king, giving credit to Mordecai. ²³And when the report was... found to be true, the two officials were hanged on a gallows. All this was recorded in the book of the annals in the presence of the king.

Esther's cousin, Mordecai, overhears a plot to kill Xerxes

CHAPTER 2 VERSE 19
"At the king's gate"
This was the administrative centre of the Susan court. Mordecai, who descended from Jerusalem's nobility, was most probably a high official in the civil service. A cuneiform tablet of the time lists a Susan minister called "Mardukaia", which derives from "Marduk" – the chief god of the Babylonians. "Mordecai" is the Hebrew rendering of the name.

Esther tells the king about the plot, and the conspirators are hanged

ESTHER 3–7

THE DAYS OF PURIM

THE FESTIVAL OF PURIM
Every year, Jews celebrate Purim to commemorate the events in this story. It is a joyful, noisy occasion, during which the Book of Esther is read out loud.

✛

CHAPTER 3 VERSE 1
"Haman… the Agagite"
King Agag was the Amalekite king put to death by the prophet Samuel (1 Samuel: 15). The Amalekites and Israelites had been fierce enemies from the time of the Exodus. In Hezekiah's reign, the Amalekites were defeated by the tribe of Simeon and their land taken (1 Chronicles 4: 39–43). From then on they were a nation of dispossessed people. Haman's Amalekite ancestry would explain his hatred of the Jews.

✛

CHAPTER 3 VERSE 7
"Month of Nisan"
The diaries of the Persian court were drawn up in Nisan, the first month of the year – which fell in March. The Persians were superstitious and believed in fate. Therefore the dates of specific occasions were determined by various methods of divination.

THE KING'S SEAL
The king's word was law. A decree issued in his name and authorized by his seal could not be revoked.

THE ROYAL POST
King Cyrus introduced a swift and efficient postal system. Letters were carried by royal couriers via relays of horses and other animals, kept at allotted stations across the empire.

3 K ING[1] XERXES honoured *Haman… the Agagite,* elevating him… [2]All the royal officials at the king's gate knelt down and paid honour to Haman… [5]When Haman saw that Mordecai would not kneel down or pay him honour, he was enraged. [6]Yet having learned who Mordecai's people were, he scorned the idea of killing only Mordecai. Instead Haman looked for a way to destroy all Mordecai's people, the Jews…

[7]In the… *month of Nisan,* [the royal officials] *cast the pur* (that is, the lot) in the presence of Haman to select a day and month. And the lot fell on the twelfth month.

Haman told the king that some of his subjects were not obeying the laws and asked him to issue a decree to plunder and kill them. Xerxes agreed and gave Haman his royal seal. The edict was posted throughout the empire. When Mordecai heard the news, he sent Esther to beg for mercy.

Mordecai

Haman is outraged when Mordecai refuses to bow to him

Haman

Haman and his officials cast lots to fix a time to kill Mordecai and the whole Jewish nation

5 [1]Esther put on her royal robes and stood in the inner court of the palace… The king was sitting on his royal throne [and he] [2]*held out to her the gold sceptre…* [3]Then the king asked, "What is it, Queen Esther?…" [4]"If it pleases the king," replied Esther, "let the king, together with Haman, come… [8]tomorrow to the banquet I will prepare for them. Then I will answer the king's question."

[9]Haman went out that day happy and in high spirits. But when he saw Mordecai at the king's gate and observed that he neither rose nor showed fear in his presence, he was filled with rage… [14][He decided to] have a gallows built… to have Mordecai hanged on.

That night the king could not sleep, so he ordered the book of records to be read to him. He discovered that Mordecai had not been rewarded for saving his life, so the next day he had him dressed in royal robes and paraded through the streets.

7   ¹So the king and Haman went to dine with Queen Esther. ²The king [asked] "Queen Esther, what is your petition?..." ³Then Queen Esther answered, "If I have found favour with you, O king... spare my people – this is my request. ⁴For I and my people have been sold for destruction and slaughter and annihilation..." ⁵King Xerxes asked Queen Esther, "Who is he? Where is the man who has dared to do such a thing?"

⁶Esther said, "The adversary and enemy is this vile Haman."... ⁹Then Harbona, one of the eunuchs attending the king, said, "A gallows seventy-five feet high stands by Haman's house. He had it made for Mordecai, who spoke up to help the king." The king said, "Hang him on it!" ¹⁰So they hanged Haman on the gallows.

A second decree was issued bearing the king's seal. This allowed the Jews to defend themselves against attack and to destroy their enemies. Supported by the king's officials, the Jews killed all those who acted on Haman's decree.

CHAPTER 3 VERSE 7
"Cast the pur"
The word "pur" appears on a die dating from the reign of Assyrian King Shalmaneser III (858–24 BC). Haman threw dice to determine a day to carry out his plan to massacre the Jews. The Jewish festival of Purim takes its name from the Hebrew plural of "pur".

LOTS
Small stones and ceramic pieces were often used as lots. These lots were found at the Masada Fortress, south of Jerusalem, where the Jews took refuge during their revolt against Rome in AD 70. The Jews decided to die rather than face capture. A name was written on each lot to decide who would kill the others.

Queen Esther arranges a feast for Haman and the king

Esther tells the king of Haman's plan to kill Mordecai and the Jews

The king is indebted to Mordecai for saving his life

The king orders Haman's execution

UNDERSTANDING THE STORY
The Book of Esther is the only book of the Bible that never mentions God by name, but the events in the story convey divine providence at work. Esther's elevation to queen and Mordecai's role in exposing a plot against the king place them in a position to be able to foil Haman's plan to exterminate the Jews.

CHAPTER 5 VERSE 2
"Held out... the gold sceptre"
To approach the king without his summons was punishable by death, unless he held out his sceptre. This protocol protected the king against assassins and maintained his dignity.

NEHEMIAH 1–2
NEHEMIAH GOES TO JERUSALEM

1 THE[1] WORDS OF NEHEMIAH son of Hacaliah... *While I was in the citadel of Susa,* [2]Hanani, one of my brothers, came from Judah with some other men... [3]They said to me, "Those who survived the exile and are back in the province are in great trouble and disgrace. The wall of Jerusalem is broken down, and its gates have been burned with fire." [4]When I heard these things, I sat down and wept... and prayed before the God of heaven. [11]["O LORD,] give your servant success today by granting him favour in the presence of this man." *I was cupbearer to the king...*

2 [1]*In the twentieth year* of King Artaxerxes, when wine was brought for him, I took the wine and gave it to the king. I had not been sad in his presence before; [2]so the king asked me, "Why does your face look so sad when you are not ill? This can be nothing but sadness of heart."

I was very much afraid, [3]but I said to the king, "May the king live for ever! Why should my face not look sad when the city where my fathers are buried lies in ruins... [5]If it pleases the king and if your servant has found favour in his sight, let him *send me to the city in Judah...* so that I can rebuild it."

[6]Then the king, with the queen sitting beside him, asked me, "How long will your journey take, and when will you get back?" It pleased the king to send me; so I set a time. [7]I also said to him, "If it pleases the king, may I have letters to the governors of Trans-Euphrates, so that they will provide me safe-conduct until I arrive in Judah? [8]And may I have a letter to Asaph, keeper of the king's forest, so he will give me timber to make beams for the gates of the citadel by the temple and for the city wall and for the residence I will occupy?" And because the gracious hand of my God was upon me, the king granted my requests... [9]The king had also sent army officers and cavalry with me...

[11]I went to Jerusalem, and after staying there three days [12]I set out during the night with a few men.

CHAPTER 1 VERSE 1
"While I was in... Susa"
Chapters 1–7 and 11–13 of the Book of Nehemiah are written in the first person. The identity of the chronicler is unknown, but Nehemiah's personal account of the times is clearly a major contribution.

CHAPTER 1 VERSE 11
"I was cupbearer to the king"
Nehemiah's privileged, if somewhat precarious, duty was to taste the king's wine to ensure that it was not poisoned. This trusted position gave Nehemiah daily access to the king.

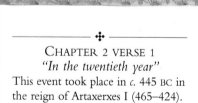

King Artaxerxes sees that his cupbearer is distressed

CHAPTER 2 VERSE 1
"In the twentieth year"
This event took place in *c.* 445 BC in the reign of Artaxerxes I (465–424).

KING ARTAXERXES
Artaxerxes, known as "Longimanus" (long hand), succeeded his father, Xerxes, who was murdered in his bedroom by a court official. King Artaxerxes was tolerant of the Jews, although earlier in his reign he had halted the rebuilding of Jerusalem's walls following a deposition from the nobles in Samaria. They had succeeded in persuading him that a strong Jerusalem would pose a threat to Persia, as the Jews had a history of rebelling against foreign kings.

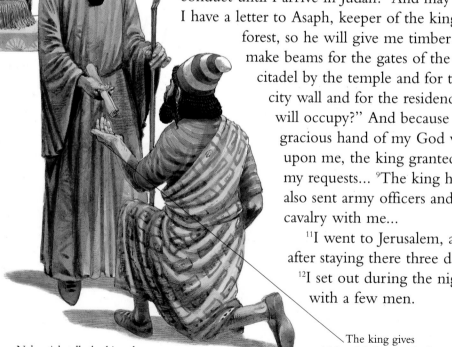

Nehemiah tells the king that Jerusalem is in ruins and asks for permission to go there

The king gives Nehemiah letters of safe-conduct and a military escort for the journey

I had not told anyone what my God had put in my heart to do for Jerusalem. There were no mounts with me except the one I was riding on.

¹³By night I went out through the Valley Gate towards the Jackal Well and the Dung Gate, examining the walls of Jerusalem... ¹⁴Then I moved on towards the Fountain Gate and the King's Pool, but there was not enough room for my mount to get through... ¹⁵Finally, I turned back and re-entered through the Valley Gate...

¹⁷Then I said to them, "You see the trouble we are in: Jerusalem lies in ruins, and its gates have been burned with fire. Come, let us rebuild the wall of Jerusalem, and we will no longer be in disgrace."

¹⁸They replied, "Let us start rebuilding." So they began this good work.

UNDERSTANDING THE STORY

During their years in a foreign land, the Jews reflect upon what happened to their country and the reasons for their exile. This experience brings many back to God. Nehemiah is among those Jews who are committed to rebuilding Jerusalem as the religious and political capital of a new Israel.

CHAPTER 2 VERSE 5
"Send me to the city in Judah"
Shortly after his arrival, Nehemiah was appointed Governor of Judah. He stayed in Jerusalem for twelve years before returning to Susa, a journey that took four months. Artaxerxes later allowed him to return (Nehemiah 13: 6–7).

DUNG GATE
This gate was in the south-western corner of Jerusalem's walls and led out to the Valley of Hinnom, where the city's refuse was burned. The present gate was built in the 16th century.

Nehemiah goes out at night to inspect the walls of Jerusalem

The gates have been burned

Nehemiah says that the Jews must start rebuilding the city

193

NEHEMIAH 4–12
JERUSALEM'S WALLS ARE REBUILT

NEHEMIAH'S OPPONENTS
The threat to stop the restoration of Jerusalem came from all sides. Like Judah, these nations were vassals of Persia. Sanballat was the governor of Samaria and Nehemiah's chief enemy. Samaritans also worshipped God and had offered to help rebuild the Temple. But the Jews had refused their help because the Samaritans were of mixed race.

4 ^{6}So we rebuilt the wall till all of it reached half its height, for the people worked with all their heart. ^{7}But when Sanballat, Tobiah, the Arabs, the Ammonites and the men of Ashdod heard that the repairs to Jerusalem's walls had gone ahead and that the gaps were being closed, they were very angry. ^{8}They all plotted together to come and fight against Jerusalem and stir up trouble against it...

^{13}Therefore I stationed some of the people behind the lowest points of the wall at the exposed places, posting them by families, with their swords, spears and bows... ^{15}When our enemies heard that we were aware of their plot and that God had frustrated it, we all returned to the wall, each to his own work.

^{16}From that day on, half of my men did the work, while the other half were equipped with spears, shields, bows and armour... ^{17}Those who carried materials did their work with one hand and held a weapon in the other, ^{18}and each of the builders wore his sword at his side as he worked. But the man who sounded the trumpet stayed with me.

The walls were completed in only fifty-two days. Judah's enemies were afraid and lost their will to fight, because they realised that God was on Judah's side.

A lookout carries a trumpet

Guards are posted

When Nehemiah starts to rebuild Jerusalem's walls, Judah's enemies try to disrupt their efforts

The builders work with swords at their sides

When the walls are finished, the Jews hold a ceremony of dedication

Ezra reads from the Book of the Law

The people bow down and worship God

"Ezra the scribe"

Ezra was both a priest and a scribe. He returned from exile in 458 BC, after the Temple was rebuilt. Scribes were royal secretaries, but during the exile they became scholars – later called "rabbis" – who studied and taught Moses' Law. Both Ezra and Nehemiah believed that the depleted Jewish nation would not survive unless it remained pure, and intermarriage was forbidden. Many Jews divorced their foreign wives.

ARAMEAN SCRIBES
In this detail from an 8th-century BC wall relief, one scribe writes on papyrus, while another writes on a clay tablet.

CHAPTER 8 VERSE 12
"They now understood the words"
Artaxerxes supported Ezra's desire to teach Moses' Law to the Jews, and he insisted that they should be accountable to a court for any transgressions. In this way, the might of the Persian empire backed a God-centred system of law in Judah.

ANCIENT CYMBALS
These cymbals date from *c.* 2100 BC. When Levites sang psalms in the Temple, they used cymbals to mark pauses and the beginnings and ends of chapters.

Cast bronze handle

8   ¹All the people assembled as one man in the square before the Water Gate. They told *Ezra the scribe* to bring out the Book of the Law of Moses, which the LORD had commanded for Israel... ⁴Ezra the scribe stood on a high wooden platform built for the occasion... ⁵Ezra opened the book [and] ⁶praised the LORD, the great God; and all the people lifted their hands and responded, "Amen! Amen!" Then they bowed down and worshipped the LORD with their faces to the ground.

⁷The Levites... ⁸read from the Book of the Law of God, making it clear and giving the meaning so that the people could understand what was being read... ¹²Then all the people went away to eat and drink, to send portions of food and to celebrate with great joy, because *they now understood the words* that had been made known to them...

12   ²⁷At the dedication of the wall of Jerusalem, the Levites were... brought to Jerusalem to celebrate joyfully the dedication with songs of thanksgiving and with the music of cymbals, harps and lyres.

UNDERSTANDING THE STORY

Nehemiah responds to the plight of the Jews who have returned to Jerusalem. His faith and commitment lifts them from despondency and restores national pride. Jerusalem's new walls bring protection and separation, and the dedication ceremony marks a new era of understanding between God and his people.

PRAISE, WISDOM, AND PROPHECY

The last 22 books of the Old Testament are grouped as "Poetry and Wisdom" and "Prophets". The first five of these (Job, Psalms, Proverbs, Ecclesiastes, and Song of Songs) make up the "Poetry and Wisdom" section. This can also be divided into "Words of Praise" and "Words of Wisdom". The last seventeen books record the lives and works of Israel's major prophets.

The 22 books vary in content, but almost all of them have one element in common – their use of poetry. Over a third of the Old Testament texts were written as poetry. Unfortunately, much of its original subtlety is lost in translation. Hebrew poetic features include rhythm, repetition of sentences, similarity of sounds, and wordplay on such things as the meanings of names. These literary devices helped the reader to memorize the texts. Hebrew poetry is rich in imagery, and the biblical writers used this to convey the deepest human feelings and to express the power of spiritual experience.

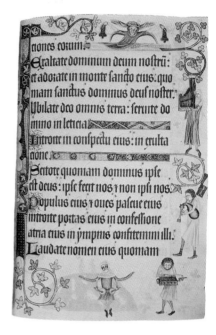

THE LUTTRELL PSALTER
Illustrated Latin text from a
14th-century collection
of psalms

PRAISE

The Book of Psalms is a collection of 150 poems and prayers. In Hebrew literature it is called "Book of Praises", reflecting its content. These psalms date from Moses' time until the period following the Jews' return from exile in Babylon. Another name for the book is "Psalter", from the Greek title meaning "songs accompanied by the harp". Nearly half the collection is attributed to King David, who was an accomplished harpist.

There are psalms both for the individual and the community, and they express the hopes and fears of the Israelite people. The book therefore gives a better understanding of Israel's spirituality during the ups and downs of its eventful history.

Jesus made many of these psalms his own prayers and quoted them often.

"I WILL PRAISE YOU WITH THE HARP, O GOD"
The words of Psalm 43 are illustrated in the 9th-century Stuttgart Psalter. A Psalter came to mean an illustrated book of psalms.

Psalms in Jewish worship

The final editing of the psalms is traditionally credited to Ezra, who reshaped religious practice in Jerusalem after the exile in the 5th century BC. The Book of Psalms is divided into five sections, which parallels the Torah, the first five books of the Hebrew Bible. Most of the psalms have a title. This gives details about the author or dedication, the occasion for which it was written, and instructions for musical accompaniment.

Psalms were usually sung or chanted alternately by two choirs, or a choir and the congregation, during religious ceremonies.

WISDOM

The books of Job, Proverbs, and Ecclesiastes are known as the "Wisdom Books". Wisdom literature was common in the ancient Middle East. Thousands of short sayings, like the proverbs, were circulated between Egypt and Mesopotamia and the lands further east. These sayings were created or collected by wise men, who were often sponsored by royal courts.

These wise men also wrote monologues or dialogues about specific human questions, such as the meaning of existence or the reason for suffering. The best-known example is the Egyptian "Instructions of Amenemope", from the first millennium BC, which is very similar to the Book of Proverbs. Many of the Israelite scholars were familiar with wisdom literature from other cultures. This is reflected in the fact that the Wisdom Books are the most cosmopolitan in the Old Testament.

Song of Songs

The Song of Songs is a love poem about a country girl, who sees her lover, a shepherd, as a dashing king. The poem's rich and sensuous imagery reflects the life and landscape of Palestine. The poem is thought to symbolize God's love for his people. Its Hebrew title means "greatest of songs".

The book is also known as "Canticles", from the Latin, "Canticum Canticorum", for "Song of Songs". The voice of love is a woman's voice. However, the poem is traditionally attributed to Solomon, which is why it is often called "Song of Solomon".

SOLOMON AND THE QUEEN OF SHEBA
An illuminated letter from the Song of Songs (Winchester Bible, c. 1165)

The suffering of Job

The Book of Job is about faith in God and the role of suffering. Satan challenges God, claiming that Job, a righteous, happy, and successful man, will reject God if his blessings are taken away.

Satan inflicts ever increasing troubles on Job, who loses his family, his possessions, and his health. He never loses his faith in God, but he is forced to question his own righteousness. Job cannot understand how God could allow the just and innocent to suffer, while evil often appears to prosper, and he curses the day he was born.

God finally speaks to Job, who is given an insight into God's infinite grace and wisdom. Job realizes that it is faith, not understanding, that is important.

JOB MOCKED BY HIS WIFE, painting by Georges de la Tour (1593–1652)

Proverbs

The Book of Proverbs is made up of nine collections of sayings by wise men and women. These people played a major role in Israelite society. They gave advice to kings and instructed the young on how to behave wisely in all circumstances in order to lead moral lives.

The underlying theme of the book is that the good will be rewarded and that the wicked will be punished. There is an emphasis on neighbourliness and its benefit to the entire community, especially where individuals are in need of help.

DRUNKARDS (3RD-CENTURY MOSAIC) "Wine is a mocker and beer a brawler" (Proverbs 20: 1).

Ecclesiastes

Ecclesiastes is a book that reflects on the meaning of life and human existence. Some scholars attribute the work to King Solomon. Its Hebrew title, "The Book of Koheleth", implies that the author is a preacher. "Ecclesiastes" is Greek for a teacher who speaks to an assembly.

The book's message is that life is ephemeral; it has no purpose or meaning when God is not at its centre.

The author concludes that life is often unfair, but that it is meant to be enjoyed, not endured. People are assured that God is the ultimate judge, and those who keep faith in him have nothing to fear.

PROPHECY

Throughout the Old Testament, a succession of charismatic preachers, called prophets, foretold God's purpose for the people of Israel.

Prophets often predicted dire punishment when the people turned away from God. They were not always heeded and were often persecuted. But the prophets also promised God's ultimate grace in the coming of a saviour, the Messiah.

The prophets came from various walks of life: Amos was a shepherd, Ezekiel a priest, and Isaiah was from an aristocratic background. Many are anonymous. The prophets who were given a book in the Bible are known as the "writing prophets". Often their message was recorded many years after their time.

A TIME TO PLANT This 15th-century rural scene from the Duc de Berry's Book of Hours illustrates the idea that "for everything there is a season" (Ecclesiastes 3: 1–2).

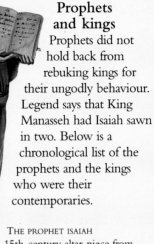

Prophets and kings

Prophets did not hold back from rebuking kings for their ungodly behaviour. Legend says that King Manasseh had Isaiah sawn in two. Below is a chronological list of the prophets and the kings who were their contemporaries.

THE PROPHET ISAIAH 15th-century altar-piece from Colmar, northern France

Date	Prophet	King
1050–10	SAMUEL	Saul
		David
	NATHAN★	David
		Solomon
870–852	ELIJAH★	Ahab
		Ahaziah
855–798	ELISHA★	Joram
		Jehu
		Jehoahaz
		Jehoash
		Joash
760–750	AMOS	Jeroboam II
760–750	JONAH	Jeroboam II
760–722	HOSEA	Jeroboam II
		Hoshea

722 BC: fall of the northern kingdom of Israel

740–680	ISAIAH	Uzziah
		Jotham
		Ahaz
		Hezekiah
		Manasseh
740–687	MICAH	Uzziah
		Jotham
		Ahaz
		Hezekiah
640–610	ZEPHANIAH	Josiah
630–612	NAHUM	Josiah
626–587	JEREMIAH	Josiah
		Jehoahaz
		Jehoiakim
		Jehoiachin
		Zedekiah
600	HABAKKUK	Jehoiakim

586 BC: fall of Judah

604–535	DANIEL	
592–570	EZEKIEL	
587	OBADIAH	
520	HAGGAI	
520	ZECHARIAH	
450	MALACHI	
DATE UNKNOWN	JOEL	

All dates are BC
★ This indicates that the prophet does not have a book in the Bible.

PSALMS 1, 8, 23, 121

WORDS OF PRAISE

PSALM 1
This introductory psalm establishes themes that recur throughout the whole book – those of devotion, thanksgiving, and unwavering faith in God. The author is unknown.

✤

CHAPTER 1 VERSE 1
"Blessed is the man"
The message is that only those who follow the path of righteousness will ultimately be blessed by God.

The good will prosper like trees planted by water

✤

CHAPTER 1 VERSE 2
"On his law he meditates"
In ancient Israel, the Law was studied every day. An intimate knowledge of the Law was a way of getting closer to God.

PSALM 8
This psalm, written by King David, celebrates humankind's dominion over the earth. The psalm is a reflection on God's greatness and recognizes humankind's insignificance when compared to the glory of God's creation.

✤

CHAPTER 8 VERSE 2
"The lips of children and infants"
This phrase underlines the father-child relationship between humans and their creator. God is the source of all human potential.

1 BLESSED[1] IS THE MAN who does not walk in the counsel of the wicked or stand in the ways of sinners or sit in the seat of mockers.
[2]But his delight is in the law of the LORD,
and *on his law he meditates* day and night.
[3]He is like a tree planted by streams of water,
which yields its fruit in season and whose leaf does not wither.
Whatever he does prospers.
[4]Not so the wicked! They are like chaff that the wind blows away.
[5]Therefore the wicked will not stand in the judgment,
nor sinners in the assembly of the righteous.
[6]For the LORD watches over the way of the righteous,
but the way of the wicked will perish.

The wicked are like chaff in the wind

God gives humankind dominion over his creation

8 [1]O LORD, OUR LORD,
how majestic is your name in all the earth!
You have set your glory above the heavens.
[2]From *the lips of children and infants*
you have ordained praise...
[3]When I consider your heavens, the work of your fingers,
the moon and the stars, which you have set in place,
[4]what is man that you are mindful of him,
the son of man that you care for him?
[5]You made him a little lower than the heavenly beings
and crowned him with glory and honour.
[6]You made him ruler over the works of your hands;
you put everything under his feet:
[7]all flocks and herds, and the beasts of the field,
[8]the birds of the air, and the fish of the sea,
all that swim the paths of the seas.

God is the good shepherd,
who watches over his flock

People need fear no evil

23 ¹THE LORD IS MY SHEPHERD, I shall not be in want.
²He makes me lie down in green pastures,
he leads me beside quiet waters,
³he restores my soul.
He guides me in paths of righteousness for his name's sake.
⁴Even though I walk through the valley of the shadow of death,
I will fear no evil, for you are with me;
your rod and your staff, they comfort me.
⁵You prepare a table before me in the presence of my enemies.
You anoint my head with oil, my cup overflows.
⁶Surely goodness and love will follow me all the days of my life,
and I will dwell in the house of the LORD for ever.

121 ¹I LIFT UP MY EYES TO THE HILLS – where does
my help come from?
²My help comes from the LORD, the Maker
of heaven and earth.
³He will not let your foot slip – he who
watches over you will not slumber;
⁴indeed, he who watches over Israel will
neither slumber nor sleep.
⁵The LORD watches over you – *the LORD is
your shade* at your right hand;
⁶The sun will not harm you by day, nor the
moon by night.
⁷The LORD will keep you from all harm – he will
watch over your life;
⁸the LORD will watch over your coming and
going both now and for evermore.

God protects his creation

PSALM 23
David's psalm is a joyful proclamation of God's providence. Humankind can live free from fear because, like the good shepherd, God will always provide, protect, and guide his flock.

CHAPTER 23 VERSE 5
"You anoint my head with oil"
When a king made a covenant with a vassal, he often sealed it by holding a banquet. During the festivities, it was customary to anoint the head of his guests with oil as a sign of friendship and protection.

PSALM 121
This is the second in a collection of fifteen psalms called "Songs of Ascents". Tradition suggests that these psalms were sung during the annual religious pilgrimages to Jerusalem. God is presented as a companion and guardian of his people.

CHAPTER 121 VERSE 5
"The LORD is your shade"
Just as a shadow never leaves a person, so the Lord remains with his people. And just as shade shelters people from excessive heat, so God sustains and protects those who depend on him.

PROVERBS 3, 9, 10, 11, 15, 17, 25, 26, 27, 30

WORDS OF WISDOM

Wisdom is personified as a woman. She is a tree of life to those who embrace her

---
❖

CHAPTER 3 VERSE 18
"She is a tree of life"
Wisdom is a life-giving source, because it leads people towards a proper relationship with God. In ancient Middle-Eastern literature, the flourishing tree was a common metaphor for continuing blessings.

❖

CHAPTER 9 VERSE 10
"The fear of the LORD is the beginning of wisdom"
Israel's wise men believed that the basis of true wisdom was "fear of God", which means reverence rather than terror. People should worship their God and live their lives according to his Law. Without this "fear", wisdom fails to bring people closer to their creator.

Benefits of wisdom

3 LET[3] LOVE AND faithfulness never leave you; bind them around your neck, write them on the tablet of your heart. [4]Then you will win favour and a good name in the sight of God and man.

[13]BLESSED IS THE man who finds wisdom, the man who gains understanding, [14]for she is more profitable than silver and yields better returns than gold. [15]She is more precious than rubies; nothing you desire can compare with her. [16]Long life is in her right hand; in her left are riches and honour. [17]Her ways are pleasant ways, and all her paths are peace. [18]*She is a tree of life* to those who embrace her; those who lay hold of her will be blessed.

9 [10]THE FEAR OF *the* LORD *is the beginning of wisdom*, and knowledge of the Holy One is understanding.

The Proverbs of Solomon

10 [11]THE MOUTH OF the righteous is a fountain of life, but violence overwhelms the mouth of the wicked.

[12]HATRED STIRS UP dissension, but love covers over all wrongs.

11 [1]THE LORD ABHORS dishonest scales, but accurate weights are his delight.

[2]WHEN PRIDE COMES, then comes disgrace, but with humility comes wisdom.

[22]LIKE A GOLD ring in a pig's snout is a beautiful woman who shows no discretion.

[27]HE WHO SEEKS good finds goodwill, but evil comes to him who searches for it.

15 [17]BETTER A MEAL of vegetables where there is love than a fattened calf with hatred.

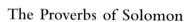

The righteous are like a fountain of life

Children share a simple meal

Love in the home is more important than wealth

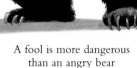

17   ¹²BETTER TO MEET a bear robbed of her cubs than a fool in his folly.

25   ²¹IF YOUR ENEMY *is hungry*, give him food to eat; if he is thirsty, give him water to drink. ²²In doing this, you will heap burning coals on his head, and the LORD will reward you.

A person who lacks self control is like a ruined city

The wise are kind to their enemies

A fool is more dangerous than an angry bear

²⁸LIKE A CITY whose walls are broken down is a man who lacks self-control.

26   ¹¹AS A DOG returns to its vomit, so a fool repeats his folly.

¹³THE SLUGGARD SAYS, "There is a lion in the road, a fierce lion roaming the streets!"

²²THE WORDS OF a gossip are like choice morsels; they go down to a man's inmost parts.

The lazy will claim there is a lion outside to avoid going out

27   ¹⁹AS WATER REFLECTS a face, so a man's heart reflects the man.

Sayings of Agur

30   ¹⁷THE EYE THAT mocks a father, that scorns obedience to a mother, will be pecked out by the ravens of the valley, will be eaten by the vultures.

²⁴FOUR THINGS ON earth are small, yet they are extremely wise:

²⁵Ants are creatures of little strength, yet they store up their food in the summer;

²⁶conies are creatures of little power, yet they make their home in the crags; ²⁷locusts have no king, yet they advance together in ranks; ²⁸a lizard can be caught in the hand, yet it is found in kings' palaces.

The humble lizard can be found in a king's palace

UNDERSTANDING THE PROVERBS

The Book of Proverbs uses a down-to-earth philosophy, often delivered in a humorous way, to give people practical advice on how to live a moral life. The proverbs imply that religion and life are inextricable. Wisdom can only lead to happiness if it is based on a reverence for God and his Law.

THE PROVERBS OF SOLOMON

King Solomon was renowned for his wisdom, and his court became an international centre of learning. Much of the wisdom literature has been attributed to him. The Bible says that "he spoke three thousand proverbs; and his songs were a thousand and five" (1 Kings 2: 23).

THE SAYINGS OF AGUR

Agur learned humility by observing the wonders of nature. He was probably an Ishmaelite from Arabia, and his sayings reflect the wisdom of the East. The people of Israel acknowledged words of wisdom, whatever their source, as long as their essence was in accordance with God's Law.

        ❖

CHAPTER 25 VERSE 21

"If your enemy is hungry"

Many proverbs stress the importance of being a good neighbour. This extends even to those who are hostile. If people repay enmity with acts of kindness, tension and strife in the community can be avoided.

THE USE OF WORDS

The proverbs rely on short, sharp phrases for effect. Words are used economically, "the fewer the better". There is also great stress on the power of the word, both written and spoken. Words can be used both for good and evil, and their effect should not be underestimated. A major theme in the book is that listening leads to wisdom, whereas chatter and gossip are for fools.

MALACHI 1–4

WORDS OF PROPHECY

Biblical scholars have placed this prophet as living *c.* 450 BC, during the post-exilic period. At this time, Israel was an economically depressed, weak vassal state. Malachi (Hebrew for "my messenger") delivered God's message to a nation whose expectations of a new kingdom of Jerusalem had not been fulfilled.

Malachi delivers God's message to an apathetic Israel

The jackals will inherit the home-land of the Edomites

CHAPTER 1 VERSES 2–3
"I have loved Jacob, but Esau I have hated"
This expression refers to when God made his covenant with Jacob (the Israelite's ancestor) and rejected Jacob's brother, Esau (the forefather of the Edomites). At this time, the Edomites seemed to be benefiting from Israel's ruin. Malachi promises that God will punish the Edomites. This prophecy was fulfilled by 400 BC, when the Nabatean Arabs forced the Edomites to leave their homeland and resettle in southern Palestine, an area later called Idumea.

CHAPTER 1 VERSE 8
"Try offering them to your governor!"
Malachi highlights the lack of respect the priests are showing God, their sovereign Lord. He asks whether they would dare to give damaged offerings to the Persian governor, their foreign oppressor.

1 AN[1] ORACLE: the word of the LORD to Israel through Malachi. [2]"I have loved you," says the LORD.

"But you ask, 'How have you loved us?'"

"Was not Esau Jacob's brother?" the LORD says. "Yet *I have loved Jacob,* [3]*but Esau I have hated*, and I have turned his mountains into a wasteland and left his inheritance to the desert jackals."

[4]Edom may say, "Though we have been crushed, we will rebuild the ruins."

But this is what the LORD Almighty says: "They may build, but I will demolish...

[6]"A son honours his father... If I am a father, where is the honour due to me?... It is you, O priests, who show contempt for my name...

[8]When you sacrifice crippled or diseased animals, is that not wrong? *Try offering them to your governor!*...

[14]"Cursed is the cheat who has an acceptable male in his flock and vows to give it, but then sacrifices a blemished animal to the LORD. For I am a great king," says the LORD Almighty, "and my name is to be feared among the nations..."

2 [11]Judah has broken faith. A detestable thing has been committed in Israel and in Jerusalem: Judah has desecrated the sanctuary the LORD loves, by marrying the daughter of a foreign god... [17]You have wearied the LORD with your words... By saying, "All who do evil are good in the eyes of the LORD, and he is pleased with them" or "Where is the God of Justice?"

3 [1]"See, I will send my messenger, who will prepare the way before me. Then suddenly *the LORD you are seeking will come* to his temple; the messenger of the covenant, whom you desire, will come," says the LORD Almighty.

God is angry because the Israelites offer him imperfect sacrifices

²But who can endure the day of his coming? Who can stand when he appears?... ³He will sit as a refiner and purifier of silver; he will purify the Levites and refine them like gold and silver. Then the LORD will have men who will bring offerings in righteousness...

Elijah will return before the judgement day

God urges the Israelites to follow the Laws he gave to Moses

The evil will be judged and burn like stubble

The good will receive salvation

⁶"I the LORD do not change. So you, O descendants of Jacob, are not destroyed... ⁷Return to me, and I will return to you..."

4 ¹"*Surely the day is coming*; it will burn like a furnace. All the arrogant and every evildoer will be stubble, and that day that is coming will set them on fire... ²But for you who revere my name, the sun of righteousness will rise with healing in its wings...

⁴"Remember the law of my servant Moses, the decrees and laws I gave him at Horeb for all Israel.

⁵"See, *I will send you the prophet Elijah* before that great and dreadful day of the LORD comes. ⁶He will turn the hearts of the fathers to their children, and the hearts of the children to their fathers; or else I will come and strike the land with a curse."

UNDERSTANDING THE STORY

Malachi confronts a Jewish community that has lapsed into apathy. His words are spoken to reawaken faith in God's people and to remind them that their dissolute state is a result of their own religious lethargy, not because God has deserted them. But Malachi offers them hope by reaffirming God's promise of a Messiah.

CHAPTER 3 VERSE 1
"The LORD... will come"
Malachi reassures the disillusioned Israelites that their expectation of a Messiah will be fulfilled.

CHAPTER 4 VERSE 1
"Surely the day is coming"
God promises a day of judgement on earth through the ministry of the Messiah. The good will find salvation and evil will be destroyed.

CHAPTER 4 VERSE 5
"I will send... Elijah"
God will send a prophet to prepare for the coming of the Messiah. This prophet is the new Elijah – later identified in the New Testament as John the Baptist (Matthew 11: 17).

MOSES AND ELIJAH
Moses and Elijah were two of Israel's most important historic figures. Both appear before the three apostles at Jesus' transfiguration. Moses was Israel's greatest leader and law-giver, and Elijah was the representative of the prophets.

THE NEW TESTAMENT

"FOR GOD SO LOVED THE WORLD
that he gave his one and only Son, that
whoever believes in him shall not perish
but have eternal life."

JOHN 3: 16

THE NEW TESTAMENT

The New Testament is a collection of writings by the apostles, who witnessed the birth of the Christian Church nearly 2,000 years ago. Jesus did not leave any writings, but some of the apostles who followed him during his ministry, or received testimonies about him after his death, kept a record of Jesus' life and the spread of Christianity. The New Testament contains 27 books of their writings. Not all of these were officially recognized by the Church until the 4th century AD.

The main events in Jesus' life and ministry took place in Palestine, around Galilee and Judea. The apostles' missionary journeys extended throughout the lands of the Mediterranean.

AERIAL VIEW OF GALILEE

STRUCTURE OF THE NEW TESTAMENT

This collection of books is divided into three sections: the Gospels, the Acts, and the Epistles. The Gospels record the life and teachings of Jesus, the Book of Acts describes the origins of the Church, and the Epistles present the beginnings of Christian teachings.

The Gospels

"Gospel" is the English translation of the Greek word "euangelion", which means "good news". The Gospels proclaim the good news that Jesus was the long-awaited Messiah. They were written over a period of about fifty years. The four Gospels of Matthew, Mark, Luke, and John were collated by the early Church and circulated towards the end of the 1st century. Each one presents the life of Jesus from a different perspective.

The Acts

Luke also wrote a sequel to his Gospel, the Acts of the Apostles. This is a record of the first thirty years of the early Church and covers the period from the ascension of Jesus Christ to Paul's ministry in Rome. The Book of Acts describes in detail the missionary work of the apostles and other disciples. It also gives an account of the problems that the early Church encountered.

The Epistles

The New Testament contains 22 letters. Some of these are addressed to communities of people, some to individuals, and some are general letters. Paul is traditionally believed to have written thirteen of them. Eight are by the apostles John, Jude, James, and Peter, and one is anonymous. The Epistles give instructions and encouragement to the early churches.

THE APOSTLE PAUL
Paul at his writing desk, painting by Rembrandt (1630)

JEWISH WORSHIP IN THE TIME OF JESUS

After the Israelites were exiled to Babylon (c. 586 BC) and their Temple was destroyed, they began to worship in sanctuaries. These became known as "synagogues". This name derives from the Greek word "sunagoge" which means "assembly" or "gathering". The Jewish people (Israelites) met in the synagogues to pray and to listen to the reading of scriptures.

In about 537 BC, when the Babylonian empire had fallen to the Persians, the Jews were allowed to return to Judah. However, many Jews did not return and dispersed throughout the areas controlled by the Persians. This led to synagogues being built throughout the Mediterranean and ancient Middle East.

By Jesus' day, the Temple had been rebuilt twice. It was still used as a place of prayer and for celebrating the main Jewish festivals, such as the Passover. The Jewish people re-established the priesthood and resumed the practice of sacrificial offerings.

SYNAGOGUE, CAPERNAUM (c. AD 200–300)

Synagogues

In New Testament times, synagogues consisted of two main rooms: the court and the basilica. These were separated from each other by a vestibule. On one wall of the synagogue was an apse (a semi-circular niche), which contained an ark where the scrolls of the Law were kept. Synagogue meetings were led by elders. One of these elders, the chief officer, supervised the services and taught children how to read. Men and women sat separately during the services.

THE GOSPELS

The first three Gospels (Matthew, Mark, and Luke) contain a great deal of similar information and are known as the "Synoptic" Gospels. They all describe Jesus' ministry in Galilee and then his journey to Jerusalem. John's Gospel, however, has very little in common with the other three. It describes a longer ministry in Judea and emphasizes the spiritual aspects of Jesus' ministry.

The Gospels are not intended to be a comprehensive history of the life of Jesus, but aim to provide a clear understanding of his ministry. Each Gospel highlights different aspects of Jesus' work and sometimes places events in a different chronological order, such as Jesus' cleansing of the Temple (John 2: 13–22). The Gospel of Mark was probably written first (*c.* AD 60–70), Matthew and Luke followed fifteen to twenty years later. John's Gospel is also thought to have been written towards the end of the 1st century.

Matthew

The author of this Gospel is believed to be the apostle Matthew, formerly a tax collector from Capernaum (Matthew 9: 9). This Gospel often uses Jewish terminology and portrays Jesus as the fulfilment of the Old Testament prophecies. However, Matthew also violently attacks the Jewish leaders (particularly the Pharisees). Matthew's account contains little narrative as its main purpose is to teach.

JESUS CLEANSING THE TEMPLE
Painting by Bruegel (1556)

John

John is traditionally believed to be the apostle John "whom Jesus loved". His Gospel focuses on Jesus' divinity and does not contain parables. John often uses symbolic opposites, such as light and dark, to illustrate his message. According to John, Jesus' ministry takes place over three years, as he mentions three Passover feasts.

CHRIST AND THE FOUR SAINTS BY THOMAS ROOKE (1842–1942)
Christ appears in the centre panel. To his left are Matthew and Mark, and to his right are Luke and John.

Mark

Mark's Gospel is the shortest account. The author has been identified as John Mark (Acts 12: 12), who worked with Paul, Barnabas, and Peter. It is written for a non-Jewish audience and explains many of the Jewish customs and words. It has a strong narrative element and makes reference to the experiences of Peter, James, and John, who all witnessed much of Jesus' ministry.

Luke

Luke, a doctor, was the companion of Paul (Colossians 4: 14). Luke's account is presented in the form of a biography of Jesus' dealings with people. It is the longest of the four accounts and describes Jesus' journey from Galilee to Jerusalem in some detail. Luke records Jesus' teaching and healing and emphasizes his compassion for the poor and needy.

Christian Holy days

After Jesus' death, his disciples continued to observe Jewish feasts and festivals. However, there was a gradual move away from these celebrations. To the apostles, the Israelite law, rituals, and festivals were no longer necessary. The apostle Paul states this in his letters to the Colossians (2: 16–17). However, even in the very early days of the Church, Christians commemorated the events that led to the birth of Christianity.

CHRISTIAN HOLY DAYS

Sunday
Sunday is a Holy day of rest for Christians. It commemorates the day that Christ rose from the dead, which is recorded in the Gospels to be the first day of the week. It is also known as the "Lord's Day".

Epiphany
Most Christians celebrate Epiphany on the 6th of January. It recalls the birth of Jesus and the visit of the Magi.

Lent
Lent is a forty-day period of penance that ends on Easter Sunday. It is a time when Christians prepare for Easter and serves as a reminder of Jesus' forty days in the wilderness. Some Christians observe Lent by fasting.

Easter Week
Easter commemorates the events leading up to Jesus' death and resurrection.

Palm Sunday is the first day of Holy Week. It recalls Jesus' entry into Jerusalem, when people lined the streets with palm leaves.

Maunday Thursday celebrates Jesus' last meal with his disciples, his arrest, and imprisonment.

Good Friday commemorates Jesus' crucifixion.

Easter Sunday observes Jesus' resurrection. It falls on the first Sunday after the full moon on or after March 21st. Orthodox churches date it differently.

Pentecost
This commemorates the apostles receiving the Holy Spirit and the birth of the early Church.

Christmas
Christmas day celebrates Jesus' birth and is observed on the 25th December. Its name derives from the Old English "Cristes Maesse", which means the Mass of Christ.

CELEBRATION OF PALM SUNDAY AT THE HOLY SEPULCHRE, JERUSALEM.

DATING THE NEW TESTAMENT

Jesus was born in Bethlehem, Judea, during the final years of Herod the Great's reign in Palestine. At this time, the country was part of the Roman empire, which was ruled over by the emperor Augustus Caesar. Very little is known about Jesus' early life; however, much was written about his ministry and the spread of Christianity. Besides the New Testament texts, the historians Josephus and Tacitus give additional information about Jesus and the political situation at that time.

TACITUS AT HIS WRITING DESK
Detail from a 17th-century
French engraving

FLAVIUS JOSEPHUS
(AD 38–100)
Engraving of the
historian, who wrote a
twenty-volume account
of the Jewish people

Non-biblical evidence

Flavius Josephus was the most important historian of the Jewish people in the New Testament period. In his works, he makes a direct reference to John the Baptist, James, and Jesus. In "Jewish Antiquities" he writes: "There lived a man called Jesus, a wise man... He was the Messiah". The Roman historian and senator Tacitus (AD 56–115) mentions Jesus' existence in his "Annals". He wrote much about Nero's persecution of the Christians. Pliny the Younger (AD 61–112), a governor in Asia Minor, mentions Jesus in letters to the emperor Trajan, describing Rome's treatment of Christians.

The political situation in Palestine

The Roman Senate allowed self-rule in many parts of the empire. The native king in Palestine, Herod the Great, ruled the Jewish people until his death in 4 BC. Palestine was then split between his three sons: Philip, Archelaus, and Herod Antipas. Judea was brought under direct Roman control in AD 6, when its ruler, Archelaus, was replaced by a Roman governor.

Herod and his family were not popular amongst the Jewish people. However, the presence of a Roman army in Judea and the heavy taxes imposed in Palestine made the Romans even less welcome. A Jewish political group known as the Zealots attempted to overthrow them in AD 66.

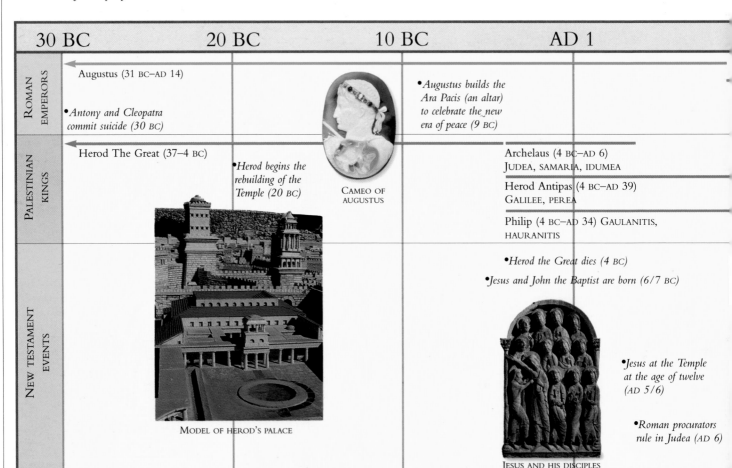

	30 BC	20 BC	10 BC	AD 1
ROMAN EMPERORS	Augustus (31 BC–AD 14) •Antony and Cleopatra commit suicide (30 BC)		CAMEO OF AUGUSTUS	•Augustus builds the Ara Pacis (an altar) to celebrate the new era of peace (9 BC)
PALESTINIAN KINGS	Herod The Great (37–4 BC)	•Herod begins the rebuilding of the Temple (20 BC)		Archelaus (4 BC–AD 6) JUDEA, SAMARIA, IDUMEA / Herod Antipas (4 BC–AD 39) GALILEE, PEREA / Philip (4 BC–AD 34) GAULANITIS, HAURANITIS
NEW TESTAMENT EVENTS	MODEL OF HEROD'S PALACE		JESUS AND HIS DISCIPLES	•Herod the Great dies (4 BC) •Jesus and John the Baptist are born (6/7 BC) •Jesus at the Temple at the age of twelve (AD 5/6) •Roman procurators rule in Judea (AD 6)

NEW TESTAMENT CHRONOLOGY: The dates contained within this chronology are all approximate. Opinions vary over the date of Jesus' birth.

ROMAN INFLUENCES

The Romans brought many benefits to the nations under their control. They built roads, bridges, amphitheatres, palaces, and many other magnificent buildings. They also introduced a just legal system. Their cultural influence was evident in the decoration of wealthy homes, and many people adopted the Roman style of dress and learned to speak Latin.

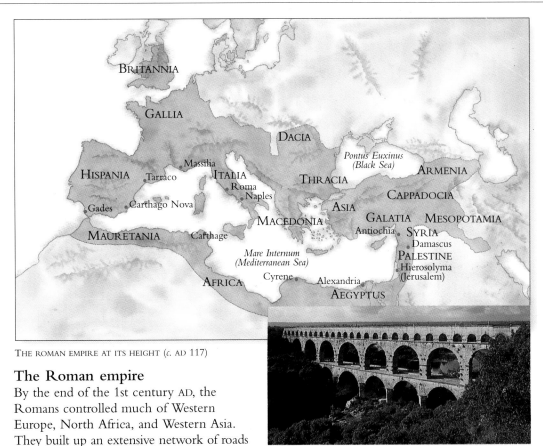

THE ROMAN EMPIRE AT ITS HEIGHT (c. AD 117)

The Roman empire

By the end of the 1st century AD, the Romans controlled much of Western Europe, North Africa, and Western Asia. They built up an extensive network of roads and ports throughout their empire, which facilitated the spread of Christianity.

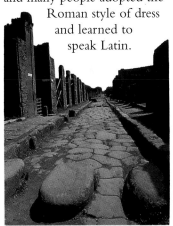

A ROMAN STREET IN POMPEII, ITALY
Roman streets had high pavements on either side and stepping stones.

THE "PONT DU GARD" AQUEDUCT, PROVENCE, FRANCE
The Romans constructed many aqueducts (waterways), such as the one above, to supply their cities with running water.

AD 20	AD 40	AD 60	AD 80
	Caligula (37–41)	Galba (68–69)	Titus (79–81)
		Otho (69)	
Tiberius (14–37)		Vitellius (69)	
•Pontius Pilate governor in Judea (26–36)	Claudius (41–54)		
		Nero (54–68)	Vespasian (69–79)	Domitian (81–96)
	Herod Agrippa I (37–44)		
	Herod Agrippa II (50–100)		

HEROD AGRIPPA BRONZE COIN

•James martyred (44)
•Peter imprisoned (44)

•Paul dies (65–67)

•John the Baptist is imprisoned (27/28)

•Jerusalem Temple destroyed (70)

•Beginning of Jesus' ministry (28)

•Paul's first missionary journey (46–48)

•John the Baptist killed (28/29)

•Jerusalem Council established (49–50)

•Paul's second missionary journey (50–52)

•Letter to the Thessalonians (51/52)

•Jesus is crucified – birth of the early Church (30)

•Paul's third missionary journey (53–57)

•Paul's letter to the Romans (57)

•Paul converted to Christian faith (34/35)

•Paul imprisoned (59–61/62)

PAUL THE APOSTLE

JESUS' EARLY YEARS

Nearly four centuries had elapsed since the last of the Israelite prophets had spoken among the Jews. The Jewish community remembered the promise of a Messiah and of a new Elijah, who was to prepare the way for him, and awaited their arrival. This messianic hope intensified over the centuries. During the Roman occupation and the reign of Herod the Great, the Jews often felt desperate; the Holy Land was occupied by ruthless foreigners, and their king, a cruel and unstable character, was not even a Jew.

It was in this rather gloomy context that two miraculous births occurred. Within the same year, two cousins, John the Baptist and Jesus, were born in Judea. Their births were mysteriously predicted by an angel.

HEROD THE GREAT
13th-century Italian mosaic

THE HERODIUM
Herod the Great's hill-top fortress of Herodium stands 12km (8 miles) south of Jerusalem. It once contained a luxurious palace and was Herod's burial place.

HEROD THE GREAT

Herod was born in about 73 BC. He was the eldest son of Antipater, an Idumean. The Idumeans were descendants of the Edomites, who inhabited an area south of Bethlehem and Jerusalem. They were proselytes (Jewish converts), as they had been forced by the Jewish king, John Hyrcanus (135–104 BC), to become circumcised Jews.

Herod the Great became governor of Galilee when he was 25 years old. His enthusiasm to wipe out the bandits terrorizing Galilee made him popular with the Romans and the Galileans, but he was not so popular with the Jewish leaders. He narrowly escaped a death sentence from Rome after executing some Jews without the consent of the Jewish elders.

Yet, ten years later (37 BC), Herod was made king of Judea by the Roman Senate. His long friendship with the Roman general Mark Antony may have helped him in his rise to power. Herod's marriage to Marianne was also seen as a calculated political move. She was a Jewish princess, and Herod hoped that she would bring him greater support from the Jewish people.

Herod's legacy

Herod undertook massive building projects during his reign. He built several new towns and cities and rebuilt old ones such as "Sebaste", which was situated on the ancient city of Samaria. "Sebaste" is Greek for "Augustus". Herod dedicated this city to the Roman emperor. King Herod also constructed the city-port of Caesarea. This was the Roman administrative centre for Palestine, and it took twelve years to complete.

Herod fortified Palestine by building seven fortresses throughout the region. His most magnificent project was the rebuilding of the Temple in Jerusalem. This was started in 19 BC but it was not completed until AD 64.

MASSACRE OF THE INNOCENTS, painting by Fra Angelico (c. 1387–1450)

MASADA THE ROCK
Herod fortified the existing buildings at Masada. He built a series of huge water cisterns, store-houses, and a palace that was constructed on three natural rock terraces.

Herod, king of the Jews

Herod's reign was marked by terror and bloodshed. Throughout his rule, Herod was fixated with the idea that members of his family (he had fifteen children) were plotting to take his throne. He executed three of his sons and his favourite wife, Marianne.

His fear of a Jewish rebellion led him to destroy all potential rivals. When Herod received the news that the awaited "Messiah" had been born in Bethlehem, he ordered all the baby boys in the vicinity to be put to death (Matthew 2: 13–16).

JOHN THE BAPTIST AND JESUS

The New Testament considers the births of John and Jesus to be the realization of Old Testament prophecies. These foretold the coming of the Messiah and the one who would pave the way for his arrival (Daniel 9: 25–26). Their births recall those of important Old Testament characters such as Isaac, Jacob, and Samson, who were born in miraculous circumstances to fulfil a special purpose.

JESUS AND JOHN
Early 17th-century painting by Paul Rubens depicting two angels with Jesus and John as babies

John's birth

John's mother, Elizabeth, was elderly and barren. However, an angel appeared to her husband, Zechariah the priest, and announced the birth of a child who would be called John. He would be "filled with the Holy Spirit even from birth". Quoting the words of the prophet Malachi, the angel added that John would "go on before the Lord, in the spirit and power of Elijah... to make ready a people prepared for the Lord" (Luke 1: 17). John would prepare the way for Jesus.

Jesus' birth

Jesus' birth was also foretold. The angel Gabriel announced to Mary, a young Israelite virgin: "The Holy Spirit will come upon you, and the power of the Most High will overshadow you. So the holy one to be born will be called the Son of God" (Luke 1: 35). Gabriel's message, also known as the Annunciation, declared that Jesus would be both human and divine and that her son would establish God's kingdom on earth. Jesus' birth was also announced to Joseph, who humbly accepted God's will and married the virgin Mary.

Jesus was born in Bethlehem, the city of King David. People from foreign countries came to see the newborn baby, the promised Messiah.

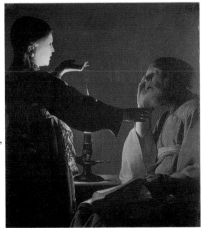

SAINT JOSEPH AND THE ANGEL
This 17th-century painting by Georges de la Tour shows Joseph receiving the news of Mary's pregnancy from the angel Gabriel.

The early years of John and Jesus

The two boys did not grow up together. John, possibly orphaned at an early age, lived in the desert of Judea, between Jerusalem and the Dead Sea; Jesus lived in Nazareth, Galilee. As Elizabeth was a relative of Mary (Luke 1: 36), Jesus and John certainly knew of each other. They may have met at festivals in Jerusalem, but the Gospels do not tell us. While Jesus grew up with siblings in a lively town, John had a more solitary existence.

JESUS IN THE TEMPLE, William Holman Hunt (1827–1910)
Jesus' childhood is mentioned only once in the Gospels, when he stayed to talk to Temple preachers and became separated from his parents (Luke 2: 43). This incident signifies Jesus' awareness of his future role at a very early age.

The ministries of John and Jesus

John started his public ministry before Jesus, urging the crowds to change their way of life, to turn away from evil and return to God because Judgement Day was near. John baptized those who repented of their sins. This earned him the name "John the Baptist". The Gospels record that John dressed like the prophet Elijah – in only a camel-skin cloak and leather belt (Mark 1: 6). John preached to people out in the desert, whereas Jesus taught in towns and cities.

John's baptism of Jesus marked the beginning of Jesus' ministry and the end of his own. Jesus' teachings would have more emphasis on love and forgiveness than John's urgent call for repentance of sins and his warning of God's impending wrath. Jesus' ministry was to be one of healing and preaching of a spiritual kingdom to the poor and underprivileged.

Baptism

The word "baptize" comes from the Greek verb "baptizo", which means "to immerse". Although baptism was practised in Judaism, it received a new meaning with the ministry of John the Baptist. In John's day, baptism was a self-administered ritual washing, which was repeated. People immersed themselves in water for purification. This ritual was practised by the Essene community of Qumran, with whom John may have had contact as a young man. However, John baptized others only once, and this served as a sign of spiritual rebirth.

RITUAL BATH, JERUSALEM
This ritual bath dates back to Old Testament times, when it was used for purification ceremonies.

LUKE 1

THE ANGEL AND THE PRIEST

✤

CHAPTER 1 VERSE 5
"Herod king of Judea"
The New Testament mentions six different Herods. At the birth of Jesus, King Herod was Herod the Great, a non-Jew from Idumea, who was appointed by the Roman Senate. He reigned between 37 and 4 BC. 1st-century Palestine was divided into three areas: Judea, Galilee, and Samaria. Herod was king of all three regions, and they were referred to generally as "Judea" in Greek.

HEROD'S KINGDOM

✤

CHAPTER 1 VERSE 5
"The priestly division of Abijah"
All Israelite priests were descended from Aaron, Moses' brother. Aaron was from the tribe of Levi, whose men were dedicated to the service of the Tabernacle in ancient Israel and, later, the Temple. King David separated them into 24 divisions.

HEROD'S TEMPLE IN JERUSALEM

✤

CHAPTER 1 VERSE 9
"He was chosen by lot"
The casting of lots, often by marked pebbles, was a common practice. In the Old Testament, lots were cast to discover God's will and to resolve difficult decisions.

1 I N[5] THE TIME OF *Herod king of Judea* there was a priest named Zechariah, who belonged to *the priestly division of Abijah*; his wife Elizabeth was also a descendant of Aaron. [6]Both of them were upright in the sight of God, observing all the Lord's commandments and regulations blamelessly. [7]But they had no children, because Elizabeth was barren; and they were both well on in years.

[8]Once when Zechariah's division was on duty and he was serving as priest before God, [9]*he was chosen by lot*, according to the custom of the priesthood, to go into the temple of the Lord and burn incense. [10]And when the time for *the burning of incense* came, all the assembled worshippers were praying outside.

[11]Then an angel of the Lord appeared to him, standing at the right side of the altar of incense. [12]When Zechariah saw him, he was startled and was gripped with fear. [13]But the angel said to him: "Do not be afraid, Zechariah; your prayer has been heard.

Elizabeth and Zechariah are old and childless

Your wife Elizabeth will bear you a son, and you are to give him the name John. [14]He will be a joy... to you, and many will rejoice because of his birth, [15]for he will be great in the sight of the Lord.

An angel appears to Zechariah in the temple

The angel tells Zechariah that Elizabeth will be blessed with a son, but Zechariah cannot believe this

He is never to take wine or other fermented drink, and he will be filled with the Holy Spirit even from birth. [16]Many of the people of Israel will he bring back to the Lord their God. [17]And he will go on before the Lord, in the spirit and power of Elijah, to turn the hearts of the fathers to their children and the disobedient to the wisdom of the righteous – to make ready a people prepared for the Lord."

[18]Zechariah asked the angel, "How can I be sure of this? I am an old man and my wife is well on in years."

[19]The angel answered, "*I am Gabriel*. I stand in the presence of God, and I have been sent to speak

When Zechariah leaves the temple, he can no longer speak

People realise that Zechariah has had a vision

to you and to tell you this good news. [20]And now you will be silent and not able to speak until the day this happens, because you did not believe my words, which will come true at their proper time."

[21]Meanwhile, the people were waiting for Zechariah and wondering why he stayed so long in the temple. [22]When he came out, he could not speak to them. They realised he had seen a vision in the temple, for he kept making signs to them but remained unable to speak.

[23]When his time of service was completed, he returned home. [24]After this his wife Elizabeth became pregnant and for five months remained in seclusion. [25]"*The Lord has* done this for me," she said. "In these days he has shown his favour and *taken away my disgrace* among the people."

UNDERSTANDING THE STORY

John is the only character in the New Testament besides Jesus to be filled with the Holy Spirit from birth. His mission in life is to prepare the way for the Messiah.

Luke 1
MARY AND THE ANGEL

THE TOWN OF NAZARETH
19th-century painting by David Roberts

CHAPTER 1 VERSE 28
"Greetings"
"Greetings" was translated as "Ave" in the first Latin version of the Bible – hence "Ave Maria".

CHAPTER 1 VERSE 35
"The Holy Spirit will come upon you"
Gabriel announces to Mary that her child will be the divine Son of God. Gabriel's message to Mary is known as the Annunciation. This painting shows the Holy Spirit in the form of a dove descending on Mary.

THE ANNUNCIATION (15TH CENTURY)

1 IN[26] THE SIXTH MONTH, God sent the angel Gabriel to *Nazareth, a town in Galilee,* [27]to a virgin pledged to be married to a man named Joseph, a descendant of David. The virgin's name was Mary. [28]The angel went to her and said, "*Greetings,* you who are highly favoured! The Lord is with you."

[29]Mary was greatly troubled at his words and wondered what kind of greeting this might be. [30]But the angel said to her, "Do not be afraid, Mary, you have found favour with God. [31]You will be with child and give birth to a son, and you are to give him the name Jesus.

The angel Gabriel tells Mary not to be afraid. He has a message from God

Mary hears that God has chosen her to be the mother of his Son

[32]He will be great and will be called the Son of the Most High. The Lord God will give him the throne of his father David, [33]and he will reign over the house of Jacob for ever; his kingdom will never end."

[34]"How will this be," Mary asked the angel, "since I am a virgin?"

[35]The angel answered, "*The Holy Spirit will come upon you,* and the power of the Most High will overshadow you.

So the holy one to be born will be called the Son of God. ³⁶Even *Elizabeth your relative* is going to have a child in her old age, and she who was said to be barren is in her sixth month. ³⁷For nothing is impossible with God."

³⁸"I am the Lord's servant," Mary answered. "May it be to me as you have said." Then the angel left her.

³⁹At that time Mary got ready and hurried to a town in the hill country of Judea, ⁴⁰where she entered Zechariah's home and greeted Elizabeth. ⁴¹When Elizabeth heard Mary's greeting, the baby leaped in her womb, and Elizabeth was filled with the Holy Spirit. ⁴²In a loud voice she exclaimed: "Blessed are you among women, and blessed is the child you will bear! ⁴³But why am I so favoured, that the mother of my Lord should come to me? ⁴⁴As soon as the sound of your greeting reached my ears, the baby in my womb leaped for joy. ⁴⁵Blessed is she who has believed that what the Lord has said to her will be accomplished!"

⁴⁶And Mary said: "*My soul glorifies the Lord* ⁴⁷and my spirit rejoices in God my Saviour, ⁴⁸for he has been mindful of the humble state of his servant. From now on all generations will call me blessed, ⁴⁹for the Mighty One has done great things for me – holy is his name. ⁵⁰His mercy extends to those who fear him, from generation to generation. ⁵¹He has performed mighty deeds with his arm; he has scattered those who are proud in their inmost thoughts. ⁵²He has brought down rulers from their thrones but has lifted up the humble. ⁵³He has filled the hungry with good things but has sent the rich away empty. ⁵⁴He has helped his servant Israel, remembering to be merciful ⁵⁵to Abraham and his descendants for ever, even as he said to our fathers."

⁵⁶Mary stayed with Elizabeth for about three months and then returned home.

UNDERSTANDING THE STORY

God has chosen a virgin to be the mother of his Son. The conception of Jesus is a miracle and the fulfilment of a prophecy (Isaiah 7: 14). Through the power of the Holy Spirit, Mary will bear a son without a human father. Jesus will be human in every sense, but also divine. Mary does not doubt what the angel tells her and rejoices in his words. Like Elizabeth, she believes that "nothing is impossible with God".

CHAPTER 1 VERSE 36
"Elizabeth your relative"
Elizabeth and Mary are both descended from Aaron, the first High Priest of Israel. The reference to "his father David" means that Mary was also a descendant of King David, Israel's first great king.

CHAPTER 1 VERSE 46
"My soul glorifies the Lord"
Mary's words of praise are known as the "Magnificat" – a hymn that takes its name from the Latin word for "glorify". Praising God through song is a role traditionally associated with angels in biblical art. This stems from their original purpose as God's messengers, who rejoice in God's creative and compassionate actions.

CHOIR OF ANGELS
Detail from a marble sculpture by
Luca della Robbia (*c.* 1435)

Mary goes to see her cousin Elizabeth and tells her the good news

The child in Elizabeth's womb leaps for joy at the sound of Mary's voice

Zechariah

Mary stays with Elizabeth for three months

LUKE 1

HIS NAME IS JOHN

CHAPTER 1 VERSE 63
"He asked for a writing tablet"
Because Zechariah doubted the
angel's message, he remained mute
during Elizabeth's pregnancy. He
was also deaf, since his relatives had
to make signs to him to find out
what name he wanted to give to
his son. The writing tablet was a
wooden board covered with wax,
written on with a pointed instrument.

WRITING TABLET

CHAPTER 1 VERSE 63
"His name is John"
The Jews followed the Greek
custom of naming the eldest son
after his father. But because of the
nature and importance of his future
mission, Zechariah's son is given
another name. In Hebrew, the name
John means "The Lord is gracious".

FIRSTBORN BOYS
A firstborn boy belonged to
God. This tradition dated from
the time of the Passover in
Egypt, when God saved the
firstborn sons of Israel. Parents
could redeem (buy back) their
son by paying the sum of five
silver pieces to the priest.

CHAPTER 1 VERSE 67
*"Zechariah was filled with the
Holy Spirit and prophesied"*
To prophesy is not just to predict
what is going to happen, it is to
proclaim God's word. When
he could speak, Zechariah
prophesied his son's mission.
Without the Holy Spirit this
would not have been possible.

1 **W**HEN[57] IT WAS TIME for Elizabeth to have her baby, she gave birth to a son. [58]Her neighbours and relatives heard that the Lord had shown her great mercy, and they shared her joy.

[59]On the eighth day they came to circumcise the child, and they were going to name him after his father Zechariah, [60]but his mother spoke up and said, "No! He is to be called John."

[61]They said to her, "There is no-one among your relatives who has that name."

[62]Then they made signs to his father, to find out what he would like to name the child. [63]*He asked for a writing tablet*, and to everyone's astonishment he wrote, *"His name is John."* [64]Immediately his mouth was opened and his tongue was loosed, and he began to speak, praising God. [65]The neighbours were all filled with awe, and throughout the hill country of Judea people were talking about all these things. [66]Everyone who heard this wondered about it, asking, "What then is this child going to be?" For the Lord's hand was with him.

[67]His father *Zechariah was filled with the Holy Spirit and prophesied*:

Family and friends expect
Elizabeth's child to be called
Zechariah, after his father

They make signs to
Zechariah to ask what
name to give his son

They wait to see what name
Zechariah will write on the tablet

[68]*"Praise be to the Lord*, the God of Israel, because he has come and has redeemed his people... [76]And you, my child, will be called a prophet of the Most High; for you will go on before the Lord to prepare the way for him, [77]to give his people the knowledge of salvation through the forgiveness of their sins, [78]because of the tender mercy of our God, by which the rising sun will come to us from heaven [79]to shine on those living in darkness and in the shadow of death, to guide our feet into the path of peace."

[80]And the child grew and became strong in spirit; *and he lived in the desert* until he appeared publicly to Israel.

UNDERSTANDING THE STORY

When God established his covenant with Abraham, the forefather of the Israelites, God promised that through the descendants of Abraham all nations would be blessed. This pledge – often confirmed by the prophets – was to be fulfilled during John's ministry. John's mission in life would be to prepare the way for the promised Messiah.

CHAPTER 1 VERSE 68
"Praise be to the Lord"
Zechariah's poetic prophecy has become known as the "Benedictus" because the Latin version begins with this word, which means "praise be". It is similar to Hannah's song of praise (1 Samuel 2: 1–10), which predicts God's will. Many leading religious figures have been named Benedict, including fourteen popes. Saint Benedict founded the first monastery in Italy in 529. The Benedictines are known for their encouragement of art and education.

BENEDICTINE MONKS

CHAPTER 1 VERSE 80
"And he lived in the desert"
John's parents, old at his birth, probably died when he was young. He grew up in the Judean desert, situated between Jerusalem and the Dead Sea. Although this desert was a desolate place, it was not sandy and waterless. The Judean desert included steppe-lands and pastoral areas. In John's time some religious communities lived in this desert, such as the Essenes, whose writings – the Dead Sea Scrolls – were discovered in 1946.

News about the child soon spreads around the neighbourhood

People come to hear what Zechariah has to say about his new son

Elizabeth says the baby's name is John

When he writes down the name John, Zechariah can speak again

JUDEAN DESERT
Spring flowers blossom in pastureland.

MATTHEW 1, LUKE 2

JESUS IS BORN

1 THIS[18] IS HOW the birth of Jesus Christ came about: His mother Mary was *pledged to be married* to Joseph, but before they came together, she was found to be with child through the Holy Spirit. [19]Because Joseph her husband was a righteous man and did not want to expose her to public disgrace, he had in mind *to divorce her quietly*.

[20]But after he had considered this, an angel of the Lord appeared to him in a dream and said, "*Joseph son of David*, do not be afraid to take Mary home as your wife, because what is conceived in her is from the Holy Spirit. [21]She will give birth to a son, and you are to give him the name Jesus, because he will save his people from their sins."

[22]All this took place to fulfil what the Lord had said through the prophet: [23]"The virgin will be with child and will give birth to a son, and *they will call him Immanuel*" – which means, "God with us."

[24]When Joseph woke up, he did what the angel of the Lord had commanded him and took Mary home as his wife.

2 [1]In those days *Caesar Augustus issued a decree* that a census should be taken of the entire Roman world. ([2]This was the first census that took place while Quirinius was governor of Syria.) [3]And everyone went to his own town to register.

CHAPTER 1 VERSE 18
"Pledged to be married"
In Israel, to be engaged to someone was a form of marriage. Although the couple did not live together, they needed a divorce to break their relationship. In the Bible, a woman pledged to be married is called a wife, and Matthew calls Joseph and Mary "husband and wife" before they are married.

MARRIAGE OF MARY AND JOSEPH
Altar-piece by Fra Angelico, Prado, Madrid (*c.* 1387–1455)

CHAPTER 1 VERSE 19
"To divorce her quietly"
Joseph could not see how he could marry a woman who was pregnant by someone else. No one would believe what had happened to Mary and, according to the Law, she might even be stoned to death. Joseph was too kind to expose her.

CHAPTER 1 VERSE 20
"Joseph son of David"
The Gospel of Matthew ends a genealogy of Jesus Christ the Son of David, by listing Joseph "the husband of Mary, of whom was born Jesus, who is called Christ". Jesus was the legal son of Joseph, who was a descendant of David.

CHAPTER 1 VERSE 23
"They will call him Immanuel"
The prophecy Matthew refers to comes from Isaiah (Isaiah 7: 14). The Gospels see Jesus fulfilling this prophecy – Immanuel means "God with us".

An angel tells Joseph that the child Mary is carrying is the Son of God

Mary and Joseph travel to Bethlehem to register for the Roman census

Joseph no longer thinks about divorcing Mary

⁴So Joseph also went up from the town of Nazareth in Galilee to Judea, to Bethlehem the town of David, because he belonged to the house and line of David. ⁵He went there to register with Mary, who was pledged to be married to him and was expecting a child.

⁶While they were there, the time came for the baby to be born, ⁷and she gave birth to her firstborn, a son. She wrapped him in cloths and *placed him in a manger*, because there was no room for them in the inn.

UNDERSTANDING THE STORY

By marrying Mary, Joseph fulfils the prophecy that the Messiah will be the "Son of David", because his adopted son becomes a descendant of King David. The Messiah will not be the political or military figure so many Jews expected, but the saviour who will deliver his people from evil.

CHAPTER 2 VERSE 1
"Caesar Augustus issued a decree"
Augustus was the first Roman emperor, ruling from 31 BC until AD 14. A census was conducted every fourteen years for military and taxation purposes, although Jews were exempt from military service. Women AUGUSTUS had to pay a poll tax from the age of twelve, so Mary as well as Joseph had to register for the census.

CHAPTER 2 VERSE 7
"Placed him in a manger"
Jesus may have been born in a stable, but the birth could also have taken place in the home of a poor family, where animals were kept under the same roof. Early Christian tradition suggests that Jesus was born in a cave that was used as a stable.

Bethlehem is crowded because of the census, and Joseph can find no room at an inn

Mary wraps the baby in swaddling clothes and places him in the manger

Stabled animals witness the birth of Jesus

THE BIRTH DATE OF JESUS
Herod the Great died in 4 BC. Jesus was probably born a few years before, in 6 or 7 BC. This discrepancy is due to a mistake made by Denys-the-Small, a 6th-century monk, who established the Christian calendar.

LUKE 2
THE SHEPHERDS AND THE ANGELS

2

AND[8] THERE WERE *shepherds living out in the fields* near by, keeping *watch over their flocks at night*. [9]An angel of the Lord appeared to them, and the glory of the Lord shone around them, and they were terrified. [10]But the angel said to them, "*Do not be afraid*. I bring you good news of great joy that will be for all the people. [11]Today in the town of David *a Saviour has been born* to you; he is Christ the Lord. [12]This will be a sign to you: You will find a baby wrapped in cloths and lying in a manger."

[13]Suddenly a great company of the heavenly host appeared with the angel, praising God and saying,

[14]"*Glory to God in the highest*, and on earth peace to men on whom his favour rests."

[15]When the angels had left them and gone into heaven, the shepherds said to one another, "Let's go to Bethlehem and see this thing that has happened, which the Lord has told us about."

CHAPTER 2 VERSE 8
"Shepherds living out in the fields"
The angel appeared to people who were very lowly in the eyes of society. Shepherds roamed year long with their flocks, which made it impossible for them to keep the ceremonial law. Considered unreliable and often regarded as thieves, shepherds were not allowed to give evidence in the courts.

FIELD NEAR BETHLEHEM
This is the field where it is traditionally believed that the angels appeared to the shepherds.

CHAPTER 2 VERSE 8
"Watch over their flocks at night"
It was not necessarily a warm time of year. Animals reserved for temple sacrifices were kept outdoors even in winter, and shepherds watched over flocks to protect them from thieves and wild animals.

CHAPTER 2 VERSE 10
"Do not be afraid"
Angels always offered a word of reassurance to those they visited unexpectedly, understanding that people would be afraid.

CHAPTER 2 VERSE 11
"A Saviour has been born"
The prophets had taught the people of Israel to expect a saviour. Many expected him to deliver them from Roman oppression, others wanted to be cured of disease. Jesus the saviour will be much more than a political leader or a healer, he "will save his people from their sins".

An angel tells them that the Messiah has been born that night

Shepherds tending their flocks in the fields near Bethlehem are terrified

Then, a great company of angels appears, all praising God

The heavens ring with the sound of angels singing

✦

CHAPTER 2 VERSE 11
"He is Christ the Lord"
The Greek name "Christ" has the same meaning as the Hebrew word "Messiah", which means "The Anointed One". The priests, prophets, and kings of the Old Testament were anointed with a sacred oil to signify their consecration to God. A "Messiah" was appointed to accomplish acts in favour of his people, under God's authority and on his behalf. This was to be the calling of Jesus.

✦

CHAPTER 2 VERSE 14
"Glory to God in the highest"
The angels' words are celebrated by the Christian Church in the hymn "Gloria in Excelsis Deo". Most hymns were originally written as poems and later set to music. In medieval times, hymns were sung by a small choir made up of male singers only, who sang in unison (plainsong).

¹⁶So they hurried off and found Mary and Joseph, and the baby, who was lying in the manger. ¹⁷When they had seen him, they spread the word concerning what had been told them about this child, ¹⁸and all who heard it were amazed at what the shepherds said to them. ¹⁹But Mary treasured up all these things and pondered them in her heart. ²⁰The shepherds returned, glorifying and praising God for all the things they had heard and seen, which were just as they had been told.

The shepherds worship the new Messiah

The shepherds go to Bethlehem and find baby Jesus lying in a manger, just as the angel had told them

CHOIR BOYS
St Albans Abbey, England

NOËL: THE FIRST CHRISTMAS
The word "Christmas" comes from the old English "Cristes Maesse" which means Mass of Christ. In carols, Christmas is often called Noël, taken from the French word for "birthday", which also gives "Nativity". Since the 4th century, Christmas has been celebrated on the 25th of December, but the exact date of Jesus' birth is not known.

UNDERSTANDING THE STORY

Poor and scorned by society, the shepherds are nevertheless highly honoured. God chooses them as the first to hear about the birth of Jesus. The baby they go to worship is a descendant of David, who had been a humble shepherd in Bethlehem before becoming a great king.

LUKE 2

SIMEON AND ANNA BLESS JESUS

2 ON[21] THE EIGHTH DAY, when it was time to circumcise him, he was named Jesus, the name the angel had given him before he had been conceived.

Mary and Joseph travel to Jerusalem, because Jesus must be taken to the temple to be dedicated to God

---

CHAPTER 2 VERSE 22
"The time of their purification"
Under Moses' Law, a mother who gave birth to a boy had to wait forty days before entering the Temple.

CHAPTER 2 VERSE 22
"Present him to the Lord"
Firstborn boys were dedicated to God's service. However, since the time of Moses, the Levites performed the religious duties of firstborn boys.

TRAVELLING BY DONKEY
The journey from Bethlehem to Jerusalem is about 8km (5 miles). Mary and Joseph rode by donkey, still a common mode of transport.

[22]When *the time of their purification* according to the Law of Moses had been completed, Joseph and Mary took him to Jerusalem to *present him to the Lord* [23](as it is written in the Law of the Lord, "Every firstborn male is to be consecrated to the Lord"), [24]*and to offer a sacrifice* in keeping with what is said in the Law of the Lord: "a pair of doves or two young pigeons."

At that time in Jerusalem, there lived a virtuous and devout man called Simeon. He had been told by God that he would not die before he had seen the Messiah. Simeon was present at the temple when Mary and Joseph brought their child to be blessed. When he saw Jesus, Simeon knew at once that this was the Saviour he had been waiting for.

[28]Simeon took him in his arms and praised God, saying:
[29]"Sovereign Lord, as you have promised, you now dismiss your servant in peace. [30]For *my eyes have seen your salvation,* [31]which you have prepared in the sight of all people, [32]a light for revelation to the Gentiles and for glory to your people Israel."

[33]The child's father and mother marvelled at what was said about him. [34]Then Simeon blessed them and said to Mary, his mother: *"This child is destined to cause the falling and rising of many in Israel, and to be a sign that will be spoken against,* [35]so that the thoughts of many hearts will be revealed. And *a sword will pierce your own soul* too."

[36]There was also a prophetess, Anna, the daughter of Phanuel,

of the tribe of Asher. She was very old; she had lived with her husband seven years after her marriage, [37]and then was a widow until she was eighty-four. She never left the temple but worshipped night and day, fasting and praying. [38]Coming up to them at that very moment, she gave thanks to God and spoke about the child to all who were looking forward to the redemption of Jerusalem.

Simeon recognises that Jesus is the Messiah and praises God

Mary and Joseph are amazed by Simeon's words

Simeon blesses the infant Messiah

Anna, the prophetess, gives thanks to God

❖
CHAPTER 2 VERSE 24
"And to offer a sacrifice"
The birth of a child was considered a gift from God and an important event in a mother's life. This is why she was asked to offer two animals, one to express her thanks to God, and one to receive God's forgiveness for any sin she may have committed. Mary offered the sacrifice of the poor, two birds, instead of a lamb and a bird.

A PAIR OF DOVES

❖
CHAPTER 2 VERSE 30
"My eyes have seen your salvation"
Simeon recognizes that God has sent his Son into the world to bring salvation to the people of all nations, and not just to the Israelites.

❖
CHAPTER 2 VERSE 34
"This child is destined… to be a sign that will be spoken against"
In his prophecy, Simeon tells Mary that her son's ministry will be a turning point in the life of Israel. By revealing the true nature of people, Jesus will make powerful enemies, who will do their utmost to cause his downfall.

❖
CHAPTER 2 VERSE 35
"A sword will pierce your… soul"
In the final words of his prophecy, Simeon foretells Mary's own pain and anguish at the death of her son, which is depicted in this detail from a 15th-century altar-piece.

MARY WEEPS FOR HER SON

UNDERSTANDING THE STORY
An ordinary Jewish custom leads to an event of great significance. Among the crowds of people and important religious leaders at the Temple, only Simeon and Anna recognize that the infant Jesus is the Messiah. God has chosen these two humble people because they are truly devout and so worthy of this special privilege.

MATTHEW 2

THE VISIT OF THE MAGI

CHAPTER 2 VERSE 1
"Magi from the east"
In the Book of Daniel, the Magi were "wise men" or astrologers who interpreted dreams and signs and were court advisers. The Greek word "Magos" means a sorcerer or magician.

STUDYING THE STARS
In ancient times, astrologers often interpreted the rising of a new star in the sky as the birth of a king. The Greek star catalogues were improved by Arabic astronomers, such as al-Sufi (903–986), pictured in this engraving.

✢

CHAPTER 2 VERSE 2
"We... come to worship him"
The Magi were non-Jews. Their homage to the "king of the Jews" represents the joy of all nations who recognize Jesus as their saviour. The Magi went to Jerusalem, the capital of the Jews, which was where they would expect to find a king. The Bible does not say that they were three. This 15th-century French painting shows fifteen Magi.

THE MAGI COME TO WORSHIP JESUS

2 AFTER[1] JESUS WAS BORN in Bethlehem in Judea, during the time of King Herod, *Magi from the east* came to Jerusalem ²and asked, "Where is the one who has been born king of the Jews? *We saw his star in the east and have come to worship him.*"

³When King Herod heard this he was disturbed, and all Jerusalem with him. ⁴When he had called together all the people's chief priests and teachers of the law, he asked them where the Christ was to be born. ⁵"In Bethlehem in Judea," they replied, "for this is what the prophet has written:

⁶" 'But you, Bethelehem, in the land of Judah, are by no means least among the rulers of Judah; for out of you will come a ruler who will be the shepherd of my people Israel.' "

King Herod

King Herod's priests tell him that the "king of the Jews" will be born in Bethlehem

⁷Then Herod called the Magi secretly and found out from them the exact time the star had appeared.

⁸He sent them to Bethlehem and said, "Go and make a careful search for the child. As soon as you find him, report to me, so that I too may go and worship him."

⁹After they had heard the king, they went on their way, and the star they had seen in the east went ahead of them until it stopped over the place where the child was. ¹⁰When they saw the star, they were overjoyed.

King Herod fears that a new king will be a threat to his power

[11]On coming to the house, *they saw the child* with his mother Mary, and they bowed down and worshipped him. Then they opened their treasures and presented him with gifts of gold and of incense and of myrrh.

[12]And having been warned in a dream not to go back to Herod, they returned to their country by another route.

UNDERSTANDING THE STORY

Although a child was considered a gift from God, very little importance was given to babies and children during this period in history. Childhood was regarded as the preparation for becoming an adult. But for the Gospel writers, Jesus the baby was as important as Jesus the adult. His birth had been prophesied, and people of all nations recognized his divinity and worshipped him.

THE GIFTS OF THE MAGI

It is traditionally believed that there were three Magi because three gifts are mentioned. In the ancient East, the presentation of gifts was a sign of allegiance and submission. The gifts that the Magi offered were very valuable in those days, and the Early Church leaders saw in them the symbols of kingship (gold), of divinity (incense), and of the burial to come (myrrh).

INCENSE

GOLD

MYRRH

CHAPTER 2 VERSE 11
"They saw the child"
The Magi did not visit Jesus on the day of his birth as is often believed. Jesus had already been circumcised and then presented in the Temple forty days after his birth. The Magi find Jesus in "the house", not in a manger.

The Magi leave Herod's palace in Jerusalem and travel to the small town of Bethlehem

The star stops over the place where the Magi will find the infant Messiah

Mary holds Jesus

The Magi promise to tell King Herod where he can find the baby Jesus

The Magi offer gifts to the new Messiah and then return home without informing Herod

MATTHEW 2, LUKE 2

FROM EGYPT TO NAZARETH

CHAPTER 2 VERSE 15

"Out of Egypt I called my son"
During times of famine or political unrest, Egypt was a country of asylum for Jews. These words refer to the Exodus, when God called the young nation of Israel out of Egypt (Hosea 11: 1). God now calls his Son, the young Jesus, whose destiny is closely linked to that of Israel.

THE PYRAMIDS AND SPHINX, EGYPT

CHAPTER 2 VERSE 16

"Kill all the boys in Bethlehem"
It would not have been out of character for Herod the Great to have committed this atrocity. His thirst for power led him to kill many people, including his favourite wife and three of his sons.

CHAPTER 2 VERSE 22

"Archelaus was reigning in Judea"
After Herod the Great's death, his kingdom was divided between his three sons. In AD 6, after complaints about Archelaus' cruelty, Emperor Augustus ousted him and turned his territories into a Roman province.

THE DIVIDED KINGDOM

2 WHEN[13] THEY [the Magi] had gone, an angel of the Lord appeared to Joseph in a dream. "Get up," he said, "take the child and his mother and escape to Egypt. Stay there until I tell you, for Herod is going to search for the child to kill him."

[14]So he got up, took the child and his mother during the night and left for Egypt, [15]where he stayed until the death of Herod. And so was fulfilled what the Lord had said through the prophet: *"Out of Egypt I called my son."*

An angel warns Joseph that Jesus is in danger

Joseph takes his family to safety in Egypt

[16]When Herod realised that he had been outwitted by the Magi, he was furious, and he gave orders to *kill all the boys in Bethlehem* and its vicinity who were two years old and under, in accordance with the time he had learned from the Magi. [17]Then what was said through the prophet Jeremiah was fulfilled: [18]"A voice is heard in Ramah, weeping and great mourning, Rachel weeping for her children and refusing to be comforted, because they are no more."

[19]After Herod died... [21][Joseph] took the child and his mother and went to the land of Israel. [22]But when he heard that *Archelaus was reigning in Judea* in place of his father Herod, he was afraid to go there. Having been warned in a dream, he withdrew to the district of Galilee, [23]and he went and lived in a town called Nazareth. So was fufilled what was said through the prophets: "He will be called a Nazarene."

Herod's soldier

A mother pleads for her baby

King Herod gives orders to kill all the boys in Bethlehem under the age of two

FROM EGYPT TO NAZARETH

Every year, the family go to the
temple for the Feast of the Passover

2 ⁴¹Every year his parents went to Jerusalem for the Feast of the Passover. ⁴²*When he was twelve years old*, they went up to the Feast, according to the custom. ⁴³After the Feast was over, while his parents were returning home, the boy Jesus stayed behind in Jerusalem, but they were unaware of it. ⁴⁴Thinking he was in their company, they travelled on for a day. Then they began looking for him among their relatives and friends. ⁴⁵When they did not find him, they went back to Jerusalem to look for him.

⁴⁶After three days they found him in the temple courts, sitting among the teachers, listening to them and asking them questions. ⁴⁷Everyone who heard him was amazed at his understanding and his answers. ⁴⁸When his parents saw him, they were astonished. His mother said to him, "Son, why have you treated us like this? Your father and I have been anxiously searching for you."

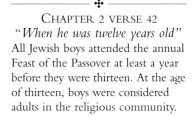

CHAPTER 2 VERSE 42
"When he was twelve years old"
All Jewish boys attended the annual Feast of the Passover at least a year before they were thirteen. At the age of thirteen, boys were considered adults in the religious community.

CHAPTER 2 VERSE 49
"I had to be in my Father's house"
Jews called God "our Father" or "Father in heaven", but rarely "my Father". As a child, Jesus is already aware of his unique relationship with God the Father. Jesus is obedient to Joseph and Mary, but he puts his duty to his Father in heaven first.

During one journey home, Mary and Joseph discover that Jesus is not with them

His parents are relieved to find Jesus in the temple courts

People who hear Jesus talking to the religious teachers are amazed at his understanding

CHAPTER 2 VERSE 52
"And Jesus grew"
Jesus was not born with complete knowledge and understanding. He grew up in a perfect way, and his wisdom and spirituality developed progressively.

⁴⁹"Why were you searching for me?" he asked. "Didn't you know *I had to be in my Father's house?*" ⁵⁰But they did not understand what he was saying to them.

⁵¹Then he went down to Nazareth with them and was obedient to them. But his mother treasured all these things in her heart. ⁵²*And Jesus grew* in wisdom and stature, and in favour with God and men.

UNDERSTANDING THE STORY

There is a parallel between the inner and outer events of Jesus' life in this story. Outside intervention protects Jesus from harm and provides him with a safe childhood environment. As Jesus grows, he is guided by an inner understanding of his special relationship with God.

MARY, JOSEPH, AND INFANT JESUS
This statue is from the Church of Saint Joseph, Nazareth.

LUKE 3
PREPARE THE WAY

CHAPTER 3 VERSE 1
"The reign of Tiberius Caesar"
Tiberius became Rome's second emperor in AD 14, succeeding his stepfather, Augustus. At first Tiberius was an able administrator, but later he isolated himself, convinced people were plotting to kill him.

EMPEROR
TIBERIUS
(AD 14–37)

CHAPTER 3 VERSE 1
"Pontius Pilate was governor"
When Archelaus was deposed, the Romans appointed their own governors in Judea, Samaria, and Idumea. Pontius Pilate, the fifth governor, ruled from AD 26–36.

CHAPTER 3 VERSE 1
"Herod tetrarch of Galilee"
Tetrarchs were minor princes. After their brother Archelaus was exiled, Herod Antipas and Philip continued to rule their portions of Herod the Great's divided kingdom. Lysanias ruled an area to the north-west.

CHAPTER 3 VERSE 2
"The high priesthood of Annas and Caiaphas"
There was only one High Priest at a time. Caiaphas, the official High Priest, was appointed by the Romans. He replaced the deposed Annas, his father-in-law, who had ceased to act officially, but whose authority was still recognized.

3 IN[1] THE FIFTEENTH YEAR of *the reign of Tiberius Caesar* – when *Pontius Pilate was governor* of Judea, *Herod tetrarch of Galilee*, his brother Philip tetrarch of Iturea and Traconitis, and Lysanias tetrarch of Abilene – [2]during *the high priesthood of Annas and Caiaphas*, the word of God came to John son of Zechariah in the desert. [3]He went into all the country around the Jordan, preaching *a baptism of repentance for the forgiveness of sins.*

[4]As is written in the book of the words of Isaiah the prophet: "A voice of one calling in the desert, *'Prepare the way* for the Lord, make straight paths for him. [5]Every valley shall be filled in, every mountain and hill made low. The crooked roads shall become straight, the rough ways smooth. [6]And all mankind will see God's salvation.' "

People ask what they must do to be saved

John calls people to repent and be baptised. He wants to prepare the way for Jesus

[7]John said to the crowds coming out to be baptised by him, "You brood of vipers! Who warned you to flee from the coming wrath? [8]Produce fruit in keeping with repentance. And do not begin to say to yourselves, 'We have Abraham as our father.' For I tell you that out of these stones God can raise up children for Abraham. [9]The axe is already at the root of the trees, and every tree that does not produce good fruit will be cut down and thrown into the fire."

[10]"What should we do then?" the crowd asked.

[11]John answered, "The man with two tunics should share with him who has none, and the one who has food should do the same."

[12]Tax collectors also came to be baptised. "Teacher," they asked, "what should we do?"

[13]"Don't collect any more than you are required to," he told them.

Tax collectors listen to John's message

¹⁴Then some soldiers asked him, "And what should we do?"

He replied, "Don't extort money and don't accuse people falsely – be content with your pay."

¹⁵The people were waiting expectantly and were all wondering in their hearts if John might possibly be the Christ. ¹⁶John answered them all, "I baptise you with water. But one more powerful than I will come, the thongs of whose sandals I am not worthy to untie. He will baptise you with the Holy Spirit and with fire. ¹⁷His winnowing fork is in his hand to clear his threshing-floor and to gather the wheat into his barn, but he will burn up the chaff with unquenchable fire." ¹⁸And with many other words John exhorted the people and preached the good news to them.

John tells people how they can lead better lives

John baptises people in the River Jordan

Soldiers hear that they must not abuse their authority

UNDERSTANDING THE STORY

John's message is that God offers forgiveness to all who are truly sorry for their sins, regardless of race. But repentance alone will not bring salvation. John wants people to understand that the baptism he offers is a commitment to change their ways and to live good lives.

CHAPTER 3 VERSE 3
"A baptism of repentance for the forgiveness of sins"

The act of baptism symbolized the cleansing of the sinner, who was totally immersed in the water. The Jews traditionally baptized non-Jews who wanted to join their community. John tells the Jews that they also need God's forgiveness and urges them to be baptized as well.

RIVER JORDAN
This section of the river is believed to be the site where Jesus was baptized.

CHAPTER 3 VERSE 4
"Prepare the way"

When a king went on a journey, the roads he would be travelling on were improved. In the same way, John is preparing the way for Jesus. John wants people to be spiritually and morally ready for the Messiah.

THE PROPHET IN THE DESERT

John was dressed like Elijah, the Old Testament prophet who also called his people to return to God. The Gospel of Matthew (3: 4) says that "John's clothes were made of camel's hair, and he had a leather belt around his waist. His food was locusts and wild honey". The Jews considered locusts a clean food (Leviticus 11: 22).

LOCUST

MATTHEW 3–4
THE DOVE AND THE DEVIL

CHAPTER 3 VERSE 14
"John tried to deter him"
John felt unfit to baptize Jesus, because he knew that the Messiah had no need for repentance. John wanted Jesus to baptize him with the power of the Holy Spirit.

BAPTISM IN THE RIVER JORDAN

CHAPTER 3 VERSE 15
"It is proper for us to do this"
John and Jesus were both guided by God's will. Jesus already identified himself with the sins of his people and his baptism was to be an example to his followers.

CHAPTER 3 VERSE 16
"He saw the Spirit of God descending like a dove"
In the Creation story (Genesis 1: 2), the Spirit of God hovered like a bird over the waters. The dove that Noah sent out from the ark signalled a new beginning for the world. The dove over the water at Jesus' baptism is symbolic of a new era.

3 Then[13] Jesus came from Galilee to the Jordan to be baptised by John. [14]But *John tried to deter him*, saying, "I need to be baptised by you, and do you come to me?"

[15]Jesus replied, "Let it be so now; *it is proper for us to do this* to fulfil all righteousness." Then John consented.

[16]As soon as Jesus was baptised, he went up out of the water. At that moment heaven was opened, and *he saw the Spirit of God descending like a dove* and lighting on him. [17]And a voice from heaven said, "This is my Son, whom I love; with him I am well pleased."

4 [1]Then *Jesus was led by the Spirit into the desert to be tempted* by the devil. [2]After fasting for forty days and forty nights, he was hungry. [3]The tempter came to him and said, "If you are the Son of God, tell these stones to become bread."

John baptizes Jesus in the River Jordan

As Jesus comes out of the water, the heavens open and a voice says, "This is my Son"

The Holy Spirit, in the form of a dove, descends from heaven and alights on Jesus

4Jesus answered, "It is written: 'Man does not live on bread alone, but on every word that comes from the mouth of God.' "

5Then *the devil took him* to the holy city and had him stand on the highest point of the temple. 6"If you are the Son of God," he said, "throw yourself down. For it is written: 'He will command his angels concerning you, and they will lift you up in their hands, so that you will not strike your foot against a stone.' "

7Jesus answered him, "It is also written: 'Do not put the Lord your God to the test.' "

8Again, the devil took him to a very high mountain and showed him all the kingdoms of the world and their splendour. 9"All this I will give you," he said, "if you will bow down and worship me."

10Jesus said to him, "Away from me, Satan! For it is written: 'Worship the Lord your God, and serve him only.' "

11Then the devil left him, and angels came and attended him.

CHAPTER 4 VERSE 1
"Jesus was led by the Spirit into the desert to be tempted"
Just as God led the Israelites into the desert, where they were tested for forty years before entering the Promised Land, Jesus was led into the desert to be tested for forty days before beginning his ministry. But, unlike some of the Israelites, Jesus did not give in to temptation.

God leads Jesus into the desert to be tempted

The devil promises Jesus all the kingdoms of the world if he will worship him instead of God

The devil asks Jesus to prove he is the Son of God by throwing himself off the temple roof

Jesus resists all of the devil's temptations, and angels appear

Jesus stays in the desert for forty days

When Jesus is hungry, the devil tempts him to turn stones into bread

CHAPTER 4 VERSE 5
"The devil took him"
We do not know how the devil came to Jesus, but the temptations he resisted were very real.

SATAN
19th-century engraving

UNDERSTANDING THE STORY

Jesus knows that he can perform miracles, but he will not use this power for selfish motives. He answers the devil's temptations by quoting from Deuteronomy (6–8), chapters relating to Israel's testing in the desert. Jesus' total dedication to God shows that he is ready to start his ministry.

JESUS' EARLY MINISTRY

Jesus grew up in Galilee, and it was here that he started his public ministry and performed many of his miracles. Galilee was the most northern of the three provinces of Palestine – Galilee, Samaria, and Judea. A small region about 70km (44 miles) long and 40km (25 miles) wide, Galilee was an area of dense forests and fertile farmlands. Its eastern side was bordered by the River Jordan and the Sea of Galilee.

Jesus was brought up in Nazareth, but most of the events described in the first three Gospels occurred near Capernaum, a town situated near the banks of the Sea of Galilee.

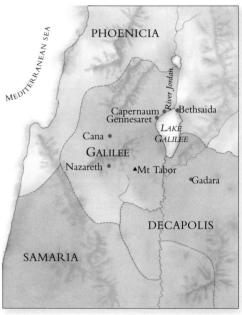

GALILEE AND THE SURROUNDING AREAS
The map indicates the main towns and villages in Galilee that Jesus visited during his early ministry. Capernaum became his base (Matthew 4: 13).

THE GALILEANS

Galilee had a mixed population of Jews and Gentiles. It was sometimes even referred to as "Galilee of the Gentiles" (Matthew 4: 15). Galilee was a fairly isolated region, cut off from Judea by Samaria, which was inhabited mostly by non-Jews. The Galileans had a very broad accent, which made them easily recognizable (Mark 14: 70). Judeans believed themselves to have purer Jewish blood than the Galileans and regarded their accent with contempt. Many people did not believe that the Messiah could come from Galilee (John 7: 41).

NIGHT FISHING ON LAKE GALILEE
Galilee is a fresh-water lake fed by the River Jordan. In Jesus' day, fishing was one of Galilee's main industries.

Lake Galilee provided an important source of food and work. Many Galileans were fishermen and, by Jesus' days, there were nine large settlements around the lake. The most important of these were Bethsaida, Tiberias, and Capernaum.

The political situation

Palestine was deeply affected by the Roman presence. The country was subjected to heavy taxes levied by the Romans and suffered the humiliation of an army of occupation. At the time of Jesus' ministry, Galilee was a Roman province but was governed by a Palestinian ruler, Herod Antipas. Judea, however, was ruled by the Roman governor Pontius Pilate.

Judea had returned to Roman control in AD 6, when Jesus was a boy. This had led to an uprising by a group of Jewish nationalists, who called themselves the "Zealots". This group organized terrorist activities against the occupying force. Their leader was Judas the Galilean. He and his militant followers refused to pay taxes to the Roman emperor and fought for Palestine's independence.

COINS
These Roman coins date to the reigns of Herod Antipas and his brother, Herod Archelaus.

JESUS' MINISTRY

Jesus preached to the Jewish people about the "kingdom of God" and the "kingdom of Heaven". These terms refer to God's reign on earth. Jesus taught that to enter God's kingdom, people needed to undergo a spiritual rebirth (John 3: 5) and commit themselves totally to God. By doing so, they would receive the promise of eternal life.

THE MIRACLE OF THE TEN LEPERS
Luke's Gospel describes how Jesus healed ten lepers, but only one returned to thank Jesus (Luke 17: 11–15). 13th-century mosaic, Monreale Cathedral, Sicily

Parables and miracles

Like other teachers of his time, Jesus used simple stories about daily life, also known as parables, to illustrate a religious principle or moral lesson. These often highlighted the importance of love and compassion for the less fortunate.

Jesus also performed many miracles. He stressed that they were not for his own glorification, but to demonstrate the truth of his message. The Gospels record about 35 miraculous events. The miracles brought salvation to the rejected, the ill, and the dying.

THE TWELVE DISCIPLES

Jesus chose twelve men from his disciples to be his special messengers. These twelve were also known as "apostles" (Mark 3: 14). They were ordinary people – mainly labourers and fishermen – who came from the Galilean countryside.

The apostles travelled everywhere with Jesus, witnessing his miracles and learning from his teachings. Jesus then sent them out to spread his ministry of teaching and healing. Jesus also taught the apostles in private, away from the crowds of followers, in order to prepare them for his death and resurrection.

THE APOSTLES, Italian mosaic from San Frediano Church, Lucca

MATTHEW
Matthew is believed to be "Levi", who worked as a tax collector in and around Capernaum. The Jewish people despised tax collectors, not just because they were corrupt, but because they collected money for the Romans. It is thought that Matthew was also a Gospel author.

THOMAS
In John's Gospel, Thomas was known as "Didymus", which is Greek for "twin" (John 11: 16).

ANDREW
Andrew was the brother of Peter and a fisherman from Bethsaida. He had originally been a disciple of John the Baptist before he joined Jesus (John 1: 35–40).

JAMES, JUDAS, AND SIMON
The New Testament lists three remaining disciples. They were James son of Alphaeus, Judas son of James, and Simon the Zealot. Simon possibly belonged to the fanatical religious sect of "Zealots".

SIMON PETER
Simon Peter, the brother of the disciple Andrew, was a fisherman in Galilee. He was one of the first to be asked to join Jesus and became the apostles' recognized leader and spokesman. Jesus changed Simon's name to "Peter". According to Matthew's Gospel, this was because Simon had acknowledged Jesus as the Messiah (Matthew 16: 15). He was the leader of the inner circle of three apostles – Peter, James, and John – who were particularly close to Jesus. Peter had an impetuous temperament, but an unwavering faith in Jesus.

JAMES
James, another fisherman, was the son of Zebedee and the brother of John. Jesus gave the two brothers the nickname "Sons of Thunder", because of their impulsive natures. Their mother, Salome, was also a disciple of Jesus (Matthew 27: 56).

JOHN
John is believed to be James' younger brother, as he is always mentioned second. He is referred to as the disciple "whom Jesus loved" (John 13: 23). John is traditionally believed to be the Gospel author.

BARTHOLOMEW
Bartholomew's name only appears in the lists of the apostles. He is believed to be Nathanael, mentioned in John's Gospel (John 1: 45–49).

PHILIP
Philip came from Bethsaida, as did Andrew and Peter. He joined Jesus at the same time as Nathanael.

JUDAS ISCARIOT
Judas was the only apostle not from Galilee; his home-town was Kerioth, in southern Judea. Judas is always mentioned last in the list of apostles in the Bible and is referred to as the one "who betrayed him" (Matthew 10: 4). He was probably an important apostle, because he was treasurer of the group.

FAMILY AND FRIENDS

There is no mention of Joseph during Jesus' ministry, but his mother Mary is referred to twice – once when Jesus turned the water into wine at Cana, and the second time when Jesus was teaching a crowd of followers. On the latter occasion, Mary went to see Jesus but he rebuked her, telling her that his disciples had become his new family (Luke 8: 19–21).

According to the scriptures, Jesus had four "brothers", James, Joseph, Simon, and Judas, as well as "sisters" (Matthew 13: 55–56). It is not clear whether these were his real brothers and sisters, just cousins, or Joseph's children from an earlier marriage.

Jesus' closest friends were Lazarus and his sisters, Mary and Martha, who lived in Bethany, just outside Jerusalem (John 11: 3, 5, 36). Jesus visited them on several occasions when he travelled to Jerusalem. John's Gospel records how Jesus brought Lazarus back to life, four days after Lazarus' death (John 11).

CHRIST IN THE HOUSE OF MARTHA AND MARY, Jan Vermeer (1632–75)

233

LUKE 4
JESUS AT NAZARETH

CHAPTER 4 VERSE 14
"Jesus returned to Galilee"
Jesus began his ministry in Judea, where he met some of his disciples. He then taught in Galilee and went back to his home town, Nazareth.

NAZARETH TODAY

CHAPTER 4 VERSE 15
"He taught in their synagogues"
There was only one temple, which was in Jerusalem, but most Jewish towns had a synagogue. Its origin goes back to the Exile – "synagogue" coming from the Greek word for "gathering". The building was a meeting place and school, but mainly it was a place of worship. Leaders often invited visiting teachers to take part in services.

CHAPTER 4 VERSE 16
"He stood up to read"
As a mark of respect for God's word, readers stood up in the synagogue and then sat down for the sermon. The reading was always in Hebrew, but the sermon was in Aramaic, a common language that was close to Hebrew and spoken by Jews of the time.

RABBI HOLDING TORAH SCROLL
In synagogues today, readings from the Torah scroll are still in Hebrew. This synagogue was built in the 18th century.

4 J ESUS[14] RETURNED *to Galilee* in the power of the Spirit, and news about him spread through the whole countryside. [15]*He taught in their synagogues*, and everyone praised him.

[16]He went to Nazareth, where he had been brought up, and on the Sabbath day he went into the synagogue, as was his custom. And *he stood up to read*. [17]*The scroll of the prophet Isaiah was handed to him.* Unrolling it, he found the place where it is written:

[18]"The Spirit of the Lord is on me, because he has anointed me to preach good news to the poor. He has sent me to proclaim freedom for the prisoners and recovery of sight for the blind, to release the oppressed, [19]to proclaim *the year of the Lord's favour.*"

Jesus stands up to read in the synagogue at Nazareth

An attendant hands Jesus the scroll of the prophet Isaiah

Jesus reads a passage that prophesies a time when Israel will be free from misery

People are surprised that Joseph's son speaks with such authority

Some Jews become angry when they hear that God offers salvation to all nations

[20]Then he rolled up the scroll, gave it back to the attendant and sat down. The eyes of everyone in the synagogue were fastened on him, [21]and he began by saying to them, *"Today this scripture is fulfilled in your hearing."*

[22]All spoke well of him and were amazed at the gracious words that came from his lips. "Isn't this Joseph's son?" they asked.

[23]Jesus said to them, "Surely you will quote this proverb to me: 'Physician, heal yourself! Do here in your home town what we have heard that you did in Capernaum.' "

²⁴"I tell you the truth," he continued, "no prophet is accepted in his home town. ²⁵I assure you that there were many widows in Israel in Elijah's time, when the sky was shut for three and a half years and there was a severe famine throughout the land. ²⁶Yet Elijah was not sent to any of them, but to a widow in Zarephath in the region of Sidon. ²⁷And there were many in Israel with leprosy in the time of Elisha the prophet, yet not one of them was cleansed – only Naaman the Syrian."

²⁸All the people in the synagogue were furious when they heard this. ²⁹They got up, drove him out of the town, and took him to the brow of the hill on which the town was built, in order to throw him down the cliff. ³⁰But he walked right through the crowd and went on his way.

The people drive
Jesus out of town

They force him to
the edge of a hill

Jesus walks
unharmed
through
the crowd

UNDERSTANDING THE STORY

This is the first time Jesus teaches in his home town. He reads from the book of Isaiah, which contains many promises of a Messiah and a new age. Jesus says that this time has come, but knows that in Nazareth especially he will encounter disbelief. His message is that God offers salvation to all people, not just to the Jews, and this makes the Nazarenes very angry.

CHAPTER 4 VERSE 17
"The scroll of the prophet Isaiah was handed to him"
The Hebrew texts of the Old Testament, written on parchment scrolls, were kept in special coffers at the back of the synagogue. Every Sabbath an attendant handed the selected scrolls to the reader, who read out a text from the Law and a text from the Prophets.

HEBREW SCROLL
Scribes meticulously copied out the text of the Old Testament.

Ivory handle

CHAPTER 4 VERSE 19
"The year of the Lord's favour"
Every 49 years the Jews celebrated the Year of Jubilee, when slaves were freed, mortgaged land was returned, and debts were cancelled. Isaiah speaks of a future golden age, when the people of Israel would be released from their misery (Isaiah 61).

CHAPTER 4 VERSE 21
"Today this scripture is fulfilled"
Jesus tells the audience that he is the fulfilment of Isaiah's prophecy.

ELIJAH AND ELISHA
These famous prophets lived at a time when the people of Israel refused to follow God's will. The Israelites rejected Elijah and Elisha as God's messengers (1 Kings 17; 2 Kings 5).

ELISHA
17th-century painting

LUKE 5–6

JESUS CHOOSES HIS APOSTLES

JESUS' DISCIPLES
Many teachers had disciples who followed them. These disciples were pupils, who selected their master, learned the Torah from them, and then followed their strict teaching. Jesus broke with this tradition. From the many disciples who followed him, he chose twelve. The apostles are this inner circle of disciples.

✥

CHAPTER 5 VERSE 1
"Lake of Gennesaret"
This was another name for the Sea of Galilee, also called the Sea of Tiberias (in the Gospel of John) and Chinnereth (in the Old Testament). This fresh-water lake is about 20km (13 miles) long and 11km (7 miles) wide, and the River Jordan runs through it.

SEA OF GALILEE

✥

CHAPTER 5 VERSE 4
"Let down the nets for a catch"
Fishing was the main occupation in the towns and villages that bordered the lake. Much of Jesus' ministry was based in this area, and at least four of his apostles were fishermen.

TILAPIA (ST PETER'S FISH)
The Sea of Galilee was a rich fishing ground. Its principal catch was tilapia.

5 ONE[1] DAY AS JESUS was standing by the *Lake of Gennesaret...* [2]he saw at the water's edge two boats... [3]He got into one of the boats, the one belonging to Simon... [4]He said to Simon, "Put out into deep water, and *let down the nets for a catch.*"

[5]Simon answered, "Master, we've worked hard all night and haven't caught anything. But because you say so, I will let down the nets."

[6]When they had done so, they caught such a large number of fish that their nets began to break. [7]So they signalled to their partners in the other boat to come and help them, and they came and filled both boats so full that they began to sink.

[8]When Simon Peter saw this, he fell at Jesus' knees and said, "Go away from me, Lord; I am a sinful man!" [9]For he and all his companions were astonished at the catch of fish they had taken, [10]and so were James and John, the sons of Zebedee, Simon's partners. Then Jesus said to Simon, "Don't be afraid; from now on you will catch men." [11]So they pulled their boats up on shore, *left everything and followed him...*

Jesus tells the fishermen to let down their nets, and they catch a huge quantity of fish

Bartholomew (Nathanael)

Philip

James

John

Peter (Simon)

Matthew (Levi)

Andrew

Jesus calls together his disciples and chooses twelve

²⁷[Jesus] saw a tax collector by the name of Levi sitting at his tax booth. "Follow me," Jesus said to him, ²⁸and Levi got up, left everything and followed him.

²⁹Then Levi held a great banquet for Jesus at his house, and a large crowd of tax collectors and others were eating with them. ³⁰But the Pharisees and the teachers of the law who belonged to their sect complained to his disciples, "Why do you eat and drink with tax collectors and 'sinners'?"

³¹Jesus answered them, "It is not the healthy who need a doctor, but the sick. ³²I have not come to call the righteous, but sinners to repentance."...

6   ¹²One of those days Jesus went out to a mountainside to pray, and spent the night praying to God. ¹³When morning came, he called his disciples to him and *chose twelve* of them, whom he also designated apostles: ¹⁴Simon (whom he named Peter), his brother Andrew, James, John, Philip, Bartholomew, ¹⁵Matthew, Thomas, James son of Alphaeus, Simon who was called the Zealot, ¹⁶Judas son of James, and Judas Iscariot, who became a traitor.

Jesus tells Levi, a tax collector, to follow him

CHAPTER 5 VERSE 11
"[They] left everything and followed him"
The Gospel of John says that some of the disciples had already met Jesus shortly after his baptism. These disciples had followed John the Baptist and heard him name Jesus as the Messiah. They believed in Jesus and returned with him to Galilee (John 1: 32–46).

WOMEN DISCIPLES
Jesus' group of disciples included women, which was unheard of at the time. The Gospel of Luke says "The Twelve were with him and also some women... Mary (called Magdalene)...; Joanna the wife of Chuza...; Susanna; and many others. These women were helping to support them out of their own means" (Luke 8: 2–3).

James

Thaddaeus (Judas)

Jesus

Thomas

Simon the Zealot

Judas Iscariot

THREE WOMEN DISCIPLES
This 16th-century church panel from Troyes, France, shows Mary Magdalene, Mary mother of James, and Salome, taking spices to anoint Jesus' body in the tomb.

UNDERSTANDING THE STORY

The number of apostles – twelve – corresponds to the number of tribes that founded Israel. The word apostle means "messenger", and Jesus' apostles will take his message to people of all nations. The new "Israel" they are to establish will be God's kingdom on earth.

CHAPTER 6 VERSE 13
"[Jesus] chose twelve"
Jesus chose people with ordinary human weaknesses. The twelve apostles had no special training, but they would follow Jesus everywhere and learn from him.

JOHN 2
THE WEDDING AT CANA

CHAPTER 2 VERSE 3
"When the wine was gone"
Wedding festivities usually lasted for seven days. The guests feasted and drank wine, which the bridegroom provided. For the wine to run out before the end of the celebrations was a serious social embarrassment.

Mary tells Jesus that there is no more wine for the guests

CHAPTER 2 VERSE 4
"My time has not yet come"
In the Gospel of John, Jesus' "time" comes when he dies on the cross and rises from the dead, and this is the first of eight mentions. All Jesus' actions are guided by his sense of mission and destiny. Jesus wants his mother to understand that what he is about to do will serve this purpose. His action is not purely for the benefit of the guests.

CHAPTER 2 VERSE 5
"Do whatever he tells you"
Although Mary was aware of her son's unusual power, she would not have expected him to perform a miracle. Her faith in his ability to resolve this domestic crisis is rewarded in an extraordinary way.

2 ON[1] THE THIRD DAY a wedding took place at Cana in Galilee. Jesus' mother was there, [2]and Jesus and his disciples had also been invited to the wedding. [3]*When the wine was gone*, Jesus' mother said to him, "They have no more wine."

[4]"Dear woman, why do you involve me?" Jesus replied. "*My time has not yet come.*"

[5]His mother said to the servants, "*Do whatever he tells you.*"

Jesus, his mother, and some of the disciples are invited to a wedding in Cana

Jesus tells the servants to fill the jars to the brim with water and then draw some for the master of the banquet

Nearby stand large stone jars that are used for ceremonial washing

[6]Nearby stood six stone water *jars, the kind used by the Jews for ceremonial washing*, each holding from twenty to thirty gallons.

[7]Jesus said to the servants, "Fill the jars with water"; so they filled them to the brim. [8]Then he told them, "Now draw some out and take it to the master of the banquet."

They did so, [9]and the master of the banquet tasted the water that had been turned into wine. He did not realise where it had come from, though the servants who had drawn the water knew. Then he called the bridegroom [10]aside and said, "Everyone brings out the choice wine first and then the cheaper wine after the guests have had too much to drink; but you have saved the best till now."

CHAPTER 2 VERSE 6
"Jars... for ceremonial washing"
The ritual requirement of the Law called for Jews to cleanse themselves of impurity, especially before a meal or a religious ceremony. The water was kept in large stone or pottery jars, which held up to 140 litres (thirty gallons). Rich people often had pools for ritual bathing.

STONE WATER JAR
This ceremonial water container from St. George's Church at Kfar Kanna dates from the time of Jesus.

The master of the banquet congratulates the bridegroom for saving the best wine until last

The servant knows that his jar was filled with water

CHAPTER 2 VERSE 11
"The first of his miraculous signs"
The miracles recorded in the Gospel of John are called signs. All Jesus' miracles have a deep significance.

CHAPTER 2 VERSE 11
"He thus revealed his glory"
In the Bible, "glory" refers to God in all his power and strength. The miracle is proof to the disciples of Jesus' special relationship with God.

CANA IN GALILEE
Cana was the home town of the disciple Bartholomew. This is believed to be Kfar Kanna, where two churches have been erected to commemorate Jesus' first miracle.

[11]This, *the first of his miraculous signs*, Jesus performed in Cana of Galilee. *He thus revealed his glory*, and his disciples put their faith in him. [12]After this he went down to Capernaum with his mother and brothers and his disciples. There they stayed for a few days.

UNDERSTANDING THE STORY

Ritual cleansing was a fundamental religious practice. In this miracle, the water can be interpreted as the Jewish religion of Jesus' day. By turning the water into wine, Jesus is saying he will bring change. The wine may represent his own blood, which he will spill to bring people closer to God.

KFAR KANNA, NEAR NAZARETH
Kfar Kanna lies 2.5km (4 miles) along the road from Nazareth to Tiberias.

MATTHEW 4, LUKE 5, MARK 2

JESUS HEALS AND FORGIVES

CHAPTER 4 VERSE 23
"Teaching in their synagogues"
Every Sabbath, Jesus taught in the synagogues, explaining the meaning of the texts that were read. On other days, he taught his disciples and preached in the open air to the large crowds who came to see him. His ability to heal was a sign that God was working through him.

CHAPTER 4 VERSE 24
"News about him spread"
The mission of Jesus was a real success. His popularity grew and spread quickly beyond Galilee.

CHAPTER 5 VERSE 12
"Covered with leprosy"
In the Bible, the word "leprosy" describes a variety of skin diseases. Lepers were confined to isolated places, and someone who touched a leper was considered unclean. Jesus ignored this restriction – he touched and healed a leper.

MAN SUFFERING FROM LEPROSY
Today leprosy can be treated.

CHAPTER 5 VERSE 14
"Show yourself to the priest"
A priest had to confirm that someone was healed from a skin disease before the person could be reinstated into the community. By respecting this requirement, Jesus knew that the authorities would have to recognize his healing powers.

---

4 JESUS[23] WENT throughout Galilee, *teaching in their synagogues*, preaching the good news of the kingdom, and healing every disease and sickness among the people. [24]*News about him spread* all over Syria, and people brought to him all who were ill with various diseases, those suffering severe pain, the demon-possessed, those having seizures, and the paralysed, and he healed them. [25]Large crowds from Galilee, the Decapolis, Jerusalem, Judea and the region across the Jordan followed him.

People suffering and in pain come to Jesus to be healed

5 [12]While Jesus was in one of the towns, a man came along who was *covered with leprosy*. When he saw Jesus, he fell with his face to the ground and begged him, "Lord, if you are willing, you can make me clean."

Jesus touches a leper, who is healed immediately

The leper presents himself to the priest to confirm that he is cured

[13]Jesus reached out his hand and touched the man. "I am willing," he said. "Be clean!" And immediately the leprosy left him. [14]Then Jesus ordered him, "Don't tell anyone, but go, *show yourself to the priest* and offer the sacrifices that Moses commanded for your cleansing, as a testimony to them."

[15]Yet the news about him spread all the more, so that crowds of people came to hear him and to be healed of their sicknesses. [16]But Jesus often withdrew to lonely places and prayed.

2 ¹A few days later, when Jesus again entered Capernaum, the people heard that he had come home. ²So many gathered that there was no room left, not even outside the door, and he preached the word to them.

³Some men came, bringing to him a paralytic, carried by four of them. ⁴Since they could not get him to Jesus because of the crowd, they made *an opening in the roof* above Jesus and, after digging through it, lowered the mat the paralysed man was lying on. ⁵When Jesus saw their faith, he said to the paralytic, "Son, your sins are forgiven."

⁶Now some *teachers of the law* were sitting there, thinking to themselves, ⁷"Why does this fellow talk like that? He's blaspheming! Who can forgive sins but God alone?"

⁸Immediately Jesus knew in his spirit that this was what they were thinking in their hearts, and he said to them, "Why are you thinking these things? ⁹Which is easier: to say to the paralytic, 'Your sins are forgiven,' or to say, 'Get up, take your mat and walk'? ¹⁰But that you may know that the Son of Man has authority on earth to forgive sins..." He said to the paralytic, ¹¹"I tell you, get up, *take your mat* and go home."

¹²He got up, took his mat and walked out in full view of them all. This amazed everyone and they praised God, saying, "We have never seen anything like this!"

People throng to see Jesus. Friends lower a paralysed man through the roof because they cannot get through the crowd

The teachers of the law accuse Jesus of blasphemy

People are astonished when the paralysed man picks up his mat and walks

UNDERSTANDING THE STORY

The miracles that accompany the teachings of Jesus are evidence of his special relationship with God. A healing could be witnessed and confirmed, but not the forgiveness of sins. The healings of the leper and the paralytic are proof that God has given Jesus the power and authority to forgive sins.

✢

CHAPTER 2 VERSE 4
"An opening in the roof"
A typical country house had a flat clay roof, with rush matting laid over supporting wooden beams. A flight of outside stairs led up to the roof. Most houses were mud-brick.

FLAT-ROOFED HOUSES, JORDAN
These have changed little since Jesus' days.

✢

CHAPTER 2 VERSE 6
"Teachers of the law"
This group of people, mostly Pharisees, studied and interpreted the Law. They believed that only God could forgive sins. This is why they accused Jesus of committing blasphemy, the worst sin of all.

✢

CHAPTER 2 VERSE 11
"Take your mat"
Most people did not have beds, they slept on the floor on mats, which were rolled up during the day.

LUKE 6
THE LORD OF THE SABBATH

CHAPTER 6 VERSE 2
*"Why are you doing what is
unlawful on the Sabbath?"*
The Sabbath was a day of rest
intended to be a time for physical,
mental, and spiritual restoration. The
Pharisees added many restrictive
rules to this commandment. The
Old Testament did not forbid
picking grain for eating, but the
Pharisees considered this to
be harvesting.

Jesus' disciples pick
ears of corn and eat
the grain

CHAPTER 6 VERSE 5
"The Son of Man"
Jesus often used this title when
referring to himself. The phrase
would have been familiar to Jews,
because the prophet Daniel used it
to describe his vision of one who
looked like a man, but who had the
authority of God (Daniel 7: 13–14).

CHAPTER 6 VERSE 9
*"Which is lawful on
the Sabbath?"*
Healing on the Sabbath was not
forbidden by the Law of Moses. But
religious leaders dictated that only
people in life-threatening situations
could be helped on the Sabbath.

Prayer shawl

Phylactery

PRAYER
The Sabbath was a time for people to
gather together in public worship.
During prayer, Jewish men wore shawls
and two small boxes (phylacteries), which
contained passages from the Torah.

6 ONE[1] SABBATH Jesus was going through the cornfields, and his disciples began to pick some ears of corn, rub them in their hands and eat the grain. [2]Some of the Pharisees asked, *"Why are you doing what is unlawful on the Sabbath?"*

[3]Jesus answered them, "Have you never read what David did when he and his companions were hungry? [4]He entered the house of God, and taking the consecrated bread, he ate what is lawful only for priests to eat. And he also gave some to his companions." [5]Then Jesus said to them, *"The Son of Man is Lord of the Sabbath."*

[6]On another Sabbath he went into the synagogue and was teaching, and a man was there whose right hand was shrivelled. [7]The Pharisees and the teachers of the law were looking for a reason to accuse Jesus, so they watched him closely to see if he would heal on the Sabbath. [8]But Jesus knew what they were thinking and said to the man with the shrivelled hand, "Get up and stand in front of everyone." So he got up and stood there.

[9]Then Jesus said to them, "I ask you, *which is lawful on the Sabbath*: to do good or to do evil, to save life or to destroy it?"

[10]He looked round at them all, and then said to the man, "Stretch out your hand." He did so, and his hand was completely restored. [11]But they were furious and began to discuss with one another what they might do to Jesus.

Jesus tells the Pharisees that
they have misinterpreted the
meaning of the Sabbath

He heals a
man with a
withered hand

The Pharisees accuse Jesus of
disobeying the Sabbath laws

UNDERSTANDING THE STORY
The Sabbath was meant to be a joyful day to praise and thank God for all his creation, but it became burdensome. Jesus has the authority to overrule the intolerable restrictions imposed by the Jewish tradition. The religious leaders see their own authority undermined by Jesus' teaching and his power to heal.

JOHN 2

JESUS CLEARS THE TEMPLE

2 **W**HEN[13] IT WAS ALMOST TIME for the Jewish Passover, *Jesus went up to Jerusalem.* [14]In the temple courts he found men selling cattle, sheep and doves, and others sitting at tables exchanging money. [15]So he made a whip out of cords, and drove all from the temple area, both sheep and cattle; he scattered the coins of the money-changers and overturned their tables. [16]To those who sold doves he said, "Get these out of here! *How dare you turn my Father's house into a market!*"

[17]His disciples remembered that it is written: "Zeal for your house will consume me."

[18]Then the Jews demanded of him, "What miraculous sign can you show us to prove your authority to do all this?"

[19]Jesus answered them, "Destroy this temple, and I will raise it again in three days."

[20]The Jews replied, "*It has taken forty-six years to build this temple*, and you are going to raise it in three days?" [21]But the temple he had spoken of was his body.

CHAPTER 2 VERSE 13
"Jesus went up to Jerusalem"
According to the Gospels of Matthew, Mark, and Luke, Jesus does not go to Jerusalem until the end of his ministry. They mention a cleansing of the Temple at this later date, although the context and some details are different.

CHAPTER 2 VERSE 16
"How dare you turn my Father's house into a market!"
The outer court of the Temple had become a place of trade, where priests sold to pilgrims certified sacrificial animals, such as cattle, sheep, and doves, at exorbitant prices. The same pilgrims were swindled by the money-changers, who changed money into Tyrian coinage – the currency required for temple taxes.

The temple courts are like a market

Jesus is angry with the money-changers

Bronze pyxis

Silver shekel

BOX OF COINS
This box (pyxis) and the Tyrian and Jewish shekels it contained date from the 1st century AD.

UNDERSTANDING THE STORY

Jesus is outraged that those who go to the Temple to worship God are being cheated by unscrupulous traders. When his authority is questioned, Jesus' answer is not understood. He is saying that his own body is a living temple where God dwells, and his death and resurrection will be the final proof.

CHAPTER 2 VERSE 20
"It has taken forty-six years to build this temple"
Herod the Great started to build the Temple in about 19 BC. The Temple was still being built in Jesus' time and was not completed until AD 63.

MATTHEW 5

THE SERMON ON THE MOUNT

✤

CHAPTER 5 VERSE 1
"He went up on a mountainside and sat down"
The "mountainside" was the steeply rising ground on the western side of the Sea of Galilee. Jesus was about to give his disciples a formal lesson, so he sat down to speak as was appropriate for teachers of his day. Crowds listened to the sermon from a distance.

THE CHURCH OF MOUNT BEATITUDES
The Fransiscans built a church on the site where Jesus gave his sermon.

✤

CHAPTER 5 VERSE 3
"Blessed are"
Jesus' words are known as the "Beatitudes", latin for "blessed", or "fortunate". People who put the will of God above personal success, even when it means that they may suffer on earth, are fortunate because they will be rewarded in heaven.

5 WHEN[1] [JESUS] SAW THE CROWDS, *he went up on a mountainside and sat down.* His disciples came to him, [2]and he began to teach them, saying:

[3]*"Blessed are* the poor in spirit, for theirs is the kingdom of heaven. [4]Blessed are those who mourn, for they will be comforted. [5]Blessed are the meek, for they will inherit the earth. [6]Blessed are those who hunger and thirst for righteousness, for they will be filled. [7]Blessed are the merciful, for they will be shown mercy. [8]Blessed are the pure in heart, for they will see God. [9]Blessed are the peacemakers, for they will be called sons of God. [10]Blessed are those who are persecuted because of righteousness, for theirs is the kingdom of heaven. [11]Blessed are you when people insult you, persecute you and falsely say all kinds of evil against you because of me. [12]Rejoice and be glad, because great is your reward in heaven, for in the same way they persecuted the prophets who were before you.

[13]*"You are the salt* of the earth. But if the salt loses its saltiness, how can it be made salty again?... [14]*You are the light* of the world. A city on a hill cannot be hidden. [15]Neither do people light a lamp and put it under a bowl. Instead they put it on its stand, and it gives light to everyone in the house. [16]In the same way, let your light shine before men, that they may see your good deeds and praise your Father in heaven.

When Jesus sees the crowds, he walks up the mountainside

Many people listen to Jesus' sermon from a distance

244

Jesus explains that he has not come to change the Law but to teach people its true meaning

He says that those who recognise their spiritual needs and put God first in their lives are fortunate

His twelve disciples and other close followers are gathered around him

Jesus tells his disciples to love their enemies and to forgive people for wrongdoings

CHAPTER 5 VERSES 13–14
"You are the salt... the light"
Salt purifies and stops corruption. True disciples bring these qualities into the world. Like light in the dark, Jesus' disciples will enlighten ignorant minds and be a shining example for others to follow.

SAINT BONIFACE (*c*. AD 680–755)
St Boniface dedicated his life to spreading the Christian message in Germany. This engraving depicts him destroying the sacred oak of a pagan god.

17"Do not think that I have come to abolish *the Law or the Prophets*; I have not come to abolish them but to fulfil them. 18I tell you the truth, until heaven and earth disappear, not the smallest letter, not the least stroke of a pen, will by any means disappear from the Law until everything is accomplished. 19Anyone who breaks one of the least of these commandments and teaches others to do the same will be called least in the kingdom of heaven, but whoever practises and teaches these commands will be called great in the kingdom of heaven. 20For I tell you that unless your righteousness surpasses that of the Pharisees and the teachers of the law, you will certainly not enter the kingdom of heaven..."

Jesus gave some examples of how to follow the spirit of the Law. It was true that murder and adultery were unlawful, but it was also wrong to harbour the sinful thoughts that might lead to these acts. He explained that sometimes the Law had been misinterpreted.

38"You have heard that it was said, '*Eye for eye, and tooth for tooth.*' 39But I tell you, Do not resist an evil person. If someone strikes you on the right cheek, turn to him the other also. 40And if someone wants to sue you and take your tunic, let him have your cloak as well... 43"You have heard that it was said, 'Love your neighbour and hate your enemy.' 44But I tell you: Love your enemies and pray for those who persecute you, 45that you may be sons of your Father in heaven... 48Be perfect, therefore, as your heavenly Father is perfect."

CHAPTER 5 VERSE 17
"The Law or the Prophets"
The Jewish Bible is divided into the Law, the Prophets, and the Writings. Jesus is the fulfilment of the Old Testament prophecies. The religious leaders have distorted and misinterpreted God's Law. Jesus' teachings reveal its true meaning.

JEWISH TORAH SCROLL
"Torah" is Hebrew for "law" or "instruction". The Torah is the first five books of the Bible and contains the Jewish laws and other writings.

CHAPTER 5 VERSE 38
"Eye for eye... tooth for tooth"
Jesus urges people not to avenge wrongdoings. God will be the final judge and will punish those who have sinned and not repented.

MATTHEW 6–7

CHAPTER 6 VERSE 1
"Acts of righteousness"
Giving, praying, and fasting were the three main religious activities. Jesus stresses that rather than be a public display of false piety, these acts should be sincere.

QUIET PRAYER
Watercolour by Richard Moser of a synagogue in Vienna

CHAPTER 6 VERSE 5
"When you pray, do not be like the hypocrites"
A man was invited to stand at the front of the synagogue and lead the prayers. To be chosen was an honour, and some used this as an opportunity for self-glory. Prayer is a personal approach to God, and so people should pray privately and with humility.

CHAPTER 6 VERSE 9
"This... is how you should pray"
Jesus gives a prayer for the disciples to use as a group. It begins with three petitions for heavenly glory and ends with three petitions for God's help in earthly life. This model for praying has become central to Christian worship and is known as the Lord's Prayer.

6 "Be[1] careful not to do your *'acts of righteousness'* before men, to be seen by them. If you do, you will have no reward from your Father in heaven.

2"So when you give to the needy, do not announce it with trumpets, as the hypocrites do in the synagogues and on the streets, to be honoured by men... 3Do not let your left hand know what your right hand is doing, 4so that your giving may be in secret...

5"And *when you pray, do not be like the hypocrites,* for they love to pray standing in the synagogues and on the street corners to be seen by men... 6Go into your room, close the door and pray to your Father, who is unseen... 7Do not keep on babbling like pagans, for they think they will be heard because of their many words... 9*This, then, is how you should pray*:

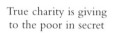

True charity is giving to the poor in secret

" 'Our Father in heaven, hallowed be your name, 10your kingdom come, your will be done on earth as it is in heaven. 11Give us today our daily bread. 12Forgive us our debts, as we also have forgiven our debtors. 13And lead us not into temptation, but deliver us from the evil one.'...

19"Do not store up for yourselves *treasures on earth...* 20But store up for yourselves *treasures in heaven,* where moth and rust do not destroy, and where thieves do not break in and steal... 25Do not worry about your life, what you will eat or drink; or about your body, what you will wear... 32For the pagans run after all these things, and your heavenly Father knows that you need them.

Those who pray alone and unobserved are closer to God

33But seek first his kingdom and his righteousness, and all these things will be given to you as well...

7 1"Do not judge, or you too will be judged...

¹²In everything, *do to others what you would have them do to you*, for this sums up the Law and the Prophets.

¹³"Enter through the narrow gate. For wide is the gate and broad the road that leads to destruction, and many enter through it. ¹⁴But small is the gate and narrow the road that leads to life, and only a few find it... ²¹Not everyone who says to me, 'Lord, Lord,' will enter the kingdom of heaven, but only he who does the will of my Father who is in heaven...

²⁴"Therefore everyone who hears these words of mine and puts them into practice is *like a wise man who built his house on the rock*. ²⁵The rain came down, the streams rose, and the winds blew and beat against that house; yet it did not fall, because it had its foundation on the rock. ²⁶But everyone who hears these words of mine and does not put them into practice is like a foolish man who built his house on sand. ²⁷The rain came down, the streams rose, and the winds blew and beat against that house, and it fell with a great crash."

Those who do good works are gaining heavenly wealth

UNDERSTANDING THE STORY

Jesus wants his disciples to have a clear understanding of God's will. The examples set by many religious leaders are confusing, because these men are highly respected by society, and Jesus exposes the hypocrisy behind their shallow "righteousness". The Sermon on the Mount is a guide for the disciples as they spread Jesus' teachings throughout the world.

The house built on firm foundations withstands the storm

The house built on sand is destroyed

❖

CHAPTER 6 VERSES 19–20
"Treasures on earth... treasures in heaven"
People should not be motivated by material gain because earthly wealth has no permanence. If they strive to live righteous lives, they will find their reward in heaven.

❖

CHAPTER 7 VERSE 12
"Do to others what you would have them do to you"
Two hundred years after Jesus spoke these words, the Roman emperor Alexander Severus wrote them in gold on his wall. Jesus' "golden rule" is a simple and practical guide that everyone can consider when relating to other people.

ALEXANDER SEVERUS
(Ruled AD 222–35)

❖

CHAPTER 7 VERSE 24
"Like a wise man who built his house on the rock"
Many will listen and agree with Jesus, but only those who apply his teachings to their daily lives will survive the pressures of life and pass the test of God's judgement.

LUKE 7

FAITH AND THE POWER TO SAVE

CHAPTER 7 VERSE 1
"He entered Capernaum"
Capernaum was Jesus' base during his ministry in Galilee. This large, busy town was the centre of the fishing industry and the home of Peter and other fishermen disciples. When the people of Capernaum refused to follow Jesus, he predicted its ruin. The town of Tell Houm now stands on the ancient site.

CAPERNAUM
This 4th-century synagogue was built over the ruins of the synagogue where Jesus often taught.

CHAPTER 7 VERSE 3
"The centurion heard of Jesus"
A centurion was normally a Roman military officer in charge of about eighty men. This centurion was probably a non-Jewish officer in the auxiliary forces under the command of Herod Antipas, the ruler of Galilee. His forces were organized like the Roman army.

GREAVES
Leg protectors (greaves) of leather or metal were worn only by army officers. This highly ornate pair was probably made for ceremonial purposes.

7 WHEN[1] JESUS HAD FINISHED saying all this in the hearing of the people, *he entered Capernaum.* ²There a centurion's servant, whom his master valued highly, was sick and about to die. ³*The centurion heard of Jesus* and sent some elders of the Jews to him, asking him to come and heal his servant. ⁴When they came to Jesus, they pleaded earnestly with him, "This man deserves to have you do this, ⁵because he loves our nation and has built our synagogue."...

⁶He was not far from the house when the centurion sent friends to say to him: "Lord, don't trouble yourself, for I do not deserve to have you come under my roof... ⁷But say the word, and my servant will be healed. ⁸For I myself am a man under authority, with soldiers under me. I tell this one, 'Go', and he goes; and that one, 'Come', and he comes. I say to my servant, 'Do this', and he does it."

Jesus is on his way to to heal a centurion's dying servant

The centurion sends friends to stop Jesus

They ask Jesus to say the word and the servant will be healed

The centurion sees that his faith has healed his servant

⁹When Jesus heard this, he was amazed at him, and turning to the crowd following him, he said, "I tell you, I have not found such great faith even in Israel." ¹⁰Then the men who had been sent returned to the house and found the servant well...

³⁶Now one of the Pharisees invited Jesus to have dinner with him, so *he went to the Pharisee's house and reclined at the table.* ³⁷When a woman who had lived a sinful life in that town learned that Jesus was eating at the Pharisee's house, she brought *an alabaster jar of perfume,* ³⁸and as she stood behind him at his feet weeping, she began to wet his feet with her tears. Then she wiped them with her hair, kissed them and poured perfume on them.

³⁹When the Pharisee who had invited him saw this, he said to himself, "If this man were a prophet, he would know who is touching him and what kind of woman she is – that she is a sinner."

⁴⁰Jesus answered him, "Simon, I have something to tell you."

"Tell me, teacher," he said.

⁴¹"Two men owed money to a certain money-lender. One owed him five hundred denarii, and the other fifty. ⁴²Neither of them had the money to pay him back, so he cancelled the debts of both. Now which of them will love him more?"

The Pharisee thinks Jesus is wrong to let a sinner touch him

The woman who has sinned shows Jesus more hospitality than his host

Jesus' feet are wet with her tears

She dries Jesus' feet with her hair and pours perfume on them

The woman's sins are forgiven because of her faith

⁴³Simon replied, "I suppose the one who had the bigger debt..."

"You have judged correctly," Jesus said.

⁴⁴Then he turned towards the woman and said to Simon, "Do you see this woman? I came into your house. You did not give me any water for my feet, but she wet my feet with her tears and wiped them with her hair. ⁴⁵You did not give me a kiss, but this woman, from the time I entered has not stopped kissing my feet. ⁴⁶You did not put oil on my head, but she has poured perfume on my feet. ⁴⁷Therefore, I tell you, her many sins have been forgiven – *for she loved much*. But he who has been forgiven little loves little."

⁴⁸Then Jesus said to her, "Your sins are forgiven."

⁴⁹The other guests began to say among themselves, "Who is this who even forgives sins?"

⁵⁰Jesus said to the woman, "Your faith has saved you; go in peace."

UNDERSTANDING THE STORIES

Faith has the power to change any situation. The centurion's belief in Jesus saves the life of his servant. The woman's unquestioning faith is shown in her spontaneous display of gratitude. Her humility highlights the Pharisee's pride. Jesus wants people to realize that the wrong attitude will prevent salvation.

CHAPTER 7 VERSE 36
"He... reclined at the table"
Wealthy Jews would probably have adopted the Roman practice of eating their meals reclining on a couch (triclinium). Diners leaned on their left sides, with feet extended away from the table, and took the food with their right hands.

A ROMAN BANQUET
From "The Roses of Heliogabalus"
by Sir Lawrence Alma-Tadema (1888)

CHAPTER 7 VERSE 37
"An alabaster jar of perfume"
Perfumes were made from a variety of plants, herbs, and spices, imported from India, Egypt, Persia, and Arabia. Only the most expensive perfumes were kept in alabaster jars. Cheaper fragrances for daily use were kept in pottery flasks.

ALABASTER
Alabaster is a soft, translucent stone that can be carved and polished. The best quality alabaster was imported from Egypt.

CHAPTER 7 VERSE 47
"For she loved much"
In Hebrew, "to love" was an expression that meant "to show gratitude". A person with a large debt will show more gratitude than one with a small debt if the debt is cancelled. The woman is a much greater sinner than the Pharisee, but she is truly repentant and her faith in Jesus brings forgiveness.

MARK 4

THE SOWER

❖

CHAPTER 4 VERSE 2
"He taught… by parables"
Jesus taught by using stories of everyday life in order to illustrate spiritual or moral truths. The stories often contained hidden meanings. They were called parables, which is from the Greek word "parabole" meaning "a placing beside" or comparison. About thirty of Jesus' parables are recorded in the Gospels.

BARLEY

WHEAT

MILLET

GRAINS FOR BREAD
Barley, wheat, and millet were all harvested, although barley was the most widely grown as it flourished on poorer soils. Bread, baked as flat cakes, was most people's staple diet.

4 JESUS[1] BEGAN to teach by the lake. The crowd that gathered round him was so large that he got into a boat and sat in it out on the lake, while all the people were along the shore at the water's edge. [2]*He taught them many things by parables*, and in his teaching said: [3]"Listen! A farmer went out to sow his seed. [4]As he was scattering the seed, some fell along the path, and the birds came and ate it up. [5]Some fell on rocky places, where it did not have much soil. It sprang up quickly, because the soil was shallow. [6]But when the sun came up, the plants were scorched, and they withered because they had no root. [7]Other seed fell among thorns, which grew up and choked the plants, so that they did not bear grain. [8]Still other seed fell on good soil. It came up, grew and produced a crop, multiplying thirty, sixty, or even a hundred times."

Jesus teaches his followers from a boat by the lake

Seed that grows in good soil produces a healthy crop many times over

Seed that lands amongst thorns is choked and prevented from growing

Seed scattered along the path is eaten by birds

⁹Then Jesus said, "He who has ears to hear, let him hear."
¹⁰When he was alone, the Twelve and the others around him asked him about the parables. ¹¹He told them, "*The secret of the kingdom of God has been given to you*. But to those on the outside everything is said in parables…"

¹³Then Jesus said to them, "Don't you understand this parable? How then will you understand any parable? ¹⁴*The farmer sows the word.* ¹⁵Some people are like seed along the path, where the word is sown. As soon as they hear it, Satan comes and takes away the word that was sown in them. ¹⁶Others, like seed sown on rocky places, hear the word and at once receive it with joy. ¹⁷But since they have no root, they last only a short time. When trouble or persecution comes because of the word, they quickly fall away. ¹⁸Still others, like seed sown among thorns, hear the word; ¹⁹but the worries of this life, the deceitfulness of wealth and the desires for other things come in and choke the word, making it unfruitful. ²⁰Others, like seed sown on good soil, hear the word, accept it, and produce a crop – thirty, sixty or even a hundred times what was sown…

²²"For *whatever is hidden is meant to be disclosed*, and whatever is concealed is meant to be brought out into the open. ²³If anyone has ears to hear, let him hear."…

³³With many similar parables Jesus spoke the word to them, as much as they could understand. ³⁴He did not say anything to them without using a parable. But when he was alone with his own disciples, he explained everything.

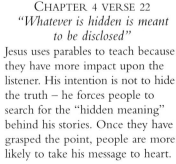

Jesus explains the parable to his disciples

UNDERSTANDING THE STORY

Just like the sower, who faces many difficulties as he tries to establish his crop, Jesus knows that it will not be easy to persuade people to accept his teachings. The significance of this parable is the importance of the "soil". People need to listen with open minds and receptive hearts for the message to take root.

✤

CHAPTER 4 VERSE 11
"The secret… given to you"
Even the disciples did not always understand Jesus' words. Jesus took trouble to explain, knowing that his ministry would soon pass to them.

✤

CHAPTER 4 VERSE 14
"The farmer sows the word"
Jesus is the farmer, who sows words instead of seeds. His teachings meet many obstacles. The message he brings is ignored, misunderstood, and sometimes abandoned because of the temptations of material things. "Seeds" can only grow in those who accept and live by Jesus' teachings.

✤

CHAPTER 4 VERSE 22
"Whatever is hidden is meant to be disclosed"
Jesus uses parables to teach because they have more impact upon the listener. His intention is not to hide the truth – he forces people to search for the "hidden meaning" behind his stories. Once they have grasped the point, people are more likely to take his message to heart.

Seed that falls on shallow soil grows quickly but is soon scorched by the sun

STRONGER THAN THE STORM

CHAPTER 4 VERSE 37
"A furious squall came up"
The Sea of Galilee is situated in a basin surrounded by mountains. It is notorious for sudden and violent storms. Squalls like this one happen because cool air from the Mediterranean clashes with the hot and humid air above the lake.

STORM OVER LAKE GALILEE

CHAPTER 5 VERSE 1
"The region of Gerasenes"
Jesus goes to the Decapolis, a region with ten Greek city-states. (Decapolis is Greek for ten cities.) One of these – Gerasa – controlled the area up to the shore of the lake.

Jesus and the disciples are crossing the lake when a storm breaks

The disciples fear they will drown and wake Jesus, who is asleep in the stern

CHAPTER 5 VERSE 3
"This man lived in the tombs"
He was probably a Gentile, who was poor and isolated from his family and community. Very poor people sometimes lived in cavern tombs, which can still be seen today near the modern village of Kursi.

4 THAT[35] DAY when evening came, [Jesus] said to his disciples, "Let us go over to the other side." [36]Leaving the crowd behind, they took him along, just as he was, in the boat. There were also other boats with him. [37]*A furious squall came up*, and the waves broke over the boat, so that it was nearly swamped. [38]Jesus was in the stern, sleeping on a cushion. The disciples woke him and said to him, "Teacher, don't you care if we drown?"

[39]He got up, rebuked the wind and said to the waves, "Quiet! Be still!" Then the wind died down and it was completely calm.

[40]He said to his disciples, "Why are you so afraid? Do you still have no faith?"

[41]They were terrified and asked each other, "Who is this? Even the wind and the waves obey him!"

5 [1]They went across the lake to *the region of Gerasenes*. [2]When Jesus got out of the boat, a man with an evil spirit came from the tombs to meet him. [3]*This man lived in the tombs*, and no-one could bind him any more, not even with a chain. [4]For he had often been chained hand and foot, but he tore the chains apart and broke the irons on his feet. No-one was strong enough to subdue him. [5]Night and day among the tombs and in the hills he would cry out and cut himself with stones.

[6]When he saw Jesus from a distance, he ran and fell on his knees in front of him. [7]He shouted at the top of his voice, "What do you want with me, Jesus, Son of the Most High God?

Jesus commands the wind and the waves to be still

The disciples are afraid of Jesus' power

Swear to God that you won't torture me!" ⁸For Jesus had said to him, "Come out of this man, you evil spirit!"

⁹Then Jesus asked him, "What is your name?"

"*My name is Legion,*" he replied, "*for we are many.*" ¹⁰And he begged Jesus again and again not to send them out of the area.

¹¹*A large herd of pigs was feeding on the nearby hillside.* ¹²The demons begged Jesus, "Send us among the pigs; allow us to go into them." ¹³He gave them permission, and the evil spirits came out and went into the pigs. The herd, about two thousand in number, rushed down the steep bank into the lake and were drowned.

¹⁴Those tending the pigs ran off and reported this in the town and countryside, and the people went out to see what had happened.

When they arrived, the man was dressed and sitting quietly with Jesus. Those who had witnessed the miracle told them about the demons and the pigs. The people were amazed and realized that Jesus was a man with great powers. They became afraid of him and begged him to leave.

¹⁸As Jesus was getting into the boat, the man who had been demon-possessed begged to go with him. ¹⁹Jesus did not let him, but said, "Go home to your family and tell them how much the Lord has done for you, and how he has had mercy on you." ²⁰So the man went away and began to tell in the Decapolis how much Jesus had done for him. And all the people were amazed.

✛
CHAPTER 5 VERSE 9
*"My name is Legion…
for we are many"*
A Roman legion consisted of about 5,000 men. The multitude of demons possessing the man recognized Jesus' power over them.

MONASTERY AT KURSI
This Byzantine monastery was built on the traditional site where Jesus cast out the demons. The location remained a mystery until shortly after the Six Day War (1967), when it was discovered during excavations for a new road.

On the shore, Jesus is greeted by a demon-possessed man

The herd of pigs rushes into the lake

Jesus tells the evil spirits to leave the man

The demons inside the man beg to be sent into the herd of pigs

UNDERSTANDING THE STORY

Jesus demonstrates his authority over natural and supernatural powers so that the faith of his disciples can grow progressively. The mixed population of the Decapolis area witnesses the miraculous transformation of the demon-possessed man, who becomes the first missionary to a Gentile audience.

✛
CHAPTER 5 VERSE 11
"A large herd of pigs was feeding on the nearby hillside"
Many non-Jews lived in Galilee and in the Decapolis. Jews did not raise pigs because they considered these animals the most unclean of all. The pigs' destruction symbolizes the removal of the man's uncleanliness.

MARK 5
STRONGER THAN DEATH

THE REGION OF GALILEE

CHAPTER 5 VERSE 21
"Crossed… to the other side"
Jesus and his disciples left the
Decapolis region and crossed the
lake to Galilee in the north.

❖

CHAPTER 5 VERSE 22
"One of the synagogue rulers"
A layman was usually responsible
for synagogue administration, which
involved looking after the building
and organizing religious services.

❖

CHAPTER 5 VERSE 25
"Subject to bleeding"
The woman's illness made her life
miserable. She could not marry (or
even socialize) because the bleeding
meant she was considered unclean.

❖

CHAPTER 5 VERSE 27
"Touched his cloak"
The Gospel of Matthew says that
the woman "touched the edge of
his cloak". Jesus wore tassels on the
edge of his cloak as a reminder of
God's commandments (Numbers
15: 38). Artists have often depicted
Jesus wearing a blue cloak. The
colour blue represents the sky and
heaven, which symbolize "hope".

JESUS DRESSED IN BLUE
Mosaic from the Hosias Loukas
Monastery, Greece

5 **W**HEN[21] JESUS had again *crossed over by boat to the other side* of
the lake, a large crowd gathered round him while he was by
the lake. [22]Then *one of the synagogue rulers*, named Jairus, came
there. Seeing Jesus, he fell at his feet [23]and pleaded earnestly with him,
"My little daughter is dying. Please come and put your hands on her so
that she will be healed and live." [24]So Jesus went with him.

A large crowd followed and pressed around him. [25]And a woman
was there who had been *subject to
bleeding* for twelve years. [26]She had
suffered a great deal under the
care of many doctors and had
spent all she had, yet instead of
getting better she grew worse.
[27]When she heard about Jesus, she
came up behind him in the crowd
and *touched his cloak*, [28]because she
thought, "If I just touch his clothes,
I will be healed." [29]Immediately
her bleeding stopped and she felt
in her body that she was freed
from her suffering.

Jesus is on his way to heal a sick child
when a woman touches his cloak

[30]At once Jesus realised that power had
gone out from him. He turned around in
the crowd and asked, "Who touched
my clothes?"

[31]"You see the people crowding
against you," his disciples answered,
"and yet you can ask,
'Who touched me?' "

[32]But Jesus kept looking
around to see who had done
it. [33]Then the woman,
knowing what had happened
to her, came and fell at his
feet and, trembling with
fear, told him the whole
truth. [34]He said to her,
"Daughter, your faith has
healed you. Go in peace
and be freed from
your suffering."

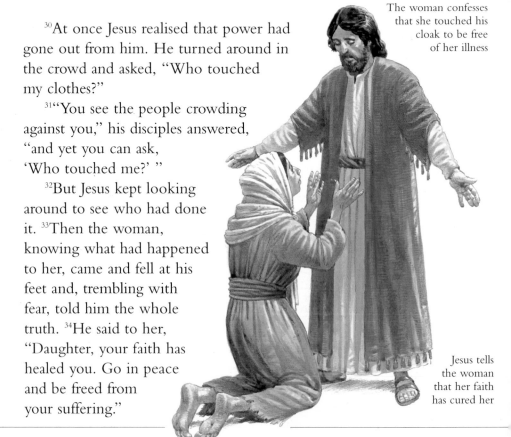

The woman confesses
that she touched his
cloak to be free
of her illness

Jesus tells
the woman
that her faith
has cured her

Jesus enters the house where Jairus' daughter lies dead

Jesus tells the dead child to get up

The disciples Peter, James, and John witness a miracle

CHAPTER 5 VERSE 38
"People crying and wailing"
When someone died, family and friends would express their sorrow with a public display of grief. As in all Middle-Eastern cultures, burial took place within 24 hours. Families often hired flute players and professional mourners. Matthew (9: 23) records, "Jesus... saw the flute players and the noisy crowds". The period of mourning lasted for seven days.

Twin pipes

PIPES
The reed pipe produces a high-pitched, wailing sound, which is why this instrument was played during the mourning period.

³⁵While Jesus was still speaking, some men came from the house of Jairus, the synagogue ruler. "Your daughter is dead," they said. "Why bother the teacher any more?"

³⁶Ignoring what they said, Jesus told the synagogue ruler, "Don't be afraid; just believe."

³⁷He did not let anyone follow him except Peter, James and John the brother of James. ³⁸When they came to the home of the synagogue ruler, Jesus saw a commotion, with *people crying and wailing* loudly.

³⁹He went in and said to them, "Why all this commotion and wailing? The child is not dead but asleep." ⁴⁰But they laughed at him.

After he put them all out, he took the child's father and mother and the disciples who were with him, and went in where the child was. ⁴¹He took her by the hand and said to her, "Talitha koum!" (which means, "Little girl, I say to you, get up!").

⁴²Immediately the girl stood up and walked around (she was twelve years old). At this they were completely astonished. ⁴³He gave strict orders not to let anyone know about this, and told them to give her something to eat.

UNDERSTANDING THE STORIES

The miracles in these stories demonstrate that the power of faith can overcome illness and death. The woman believes that she will be cured if she can just touch Jesus, and her faith is rewarded. Jesus tells her, "Your faith has healed you". Jairus knows that his daughter is dead. Jesus tells him, "Just believe", and then brings the child back to life.

Immediately the girl stands up and walks around

Jairus and his wife are overjoyed that their daughter is alive

MATTHEW 14

DEATH OF JOHN THE BAPTIST

KING HEROD
Herod Antipas was a son of Herod the Great and had inherited a part of his father's kingdom. Antipas was not a king but a tetrarch, who ruled Galilee and Perea from 4 BC until AD 39. King Herod was his popular title.

14 N OW[3] HEROD had arrested John and bound him and put him in prison *because of Herodias*, his brother Philip's wife, [4]for John had been saying to him: "It is not lawful for you to have her." [5]Herod wanted to kill John, but he was afraid of the people, because they considered him a prophet.

[6]On Herod's birthday the daughter of Herodias danced for them and pleased Herod so much [7]that he promised with an oath to give her whatever she asked. [8]Prompted by her mother, she said, "Give me here on a platter the head of John the Baptist."

Salome dances for King Herod, and he promises her anything she wants

Salome's mother hates John the Baptist because he denounced her marriage to King Herod

King Herod is distressed by Salome's request

Salome demands the head of John the Baptist

CHAPTER 14 VERSE 3
"Because of Herodias"
Herodias was a granddaughter of Herod the Great. She first married her uncle Philip and they had a daughter, Salome. Herodias left Philip to marry his brother, Herod Antipas. This second marriage was contrary to Old Testament Law.

CHAPTER 14 VERSE 10
"Beheaded in the prison"
John was imprisoned at Machaerus, a desert fortress on the border of Perea and Nabatea. Herod spent time there because he feared an attack by the Nabatean king, whose daughter had been Herod's first wife.

King Herod cannot refuse Salome's request because he has sworn an oath to keep his promise

THE BEHEADING OF JOHN THE BAPTIST
Schnorr von Carolsfeld's 19th-century engraving depicts Herod's atrocity.

[9]The king was distressed, but because of his oaths and his dinner guests, he ordered that her request be granted [10]and had John *beheaded in the prison*. [11]His head was brought in on a platter and given to the girl, who carried it to her mother. [12]John's disciples came and took his body and buried it. Then they went and told Jesus.

MARK 6
MISSION OF THE TWELVE

6 THEN[6] JESUS WENT round teaching from village to village. [7]Calling the Twelve to him, he sent them out two by two and gave them authority over evil spirits.

[8]These were his instructions: "*Take nothing for the journey* except a staff – no bread, no bag, no money in your belts. [9]Wear sandals but not an extra tunic. [10]Whenever you enter in a house, stay there until you leave that town. [11]And if any place will not welcome you or listen to you, *shake the dust off your feet* when you leave, as a testimony against them."

[12]They went out and preached that people should repent. [13]They drove out many demons and *anointed many sick people with oil* and healed them.

CHAPTER 6 VERSE 8
"Take nothing for the journey"
Jesus is telling his disciples that God will provide for their material needs. The disciples are to rely on the hospitality of others, which will bring them into close contact with the people they will be teaching.

FIG CAKES
Dried figs compacted into cakes made an excellent convenience food for travellers.

Jesus sends out his disciples two by two to preach repentance

The disciples carry staffs. They must travel everywhere by foot

CHAPTER 6 VERSE 11
"Shake the dust off your feet"
Jews performed this ritual whenever they returned home from travelling abroad. It meant that they would not contaminate God's Holy Land with heathen soil. Those who rejected the disciples would understand that they were being marked as heathens.

CHAPTER 6 VERSE 13
"Anointed many sick people with oil"
In Jesus' time, oil was commonly used for its medicinal properties. However, the disciples' anointing of the sick was a symbolic gesture. The oil was an aid to faith for those who were being healed.

[14]King Herod heard about this, for Jesus' name had become well known. Some were saying, "John the Baptist has been raised from the dead, and that is why miraculous powers are at work in him."

[15]Others said, "He is Elijah."

And still others claimed, "He is a prophet, like one of the prophets of long ago."

[16]But when Herod heard this, he said, "John, the man I beheaded, has been raised from the dead!"

UNDERSTANDING THE STORIES

The death of John marks the beginning of a new phase in Jesus' ministry. He sends out his disciples to do the task for which they were chosen. They are to preach the same message as John, but they have Jesus' authority to perform miracles. Jesus sends them out in pairs for moral support during this training.

IN THE NAME OF JESUS CHRIST
This engraving, dated 1847, shows the disciples healing the sick.

257

MATTHEW 14
JESUS FEEDS THE CROWDS

CHAPTER 14 VERSE 13
"He withdrew by boat"
Jesus left for a deserted place when he heard that Antipas, the ruler of Galilee who killed John the Baptist, was questioning his popularity. The disciples had just returned from their first mission, and Jesus wanted to concentrate on their training, away from crowds and political problems.

LOAVES AND FISH
The feeding of the crowds is recorded on this 4th-century mosaic in the Church of the Multiplication, Tabgha, the traditional site of the miracle.

CHAPTER 14 VERSE 20
"The disciples picked up twelve basketfuls of broken pieces"
Jesus respected the Jewish tradition that considered bread as a gift of God not to be wasted. The baskets of leftover bread gave the disciples material proof of their master's godly powers.

Jesus' followers wonder how so many can be fed with so little food

CHAPTER 14
VERSE 21
"Five thousand men"
The crowd eating together symbolizes the unity of the new religious community gathered around the Messiah.

14 WHEN[13] JESUS HEARD what had happened, *he withdrew by boat* privately to a solitary place. Hearing of this, the crowds followed him on foot from the towns. [14]When Jesus landed and saw a large crowd, he had compassion on them and healed their sick.

[15]As evening approached, the disciples came to him and said, "This is a remote place, and it's already getting late. Send the crowds away, so that they can go to the villages and buy themselves some food."

[16]Jesus replied, "They do not need to go away. You give them something to eat."

[17]"We have here only five loaves of bread and two fish," they answered.

[18]"Bring them here to me," he said. [19]And he directed the people to sit down on the grass. Taking the five loaves and the two fish and looking up to heaven, he gave thanks and broke the loaves. Then he gave them to the disciples, and the disciples gave them to the people. [20]They all ate and were satisfied, and *the disciples picked up twelve basketfuls of broken pieces* that were left over. [21]The number of those who ate was about *five thousand men*, besides women and children.

[22]Immediately Jesus made the disciples get into the boat and go on ahead of him to the other side, while he dismissed the crowd.

Jesus gives thanks to God and breaks the bread

The crowd has been listening to Jesus all day, and there is nowhere for them to buy food

The disciples are amazed to see the food multiply

Five loaves and two fish

MATTHEW 14

JESUS WALKS ON WATER

14 AFTER[23] HE HAD *dismissed [the crowd]*, he went up on a mountainside by himself to pray. When evening came, he was there alone, [24]but the boat was already a considerable distance from land, buffeted by the waves because the wind was against it.

[25]*During the fourth watch of the night* Jesus went out to them, walking on the lake. [26]When the disciples saw him walking on the lake, they were terrified. "It's a ghost," they said, and cried out in fear.

[27]But Jesus immediately said to them: "Take courage! It is I. Don't be afraid."

[28]"Lord, if it's you," Peter replied, "tell me to come to you on the water."

[29]"Come," he said. Then Peter got down out of the boat, walked on the water and came towards Jesus. [30]But when he saw the wind, he was afraid and, beginning to sink, cried out, "Lord, save me!"

[31]Immediately Jesus reached out his hand and caught him. "*You of little faith*," he said, "why did you doubt?"...

[33]Then those who were in the boat worshipped him, saying, "Truly you are the Son of God." [34]When they had crossed over, they landed at Gennesaret. [35]And when the men of that place recognised Jesus, they sent word to all the surrounding country. People brought all their sick to him... and all who touched him were healed.

UNDERSTANDING THE STORIES

Jesus is the host at the gathering; he provides for the physical and the spiritual needs of the crowd. Peter's first steps across the water demonstrate that faith can achieve the seemingly impossible. Both miracles serve to strengthen the disciples' belief in Jesus.

CHAPTER 14 VERSE 23
"Dismissed [the crowd]"
The Gospel of John records that the crowd "intended to come and make him king by force" (6: 15). Crowds followed Jesus wherever he went, seeing in him the promised Messiah. But they misunderstood his ministry. They wanted a king to deliver Israel from foreign rule.

CHAPTER 14 VERSE 25
"During the fourth watch of the night"
The Romans divided the night into four watches. The last, or fourth, was from 3am to 6am. Jews only had three watches, from sunset to 10pm, from 10pm to 2am, and from 2am to sunrise.

MEASURING TIME
Divisions of time were calculated using water-clocks and sundials. Water-clocks worked by slowly dripping water, which was then measured.

WATER-CLOCK

CHAPTER 14 VERSE 31
"You of little faith"
Peter began to sink as soon as he doubted Jesus. Peter wanted to share his master's power, but his faith still needed to grow.

Jesus walks across the lake towards the boat

The storm subsides, and the disciples in the boat worship Jesus

Peter is afraid and starts to sink

MATTHEW 16–17
THE TRANSFIGURATION

*Jesus asks his disciples who they think he is.
Peter replies, "You are the Son of God"*

16 WHEN[13] JESUS CAME TO THE REGION of *Caesarea Philippi*, he asked his disciples, "Who do people say the Son of Man is?" [14]They replied, "Some say John the Baptist; others say Elijah; and still others, Jeremiah or one of the prophets."

[15]"But what about you?" he asked. "Who do you say I am?"

[16]Simon Peter answered, "You are the Christ, the Son of the living God."

[17]Jesus replied, "Blessed are you, Simon son of Jonah, for this was not revealed to you by man, but by my Father in heaven. [18]And I tell you that *you are Peter, and on this rock I will build my church*, and *the gates of Hades* will not overcome it. [19]*I will give you the keys of the kingdom of heaven*; whatever you bind on earth will be bound in heaven, and whatever you loose on earth will be loosed in heaven." [20]Then he warned his disciples not to tell anyone that he was the Christ.

[21]From that time on Jesus began to explain to his disciples that he must go to Jerusalem and suffer many things at the hands of the elders, chief priests and teachers of the law, and that he must be killed and on the third day be raised to life.

[22]Peter took him aside and began to rebuke him. "Never, Lord!" he said. "This shall never happen to you!"

[23]Jesus turned and said to Peter, "*Get behind me, Satan!* You are a stumbling-block to me; you do not have in mind the things of God, but the things of men."

[24]Then Jesus said to his disciples, "If anyone would come after me, he must deny himself and take up his cross and follow me. [25]For whoever wants to save his life will lose it, but whoever loses his life for me will find it. [26]What good will it be for a man if he gains the whole world, yet forfeits his soul?... [27]For the Son of Man is going to come in his Father's glory with his angels,

---

❖

CHAPTER 16 VERSE 13
"Caesarea Philippi"
Originally called Paneas after the Greek god Pan, this city was rebuilt by Herod the Great. His son Philip renamed it in honour of Tiberius Caesar. It was called Philip's Caesarea to distinguish it from the port of Caesarea.

PAN, GOD OF NATURE
Roman mosaic

❖

CHAPTER 16 VERSE 18
"You are Peter, and on this rock I will build my church"
Jesus gives Simon the new name "Peter", which is Greek for "stone" or "rock". Peter, the apostles' leader, will be the founder of the Christian community.

❖

CHAPTER 16 VERSE 18
"The gates of Hades"
This expression means "the power of death". In Bible times, the gates represented a city's power. Hades is the Greek name for the place of the dead. The Old Testament name is "Sheol". No power will be strong enough to defeat Christianity.

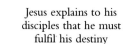

Jesus explains to his disciples that he must fulfil his destiny

Peter cannot accept that the Messiah has to suffer and die

Jesus tells Peter that the will of God must always come before earthly needs

Moses

Elijah

Jesus is transformed from a
man into a heavenly being

God's voice declares, "This is my
Son", and the disciples are terrified

and then he will reward each person according to what he has done. ²⁸I
tell you the truth, some who are standing here will not taste death
before they see the Son of Man coming in his kingdom."

17 ¹After six days Jesus took with him Peter, James and John the
brother of James, and *led them up a high mountain* by themselves. ²There
he was transfigured before them. His face shone like the sun, and his
clothes became as white as the light. ³Just then there appeared before
them *Moses and Elijah, talking with Jesus.*

⁴Peter said to Jesus, "Lord, it is good for us to be here. If you wish, I
will put up three shelters – one for you, one for Moses and one for Elijah."

⁵While he was still speaking, a bright cloud enveloped them, and a
voice from the cloud said, "This is my Son, whom I love; with him I
am well pleased. Listen to him!"

⁶When the disciples heard this, they fell face down to the ground,
terrified. ⁷But Jesus came and touched them. "Get up," he said. "Don't
be afraid." ⁸When they looked up, they saw no-one except Jesus.

UNDERSTANDING THE STORY

The disciples' recognition that Jesus is the Son of God is a turning-point in
Jesus' ministry. He must now prepare them for his suffering and death on the
cross. The vision of their transformed master helps the discouraged followers
to believe that he will indeed rise from the dead.

CHAPTER 16 VERSE 19
"I will give you the keys of the kingdom of heaven"
Led by Peter, the apostles will
continue Jesus' work. The church
they establish will proclaim eternal
life to those who follow Jesus'
teachings. "Bind" and "loose" are
legal terms for the authority to make
and to keep laws. The apostles will
set the standards for the new church.

ST PETER RECEIVES THE KEYS
15th-century German painting

CHAPTER 16 VERSE 23
"Get behind me, Satan!"
The "rock" is now a "stumbling-
block" to Jesus, because Peter does
not want to accept the fate of his
master. Jesus used these same words
in the desert when the devil tried
to tempt him from his mission.

CHAPTER 17 VERSE 1
"Led them up a high mountain"
The traditional location for the
transfiguration is Mount Tabor in
Galilee, although Mount Hermon
is much closer to Caesarea Philippi.

MOUNT TABOR

CHAPTER 17 VERSE 3
"Moses and Elijah... with Jesus"
Moses represents God's Law, which
Jesus upholds. Elijah represents the
prophets who spoke about a Messiah.

JESUS JOURNEYS TO JERUSALEM

After a time of popularity, opposition to Jesus' ministry was growing. The transfiguration had begun to prepare the disciples for their master's death. Jesus knew that this was to be in Jerusalem. At the beginning of AD 30, Jesus started out on his last trip to the Holy City. In his Gospel, Luke presents the closing days of Jesus' ministry as a long journey that started in Galilee, continued through Samaria, Judea, and Perea and ended in Jerusalem – a slow progression towards his ultimate destiny. Many of the events that Luke describes are found in different settings in the other Gospels. This may be because Jesus repeated the same teachings on more than one occasion.

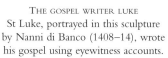

JERUSALEM
View of the Holy
City from the
Mount of Olives

THE GOSPEL WRITER LUKE
St Luke, portrayed in this sculpture
by Nanni di Banco (1408–14), wrote
his gospel using eyewitness accounts.

Samaria

Samaria was the hilly central region of Palestine, bounded by Galilee in the north, Judea in the south, the River Jordan in the east, and the sea in the west. The fertility of its soil and its strategic location meant that Samaria was invaded many times.

During the Israelite monarchy, Samaria was inhabited by the northern tribes of Israel. But after the Assyrian conquest in the 8th century BC, the Israelites intermarried with Babylonians and other foreign peoples imported by the Assyrians. Two centuries later, after the exile of the southern tribes of Judah, the Jews who resettled in Judah (Judea) and rebuilt Jerusalem regarded the Samaritans as an impure race. Over the centuries there was much enmity between the two peoples. By Jesus' time, many Jews would bypass Samaria by crossing the Jordan and travelling through Perea. Jesus, however, went into Samaria, and many Samaritans became his followers.

JEZREEL VALLEY
This fertile valley, also known as the plain of Esdraelon, separated Samaria and Galilee. The plain was an important trade route between the Mediterranean and the lands across the Jordan. Today, it is still the most fertile plain in Israel.

Perea

The name of this small region that ran along the east side of the Jordan means "beyond". It was 16km (10 miles) wide and stretched from the River Yarmuk in the north to the River Arnon in the south.

This area was inhabited by Jews during the Roman occupation. It corresponded to the land of Gilead in the Old Testament and is mentioned in the New Testament as the region "beyond the Jordan".

Perea was an attractive highland region, with plantations of olive trees, vineyards, and wheat and barley fields. Its lower lands were also known for their steppe pastures. In Jesus' time, it was a part of the Roman empire and ruled by Herod Antipas.

SAMARITAN PILGRIMAGE
A very small remnant of the Samaritan sect still exists in Israel. Mount Gerizim, rather than Jerusalem, is their holy place. These Samaritan pilgrims on Mount Gerizim are preparing sacrificial lambs for the Passover meal.

Judea

The hill-country and desert of Judea contrasted sharply with the rich agricultural lands of Samaria and Galilee. However, Judea had its own vineyards, and olive and fig tree plantations, and the area produced a variety of cereal crops. There were also pasture lands, where shepherds tended sheep. The Dead Sea was mined for salt, both for local use and export.

The Judean population was mainly concentrated in and around Jerusalem, while farming communities lived in small villages and towns. Jesus passed through such places, following the main roads or walkways across the fields, and preached in many of them with his disciples.

MARKET STREET IN JERUSALEM
This busy street market echoes the bustle of biblical times. In Jesus' day, Jerusalem had a population of 60,000.

SALT CLUSTERS ON THE DEAD SEA
In Old Testament times, this large salt-water lake was known as the "Salt Sea". It was mined extensively for salt, a valuable commodity in the ancient world.

How Jesus travelled

Travelling by land was often dangerous because of bandits. To travel alone was very risky, and people usually joined caravans or groups. Jesus travelled with his disciples, and some of them carried swords. People usually journeyed during the morning and evening to avoid the midday heat. They had to pay tolls whenever they passed through a new tax district.

The Romans built a comprehensive network of well-engineered roads throughout their empire. These roads were straight, levelled, and had proper drainage. Roads leading to cities had raised walkways for pedestrians. However, even in Roman times, the smaller roads were very poor.

Inns were dubious places where prostitution was sometimes part of the service. Travellers tended to stay in private dwellings. Hospitality was regarded as a sacred duty in Israel. Accommodation was usually free, but food for the journey was packed or bought on the way.

MILESTONE TO JERUSALEM
The Roman army built roads as a means of moving swiftly across the empire. This milestone marks the distance to Jerusalem.

Housing

The homes where Jesus and his disciples stayed were usually modest. Poorer people lived in single-roomed houses with flat roofs reached by an outside stairway. Townspeople often exchanged news by shouting at each other from their rooftops, above the noise of the streets below. In summer, the roofs were used for sleeping and also for drying flax and ripening fruits and vegetables. An extra room was often built on top.

The wealthy lived in pillared houses consisting of several rooms around a central courtyard, where animals were often kept.

JERICHO ROOFSCAPE
Flat-topped roofs dominate the skyline of old Jericho. The architecture of these houses in Israel has changed little since the time of Jesus.

Opposition to Jesus

Jesus met with much opposition during this time from the powerful religious groups. The Pharisees were purists, upholding the Law in its minutest detail. Most scribes, scholars who studied and interpreted the Law, belonged to this group. The Sadducees were mainly wealthy landowners from aristocratic families. Many High Priests were Sadducees.

The Sadducees rejected concepts such as resurrection, the soul, angels, and demons; whereas the Pharisees believed in them. The opposition to Jesus, therefore, was not unified. The Pharisees rejected Jesus' messianic claims, but they agreed on much of his teaching. The priests would not accept that Jesus could forgive sins, as they were entrusted with the sacrificial rituals for forgiveness.

THE PHARISEES AND THE HERODIANS
J J Tissot (1836–1902) shows the Pharisees and Herodians conferring over Jesus' teaching. The Herodians are thought to have been Sadducees. Both parties opposed Jesus' teachings, but not always for the same reasons.

263

LUKE 9, JOHN 4
JESUS AND THE SAMARITANS

Jesus and his disciples set out on their journey to Jerusalem

9 A**S**[51] THE TIME APPROACHED for him to be taken up to heaven, Jesus resolutely *set out for Jerusalem*. [52]And *he sent messengers on ahead*, who went into a Samaritan village to get things ready for him; [53]but the people there did not welcome him, because he was heading for Jerusalem.

[54]When the disciples James and John saw this, they asked, "Lord, do you want us to *call fire down from heaven* to destroy them?" [55]But Jesus turned and rebuked them, [56]and they went to another village.

Jesus was not always rejected by the Samaritans. He often travelled through Samaria, and on one occasion earlier in his ministry, he was welcomed into a Samaritan town called Sychar.

SAMARIA
The journey from Galilee to Jerusalem through Samaria took a few days. Jewish pilgrims avoided Samaria. They travelled on the east side of the River Jordan because the Samaritans were their enemies and would not receive them.

❖

CHAPTER 9 VERSE 51
"Set out for Jerusalem"
This marks the beginning of Jesus' ministry in Judea. His mission ends in Jerusalem, where he dies and is resurrected.

❖

CHAPTER 9 VERSE 52
"He sent messengers on ahead"
Jesus was travelling with his disciples and many other followers. A small village would not be able to provide hospitality for all these people, and so a group went on ahead to prepare for them.

4 [5]So he came to a town in Samaria called Sychar, near the plot of ground Jacob had given to his son Joseph. [6]Jacob's well was there, and Jesus, tired as he was from the journey, sat down by the well... [7]When a Samaritan woman came to draw water, Jesus said to her, "Will you give me a drink?" [8](His disciples had gone into the town to buy food.)

[9]The Samaritan woman said to him, "You are a Jew and I am a Samaritan woman. How can you ask me for a drink?" (For Jews do not associate with Samaritans.)

[10]Jesus answered her, "If you knew the gift of God and who it is that asks you for a drink, you would have asked him and he would have given you *living water*." [11]"Sir," the woman said, "you have nothing to draw with and the well is deep. Where can you get this living water?

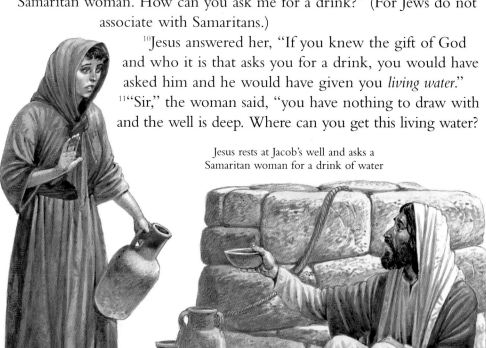

Jesus rests at Jacob's well and asks a Samaritan woman for a drink of water

A SMALL VILLAGE IN JUDEA
Isolated villages exist in rural parts of modern-day Judea and Samaria.

¹²Are you greater than our father Jacob, who gave us the well...?

¹³Jesus answered "Everyone who drinks this water will be thirsty again, ¹⁴but whoever drinks the water I give him will never thirst. Indeed, the water I give him will become in him a spring of water welling up to eternal life."

¹⁵The woman said to him, "Sir, give me this water so that I won't get thirsty and have to keep coming here to draw water."

¹⁶He told her, "Go, call your husband and come back."

¹⁷"I have no husband," she replied.

Jesus said to her... "¹⁸The fact is, you have had five husbands, and the man you now have is not your husband..."

¹⁹"Sir," the woman said, "I can see that you are a prophet. ²⁰*Our fathers worshipped on this mountain*, but you Jews claim that the place where we must worship is in Jerusalem."

²¹Jesus declared, "Believe me, woman, a time is coming when you will worship the Father neither on this mountain nor in Jerusalem... ²³The true worshippers will worship the Father in spirit and truth... ²⁴God is spirit, and his worshippers must worship in spirit and in truth..."

The Samaritan woman went back to the town and told people all the things that Jesus had said. Many of them went to listen to Jesus at the well.

✛

CHAPTER 9 VERSE 54
"Call fire down from heaven"
James and John were also known as the "Sons of Thunder". Their words recall the words of Elijah, who sent flames from heaven to consume the messengers of Ahaziah, the ungodly king of Samaria (2 Kings 1: 10).

JUDEAN VILLAGE WELL
Wells are important in Palestine today, as water dries up in summer months.

✛

CHAPTER 4 VERSE 10
"Living water"
The water that Jesus offers is the gift of eternal life. Those who follow Jesus' teaching will no longer thirst for spiritual fulfilment.

✛

CHAPTER 4 VERSE 20
"Our fathers worshipped on this mountain"
This is Mount Gerizim, a sacred place for the Samaritans. Moses told the people to pronounce God's blessing from there (Deuteronomy 11: 29). Samaritans worshipped the God of Israel, and in *c.* 400 BC they built a temple on Mount Gerizim to rival the Jewish temple in Jerusalem.

The Samaritans invite Jesus to stay in their town

³⁹Many of the Samaritans from that town believed in him because of the woman's testimony, "He told me everything I ever did." ⁴⁰So when the Samaritans came to him, they urged him to stay with them, and he stayed two days. ⁴¹And because of his words many more became believers.

UNDERSTANDING THE STORY

Jewish people considered the Samaritans to be impure and refused to associate with them. Jesus breaks with the Jewish tradition and openly enjoys their hospitality. His mission is to remove the barrier between Jews and non-Jews and to introduce Christianity to all people.

MOUNT GERIZIM

LUKE 10

THE GOOD SAMARITAN

CHAPTER 10 VERSE 25
"An expert in the law stood up to test Jesus"
Jesus was changing the traditional understanding of the Law, and so contradicted many cherished beliefs of the Jews. The religious leaders of the time felt threatened by Jesus and, naturally, challenged him.

CHAPTER 10 VERSE 29
"Who is my neighbour?"
Religious leaders viewed only a small minority as neighbours – the Jews who respected the Law and the proselytes (Gentiles who had converted to Judaism). Many people shunned those who were not of their faith and found it hard to accept Jesus' teachings that they should embrace all people.

CHAPTER 10 VERSE 30
"From Jerusalem to Jericho"
The distance from Jerusalem to Jericho is 27km (17 miles), and the road descends steeply. This rocky, desolate landscape provided many hiding places for robbers. In Jesus' time, priests lived in Jericho when not doing temple duty.

ROAD FROM JERUSALEM TO JERICHO

CHAPTER 10 VERSES 31–32
"A priest... [and] a Levite... passed by on the other side"
Jesus' audience was not shocked by the action of these religious men. The man they saw may have been dead, and the Law forbade priests and Levites to approach dead bodies so they would always remain pure.

10 O N[25] ONE OCCASION *an expert in the law stood up to test Jesus.* "Teacher," he asked, "what must I do to inherit eternal life?" [26]"What is written in the Law?" he replied. "How do you read it?"

[27]He answered: " 'Love the Lord your God with all your heart and with all your soul and with all your strength and with all your mind'; and, 'Love your neighbour as yourself.' "

[28]"You have answered correctly," Jesus replied. "Do this and you will live." [29]But he wanted to justify himself, so he asked Jesus, "And *who is my neighbour?"*

Robbers attack a man as he travels to Jericho

The robbers leave the man for dead

A priest sees the man but does not stop

A Levite walks by on the other side of the road

[30]In reply Jesus said: "A man was going down *from Jerusalem to Jericho,* when he fell into the hands of robbers. They stripped him of his clothes, beat him and went away, leaving him half-dead. [31]*A priest* happened to be going down the same road, and when he saw the man, he passed by on the other side. [32]So too, *a Levite, when he came to the place and saw him, passed by on the other side.*

³³But *a Samaritan, as he travelled, came where the man was*; and when he saw him, he took pity on him. ³⁴He went to him *and bandaged his wounds, pouring on oil and wine*. Then he put the man on his own donkey, brought him to an inn and took care of him. ³⁵The next day *he took out two silver coins* and gave them to the innkeeper. 'Look after him,' he said, 'and when I return, I will reimburse you for any extra expense you may have.'

³⁶"Which of these three do you think was a neighbour to the man who fell into the hands of robbers?"

³⁷The expert in the law replied, "The one who had mercy on him." Jesus told him, "Go and do likewise."

The injured man rides on the Samaritan's donkey

Wine

Linen bandages

Oil

The Samaritan takes the man to an inn and pays for his care

The Samaritan stops and tries to help the injured man by tending his wounds

CHAPTER 10 VERSE 33
"A Samaritan… came where the man was"
The injured man was a Jew from Jerusalem. Jesus' listeners were also Jews, and they were surprised to hear that a Samaritan – an enemy of the Jews – would show compassion. Samaritans were inhabitants of Samaria. Many people from the Assyrian empire settled in Samaria after besieging the capital city in 724 BC. They intermarried with the Jews living there, and the Samaritans became a mixed race. The Jews would have little to do with them.

SAMARITANS
The Samaritan community bases its religious practices on the first five books of the Bible (the Torah).

CHAPTER 10 VERSE 34
"And bandaged his wounds, pouring on oil and wine"
Olive oil and wine were common remedies. Wine was used as an antiseptic, sometimes mixed with herbs to relieve pain. Once the wounds were clean, oil was poured over them to soothe and protect.

CHAPTER 10 VERSE 35
"He took out two silver coins"
Two denarii was the standard wage for a manual labourer for two days' work. This sum was enough for about two months' stay in an inn.

INN OF THE GOOD SAMARITAN

UNDERSTANDING THE STORY
Jesus is saying that people should not limit their love and compassion. People should give their love wholeheartedly, just as God does. By helping a Jew, who would normally despise him, the Samaritan shows true love. The actions of the priest and the Levite show that they are following the letter, rather than the spirit, of religious law.

LUKE 11, JOHN 3

JESUS AND THE PHARISEES

CHAPTER 11 VERSE 42
"You give God a tenth"
Jews had to give one tenth of their income to God. Jesus ridicules the Pharisees for rigidly following this law of tithing, yet failing to teach the spirit in which this law was made. Tithing was meant to be an opportunity to show gratitude to God and to experience the joy of giving. The Pharisees turned tithing into a hardship and a duty.

MINT
The tithe of the land included cultivated herbs.

✣

CHAPTER 11 VERSE 44
"You are like unmarked graves"
Tombs were usually whitewashed to warn of their presence, so people would not touch them and become unclean. Jesus compares the Pharisees to hidden graves, because people did not suspect the moral impurity of their religious leaders.

✣

CHAPTER 11 VERSE 54
"Waiting to catch him"
Jesus' criticism outraged the religious leaders. They sent agents to pose as Jesus' followers and to ask him trick questions. One plan was to brand him as a political activist, knowing that the Romans feared a Jewish uprising. Jesus always saw through these attempts to discredit him.

CAESAR'S COIN
One of the Pharisees in this 15th-century painting holds a Roman coin. The Pharisees asked whether Jews should pay taxes to Rome. Jesus replied, "Give to Caesar what is Caesar's and to God what is God's".

11 WHEN[37] JESUS HAD finished speaking, a Pharisee invited him to eat with him; so he went in and reclined at the table. [38]But the Pharisee, noticing that Jesus did not first wash before the meal, was surprised.

[39]Then the Lord said to him, "Now then, you Pharisees clean the outside of the cup and dish, but inside you are full of greed... [41]Give what is inside the dish to the poor, and everything will be clean for you.

Ritual water

Jesus tells the Pharisees that they should follow the spirit, not the letter, of the law

The Pharisees resent his criticism

[42]"Woe to you Pharisees, because *you give God a tenth* of your mint, rue and all other kinds of garden herbs, but you neglect justice and the love of God...

[43]"Woe to you Pharisees, because you love the most important seats in the synagogues and greetings in the market-places.

[44]"Woe to you, because *you are like unmarked graves*, which men walk over without knowing it."

[45]One of the experts in the law answered him, "Teacher, when you say these things, you insult us also."

[46]Jesus replied, "And you experts in the law, woe to you, because you load people down with burdens they can hardly carry, and you yourselves will not lift one finger to help them.

[47]"Woe to you, because you build tombs for the prophets, and it was your forefathers who killed them. [48]So you testify that you approve of what your forefathers did..."

[53]When Jesus left there, the Pharisees and the teachers of the law began to oppose him fiercely and to besiege him with questions, [54]*waiting to catch him* in something he might say.

A Pharisee called Nicodemus wanted to know more about Jesus' teaching and went to see him in secret. He was a member of the Jewish ruling council.

3   ²*He came to Jesus at night* and said, "Rabbi, we know you are a teacher who has come from God. For no-one could perform the miraculous signs you are doing if God were not with him."

³In reply Jesus declared, "I tell you the truth, no-one can see the kingdom of God *unless he is born again.*"

⁴"How can a man be born when he is old?" Nicodemus asked. "Surely he cannot enter a second time into his mother's womb to be born!"

⁵Jesus answered, "I tell you the truth, no-one can enter the kingdom of God unless he is born of water and the Spirit. ⁶Flesh gives birth to flesh, but the Spirit gives birth to spirit... ¹³No-one has ever gone into heaven except the one who came from heaven – the Son of Man. ¹⁴*Just as Moses lifted up the snake in the desert,* so *the Son of Man must be lifted up,* ¹⁵that everyone who believes in him may have eternal life.

¹⁶"For God so loved the world that he gave his one and only Son, that whoever believes in him shall not perish but have eternal life. ¹⁷For God did not send his Son into the world to condemn the world, but to save the world through him. ¹⁸Whoever believes in him is not condemned, but whoever does not believe stands condemned already because he has not believed in the name of God's one and only Son."

Nicodemus, a Pharisee, goes to see Jesus privately

Jesus tells Nicodemus that he must be reborn spiritually before he can inherit eternal life

Nicodemus is a member of the Jewish ruling council

UNDERSTANDING THE STORY

People admire the piety of the Pharisees; this is the reason why Jesus criticizes them so harshly. The example set by the Pharisees is leading people away from the path towards salvation. Jesus tries to make the religious leaders understand this, so that they too can be spiritually reborn.

CHAPTER 3 VERSE 2
"He came to Jesus at night"
Not all the Pharisees were opposed to Jesus' teachings, and Jesus recognizes Nicodemus' genuine desire to know more. The fact that Nicodemus went at night and in secret indicates that he did not wish other Pharisees to know about his private conversation with Jesus.

CHAPTER 3 VERSE 3
"Unless he is born again"
This expression also means to be "born from above". When people commit themselves to living their lives according to God's will, their sins are forgiven and they experience a new, spiritual birth.

CHAPTER 3 VERSE 14
"Just as Moses lifted up the snake in the desert"
During their time in the desert, the Israelites rebelled against God, who sent fiery snakes to punish them. The only ones saved were those who looked at a bronze snake, raised up by Moses on a pole (Numbers 21: 4-9). People must look to Jesus and his teachings for their salvation.

MOSES AND THE SNAKE
The desert scene depicted in a 13th-century stained-glass panel

---

CHAPTER 3 VERSE 14
"The Son of Man must be lifted up"
The words Jesus uses have a double meaning – he knows that his death on the cross and his resurrection are part of God's mysterious plan for the salvation of humanity.

LUKE 9, 14, 18

THE COST OF FOLLOWING JESUS

9 AS⁵⁷ THEY WERE WALKING along the road, a man said to [Jesus], "I will follow you wherever you go." ⁵⁸Jesus replied, "Foxes have holes and birds of the air have nests, but the Son of Man has *nowhere to lay his head.*"

⁵⁹He said to another man, "Follow me."

But the man replied, "Lord, *first let me go and bury my father.*"

⁶⁰Jesus said to him, "Let the dead bury their own dead, but you go and proclaim the kingdom of God."

⁶¹Still another said, "I will follow you, Lord; but first let me go back and say good-bye to my family."

⁶² Jesus replied, "No-one who puts his hand to the plough and looks back is fit for service in the kingdom of God."

14 ²⁵Large crowds were travelling with Jesus, and turning to them he said: ²⁶"*If anyone comes to me and does not hate* his father and mother, his wife and children, his brother and sisters – yes, even his own life – he cannot be my disciple. ²⁷And anyone who does not *carry his cross* and follow me cannot be my disciple.

²⁸"Suppose one of you wants to build a tower. Will he not first *sit down and estimate the cost* to see if he has enough money to complete it?

CHAPTER 9 VERSE 58
"Nowhere to lay his head"
A disciple's life was very demanding. Jesus had no home of his own and had to rely on other people's hospitality. He expected his disciples to do the same.

SLEEPING DISCIPLES
This detail of a painting by Botticelli shows three of Jesus' disciples sleeping out in the open.

CHAPTER 9 VERSE 59
"First let me... bury my father"
In Jesus' time "to bury" also meant "to look after until death", which could mean many years. This man is saying that he has too many other commitments to be a disciple just yet. Jesus says it is not something that can be put off.

Jesus warns a follower that a disciple's life is difficult

CHAPTER 14 VERSE 26
"If anyone comes to me and does not hate"
The Gospel of Matthew explains the meaning of this Middle-Eastern expression. Jesus says, "Anyone who loves his father or mother more than me is not worthy of me" (Matthew 10: 37–38). Jesus is not asking his followers to hate their families. On the contrary, he urges people to take care of their parents (Mark 7: 9–13) and couples to stay together (Mark 10: 2–12).

Another man wants to be a disciple, but he is too busy at that moment

Jesus tells another that he must put God first

²⁹For if he lays the foundation and is not able to finish it, everyone who sees it will ridicule him, ³⁰saying, 'This fellow began to build and was not able to finish.' "

A rich ruler asked Jesus what he should do to inherit eternal life. Jesus told him to follow the commandments. The ruler replied that he had always done this. Jesus told him that there was one more thing he must do – give away all his wealth to the poor. Only then could the rich man be a true disciple of Jesus.

18   ²³When he heard this, he became very sad, because he was a man of great wealth. ²⁴Jesus looked at him and said, "How hard it is for the rich to enter the kingdom of God! ²⁵Indeed, *it is easier for a camel to go through the eye of a needle* than for a rich man to enter the kingdom of God."

²⁶Those who heard this asked, "Who then can be saved?"

²⁷Jesus replied, "What is impossible with men is possible with God."

²⁸Peter said to him, "We have left all we had to follow you!"

²⁹"I tell you the truth," Jesus said to them, "no-one who has left home or wife or brothers or parents or children for the sake of the kingdom of God ³⁰ will fail to receive many times as much in this age and, in the age to come, eternal life."

A rich ruler asks Jesus what he must do to inherit eternal life

Jesus tells the rich man that it is not enough to keep the commandments, he must give everything he has to the poor

UNDERSTANDING THE STORY

Jesus stresses the sacrifices that a disciple will need to make. He is not asking people to abandon their families or to give up everything. Jesus tells the rich man to give away his money because material things should never take priority. True disciples must always put God first in their lives.

CHAPTER 14 VERSE 27
"Carry his cross"
People condemned to be crucified had to carry their cross to the place of crucifixion. Symbolically, the cross-bearing means "total commitment". Jesus' followers renounce all selfish ambition and serve God, whatever the cost, until the end of their lives.

BYZANTINE CROSS
Some Christians wear a cross as a sign of their commitment to Jesus.

CHAPTER 14 VERSE 28
"Sit down and estimate the cost"
Many were impressed with Jesus' teachings and wanted to follow him. Jesus wants them to consider carefully the commitment involved.

CHAPTER 18 VERSE 25
"It is easier for a camel to go through the eye of a needle"
Jews considered the wealthy to be blessed and approved by God and therefore the likeliest candidates for heaven. Jesus does not reject the rich, but he wants them to be aware that worldly wealth can prevent a close relationship with God.

ONE-HUMPED ARABIAN CAMEL
Jesus uses the camel to illustrate his point because his audience would have been familiar with this desert animal. Camels can carry heavy loads over great distances and travel for days without water.

LUKE 14

THE PHARISEE'S DINNER

14 ONE[1] SABBATH, *when Jesus went to eat* in the house of a prominent Pharisee, he was being carefully watched... [7]When he noticed how the guests picked *the places of honour* at the table, he told them this parable:

[8]"When someone invites you to a wedding feast, do not take the place of honour, for a person more distinguished than you may have been invited. [9]If so, the host who invited both of you will come and say to you, 'Give this man your seat.' Then, humiliated, you will have to take the least important place. [10]But when you are invited, take the lowest place, so that when your host comes, he will say to you, 'Friend, move up to a better place.' Then you will be honoured in the presence of all your fellow guests. [11]For everyone who exalts himself will be humbled, and he who humbles himself will be exalted."

CHAPTER 14 VERSE 1
"One Sabbath, when Jesus went to eat"
It was customary not to eat on the Sabbath until after the synagogue service, which was at midday. The most important meal of the day was the evening meal.

CHAPTER 14 VERSE 7
"The places of honour"
At a formal dinner, three couches would be arranged around a table, leaving one side empty for serving. The nearer a guest was to his host, the more highly he was honoured.

COUCHES
These were often made of finely carved wood and inlaid with ivory.

CHAPTER 14 VERSE 15
"Feast in the kingdom of God"
In the Middle East, feasts were important social occasions, and Jesus often used them to illustrate God's kingdom. Eating was an expression of spiritual communion with God, as well as a time for sharing and rejoicing with others. Official religious feasts involved the sacrifice and eating of animals.

EDIBLE PLATES
Food was often served on round, flat bread, made by pressing the dough up against the wall of a cylindrical oven.

Jesus is invited to dinner at the house of an important Pharisee

He notices the guests arguing about where they should sit

Host

Jesus tells the guests to choose the least-important seat, and then they may be asked to sit in a better place

Jesus explained to his host that he should not invite friends and relatives to dinner or lunch because they can repay him by inviting him back. Instead, he should invite the poor and the ill, who cannot return the invitation. These selfless acts will be repaid in heaven.

[15]When one of those at the table with him heard this, he said to Jesus, "Blessed is the man who will eat at the *feast in the kingdom of God.*"

LUKE 14

THE GREAT BANQUET

14 JESUS[16] REPLIED: "A certain man was preparing a great banquet and invited many guests. [17]At the time of the banquet he sent his servant to tell those who had been invited, 'Come, for everything is now ready.'

[18]"But they all alike *began to make excuses*. The first said, 'I have just bought a field, and I must go and see it...'

[19]"Another said, 'I have just bought five yoke of oxen, and I'm on my way to try them out. Please excuse me.'

[20]"Still another said, 'I have just got married, so I can't come.'

[21]"The servant came back and reported this to his master. Then *the owner of the house became angry* and ordered his servant, 'Go out quickly into the streets and alleys of the town and *bring in the poor, the crippled, the blind and the lame.*' [22]" 'Sir', the servant said, 'what you ordered has been done, but there is still room.'

[23]"Then the master told his servant, 'Go out to the roads and country lanes and make them come in, so that my house will be full. [24]I tell you, not one of those men who were invited will get a taste of my banquet.' "

This guest needs to try out his new oxen

This guest has to inspect his fields

This guest has just got married

A servant goes to tell the guests that his master's banquet is ready

The guests all give excuses for not attending

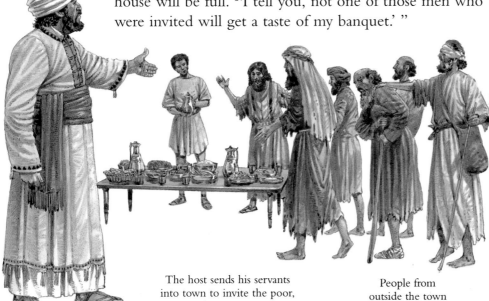

The host sends his servants into town to invite the poor, the blind, and the crippled

People from outside the town are also invited

UNDERSTANDING THE STORIES

In the first story, Jesus illustrates the importance of humility and charity. In the second, he warns the Pharisees that they may be left outside God's kingdom. These religious leaders are invited first, because they can set an example to others. But the Pharisees refuse, and the least expected in society are welcomed.

CHAPTER 14 VERSE 18
"Began to make excuses"
The guests would have already accepted the host's invitation, and so they were breaking a commitment to him. They represent the religious leaders, who uphold high standards in public, but fail to keep these standards themselves. The servant represents Jesus, who carries out God's work on earth.

CHAPTER 14 VERSE 21
"The owner... became angry"
It was very rude to turn down an invitation at the last minute. None of the guests' excuses are honest: a field or an ox would never have been bought before they were inspected, and newly married men would be excused from military service, but not from attending formal social gatherings.

CHAPTER 14 VERSE 21
"Bring in the poor... the blind and the lame"
These people would have been excluded from the Temple and all religious meetings because of their infirmities. They represent the Jews who are spiritually or socially outcast but who welcome Jesus' teachings. Even people outside the community respond to his word and are invited into God's kingdom.

LUKE 9, MATTHEW 18

THE GREATEST IN THE KINGDOM

CHAPTER 18 VERSE 3
"Become like little children"
Children were under the authority of parents and elders and dependent on them for their well-being. Jesus' followers must adopt this attitude and not allow self-reliance to create a barrier between them and God.

CHAPTER 18 VERSE 6
"Little ones who believe in me"
These are people who accept that their lives are of no value without God. They have complete trust in Jesus' teachings, knowing that he has their best interests at heart.

CHAPTER 18 VERSE 8
"Cut it off and throw it away"
Jesus' words are not to be taken literally. He uses vivid language to illustrate his point. The cause of sin should be investigated and removed, because it cuts people off from God.

CHAPTER 18 VERSE 9
"Thrown into the fire of hell"
Hell was "Gehenna", Greek for a deep ravine near Jerusalem called the "Valley of Hinnom". In this valley, children were once sacrificed to pagan gods. Even some of Judah's kings were guilty of this evil practice. In Jesus' time, it was a continually burning rubbish dump.

THE VALLEY OF HINNOM TODAY

9 AN[46] ARGUMENT STARTED among the disciples as to which of them would be the greatest. [47]Jesus, knowing their thoughts, took a little child and made him stand beside him. [48]Then he said to them, "Whoever welcomes this little child in my name welcomes me; and whoever welcomes me welcomes the one who sent me. For he who is least among you all – he is the greatest."

The disciples ask Jesus who is the greatest in the kingdom

Jesus tells the disciples that they must change and become as humble and trusting as children

18 [3]And he said: "I tell you the truth, unless you change and *become like little children*, you will never enter the kingdom of heaven...

[5]"And whoever welcomes a little child like this in my name welcomes me. [6]But if anyone causes one of these *little ones who believe in me* to sin, it would be better for him to have a large millstone hung around his neck and to be drowned in the depths of the sea.

[7]"Woe to the world because of the things that cause people to sin! Such things must come, but woe to the man through whom they come! [8]If your hand or your foot causes you to sin, *cut it off and throw it away*. It is better for you to enter life maimed or crippled than to have two hands or two feet and be thrown into eternal fire. [9]And if your eye causes you to sin, gouge it out and throw it away. It is better for you to enter life with one eye than to have two eyes and be *thrown into the fire of hell*."

[10]"See that you do not look down on one of these little ones. For I tell you that *their angels in heaven* always see the face of my Father in heaven.

The shepherd goes to look for a lost sheep, leaving the rest of his flock grazing on the hillside

When the shepherd finds the stray sheep, he is overjoyed

CHAPTER 18 VERSE 10
"Their angels in heaven"
The Bible speaks of guardian angels as heavenly representatives of nations, churches, and individuals. The angels "always see the face of God", which derives from a courtly expression meaning direct access to the king. Everyone, whatever their status, has constant personal access to God.

CHAPTER 18 VERSE 12
"If a man owns a hundred sheep"
The image of a shepherd nurturing his flock is frequent throughout the Bible. Sheep are helpless animals, who rely on a shepherd to provide them with food and water and to protect them from harm. This relationship is used to symbolize God's love and care for humanity.

The lost sheep is taken back to the flock

CHAPTER 18 VERSE 13
"Happier about that one sheep than about the ninety-nine"
Jesus identified himself with the role of a shepherd, whose duty it was to look after every sheep in a flock. Jesus is concerned with the fate of each individual. His words do not mean that one sheep is more important than the other 99. He is saying that God understands and forgives those who stray, and it causes special joy when they are brought back into the fold.

[12]"What do you think? *If a man owns a hundred sheep*, and one of them wanders away, will he not leave the ninety-nine on the hills and go to look for the one that wandered off? [13]And if he finds it, I tell you the truth, he is *happier about that one sheep than about the ninety-nine* that did not wander off. [14]In the same way your Father in heaven is not willing that any of these little ones should be lost."

UNDERSTANDING THE STORY

The chosen twelve have become proud of their status and are quarrelling about their roles in the new kingdom. Jesus uses the example of the shepherd and his flock to illustrate the reality of God's kingdom. The parable of the lost sheep is a model for the disciples. Their mission is to save lost souls. But the disciples must first deal with their own vices. They need to work together to carry out God's will. Those who humbly serve others are on the path to true greatness.

JESUS, THE GOOD SHEPHERD
5th-century Byzantine mosaic, Mausoleo di Galla Placidia, Ravenna, Italy

LUKE 15

THE PRODIGAL SON

15

CHAPTER 15 VERSE 12
"Give me my share"
In Jesus' time, for a son to demand a share of his family's estate while his father was still alive and well was to wish his death.

CHAPTER 15 VERSE 13
"Set off for a distant country"
By leaving the family estate with all his belongings, the younger son is saying that he has no intention of coming back. For the father, it is a sign of rejection and as if his son were dead.

CHAPTER 15 VERSE 15
"Sent him to his fields to feed pigs"
Jews never fed pigs and to do so was degrading. The Jewish people considered pigs to be impure, unclean animals, and they were not supposed to approach them or to eat their meat.

CHAPTER 15 VERSE 20
"He ran to his son"
In biblical times it would have been considered humiliating for a wealthy man wearing heavy robes to run anywhere. In this story, the father runs to his errant son, welcoming him back despite his behaviour.

The younger son leaves home, taking his share of the property

The son squanders his money on wild living and goes in search of work

Poor and starving, the errant son is sent to feed pigs

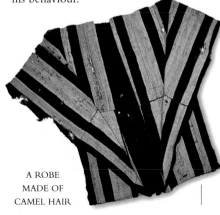

A ROBE
MADE OF
CAMEL HAIR

THERE[11] WAS A MAN who had two sons. [12]The younger one said to his father, 'Father, *give me my share* of the estate.' So he divided his property between them.

[13]"Not long after that, the younger son got together all he had, *set off for a distant country* and there squandered his wealth in wild living. [14]After he had spent everything, there was a severe famine in that whole country, and he began to be in need. [15]So he went and hired himself out to a citizen of that country, who *sent him to his fields to feed pigs*. [16]He longed to fill his stomach with the pods that the pigs were eating, but no-one gave him anything.

[17]"When he came to his senses, he said, 'How many of my father's hired men have food to spare, and here I am starving to death! [18]I will set out and go back to my father and say to him: Father, I have sinned against heaven and against you. [19]I am no longer worthy to be called your son; make me like one of your hired men.' [20]So he got up and went to his father.

"But while he was still a long way off, his father saw him and was filled with compassion for him; *he ran to his son*, threw his arms around him and kissed him.

[21]"The son said to him, 'Father, I have sinned against heaven and against you. I am no longer worthy to be called your son.'

[22]"But the father said to his servants, 'Quick! *Bring the best robe* and put it on him. Put a ring on his finger and sandals on his feet. [23]*Bring the fattened calf* and kill it. Let's have a feast and celebrate.

²⁴For this son of mine was dead and is alive again; he was lost and is found.' So they began to celebrate.

²⁵"Meanwhile, the older son was in the field. When he came near the house, he heard music and dancing. ²⁶So he called one of the servants and asked him what was going on. ²⁷'Your brother has come,' he replied, 'and your father has killed the fattened calf because he has him back safe and sound.'

²⁸"*The older brother became angry* and refused to go in. So *his father went out and pleaded with him*. ²⁹But he answered his father, 'Look! All these years I've been slaving for you and never disobeyed your orders. Yet you never gave me even a young goat so I could celebrate with my friends.

✣

CHAPTER 15 VERSE 22
"Bring the best robe"
The best robe traditionally belongs to the head of the family. The ring the father gives his son symbolizes his power over the servants, and the sandals indicate freedom. Sandals are worn by the family, but not by servants. Even guests would take off their sandals when invited into a house. The young rebel is accepted back as a member of the family.

SANDALS

RING

The younger son decides to return home

His father welcomes him back and holds a feast to celebrate his return

The elder son resents his brother and refuses to join in the celebrations

✣

CHAPTER 15 VERSE 23
"Bring the fattened calf"
In wealthy families, a calf fattened on milk was killed for very special occasions or feasts – as is the custom today with turkeys and geese.

CALF

³⁰But when this son of yours who has squandered your property with prostitutes comes home, you kill the fattened calf for him!'

³¹" 'My son,' the father said, 'you are always with me, and everything I have is yours. ³²But we had to celebrate and be glad, because this brother of yours was dead and is alive again; he was lost and is found.' "

UNDERSTANDING THE STORY

Just as the father in this story welcomes his errant son, God opens his arms to those who repent. The elder brother believes he has been a good son, but his inability to accept his brother's repentance is a warning to those, like the Pharisees, who follow religious rules but show no compassion.

✣

CHAPTER 15 VERSE 28
"The older brother became angry"
The father has forgiven the guilty son, but his elder son is jealous and feels unable to rejoice with the rest of the household. His self-righteousness prevents him from accepting his younger brother.

✣

CHAPTER 15 VERSE 28
"His father… pleaded with him"
In Middle-Eastern tradition, a father would never normally discuss domestic matters with his children. By doing so, the father demonstrates his love for the unforgiving son.

LUKE 16

THE SHREWD MANAGER

CHAPTER 16 VERSE 2
"Give me an account"
The rich man is not asking for an explanation. He wants a full report of his manager's actions, together with the relevant accounts.

CHAPTER 16 VERSE 4
"I know what I'll do"
Rather than repenting and relying on his master's mercy, the manager decides to falsify his accounts to gain favour with people who might help him when he loses his job.

CHAPTER 16 VERSE 6
"Eight hundred gallons of olive oil"
This amount was the product of about 450 olive trees. Olive oil was used in food preparation, as a fuel, a medicine, and a hair dressing. It was also the base of many lotions.

OLIVE PRESS

CHAPTER 16 VERSE 7
"A thousand bushels of wheat"
The second debtor owed the equivalent of about forty hectares (100 acres) of harvested crop.

BUSHEL OF WHEAT

16 JESUS[1] TOLD HIS DISCIPLES: "There was a rich man whose manager was accused of wasting his possessions. [2]So he called him in and asked him, 'What is this I hear about you? *Give me an account* of your management, because you cannot be manager any longer.'

[3]"The manager said to himself, 'What shall I do now? My master is taking away my job. I'm not strong enough to dig, and I'm ashamed to beg – [4]*I know what I'll do* so that, when I lose my job here, people will welcome me into their houses.'

[5]"So he called in each of his master's debtors. He asked the first, 'How much do you owe my master?'

[6]" *'Eight hundred gallons of olive oil,'* he replied.

"The manager told him, 'Take your bill, sit down quickly, and make it four hundred.'

[7]"Then he asked the second, 'And how much do you owe?'

A manager fears that he will lose his job

His master hears that his wealth is being wasted. He asks the manager for a full account of his management

" *'A thousand bushels of wheat,'* he replied.

"He told him, *'Take your bill and make it eight hundred.'*

[8]"*The master commended the dishonest manager* because he had acted shrewdly. For the people of this world are more shrewd in dealing with their own kind than are the people of the light.

⁹I tell you, *use worldly wealth to gain friends for yourselves*, so that when it is gone, you will be welcomed into eternal dwellings.

¹⁰"Whoever can be trusted with very little can also be trusted with much, and whoever is dishonest with very little will also be dishonest with much. ¹¹So if you have not been trustworthy in handling worldly wealth, *who will trust you with true riches*? ¹²And if you have not been trustworthy with someone else's property, who will give you property of your own?

¹³"No servant can serve two masters. Either he will hate the one and love the other, or he will be devoted to the one and despise the other. You cannot serve both God and Money."

¹⁴The Pharisees, who loved money, heard all this and were sneering at Jesus. ¹⁵He said to them, "You are the ones who justify yourselves in the eyes of men, but God knows your hearts. What is highly valued among men is detestable in God's sight."

The master acknowledges that his manager has been clever, but he realises that he can no longer trust him

A man who owes a thousand bushels of wheat is delighted when the manager tells him to reduce his bill

The manager knows that the debtors will befriend him when he loses his job

Oil amphorae

The manager tells the first debtor to cut his oil debt in half

UNDERSTANDING THE STORY

Jesus teaches that those who misuse money and power are not serving God. Like the manager in this story, the Pharisees are using their position for their own gain. As respected members of the religious community, the Pharisees use their status to justify their actions, but they cannot conceal their real motives from God.

✣

CHAPTER 16 VERSE 7
"Take your bill and make it eight hundred"
Debtors did not receive an invoice like today. By writing down the amount owed in front of a witness (the manager), the debtors were officially recognizing their debts. In Jesus' times, accounts were often recorded on papyrus scrolls, which were made from crushing the stem of the papyrus plant.

PAPYRUS
SCROLL

✣

CHAPTER 16 VERSE 8
"The master commended the dishonest manager"
The master lets the manager know that he is aware of his deceit and that he recognizes his shrewdness in turning the situation to his best advantage. But the master is not praising the manager's dishonesty.

✣

CHAPTER 16 VERSE 9
"Use worldly wealth to gain friends for yourselves"
Jesus is not saying that people should behave like the manager, who reduced the debts to gain friends for selfish reasons. He is telling them that they should use their wealth for unselfish acts, which will gain them friends on earth and in heaven.

✣

CHAPTER 16 VERSE 11
"Who will trust you with true riches?"
The manager has misused both his own abilities and his master's wealth to make life easier for himself. He has shown that he is unworthy of what was entrusted to him.

LUKE 18–19

JESUS AND THE HUMBLE

CHAPTER 18 VERSE 11

"The Pharisee stood up"

Worshippers could pray in the Temple at any time of day. People normally stood and prayed aloud. Jews respected the piety of the Pharisees, and so Jesus' criticism of their "holier than thou" behaviour shocked everyone.

The Pharisee parades his piety

The tax collector dares not even look up to heaven

CHAPTER 18 VERSE 13

"The tax collector stood at a distance"

Jewish society looked down on tax collectors because they were dishonest and collaborated with the Romans. Many considered these men too impure to approach God.

CHAPTER 18 VERSE 16

"Let the little children come to me"

To Jesus, children are not a nuisance or less important than adults. Jesus urges his disciples to welcome all members of the community.

CHILDREN TODAY
These Jewish children are eating matzot, an unleavened bread traditionally eaten at Passover.

CHAPTER 18 VERSE 35

"As Jesus approached Jericho"

Jesus visited the new city of Jericho, which Herod the Great built 1.6km (one mile) south of the ruins of the Old Testament city.

18 TO⁹ SOME WHO were confident of their own righteousness and looked down on everybody else, Jesus told this parable: ¹⁰"Two men went up to the temple to pray, one a Pharisee and the other a tax collector. ¹¹*The Pharisee stood up* and prayed about himself: 'God, I thank you that I am not like other men – robbers, evildoers, adulterers – or even like this tax collector. ¹²I fast twice a week and give a tenth of all I get.'

¹³"But *the tax collector stood at a distance*. He would not even look up to heaven, but beat his breast and said, 'God, have mercy on me, a sinner.'

¹⁴"I tell you that this man, rather than the other, went home justified before God. For everyone who exalts himself will be humbled, and he who humbles himself will be exalted."

¹⁵People were also bringing babies to Jesus to have him touch them. When the disciples saw this, they rebuked them. ¹⁶But Jesus called the children to him and said, "*Let the little children come to me*, and do not hinder them, for the kingdom of God belongs to such as these. ¹⁷I tell you the truth, anyone who will not receive the kingdom like a little child will never enter it."...

³⁵*As Jesus approached Jericho, a blind man was sitting by the roadside begging.* ³⁶When he heard the crowd going by, he asked what was happening. ³⁷They told him, "Jesus of Nazareth is passing by."

³⁸He called out, "Jesus, Son of David, have mercy on me!"

³⁹Those who led the way rebuked him and told him to be quiet, but he shouted all the more,

People bring their children to Jesus

The disciples want to send them away

Jesus says, "Let the children come to me"

"Son of David, have mercy on me!" [40]Jesus stopped and ordered the man to be brought to him. When he came near, Jesus asked him, [41]"What do you want me to do for you?"

"Lord, I want to see," he replied.

[42]Jesus said to him, "Receive your sight; your faith has healed you." [43]Immediately he received his sight and followed Jesus, praising God. When all the people saw it, they also praised God.

19 [1]Jesus entered Jericho and was passing through. [2]A man was there by the name of Zacchaeus; he was a chief tax collector and was wealthy. [3]He wanted to see who Jesus was, but being a short man he could not, because of the crowd. [4]So he ran ahead and *climbed a sycamore-fig tree* to see him, since Jesus was coming that way.

[5]When Jesus reached the spot, he looked up and said to him, "Zacchaeus, come down immediately. I must stay at your house today." [6]So he came down at once and welcomed him gladly.

[7]All the people saw this and began to mutter, "He has gone to be the guest of a 'sinner'."

[8]But Zacchaeus stood up and said to the Lord, "Look, Lord! Here and now I give half of my possessions to the poor, and if I have cheated anybody out of anything, *I will pay back four times the amount.*"

[9]Jesus said to him, "Today salvation has come to this house, because *this man, too, is a son of Abraham.* [10]For the Son of Man came to seek and to save what was lost."

Jesus restores the blind man's sight

Zacchaeus climbs up a fig tree so he can see Jesus

Jesus calls Zacchaeus down

FRESH FIGS
Figs were eaten fresh or pressed into cakes. Medicinally, they were used as a poultice.

The crowd is angry that Jesus talks to a tax collector

CHAPTER 18 VERSE 35
"A blind man was sitting by the roadside begging"
Jericho was on a road used by pilgrims on their way to Jerusalem. Beggars were a common sight outside the gates of large towns.

CHAPTER 19 VERSE 4
"Climbed a sycamore-fig tree"
With short trunks and spreading branches, sycamore-fig trees are easy to climb. They were often planted by the roadside to provide shade.

CHAPTER 19 VERSE 8
"I will pay back four times the amount"
In Jesus' time, thieves had to repay the total amount they had stolen plus a fifth. Zacchaeus shows his repentance by far exceeding this.

CHAPTER 19 VERSE 9
"This man, too, is a son of Abraham"
Religious leaders saw Zacchaeus as a parasite who betrayed his community. In their eyes, he was not a true Jew. This is why the crowd was shocked that Jesus would go to his house. Jesus welcomes the remorseful tax collector back into Jewish society.

UNDERSTANDING THE STORY

Jesus uses conventional attitudes to illustrate the importance of humility. It is not the self-righteous Pharisee who is on the right path to heaven; it is the repentant tax collector, who loses his dignity by climbing a fig tree to see Jesus. To enter God's kingdom, people must be as trusting as children.

JOHN 11

THE RAISING OF LAZARUS

CHAPTER 11 VERSE 11
"Lazarus has fallen asleep"
In the Bible, death is often represented as sleep. Jesus uses this image to teach his disciples that physical death is not final, but leads to a new spiritual life.

CHAPTER 11 VERSE 17
"Lazarus had already been in the tomb for four days"
Many Jews believed that the souls of the dead could return to their bodies within three days of dying. After four days, Lazarus' body would have started to decay, and there was no hope of seeing him alive again.

LAZARUS' TOMB
This 2,000-year-old burial site at Bethany is the traditional tomb of Lazarus.

CHAPTER 11 VERSE 27
"I believe that you are the Christ, the Son of God"
Martha declares her faith in Jesus. She knows that he who has the power to give eternal life also has the power to bring her brother back from the dead.

11 NOW[1] A MAN NAMED LAZARUS was sick. He was from Bethany, the village of Mary and her sister Martha... [3]So the sisters sent word to Jesus, "Lord, the one you love is sick."

[4]When he heard this, Jesus said, "This sickness will not end in death. No, it is for God's glory so that God's Son may be glorified through it." [5]Jesus loved Martha and her sister and Lazarus. [6]Yet when he heard that Lazarus was sick, he stayed where he was two more days. [7]Then he said to his disciples, "Let us go back to Judea... [11]Our friend *Lazarus has fallen asleep*; but I am going there to wake him up."

[17][When he arrived in Bethany], Jesus found that *Lazarus had already been in the tomb for four days...* [20]When Martha heard that Jesus was coming, she went out to meet him, but Mary stayed at home.

[21]"Lord," Martha said to Jesus, "if you had been here, my brother would not have died. [22]But I know that even now God will give you whatever you ask."

[23]Jesus said to her, "Your brother will rise again."

[24]Martha answered, "I know he will rise again in the resurrection at the last day." [25]Jesus said to her, "I am the resurrection and the life. He who believes in me will live, even though he dies; [26]and whoever lives and believes in me will never die. Do you believe this?"

Martha knows that Jesus has the power to heal their sick brother

Martha greets Jesus with the news that Lazarus is dead

Mary

Lazarus is near to death

Mary weeps at Jesus' feet

Jesus is moved to tears by the depth of their grief

[27]"Yes, Lord," she told him, "*I believe that you are the Christ, the Son of God*, who was to come into the world."

[28]And after she had said this, she went back and called her sister Mary aside. "The Teacher is here," she said, "and is asking for you."...

[32]When Mary reached the place where Jesus was and saw him, she fell at his feet and said, "Lord, if you had been here, my brother would not have died."

[33]When Jesus saw her weeping, and the Jews who had come along with her also weeping, he was deeply moved in spirit and... [35]*Jesus wept*...

[38][He] came to the tomb. It was a cave with a stone laid across the entrance. [39]"Take away the stone... [40]Did I not tell you that if you believed, you would see the glory of God?"

[41]So they took away the stone. Then Jesus looked up and said, "*Father, I thank you* that you have heard me..."

[43]When he had said this, Jesus called in a loud voice, "Lazarus, come out!" [44]The dead man came out, his hands and feet wrapped with strips of linen...

Jesus said to them, "Take off the grave clothes and let him go."

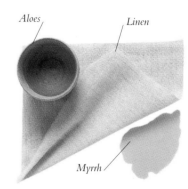

CHAPTER 11 VERSE 35
"Jesus wept"
Jesus wept because he was moved by the suffering of those who grieved for Lazarus. This is the shortest verse in the Bible.

Aloes   *Linen*

Myrrh

EMBALMING THE BODY
The bodies of the dead were washed and wrapped in a sheet or bandages. The wealthy were placed in linen, which often contained aloes and myrrh.

Jesus calls to Lazarus to come out of the tomb

People watch in amazement

Lazarus rises from the dead and walks out of the tomb. His body is still wrapped in linen

UNDERSTANDING THE STORY

Jesus shows compassion for the people suffering around him, but his miracle has a deeper significance. Jesus brings Lazarus back to life to prove to his followers that he is the Son of God. Jesus does not want people to fear physical death, but to understand that he has the power to give them eternal life.

CHAPTER 11 VERSE 41
"Father, I thank you"
Jesus never doubted that God would help him. He gave thanks aloud so that people would believe that his authority was from God.

JESUS' LAST DAYS

On the Sunday before Passover, Jesus rode into Jerusalem. Thousands of Jews had gathered there to celebrate this religious festival. The city had become the political and religious centre of Israel around 1000 BC. However, the Babylonian king, Nebuchadnezzar, destroyed it in 586 BC. When the Jews returned from exile in Babylon, they rebuilt Jerusalem. In Jesus' time, Herod the Great had greatly expanded and beautified the city. Jesus knew he would shortly die there, and that Jerusalem would be destroyed once again.

THE GROWTH OF JERUSALEM
David made Jerusalem his capital, and Solomon built the Temple there. By the time of Jesus, the city had a population of 60,000.

PRESENT WALL (OLD CITY)

DAVID'S JERUSALEM
(11TH CENTURY BC)

SOLOMON'S JERUSALEM
(10TH CENTURY BC)

HEROD'S JERUSALEM
(1ST CENTURY AD)

How people viewed Jesus

When Jesus drew near to Jerusalem, he called for a donkey and rode into the city on it. The significance of this was not lost on the Jewish people. They recalled the prophecy of Zechariah: "Lo, your king comes… riding on the foal of an ass" (Zechariah 9: 9). The Jews had suffered centuries of foreign oppression. Now under Roman rule, they were awaiting the promised king who would restore them to their former glory. They acclaimed Jesus as the Messiah, or the Anointed One – the new King David.

This alarmed the Jewish religious leaders. They knew that if the people revolted the Romans would hold them responsible. Furthermore, Jesus condemned the commercial practices held in the Temple. The priests, therefore, feared they would lose their income and their authority as guardians of Moses' Law.

Jesus proclaimed the coming of the Kingdom of God, but even the apostles thought the kingdom he spoke of was political rather than spiritual.

The Sanhedrin

The highest court of the Jews was the Sanhedrin in Jerusalem. Its 71 members were made up of Pharisees and Sadducees, presided over by the High Priest. During Roman rule, the High Priest was appointed by the Roman governor.

When Jesus was arrested, he was taken to the High Priest's house and tried before the Sanhedrin, who pronounced him guilty of blasphemy. Although the Sanhedrin could administer justice in Judea, it could not impose the death penalty. This could be done only by the Roman governor – in Jesus' case, Pontius Pilate. Under Roman law, blasphemy was not a crime. And so, when Jesus was handed over to Pontius Pilate, the Sanhedrin accused him of treason against Rome.

JESUS BEFORE
THE SANHEDRIN
(6th-century mosaic)
The Gospels' account of Jesus' trial records that there were many irregularities in the procedures and a gross miscarriage of justice.

JESUS RIDES INTO JERUSALEM ON A DONKEY
This 13th-century illustration shows Jesus being greeted by the pilgrims on their way to Jerusalem.

MAP OF JERUSALEM
This map of Jerusalem shows the location of the events leading up to Jesus' death and resurrection. They are numbered chronologically.

5. Herod's Palace, possible site of Jesus' trial before Pilate

2. The "Upper Room", possible location of the Last Supper

The letters SPQR stand for "the Senate and people of Rome". This emblem of Roman power could be found on army standards, coins, and buildings across the entire Roman empire. In Judea and other occupied territories, the emblem was a symbol of Roman oppression.

Pontius Pilate, Roman governor of Judea

Pilate's official title was "procurator". This was a financial and military administrator of a Roman province.

Pilate's headquarters were in Caesarea, although he had a residence at the Antonia Fortress in Jerusalem. He was probably in the city for the Passover. The Gospels depict Pilate as a weak man, who condemned Jesus to death to please the religious leaders, despite his own conviction that Jesus was innocent. Historians such as Tacitus and Josephus paint a different picture, viewing him as an ambitious, ruthless, and insensitive person. He offended and antagonized the Jews on a number of occasions. His attempt to use Temple funds to build an aqueduct caused mass protests. Pilate dealt with the situation by sending in troops, and many Jews were killed.

JESUS BEFORE PILATE
The carving on this 4th-century marble sarcophagus shows Pilate washing his hands of responsibility for Jesus' death.

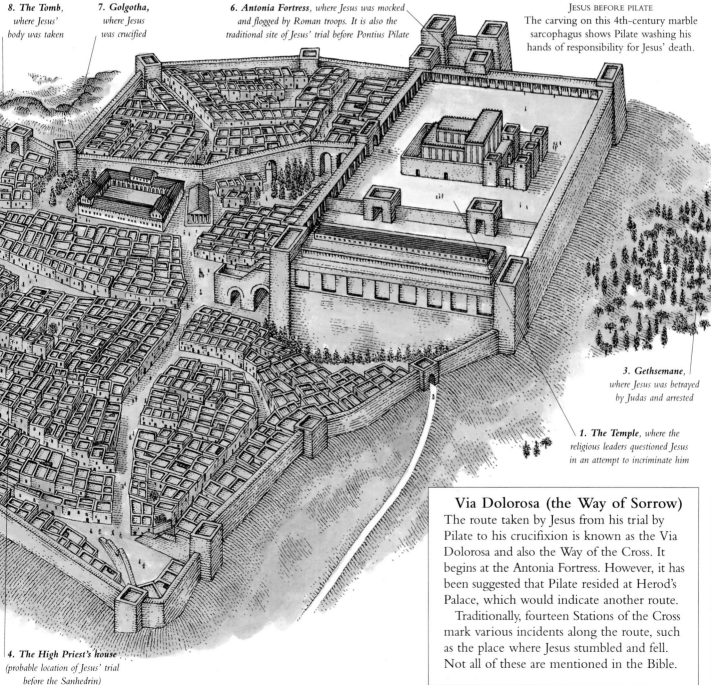

8. The Tomb, where Jesus' body was taken

7. Golgotha, where Jesus was crucified

6. Antonia Fortress, where Jesus was mocked and flogged by Roman troops. It is also the traditional site of Jesus' trial before Pontius Pilate

3. Gethsemane, where Jesus was betrayed by Judas and arrested

1. The Temple, where the religious leaders questioned Jesus in an attempt to incriminate him

4. The High Priest's house (probable location of Jesus' trial before the Sanhedrin)

Via Dolorosa (the Way of Sorrow)

The route taken by Jesus from his trial by Pilate to his crucifixion is known as the Via Dolorosa and also the Way of the Cross. It begins at the Antonia Fortress. However, it has been suggested that Pilate resided at Herod's Palace, which would indicate another route.

Traditionally, fourteen Stations of the Cross mark various incidents along the route, such as the place where Jesus stumbled and fell. Not all of these are mentioned in the Bible.

MATTHEW 21
JESUS ENTERS JERUSALEM

CHAPTER 21 VERSE 5

"See, your king comes to you, gentle and riding on a donkey"
This prophecy is from Zechariah (9: 9–10), who foretells the coming of the Messiah: "He will proclaim peace to the nations. His rule will extend... to the ends of the earth." By riding on the colt, Jesus demonstrates his fulfilment of the prophecy.

Jesus sends two disciples ahead of him to collect a donkey and her colt

CHAPTER 21 VERSE 8

"Spread their cloaks"
Jesus' entry on a donkey was a clear declaration, and the thousands of pilgrims on their way to Jerusalem were in no doubt of its meaning: Jesus was the prophesied Messiah. The cloaks and palm leaves on the road were the equivalent of today's red carpet. The crowds welcomed Jesus as the new King David.

PALM SUNDAY IN TANZANIA
These Christians from the Buhangija Mission, Shinyanga, commemorate Jesus' triumphal entry into Jerusalem. Although most people on mainland Tanzania follow traditional African religions, Christianity is taught in many missionary schools there.

21 AS[1] THEY APPROACHED Jerusalem and came to Bethphage on the Mount of Olives, Jesus sent two disciples, [2]saying to them, "Go to the village ahead of you, and at once you will find a donkey tied there, with her colt by her. Untie them and bring them to me. [3]If anyone says anything to you, tell him that the Lord needs them, and he will send them right away."

[4]This took place to fulfil what was spoken through the prophet: [5]"Say to the Daughter of Zion, '*See, your king comes to you, gentle and riding on a donkey*, on a colt, the foal of a donkey.' "

[6]The disciples went and did as Jesus had instructed them. [7]They brought the donkey and the colt, placed their cloaks on them, and Jesus sat on them. [8]A very large crowd *spread their cloaks* on the road, while others cut branches from the trees and spread them on the road. [9]The crowds that went ahead of him and those that followed shouted, "Hosanna to the Son of David! Blessed is he who comes in the name of the Lord! *Hosanna in the highest!*"

[10]When Jesus entered Jerusalem, the whole city was stirred and asked, "Who is this?"

Jesus enters Jerusalem on a donkey

Children sing "Hosanna to the king"

People lay cloaks and palm leaves in Jesus' path

¹¹The crowds answered, "This is Jesus, the prophet from Nazareth in Galilee."...

¹⁴The blind and the lame came to him at the temple, and he healed them. ¹⁵But when the chief priests and the teachers of the law saw the wonderful things he did and the children shouting in the temple area, "Hosanna to the Son of David," they were indignant.

¹⁶"Do you hear what these children are saying?" they asked him. "Yes," replied Jesus, "have you never read, '*From the lips of children* and infants you have ordained praise'?"

¹⁷And he left them and went out of the city to Bethany, where he spent the night.

¹⁸Early in the morning, as he was on his way back to the city, he was hungry. ¹⁹Seeing a fig-tree by the road, he went up to it but found nothing on it except leaves.

Then he said to it, "May you never bear fruit again!" *Immediately the tree withered.*

²⁰When the disciples saw this, they were amazed.

Jesus shows the disciples the power of true faith

The disciples are amazed when the fig-tree immediately withers

Jesus says that the fig-tree will never bear fruit again

"How did the fig-tree wither so quickly?" they asked.

²¹Jesus replied, "I tell you the truth, if you have faith and do not doubt, not only can you do what was done to the fig-tree, but also you can say to this mountain, 'Go, throw yourself into the sea,' and it will be done. ²²If you believe, you will receive whatever you ask for in prayer."

UNDERSTANDING THE STORY

Jesus' entry into Jerusalem on a colt is a symbolic act, and the crowds are ecstatic. All their expectations will be fulfilled in Israel's new king, who will deliver them from Roman oppression. They recognize Jesus as the Messiah they have been promised, but they still misunderstand his mission of salvation.

CHAPTER 21 VERSE 9
"Hosanna in the highest!"
Hosanna is Greek for the Hebrew words "save us" and comes from a Psalm (118: 25). It was sung during a festival of thanksgiving, when people waved palms and cried out for God to save them by sending the Messiah.

PASSOVER MEAL
The crowds who greeted Jesus were on their way to Jerusalem for the Passover celebrations. The focal event was the Passover feast, when every Jewish family sat down to a special meal. This 15th-century painting depicts the traditional bitter herbs and unleavened bread.

CHAPTER 21 VERSE 16
"From the lips of children"
Jesus confirms his divinity by quoting the words of a Psalm (8: 2), in which children give praise to God.

CHAPTER 21 VERSE 19
"Immediately the tree withered"
The fig-tree was in full leaf but bore no fruit. This event is a visual parable relating to Temple worship. Despite outward appearances, the practices tolerated by the religious leaders were as fruitless as the tree and destined to wither and die.

FIG-TREE
The slow-growing fig-tree can produce fruit for nine months each year.

MATTHEW 21
JESUS' AUTHORITY

CHAPTER 21 VERSE 25
*"John's baptism – where
did it come from?"*

Jesus replied with another question, which was a traditional practice of rabbis. He knew that the Pharisees would be unable to answer him, and so they would be discredited in front of all the people listening.

BAPTISM OF CHRIST
This 12th-century Austrian altar-piece depicts John baptizing Christ.

CHAPTER 21 VERSES 29–30
"I will not... I will, sir"

The "first son" in Jesus' parable represents the sinners, who heard John's message and changed their way of life. The "second son" represents the religious leaders, who outwardly displayed piety, but rejected John's call for repentance.

CHAPTER 21 VERSE 33
"Built a watchtower"

Watchtowers were often built to overlook the vineyards. Family members would stay in these towers during the growing season to protect their vines from robbers.

STONE WATCHTOWER, ISRAEL

21 JESUS[23] ENTERED the temple courts, and, while he was teaching, the chief priests and the elders of the people came to him. "By what authority are you doing these things?" they asked. "And who gave you this authority?"

[24]Jesus replied, "I will also ask you one question. If you answer me, I will tell you by what authority I am doing these things. [25]*John's baptism – where did it come from?* Was it from heaven, or from men?"

They discussed it among themselves and said, "If we say, 'From heaven', he will ask, 'Then why didn't you believe him?' [26]But if we say, 'From men' – we are afraid of the people, for they all hold that John was a prophet." [27]So they answered Jesus, "We don't know."

Then he said, "Neither will I tell you by what authority I am doing these things. [28]What do you think? There was a man who had two sons. He went to the first and said, 'Son, go and work today in the vineyard.' [29]*'I will not,'* he answered, but later he changed his mind and went. [30]Then the father went to the other son and said the same thing. He answered, *'I will, sir,'* but he did not go. [31]Which of the two did what the father wanted?" "The first," they answered.

The religious leaders question Jesus' authority. Jesus tells them two parables

A father asks his first son to work in his vineyard, but he refuses

Son

The first son changes his mind and does as his father asks

The father then asks his second son to work in the vineyard

This son agrees to work, then hides out of sight

Jesus told the Pharisees that tax collectors and prostitutes would enter the kingdom of God before them, for these sinners had believed John's words and repented.

³³"Listen to another parable: There was a landowner who planted a vineyard. He put a wall around it, dug a winepress in it and *built a watchtower.* Then he rented the vineyard to some farmers and went away on a journey. ³⁴When the harvest time approached, he sent his servants to the tenants to collect his fruit.

The tenants seized his servants, beat one, stoned another, and killed the third. Then he sent other servants to them, whom they treated in the same way. Finally he sent his own son to them. The tenants decided to take the son's inheritance, and so they threw him out of the vineyard and then killed him.

⁴⁰"Therefore, when the owner of the vineyard comes, what will he do to those tenants?"

⁴¹"He will bring those wretches to a wretched end," they replied, "and he will rent the vineyard to other tenants, who will give him his share of the crop at harvest time."

⁴²Jesus said to them, "Have you never read in the Scriptures: '*The stone the builders rejected* has become the capstone; the Lord has done this, and it is marvellous in our eyes?' ⁴³Therefore I tell you that the kingdom of God will be taken away from you and given to a people who will produce its fruit. ⁴⁴He who falls on this stone will be broken to pieces, but he on whom it falls will be crushed."

⁴⁵When the chief priests and the Pharisees heard Jesus' parables, they knew he was talking about them. ⁴⁶They looked for a way to arrest him, but they were afraid... because the people held that he was a prophet.

VINEYARDS
Grapes were a basic crop in Palestine, together with grain and olives. During harvesting, the grapes were gathered and taken to the winepress to be trampled.

THE TENANTS, THE SERVANTS, AND THE OTHER TENANTS
The "tenants" represent the religious leaders, and the "servants" are those persecuted for their religious beliefs. Jesus is the "son", who will be condemned to death. The "other tenants" refer to all those who already follow Jesus' teachings and who will grow to become the Christian community.

The landowner sends more servants, and the tenants treat them in the same way

A landowner rents his vineyard

At harvest time, he sends three servants to collect fruit from his tenants

This servant is beaten

Finally, the owner sends his son, but the tenants kill him as well

This servant is stoned

This servant is killed

UNDERSTANDING THE STORY

The chief priests and elders are looking for a way to destroy Jesus' reputation with the crowds. Instead, Jesus manages to discredit the religious leaders. Through his parables, Jesus attacks their insincere displays of faith and warns them that if they reject him, they also reject God.

CHAPTER 21 VERSE 42
"The stone the builders rejected"
In Hebrew, the word for "stone" (eben) is very similar to the word for "son" (ben). Jesus is alluding to himself. He is the "stone" rejected by the religious leaders, but God will reinstate him as the crowning glory of the Church.

MATTHEW 24

THE END OF THE AGE

CHAPTER 24 VERSE 2
"Not one stone here will be left"
In Jesus' time, Herod's Temple was a magnificent building, even though it was not completed until AD 64. Jesus' prediction was fulfilled in AD 70, when the Romans besieged Jerusalem and destroyed the Temple. Its destruction symbolized the end of the old order. The Church was to replace it as the new, living Temple.

DESTRUCTION OF JERUSALEM
This relief on the Arch of Titus, Rome, depicts the Romans plundering the Temple in Jerusalem.

24 ᴶESUS[1] LEFT THE TEMPLE and was walking away when his disciples came up to him to call his attention to its buildings. [2]"Do you see all these things?" he asked. "I tell you the truth, *not one stone here will be left* on another; every one will be thrown down."

[3]As Jesus was sitting on *the Mount of Olives,* the disciples came to him privately. "Tell us," they said, "when will this happen, and what will be the sign of your coming and of the end of the age?"

[4]Jesus answered: "*Watch out that no-one deceives you.* [5]For many will come in my name, claiming, 'I am the Christ', and will deceive many. [6]You will hear of wars and rumours of wars... [7]Nation will rise against nation, and kingdom against kingdom. There will be famines and earthquakes in various places.

[26]"So if anyone tells you, 'There he is, out in the desert,' do not go out; or, 'Here he is, in the inner rooms,' do not believe it. [27]For as lightning that comes from the east is visible even in the west, so will be the coming of the Son of Man...

[29]"Immediately after the distress of those days 'the sun will be darkened, and the moon will not give its light; the stars will fall from the sky, and the heavenly bodies will be shaken.' "

CHAPTER 24 VERSE 3
"The Mount of Olives"
The Mount of Olives is a ridge of hills beyond the Kidron Valley. They rise to a height of about 830m (2,676ft) and provide an excellent view of Jerusalem. It was there that, in his vision, the prophet Ezekiel saw "the glory of the Lord" (Ezekiel 11: 23).

CHAPTER 24 VERSE 4
"Watch out that no-one deceives you"
In the turbulent years before the Jewish rebellion (AD 66), many people set themselves up as deliverers from Roman rule. Jesus warned his disciples to beware of these false leaders, and not to confuse the role of the Messiah with that of a political saviour.

Jesus predicts the destruction of Jerusalem

The disciples ask Jesus about the end of the age

He says there will be wars, famines, and earthquakes before God's final judgement

Jesus warns his disciples to beware of false prophets

290

At the end of the age the sun and moon will darken, and the stars will fall from the sky

Jesus will appear in power and glory on the clouds

People will be working as usual, when one may be taken up to heaven and the other left

[30]"At that time *the sign of the Son of Man* will appear in the sky, and all the nations of the earth will mourn. They will see the Son of Man coming on the clouds of the sky, with power and great glory. [31]And *he will send his angels with a loud trumpet call*, and they will gather his elect from the four winds, from one end of the heavens to the other.

[32]"Now learn this lesson from the fig-tree: As soon as its twigs get tender and its leaves come out, you know that summer is near. [33]Even so, when you see all these things, you know that it is near, right at the door. [34]I tell you the truth, this generation will certainly not pass away until all these things have happened. [35]Heaven and earth will pass away, but my words will never pass away.

[36]"No-one knows about that day or hour, not even the angels in heaven, nor the Son, but only the Father. [37]As it was in the days of Noah, so it will be at the coming of the Son of Man. [38]For in the days before the flood, people... [39]knew nothing about what would happen until the flood came and took them all away. That is how it will be at the coming of the Son of Man... [40]Two men will be in the field; one will be taken and the other left. [41]Two women will be grinding with a hand mill; *one will be taken and the other left*."

UNDERSTANDING THE STORY

The disciples do not distinguish between the two events that Jesus talks about. The first "end of the age" is the imminent destruction of Jerusalem. The second is God's final day of judgement. Jesus tells his disciples to be ready at all times, for the end of the world will come without any warning.

CHAPTER 24 VERSE 30
"The sign of the Son of Man"
This describes Jesus' final return to earth. The passage recalls the traditional imagery used in the Old Testament prophecy of Daniel (7: 13–14), who foresaw God's judgement at the end of time.

CHAPTER 24 VERSE 31
"He will send his angels with a loud trumpet call"
The word "angel" means "messenger". The angels serve as God's agents. They will be sent with divine power to announce his final judgement throughout the world.

ANGEL
Detail from church window by Burne-Jones (1876)

CHAPTER 24 VERSE 41
"One will be taken... the other left"
At the end of time, people will be separated. The faithful and the righteous will receive spiritual salvation; those who are left will be condemned to eternal damnation.

MATTHEW 24

THE WISE AND WICKED SERVANTS

✣

CHAPTER 24 VERSE 42
*"You do not know on what day
your Lord will come"*
Jesus urges his followers always to be
ready for "Judgement Day". Even he
does not know when this will be.

✣

CHAPTER 24 VERSE 43
*"If the owner of the house had
known... the thief was coming"*
The "thief" is death. People will be
judged according to their lives at the
time of their deaths. No one can
know for certain when this will be
and should therefore
always be ready.

✣

CHAPTER 24 VERSE 48
*"Away a long
time"*
Jesus' followers will not
always have his presence
to guide them. Jesus warns
his disciples that his final
return on Judgement Day
may be a long way off.
They must not be like the
"wicked servant", who
only serves his master well
under constant supervision.

✣

CHAPTER 24 VERSE 51
"Gnashing of teeth"
Jesus is describing a vision of hell,
probably based on Jerusalem's
Hinnom Valley rubbish dump,
where fires burned constantly and
wild dogs "gnashed their teeth"
as they fought over scraps.

WILD DOGS
Jews regarded dogs as lowly scavengers
and never kept them as pets.

24 "KEEP[42] WATCH, because *you do not know on what day your Lord will come.* [43]But understand this: *If the owner of the house had known at what time of night the thief was coming,* he would have kept watch and would not have let his house be broken into. [44]So you also must be ready, because the Son of Man will come at an hour when you do not expect him.

[45]"Who then is the faithful and wise servant, whom the master has put in charge of the servants of his household to give them their food at the proper time? [46]It will be good for that servant whose master finds him doing so when he returns. [47]I tell you the truth, he will put him in charge of all his possessions. [48]But suppose that servant is wicked and says to himself, 'My master is staying *away a long time,*' [49]and he then begins to beat his fellow-servants and to eat and drink with drunkards.

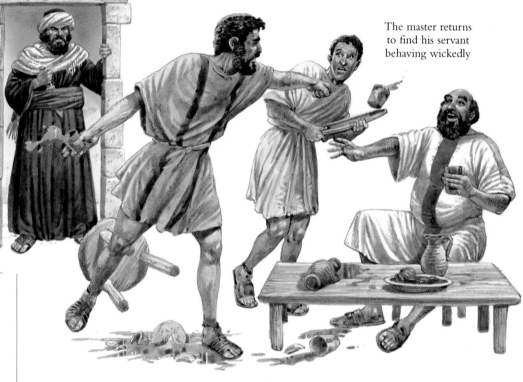

The master returns
to find his servant
behaving wickedly

[50]The master of that servant will come on a day when he does not expect him and at an hour he is not aware of. [51]He will cut him to pieces and assign him a place with the hypocrites, where there will be weeping and *gnashing of teeth.*"

UNDERSTANDING THE STORY

Jesus will return at "the end of the age", and God will make his final judgement. But Jesus does not want people to be preoccupied with this. His message is to "live every day as if it were the last", because people will be judged on how they live their lives, and no one knows when death will come.

MATTHEW 25

THE TEN VIRGINS

25 "THE[1] KINGDOM OF HEAVEN will be like ten virgins who took their lamps and went out to meet the bridegroom. [2]Five of them were foolish and five were wise. [3]The foolish ones took their lamps but did not take any oil with them. [4]The wise, however, took *oil in jars along with their lamps.* [5]The bridegroom was a long time in coming, and they all became drowsy and fell asleep.

[6]"At midnight the cry rang out: 'Here's the bridegroom! Come out to meet him!'

[7]"Then all the virgins woke up and trimmed their lamps. [8]The foolish ones said to the wise, 'Give us some of your oil; our lamps are going out.'

[9]" 'No,' they replied, *'there may not be enough for both us and you.* Instead, go to those who sell oil and buy some for yourselves.'

❖

CHAPTER 25 VERSE 4
"Oil in jars... with their lamps"
Lamps used for outdoor processions were torches made from oil-soaked rags fixed to the top of a long, wooden pole. They provided a lot of light, but only for a short time. Then the charred ends of the rags were trimmed and more oil added.

OIL JUG
Oil was poured from large storage jars into small jugs for daily use.

The bridesmaids who brought oil for their lamps escort the bridegroom to the wedding feast

The bridesmaids are all asleep when the bridegroom arrives

THE TEN VIRGINS
These unmarried women were bridesmaids, who helped the bride prepare for her wedding. This was always held at night. The bridesmaids were responsible for meeting the bridegroom and escorting him to the wedding ceremony.

[10]"But while they were on their way to buy the oil, the bridegroom arrived. The virgins who were ready went in with him to the wedding banquet. And the door was shut.

[11]"Later the others also came. 'Sir! Sir!' they said. 'Open the door for us!'

[12]"But he replied, 'I tell you the truth, I don't know you.'

[13]"Therefore keep watch, because you do not know the day or the hour."

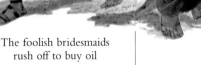

The foolish bridesmaids rush off to buy oil

When they arrive at the wedding feast, they find themselves shut out

UNDERSTANDING THE STORY

This parable conveys a similar message to "The Wise and Wicked Servants". Individuals are responsible for their own actions; they cannot borrow from others to get themselves out of trouble. Jesus asks his followers to be prepared and vigilant for his return, or they run the risk of being excluded from heaven.

❖

CHAPTER 25 VERSE 9
"There may not be enough for both us and you"
The "wise" bridesmaids are not being selfish. They know that if they share their oil with the other bridesmaids the whole procession could be plunged into darkness.

MATTHEW 25

THE MASTER'S FORTUNE

The servant digs a large
hole to bury his talent

❖

CHAPTER 25 VERSE 15
"He gave five talents of money"
The word "talent" derives from
this story. It means aptitude. The
master entrusts varying amounts to
each of his servants according to
their natural abilites. He did not
trust one more than another.

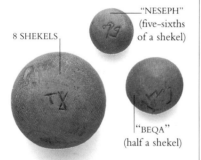

"NESEPH"
(five-sixths
of a shekel)

8 SHEKELS

"BEQA"
(half a shekel)

WEIGHTS AND MONEY
Three different currencies were in
use in Palestine at the time of Jesus.
Money-changers changed coinage
by using a system of weights based
on the shekel. The heaviest weight
was a talent. It represented about
3,000 shekels, the equivalent of
12,000 denarii. People often used
these weights instead of coins.

The master returns and wants
to know what his servants
have done with his money

❖

CHAPTER 25 VERSE 26
"You wicked, lazy servant!"
The servant did not squander what
the master had given him, but he
failed to put his talent to good use.
He chose security and did nothing
at all rather than risk failure.

25 " **T**HE[1] KINGDOM OF HEAVEN will be like...[14]a man going on a journey, who called his servants and entrusted his property to them. [15]To one *he gave five talents of money*, to another two talents, and to another one talent, each according to his ability. Then he went on his journey. [16]The man who had received the five talents went at once and put his money to work and gained five more. [17]So also, the one with the two talents gained two more. [18]But the man who had received the one talent went off, dug a hole in the ground and hid his master's money."

When the master returned, he wanted to know what his servants had done with the talents he had left them. He was equally pleased with the two men who had doubled his investment. He said the same to both.

[21]" 'Well done... You have been faithful with a few things; I will put you in charge of many things. Come and share your master's happiness!'
[24]"Then the man who had received the one talent came. 'Master,' he said, 'I knew that you are a hard man... [25]So I was afraid and went out and hid your talent in the ground. See, here is what belongs to you.'
[26]"His master replied, 'You wicked, lazy servant! So you knew that I harvest where I have not sown and gather where I have not scattered seed? [27]Well then, you should have put my money on deposit with the bankers, so that when I returned I would have received it back with interest.
[28]" 'Take the talent from him and give it to the one who has the ten talents. [29]For everyone who has will be given more, and he will have an abundance. Whoever does not have, even what he has will be taken from him... [30]Throw that worthless servant outside, into the darkness...' "

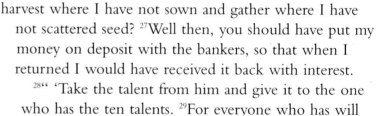

The master
praises the two
who put their
talents to work

The one who buried his talent
finds that his master is furious

UNDERSTANDING THE STORY

In the kingdom of God, success is not the amount that people achieve, it is each person using their abilities to the full. The servants knew that one day they would have to account to their master. The two who use their abilities productively to benefit their master are rewarded; the other loses everything.

MATTHEW 25

THE SHEEP AND THE GOATS

25 "WHEN[31] THE SON OF MAN comes in his glory, and all the angels with him, he will sit on his throne in heavenly glory. [32]All the nations will be gathered before him, and he will separate the people one from another as a shepherd separates the sheep from the goats. [33]He will put *the sheep on his right and the goats on his left.*

[34]"Then the King will say to those on his right, 'Come, you who are blessed by my Father; take your inheritance, the kingdom prepared for you since the creation of the world. [35]For I was hungry and you gave me something to eat, I was thirsty and you gave me something to drink, I was a stranger and you invited me in, [36]I needed clothes and you clothed me, I was sick and you looked after me, I was in prison and you came to visit me... [40]Whatever you did for one of *the least of these brothers of mine*, you did for me.'

[41]"Then he will say to those on his left, 'Depart from me, you who are cursed, into the eternal fire prepared for the devil and his angels... [45]Whatever you did not do for one of the least of these, you did not do for me.' [46]Then they will go away to eternal punishment, but the righteous to eternal life."

CHAPTER 25 VERSE 33
"The sheep on his right and the goats on his left"
In the Bible, "sheep" represent God's people. Middle-Eastern shepherds tended mixed flocks of sheep and goats. At first sight, it was not easy to distinguish one from the other. As in many cultures, right and left symbolize good and bad.

Goat

The shepherd separates the sheep from the goats: sheep on the right and goats on the left

Sheep

CHAPTER 25 VERSE 40
"The least of these brothers of mine"
Jesus calls on those who follow him to do all they can to help the poor, the humble, and the deprived. Whatever people do to alleviate the suffering of those less fortunate, they do for God.

UNDERSTANDING THE STORY

One day, God will judge the whole world, Jews and non-Jews alike. Those who have served the needs of others for Jesus' sake will be rewarded in abundance. These fortunate people will enjoy a never-ending life in God's presence. But those who fail God's judgement will be eternally damned.

SHEPHERDESS
The practice of keeping mixed flocks continues in Israel. This girl is tending sheep and goats in the Judean hills.

LUKE 22, MARK 14, JOHN 13, MATTHEW 26
THE LORD'S SUPPER

CHAPTER 22 VERSE 5
"Agreed to give him money"
Judas received thirty pieces of silver (Matthew 26: 15). As he was in charge of the disciples' treasury, it is unlikely he betrayed Jesus for money alone. Judas was the only apostle from Judea, which was under direct Roman rule. Judas probably betrayed Jesus when he realized his master would not overthrow the Romans.

JUDAS BETRAYS JESUS
Judas receives thirty pieces of silver. A painting by Duccio di Buoninsegna (*c.* 1278–1318), from the Museo dell'Opera del Duomo, Siena

CHAPTER 14 VERSE 12
"The Feast of Unleavened Bread"
This Jewish festival is an annual commemoration of the Israelites' escape from Egypt. They left in the middle of the night and did not have time to wait for their bread to rise (Exodus 12: 34). Every family eats unleavened bread for the week following the Passover meal.

CHAPTER 14 VERSE 12
"The Passover lamb"
Lamb is eaten at Passover as a reminder of the Exodus, when God protected his people. Each Israelite family sacrificed a lamb and the plague "passed over" their homes (Exodus 12: 21–30). In John's Gospel, the Last Supper was not the Passover meal. According to John, Jesus was crucified on the day of Passover, at the same time as the slaughter of the lambs. Jesus was the "lamb of God" (John 1: 29).

22 T[2]HE CHIEF PRIESTS and the teachers of the law were looking for some way to get rid of Jesus, for they were afraid of the people. [3]Then Satan entered Judas, called Iscariot, one of the Twelve. [4]And Judas went to the chief priests and the officers of the temple guard and discussed with them how he might betray Jesus. [5]They were delighted and *agreed to give him money*. [6]He consented, and watched for an opportunity to hand Jesus over to them when no crowd was present.

14 [12]On the first day of *the Feast of Unleavened Bread*, when it was customary to sacrifice *the Passover lamb*, Jesus' disciples asked him, "Where do you want us to go and make preparations... to eat the Passover?"

Jesus told two of his disciples to go into the city and to follow a man carrying a jar of water. He would lead them to a house, where they were to prepare the upper room for the Passover Feast. That evening, Jesus and the disciples went to the upper room. While they were eating, he said that one of them would betray him. They were saddened and asked who it would be.

[20]"It is one of the Twelve," he replied, "one who dips bread into the bowl with me. [21]*The Son of Man will go just as it is written about him. But woe to that man who betrays the Son of Man!*

Jesus and the disciples eat the Passover meal together

Thaddaeus

James

Matthew

Simon

Bartholomew

Philip

Andrew

It would be better for him if he had not been born."

13 ²⁶Then, *dipping the piece of bread, he gave it to Judas Iscariot*, son of Simon. ²⁷As soon as Judas took the bread, Satan entered into him.

"What you are about to do, do quickly," Jesus told him, ²⁸but no one at the meal understood why Jesus said this to him. ²⁹Since Judas had charge of the money, some thought Jesus was telling him to buy what was needed for the Feast, or to give something to the poor. ³⁰As soon as Judas had taken the bread, he went out. And it was night.

26 ²⁶While they were eating, Jesus took bread, gave thanks and broke it, and gave it to his disciples, saying, *"Take and eat; this is my body."*

²⁷Then he took the cup, gave thanks and offered it to them, saying, "Drink from it, all of you. ²⁸This is *my blood of the covenant*, which is poured out for many for the forgiveness of sins. ²⁹I tell you, I will not drink of this fruit of the vine from now on until that day when I drink it anew with you in my Father's kingdom."

³⁰When they had sung a hymn, they went out to the Mount of Olives.

UNDERSTANDING THE STORY

The Passover meal commemorates the deliverance of Israel at the time of the Exodus by the sacrificing of a lamb. The Lord's Supper inaugerates a new era, the era of the Church. Jesus will offer himself as a final sacrifice. He is the "Passover lamb", who will die to deliver people from their sins.

THE UPPER ROOM
The Coenaculum on Mt Zion in Jerusalem is the traditional site of the Lord's Supper.

✤

CHAPTER 14 VERSE 21
"The Son of Man will go just as it is written"
Jesus is referring to the Scriptures, which prophesied his death: "He was despised and rejected by men... he was led like a lamb to the slaughter" (Isaiah 53: 3–7). Jesus knew that his death was inevitable.

✤

CHAPTER 13 VERSE 26
"Dipping the piece of bread, he gave it to Judas Iscariot"
It is still a custom in the Middle East to dip a piece of bread, or meat wrapped in bread, into a bowl of stewed fruit. It is considered an honour to be handed a piece of food from the host. Jesus' gesture of friendship was a final appeal to Judas to change his mind.

✤

CHAPTER 26 VERSE 26
"Take and eat; this is my body"
The Gospel of Luke adds: "This is my body given for you; do this in remembrance of me" (22: 19). In the Christian Church, this meal is a service of memorial called "Holy Communion" (the Lord's Supper). It is also known as the "Eucharist", from the Greek for "thanksgiving", because Jesus "gave thanks" before he shared the bread and wine.

✤

CHAPTER 26 VERSE 28
"My blood of the covenant"
God's covenant with Moses required the Israelites to offer sacrifices to atone for their sins. Jesus announces a new covenant in which his own death will be the final sacrifice to deliver everyone from sin.

John

Jesus says the bread and wine are his body and blood

Jesus dips a piece of bread and gives it to Judas

Peter

Judas is about to betray Jesus

Thomas

Judas

James

MARK 14, MATTHEW 26
JESUS IS ARRESTED

CHAPTER 14 VERSE 27
"I will strike the shepherd, and the sheep will be scattered"
Jesus quotes the prophet Zechariah (Zechariah 13: 7). Jesus knows that the apostles will all abandon him.

CHAPTER 14 VERSE 34
"My soul is overwhelmed with sorrow to the point of death"
As the time of his suffering draws close, Jesus shows his human side. It is the mental anguish that he must endure, rather than the physical pain, that so deeply distresses Jesus. The Gospel of Luke records that "his sweat was like drops of blood falling to the ground" (2: 44).

CHAPTER 14
VERSE 36
"Abba"
This is the Aramaic word that children used for "father". It expresses the close relationship between Jesus the Son and God the Father.

Jesus asks the disciples to keep watch while he prays

The disciples cannot stay awake

CHAPTER 14 VERSE 36
"Take this cup from me"
To "drink the cup" is an Old Testament expression that means to experience the wrath of God. Jesus must suffer for the sins of the world, and when the full force of God's anger falls on his innocent shoulders, Jesus knows that he will be cut off from his heavenly Father.

Jesus is deeply anguished by the ordeal he must face

He asks God to help him

14 "YOU[27] WILL ALL FALL AWAY," Jesus told [his disciples], "for it is written: *'I will strike the shepherd, and the sheep will be scattered.'* [28]But after I have risen, I will go ahead of you into Galilee."

[29]Peter declared, "Even if all fall away, I will not."

[30]"I tell you the truth," Jesus answered, "today – yes, tonight – before the cock crows twice you yourself will disown me three times."

[31]But Peter insisted emphatically, "Even if I have to die with you, I will never disown you." And all the others said the same.

[32]They went to a place called Gethsemane, and Jesus said to his disciples, "Sit here while I pray." [33]He took Peter, James and John along with him, and he began to be deeply distressed and troubled. [34]*"My soul is overwhelmed with sorrow to the point of death,"* he said to them. "Stay here and keep watch."

[35]Going a little further, he fell to the ground and prayed that if possible the hour might pass from him. [36]*"Abba*, Father," he said, "everything is possible for you. *Take this cup from me.* Yet not what I will, but what you will."

[37]Then he returned to his disciples and found them sleeping. "Simon," he said to Peter, "are you asleep? Could you not keep watch for one hour? [38]Watch and pray so that you will not fall into temptation. The spirit is willing, but the body is weak."

[39]Once more he went away and prayed the same thing. [40]When he came back, he again found them sleeping, because their eyes were heavy. They did not know what to say to him.

[41]Returning the third time, he said to them, "Are you still sleeping and resting? Enough! The hour has come. Look, the Son of Man is betrayed into the hands of sinners. [42]Rise! Let us go! Here comes my betrayer!"

⁴³Just as he was speaking, Judas, one of the Twelve, appeared. With him was a crowd armed with swords and clubs, sent from the chief priests, the teachers of the law, and the elders.

⁴⁴Now the betrayer had arranged a signal with them: "The one I kiss is the man; arrest him and lead him away under guard."

⁴⁵Going at once to Jesus, *Judas said, "Rabbi!" and kissed him.* ⁴⁶*The men seized Jesus and arrested him.* ⁴⁷Then one of those standing near drew his sword and struck the servant of the high priest, cutting off his ear.

26   ⁵²"Put your sword back in its place," Jesus said to him, "for *all who draw the sword will die by the sword*. ⁵³Do you think I cannot call on my Father, and he will at once put at my disposal more than twelve legions of angels?..."

⁵⁵At that time Jesus said to the crowd, "Am I leading a rebellion, that you have come out with swords and clubs to capture me? Every day I sat in the temple courts teaching, and you did not arrest me. ⁵⁶But this has all taken place that the writings of the prophets might be fulfilled." Then all the disciples deserted him and fled.

An armed crowd comes looking for Jesus

Jesus faces his enemies without fear

Judas betrays his master with a kiss

UNDERSTANDING THE STORY

Jesus is fully aware of God's purpose in sending him into the world. He is the divine Son of God, yet he was born a man. Jesus' anguish at Gethsemane highlights his humanity, he faces his fear and goes willingly to his fate. Despite his own personal agony, Jesus expresses deep concern for his disciples.

CHAPTER 14 VERSE 45
"Judas said, 'Rabbi!' and kissed him"

Only someone close to Jesus knew where he could be found without the usual following crowds. A kiss as a greeting was either a show of affection between friends or a sign of respect that a disciple would give to his teacher. Jesus the teacher had offered Judas friendship. Yet Judas chose to betray him with a kiss.

CHAPTER 14 VERSE 46
"The men seized Jesus and arrested him"

The High Priest and his ruling council had their own security forces at their disposal. These Temple police, "armed with swords and clubs", had the power to arrest suspected criminals.

ROMAN SWORD
This short sword (gladius) was easy to wield, making it an effective stabbing weapon in the crush of battle.

CHAPTER 26 VERSE 52
"All who draw the sword will die by the sword"

Jesus was totally opposed to violence. He always preached peace and submission. He urged his followers to "turn the other cheek" when faced with physical assault. He did not approve of the attack on the High Priest's servant. Luke records that "he touched the man's ear and healed him" (22: 51).

THE GARDEN OF GETHSEMANE
This was one of Jesus' favourite places. The Hebrew name "Gethsemane" means "olive press". Situated on the lower slopes of the Mount of Olives, Gethsemane was where the olives were brought to be pressed for oil.

MARK 14
JESUS IS TRIED BY THE PRIESTS

---❖---
CHAPTER 14 VERSE 53
"The high priest"
The High Priest was the supreme leader of Israel. By Jesus' time, the office had become unpopular with many Jews because the High Priest was appointed by the Romans.

---❖---
CHAPTER 14 VERSE 54
"The courtyard of the high priest"
Court sessions were held during the day in a public area near the Temple, although never on Holy days. Jesus was tried at night in a private residence during Passover.

---❖---
CHAPTER 14 VERSE 55
"The whole Sanhedrin"
The Sanhedrin – from the Greek word for "council" – was the Jewish high court. It consisted of seventy members (chief priests, teachers of the Law, and elders), who were presided over by the High Priest.

---❖---
CHAPTER 14 VERSE 63
"The high priest tore his clothes"
The Sanhedrin considered Jesus' answer to be blasphemy. The High Priest tore his clothes in a traditional display of grief, although the Law forbade this (Leviticus 10: 6).

CLOTHES OF OFFICE
The High Priest wore special clothes, including a "Breastplate of Judgement" on which the names of the twelve tribes of Israel were inscribed on twelve precious stones.

14 THEY[53] TOOK JESUS to *the high priest*, and all the chief priests, elders and teachers of the law came together. [54]Peter followed him at a distance, right into *the courtyard of the high priest*. There he sat with the guards and warmed himself at the fire.

[55]The chief priests and *the whole Sanhedrin* were looking for evidence against Jesus so that they could put him to death, but they did not find any. [56]Many testified falsely against him, but their statements did not agree.

Jesus remains silent as witnesses give false evidence against him

The high priest asks if Jesus is the Son of God

Jesus replies, "I am"

The high priest accuses Jesus of blasphemy

[57]Then some stood up and gave this false testimony against him: [58]"We heard him say, 'I will destroy this man-made temple and in three days will build another, not made by man.' " [59]Yet even then their testimony did not agree.

[60]Then the high priest stood up before them and asked Jesus, "Are you not going to answer? What is this testimony that these men are bringing against you?" [61]But Jesus remained silent and gave no answer.

Again the high priest asked him, "Are you the Christ, the Son of the Blessed One?"

[62]"I am," said Jesus. "And you will see the Son of Man sitting at the right hand of the Mighty One and coming on the clouds of heaven."

[63]*The high priest tore his clothes.* "Why do we need any more witnesses?... [64]You have heard the blasphemy. What do you think?"

They all *condemned him* as worthy of death. ⁶⁵Then *some began to spit at him*; they blindfolded him, *struck him with their fists*, and said, "Prophesy!" And the guards took him and beat him.

⁶⁶While Peter was below in the courtyard, one of the servant girls of the high priest came by. ⁶⁷When she saw Peter warming himself, she looked closely at him.

"You also were with that Nazarene, Jesus," she said.

⁶⁸But he denied it. "I don't know... what you are talking about," he said, and went out into the entrance [and the cock crowed].

Outside in the courtyard, a servant girl recognises Peter

Three times Peter denies that he knows Jesus

People can hear that Peter has a Galilean accent

⁶⁹When the servant girl saw him there, she said again to those standing around, "This fellow is one of them." ⁷⁰Again he denied it.

After a while, those standing near said to Peter, "Surely you are one of them, for you are a Galilean."

⁷¹He began to call curses on himself, and swore to them, "*I don't know this man* you're talking about."

⁷²Immediately *the cock crowed the second time*... Peter remembered the words Jesus had spoken to him: "Before the cock crows twice you will disown me three times." And he broke down and wept.

UNDERSTANDING THE STORY

Jesus had once asked his disciples to tell no one that he was the Son of God, because he did not want to be the focus of a political uprising. Now his time has come, and he confesses his divinity without fear. His mission can now be fulfilled. He is the Messiah who will save people from their sins.

CHAPTER 14 VERSE 64
"Condemned him"
The Sanhedrin found Jesus guilty of blasphemy, which carried the death penalty by stoning. However, their procedure meant that Jesus' trial was illegal. Jewish Law decreed that testimonies against the accused must always agree, and that a death penalty could not be pronounced on the same day as the trial.

CHAPTER 14 VERSE 65
"Some began to spit at him... struck him with their fists"
This was an expression of rejection and condemnation in Bible times. But it was unlawful for members of the Sanhedrin to strike the accused.

CHAPTER 14 VERSE 71
"I don't know this man"
All four gospels record this moment of human weakness. Jesus had warned Peter just a short time earlier: "Watch and pray so that you will not fall into temptation. The spirit is willing, but the body is weak". Peter had been certain that he would never disown Jesus, yet, when his loyalty is put to the test, his courage fails him.

CHAPTER 14 VERSE 72
"The cock crowed the second time"
This was a dramatic reminder to Peter of Jesus' prophetic words. Many households kept poultry, and the crowing of roosters announced the approaching day. The night had ended and the full horror of his denial dawned on Peter.

COCKCROWING
Cockcrowing is an ancient means of telling the time. The Romans named the third watch of the night "cockcrowing" (midnight to 3am).

MATTHEW 27

JESUS IS TRIED BY THE ROMANS

27

CHAPTER 27 VERSE 2
"Handed him over to Pilate, the governor"
The Romans did not allow the Sanhedrin to sentence people to death. This is why Jesus was sent to Pontius Pilate, the Roman governor of Judea from AD 26 to 36, who stayed in Jerusalem during the Passover. His official residence was at Caesarea, on the Mediterranean coast.

Judas returns the money to the priests

CHAPTER 27 VERSE 3
"[Judas] was seized with remorse"
Judas realized the consequences of his betrayal when he saw his innocent master being unjustly condemned, but it was too late. In a state of total despair, Judas took his own life. His suicide was a tragic confession of his guilt and shame.

THE DEATH OF JUDAS
This 14th-century fresco by Pietro Lorenzetti depicts Judas' suicide.

The crowd calls for Jesus to be crucified

E ARLY[1] IN THE MORNING, all the chief priests and the elders of the people came to the decision to put Jesus to death. [2]They... *handed him over to Pilate, the governor.*

[3]When Judas, who had betrayed him, saw that Jesus was condemned, he *was seized with remorse* and returned the thirty silver coins to the chief priests and the elders. [4]"I have sinned", he said, "for I have betrayed innocent blood."... [5]Then he went away and hanged himself.

The priests could not put the coins into the temple treasury because it was blood money. Instead, they spent it on a plot of land to be used as a cemetery for foreigners.

[11]Meanwhile Jesus stood before the governor, and the governor asked him, "Are you the king of the Jews?"

"Yes, it is as you say," Jesus replied.

[12]When he was accused by the chief priests and the elders, he gave no answer. [13]Then Pilate asked him, "Don't you hear *the testimony they are bringing against you*?" [14]But Jesus made no reply...

[15]Now it was the governor's custom at the Feast to release a prisoner chosen by the crowd. [16]At that time they had a notorious prisoner, called *Barabbas.*

Pilate's wife sends him a message saying Jesus is innocent

Pontius Pilate wants to free Jesus

Jesus will not answer his accusers

The Jewish leaders accuse Jesus of challenging the authority of Rome

Pilate calls for water to wash his hands of any responsibility

[17]So when the crowd had gathered, Pilate asked them, "Which one do you want me to release to you: Barabbas, or Jesus who is called Christ?" [18]For he knew it was out of envy that they had handed Jesus over to him.

[19]While Pilate was sitting on the judge's seat, his wife sent him this message: "Don't have anything to do with that innocent man, for I have suffered a great deal today in a dream because of him."

[20]But the chief priests and the elders persuaded the crowd to ask for Barabbas and to have Jesus executed.

[21]"Which of the two do you want me to release to you?" asked the governor.

"Barabbas," they answered.

[22]"What shall I do, then, with Jesus who is called Christ?" Pilate asked. They all answered, "*Crucify him!*"

[23]"Why? What crime has he commited?" asked Pilate.

But they shouted all the louder, "Crucify him!"

[24]When Pilate saw that he was getting nowhere, but that instead an uproar was starting, *he took water and washed his hands* in front of the crowd. "I am innocent of this man's blood," he said. "It is your responsibility!"...

[26]Then he released Barabbas to them. But he had Jesus flogged, and handed him over to be crucified.

[27]Then the governor's soldiers took Jesus into the Praetorium and gathered the whole company

Crown of thorns

A soldier dresses Jesus in a scarlet robe

The Roman soldiers mock Jesus, bowing down to the "king of the Jews"

of soldiers around him. [28]They stripped him and put a scarlet robe on him, [29]and then twisted together a crown of thorns and set it on his head. They put a staff in his right hand and knelt in front of him and mocked him. "Hail, king of the Jews!" they said. [30]They spat on him, and took the staff and struck him on the head again and again. [31]After they had mocked him, they took off the robe and put his own clothes on him. Then they led him away to crucify him.

UNDERSTANDING THE STORY

Jesus is tried before the Roman governor because this is the only way that the religious leaders can secure a death sentence. They have no qualms about altering the charges against Jesus from religious to political. Pilate knows that the charges are unfounded, but he succumbs to pressure and crucifies an innocent man.

CHAPTER 27 VERSE 13
"The testimony... against you"
The death sentence for blasphemy was not recognized under Roman Law. To persuade Pilate to pass the death penalty, the religious leaders presented Jesus as a political activist. They told Pilate, "We have found this man subverting our nation. He opposes payment of taxes to Caesar and claims to be a king" (Luke 23: 2).

CHAPTER 27 VERSE 16
"Barabbas"
Barabbas had been imprisoned for insurrection and murder. This Aramaic name means "son of the father". Ironically, Jesus, the Son of God the Father, died in his place.

CHAPTER 27 VERSE 22
"Crucify him!"
Crucifixion was an ancient method of execution that the Romans adopted from the Greeks. It was used only for the most serious crimes, such as treason. Death was agonizing. The body gradually collapsed under its own weight, and the victims found it increasingly difficult to breathe.

CHAPTER 27 VERSE 24
"He... washed his hands"
Pilate performed a symbolic Jewish ritual of cleansing (Deuteronomy 21: 6–9). Those present knew that he was exonerating himself from blame.

PRAETORIUM (ANTONIA FORTRESS)
The soldiers took Jesus to the Praetorium, Pilate's palace and military headquarters in Jerusalem. The fortress was rectangular with a tower at each corner, two of which overlooked the Temple.

MARK 15
JESUS IS CRUCIFIED

Jesus stumbles, and a passer-by is forced to carry the cross

15

A ²¹ CERTAIN MAN *from Cyrene*, Simon, the father of Alexander and Rufus, was passing by on his way in from the country, and they *forced him to carry the cross*. ²²They brought Jesus to the place called Golgotha (which means The Place of the Skull). ²³Then they offered him *wine mixed with myrrh*, but he did not take it. ²⁴And they crucified him. Dividing up his clothes, they cast lots to see what each would get.

²⁵It was the third hour when they crucified him.

²⁶The written notice of the charge against him read: THE KING OF THE JEWS. ²⁷They crucified two robbers with him, one on his right and one on his left. ²⁹Those who passed by hurled insults at him, shaking their heads and saying, "So! You who are going to destroy the temple and build it in three days, ³⁰come down from the cross and save yourself!"

³¹In the same way the chief priests and the teachers of the law mocked him among themselves. "He saved others," they said, "but he can't save himself! ³²Let this Christ, this King of Israel, come down now from the cross, that we may see and believe." Those crucified with him also heaped insults on him.

³³At the sixth hour darkness came over the whole land until the ninth hour. ³⁴And in the ninth hour Jesus cried out in a loud voice, "Eloi, Eloi, lama sabachthani?" – which means, *"My God, my God, why have you forsaken me?"*

³⁵When some of those standing near heard this, they said, "Listen, he's calling Elijah."

³⁶One man ran, filled a sponge with wine vinegar, put it on a stick, and offered it to Jesus to drink. "Now leave him alone. Let's see if Elijah comes to take him down," he said.

³⁷With a loud cry, Jesus breathed his last.

³⁸*The curtain of the temple was torn in two from top to bottom.* ³⁹And when the centurion, who stood there in front of Jesus, heard his cry and saw how he died, he said, "Surely this man was the Son of God!"

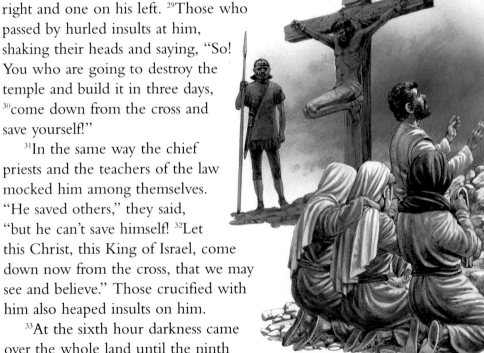

Darkness falls over the whole land

Those who are disciples of Jesus watch helplessly as he suffers on the cross

---

CHAPTER 15 VERSE 21
"A certain man from Cyrene"
Cyrene was a large city in North Africa (modern-day Tripoli). It had a large Jewish population. Simon was probably a pilgrim who had come to Jerusalem for the Passover.

CHAPTER 15 VERSE 21
"Forced him to carry the cross"
The condemned were often flogged and then made to carry the heavy crossbeam to the place of execution. The beating made them so weak that the load was often too much to bear.

VIA DOLOROSA
The "Way of Sorrow" is the traditional journey that Jesus made to Golgotha. It is marked by fourteen stations – places of special significance. This is the fourth station, where Jesus met his mother.

CHAPTER 15 VERSE 23
"Wine mixed with myrrh"
This was not the spice commonly used in perfumes. This variety of myrrh was similar to laudanum and known for its painkilling properties.

not middle

⁴⁰Some women were watching from a distance. Among them were Mary Magdalene, Mary the mother of James the younger and of Joses, and Salome. ⁴¹In Galilee these women had followed him and cared for his needs. Many other women who had come up with him to Jerusalem were also there.

⁴²It was Preparation Day (that is, the day before the Sabbath). So as evening approached, ⁴³Joseph of Arimathea, a prominent member of the Council, who was himself waiting for the kingdom of God, went boldly to Pilate and asked for Jesus' body. ⁴⁴Pilate was surprised to hear that he was already dead... ⁴⁶So Joseph bought some linen cloth, took down the body, wrapped it in the linen, and placed it in a tomb cut out of rock. Then he rolled a stone against the entrance of the tomb.

Jesus calls out to God and then breathes his last

A watching centurion is convinced that Jesus is the Son of God

Two robbers are crucified with Jesus

The religious leaders mock Jesus, saying that if he really were the Son of God, he could save himself

Roman soldiers cast lots for Jesus' clothes

GOLGOTHA (CALVARY)
This rocky outcrop is one of two possible sites for Golgotha. It is known as Gordon's Calvary, after the British General who identified it. The other site, from an earlier Christian tradition, is the Church of the Holy Sepulchre.

CHAPTER 15 VERSE 34
"My God, my God, why have you forsaken me?"
As the sins of the world fall on Jesus, he is cut off from God. He murmurs the beginning of Psalm 22. The psalm has many parallels with events that took place at Golgotha, and it uncannily describes Jesus' mental and physical agony. But the main theme of this psalm is hope for salvation and absolute trust in God.

CHAPTER 15 VERSE 38
"The curtain of the temple was torn in two from top to bottom"
This curtain separated the Holy of Holies from the rest of the Temple, symbolizing God's unapproachability. The death of Jesus removed this barrier and opened the way to God.

Joseph of Arimathea receives Pilate's permission to take Jesus' body for burial

UNDERSTANDING THE STORY

Jesus' horrific death by crucifixion brings to fulfilment many of the Old Testament prophecies. It is the ultimate act of self-sacrifice. He came into the world to remove the barrier of sin between God and humanity, and he suffers as a man to accomplish God's will. His death is not a defeat, but a triumph.

MATTHEW 27–28

JESUS IS RISEN

CHAPTER 27 VERSE 62
*"The next day, the one after
Preparation Day"*

Jesus died on Preparation Day, which
was the day before the Sabbath.
Instead of simply saying it was the
Sabbath, Matthew uses this phrase
because of the importance of the
actual day that Jesus was crucified.

CHAPTER 27 VERSE 64
"The tomb"

Joseph of Arimathea
had asked Pilate's
permission to bury
Jesus. Joseph washed
the body, wrapped it
in linen, and then
placed it in his
own unused tomb.

JOSEPH OF ARIMATHEA
This stained-glass window
from St Thomas' Church,
Glastonbury, depicts Joseph
carrying two flasks containing
Jesus' sweat and blood.

CHAPTER 27 VERSE 64
"This last deception"

The Messiah's resurrection was
prophesied in the Old Testament:
"You will not abandon me to the
grave" (Psalm 16: 10). The religious
leaders feared that the disciples
would fake Jesus' resurrection
in order to reinforce his
claim that he was the
Son of God.

27 THE[62] NEXT DAY, *the one after Preparation Day*, the chief priests and the Pharisees went to Pilate. [63]"Sir," they said, "we remember that while he was still alive that deceiver said, 'After three days I will rise again.' [64]So give the order for *the tomb* to be made secure until the third day. Otherwise, his disciples may come and steal the body and tell the people that he has been raised from the dead. *This last deception* will be worse than the first."

[65]"Take a guard," Pilate answered. "Go, make the tomb as secure as you know how." [66]So they went and made the tomb secure by putting a seal on the stone and posting the guard.

28 [1]After the Sabbath, at dawn on the first day of the week, Mary Magdalene and the other Mary went to look at the tomb.

[2]There was a violent earthquake, for an angel of the Lord came down from heaven and, going to the tomb, rolled back the stone and sat on it. [3]His appearance was like lightning, and *his clothes were white as snow*. [4]The guards were so afraid of him that they shook and became like dead men.

Pontius
Pilate

Pilate gives
orders to
secure
Jesus' tomb

An angel appears at Jesus'
tomb and tells the women
that Jesus has risen

The two Marys have come
to anoint Jesus' body. They
see the tomb is empty and
rush off to tell the
disciples the
good news

The guards
faint with fear

⁵The angel said to the women, "Do not be afraid, for I know that you are looking for Jesus, who was crucified. ⁶He is not here; he has risen, just as he said. Come and see *the place where he lay*. ⁷Then go quickly and tell his disciples: 'He has risen from the dead and is *going ahead of you into Galilee*. There you will see him.' Now I have told you."

⁸So the women hurried away from the tomb, afraid yet filled with joy, and ran to tell his disciples. ⁹Suddenly Jesus met them. "Greetings," he said. They came to him, clasped his feet and worshipped him. ¹⁰Then Jesus said to them, "Do not be afraid. Go and tell my brothers to go to Galilee; there they will see me."

¹¹While the women were on their way, some of the guards went into the city and reported to the chief priests everything that had happened. ¹²When the chief priests had met with the elders and devised a plan,

they gave the soldiers a large sum of money, ¹³telling them, "You are to say, 'His disciples came during the night and stole him away while we were asleep.' ¹⁴If this report gets to the governor, we will satisfy him and keep you out of trouble." ¹⁵So the soldiers took the money and did as they were instructed. And this story has been widely circulated among the Jews.

The guards tell the chief priests what they saw at the tomb

The chief priests bribe the guards to spread the news that Jesus' disciples stole his body

Jesus appears to the women

The women bow down and worship at his feet

Mary, mother of James and Joses

Mary Magdalene

CHAPTER 28 VERSE 3
"His clothes were white as snow"
This description of the angel recalls the words of the prophet Daniel, who had a vision of God himself: "The Ancient of Days took his seat. His clothing was as white as snow" (Daniel 7: 9). The angel of the Lord appears to the women with all the majesty of God.

CHAPTER 28 VERSE 6
"The place where he lay"
The exact site of Jesus' tomb is unknown. The Gospels tell us that Jesus' burial place was cut out of the rock and in a garden close to the place of crucifixion. Early testimonies suggest the original site is under the Church of the Holy Sepulchre, but since the 19th century, the Garden Tomb has been the preferred site for many Christians.

THE GARDEN TOMB, JERUSALEM

UNDERSTANDING THE STORY
Jesus is raised from the dead on the third day after his crucifixion. He appears to several people, but no one witnesses his actual resurrection. When the two women arrive at the tomb, it is already empty. The disciples' faith in Jesus' resurrection is not confirmed until they meet him face to face.

CHAPTER 28 VERSE 7
"Going ahead of you into Galilee"
In the Gospel of Matthew, Jesus reappears to his disciples only in Galilee (Matthew 28: 16).

LUKE 24

ON THE ROAD TO EMMAUS

Jesus meets
two disciples
going to Emmaus

24 **N**OW[13] THAT SAME DAY two of [the disciples] were going to a village called Emmaus, about seven miles from Jersusalem. [14]They were talking with each other about everything that had happened. [15]As they talked... Jesus himself came up and walked along with them; [16]but they were kept from recognising him.

[17]He asked them, "What are you discussing...?"

They stood still, their faces downcast. [18]*One of them, named Cleopas,* asked him, "Are you only a visitor to Jerusalem and do not know the things that have happened there in these days?"

[19]"What things?" he asked. "About Jesus of Nazareth," they replied. "He was a prophet, powerful in word and deed before God and all the people. [20]*The chief priests and our rulers* handed him over to be sentenced to death, and they crucified him; [21]but we had hoped that he was *the one who was going to redeem Israel.*"

The disciples told him all that had happened. As Jesus explained the Old Testament prophecies and how everything had been foretold, their spirits began to lift. When they reached Emmaus, the disciples urged him to stay with them.

[30]When he was at the table with them, he took bread, gave thanks, broke it and began to give it to them. [31]Then their eyes were opened and they recognised him, and he disappeared from their sight...

❖

CHAPTER 24 VERSE 18
"One of them, named Cleopas"
Jesus appeared to two disciples who belonged to the wider group of his followers. Cleopas, who is not mentioned elsewhere in the Bible, was one of them.

❖

CHAPTER 24 VERSE 20
"The chief priests and our rulers"
In the eyes of the disciples, the main responsibility for their master's death did not fall on the Romans, but on their own people.

THE ROAD TO EMMAUS
The foreground ruins mark the possible site of Emmaus on the ancient Jerusalem-to-Joppa road. The road is still used.

❖

CHAPTER 24 VERSE 21
"The one... to redeem Israel"
Many of those who had followed Jesus did so in the belief that the Messiah would be a political saviour who would overthrow the Romans.

The despondent disciples are kept from recognising Jesus, but his words comfort them

When Jesus breaks bread and gives thanks for the meal, the disciples realise who he is. Then Jesus disappears

Jesus shares a meal with the disciples

Jesus explains that the death of the Messiah was foretold by the prophets

JOHN 20

DOUBTING THOMAS

20 ON¹⁹ THE EVENING of that first day of the week, when the disciples were together, *with the doors locked* for fear of the Jews, Jesus came and stood among them and said, *"Peace be with you!"* ²⁰After he said this, he showed them his hands and side. The disciples were overjoyed when they saw the Lord. ²¹Again Jesus said, "Peace be with you! As the Father has sent me, I am sending you." And with that he breathed on them and said, "Receive the Holy Spirit..."

²⁴Now Thomas (called Didymus), one of the Twelve, was not with the disciples when Jesus came. ²⁵So the other disciples told him, "We have seen the Lord!"

But he said to them, *"Unless I see the nail marks* in his hands and put my finger where the nails were, and *put my hand into his side,* I will not believe it."

²⁶A week later his disciples were in the house again, and Thomas was with them. Though the doors were locked, Jesus came and stood among them and said, "Peace be with you!" ²⁷Then he said to Thomas, "Put your finger here; see my hands. Reach out your hand and put it into my side. Stop doubting and believe."

²⁸Thomas said to him, "My Lord and my God!"

²⁹Then Jesus told him, "Because you have seen me, you have believed; blessed are those who have not seen and yet have believed."

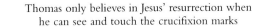

Thomas only believes in Jesus' resurrection when he can see and touch the crucifixion marks

---

✦ CHAPTER 20 VERSE 19
"With the doors locked"
The body of Jesus is transformed by his resurrection. He appeared like a spirit, but he was as solid as a mortal. Luke's Gospel records that Jesus asked for food and ate it (24: 41–43).

Jesus says that those who believe without seeing are blessed, because they are showing true faith

Jesus shows Thomas the nail marks

Jesus tells Thomas to reach out and put his hand in his side

✦ CHAPTER 20 VERSE 19
"Peace be with you!"
Jesus did not rebuke the disciples, who must have agonized over letting him down. His familiar Hebrew greeting comforted them.

✦ CHAPTER 20 VERSE 25
"Unless I see the nail marks"
These marks are traditionally depicted on Jesus' palms. In reality, the nails were driven through the wrists and sideways through the ankles of those sentenced to die on the cross.

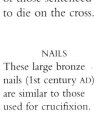

NAILS
These large bronze nails (1st century AD) are similar to those used for crucifixion.

✦ CHAPTER 20 VERSE 25
"Put my hand into his side"
John's Gospel says that when Jesus' body was taken down from the cross, "one of the soldiers pierced Jesus' side with a spear" (19: 34).

UNDERSTANDING THE STORIES

Jesus had told the disciples that they would "all fall away" when he was killed, fulfilling Zechariah's prophecy: "Strike the shepherd, and the sheep will be scattered". The disciples on their way to Emmaus and the eleven apostles are lost sheep. Jesus comforts and reassures them, renewing their faith. Jesus has not abandoned them, and this knowledge will enable them to carry on his work.

JOHN 21
THE LAST BREAKFAST

21 AFTERWARDS[1] JESUS APPEARED again to his disciples, by the Sea of Tiberias. It happened this way: [2]Simon Peter, Thomas (called Didymus), Nathanael from Cana in Galilee, [and] the sons of Zebedee... were together. [3]"I'm going out to fish," Simon Peter told them, and they said, "We'll go with you." So they went out and got into the boat, but that night they caught nothing.

[4]Early in the morning, Jesus stood on the shore, but the disciples did not realise that it was Jesus.

[5]He called out to them, "Friends, haven't you any fish?"

"No," they answered.

Most fishermen worked at night in wooden boats. They occasionally used lines and hooks, but usually fished with nets. After landing their catch, the men had to sort the fish and mend their nets.

A man appears on the shore and tells the disciples to cast their nets on the other side

The disciples fish all night on Lake Galilee, but they catch nothing

They cast the net again, and it fills with fish

The disciples recognise Jesus, and Peter swims across the lake to him

---
❖

CHAPTER 21 VERSE 7
"He wrapped his outer garment around him"
Fishing was heavy, strenuous work, and the disciples would have taken off their garments to make the task easier. Peter put his clothes back on as a sign of respect for Jesus.

❖

CHAPTER 21 VERSE 15
"Do you truly love me"
Peter once said to Jesus: "Even if all fall away, I will not" (Mark 14: 29), but later disowned him three times. Peter has changed. Three times he declares his love, no longer placing himself above others. This humility shows the correct attitude for his new role. Jesus' words, "Feed my sheep", confirm that Peter is still his chosen leader and is forgiven.

[6]He said, "Throw your net on the right side of the boat and you will find some." When they did, they were unable to haul the net in because of the large number of fish.

[7]Then the disciple whom Jesus loved said to Peter, "It is the Lord!" As soon as Simon Peter heard him say, "It is the Lord," *he wrapped his outer garment around him...* and jumped into the water. [8]The other disciples followed in the boat, towing the net full of fish, for they were not far from the shore... [9]When they landed, they saw a fire of burning coals there with fish on it, and some bread.

[10]Jesus said to them, "Bring some of the fish you have just caught."

[11]Simon Peter climbed aboard and dragged the net ashore. It was full of large fish, 153, but even with so many the net was not torn. [12]Jesus said to them, "Come and have breakfast."... [14]This was now the third time Jesus appeared to his disciples after he was raised from the dead.

[15]When they had finished eating, Jesus said to Simon Peter, "Simon son of John, *do you truly love me* more than these?"

"Yes, Lord," he said, "you know that I love you."

Jesus said, "Feed my lambs."

[16]Again Jesus said, "Simon son of John, do you truly love me?"

He answered, "Yes, Lord, you know that I love you."

Jesus said, "Take care of my sheep."

[17]The third time he said to him, "Simon son of John, do you love me?"

Peter was hurt because Jesus asked him the third time, "Do you love me?" He said, "Lord, you know all things; you know that I love you."

Jesus said, "Feed my sheep. [18]I tell you the truth, when you were younger you dressed yourself and went where you wanted; but when you are old you will *stretch out your hands*, and someone else will dress you and lead you where you do not want to go." [19]Jesus said this to indicate the kind of death by which Peter would glorify God. Then he said to him, "*Follow me!*"

CHAPTER 21 VERSE 18
"Stretch out your hands"
Jesus is foretelling Peter's martyrdom. According to a tradition dating from the 3rd century, Peter was crucified in Rome. He told his executioners that he was not worthy of dying in the same way as Jesus, so they crucified Peter upside down.

PETER'S CRUCIFIXION
Detail from a 16th-century French stained-glass window

UNDERSTANDING THE STORY

This same miracle happened three years earlier, when Jesus called his first disciples. He appears to his disciples in this familiar setting because he wants to reassure them. They no longer have their leader to counsel and strengthen them. Jesus hands over this responsibility to Peter, saying, "Take care of my sheep". Jesus is referring to the new Christian community, not just to the disciples.

CHAPTER 21 VERSE 19
"Follow me!"
These words recall the way Jesus recruited his disciples three years earlier, when they also caught a miraculous amount of fish on Lake Galilee. Then, Jesus asked the fishermen to follow him; now he is asking Peter to take on a special role. Peter will be the disciples' new leader and will supervise the establishment of the early Church.

Jesus invites the disciples to have breakfast with him

Jesus confirms that Peter will be the leader of the Church

Peter affirms his love for Jesus three times

MATTHEW 28, ACTS 1

JESUS IS TAKEN UP TO HEAVEN

CHAPTER 28 VERSE 18
"All authority... given to me"
Jesus' words recall Daniel's prophecy of a future Messiah: "He was given authority, glory and sovereign power; all peoples, nations and men of every language worshipped him. His dominion is an everlasting dominion that will not pass away, and his kingdom is one that will never be destroyed" (Daniel 7: 13–14).

THE PROPHET DANIEL
Daniel was thrown into a lions' den because of his faith. God sent an angel to close the lions' mouths, as depicted in this church window (1879).

CHAPTER 1 VERSE 3
"Over a period of forty days"
The period between the resurrection and the ascension was a time for the apostles to prepare for their new ministry, when they would no longer have Jesus' physical presence.

CHAPTER 1 VERSE 4
"The gift my Father promised"
Jesus is referring to the Holy Spirit, the spirit of God on earth, which will give the disciples the power to carry out their work.

CHAPTER 1 VERSE 6
"Are you at this time going to restore the kingdom of Israel?"
The disciples are still thinking in nationalistic terms. Jesus says that God's kingdom is for all nations.

28 THE[16] ELEVEN DISCIPLES went to Galilee, to the mountain where Jesus had told them to go. [17]When they saw him, they worshipped him; but some doubted. [18]Then Jesus came to them and said: "*All authority in heaven and on earth has been given to me.* [19]Therefore go and make disciples of all nations, baptising them in the name of the Father and of the Son and of the Holy Spirit, and [20]teaching them to obey everything I have commanded you. And surely I am with you always, to the very end of the age."

1 [3][Jesus] gave many convincing proofs that he was alive. He appeared to them *over a period of forty days* and spoke about the kingdom of God. [4]On one occasion, while he was eating with them, he gave them this command: "Do not leave Jerusalem, but wait for *the gift my Father promised*, which you have heard me speak about. [5]For John baptised with water, but in a few days you will be baptised with the Holy Spirit."

[6]So when they met together, they asked him, "Lord, *are you at this time going to restore the kingdom of Israel?*" [7]He said to them: "It is not for you to know the times or dates the Father has set by his own authority. [8]But you will receive power when the Holy Spirit comes on you; and you will be my witnesses in Jerusalem,

The disciples ask when Jesus will reestablish the kingdom of Israel

and in all Judea and Samaria, and to the ends of the earth."

⁹After he said this, he was taken up before their very eyes, and a cloud hid him from their sight.

¹⁰They were looking intently up into the sky as he was going, when suddenly two men dressed in white stood beside them. ¹¹"Men of Galilee," they said, "why do you stand here looking into the sky? This same Jesus, who has been taken from you into heaven, will come back in the same way you have seen him go into heaven." ¹²Then they returned to Jerusalem from the hill called the Mount of Olives, *a Sabbath day's walk* from the city. ¹³When they arrived, they went upstairs to the room where they were staying... ¹⁴They all *joined together constantly in prayer*, along with the women and Mary the mother of Jesus, and with his brothers.

As Jesus is taken up to heaven on the clouds, he tells the disciples that they will soon receive the power of the Holy Spirit

DOME OF THE ASCENSION
This 12th-century chapel was built by the Crusaders. It stands at the traditional site where Jesus ascended to heaven.

✦

CHAPTER 1 VERSE 12
"A Sabbath day's walk"
The Mount of Olives was nearly 1km (half a mile) from Jerusalem. A Sabbath day's journey was the maximum a person could walk and still honour the Sabbath.

✦

CHAPTER 1 VERSE 14
"Joined together... in prayer"
For the first time, men and women gathered together in one room to pray as a community.

UNDERSTANDING THE STORY

The number forty is symbolic of completion. The disciples' apprenticeship is over, and their master leaves the earth and ascends to heaven. But Jesus assures them that he will remain with them in the form of the Holy Spirit, to guide them as they take his message out into the world.

Two angels appear and say that Jesus will one day return to earth in the same way

The disciples see Jesus ascend

THE BIRTH OF THE CHURCH

Jesus chose twelve men from his many followers to be especially close to him and to spread his message after him. They are known as the "apostles", from the Greek word meaning "envoy". After Judas Iscariot's suicide, Matthias was chosen to replace him and to maintain the original number. It is thought that Jesus chose twelve men, because of the twelve tribes of Israel, the implication being that his ministry would unite the tribes into a new Israel – the Church.

ST LUKE
14th-century painting from a Serbian monastery

The Gift of the Holy Spirit

There was now no doubt among the twelve apostles and the other disciples that Jesus was alive. However, the many "convincing proofs" (Acts 1: 3) of his resurrection were not sufficient to enable the disciples to understand fully that the kingdom that Jesus offered was a spiritual kingdom and not the restoration of the Israelite nation. They needed the gift that Jesus promised, the Holy Spirit, to enable them to spread the "Good News" about Jesus around the world and make disciples from all nations. Ten days after their master's ascension to heaven, the day of Pentecost, the apostles received the gift of the Holy Spirit, and they spoke in many languages. Unlike the episode of Babel, where pride and arrogance led to the scattering of people and the confusion of languages, the pouring out of the Holy Spirit untied tongues and created understanding and unity. The apostles spoke, and three thousand people joined the disciples that day. The Church was born.

THE APOSTLES ON THE DAY OF PENTECOST
This detail is from the Verdun altar, Austria, and dates from 1181. It is an example of cloisonné work (enamel on gilded copper) and depicts the apostles receiving the gift of the Holy Spirit.

The Acts

Most of our knowledge about the events following Jesus' resurrection comes from Acts, written by Luke, a Greek doctor. He also wrote the Gospel of Luke, a well-documented account of Jesus' life. Following his conversion to Christianity, Luke travelled with the apostles for at least three decades and was in close contact with many eye-witnesses of Jesus' ministry. Luke had access to various documents, among them the Gospel of Mark.

Peter, the leader of the apostles

Peter's name in Greek means "rock". He was given this name by Jesus because he would be the rock on which the Church would be built. Peter was one of the "inner circle" of Jesus' disciples, and he was a witness to all the major events of Jesus' ministry. In a moment of human weakness after Jesus' arrest, he denied knowing his master. Peter was devastated by this failing. Jesus appeared after his resurrection especially to reassure Peter. Jesus told him, "Take care of my sheep" (John 21: 16), reaffirming Peter as his appointed leader. After receiving the gift of the Holy Spirit at Pentecost, Peter gave the first Christian sermon (Acts 2: 14–40).

ST PETER HOLDING THE KEYS TO HEAVEN
Peter's leadership is acknowledged by the Gospel writers, who always place him first when listing the apostles. This statue of Peter stands in Prague.

THE ACTS OF THE APOSTLES
A detail of the Brussels Tapestries from the Palazzo Ducale in Mantua, Italy, shows the apostles Peter and John healing a crippled man at the Temple in Jerusalem. This was the first recorded healing by the apostles after Jesus' death.

LORD'S SUPPER (wall painting from a catacomb in Rome)
From the earliest years, Christians ate a ritual meal to remember Jesus' death.

Early Christian belief and worship

Early Christian theology was mainly Jewish, using Old Testament language and concepts, such as the Passover lamb for Jesus. As all the first converts were Jews, they already believed in God. The early Christians used the Scriptures to prove that Jesus had fulfilled the prophecies.

ST PETER BAPTIZING (ITALIAN FRESCO)
Baptism was considered an essential step in conversion to Christianity. It symbolized a new birth.

They formed one big community in Jerusalem, and shared everything. They still respected Jewish dietary laws and went to the Temple every day to worship and preach. Christians also worshipped together in each other's homes. They still kept the Sabbath, but services were held on Sunday (Lord's day), commemorating Jesus' resurrection.

Opposition from the Jewish leaders

The early Christians soon met opposition from the Jewish religious leaders. Although some of the believers continued sacrificing at the Temple, they all considered Jesus' crucifixion to be the ultimate sacrifice. This was unacceptable to many Jews, who began to persecute the apostles. Much of the opposition came from the Sadducees, who did not believe in the resurrection of the dead. The Sadducees accepted only the first five books of the Bible, and the concept of resurrection appears in books written after the Jews' exile in Babylon.

Hellenic Jews and Christians

By the 1st century AD, Jews fell broadly into two groups: the Hebraic Jews (who lived in Judea and formed the greater population) and the Hellenic Jews (who were scattered throughout the Roman world). Hellenic Jews were descendants of exiles deported from Israel to Babylon and Egypt during the 8th–6th centuries BC. These dispersed Jews were united by the common culture of Hellenism and the koine dialect of Greek that Alexander the Great had imposed on the lands he had conquered. The Hellenic Jews had a different cultural identity, but their religious beliefs were unchanged. Many came to Jerusalem on pilgrimage and worshipped in the Greek synagogues. The new Christian faith spread rapidly throughout the Roman empire through the Hellenic Jews.

THE STONING OF STEPHEN
Stephen, one of seven chosen to be a deacon, was stoned to death for his faith. He became the first Christian martyr.

Deacons

The community of believers grew rapidly, which caused many practical problems. The Hellenists among the early Christians complained that common funds were being distributed unfairly at their expense. To solve this problem, seven men were chosen from the Hellenic community to be in charge of the Church's administration. They were called "deacons" from the Greek "to serve".

DEACON OF THE COPTIC CHURCH
A deacon is an ordained minister in the Christian church, whose main duty is secular administration.

Early Christian symbols

From AD 64 onwards, Christians faced harsh persecution from the Roman authorities. This led to the adoption of various symbols, such as fish, doves, and ships, that were not incriminating to followers of the Christian faith.

A fish was one of the earliest symbols, recalling the time when Jesus told his disciples that they would be "fishers of men" (Matthew 4: 19). The cross did not become a symbol of Christianity until the reign of Constantine, the first Christian emperor (306–37).

The cross recalls Jesus' crucifixion

The fish was one of the first symbols

The fish appeared on the tombs of many of the first Christians. A fish and cross are combined in this carving from a Coptic (Christian) cemetery in Egypt.

The three concentric circles on this mosaic from a baptistery in Italy probably represent the Holy Trinity: The Father, the Son, and the Holy Spirit.

Circular cross

The design is divided into three

This carving comes from the Basilica of St John at Ephesus. The design is a blend of a cross and a circle. It represents the sun in the sky and the Son of God, both givers of life.

ACTS 2
THE FIRST BELIEVERS

CHAPTER 2 VERSE 1
"The day of Pentecost"
The name Pentecost comes from the Greek word for "fifty". It was one of the most important Jewish festivals of the year, held on the fiftieth day after Passover. In the Old Testament, Pentecost is called the Feast of Harvest. It celebrated the end of the grain harvest, and Jews gave thanks to God for his blessing. In the apostles' times, the festival was mainly to commemorate God giving the Law to Moses.

CHAPTER 2 VERSE 2
"The blowing of a violent wind"
The word for "wind" is the same as the word for "spirit" in both Hebrew (ruah) and Greek (pneuma).

CHAPTER 2 VERSE 2
"Filled the whole house"
The "house" was possibly the Temple, since the Hebrew and Greek can also be translated as such.

CHAPTER 2 VERSE 3
"Tongues of fire"
Fire symbolizes the purification and enlightenment that the apostles must bring to the world in Jesus' name. In the Bible, fire is often a manifestation of God's presence. When God called Moses to lead the Israelites out of Egypt, he spoke to him from a burning bush.

MOSES AND THE BURNING BUSH
Hand-painted illustration from the
Nuremberg Bible (1483), Germany

2 **W**HEN[1] THE DAY *of Pentecost* came, they were all together in one place. [2]Suddenly a sound like *the blowing of a violent wind* came from heaven and *filled the whole house* where they were sitting. [3]They saw what seemed to be *tongues of fire* that separated and came to rest on each of them. [4]All of them were filled with the Holy Spirit and began to speak in other tongues as the Spirit enabled them.

Tongues of fire

On the day of Pentecost, the apostles receive the Holy
Spirit. This is the gift that Jesus had promised

[5]Now there were staying in Jerusalem God-fearing Jews from every nation under heaven. [6]When they heard this sound, a crowd came together in bewilderment, because *each one heard them speaking in his own language.* [7]Utterly amazed, they asked: "Are not all these men who are speaking Galileans? [8]Then how is it that each of us hears them in his own native language? [9]Parthians, Medes and Elamites; residents of Mesopotamia, Judea and Cappadocia, Pontus and Asia, [10]Phrygia and Pamphylia, Egypt and the parts of Libya near Cyrene; visitors from Rome [11](both Jews and converts to Judaism); Cretans and Arabs – we hear them declaring the wonders of God in our own tongues!" [12]Amazed and perplexed, they asked one another, "What does this mean?"

[13]Some, however, made fun of them and said, "They have had too much wine."

[14]Then *Peter stood up with the Eleven*, raised his voice and addressed the crowd: "Fellow Jews and all of you who live in Jerusalem, let me explain this to you; listen carefully to what I say. [15]These men are not drunk, as you suppose. It's only nine in the morning!

¹⁶"No, this is what was spoken by the prophet Joel:

¹⁷" 'In the last days, God says, I will pour out my Spirit on all people. Your sons and daughters will prophesy, your young men will see visions, your old men will dream dreams. ¹⁸Even on my servants, both men and women, I will pour out my Spirit in those days, and they will prophesy... ²¹And everyone who calls on the name of the Lord will be saved.'

²²"Men of Israel, listen to this: Jesus of Nazareth was a man accredited by God to you by miracles, wonders and signs, which God did among you through him, as you yourselves know. ²³This man was handed over to you by God's set purpose and foreknowledge; and you, with the help of wicked men, put him to death by nailing him to the cross. ²⁴But God raised him from the dead, freeing him from the agony of death, because it was impossible for death to keep its hold on him...

³⁶"Therefore let all Israel be assured of this: God has made this Jesus, whom you crucified, both Lord and Christ." ³⁷When the people heard this, they were cut to the heart and said to Peter and the other apostles, "Brothers, what shall we do?"

³⁸Peter replied, "*Repent and be baptised*, every one of you, in the name of Jesus Christ for the forgiveness of your sins. And you will receive the gift of the Holy Spirit. ³⁹The promise is for you and your children and for all who are far off – for all whom the Lord our God will call."

⁴¹Those who accepted his message were baptised, and about three thousand were added to their number that day.

Peter tells the festival crowds about Jesus' resurrection

Many accept Peter's invitation to repent and be baptised

Three thousand people become Christians that same day

UNDERSTANDING THE STORY

The apostles are no longer fearful and alone. The descent of the Holy Spirit gives them the strength to take up the role for which Jesus trained them. The event is generally recognized as the founding of the Christian Church. Its doors are open to people of all nations who believe in Jesus and follow his teachings.

CHAPTER 2 VERSE 6
"Each one heard them speaking in his own language"
Pentecost was a pilgrimage festival, and so Jerusalem was packed with foreigners. The descent of the Holy Spirit as "tongues of fire" had a dramatic effect on the apostles' own tongues. They were speaking the word of God, and this broke down the usual barrier of language. It is a reversal of what happened at Babel, when God's punishment meant that the people could no longer understand each other.

CHAPTER 2 VERSE 14
"Peter stood up with the Eleven"
Judas' place was taken by Matthias, who had been a disciple since the beginning of Jesus' ministry. The apostles had prayed for guidance and then chosen Matthias by lot.

A RIVER BAPTISM IN MOZAMBIQUE

CHAPTER 2 VERSE 38
"Repent and be baptised"
These words were used by John the Baptist, who was the first to preach this message. Believers repented and asked for God's forgiveness. Then they were baptized by immersion in water. This signified their spiritual cleansing and the beginning of a new life of unity with God.

THE GIFT OF THE HOLY SPIRIT
The Holy Spirit is the third person of the Trinity. The God of the New Testament is a unique God in three persons: God the Father, God the Son (Jesus), and God the Holy Spirit.

ACTS 3–4

PETER AND JOHN

3

ONE[1] DAY *Peter and John* were going up to the temple at *the time of prayer* – at three in the afternoon. [2]Now a man crippled from birth was being carried to *the temple gate called Beautiful*, where he was put every day to beg from those going into the temple courts. [3]When he saw Peter and John about to enter, he asked them for money. [4]Peter looked straight at him, as did John. Then Peter said, "Look at us!" [5]So the man gave them his attention, expecting to get something from them.

[6]Then Peter said, "Silver or gold I do not have, but what I have I give you. In the name of Jesus Christ of Nazareth, walk."

Peter helped the beggar to his feet. The man's legs became strong, and he followed the apostles into the temple courts, walking and jumping and praising God. People who recognised him could not believe it.

[11]While the beggar held on to Peter and John, all the people were astonished and came running to them in the place called *Solomon's Colonnade*. [12]When Peter saw this, he said to them: "Men of Israel, why does this surprise you? Why do you stare at us as if by our own power or godliness we had made this man walk?... [16]By faith in the name of Jesus, this man whom you see and know was made strong. It is Jesus' name and the faith that comes through him that has given this complete healing to him, as you can all see... [24]Indeed, all *the prophets from Samuel on...* have foretold these days..."

CHAPTER 3 VERSE 1
"Peter and John"

These apostles often partnered each other. Jesus had sent out his disciples "two by two" during their apprenticeship. Peter and John, together with John's brother James, were very close to Jesus. They are now the leading apostles.

John

A lame man begs for money

Peter helps the beggar to his feet

CHAPTER 3 VERSE 1
"The time of prayer"

The Temple at this period had three set times of prayer: 9am and 3pm, coinciding with the morning and evening sacrifices, and then sunset.

THE WESTERN WALL
This is the only part of Herod's Temple to remain and is commonly known as the Wailing Wall. Jews go there to mourn the destruction of the Temple and to pray.

CHAPTER 3 VERSE 2
"The temple gate called Beautiful"

This gate of Corinthian bronze was probably one of three that led from the Court of the Gentiles into the Women's Court. The gate stood on the east side of the Temple complex and faced Solomon's Colonnade.

People are amazed to see the lame man walking and jumping

The beggar follows Peter and John into the temple court, praising God

4 ¹The priests and the captain of the temple guard and the Sadducees came up to Peter and John while they were speaking to the people. ²*They were greatly disturbed* because the apostles were teaching the people and proclaiming in Jesus the resurrection of the dead. ³They seized Peter and John, and *because it was evening*, they put them in jail until the next day. ⁴But many who heard the message believed, and the number of men grew to about five thousand.

⁵The next day [members of the council] met in Jerusalem... ⁷They had Peter and John brought before them and began to question them: "By what power or what name did you do this?" ⁸Then Peter, filled with the Holy Spirit, said to them... "¹⁰It is by the name of Jesus Christ of Nazareth, whom you crucified but whom God raised from the dead, that this man stands before you healed...

"¹²Salvation is found in no-one else, for there is no other name under heaven given to men by which we must be saved."

¹³When they saw the courage of Peter and John and realised that they were unschooled, ordinary men, they were astonished... ¹⁸Then they... commanded them not to speak or teach at all in the name of Jesus. ¹⁹But Peter and John replied, "Judge for yourselves whether it is right in God's sight to obey you rather than God. ²⁰For we cannot help speaking about what we have seen and heard."

²¹After further threats they let them go.

Many listening in the temple courts are converted

Peter preaches about the resurrection of Jesus

Temple guards

The religious leaders order the apostles' arrest

UNDERSTANDING THE STORY

The courage and authority of the apostles is not learned in schools, but comes from the power of the Holy Spirit, working through them. Peter repeatedly tells his audience that faith in Jesus is the source of the miraculous healing. The truth of Jesus' death on the cross and resurrection is the key message of the new Church.

CHAPTER 3 VERSE 11
"Solomon's Colonnade"
The inner courts of the Temple were surrounded on all four sides by the Court of the Gentiles. Along the eastern side of this outer court was Solomon's Colonnade – two rows of high stone columns supporting a cedar roof. This porch was where Jesus often taught, and it became a favourite meeting place for the early Christians.

RUINS OF SOLOMON'S COLONNADE
The colonnade faces across the Kidron Valley towards the Mount of Olives.

CHAPTER 3 VERSE 24
"The prophets from Samuel on"
Samuel, last of the Judges, was the prophet who anointed King Saul and King David. Samuel's prophecies, and those of the prophets after him, were regarded as "Messianic", because they prophesied the coming of the Messiah. Jesus Christ was the fulfilment of their prophecies.

CHAPTER 4 VERSE 2
"They were greatly disturbed"
Many priests, including the High Priest, were Sadducees. This elite political party was opposed to the idea of resurrection of the dead.

CHAPTER 4 VERSE 3
"Because it was evening"
At about 4pm, when the evening sacrifices were over, the Temple gates were closed. Any official matter for the Sanhedrin could only be dealt with in daylight.

ACTS 4–5

THE EARLY CHURCH

4

O**N**[23] **THEIR RELEASE,** Peter and John went back to their own people and reported all that the chief priests and elders had said to them. [24]When they heard this, they raised their voices together in prayer to God...

[31]After they prayed, *the place where they were meeting was shaken.* And they were all filled with the Holy Spirit and spoke the word of God boldly.

[32]All the believers were one in heart and mind. No-one claimed that any of his possessions was his own, but *they shared everything* they had. [33]With great power the apostles continued to testify to the resurrection of the Lord Jesus, and much grace was upon them all. [34]There were no needy persons among them. For from time to time those who owned lands or houses sold them, brought the money from the sales [35]and put it at the apostles' feet, and it was distributed to anyone as he had need.

[36]*Joseph, a Levite from Cyprus*, whom the apostles called Barnabas (which means Son of Encouragement), [37]sold a field he owned and brought the money and put it at the apostles' feet.

CHAPTER 4 VERSE 31
"The place... was shaken"
God demonstrates his presence through a supernatural force. He answers the disciples' prayer by giving them the strength to continue preaching Jesus' words.

CHAPTER 4 VERSE 32
"They shared everything"
The early Church established a community that provided for the needs of its members. The pooling of property and land was voluntary. In Israel today, a community of people live on kibbutzim, working together and sharing resources.

QUETARA KIBBUTZ, ISRAEL
These kibbutz members are sorting peppers. They are paid in goods and services rather than in wages.

CHAPTER 4 VERSE 36
"Joseph, a Levite from Cyprus"
When the Israelites conquered Canaan, the Levites did not inherit any tribal land but were allotted various cities. The fact that Joseph (Barnabas) owned land indicates that the Old Testament division of land had broken down by this time.

ST BARNABAS
15th-century mural from the Church of the Holy Cross, Platanistasa in Cyprus

Peter

Many believers sell their possessions and give the money to the Church

Barnabas

Barnabas sells a field and gives all the money to Peter

Ananias gives Peter half the money from the sale of his land, saying that it is all he received

Ananias is punished by God for his deception and falls down dead

5 ¹Now a man named Ananias, together with his wife Sapphira, also sold a piece of property. ²With his wife's full knowledge he kept back part of the money for himself, but brought the rest and put it at the apostles' feet.

³Then Peter said, "Ananias, how is it that Satan has so filled your heart that you have lied to the Holy Spirit and have kept for yourself some of the money you received for the land? ⁴Didn't it belong to you before it was sold? And after it was sold, wasn't the money at your disposal? What made you think of doing such a thing? You have not lied to men but to God."

Then Ananias fell down and died. When people heard what had happened they were seized with fear. Some young men came forward, wrapped up his body, and carried him out to be buried. Then Ananias' wife came to Peter and the disciples, unaware of what had happened. Peter asked her if the money her husband had given him was the total amount from the sale of the land.

Some young men wrap up Ananias' body and take it away to be buried

⁸"Yes," she said, "that is the price." ⁹Peter said to her: "How could you agree to test the Spirit of the Lord? Look! The feet of the men who buried your husband are at the door, and they will carry you out also."

¹⁰At that moment *she fell down at his feet and died.* Then the young men came in and, finding her dead, carried her out and buried her beside her husband. ¹¹Great fear seized the whole church and all who heard about these events.

Sapphira

Peter asks about the money

¹²The apostles performed many miraculous signs and wonders among the people. And... ¹⁴more and more men and women believed in the Lord... ¹⁵As a result, people brought the sick into the streets and laid them on beds and mats so that at least *Peter's shadow might fall on some of them* as he passed by.

UNDERSTANDING THE STORY

Jesus' disciples refuse to be silenced and, despite attacks from the Jewish religious leaders, the early Church is growing. The apostles are establishing a community that looks after the needs of its people. The fate of Ananias and his wife is a warning that there is no place in the Church for hypocrisy or deceit.

✛

CHAPTER 5 VERSE 10
"She fell down at his feet and died"
Sapphira and Ananias are judged harshly because they lied to God, not because they failed to give everything they owned. Their offering to the Church was motivated by the desire to impress people, and provides a sharp contrast with Barnabas' selfless generosity. Their terrible punishment serves as a reminder to others of the need to be honest with God.

Ananias' wife, Sapphira, goes to see Peter, unaware of what has happened

Sapphira lies to Peter, telling the same story as Ananias

Peter warns Sapphira that the men who buried her husband are coming back for her

✛

CHAPTER 5 VERSE 15
"Peter's shadow might fall on some of them"
Peter has taken over Jesus' role of healer and teacher. The people have such faith in Peter that they believe even his shadow can cure them. This recalls Luke's account of a woman who believed she would be healed just by touching Jesus' cloak (Luke 8: 43–48).

ACTS 5

THE APOSTLES ARE PERSECUTED

CHAPTER 5 VERSE 30
"By hanging him on a tree"
Peter's words refer to the stake
that Jesus was crucified on, which
was probably part of a tree-trunk.
This phrase also recalls Old
Testament scriptures, which stated
that criminals were to be stoned
and then publicly hung from a tree
(Deuteronomy 21: 22). Jesus was
treated like a common criminal.

The apostles are arrested
and imprisoned

An angel appears and
opens their prison door

CHAPTER 5 VERSE 34
"A Pharisee named Gamaliel"
Gamaliel was a well-known and
respected rabbi. He taught in the
school of Hillel, whose views
on Jewish Law were
fairly moderate.

5 **T**HEN[17] THE HIGH PRIEST and all his associates, who were members of the party of the Sadducees, were filled with jealousy. [18]They arrested the apostles and put them in the public jail. [19]But during the night an angel of the Lord opened the doors of the jail and brought them out. [20]"Go, stand in the temple courts," he said, "and tell the people the full message of this new life."

[21]At daybreak they entered the temple courts, as they had been told, and began to teach the people.

When the high priest and his associates arrived, they called together the Sanhedrin – the full assembly of the elders of Israel – and sent to the jail for the apostles. [22]But on arriving at the jail, the officers did not find them there. So they went back and reported, [23]"We found the jail securely locked, with the guards standing at the doors; but when we opened them, we found no-one inside." [24]On hearing this report, the captain of the temple guard and the chief priests were puzzled, wondering what would come of this.

[25]Then someone came and said, "Look! The men you put in jail are standing in the temple courts teaching the people." [26]At that, the captain went with his officers and brought the apostles. They did not use force, because they feared that the people would stone them.

[27]Having brought the apostles, they made them appear before the Sanhedrin to be questioned by the high priest.

The apostles return to the temple
courts and continue to preach

The High Priest questions
the apostles

The apostles are arrested
again and taken before
the full assembly of
the Sanhedrin

Peter tells the
Sanhedrin that he
will obey only God,
and not men

The religious
leaders are furious

[28]"We gave you strict orders not to teach in this name," he said. "Yet you have filled Jerusalem with your teaching and are determined to make us guilty of this man's blood."

[29]Peter and the other apostles replied: "We must obey God rather than men! [30]The God of our fathers raised Jesus from the dead – whom you had killed *by hanging him on a tree.* [31]God exalted him to his own right hand as Prince and Saviour that he might give repentance and forgiveness of sins to Israel. [32]We are witnesses of these things, and so is the Holy Spirit, whom God has given to those who obey him."

[33]When they heard this, they were furious and wanted to put them to death. [34]But *a Pharisee named Gamaliel*, a teacher of the law, who was honoured by all the people, stood up in the Sanhedrin and ordered that the men be put outside for a little while.

The Sanhedrin wants the apostles put to death

[35]Then he addressed them: "Men of Israel, consider carefully what you intend to do to these men. [36]Some time ago *Theudas* appeared, claiming to be somebody, and about four hundred men rallied to him. He was killed, all his followers were dispersed, and it all came to nothing. [37]After him, *Judas* the Galilean appeared *in the days of the census* and led a band of people in revolt. He too was killed, and all his followers were scattered. [38]Therefore, in the present case I advise you: Leave these men alone! Let them go! For if their purpose or activity is of human origin, it will fail. [39]But if it is from God, you will not be able to stop these men; you will only find yourselves fighting against God."

Gamaliel reasons with them, and so the apostles are flogged and sent away

[40]His speech persuaded them. *They called the apostles in and had them flogged.* Then they ordered them not to speak in the name of Jesus, and let them go.

[41]The apostles left the Sanhedrin, rejoicing because they had been counted worthy of suffering disgrace for the Name. [42]Day after day, in the temple courts and from house to house, they never stopped teaching and proclaiming the good news that Jesus is the Christ.

The apostles are glad to suffer in Jesus' name

UNDERSTANDING THE STORY

The Sanhedrin is infuriated by the popularity of the apostles, whom they see as uneducated, ordinary men. They pose a threat to the religious leaders, who want to destroy them. Instead of being deterred by their persecutors, the apostles consider it a privilege to be able to suffer for Jesus' sake.

❖

CHAPTER 5 VERSES 36, 37
"Theudas [and]... Judas"
In early New Testament times, several men claimed to have received revelations and miraculous powers from God. These people refused to pay taxes to Caesar and stirred up revolts to try to overthrow the Romans. According to Josephus, a Jewish historian, Theudas lived forty years after Judas, not before. It is possible that there were two rebels named Theudas.

❖

CHAPTER 5 VERSE 37
"In the days of the census"
The Roman government conducted an official registration of people about every fourteen years. The New Testament mentions two censuses. The first was taken at the time of Jesus' birth, and all citizens had to return to their home towns. This was the second, and it took place in AD 6 to assess the amount of property in Judea.

❖

CHAPTER 5 VERSE 40
"They... had them flogged"
Flogging was a traditional form of punishment. Mosaic law forbade more than forty lashes to be given (Deuteronomy 25: 2–3). The whips used in crucifixion beatings were made of leather cords attached to a handle. Sometimes these cords were knotted or strung with pieces of metal and bone to make the scourging more painful.

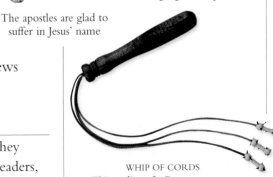

WHIP OF CORDS
This replica of a Roman scourge is similar to the one used to whip Jesus before his crucifixion.

ACTS 6–8

STEPHEN, THE FIRST MARTYR

❖

CHAPTER 6 VERSE 1
"Grecian Jews... Hebraic Jews"

At this stage, the believers were all Jewish, but from various cultural backgrounds. The "Grecian Jews" had settled in Jerusalem, but their outlook was influenced by their Hellenistic roots, and they worshipped God in their own language. The "Hebraic Jews" were born in Palestine and spoke Hebrew and Aramaic.

❖

CHAPTER 6 VERSE 1
"Their widows were being overlooked"

These widows in Jerusalem had probably given away their capital in the early days of the Church and now needed support. The majority of the early Church's members were Hebraic, and the Grecian minority were concerned that their poor were not receiving a fair share of food.

❖

CHAPTER 6 VERSE 3
"Choose seven men"

It was common Jewish practice to set up committees of seven. These seven men were chosen from the Greek congregation in order to serve the needs of their community. The word "deacon" comes from the Greek translation of the verb "to serve". These "servants" of the early Church were the first deacons.

ST STEPHEN
This is a 12th-century mural from a monastery near Cappadocia in Turkey. The word "saint" comes from the Latin for "purity" and "consecration". It originally referred to all followers of Jesus.

6 IN[1] THOSE DAYS when the number of disciples was increasing, the *Grecian Jews* among them complained against the *Hebraic Jews* because *their widows were being overlooked* in the daily distribution of food. [2]So the Twelve gathered all the disciples together and said, "It would not be right for us to neglect the ministry of the word of God in order to wait on tables. [3]Brothers, *choose seven men* from among you who are known to be full of the Spirit and wisdom. We will turn this responsibility over to them [4]and will give our attention to prayer and the ministry of the word."

Members of the Church choose seven men to help distribute food

The apostles bless each of the seven

Stephen

[5]This proposal pleased the whole group. They chose Stephen, a man full of faith and of the Holy Spirit; also Philip, Procorus, Nicanor, Timon, Parmenas, and Nicolas from Antioch, a convert to Judaism. [6]They presented these men to the apostles, who prayed and laid their hands on them. [7]So the word of God spread. The number of disciples in Jerusalem increased rapidly, and a large number of priests became obedient to the faith.

[8]Now Stephen... did great wonders and miraculous signs among the people. [9]Opposition arose, however, from members of the Synagogue of the *Freedmen*... These men began to argue with Stephen, [10]but they could not stand up against his wisdom... [12]So they stirred up the people and the elders and the teachers of the law. They seized Stephen and brought him before the Sanhedrin. [13]They produced false witnesses, who testified, "This fellow never stops speaking against this holy place and against the law..."

The high priest asked Stephen if the accusations were true. In an eloquent reply, Stephen reminded the Sanhedrin that true worship did not depend on ritual or a specific place. Finally, after trying to explain the Christian view, he attacked their narrow-mindedness and gave them a warning.

7 ⁵¹"You are just like your fathers... ⁵²Was there ever a prophet your fathers did not persecute? They even killed those who predicted the coming of the Righteous One. And now you have betrayed and murdered him – ⁵³you who have received the law... but have not obeyed it."

⁵⁴When they heard this, they were furious and gnashed their teeth at him. ⁵⁵But Stephen, full of the Holy Spirit, looked up to heaven and saw the glory of God, and Jesus standing at the right hand of God.

Stephen is accused of blasphemy and taken before the Sanhedrin

Stephen's defence enrages the Sanhedrin

High priest

Stephen looks up and sees a vision of God and Jesus

CHAPTER 6 VERSE 9
"Freedmen"
These Jews were former Roman prisoners or slaves who had formed their own synagogue in Jerusalem. They came from Greek-speaking areas such as Cyrene (in North Africa), Alexandria (in Egypt), and Cilicia (in Asia Minor).

ST STEPHEN'S GATE
This is the traditional site where Stephen was stoned. The gate is also known as Lion's Gate.

CHAPTER 7 VERSE 58
"The witnesses"
By law, prosecuting witnesses had to cast the first stone. The word "martyr" derives from the Greek word for "witness". Stephen bore witness to Jesus' resurrection and became the first Christian martyr. It is ironic that he was killed by those who "witnessed" his confession.

⁵⁶"Look," he said, "I see heaven open and the Son of Man standing at the right hand of God." ⁵⁷At this they covered their ears and, yelling at the top of their voices, they all rushed at him, ⁵⁸dragged him out of the city and began to stone him. Meanwhile, *the witnesses* laid their clothes at the feet of a young man named Saul.

⁵⁹While they were stoning him, Stephen prayed, "Lord Jesus, receive my Spirit." ⁶⁰Then he fell on his knees and cried out, "Lord, do not hold this sin against them." When he had said this, he fell asleep.

8 ¹And Saul was there, giving approval to his death.

UNDERSTANDING THE STORY

The Church is growing rapidly, and the apostles need practical help with the increasing day-to-day administrative duties. Stephen is one of seven who are chosen. He is the first believer to die for his faith. Like Jesus, his ability to forgive those who persecute him is an example to others.

Saul looks on with approval

Stephen is dragged out of the city and stoned to death

THE GROWTH OF THE CHURCH

Despite opposition from the Jewish religious leaders, the early Church continued to grow. Persecution caused many Christians to leave Jerusalem, and so the Gospel message began to spread to other communities. However, the first Christians still lived according to the Jewish religious customs. This caused difficulty when non-Jews (Gentiles) wanted to be baptized into the new faith. The early Church struggled with this dilemma. It was Paul – formerly the zealous persecutor Saul – who realized that the Church's whole future depended on the conversion of Gentiles.

ST PHILIP, Albrecht Dürer (1471–1528) Philip was one of the seven deacons.

The evangelists

As witnesses of the resurrection of Jesus, the apostles were the pillars of the early Church. Their main role was to ensure that the Gospel was preached in total accordance with Jesus' teachings. They remained in Jerusalem as a source of encouragement to those who were being imprisoned for their faith. The believers who left Jerusalem were not silenced by the persecution. They preached the Good News about Jesus wherever they went. These disciples became known as "evangelists"; their aim was to spread the Gospel. Two of the most prominent early evangelists were Philip and Barnabas.

ST PAUL'S CONVERSION Paul became a Christian when Jesus spoke to him. Painting by Caravaggio (1573-1610)

Gamaliel

As a young man, Paul went to Jerusalem and studied with Gamaliel, who was one of the most famous Pharisaic teachers of his time and who belonged to a school of thought that emphasized tradition over the Law. Gamaliel was a member of the Sanhedrin, and he advised his colleagues to treat the early Christians more moderately. His argument was that, if Jesus was a false prophet, like so many before, his followers would soon fade into obscurity.

TEMPLE STEPS Gamaliel once taught on these recently excavated steps of the Temple court.

TARSUS: THE BIRTHPLACE OF ST PAUL, hand-painted engraving (1840)

Paul's upbringing

Paul was a Jew from the tribe of Benjamin. He grew up in the Hellenistic city of Tarsus, a port at the crossroads of important trade routes in Asia Minor. Greek was his native language, and he was greatly influenced by Greek culture and philosophy.

Paul trained as a Pharisee and learnt Hebrew and Aramaic. He had a passionate temperament and was proud of his Jewish heritage. He adhered strictly to the Jewish laws and customs. At first, he viewed Christian teachings as heretical.

Paul the persecutor

In his zeal to eradicate what he saw as heresy, Paul set out to arrest Christians in Judea and Damascus. He acted for the High Priest, who the Romans allowed to arrest Jewish criminals. Both Judea and Damascus were in the Roman province of Syria. The High Priest's jurisdiction extended to Damascus, which had a large Jewish population. However, Paul could not arrest those Christians who fled to Samaria, because of the long enmity between the Jews and Samaritans. Nor could he arrest Christians in Caesarea, as the High Priest's authority did not extend there.

Roman citizenship

Paul held Roman citizenship. He probably inherited this from his father or an ancestor, who may have received it for services to the empire. Roman citizenship provided protection and many privileges. A Roman citizen could not be beaten to extract a confession or be imprisoned without trial. As a citizen, Paul could also demand to be tried in a Roman court.

ROMAN CITIZEN
Only Roman citizens could wear a toga – a single piece of cloth wrapped around the body.

GENTILES NOT ADMITTED
A notice in Greek warning Gentiles not to enter the inner Temple

The Jews and the Gentiles

After God's covenant with Abraham, the Israelites considered all those not descended from Isaac and Jacob as "Gentiles". The word means "nations", meaning nations other than Israel. Jews maintained their separate identity by forbidding intermarriage, observing dietary laws, and practising circumcision. By the 1st century AD, many Gentiles had embraced the Jewish faith. These converts to Judaism were known as proselytes. Initially, the apostles and evangelists preached in synagogues to Jews and proselytes. However, when Christianity began to spread outside Jerusalem into pagan cities such as Antioch, many Gentiles responded to the Christian message. The Hebraic Christians argued that Gentiles could not be accepted into the faith because they were uncircumcised and did not observe Jewish dietary laws. The Council of Jerusalem finally resolved this controversy in AD 49, when it was decided that Gentiles need not be circumcised to enter the new faith. Jewish Christians took some years to accept that the old rituals were no longer necessary.

CIRCUMCISION
God's covenant with Abraham was symbolized by the rite of circumcision. Gentiles were considered unclean because they were not circumcised.

The Church at Antioch

The Greek city of Antioch became the main base for spreading the Gospel message to the Gentiles. It was founded in 300 BC by Seleucus Nicator and named in honour of his father, Antiochus. In 64 BC, it became the capital of the Roman province of Syria. Antioch was a river port of the Mediterranean, and many trade routes passed through the city. This made it a busy commercial and cosmopolitan centre of Hellenistic culture, open to receiving new ideas.

The city had a large Jewish population, which was allowed to observe its own customs. Many Gentiles in Antioch had already become converts to Judaism. The Church sent Barnabas to the city, where he became a missionary among the Gentiles. It was at Antioch that Christians converted Gentiles without first making them undergo circumcision – one of the requirements of a converted Jew.

Jerusalem had been the birthplace of the Church, but Antioch was where the Church began to diverge from its Hebraic roots. The name "Christian", meaning "follower of Christ", was first used in Antioch.

ANTIOCH (MODERN HATAY), TURKEY
With its favourable location, Antioch became the centre from which the Church spread rapidly.

ST PAUL PREACHING AT ATHENS, Raphael di Sanzio (1483–1520)
Paul's initiative was a major force in spreading the Gospel beyond the Jews.

The Gospel for all

The apostles and the evangelists varied the way they preached the Gospel, depending on their audience.

When speaking to Jews, they emphasized that Jesus was the Messiah prophesied in the Scriptures. To the Gentiles, the evangelists stressed that there was only one God, and that Jesus was their deliverer from demons and the conqueror of all evil. Only the Jews were familiar with such concepts as the "kingdom of God" and the "Son of Man". Gentiles were taught about "eternal life" (or personal salvation) and the "Son of God" or the "Lord". Both Jews and Gentiles declared their new faith and received the Holy Spirit through baptism.

ACTS 8

PHILIP IN SAMARIA

Saul tries to destroy the new Church in Jerusalem

Many Christians are sent to prison

8 O N[1] THAT DAY a great persecution broke out against the church at Jerusalem, and all except the apostles were scattered throughout Judea and Samaria. [2]Godly men buried Stephen and mourned deeply for him. [3]But Saul began to destroy the church. Going from house to house, he dragged off men and women and put them in prison.

[4]Those who had been scattered preached the word wherever they went. [5]*Philip went down to a city in Samaria and proclaimed the Christ* there. [6]When the crowds heard Philip and saw the miraculous signs he did, they all paid close attention to what he said.

[7]With shrieks, evil spirits came out of many, and many paralytics and cripples were healed. [8]So there was great joy in that city.

[9]Now for some time *a man named Simon* had practised sorcery in the city and amazed all the people of Samaria. He boasted that he was someone great, [10]and all the people... [11]followed him...

Philip goes to Samaria, where he performs miraculous acts

Simon envies Philip's power

Many who see the miracles are converted

Philip heals the sick and casts out evil spirits

CHAPTER 8 VERSE 5
"Philip... proclaimed the Christ"
Philip is one of many who fled persecution, but he did not hide. Philip became an "evangelist", a word deriving from the Greek "euangelion", which means "good news". The good news he spoke of was that Jesus is the Son of God.

CHAPTER 8 VERSE 9
"A man named Simon"
Simon's conversion was short-lived. He is known in early Christian literature as "Simon Magus" – Simon the Sorcerer. He became a Christian because he wanted to obtain the spiritual power he saw in Philip's miracles. His shameful act is still known as "Simony".

ST PHILIP, EXORCIST OF DEMONS
This 12th-century mosaic from St Mark's Church in Venice shows Philip casting out a devil from a possessed man.

[12]But when they believed Philip as he preached the good news of the kingdom of God and the name of Jesus Christ, they were baptised, both men and women. [13]Simon himself believed and was baptised. And he followed Philip everywhere, astonished by the great signs and miracles he saw.

The apostles sent Peter and John to Samaria. When they arrived, Peter and John confirmed those who had been baptised by placing their hands on them so that they would receive the Holy Spirit. When he saw this, Simon offered the apostles money, because he wanted to buy the gift of the Holy Spirit. Peter refused and told Simon to ask God for forgiveness. On the way back to Jerusalem, Peter and John preached in many Samaritan villages.

[26]Now an angel of the Lord said to Philip, "Go south to the road – the desert road – that goes from Jerusalem to Gaza." [27]So he started out, and on his way he met an Ethiopian eunuch, an important official in charge of all the treasury of *Candace, queen of the Ethiopians*. This man had gone to Jerusalem to worship, [28]and on his way home was sitting in his chariot reading the book of Isaiah the prophet. [29]The Spirit told Philip, "Go to that chariot and stay near it."

So Philip asked the eunuch if he understood the passage he was reading. The man invited Philip to ride with him and to explain it. Philip accepted and went on to tell him about Jesus. As they rode along they came to some water, and the man asked to be baptised.

THE SPREAD OF CHRISTIANITY
Philip left Jerusalem and preached in Samaria before settling in Caesarea.

CHAPTER 8 VERSE 27
"Candace... of the Ethiopians"
"Candace" was the title of the queen mother in Ethiopia. She ruled in place of her son the king, who was considered too sacred to be involved in the affairs of his country. At this time, Ethiopia was a region to the south of Egypt that included parts of modern Ethiopia and Sudan. The area was also known as "Cush".

Philip meets an Ethiopian eunuch, who is reading the Book of Isaiah

The man asks Philip to explain the passage he is reading

Philip tells him about Jesus, and the man asks to be baptised

Philip baptises the Ethiopian, then disappears

[38]Then both Philip and the eunuch went down into the water and Philip baptised him. [39]When they came up out of the water, the Spirit of the Lord suddenly took Philip away, and the eunuch did not see him again, but went on his way rejoicing. [40]Philip, however, appeared at Azotus and travelled about, preaching the gospel in all the towns *until he reached Caesarea*.

CHAPTER 8 VERSE 40
"Until he reached Caesarea"
Caesarea was transformed into a beautiful marble city by Herod the Great. It became the capital of Roman Judea. Philip settled in Caesarea, and its prosperous harbour helped to spread the Christian message out into the world.

UNDERSTANDING THE STORY

Persecution forces many to leave Jerusalem, but the early Christians are determined to fulfil Jesus' words: "You will be my witnesses in Jerusalem, and in all Judea and Samaria, and to the end of the earth" (Acts 1: 8). Philip's baptism of the eunuch – a class excluded from Jewish worship – demonstrates that there are no barriers in the Christian Church to those who believe.

329

ACTS 9

SAUL'S CONVERSION

Saul – later called by his Roman name, Paul – was a Pharisee as well as a Roman citizen. His wealthy parents sent him to Jerusalem to be educated as an orthodox Jew. Saul was renowned for his zealous nature. His persecution of the Christians threatened to destroy the early Church. But it also resulted in the initial spread of Christianity from Jerusalem.

✢

CHAPTER 9 VERSE 2
"Damascus"
Damascus developed as a trading and religious centre due to its ideal location at the intersection of major highways. The city was named after its exports of a patterned cloth called "damask". Damascus was the capital of the Roman province of Syria and had a large Jewish population. It would have taken Saul about six days to travel there from Jerusalem.

✢

CHAPTER 9 VERSE 2
"The Way"
Christianity was known as "The Way" and was viewed as a sect of Judaism for many years. Jesus called himself "The Way" (John 14: 6).

THE LIGHT OF THE WORLD
19th-century painting by W. Holman Hunt representing Jesus as "The Way"

9 **M**EANWHILE[1], Saul was still breathing out murderous threats against the Lord's disciples. He went to the high priest [2]and asked him for letters to the synagogues in *Damascus*, so that if if he found any there who belonged to *the Way*, whether men or women, he might take them as prisoners to Jerusalem. [3]As he neared Damascus on his journey, suddenly a light from heaven flashed around him. [4]He fell to the ground and heard a voice say to him, "Saul, Saul, why do you persecute me?"

A heavenly light blinds Saul

Jesus' voice asks Saul why he is persecuting him

Saul is carrying letters permitting him to imprison any Christians in Damascus

Saul's companions see nothing

[5]"Who are you, Lord?" Saul asked. "I am Jesus, whom you are persecuting," he replied. [6]"Now get up and go into the city, and you will be told what you must do."

[7]The men travelling with Saul stood there speechless; they heard the sound but did not see anyone. [8]Saul got up from the ground, but when he opened his eyes he could see nothing. So they led him by the hand into Damascus. [9]For three days he was blind, and did not eat or drink anything.

[10]In Damascus there was a disciple named Ananias. The Lord [Jesus] called to him in a vision.

Jesus told Ananias to go to Saul. At first, Ananias was unwilling because of Saul's reputation. But Jesus told him that he had chosen Saul to be his missionary to the Gentiles. So Ananias went to the house where Saul was staying and, placing his hands on him, explained that Jesus had sent him to restore his sight.

[18]Immediately, something like scales fell from Saul's eyes, and he could see again. He got up and was baptised...

In Damascus, Jesus sends Ananias to Saul to restore his sight

Saul... ²⁰began to preach in the synagogues that Jesus is the Son of God. ²¹All those who heard him were astonished and asked, "Isn't he the man who caused havoc in Jerusalem among those who call on this name? And hasn't he come here to take them as prisoners to the chief priests?" ²²Yet Saul grew more and more powerful and baffled the Jews living in Damascus by proving that Jesus is the Christ.

Saul preaches the Christian message to the Jews in Damascus

Saul

The Jews are astonished by Saul's conversion

Some of the Jews plot to kill Saul

²³After many days had gone by, *the Jews conspired to kill him,* ²⁴but Saul learned of their plan. Day and night they kept close watch on the city gates in order to kill him. ²⁵But his followers took him by night and lowered him in a basket through an opening in the wall.

²⁶When he came to Jerusalem, he tried to join the disciples, but they were all afraid of him... ²⁷But Barnabas took him and brought him to the apostles. He told them how Saul on his journey had seen the Lord and that the Lord had spoken to him, and how in Damascus he had preached fearlessly in the name of Jesus. ²⁸So Saul stayed with them and... ²⁹talked and debated with the Grecian Jews, but they tried to kill him. ³⁰When the brothers learned of this, they took him down to Caesarea and sent him off to *Tarsus.*

³¹Then the church throughout Judea, Galilee and Samaria enjoyed a time of peace. It was strengthened; and encouraged by the Holy Spirit, it grew in numbers, living in the fear of the Lord.

UNDERSTANDING THE STORY

The conversion of Saul, with his high social position and forceful personality, has a dramatic impact on the early Church. Saul sets out to fulfil the mission Jesus has given him: "I am sending you to [the Gentiles] to open their eyes and turn them from darkness to light" (Acts 26: 17–18).

✤

CHAPTER 9 VERSE 23
"The Jews conspired to kill him"
From this point onwards, the early Church faced intensifying persecution from the Sadducees and Pharisees, as well as the Romans. Paul recalls this event: "In Damascus the governor under king Aretas had the city of the Damascenes guarded in order to arrest me..." (2 Corinthians 11: 32).

Saul's followers hear of the plot to kill Saul and help him escape

Saul is lowered down the city walls in a basket

✤

CHAPTER 9 VERSE 30
"Tarsus"
Saul was born in Tarsus, a major city in south-east Asia Minor. It had become a prosperous city because of its favourable position on a trade route between Syria and Asia Minor. By Roman times, Tarsus was also an established centre of Greek culture and learning. Saul regarded Tarsus as his home city.

ACTS 9–10
PETER'S MIRACLES

CHAPTER 9 VERSE 35
"Lydda and Sharon"
Lydda is a town about 16km (10 miles) inland from Joppa. The Sharon plain is an extremely fertile area, stretching along the Mediterranean coast from Joppa to Caesarea. In New Testament times, the plain was mostly pasture land. Today it is one of the richest agricultural areas in Israel.

LYDDA
This is an early 20th-century view of Lydda. Today it is a modern city.

CHAPTER 9 VERSE 37
"Her body was washed and placed in an upstairs room"
Ritual purification of the dead required the body to be washed. It was then wrapped in cloth – the wealthy used linen containing aloes and myrrh. In Jerusalem, the dead were always buried within 24 hours. In other areas of Israel, if burial was delayed, the body was kept in an upper room.

JOPPA
The ancient city of Joppa (modern Jaffa) was built on a rocky ledge looking over the Mediterranean. It was traditionally founded by Japheth, who was a son of Noah. In Bible times, Joppa was the seaport for Jerusalem. It is the only natural harbour between Eygpt and Mount Carmel. In 1950, the city amalgamated with modern Tel-Aviv.

9 A**S**[32] PETER TRAVELLED about the country, he went to visit the saints in Lydda. [33]There he found a man named Aeneas, a paralytic who had been bedridden for eight years. [34]"Aeneas," Peter said to him, "Jesus Christ heals you. Get up and tidy up your mat." Immediately Aeneas got up. [35]All those who lived in *Lydda and Sharon* saw him and turned to the Lord.

[36]In Joppa there was a disciple named Tabitha (which, when translated, is Dorcas), who was always doing good and helping the poor. [37]About that time she became sick and died, and *her body was washed and placed in an upstairs room*. [38]Lydda was near Joppa; so when the disciples heard that Peter was in Lydda, they sent two men to him and urged him, "Please come at once!" [39]Peter went with them, and when he arrived he was taken upstairs to the room. All the widows stood around him, crying and showing him the robes and other clothing that Dorcas had made while she was still with them. [40]Peter sent them all out of the room; then he got down on his knees and prayed. Turning towards the dead woman, he said, "Tabitha, get up." She opened her eyes, and seeing Peter she sat up. [41]He took her by the hand and helped her to her feet.

Tabitha's friends mourn her death

They send for Peter

The women show Peter some clothes that Tabitha had made for the poor

Peter tells everyone to leave the room

Peter prays for Tabitha and she opens her eyes

Then he called the believers and the widows and presented her to them alive. [42]This became known all over Joppa, and many people believed in the Lord. [43]Peter stayed in Joppa for some time with a tanner named Simon.

10 At[1] Caesarea there was a man named Cornelius, *a centurion in what was known as the Italian Regiment*. [2]He and all his family were devout and God-fearing; he gave generously to those in need and prayed to God regularly. [3]One day at about three in the afternoon he had a vision.

Cornelius saw an angel, who told him to send men to Joppa to bring back Peter. In Joppa, Peter had a vision as he sat praying. It showed him that nothing created by God could be impure. Then a voice told him about the arrival of Cornelius' men. The following morning, Peter went with the men to Caesarea.

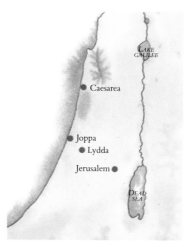

An angel tells Cornelius to bring Peter to Caesarea

²⁵Cornelius met him and fell at his feet in reverence. ²⁶But Peter made him get up. "Stand up," he said, "I am only a man myself."

²⁷Talking with him, Peter went inside and found a large gathering of people. ²⁸He said to them: "You are well aware that it is against our law for a Jew to associate with a Gentile or visit him. But God has shown me that I should not call any man impure or unclean"...

⁴⁴While Peter was still speaking these words, the Holy Spirit came on all who heard the message. ⁴⁵The circumcised believers who had come with Peter were astonished that the gift of the Holy Spirit had been poured out even on the Gentiles. ⁴⁶For they heard them speaking in tongues and praising God.

Then Peter said: ⁴⁷"Can anyone keep these people from being baptised with water? They have received the Holy Spirit just as we have." ⁴⁸So he ordered that they be baptised in the name of Jesus Christ.

PETER'S TRAVELS
Peter healed the sick and baptized both Jews and Gentiles throughout the region shown above.

CHAPTER 10 VERSE 1
*"A centurion in...
the Italian Regiment"*
The Italian Regiment was made up of men enlisted in Italy. A "Regiment" was the Greek translation of a Roman "Cohort", which was a unit of the Roman army consisting of six centuries (about 500 men). Centurions were officers chosen from the ranks. They are often favourably recorded in the New Testament for their tolerance.

Peter arrives at Cornelius' house

Cornelius kneels at Peter's feet, but Peter tells him to stand up

As a strict Jew, Peter is forbidden to enter Gentile houses, but God has told him that this attitude is wrong

Inside the house is a large gathering of non-Jews

UNDERSTANDING THE STORY

Peter now takes on the power to perform miracles and becomes the "rock" on which the Church can be built. In Peter's vision, the Holy Spirit initiates the new direction for the early Church: Gentiles, like Cornelius and his family, can be baptized without becoming Jews.

While Peter is speaking to the Gentiles, they receive the Holy Spirit and start to praise God

ACTS 11
THE GOSPEL FOR ALL

The Jewish disciples criticise
Peter for eating with Gentiles

Peter says that the
Holy Spirit spoke to
him in a vision

❖

CHAPTER 11 VERSE 8
"Nothing impure or unclean"
Strict obedience to the ritual laws
was a major part of day-to-day
life, and so it was very difficult
for Jewish believers to come to
terms with the end of their
religious practices. Moses' Law
had instructed that only clean
animals – "any animal that has a
split hoof divided in two and that
chews the cud" – could be eaten.
All meat had to be killed in a
special way to rid the flesh of blood
before being cooked. Peter's vision
initiates a debate about the
importance of these food laws.

❖

CHAPTER 11 VERSE 19
"Phoenicia"
This was the narrow strip of land
along the Mediterranean coast that
is now part of Lebanon and Syria.
"Phoenicia" means "Land of
Purple", because it was famous
for purple dyes produced from
shellfish. Phoenicia was also known
for its wooded slopes and fertile
plains. Many early Christians fled
to this area to escape persecution.

11 THE[1] APOSTLES and the brothers throughout Judea heard that the Gentiles also had received the word of God. [2]So when Peter went up to Jerusalem, the circumcised believers criticised him [3]and said, "You went into the house of uncircumcised men and ate with them."

[4]Peter began and explained everything to them precisely as it had happened: [5]"I was in the city of Joppa praying, and in a trance I saw a vision. I saw something like a large sheet being let down from heaven by its four corners, and it came down to where I was. [6]I looked into it and saw four-footed animals of the earth, wild beasts, reptiles, and birds of the air. [7]Then I heard a voice telling me, 'Get up, Peter. Kill and eat.' [8]"I replied, 'Surely not, Lord! *Nothing impure or unclean* has ever entered my mouth.' [9]"The voice spoke from heaven a second time, 'Do not call anything impure that God has made clean.' [10]This happened three times, and then it was all pulled up to heaven again.

He saw unclean
animals in his vision

Peter heard a voice telling him
that nothing created by God
could be impure

Peter explained that the Holy Spirit had instructed him to go to a Centurion's house in Caesarea, and that when he arrived he had found a large gathering of Gentile believers. Peter told them that he had spoken to the Gentiles and then witnessed the Holy Spirit descending upon them.

[18]When they heard this, they had no further objections and praised God, saying, "So then, God has granted even the Gentiles repentance unto life." [19]Now those who had been scattered by the persecution in connection with Stephen travelled as far as *Phoenicia,* Cyprus and *Antioch,* telling the message only to Jews. [20]Some of them, however, men from Cyprus and Cyrene, went to Antioch and began to speak to Greeks also, telling them the good news about the Lord Jesus. [21]The Lord's hand was with them, and a great number of people believed and turned to the Lord.

[22]News of this reached the ears of the church at Jerusalem, and they sent Barnabas to Antioch. [23]When he arrived and saw the evidence of the grace of God, he was glad and encouraged them all to remain true to the Lord with all their hearts. [24]He was a good man, full of the Holy Spirit and faith and a great number of people were brought to the Lord.

²⁵Then Barnabas went to Tarsus to look for Saul, ²⁶and when he found him, he brought him to Antioch. So for a whole year Barnabas and Saul met with the church and taught great numbers of people. The *disciples were called Christians* first at Antioch. ²⁷During this time some prophets came down from Jerusalem to Antioch. ²⁸One of them, named Agabus, stood up and through the Spirit predicted that a severe famine would spread over the entire Roman world. (This happened during the reign of Claudius.) ²⁹The disciples, each according to his ability, decided to provide help for the brothers living in Judea. ³⁰This they did, sending their gift to *the elders* by Barnabas and Saul.

The Church leaders in Jerusalem hear that many people in Antioch are becoming Christians

Saul

Saul and Barnabas go to Antioch to teach the people about Jesus' message

Many others are converted

Barnabas

UNDERSTANDING THE STORY

Peter's vision convinces him that the ancient rituals of Israel can be over-ruled. As head of the Church, Peter knows that it is his duty to lead the people in a new direction. But it is Paul (Saul) who becomes the leading missionary. Paul spreads a new message: God welcomes all into his Church.

❖

CHAPTER 11 VERSE 19
"Antioch"
Capital of Syria, Antioch was the third largest city in the Roman empire, after Rome and Alexandria. Antioch was a cosmopolitan city with a population of 500,000. The Jews who had settled there had developed good relations with their Gentile neighbours. This made Antioch an ideal centre for the early Church.

ST PETER'S
This church in Antioch was the first Christian church to be built.

❖

CHAPTER 11 VERSE 26
"Disciples were called Christians"
The name "Christian" comes from the Greek and Latin "Christianos", which means "belonging to Christ", and was probably first used as a term of abuse. In one of his letters, Peter said to the persecuted Christians: "If you suffer as a Christian, do not be ashamed, but praise God that you bear that name" (1 Peter 4: 16). This oil lamp (*c.* AD 400) has a Greek symbol of Christianity.

❖

CHAPTER 11 VERSE 30
"The elders"
"Elders" was the title given to the leaders of the synagogues. The Church retained this Jewish principle of a shared leadership and called its leaders "the elders". They were elected by their congregations. These men were chosen because of their spiritual and moral standing, not because of their age. Some elders, like Timothy, were young.

ACTS 12
PETER'S ESCAPE

Herod's men put
James to death

12 I[T] WAS ABOUT THIS TIME that *King Herod* arrested some who belonged to the church, intending to persecute them. [2]He had *James, the brother of John*, put to death with the sword. [3]When he saw that this pleased the Jews, he proceeded to seize Peter also. This happened during the Feast of Unleavened Bread. [4]After arresting him, he put him in prison, handing him over to be guarded by four squads of four soldiers each. Herod intended to bring him out for public trial after the Passover. [5]So Peter was kept in prison, but the church was earnestly praying to God for him.

[6]The night before Herod was to bring him to trial, Peter was sleeping between two soldiers, bound with two chains, and sentries stood guard at the entrance. [7]Suddenly an angel of the Lord appeared and a light shone in the cell. He struck Peter on the side and woke him up. "Quick, get up!" he said, and the chains fell off Peter's wrists.

[8]Then the angel said to him... "Wrap your cloak around you and follow me"... [9]Peter followed him out of the prison, but he had no idea that what the angel was doing was really happening; he thought he was seeing a vision.

CHAPTER 12 VERSE 1
"King Herod"
This king was Agrippa I and he ruled over Galilee, Perea, Judea, and Samaria. His grandfather was Herod the Great, who had attempted to kill the baby Jesus. His uncle, Herod Antipas, beheaded John the Baptist and tried Jesus. Agrippa won favour with the Jews, particularly the Pharisees, by opposing the early Church.

HEAD OF AGRIPPA
Coin (*c.* AD 37–44)

CHAPTER 12 VERSE 2
"James, the brother of John"
James and John were Galilean fishermen. Their mother, Salome, was one of the women who followed Jesus, cared for his needs, and watched him die. Jesus named the brothers "Sons of Thunder" (Mark 3: 17) because of their spirited characters. Despite rebuking James and John for their over-zealous behaviour, Jesus remained close to them. Together with Peter, the brothers formed an inner circle within the apostles.

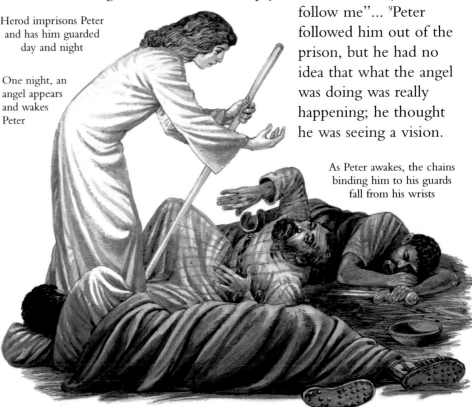

Herod imprisons Peter and has him guarded day and night

One night, an angel appears and wakes Peter

As Peter awakes, the chains binding him to his guards fall from his wrists

[10]They passed the first and the second guards and came to the iron gate leading to the city. It opened for them by itself, and they went through it. When they had walked the length of one street, suddenly the angel left him.

[11]Then Peter came to himself and said, "Now I know without a doubt that the Lord sent an angel and rescued me from Herod's clutches and from everything the Jewish people were anticipating."

[12] When this had dawned on him, he went to the house of Mary the mother of *John, also called Mark*, where many people had gathered and were praying. [13] Peter knocked at the outer entrance, and a servant girl named Rhoda came to answer the door. [14] When she recognised Peter's voice, she was so overjoyed she ran back without opening it and exclaimed, "Peter is at the door!"

[15] "You're out of your mind," they told her. When she kept insisting that it was so, they said, "It must be his angel."

[16] But Peter kept on knocking, and when they opened the door and saw him, they were astonished. [17] Peter motioned with his hand for them to be quiet and described how the Lord had brought him out of prison. "Tell James and the brothers about this," he said, and then he left for another place.

[18] In the morning, there was no small commotion among the soldiers as to what had become of Peter. [19] After Herod had a thorough search made for him and did not find him, he cross-examined the guards and ordered that they be executed.

Then Herod went from Judea to Caesarea and stayed there a while. [20] He had been quarrelling with the people of Tyre and Sidon; they now joined together and sought an audience with him... They asked for peace, because they depended on the king's country for their food supply.

[21] On the appointed day Herod, wearing his royal robes, sat on his throne and delivered a public address to the people. [22] They shouted, "This is the voice of a god, not of a man." [23] Immediately, because Herod did not give praise to God, an angel of the Lord struck him down, and *he was eaten by worms and died*. [24] But the word of God continued to increase and spread.

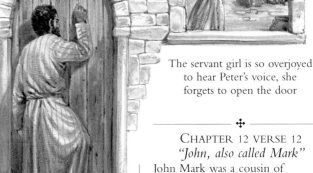

The servant girl is so overjoyed to hear Peter's voice, she forgets to open the door

❖

CHAPTER 12 VERSE 12
"John, also called Mark"
John Mark was a cousin of Barnabas and the son of an influential woman named Mary. It was in her house that the early Church met during this period. Most scholars agree that John Mark is the author of the second book of the Gospels.

❖

CHAPTER 12 VERSE 23
"He was eaten by worms and died"
This event happened in early AD 44 and was recorded by the Jewish historian Josephus. He wrote that Herod was wearing a bright silver robe during a festival in honour of Claudius Caesar. When the crowd called him a god, Herod did not deny it. Seized with violent pains, he was taken away and died five days later. The expression "eaten by worms" suggests he died of an acute intestinal disorder, but it could also describe the death of a tyrant.

Peter goes to Mary's house and knocks on the door

Herod cross-examines Peter's guards, then orders their execution

Herod is struck down by God

UNDERSTANDING OF THE STORY

Those who oppose the early Church find a new ally in Herod. The new king wants to ensure his popularity with the people by gaining favour with the Jews. But the Christian believers are not discouraged by this renewed persecution. They put their faith in prayer, and they receive miraculous assistance from God.

PAUL'S JOURNEYS

About sixteen years after Jesus' death, Paul set off on the first of his missions to convert both Jews and non-Jews to Christianity. During the next twenty years, he undertook three missionary journeys around the Mediterranean, Middle East, and into Europe, which are reported by Luke in the Book of Acts. Paul also made a fourth journey, to Rome, where he was to stand trial.

Paul often preached in synagogues, which were built by the Jews who had settled throughout the Mediterranean after the Exile. Sometimes Paul met hostility and was forced to move on to new towns and cities. But much of his work was a success, and he revisited places, giving advice and hope to the Christian converts.

THE APOSTLE PAUL
11th-century Byzantine illuminated manuscript

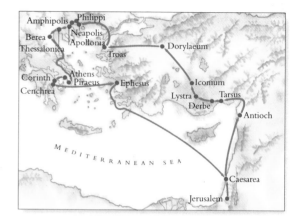

THE SECOND JOURNEY
Paul's second journey was longer. His travels took him to mainland Europe, and he stayed in Corinth for eighteen months. After three years he finally returned to Antioch.

Where did Paul travel?

Paul followed the main trade routes, going from city to city either across the sea or by road. The three main centres for his missionary activities were Antioch, Ephesus, and Corinth. By travelling to large commercial centres and provincial capitals such as these, Paul could speak to great numbers of people. The many visitors to these cosmopolitan cities would also carry the Christian message back to their homelands.

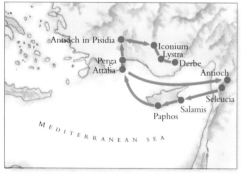

THE FIRST JOURNEY
Paul first journeyed to Salamis in Cyprus. He then crossed the sea to Perga in Asia Minor, and travelled inland. After visiting various cities, he returned home by the same route.

THE THIRD JOURNEY
Paul's third journey took him back to many cities he had previously visited, such as Derbe, Lystra, Iconium, and Pisidian Antioch. He stayed for over two years in Ephesus, the capital of the Roman province of Asia, before travelling through Macedonia and Greece on his return to Jerusalem.

Paul's companions

Paul never travelled alone. One of his most faithful companions was Luke, who records the journeys in the Book of Acts. Paul's other main disciples were Barnabas, John Mark, Silas, Timothy, and Titus. They came from a variety of backgrounds, which helped Paul when speaking to different audiences – Timothy was a Greek Jew and Titus a Gentile convert. However, relations between Paul and the missionaries were not always perfect, and on occasion, arguments caused them to split up (Acts 15: 39).

THE APOSTLE BARNABAS
This illustration from a French manuscript shows Barnabas, who accompanied Paul on his first missionary journey. Barnabas came from Cyprus.

Sea travel

Paul's voyage to Rome is covered in great detail (Acts 27). The text indicates that he travelled on a cargo ship from Alexandria to Rome. The vessel probably had two masts, six anchors, and carried 276 passengers.

MODEL OF A ROMAN CARGO SHIP

The Church under threat

Many people, both Jews and non-Jews, saw the Gospel as a threat to their own religion and traditional ways of life. As a result, Paul suffered persecution. He was stoned, tortured, and imprisoned. Paul never gave up, but not all the early Christians were such strong characters, and the Church was undermined by this persecution. Christianity was also threatened by false teaching. Each individual church probably developed its own approach to Christian teaching. Paul wrote to these communities in order to encourage the believers to keep their faith and to give guidance on correct Christian teaching.

AERIAL VIEW OF CAESAREA
Paul was imprisoned in this seaport for two years, awaiting trial by the Jewish leaders (Acts 23: 23, 33).

RUINS AT PHILIPPI
Paul and his companions were beaten and imprisoned at Philippi (Acts 16: 22–23).

PAUL'S LETTERS

Thirteen of the New Testament letters are introduced by the apostle Paul, who is traditionally believed to be the author. A fourteenth letter, Letter to the Hebrews, is also considered by some to be Paul's work. His letters were not sermons, but lively messages to specific people, individuals, or churches. The letters were composed during or after a journey. They were often handed in to a church by one of Paul's envoys, or by someone travelling to the city to which the letter was addressed. Paul wrote some while imprisoned in Rome. Sometimes he used secretaries, who added their names at the end of the letter, like Tertius, who wrote the Letter to the Romans, but usually Paul signed them himself.

Papyrus letter

Reed pen

WRITING MATERIALS
Paul's letters were all written in vernacular Greek (koine). He probably used a reed pen called a "kalamos" on paper made from papyrus. The ink, coloured black, was made by mixing carbon, water, and oil or gum (3 John 13).

The purpose of Paul's letters

Paul's letters were written to give guidance to the early Christian communities he established. He was absent from these churches for long periods, visiting other churches, or attempting to establish new ones. His letters offer encouragement, warnings, and advice.

REMAINS OF THE ANCIENT CITY AT CORINTH
Paul wrote two letters to the church in Corinth. These address the problems faced by Christians in this wealthy Greek city, which Paul first visited on his second journey.

Extract from Paul's letter to the Corinthians (1 Corinthians 13)

[1]If I speak in the tongues of men and of angels, but have not love, I am only a resounding gong or a clanging cymbal. [2]If I have the gift of prophecy and can fathom all mysteries and all knowledge, and if I have a faith that can move mountains, but have not love, I am nothing. [3]If I give all I possess to the poor and surrender my body to the flames, but have not love, I gain nothing.

[4]Love is patient, love is kind. It does not envy, it does not boast, it is not proud. [5]It is not rude, it is not self-seeking, it is not easily angered, it keeps no record of wrongs. [6]Love does not delight in evil but rejoices with the truth. [7]It always protects, always trusts, always hopes, always perseveres. [8]Love never fails... [11]When I was a child, I talked like a child, I thought like a child, I reasoned like a child. When I became a man, I put childish ways behind me. [12]Now we see but a poor reflection as in a mirror; then we shall see face to face. Now I know in part; then I shall know fully, even as I am fully known. [13]And now these three remain: faith, hope and love. But the greatest of these is love.

The Epistles

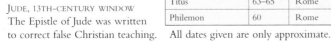

The New Testament contains seven other letters, known as the "Catholic Epistles". These letters were circulated to all the early Christians, and not just to a specific church. The word "catholic" means "universal". The Catholic Epistles are James; 1 and 2 Peter; 1, 2, and 3 John; and Jude.

JUDE, 13TH-CENTURY WINDOW
The Epistle of Jude was written to correct false Christian teaching.

Paul's letters	Date AD	Written in
Romans	57	Cenchrea/Corinth
Corinthians 1	55	Ephesus
Corinthians 2	55	Macedonia
Galatians	49	Antioch
Ephesians	60	Rome
Philippians	61	Rome
Colossians	60	Rome
Thessalonians 1	51	Corinth
Thessalonians 2	51	Corinth
Timothy 1	63–65	Philippi
Timothy 2	63–65	Rome
Titus	63–65	Rome
Philemon	60	Rome

All dates given are only approximate.

ACTS 13
THE FIRST MISSIONARIES

CHAPTER 13 VERSE 4
"Seleucia"

At this time, Seleucia was an important seaport for the Romans because of its ideal position on a trade route. It was about 25km (16 miles) from Antioch.

13 IN[1] THE CHURCH at [Syrian] Antioch there were prophets and teachers: Barnabas, Simeon called Niger, Lucius of Cyrene, Manaen... and Saul. [2]While they were worshipping the Lord and fasting, the Holy Spirit said, "Set apart for me Barnabas and Saul for the work to which I have called them."...

[4]The two of them, sent on their way by the Holy Spirit, went down to *Seleucia* and sailed from there to *Cyprus*. [5]When they arrived at Salamis, they proclaimed the word of God in the Jewish synagogues. John was with them as their helper.

[6]They travelled through the whole island until they came to Paphos. There they met a Jewish sorcerer and false prophet named Bar-Jesus, [7]who was an attendant of the proconsul, Sergius Paulus.

The proconsul's attendant is a false prophet called Bar-Jesus

Proconsul

John

Saul

Barnabas

The proconsul of Cyprus asks the apostles about God

Bar-Jesus tries to discredit the apostles

The proconsul sees this event and believes in God

Saul blinds Bar-Jesus by the power of the Holy Spirit

CHAPTER 13 VERSE 4
"Cyprus"

The island of Cyprus is visible from the port of Seleucia. Cyprus was famous for rich copper deposits. Its name comes from the Latin word for "copper". Salamis (modern Famagusta) was the capital, but the Romans used the city of Paphos as their headquarters. Cyprus had a large Jewish population.

SALAMIS, CYPRUS
Roman ruins, 2nd century AD

The proconsul, an intelligent man, sent for Barnabas and Saul because he wanted to hear the word of God. [8]But Elymas the sorcerer (for that is what his name means) opposed them and tried to turn the proconsul from the faith. [9]Then *Saul, who was also called Paul*, filled with the Holy Spirit, looked straight at Elymas and said, [10]"You are a child of the devil and an enemy of everything that is right! You are full of all kinds of deceit and trickery. Will you never stop perverting the right ways of the Lord? [11]Now the hand of the Lord is against you. You are going to be blind, and for a time you will be unable to see the light of the sun."

Immediately mist and darkness came over him, and he groped about, seeking someone to lead him by the hand. [12]When the proconsul saw what had happened, he believed, for he was amazed at the teaching about the Lord.

¹³From Paphos, Paul and his companions sailed to Perga in Pamphylia, where *John left them* to return to Jerusalem. ¹⁴From Perga they went on to Pisidian Antioch. On the Sabbath they entered the synagogue.

Paul spoke to the Jews about Jesus' death and resurrection and explained that the only way to God was through Jesus.

John returns to Jerusalem

Paul and Barnabas sail to Pisidian Antioch

⁴²As Paul and Barnabas were leaving the synagogue, the people invited them to speak further about these things on the next Sabbath...

⁴⁴On the next Sabbath almost the whole city gathered to hear the word of the Lord. ⁴⁵When the Jews saw the crowds, they were filled with jealousy and talked abusively against what Paul was saying.

⁴⁶Then Paul and Barnabas answered them boldly: "We had to speak the word of God to you first. Since you reject it and do not consider yourselves worthy of eternal life, we now turn to *the Gentiles...*"

⁴⁸When the Gentiles heard this, they were glad and honoured the word of the Lord; and all who were appointed for eternal life believed.

Paul preaches to a large crowd about Jesus

The Jews reject Paul's message

Paul decides to dedicate himself to preaching to non-Jews

UNDERSTANDING THE STORY

The Church's appointment of the first missionaries is a historic step. Paul and his companions do not set out with strategic plans; instead they rely on the Holy Spirit to guide their mission. When their message is rejected by the Jews at Pisidian Antioch, Paul decides to take the Gospel to the Gentiles.

CHAPTER 13 VERSE 9
"Saul... called Paul"

Saul (a Hebrew name) is now called Paul (a Roman name). Paul is a Jew, but as a Roman citizen he is also part of the Gentile world. This change of name highlights Paul's role as apostle to the Gentiles.

ST PAUL
12th-century church mural, Cyprus

CHAPTER 13 VERSE 13
"John left them"

This is John Mark, the probable author of the second Gospel. His role as an assistant ended when he returned to Jerusalem for an unknown reason. This later caused a rift between Paul and Barnabas, John's uncle. Barnabas wanted John to rejoin them, but Paul thought John was unreliable.

CHAPTER 13 VERSE 46
"The Gentiles"

Jews called non-Jews "Gentiles", from the Latin word "gens" meaning "nation". The word evolved at the time when the Jews had to share the Promised Land with non-Jewish nations and keep separate from them.

ROMAN AQUEDUCT, PISIDIAN ANTIOCH

ACTS 13–14
PAUL AND THE GALATIANS

The Jews expel Paul and Barnabas
from Pisidian Antioch

✤

CHAPTER 13 VERSE 51
"Shook the dust from their feet"
Jews performed this symbolic act
when they left an "unclean" Gentile
area. When Jesus sent out his
disciples, he told them to do this as a
warning to those who rejected him.

SYNAGOGUE FLOOR
This 6th-century mosaic floor is from
a synagogue in Bet she'an, Israel.

CHAPTER 14 VERSE 1
"As usual into the... synagogue"
Despite saying that he would take
the Christian message to the Gentiles
(Acts 13: 46), Paul continues to
preach in the synagogues first.

✤

CHAPTER 14 VERSE 6
"The Lycaonian cities"
Lycaonia was a remote district in
the Roman province of Galatia, in
Asia Minor. The main Lycaonian
cities were Iconium, Lystra,
Derbe, and Pisidian Antioch.
Paul later wrote to the Galatians,
urging them to remain true
to Christianity.

13 THE[49] WORD OF THE LORD spread through the whole region. [50]But the Jews incited the God-fearing women of high standing and the leading men of the city. They stirred up persecution against Paul and Barnabas, and expelled them from their region. [51]So they *shook the dust from their feet* in protest against them and went to Iconium. [52]And the disciples were filled with joy and with the Holy Spirit.

14 [1]At Iconium Paul and Barnabas went *as usual into the Jewish synagogue*... [4]The people of the city were divided; some sided with the Jews, others with the apostles. [5]There was a plot afoot among the Gentiles and Jews, together with their leaders, to ill-treat them and stone them. [6]But they found out about it and fled to *the Lycaonian cities* of Lystra and Derbe and to the surrounding country, [7]where they continued to preach the good news.

[8]In Lystra there sat a man crippled in his feet, who was lame from birth and had never walked. [9]He listened to Paul as he was speaking. Paul looked directly at him, saw that he had faith to be healed [10]and called out, "Stand up on your feet!" At that, the man jumped up and began to walk.

At Lystra, Paul
cures a lame man

The people see the miracle
and call the apostles gods

Paul and Barnabas are
appalled and tear their
clothes in distress

The priest of
Zeus wants to
offer sacrifices to
the apostles

Sacrificial bull

The apostles explain to
the people that they
are only men, not gods

Priest of
Zeus

[11]When the crowd saw what Paul had done, they shouted in the Lycaonian language, "The gods have come down to us in human form!" [12]Barnabas they called *Zeus*, and Paul they called *Hermes* because he was the chief speaker. [13]The priest of Zeus, whose temple was just outside the city, brought bulls and wreaths to the city gates because he and the crowd wanted to offer sacrifices to them.

[14]But when *the apostles* Barnabas and Paul heard of this, they tore their clothes and rushed out into the crowd, shouting: [15]"Men, why are you doing this? We too are only men, human like you. We are bringing you good news, telling you to turn from these worthless things to the living God, who made heaven and earth and sea and everything in them..." [19]Then some Jews came from Antioch and Iconium and won the crowd over. They stoned Paul and dragged him outside the city, thinking he was dead. [20]But after the disciples had gathered round him, he got up and went back into the city. The next day he and Barnabas left for Derbe.

The people stone Paul. He is dragged out of the city and left for dead

Paul and Barnabas gained a large number of disciples in Derbe. Then they returned to Lystra, Iconium, and Pisidian Antioch. They encouraged the disciples to remain true to their faith and appointed elders in every church. After travelling through Pisidia and Pamphylia, Paul and Barnabas returned to Attalia.

[26]From Attalia they sailed back to [Syrian] Antioch, where they had been committed to the grace of God for the work they had now completed. [27]On arriving there, they gathered the church together and reported all that God had done through them and how he had opened the door of faith to the Gentiles.

UNDERSTANDING THE STORY

The early missionaries face extreme hardship. Many people are hostile to their message and drive them away. But Paul and Barnabas are determined to bring the Gospel to Jews and Gentiles alike.

ROMAN SILVER
BROOCH OF ZEUS

CHAPTER 14 VERSE 12
"Zeus... Hermes"
Zeus was the chief Greek deity, and Hermes was his divine messenger. According to an ancient legend, these two gods visited Lystra and were so angered by the inhospitality of the people that they destroyed the town. This story was well-known by the people of Lystra and explains why they reacted to Paul and Barnabas in such a way.

PAUL AND BARNABAS
From this point onwards, the leadership passes from Barnabas to Paul. Earlier in their travels, Barnabas is mentioned before Paul, but it is clearly Paul who now takes control of the missionary work.

CHAPTER 14 VERSE 14
"The apostles"
The Greek word "apostolos" means "one who is sent out". In the New Testament, "apostle" is a term used for the twelve disciples. But "apostle" acquires a more general meaning in Paul's letters. He includes all those who, like himself, were chosen by Christ to establish the Church. Paul makes it clear that the apostles were given special powers, and that their authority could not be transferred to other Church members.

Paul and Barnabas travel through Galatia preaching the Gospel

THE FIRST CHURCH COUNCIL

In Jerusalem, Paul and Barnabas argue with some believers, who want all Gentiles to be circumcised before joining the Church

Paul

Barnabas

15 SOME[1] MEN CAME DOWN FROM JUDEA to Antioch and were teaching the brothers: "*Unless you are circumcised*, according to the custom taught by Moses, you cannot be saved." [2]This brought Paul and Barnabas into sharp dispute and debate with them. So Paul and Barnabas were appointed, along with some other believers, to go up to Jerusalem to see the apostles and elders about this question. [3]The church sent them on their way, and as they travelled through Phoenicia and Samaria, they told how the Gentiles had been converted... [4]When they came to Jerusalem, they were welcomed by the church and the apostles and elders, to whom they reported everything God had done through them.

[5]Then some of the believers who belonged to the party of the Pharisees stood up and said, "The Gentiles must be circumcised and required to obey the law of Moses."

[6]The apostles and elders met to consider this question.

[7]After much discussion, Peter got up and addressed them: "Brothers, you know that some time ago God made a choice among you that the Gentiles might hear from my lips the message of the gospel and believe. [8]God, who knows the heart, showed that he accepted them by giving the Holy Spirit to them, just as he did to us. [9]He made no distinction between us and them, for he purified their hearts by faith. [10]Now then, why do you try to test God by putting on the necks of the disciples a yoke that neither we nor our fathers have been able to bear? [11]No! We believe it is *through the grace of our Lord Jesus* that we are saved, just as they are." [12]The whole assembly became silent as they listened to Barnabas and Paul telling about the miraculous signs and wonders God had done among the Gentiles through them.

Peter

The Jerusalem Council meet to discuss whether Gentiles should be circumcised

Peter explains that salvation comes through Jesus Christ, not through a physical rite

❖

CHAPTER 15 VERSE 1
"Unless you are circumcised"
Many Jewish Christians believed that the new Church should follow Mosaic Law. Paul called this element in the Church the "Judaizers". He believed that circumcision went against Jesus' message. Paul wrote, "It is we who are the [true] circumcision, we who worship by the Spirit of God, who glory in Christ Jesus, and who put no confidence in the flesh" (Philippians 3: 3).

❖

CHAPTER 15 VERSE 11
"Through... our Lord Jesus"
Peter wanted freedom of choice for Gentile converts. He based his argument on the teachings of Jesus and on his vision about unclean animals (Acts 11: 7). Peter believed that salvation through Jesus was spiritual, not physical, therefore the Mosaic rules could be set aside.

THE JERUSALEM COUNCIL
This was a council of apostles and elders from the churches of Antioch and Jerusalem. The council first assembled in about AD 49 to discuss the disputes raised by a minority of Christian Jews who wanted all Gentile converts to be circumcised.

[13]When they finished, *James* spoke up: "Brothers, listen to me. [14]Simon has described to us how God at first showed his concern by taking from the Gentiles a people for himself... [19]It is my judgment, therefore, that we should not make it difficult for the Gentiles who are turning to God. [20]Instead we should write to them..."

[23]The apostles and elders, your brothers,

To the Gentile believers in Antioch, Syria and Cilicia: Greetings.

[24]We have heard that some went out from us without our authorisation and disturbed you, troubling your minds by what they said... [27]Therefore we are sending *Judas and Silas* to confirm by word of mouth what we are writing. [28]It seemed good to the Holy Spirit and to us not to burden you with anything beyond the following requirements: [29]*You are to abstain* from food sacrificed to idols, from blood, from the meat of strangled animals and from sexual immorality. You will do well to avoid these things. Farewell.

James writes a letter to the churches in Antioch, Syria, and Cilicia

Gentiles are asked to observe food laws and to avoid sexual immorality

[30]The men were sent off and went down to Antioch, where they gathered the church together and delivered the letter. [31]The people read it and were glad for its encouraging message. [32]Judas and Silas, who themselves were prophets, said much to encourage and strengthen the brothers.

Judas

Silas

Judas and Silas deliver James' letter to the Gentiles in Antioch

The Gentiles are pleased that the Council has decided not to impose circumcision

UNDERSTANDING THE STORY

The debate over Gentile circumcision highlights the differences between Mosaic and Christian teachings within the Church. The Jerusalem Council reaches an agreement. The Jews and Gentiles are asked to show mutual respect for each other's traditional values and to find a new unity in the Gospel message.

CHAPTER 15 VERSE 13
"James"
This is not James the apostle, but another disciple to whom Jesus appeared after his ascension. James later became Peter's successor.

CHAPTER 15 VERSE 27
"Judas and Silas"
This was Judas Barsabbas, who was a leader in Jerusalem. He travelled with Silas, another prominent figure in the early Church. Silas accompanied Paul on his second missionary journey. Like Paul, Silas had Roman citizenship. He also played an important role in the Christian church at Corinth.

CHAPTER 15 VERSE 29
"You are to abstain"
The Gentile believers were asked to be sensitive to the Jewish traditions. The food regulations were requested to preserve unity and prevent offence. The apostles maintained that the moral standards set up in the Old Testament applied to all Christians. But now there is a new emphasis on freedom and self-discipline. Paul wrote, "Everything is permissible – but not everything is beneficial, nor constructive" (1 Corinthians 10: 23).

SACRIFICES
This 5th-century BC Greek bowl depicts an animal being sacrificed. Sacrifice was part of ritual worship for the Jews as well as for many other nations. The early Church rejected this Jewish tradition: Paul argued that Jesus' death was the final sacrifice; Jesus had given up his life to redeem mankind.

ACTS 15–16
PAUL IN PHILIPPI

At Philippi, the Jews meet to pray by the river

Paul baptises Lydia, a Roman woman who worships God

Lydia invites Paul and his companions to her house

15 S OME[36] TIME LATER [Paul and Barnabas]... [39]had such *a sharp disagreement* that they parted company. Barnabas took Mark and sailed for Cyprus, [40]but Paul chose Silas [and they] [41]went through Syria and Cilicia, strengthening the churches.

Paul travelled to Derbe and then to Lystra, where he joined up with Timothy, another apostle. From there, he journeyed through Galatia and on to Troas. There, Paul had a vision of a man begging him to come to Macedonia.

16 [10]After Paul had seen the vision, *we got ready* at once to leave for Macedonia... [11]From Troas we [sailed to] Neapolis. [12]From there we travelled to Philippi, a Roman colony and the leading city of that district of Macedonia...

[13]On the Sabbath we went outside the city gate to the river, where we expected to find *a place of prayer*. We sat down and began to speak to the women who had gathered there. [14]One of those listening was a woman named Lydia, a dealer in purple cloth... who was a worshipper of God. The Lord opened her heart to respond to Paul's message. [15]When she and the members of her household were baptised, she invited us to her home...

[16]Once when we were going to the place of prayer, we were met by a slave girl who had a spirit by which she predicted the future.

CHAPTER 15 VERSE 39
"A sharp disagreement"
This refers to their argument over John Mark, who had returned to join the missionaries. Paul rejected Mark, who had previously deserted them. Mark later redeems himself in Paul's eyes by his devotion to missionary work.

CHAPTER 16 VERSE 10
"We got ready"
The use of the pronoun "we" suggests that Luke, the author of Acts and the second Gospel, joins the missionaries at this point.

CHAPTER 16 VERSE 13
"A place of prayer"
In those cities like Philippi where there were few Jews and no synagogues, Jews usually met outdoors near water. In Philippi, they worshipped by the River Gangite.

Paul banishes a spirit from a slave girl

Her owners can no longer make money from her

They drag the apostles to the magistrates

The girl tells fortunes

The apostles are sent to prison

She earned a great deal of money for her owners by fortune-telling. [17]This girl followed Paul and the rest of us, shouting, "These men are servants of the Most High God, who are telling you the way to be saved." [18]She kept this up for many days. Finally Paul... turned round and said to the spirit, "In the name of Jesus Christ I command you to come out of her!" At that moment the spirit left her. [19]When the owners of the slave girl realised that their hope of making money was gone, they seized Paul and Silas and dragged them into the market-place to face the authorities.

²⁰They brought them before the magistrates and said, "These men are Jews, and are throwing our city into an uproar ²¹by advocating customs unlawful for us Romans to accept or practise."

²²The crowd joined in the attack against Paul and Silas, and the magistrates ordered them to be stripped and beaten. ²³After they had been severely flogged, they were thrown into prison, and the jailer was commanded to guard them carefully...

²⁵About midnight Paul and Silas were praying and singing hymns to God, and the other prisoners were listening to them. ²⁶Suddenly there was such a violent earthquake that the foundations of the prison were shaken. At once all the prison doors flew open, and everybody's chains came loose. ²⁷The jailer woke up, and when he saw the prison doors open, he drew his sword and *was about to kill himself* because he thought the prisoners had escaped. ²⁸But Paul shouted, "Don't harm yourself! We are all here!" ²⁹The jailer called for lights, rushed in and fell trembling before Paul and Silas [and asked] ³⁰"Sirs, what must I do to be saved?" ³¹They replied, "Believe in the Lord Jesus, and you will be saved..." ³³At that hour of the night the jailer took them and washed their wounds; then immediately he and all his family were baptised...

An earthquake opens the prison doors

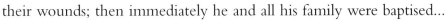

The jailer is astonished to find that Paul and Silas have not tried to escape

³⁵When it was daylight, the magistrates sent their officers to the jailer with the order: "Release those men."... ³⁷But Paul said to the officers: "They beat us publicly without a trial, even though *we are Roman citizens*, and threw us into prison. And now do they want to get rid of us quietly? No! Let them come themselves and escort us out." [When the magistrates heard this] ³⁹they came to appease them and escorted them from the prison, requesting them to leave the city.

The jailer asks Paul to baptise him

UNDERSTANDING THE STORY

In Philippi, Paul finds his first European converts. But he also faces great hostility because Christianity is seen as a threat to Roman order and is dealt with harshly. However, Paul is undeterred. He uses his Roman privileges to help him establish a church in Philippi that will remain loyal and supportive.

PHILIPPI

This ancient city in north-eastern Greece was established by Philip II of Macedonia in 356 BC. Paul arrived there in *c.* AD 50 and founded the first Christian community in Europe. Philippi was a major medical centre, and Luke – a doctor – remained there when Paul moved on.

PHILIP II
Gold medallion

LYDIA

Lydia was a wealthy Roman business woman. Although she was a Gentile, she observed Jewish law. Lydia's house later became the first church in Philippi.

THE PRISON IN PHILIPPI
These ruins of a church were built on the site where Paul was detained in prison.

❖

CHAPTER 16 VERSE 27
"Was about to kill himself"
According to Roman law, the guard in charge of a prisoner who escaped was executed. This jailer chose to kill himself rather than face shame and torture.

❖

CHAPTER 16 VERSE 37
"We are Roman citizens"
It was illegal to beat Roman citizens publicly without a proper trial. The apostles did not stop the beating by proclaiming their citizenship, because Paul wanted to establish their innocence for the sake of the Christians who would have to remain in the town.

ACTS 17

FROM PHILIPPI TO ATHENS

THESSALONICA
Capital city and main port of Macedonia, Thessalonica grew in importance under Roman control. The city lay on the Via Egnatia, a major Roman road that ran from Rome to the East. Paul used this road on his journey through Greece.

ATHENS
Athens began as a small village on a hill in 3000 BC. The city reached its height as the centre of Greek learning and culture in the 5th century BC. In Paul's time, Athens still attracted many philosophers.

17 WHEN[1] THEY HAD PASSED through Amphipolis and Apollonia, they came to Thessalonica, where there was a Jewish synagogue. [2]As his custom was, Paul went into the synagogue, and on three Sabbath days he reasoned with them from the Scriptures, [3]explaining and proving that the Christ had to suffer and rise from the dead... [4]Some of the Jews were persuaded and joined Paul and Silas, as did a large number of God-fearing Greeks and not a few prominent women.

[5]But the Jews were jealous; so they rounded up some bad characters from the market-place, formed a mob and started a riot in the city. They rushed to Jason's house in search of Paul and Silas in order to bring them out to the crowd. [6]But when they did not find them, they dragged Jason and some other brothers before the city officials, shouting: "These men who have caused trouble all over the world have now come here, [7]and Jason has welcomed them into his house. They are all defying Caesar's decrees, saying that there is another king, one called Jesus." [8]When they heard this, the crowd and the city officials were thrown into turmoil. [9]Then they put Jason and the others on bail and let them go.

[10]As soon as it was night, the brothers sent Paul and Silas away to Berea. On arriving there, they went to the Jewish synagogue.

In Thessalonica, Paul preaches the Gospel message. Some Jews are angry and start a riot

Paul's followers are persecuted

In Berea, Paul receives a better reception

CHAPTER 17 VERSE 19
"Areopagus"
"Areopagus" means "hill of Ares", the Greek god of war. It was a small hill where the council used to meet in ancient times to govern the city-state. By Roman times, the council had become a court supervising education, morality, and religion.

CHAPTER 17 VERSE 23
"TO AN UNKNOWN GOD"
According to legend, a terrible plague once raged through Athens. It was only when a flock of sheep was sacrificed on an altar dedicated to "an unknown god" that the plague came to an end.

[11]Now the Bereans were of more noble character than the Thessalonians, for they received the message with great eagerness and examined the Scriptures every day to see if what Paul said was true. [12]Many of the Jews believed, as did also a number of prominent Greek women and many Greek men.

[13]When the Jews in Thessalonica learned that Paul was preaching the word of God at Berea, they went there too, agitating the crowds and stirring them up.

Some Thessalonians arrive and try to stir up trouble

[14]The brothers immediately sent Paul to the coast, but Silas and Timothy stayed at Berea. [15]The men who escorted Paul brought him to Athens and then left with instructions for Silas and Timothy to join him as soon as possible.

[16]While Paul was waiting for them in Athens, he was greatly distressed to see that the city was full of idols. [17]So he reasoned in the synagogue with the Jews and the God-fearing Greeks, as well as in the market-place day by day with those who happened to be there. [18]A group of Epicurean and Stoic philosophers began to dispute with him. Some of them asked, "What is this babbler trying to say?" Others remarked, "He seems to be advocating foreign gods."... [19]Then they took him and brought him to a meeting of the *Areopagus,* where they said to him, "May we know what this new teaching is that you are presenting?..."

[22]Paul then stood up in the meeting of the Areopagus and said: "Men of Athens! I see that in every way you are very religious. [23]For as I walked around and looked carefully at your objects of worship, I even found an altar with this inscription: *TO AN UNKNOWN GOD.* Now what you worship as something unknown I am going to proclaim to you.

[24]"The God who made the world and everything in it is the Lord of heaven and earth and does not live in temples built by hands... [29]We should not think that the divine being is like gold or silver or stone – an image made by man's design and skill. [30]In the past God overlooked such ignorance, but now he commands all people everywhere to repent..."

[32]When they heard about the resurrection of the dead, some of them sneered, but others said, "We want to hear you again on this subject." [33]At that, Paul left the Council. [34]A few men became followers of Paul and believed.

Paul is distressed to find that the city of Athens is full of idols

Jupiter

Paul

In Athens, Paul is invited to reason with a group of philosophers

UNDERSTANDING THE STORY

As he travels farther afield, Paul encounters many different reactions to the Gospel message. He finds hostility from the Thessalonian Jews, enthusiasm from the Bereans, and scepticism from the Greek philosophers. Each time, however, Paul communicates his beliefs and brings more people to believe in Jesus.

SCHOOLS OF PHILOSOPHY IN ANCIENT ATHENS

Epicureans followed the beliefs of the philosopher Epicurus (342–270 BC), who claimed that happiness is the supreme good. He stated that people should avoid mental and physical pain and strive for contentment by living a moderate and simple life. The Stoics held the view that people should submit to their predestined, unchangeable fates without expressing joy or grief.

BUST OF EPICURUS

Epicurus was brought up in Samos, an island off the west coast of Turkey. He moved to Athens and founded a school of philosophy in 307 BC. Despite Epicurus' view that moderation led to happiness, the school was later criticized for promoting debauchery.

ACTS 18

PAUL IN CORINTH

PAUL[1] LEFT ATHENS and went to Corinth. [2]There he met a Jew named Aquila, a native of Pontus, who had recently come from Italy with his wife Priscilla, because *Claudius* had ordered all the Jews to leave Rome. *Paul* went to see them, [3]and because he *was a tentmaker* as they were, he stayed and worked with them. [4]Every Sabbath he reasoned in the synagogue, trying to persuade Jews and Greeks.

[5]When Silas and *Timothy* came from Macedonia, Paul devoted himself exclusively to preaching, testifying to the Jews that Jesus was the Christ. [6]But when the Jews opposed Paul and became abusive, he shook out his clothes in protest and said to them, "Your blood be on your own heads! I am clear of my responsibility. From now on I will go to the Gentiles."

CORINTH
Corinth was the capital of the Roman province of Achaia, 80km (55 miles) south-west of Athens. The Romans had destroyed the city in 146 BC, but in 44 BC Julius Caesar ordered it to be rebuilt. Situated between the Ionian and Aegean seas, Corinth had two large harbours. It was popular with traders and travellers as a link between Rome and the East.

CORINTH
Ruins of the Temple of Aphrodite

RELIGION AND IMMORALITY
Corinth was notorious for sexual excess, which was an accepted part of pagan religious practice. The wealthy, cosmopolitan city contained more than twelve pagan temples. The most infamous, the Temple of Aphrodite, dedicated to the Goddess of Love, had hundreds of sacred prostitutes.

CLAUDIUS CAESAR
Bronze coin from Turkey

CHAPTER 18 VERSE 2
"Claudius"
Claudius Caesar was the Roman emperor from AD 41–54. At first he was tolerant of the Jewish community, but he later expelled many of the Jews from Rome for rioting. Aquila and Priscilla, who became good friends with Paul, were among those driven out of Italy.

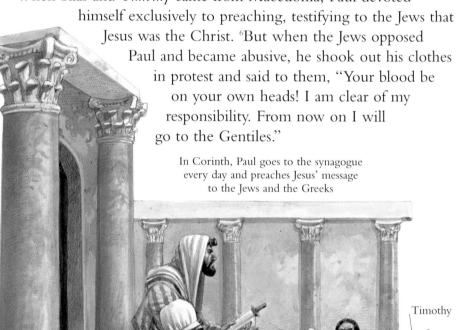

In Corinth, Paul goes to the synagogue every day and preaches Jesus' message to the Jews and the Greeks

Timothy

Silas

Paul

When the Jews oppose Paul, he shakes out his clothes and tells them he will speak only to the Gentiles

[7]Then Paul left the synagogue and went next door to the house of Titius Justus, a worshipper of God. [8]Crispus, the synagogue ruler, and his entire household believed in the Lord; and many of the Corinthians who heard him believed and were baptised.

⁹One night the Lord spoke to Paul in a vision: "Do not be afraid; keep on speaking, do not be silent. ¹⁰For I am with you, and no-one is going to attack and harm you, because I have many people in this city." ¹¹So Paul stayed for a year and a half, teaching them the word of God.

¹²While *Gallio* was proconsul of Achaia, the Jews made a united attack on Paul and brought him into court. ¹³"This man," they charged, "is persuading the people to worship God in ways contrary to the law."

One night, Paul has a vision. God urges him to stay in Corinth

¹⁴Just as Paul was about to speak, Gallio said to the Jews, "If you Jews were making a complaint about some misdemeanour or serious crime, it would be reasonable for me to listen to you. ¹⁵But since it involves questions about words and names and your own law – settle the matter yourselves. I will not be a judge of such things." ¹⁶So he had them ejected from the court. ¹⁷Then they all turned on Sosthenes the synagogue ruler and beat him in front of the court. But Gallio showed no concern whatever.

The Jews bring Paul before Gallio, the proconsul

Sosthenes

Gallio rejects the case, and the synagogue leader is beaten

Gallio

Paul stayed on in Corinth for some time, and the early Church flourished under his guidance. From Corinth, Paul went on to visit the Christian communities that he had established previously. He also wrote a series of letters to these early Churches, giving them practical advice and encouragement.

UNDERSTANDING THE STORY

Paul receives a mixed reception in Corinth: he makes both loyal friends and violent enemies. When God assures Paul's safety, any doubts he has are overcome. He realizes that his Roman citizenship gives him protection under Roman law and that he can now establish a Christian church without fear of persecution.

CHAPTER 18 VERSES 2–3
"Paul… was a tentmaker"
It was a Jewish custom for all sons to learn a manual trade. The term "tentmaker" may also refer to leather work in general, because tents were often constructed from leather. As a rabbi, Paul had to perform his religious and legal work free of charge, so he probably needed to do manual labour in order to support himself.

CHAPTER 18 VERSE 5
"Timothy"
Timothy joined Paul in Lystra (Acts 16: 1). His mother was a Jewish Christian, and his father was a Gentile. Despite his youth and inexperience, Timothy became Paul's close friend and companion, remaining with him during Paul's imprisonment in Rome. Paul wrote two letters of advice to him (1 and 2 Timothy). After serving the churches in Thessalonica, Corinth, and Philippi, Timothy became the first bishop of Ephesus.

CHAPTER 18 VERSE 12
"Gallio"
An inscription found at Delphi, Greece, mentions that Gallio was proconsul of Achaia in AD 52. At this time, Achaia was a Roman province in the Greek peninsula south of Thessalonica. During his time as proconsul, Gallio was well known for being a just administrator. He left Achaia due to illness and returned to Rome. There, he was forced to commit suicide because of his brother Seneca's involvement in a conspiracy against the emperor Nero.

BUST OF SENECA
Seneca was one of the Stoic philosophers, advocating the value of inner virtue and emotional restraint. He provided guidance for the young Nero.

ACTS 19

PAUL AND THE EPHESIANS

PAUL[1] TOOK THE ROAD through the interior and arrived at Ephesus... [8]Paul entered the synagogue and spoke boldly there for three months, arguing persuasively about the kingdom of God. [9]But some of them became obstinate; they refused to believe and publicly maligned the Way. So Paul left them. He took the disciples with him and had discussions daily in *the lecture hall of Tyrannus*. [10]This went on for two years, so that all the Jews and Greeks who lived in the province of Asia heard the word of the Lord.

[11]God did extraordinary miracles through Paul, [12]so that even *handkerchiefs and aprons* that had touched him were taken to the sick, and their illnesses were cured and the evil spirits left them.

[13]Some Jews who went around driving out evil spirits tried to invoke the name of the Lord Jesus over those who were demon-possessed. They would say, "In the name of Jesus, whom Paul preaches, I command you to come out."... [15]One day [an] evil spirit answered them, "Jesus I know, and I know about Paul, but who are you?" [16]Then the man who had the evil spirit jumped on them and overpowered them all. He gave them such a beating that they ran out of the house naked and bleeding.

[17]When this became known to the Jews and Greeks living in Ephesus, they were all seized with fear, and the name of the Lord Jesus was held in high honour. [18]Many of those who believed now came and openly confessed their evil deeds. [19]A number who had practised sorcery brought their scrolls together and burned them publicly. When they calculated the value of the scrolls, the total came to *fifty thousand drachmas*. [20]In this way the word of the Lord spread widely and grew in power...

CHAPTER 19 VERSE 9
"The lecture hall of Tyrannus"
Tyrannus was probably a philosophy teacher or a Jewish rabbi who had a private lecture hall. Early tradition records that Paul preached there in the early afternoon, during siesta time, when the hall would not have been used for lectures.

In Ephesus, Paul performs extraordinary miracles

CHAPTER 19
VERSE 12
"Handkerchiefs and aprons"
These items were "props" and not a necessary part of the healing. Paul probably used them to communicate God's power to a population deeply fascinated by magic.

JESUS' CLOAK
This mosaic from a church in Istanbul shows a woman touching Jesus' cloak to be healed. The sick and suffering found the same miraculous healing powers in Paul's aprons and handkerchiefs and in Peter's shadow (Acts 5: 12).

CHAPTER 19 VERSE 19
"Fifty thousand drachmas"
One drachma was an average day's wage, so the value of these scrolls was worth more than 135 years' wages. Sorcerers relied on the superstitions of the Ephesians for their income, yet they publicly burned their magic scrolls. This conveys the impact of Paul's message.

False healers use Jesus' name to exorcise demons

A demon-possessed man attacks the Jews and beats them

²³About that time there arose a great disturbance about the Way. ²⁴A silversmith named Demetrius, who made silver shrines of Artemis, brought in no little business for the craftsmen. ²⁵He called them together, along with the workmen in related trades, and said: "Men... ²⁶you see and hear how this fellow Paul has convinced and led astray large numbers of people here in Ephesus and in practically the whole province of Asia. He says that man-made gods are no gods at all. ²⁷There is danger not only that our trade will lose its good name, but also that *the temple of the great goddess Artemis* will be discredited, and the goddess herself, who is worshipped throughout the province of Asia and the world, will be robbed of her divine majesty."

²⁸When they heard this, they were furious and began shouting: "Great is *Artemis of the Ephesians!*"

The false healers rush from the house, naked and bleeding

Demetrius makes silver shrines of Artemis

The craftsmen fear that Paul's message will destroy their livelihoods

²⁹Soon the whole city was in an uproar... ³⁵The city clerk quietened the crowd and said... ³⁸"If, then, Demetrius and his fellow craftsmen have a grievance against anybody, the courts are open and there are proconsuls. They can press charges. ³⁹If there is anything further you want to bring up, it must be settled in a legal assembly. ⁴⁰As it is, we are in danger of being charged with rioting because of today's events..."

Following this uproar, Paul and his companions decided to leave Ephesus. They travelled back to Jerusalem, where all the missionaries were warmly welcomed.

UNDERSTANDING THE STORY

Paul finds that Ephesus is a city steeped in superstition, and he uses the Ephesians' reliance on magic as a means to demonstrate the power of his message. The profound effect of Paul's ministry is evident in the violent reactions of the craftsmen, who rely on the pagan worship of Artemis.

2ND-CENTURY TEMPLE OF HADRIAN, EPHESUS

EPHESUS

In Paul's day, Ephesus was the largest city in the Roman province of Asia (modern Turkey) and a thriving commercial centre. It was situated on an inland harbour on the Cayster River, which flowed into the Aegean Sea, and was at an intersection of major trade routes.

CHAPTER 19 VERSE 27
"The temple of... Artemis"
This temple was built in 250 BC and was considered one of the seven wonders of the ancient world. At the centre of the temple stood a statue of Artemis, carved from a meteorite. According to legend, this was hurled to earth by Zeus, king of the Greek gods.

STATUE OF ARTEMIS OF EPHESUS

CHAPTER 19 VERSE 28
"Artemis of the Ephesians!"
This Artemis had little in common with the classic Greek deity, who was goddess of the moon and hunting. When the Greeks colonized Ephesus, it was already a site of worship of an ancient fertility goddess. The Greeks named her Artemis, but she retained all the attributes of a mother earth deity.

ACTS 21-25
PAUL IS ARRESTED AND TRIED

In Jerusalem, Paul is dragged out of the temple by Jews who object to his preaching

Paul

21 SOME[27] JEWS FROM the province of Asia saw Paul at the temple. They stirred up the whole crowd and seized him, [28]shouting, "Men of Israel, help us! This is the man who teaches all men everywhere against our people and our law and this place. And besides, he has brought *Greeks into the temple area...*"

[30]The whole city was aroused, and the people came running from all directions. Seizing Paul, they dragged him from the temple, and immediately the gates were shut. [31]While they were trying to kill him, news reached *the commander of the Roman troops* that the whole city of Jerusalem was in an uproar. [32]He at once took some officers and soldiers and ran down to the crowd. When the rioters saw the commander and his soldiers, they stopped beating Paul.

Roman troops arrive to break up the riot

Paul is arrested and bound in chains

The commander is alarmed when he learns that Paul is a Roman citizen

✢
CHAPTER 21 VERSE 28
"Greeks into the temple area"
The Temple was divided into several courts. Non-Jews were allowed to enter the outer "Court of Gentiles", but access to the inner courts was strictly forbidden. Stone markers warned that any foreign trespassers would be killed. Paul was falsely accused of bringing Greeks into the inner courts. This accusation caused an uproar in the city.

✢
CHAPTER 21 VERSE 31
"The commander of the... troops"
This was Claudius Lysias, who was in charge of the Roman garrison at Fort Antonia. The fortress was connected to the northern end of the Temple. Jesus had been taken to Fort Antonia after his trial with Pontius Pilate. Paul was also taken here when he was arrested.

He decides to take Paul before the Sanhedrin

Paul was arrested and bound in chains. As he was about to be flogged, Paul told them that he was a Roman citizen. The commander was alarmed and decided to take Paul before the Sanhedrin to find out why Paul was being accused by the Jews.

23

⁶Then Paul, knowing that some of them were Sadducees and the others Pharisees, called out in the Sanhedrin, "My brothers, I am a Pharisee, the son of a Pharisee. I stand on trial because of my hope in the resurrection of the dead." ⁷When he said this, *a dispute broke out* between the Pharisees and the Sadducees, and the assembly was divided... ⁹There was a great uproar... ¹⁰The dispute became so violent that the commander was afraid Paul would be torn to pieces by them... ¹¹The following night the Lord stood near Paul and said, "Take courage! As you have testified about me in

The Pharisees and Sadducees argue about Paul's faith

Jerusalem, so you must also testify in Rome." ¹²The next morning the Jews formed a conspiracy and bound themselves with an oath not to eat or drink until they had killed Paul.

The plot was discovered and Paul was sent to Caesarea, where he was put on trial before Felix, the Roman Governor. The Jews accused Paul, but no conclusion was reached.

24 ²⁷When two years had passed, *Felix was succeeded by Porcius Festus...*

25 ¹[who] went up from Caesarea to Jerusalem, ²where the chief priests and Jewish leaders... presented the charges against Paul. ³They urgently requested Festus, as a favour to them, to have Paul transferred to Jerusalem, for they were preparing an ambush to kill him along the way. ⁴Festus answered, "Paul is being held at Caesarea... ⁵Let some of your leaders come with me and press charges against the man there..." ⁶The next day he convened the court and ordered that Paul be brought before him. ⁷When Paul appeared, the Jews who had come down from Jerusalem stood around him, bringing many serious charges against him, which they could not prove... ⁹Festus, wishing to do the Jews a favour, said to Paul, "Are you willing to go up to Jerusalem and stand trial before me there on these charges?"

¹⁰Paul answered: "I am now standing before Caesar's court, where I ought to be tried... ¹¹*I appeal to Caesar!*" ¹²After Festus had conferred with his council, he declared: "You have appealed to Caesar. To Caesar you will go!"

Paul asks the Roman Govenor to be tried in Rome

Festus agrees

UNDERSTANDING THE STORY

When the Jews in Jerusalem threaten Paul with false accusations, he uses the internal divisions of his accusers to his advantage. Persecution and imprisonment for Paul result in a new missionary journey to Rome.

CHAPTER 23 VERSE 7
"A dispute broke out"
The Sanhedrin was the supreme Jewish court. In Paul's time, it was composed of 71 Sadducees and Pharisees. These two groups emerged during the period between the Old and the New Testament and held different religious and political views. Whereas the Pharisees believed in the resurrection of the dead, the Sadducees did not.

CHAPTER 24 VERSE 27
"Felix was succeeded by... Festus"
Antonius Felix was governor of Judea from AD 52–60. Formerly a slave, Felix was a brutal and corrupt ruler. His immorality and incompetence eventually led to his dismissal. His successor, Porcius Festus, was a just and respectable man.

CHAPTER 25 VERSE 11
"I appeal to Caesar!"
Paul exercised his right as a Roman citizen to be tried before Caesar in Rome. At this time, Nero was the emperor. Nero was under the influence of Seneca, the philosopher, and had not yet begun his persecution of the Christians.

BUST OF NERO (RULED AD 54–68)
Nero became emperor at sixteen. The first years of his reign were moderate, but he soon became a brutal and debauched ruler. Nero had his wife, mother, and stepbrother murdered. It is believed that he set fire to Rome in order to build himself a new palace.

ACTS 27–28
PAUL IS SHIPWRECKED

CHAPTER 27 VERSE 2
"From Adramyttium"
Paul's ship came from a harbour situated on the north-western coast of Asia Minor. It is now modern Edremit in Turkey.

PAUL'S JOURNEY TO ROME

CHAPTER 27 VERSE 2
"Ports along the coast"
Ships often stopped at ports along the coastline of the Mediterranean Sea for commercial reasons. Boats leaving Egypt and the east coast of the Mediterranean took this longer route, rather than sailing directly to Italy, because of the strong westerly winds.

CHAPTER 27 VERSE 14
"A wind... called the 'north-easter' "
This strong wind was known as the "Euroquilo", a term used for the north-easterly wind that came down from the mountains of Crete. The word is formed from the Greek word "Euros" (the east wind) and the Latin word "Aquilo" (the north wind).

CHAPTER 27 VERSE 20
"Neither sun nor stars"
In Paul's time, sailors navigated by observing the position of the sun and stars. Deprived of this means, they were unable to gauge their position.

27 WHEN[1] IT WAS DECIDED that we would sail for Italy, Paul and some other prisoners were handed over to a centurion named Julius, who belonged to the Imperial Regiment. [2]We boarded a ship *from Adramyttium* about to sail for *ports along the coast* of the province of Asia, and we put out to sea...

[14]*A wind of hurricane force, called the "north-easter"*, swept down from the island. [15]The ship was caught by the storm and could not head into the wind; so we gave way to it and were driven along... [18]We took such a violent battering from the storm that the next day they began to throw the cargo overboard...

Paul sets sail for Rome

The ship is caught in a violent storm

The sailors throw cargo overboard

Paul urges the sailors not to give up hope

²⁰When *neither sun nor stars* appeared for many days and the storm continued raging, we finally gave up all hope of being saved.

²¹After the men had gone a long time without food, Paul stood up before them and said... ²²"I urge you to keep up your courage, because not one of you will be lost; only the ship will be destroyed. ²³Last night an angel of the God whose I am and whom I serve stood beside me ²⁴and said, 'Do not be afraid, Paul. You must stand trial before Caesar; and God has graciously given you the lives of all who sail with you.' ... ²⁶Nevertheless, we must run aground on some island."

Two weeks later, the boat approached land. The sailors had gone without food for many days, and Paul advised them to eat. He assured them that God would protect them. Then they struck a sand-bar and the ship was wrecked, but everyone reached the shore safely.

The crew is washed up on the island of Malta

Paul is bitten by a viper

When the local people see that Paul is unharmed, they think he is a god

28 ¹We found out that *the island was called Malta.* ²*The islanders* showed us unusual kindness. They built a fire and welcomed us all because it was raining and cold. ³Paul gathered a pile of brushwood and, as he put it on the fire, a viper, driven out by the heat, fastened itself on his hand. ⁴When the islanders saw the snake hanging from his hand, they said to each other, "This man must be a murderer; for though he escaped from the sea, *Justice* has not allowed him to live."... ⁶The people expected him to swell up or suddenly fall dead, but after waiting a long time and seeing nothing unusual happen to him, they changed their minds and said he was a god.

⁷There was an estate near by that belonged to Publius, the chief official of the island. He welcomed us to his home and for three days entertained us hospitably. ⁸His father was sick in bed, suffering from fever and dysentery. Paul went in to see him and... healed him. ⁹When this had happened, the rest of sick on the island came and were cured. ¹⁰They honoured us in many ways and when we were ready to sail, they furnished us with the supplies we needed.

UNDERSTANDING THE STORY

Despite the violence of the storm at sea, Paul never doubts God's promise that he will go to Rome. His faith inspires courage in those around him. The shipwreck at Malta gives Paul the opportunity to bring the Christian message to another community.

PAUL'S SEA JOURNEY
3rd-century Roman relief

✤

CHAPTER 28 VERSE 1
"The island was called Malta"
The Romans called Malta "Melita" meaning "refuge". Its natural harbours made it a haven for ships.

✤

CHAPTER 28 VERSE 2
"The islanders"
This Bible word for the people of Malta is "barbarians", which means "non-Greek speakers". Phoenicians settled in Malta *c.* 1000 BC. The islanders later came under Greek, then Roman, control, but the islanders retained their own dialect.

Paul heals the sick in Malta

✤

CHAPTER 28 VERSE 4
"Justice"
The local people may have been referring to Zeus, the king of the Greek Gods. Zeus was notoriously capricious in Greek mythology and dealt out his "justice" at random.

ACTS 28

PAUL IN ROME

"Castor and Pollux"
In Greek mythology, Castor and Pollux, the twin sons of Zeus, were transformed by their father into the constellation "Gemini". Zeus gave them control of the wind and waves. Many mariners put figureheads of the twins on the bows of their ships to protect them from bad weather.

Paul explains to the Jews what happened in Jerusalem

FROM MALTA TO ROME
First the ship sailed to Syracuse, the main city in Sicily. From there, it went to Rhegium, on the southern tip of Italy, before arriving at Puteoli (modern Pozzuoli), near the Bay of Naples. This was Italy's main port. The last stage of the journey was by land along the Appian Way, which was the main road from Rome to the south of Italy. It took Paul a week to reach Rome.

VIA APPIA
This Roman road was the first in a network of roads initiated by Appius Claudius Caesar in 312 BC. Parts of it are still visible today.

28 ^11AFTER THREE MONTHS we put out to sea in a ship that had wintered in the island. It was an Alexandrian ship with the figurehead of the twin gods *Castor and Pollux*. ^12We put in at Syracuse and stayed there three days. ^13From there we set sail and arrived at Rhegium. The next day the south wind came up, and on the following day we reached Puteoli. ^14There we found some brothers who invited us to spend a week with them. And so we came to Rome. ^15The brothers there had heard that we were coming, and *they travelled as far as the Forum of Appius and the Three Taverns to meet us*. At the sight of these men Paul thanked God and was encouraged. ^16When we got to Rome, Paul was allowed to live by himself, with a soldier to guard him.

^17Three days later *he called together the leaders of the Jews*. When they had assembled, Paul said to them: "My brothers, although I have done nothing against our people or against the customs of our ancestors, I was arrested in Jerusalem and handed over to the Romans. ^18They examined me and wanted to release me, because I was not guilty of any crime deserving death. ^19But when the Jews objected, I was compelled to appeal to Caesar – not that I had any charge to bring against my own people. ^20For this reason I have asked to see you and talk with you. It is because of the hope of Israel that I am bound with this chain."

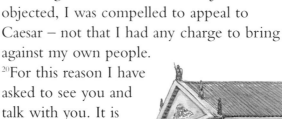

Paul is under house arrest

Paul talks to the Jews about Jesus

Some believe Paul, but others do not

[21]They replied, "We have not received any letters from Judea concerning you, and none of the brothers who have come from there has reported or said anything bad about you. [22]But we want to hear what your views are, for we know that people everywhere are talking against this sect."

[23]They arranged to meet Paul on a certain day, and came in even larger numbers to the place where he was staying. From morning till evening he explained and declared to them the kingdom of God and tried to convince them about Jesus from the Law of Moses and from the Prophets. [24]Some were convinced by what he said, but others would not believe. [25]They disagreed among themselves and began to leave after Paul had made this final statement:

"The Holy Spirit spoke the truth to your forefathers when he said through Isaiah the prophet: [26]'Go to this people and say, "You will be ever hearing but never understanding; you will be ever seeing but never perceiving." [27]For this people's heart has become calloused; they hardly hear with their ears, and they have closed their eyes. Otherwise they might see with their eyes, hear with their ears, understand with their hearts and turn, and I would heal them.'

[28]"Therefore I want you to know that God's salvation has been sent to the Gentiles, and they will listen!"

[29]After he said this, the Jews left, arguing vigorously among themselves. [30]For two whole years Paul stayed there in his own rented house and welcomed all who came to see him. [31]Boldly and without hindrance he preached the kingdom of God and taught about the Lord Jesus Christ.

For two years, Paul stays in his own rented house

Paul welcomes all visitors and teaches them about Jesus

CHAPTER 28 VERSE 15
"They travelled... to meet us"
A community of Christians was already established in Rome at this time. They were aware that Paul was on his way to the city. His fellow Christians travelled many days to welcome him at these popular meeting places midway between Puteoli and Rome.

THE COLOSSEUM IN ROME
During the years of persecution, many Christians died in this arena.

CHAPTER 28 VERSE 17
"He called together... the Jews"
Emperor Claudius had expelled the Jews from Rome in AD 50 for rioting. By this time (AD 61) many Jews had returned and were powerful in Emperor Nero's court. Paul was anxious to speak to them because he knew they could influence the outcome of his trial.

PAUL'S LAST JOURNEYS
The Bible does not mention Paul being put on trial. His letters from Rome suggest that he was released and subsequently visited churches from Asia Minor, Crete, Greece, and Spain. However, the Bible does not record these journeys or how Paul died. Modern scholars believe that he was eventually rearrested and executed during Nero's persecution of the Christians (c. AD 67).

UNDERSTANDING THE STORY

Paul takes the Christian message to the heart of the Roman empire. When his attempt to reason with the Roman Jews fails, he reiterates his belief that the future of the Christian Church lies with the Gentiles. The Book of Acts ends without recording the final years of Paul's ministry.

359

REVELATION

Revelation is the last book in the Bible. It is very different in content, tone, and style from the rest of the New Testament books. Early testimonies attribute Revelation to the apostle and Gospel writer John, who wrote it about thirty years after Paul's journeys (*c.* 90–95 AD). It describes John's vision of the final day of judgement and gives words of encouragement and support to the early Christians, who were suffering persecution under the Romans at this time. John wrote Revelation on the island of Patmos, where he had been exiled by the Roman emperor Domitian. John addresses Revelation to the Seven Churches in Asia Minor, which were under his care at this time.

The persecution of the Christians

Towards the end of the 1st century, the Christians had suffered two waves of persecution under the Romans. In AD 64, Nero blamed the Christians for the fire that destroyed much of the city of Rome, and he burned and crucified many of them. A few decades later, the emperor Domitian (AD 81–96) proclaimed that he was a god and ordered his subjects to worship him. When Jesus' followers refused, they were imprisoned, tortured, and killed. They also faced fierce opposition from Jewish leaders. Early Christian tradition says that after the Roman–Jewish war (AD 66–70) Christians were forbidden from entering synagogues. They were therefore forced to meet in secret places.

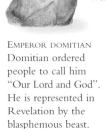

EMPEROR DOMITIAN
Domitian ordered people to call him "Our Lord and God". He is represented in Revelation by the blasphemous beast.

The purpose of Revelation

John wrote Revelation to strengthen the faith of Christians, who were repressed by the Roman authorities. His main message was that God would triumph over evil (the Roman emperors), and he assured them that Judgement Day was imminent.

THE APOSTLE JOHN
This painting by Hans Memling (*c.* 1433–1494) depicts John receiving his vision on Patmos.

The seven churches of Asia Minor

These churches were not physical places of worship, but communities of people who believed in Jesus. There were more than seven Christian communities in the Roman province of Asia Minor at this time. The reason John addresses his letter to only seven may have been because they were postal centres. Ephesus, Thyatira, Sardis, Pergamum, Philadelphia, Laodicea, and Smyrna were all situated on a circular route around the western central part of the province. It would have been easy for John's letter to be circulated to the surrounding Christian communities from these main towns.

The fate of the twelve

John was persecuted probably because he refused to worship the emperor Domitian. Several of the original twelve disciples suffered similar fates. Peter is said to have died a martyr in Rome (probably during Nero's persecution in AD 64). The Book of Acts reports that James, the brother of John, was decapitated by Herod Agrippa (12: 2). Christian tradition states that Andrew preached in Scythia, but was eventually crucified in Achaia. Other early Christian writings mention the deaths of the remaining disciples, but the historical accuracy of these accounts is uncertain.

THE ISLAND OF PATMOS
Patmos is one of the Greek islands. In John's day, it was used by the Romans to detain prisoners.

The content of Revelation

The Book of Revelation can be divided into four key visions. The first depicts Christ among the seven churches; the second shows seven trumpets, seven bowls of wrath, and a scroll with seven seals. John's next vision is of Christ's return on Judgement Day, and the last is of a new heaven and earth. The first three chapters of Revelation form an introduction to the whole book. They explain that John received his visions from an angel, who acts as an intermediary for the risen Christ.

ST JAMES
15th-century
German painting

Apocalyptic writing

Revelation has been influenced by a style of Jewish writing known as "apocalyptic", which is Greek for "revelation". Apocalyptic literature emerged about 200 BC, when the Jewish people experienced occupation and religious persecution under Syrian rulers (the Seleucids). The Seleucids forbade Jewish worship and forced the Jews to join in heathen celebrations.

ANTIOCHUS IV EPIPHANES
This Roman coin depicts the most oppressive Seleucid ruler (*c.* 175–164 BC).

THE APOCALYPSE
Illuminated manuscript (1109) showing Daniel's vision of Judgement Day (Daniel 7).

The Apocalyptic writers alluded to the Old Testament prophecies about the Messianic kingdom. They contrasted God's kingdom with their suffering and offered a vision of hope to the Jews. Apocalyptic writing often contained references and symbols taken from the Book of Daniel.

Understanding Revelation

Revelation is difficult to interpret because it uses a coded language, a common feature of Apocalyptic writing. Its message can be better understood when it is seen in relation to Old Testament events, prophecies, and symbols.

Allusions to the Old Testament

The last section of Revelation recalls the first chapters of the Old Testament (Genesis 2–3). Revelation describes paradise as a new Garden of Eden, which contains the "Tree of Life". The tree symbolizes eternal life for the followers of Jesus Christ.

John's vision of Judgement Day describes angels pouring seven bowls of wrath on the wicked (Revelation 16). Each bowl brings forth a plague. These echo the ten plagues that Moses brought upon the Egyptians (Exodus 7–11).

JESUS AND THE TREE OF LIFE
16th-century stained-glass window, depicting the cross as the Tree of Life

SYMBOLISM

Revelation relies heavily on symbolic language, most of which derives from the Old Testament scriptures. The numbers in Revelation have a symbolic significance. The number seven appears frequently. In Hebrew tradition, it represents perfection and completeness. Revelation features seven churches, seven visions, seven seals, seven trumpets, seven bowls of wrath, and seven angels.

The number six symbolizes imperfection. John describes a beast that deceives people into false worship (Revelation 13: 11–18). The beast is represented by the numbers 666, which is a code for the emperor Nero. All Greek and Hebrew letters have a numerical value. The total value of Nero's name in Hebrew is 666.

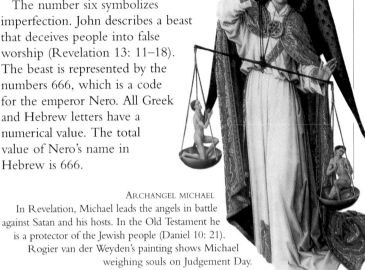

ARCHANGEL MICHAEL
In Revelation, Michael leads the angels in battle against Satan and his hosts. In the Old Testament he is a protector of the Jewish people (Daniel 10: 21). Rogier van der Weyden's painting shows Michael weighing souls on Judgement Day.

The lamb

The lamb is a recurring symbol in Revelation. It represents Jesus, who offered himself as the final sacrifice for humankind. This image recalls the Passover lamb, which was sacrificed to save the Israelites in Egypt (Exodus 12: 3).

The fall of Babylon

One of John's visions describes a harlot riding a scarlet dragon (Revelation 17: 3–5). She is referred to as "Babylon". In the Old Testament, the Babylonian empire was the enemy of Israel, and the prophets predicted its downfall. In the New Testament, "Babylon" is the enemy of the Church and represents the Roman empire.

The seven-sealed scroll

The final judgement of humankind is revealed to John through an angel, who opens seven seals on a scroll. John sees seven visions, which depict destruction, suffering, and famine. This imagery comes from Jeremiah, who foretold the end of the world: "I will destroy them with the sword, famine, and plague" (Jeremiah 14: 12).

THE BEAST OF THE SEA
This 14th-century French tapestry illustrates John's vision of a beast emerging from the sea (Revelation 13: 1–2). The beast represents the powers persecuting the Christians. It has the body of a leopard, the feet of a bear, and a lion's mouth. This recalls Daniel's vision of four beasts (Daniel 7: 1–7).

JOHN AND THE GREAT VISION

THE SEVEN CHURCHES, ASIA MINOR

✤

CHAPTER 1 VERSE 1
"The revelation"
The first word of the last book in the Bible, "revelation", is also the title of the book, just as "Genesis", (the beginning) is the title and first word of the first book. "Revelation" is the translation of the Greek word "Apokalupsis". Today, "apocalypse" suggests a catastrophic event, but in the Bible it means the disclosure of something hidden.

God sends an angel as a messenger to John

The angel tells John to write to the seven churches

1 THE[1] REVELATION of Jesus Christ, which God gave him to show his servants what must soon take place. He made it known by sending his angel to *his servant John*, [2]who testifies to everything he saw – that is, the word of God and the testimony of Jesus Christ. [3]*Blessed is the one* who reads the words of this prophecy, and blessed are those who hear it and take to heart what is written in it, because the time is near.

[4]John, to the seven churches in the province of Asia:

Grace and peace to you from him who is, and who was, and who is to come, and from the seven spirits before his throne, [5]and from Jesus Christ, who is the faithful witness, the firstborn from the dead, and the ruler of the kings of the earth. To him who loves us and has freed us from our sins by his blood, [6]and has made us to be a kingdom and priests to serve his God and Father – to him be glory and power for ever and ever! Amen.

[7]Look, he is coming with the clouds, and every eye will see him, even those who pierced him; and all the peoples of the earth will mourn because of him. So shall it be! Amen.

[8]"I am *the Alpha and the Omega*," says the Lord God, "who is, and who was, and who is to come, the Almighty."

[9]I, John, your brother and companion in the suffering and kingdom and patient endurance that are ours in Jesus, was on *the island of Patmos* because of the word of God and the testimony of Jesus. [10]On the Lord's day I was in the Spirit, and I heard behind me a loud voice like a trumpet, [11]which said: "Write on a scroll what you see and send it to the seven churches: to Ephesus, Smyrna, Pergamum, Thyatira, Sardis, Philadelphia and Laodicea."

[12]I turned round to see the voice that was speaking to me. And when I turned I saw seven golden lampstands, [13]and among the lampstands was someone "like a son of man", dressed in a robe reaching down to his feet and with a golden sash round his chest. [14]His head and hair were white like wool, as white as snow, and his eyes were like blazing fire. [15]His feet were like bronze glowing in a furnace, and his voice was like the sound of rushing waters. [16]In his right hand he held seven stars, and out of his mouth came a sharp *double-edged sword*. His face was like the sun shining in all its brilliance.

Seven stars

A double-edged sword

The keys to death and Hades

John turns to look at who is speaking to him and falls to the ground

Seven lampstands

The souls in Hades

JOHN'S VISION ON PATMOS
17th-century painting by Juan Sanchez

⊹

CHAPTER 1 VERSE 1
"His servant John"
The author of Revelation is traditionally thought to be the apostle John, the son of Zebedee, who wrote the Gospel of John and three short New Testament letters.

⊹

CHAPTER 1 VERSE 3
"Blessed is the one"
Revelation is a book of blessings to the Christian Church. This is the first of seven blessings in the book.

⊹

CHAPTER 1 VERSE 8
"The Alpha and the Omega"
Alpha is the first letter of the Greek alphabet; Omega is the last. The phrase means that God rules over his creation from the beginning to the end of time.

⊹

CHAPTER 1 VERSE 9
"The island of Patmos"
Patmos is a small rocky island in the Aegean Sea, south-west of Ephesus. During Roman times, Patmos was a penal island. John was probably sent there for preaching Jesus' message.

⊹

CHAPTER 1 VERSE 16
"Double-edged sword"
This sword can be used both to cut people free and as an instrument of judgement.

¹⁷When I saw him, I fell at his feet as though dead. Then he placed his right hand on me and said: "Do not be afraid. I am the First and the Last. ¹⁸I am the Living One; I was dead, and behold I am alive for ever and ever! And I hold the keys of death and Hades.

¹⁹"Write, therefore, what you have seen, what is now and what will take place later. ²⁰The mystery of the seven stars that you saw in my right hand and of the seven golden lampstands is this: the seven stars are the angels of the seven churches, and the seven lampstands are the seven churches."

UNDERSTANDING THE STORY

John's vision reveals the glory and majesty of the risen Jesus. The "Son of Man" has all the attributes of God and now shares his father's throne in the kingdom of heaven. The vision is a celebration of Jesus' triumph over death and his everlasting supremacy over God's creation.

THE SEVEN STARS

John writes to the seven churches

CHAPTER 2 VERSE 1
"To the angel of the church"
The seven angels – the seven stars of John's first vision (Revelation 1: 20) – refer to the leaders of the seven churches and their close relationship with God.

The church in Smyrna

Jesus promises the crown of life to those who suffer for their faith

---

CHAPTER 2 VERSES 1–5
"Ephesus... [I will] remove your lampstand"
Jesus tells the Ephesians that their religious zeal has become more important than their concern for each other. He warns them that he will remove his Church, their "lampstand", from Ephesus if they do not change their ways.

CHAPTER 2 VERSES 8–10
"Smyrna... I will give you the crown of life"
This letter gives encouragement to the Church in Smyrna, which was enduring persecution from the Jews. The battlements of the prosperous city looked like a crown. Jesus offers the crown of eternal life.

CHAPTER 2 VERSES 12–13
"Pergamum... where Satan has his throne"
Pergamum had the oldest temple dedicated to the worship of the Roman emperor. The head of the ruling empire is alluded to as the embodiment of evil.

2 To[1] THE ANGEL *of the church* in *Ephesus* write... [2]I know your deeds, your hard work and your perseverance. I know that you cannot tolerate wicked men, that you have tested those who claim to be apostles but are not... [4]Yet I hold this against you: You have forsaken your first love... [5]If you do not repent, I will come to you and *remove your lampstand* from its place...
[8]"To the angel of the church in *Smyrna* write... [9]I know your afflictions and your poverty – yet you are rich! ... [10]Do not be afraid of what you are about to suffer... Be faithful, even to the point of death, and *I will give you the crown of life...*
[12]"To the angel of the church in *Pergamum* write... [13]I know where you live – *where Satan has his throne.* Yet you remain true to my name... [14]Nevertheless, I have a few things against you: You have people there who hold to the teaching of Balaam, who taught Balak to entice the Israelites to sin by eating food sacrificed to idols and by committing sexual immorality... [16]Repent therefore! Otherwise, I will soon come to you and will fight against them with the sword of my mouth...

The church in Ephesus

Jesus threatens to remove their lampstand

The church in Pergamum

Jesus speaks about the evil of Rome

[18]"To the angel of the church in *Thyatira* write: These are the words of the Son of God, whose eyes are like blazing fire and whose feet are *like burnished bronze.* [19]I know your deeds, your love and faith... [20]Nevertheless, I have this against you: You tolerate that woman Jezebel, who calls herself a prophetess... [21]I have given her time to repent of her immorality, but she is unwilling... [24]Now I say... to you who do not hold to her teaching and have not learned Satan's so-called deep secrets... [25]Only hold on to what you have until I come...

Jesus warns against being seduced by false prophets

The church in Thyatira

The church in Sardis

Jesus tells people to wake up

3 ¹"To the angel of the church in *Sardis* write... I know your deeds; you have a reputation of being alive, but you are dead. ²Wake up!... ³Remember, therefore, what you have received and heard; obey it, and repent. But if you do not wake up, *I will come like a thief...* ⁴Yet you have a few people in Sardis who have not soiled their clothes. They will walk with me, dressed in white, for they are worthy. ⁵He who overcomes will, like them, be dressed in white...

⁷"To the angel of the church in *Philadelphia* write... ⁸I know your deeds. See, I have placed before you an open door that no-one can shut. I know that you have little strength, yet you have kept my word and have not denied my name... ⁹I will make those who are of the synagogue of Satan... come and fall down at your feet... ¹¹I am coming soon. Hold on to what you have, so that no-one will take your crown. ¹²Him who overcomes *I will make a pillar* in the temple of my God...

¹⁴"To the angel of the church in *Laodicea* write... ¹⁵I know your deeds, that you are *neither cold nor hot*. I wish you were either one or the other! ¹⁶So, because you are lukewarm... I am about to spit you out of my mouth. ¹⁷You say, 'I am rich... and do not need a thing.' But you do not realise that you are wretched, pitiful, poor, blind and naked. ¹⁸I counsel you to buy from me gold refined in the fire, so that you can become rich; and white clothes to wear, so that you can cover your shameful nakedness; and salve to put on your eyes, so that you can see... ²⁰"Here I am! I stand at the door and knock. If anyone hears my voice and opens the door, I will come in and eat with him, and he with me... ²²"He who has an ear, let him hear what the Spirit says to the churches."

The church in Philadelphia

The church in Laodicea

Jesus rejects those who are lukewarm about their faith

✤

CHAPTER 2 VERSE 18
"Thyatira... like burnished bronze"
Thyatira was famous for its trade guilds, in particular bronze workers. "Burnished bronze" was an alloy frequently used for making coins. Jesus offers a way of life brighter than the shining bronze in the city.

✤

CHAPTER 3 VERSES 1–3
"Sardis... I will come like a thief"
Sardis was once a wealthy city. It was built on a hill and was considered to be impregnable. Nevertheless, it was captured five times. Jesus warns against the same complacency within the Church.

Jesus offers the key to a better world

✤

CHAPTER 3
VERSES 7–12
"Philadelphia... I will make a pillar"
Philadelphia had suffered from many earthquakes that had left its buildings insecure. Jesus promises a secure and permanent home in the kingdom of God.

✤

CHAPTER 3 VERSES 14–15
"Laodicea... neither cold nor hot"
Laodicea was a prosperous city, but it had a poor water system. The nearby city of Colosse had clean, cold mountain water, and neighbouring Hierapolis had medicinal hot springs. But the water in Laodicea was lukewarm and polluted. Jesus urges the Church to be as refreshing as the water of Colosse and as healing as the water of Hierapolis.

LAODICEA, MODERN PAMUKKALE
Calcium carbonate formations

UNDERSTANDING THE STORY

John's letters reveal Jesus' concern for the Christian communities and his knowledge of their needs. The letters allude to the circumstances of the cities to which they are sent. Jesus offers the different communities advice, warnings, and promises so that they may become true reflections of the Universal Church.

REVELATION 12
THE WOMAN AND THE DRAGON

CHAPTER 12 VERSE 1
"A crown of twelve stars"
This woman represents the unfolding history of God's people. The twelve stars symbolize the twelve tribes of Israel, from whom Jesus, the Messiah is descended. His time on earth led to the birth of the Christian community.

In John's vision, a woman appears in heaven

A dragon waits to devour her child

CHAPTER 12 VERSE 3
"An enormous red dragon"
The dragon represents Satan, the primeval enemy of God. The sea-dragon was often depicted as a symbol of evil in ancient Near-Eastern mythologies. In this vision, the dragon has seven heads, which symbolize complete earthly knowledge, and ten horns, which symbolize great power.

CHAPTER 12 VERSE 5
"A son... with an iron sceptre"
This child is Jesus. The iron sceptre shows the strength and endurance of his reign.

CHAPTER 12 VERSE 5
"Snatched up to God"
This symbolizes Jesus' ascension to heaven to reign with God.

12 A GREAT[1] AND WONDROUS SIGN appeared in heaven: a woman clothed with the sun, with the moon under her feet and *a crown of twelve stars* on her head. [2]She was pregnant and cried out in pain as she was about to give birth. [3]Then another sign... *an enormous red dragon* with seven heads and ten horns and seven crowns on his heads. [4]His tail swept a third of the stars out of the sky and flung them to the earth. The dragon stood in front of the woman who was about to give birth, so that he might devour her child the moment it was born. [5]She gave birth to *a son, a male child, who will rule all the nations with an iron sceptre*. And her child was *snatched up to God* and to his throne. [6]The woman fled *into the desert* to a place prepared for her by God, where she might be taken care of *for 1,260 days*.

The child is taken up to heaven

There is a war in heaven

Michael and his angels fight the dragon

The dragon and its angels fall to earth

[7]And there was war in heaven. *Michael and his angels* fought against the dragon, and the dragon and his angels fought back. [8]But he was not strong enough, and they lost their place in heaven. [9]The great dragon was hurled down – that ancient serpent called the devil, or Satan, who leads the whole world astray. He was hurled to the earth, and his angels with him.

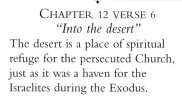

¹⁰Then I heard a loud voice in heaven say: "Now have come the salvation and the power and the kingdom of our God, and the authority of his Christ. For the accuser of our brothers, who accuses them before our God day and night, has been hurled down. ¹¹They overcame him by the blood of the Lamb and by the word of their testimony; they did not love their lives so much as to shrink from death. ¹²Therefore rejoice, you heavens and you who dwell in them! But woe to the earth and the sea, because the devil has gone down to you! He is filled with fury, because he knows that his time is short."

John hears a voice telling him that salvation has come

The dragon pursues the woman

¹³When the dragon saw that he had been hurled to the earth, he pursued the woman who had given birth to the male child. ¹⁴The woman was given the two wings of a great eagle, so that she might fly to the place prepared for her in the desert, where she would be taken care of for a time, times and half a time, out of the serpent's reach. ¹⁵Then from his mouth the serpent spewed water like a river, to overtake the woman and sweep her away with the torrent.

The woman escapes to the desert

SINAI DESERT
The Israelites lived in this desert for forty years.

CHAPTER 12 VERSE 6
"Into the desert"
The desert is a place of spiritual refuge for the persecuted Church, just as it was a haven for the Israelites during the Exodus.

CHAPTER 12 VERSE 6
"For 1,260 days"
1,260 days (three-and-a-half years) refers to the expression "a time, times and half a time" (v. 14). In the Book of Daniel, this denotes a finite period of time set by God for the rule of evil on earth before the final Judgement (Daniel 7: 25).

¹⁶But the earth helped the woman by opening its mouth and swallowing the river that the dragon had spewed out of his mouth. ¹⁷Then the dragon was enraged at the woman and went off to make war against the rest of her offspring – those who obey God's commandments and hold to the testimony of Jesus.

The dragon tries to drown the woman, but the earth swallows up the water

God gives her wings to fly to safety

CHAPTER 12 VERSE 7
"Michael and his angels"
Michael is an archangel, whose name means "who is like God?". In Daniel, Michael is referred to as the "great prince" who protects the people of God (Daniel 10: 13, 12: 1). In John's vision, the victory of Michael and his army over the dragon represents the victory of the Messiah and his followers over Satan.

UNDERSTANDING THE STORY

The characters of this vision appear in symbolic form and represent God and Satan engaged in a spiritual war. Defeated by the work of Jesus, God's enemy uses his remaining power to persecute the Church. But the Christian community is protected by Jesus, who gave his life to bring salvation.

REVELATION 20–22
THE NEW JERUSALEM

CHAPTER 20 VERSE 1
"The key to the Abyss"
The word "abyss" comes from the Greek word for "bottomless pit" and is used here to denote a place of torment. In the New Testament, the abyss is synonymous with hell.

The martyrs reign with Jesus

Satan is thrown into the abyss

20 I SAW[1] AN ANGEL coming down out of heaven, having *the key to the Abyss* and holding in his hand a great chain. [2]He seized the dragon, that ancient serpent, who is the devil, or Satan, and bound him for *a thousand years.* [3]He threw him into the Abyss, and locked and sealed it over him, to keep him from deceiving the nations any more until the thousand years were ended. After that he must be set free for a short time.

[4]I saw thrones on which were seated those who had been given authority to judge. And I saw the souls of those who had been beheaded because of their testimony for Jesus and because of the word of God... They came to life and reigned with Christ for a thousand years... [5]This is the first resurrection. [6]Blessed and holy are those who have part in the first resurrection...

[7]When the thousand years are over, Satan will be released from his prison [8]and go out to deceive the nations in the four corners of the earth − *Gog and Magog* − to gather them for battle. In number they are like the sand on the seashore. [9]They marched across the breadth of the earth and surrounded the camp of God's people, the city he loves. But fire came down from heaven and devoured them. [10]And the devil, who deceived them, was thrown into the lake of burning sulphur where the beast and the false prophet had been thrown. They will be tormented day and night for ever and ever.

The dead come out of the sea

The book of life reveals those who will inherit eternal life

CHAPTER 20 VERSE 2
"A thousand years"
This period is a time when Jesus will reign over the world, while Satan is imprisoned in the abyss.

CHAPTER 20 VERSE 8
"Gog and Magog"
These names are taken from Ezekiel's prophecy (Ezekiel 38–39), in which Gog and Magog are enemies of Israel. In Revelation, they are the last enemies of God: people from all nations who have united for a final battle against him.

CHAPTER 20 VERSE 12
"The book of life"
This book is inscribed with the names of all those who will inherit everlasting life.

The dead emerge from Hades

[11]Then I saw a great white throne and him who was seated on it. Earth and sky fled from his presence, and there was no place for them. [12]And I saw the dead, great and small, standing before the throne, and books were opened. Another book was opened, which is *the book of life*. The dead were judged according to what they had done as recorded in the books.

¹³The sea gave up the dead that were in it, and death and *Hades* gave up the dead that were in them, and each person was judged according to what he had done... ¹⁴*The lake of fire* is the second death. ¹⁵If anyone's name was not found written in the book of life, he was thrown into the lake of fire.

21 ¹Then I saw a new heaven and a new earth, for the first heaven and the first earth had passed away, and there was no longer any sea. ²I saw the Holy City, *the new Jerusalem*, coming down out of heaven from God, prepared as a bride beautifully dressed for her husband. ³And I heard a loud voice from the throne saying, "Now the dwelling of God is with men, and he will live with them. They will be his people, and God himself will be with them and be their God..."

22 ¹Then the angel showed me the river of the water of life, as clear as crystal, flowing from the throne of God and of the Lamb ²down the middle of the great street of the city. On each side of the river stood the tree of life, bearing twelve crops of fruit, yielding its fruit every month. And the leaves of the tree are for the healing of the nations... ⁶The angel said to me, "These words are trustworthy and true..."

¹⁶"I, Jesus, have sent my angel to give you this testimony for the churches. I am the Root and the Offspring of David, and the bright Morning Star."

¹⁷The Spirit and the bride say, "Come!" And let him who hears say, "Come!" Whoever is thirsty, let him come; and whoever wishes, let him take the free gift of the water of life.

The blood of life flows from the lamb

The water of life flows through the city

The tree of life

The angel shows John the new Jerusalem

UNDERSTANDING THE STORY

In John's final description of paradise, Jerusalem is a new Creation. This holy city is even more magnificent than the Garden of Eden. Evil is defeated and can no longer come between God and his people. The new Jerusalem is a place of eternal blessing, where perfect communion exists between God and his creation.

CHAPTER 20 VERSE 13
"Hades"
The Greek word "Hades" describes the realm of the dead. The Bible says very little about the state of the dead between their death and the end of the world, but it was thought that all departed spirits live in a place called "Hades" ("Sheol" in Hebrew), where they await the final judgement day.

CHAPTER 20 VERSE 14
"The lake of fire"
Fire is often used as a symbol of God's wrath. Here, the lake is the "second death" (20: 14) – a place of eternal punishment and separation from God.

CHAPTER 21 VERSE 2
"The new Jerusalem"
John describes a city with walls of jasper and gates of pearl built on foundations encrusted with jewels (Revelation 21: 18–21). There is no longer the need for a temple because the new Jerusalem is a heaven on earth, where God and humanity dwell in spiritual harmony – God's grace pervades everything.

PEOPLE OF THE OLD TESTAMENT

The Old Testament spans a vast period of time. Accurate dating is often impossible but, for those people who can be given dates, they are all BC.

AARON
Older brother of Moses. Aaron was more eloquent than Moses and became joint spokesman for the Israelites at the time of the Exodus. When Moses was on Mount Sinai, Aaron gave in to the Israelites' demand for an idol. Despite this, he was appointed High Priest and his descendants were given the responsibility for Israel's priesthood.

AARON AND MOSES

ABDON
11th-century minor Judge from a wealthy family who led Israel for eight years.

ABEDNEGO
Babylonian name given to Azariah, one of Daniel's three companions who were thrown into a furnace because they worshipped God.

ABEL
Second son of Adam and Eve. He was a shepherd who was killed by his jealous brother Cain because his offering to God was accepted, whereas Cain's was rejected. "Abel" means "breath" in Hebrew, highlighting the brevity and fragility of his life.

ABIGAIL
Beautiful wife of the wealthy Nabal, who refused David help while David was an outlaw. Abigail persuaded David not to kill her husband. She later married David.

ABIJAH
King of Judah (913–10) and son of Rehoboam and Maacah (the daughter of Absalom). He reigned during a period of continual wars between Israel and Judah.

ABISHAG
A Shunammite girl who looked after the dying King David.

ABNER
Saul's cousin and his army commander. He supported Saul's son Ish-Bosheth in his struggle against David for the monarchy.

ABRAM/ABRAHAM
Son of Terah, Abraham became the first Patriarch of Israel. He was chosen by God to be the forefather of the Israelite nation. His wife, Sarah, gave him her maidservant, Hagar, who bore him a son called Ishmael. Both Hagar and Ishmael were then driven out by the jealous Sarah. His second son by Sarah, named Isaac, inherited his father's dynasty. Abraham is seen as a model for complete faith in God.

ABSALOM
Rebellious son of King David who revolted against his father in an attempt to gain the throne. When Absalom's long hair became caught in the branches of an oak tree during a battle, he was killed by David's army chief, Joab.

ACHAN
An Israelite who broke God's commandment by looting Jericho after its defeat by Joshua. He and his family were stoned to death.

ADAM
Adam (Hebrew for "man") was the first man and husband of Eve. God gave them dominion over the world. It was their original sin that robbed humanity of its immortality.

ADONIJAH
Fourth son of David and heir to the throne. He was set aside when Solomon was proclaimed king. Adonijah was later killed by Solomon.

AGAG
Title or name of an Amalekite king. He was defeated by Saul, who spared him (despite God's instructions that Agag should be killed). Agag was later killed by Samuel the prophet.

AGUR
Probable author of Proverbs 30. In his prayer, Agur asked God for deliverance from hardship.

AHAB
Son of Omri and king of Israel (874–53). He was a successful military leader, with a strong and stable government. He was also the first king of Israel to encounter Assyrian attacks. He married the Phoenician princess Jezebel and allowed her to promote Baal-worship in Israel.

AHAZ
Eleventh king of Judah (735–15) who suffered the effects of increasing Assyrian power. He was considered an evil king. He sacrificed his own son to pagan gods.

AHAZIAH
1. Son of King Ahab by Jezebel and king of Israel (853–52). During his brief reign, he allowed the worship of Baal. When he fell ill, he turned to Baal rather than God. He died shortly afterwards.
2. Son of Jehoram, grandson of Ahab, and king of Judah (841–41). He was assassinated by Jehu, a military commander who succeeded Jehoram as king of Israel.

AMALEK
A grandson of Esau and ancestor of the Amalekites. This tribe became a bitter enemy of Israel.

AMASA
Nephew of David and commander of Absalom's army. After Absalom was murdered, he took over from his cousin Joab as commander of David's army. He was later murdered by Joab.

AMAZIAH
King of Judah (792–67) and son of Joash. He successfully defeated the Edomites, but was later assassinated.

AMNON
First-born son of David, who raped his half-sister, Tamar. His half-brother, Absalom, then killed Amnon to avenge the rape.

AMON
Son of Manasseh, father of Josiah, and king of Judah (642–40). His brief reign ended when he was assassinated by his servants.

AMOS
8th-century prophet and shepherd whose message of doom for Israel is recorded in the Book of Amos.

ANAK
A giant who was the ancestor of the Anakites (Goliath was probably an Anakite).

ARTAXERXES
Persian king (465–24) who authorized the rebuilding of the walls in Jerusalem under Nehemiah.

ASA
Son of Abijah and king of Judah (910–869), his reign was dominated by continued conflicts with Israel. He was faithful to God and denounced the worship of Baal and Asherah.

ASHER
Son of Jacob by Zilpah and ancestral head of the tribe of Asher.

ATHALIAH
Daughter of Ahab and Jezebel (of Israel) who married Jehoram (king of Judah) and became the only ruling queen of Judah (841–35). She secured her position by murdering all her grandsons except Jehoash. She was killed in a revolt led by a priest.

BALAAM

BAASHA

King of Israel (908–886) who won the throne by killing his predecessor, Nadab.

CAIN

BALAAM

Non-Israelite prophet who practised divination. He was hired by King Balak to curse Israel. God intervened, and Balaam blessed the Israelites instead. Balaam was killed when the Israelites invaded Canaan.

BALAK

King of Moab at the time when Israel entered Canaan (c. 1400). He is notable for asking the non-Israelite prophet Balaam to curse Israel.

BARAK

A military leader under the Judge Deborah. He helped defeat the Canaanites.

BATHSHEBA

Wife of Uriah the Hittite. She was seen bathing on her roof by King David, who seduced her. When her pregnancy could no longer be hidden, David ordered Uriah to be killed and married Bathsheba. God punished their adultery through the death of their baby.

BELSHAZZAR

Last king of Babylon. Notable for the mysterious writing that appeared on his palace wall, which Daniel interpreted to mean the Persian conquest of Babylon.

BENJAMIN

Youngest of the twelve sons of Jacob and Rachel and ancestral head of the tribe of Benjamin. He was the only full brother of Joseph and was favoured by Jacob.

BETHUEL

Son of Nahor and Milcah and father of Laban and Rebekah.

BILHAH

Rachel's servant who was given as a concubine to Jacob because Rachel seemed to be barren. She bore Jacob two sons, Dan and Naphthali.

BOAZ

Wealthy man from Bethlehem who married Ruth. He became the great-grandfather of King David through their son Obed.

CAIN

First son of Adam and Eve. Cain was a farmer. When his offering was rejected by God, he became jealous of his brother Abel and killed him.

CALEB

Friend of Joshua. Both were sent as spies to look over the land of Canaan. Caleb and Joshua were the only adults of the Exodus generation who inherited the Promised Land.

CANAAN

Grandson of Noah, son of Ham, and ancestor of the Canaanites.

CYRUS II

Persian emperor and founder of the Persian empire. Under his rule (549–30), the Jewish people were allowed to return to Judah from exile in Babylon. He also permitted the rebuilding of the Temple in Jerusalem.

DAN

Fifth son of Jacob and ancestral head of the tribe of Dan.

DANIEL

6th-century prophet who was taken into exile by King Nebuchadnezzar. Daniel, who trained as an administrator, gained favour with the king because of his ability to interpret dreams. He was also thrown into the lions' den by King Darius, but miraculously survived.

DARIUS

Persian king who succeeded Belshazzar (522–486). Darius is notable for throwing Daniel to the lions.

DAVID

Youngest son of Jesse, David was a shepherd who became the greatest king of Israel. His reign heralded a golden era. David defeated Israel's enemies, united his people, increased the size of the nation, and established Jerusalem as the political and religious centre of Israel. David was also a great musician. He is the accredited author of many of the psalms in the Bible.

DEBORAH

13th-century prophetess. Under her leadership, Israel was liberated from its enemies for forty years.

DELILAH

The woman who tricked Samson into revealing the secret of his strength, which was the length of his hair. She betrayed him to the rulers of the Philistines, who each offered her 1,100 silver shekels.

DINAH

The daughter of Jacob and Leah. She was raped by Shechem, a neighbouring prince.

EDOM (see ESAU)

Another name for Esau, which means "red" – Esau sold his inheritance for a red stew.

EHUD

13th-century Benjamite Judge who was chosen by God to bring the Israelites out of the control of Eglon, the king of Moab. Ehud killed Eglon with a dagger under the guise of bringing him presents.

ELAH

King of Israel (886–85) and son of Baasha. Elah was murdered after only a brief period as king.

ELI

High Priest during the period of the Judges who trained Samuel during his childhood. Eli's own sons were disobedient and sinful, and were eventually killed. Samuel took over from Eli as the next High Priest.

ELIEZER

Head servant who was sent by Abraham to find a suitable wife for his son Isaac.

ELIJAH

9th-century Israelite prophet. He confronted Ahab when Ahab tried to establish Baal-worship and publicly proved that Baal was a false god. His prophetic message emphasized unconditional loyalty and responsibility to God. Elijah is the only Old Testament character, other than Enoch, who did not die. Instead he was taken up to heaven in a whirlwind.

ELIMELECH

Husband of Naomi. He was from Bethlehem but died in Moab.

ELISHA

Successor and disciple of Elijah, Elisha was the leading 9th-century prophet in Israel during the reigns of Joram, Jehu, Jehoahaz, and Jehoash. He worked many miracles for both the nation and for individuals.

ELKANAH

Levite husband of Hannah and father of Samuel.

ELON

12th-century Judge from the tribe of Zebulun who led Israel for ten years.

ENOCH

Seventh son of Adam. He lived for 365 years. Like Elijah, he was taken up to heaven.

EPHRAIM

Younger and more favoured son of Joseph by Asenath and the ancestral head of the tribes of Ephraim.

ESAU (see EDOM)

Son of Isaac and Rebekah and twin brother of Jacob. Esau despised his birthright and gave it away to Jacob for a bowl of stew. He was tricked out of his father's blessing by Rebekah and Jacob. Esau was also known as Edom (which means "red") and became the ancestral head of the tribe of Edom.

DAVID AND BATHSHEBA

EVE

First woman created by God and the wife of Adam. Eve was deceived by a serpent and ate from the forbidden Tree of Knowledge. She then persuaded Adam to eat from the same tree. For their disobedience, God banished them from Eden, and sin and death came into the world.

EZEKIEL

6th-century prophet and priest during the period of Babylonian exile whose prophetic message is recorded in the Book of Ezekiel. He foretold the fall of Jerusalem. Later his message was more hopeful, and he spoke about the coming of the Messiah.

EZRA

Priest during the time of Artaxerxes and Nehemiah whose words are recorded in the Book of Ezra.

GAD

Eldest son of Jacob by Leah's maidservant Zilpah and ancestral father of the tribe of Gad.

GIDEON

12th-century Judge who delivered Israel from the Midianites and the Amalekites.

GILEAD

Grandson of Manasseh (Joseph's elder son) and ancestral founder of the Gileadite clan.

GOLIATH

Giant of Gath at the time of King David. He was the leading warrior of the Philistine army and challenged the Israelites to fight with him. The young David took up the challenge and slew him with a stone and sling.

HABAKKUK

7th-century minor prophet who lived through the Babylonian conquests. His message is recorded in the Book of Habakkuk. He called for the corruption of Judah to be judged and urged the Israelites to be more faithful to God.

HAGAR

Egyptian maidservant of Sarah (Abraham's wife) who was given to Abraham as a concubine. She bore a son called Ishmael.

GIDEON

HAGGAI

Late 6th-century prophet who lived in Babylon. His prophecies are recorded in the Book of Haggai. He urged the Jewish people to return to Jerusalem and finish the rebuilding of the Temple.

HAM

Second son of Noah, who saw his father lying drunk and naked in his tent. Noah was furious and cursed Ham's descendants through Ham's son Canaan.

GOLIATH

HAMAN

Favoured nobleman of King Xerxes. He plotted to massacre the Jews because he wanted to punish a Jew called Mordecai, who refused to honour him. Haman's plans were discovered and defeated by Esther, and he died on the gallows he had built for Mordecai.

HANNAH

Wife of Elkanah and mother of Samuel. She was blessed by the High Priest Eli as she prayed for a child in the Temple. When she bore a son, Samuel, she was so grateful that she dedicated him to God.

HEZEKIAH

King of Judah (715–686) and son of Ahaz, Hezekiah inherited a kingdom that was under the control of the Assyrians. Despite these difficulties, Hezekiah reestablished worship at the Temple in Jerusalem and banned many pagan practices.

HIRAM

King of Tyre (987–44) and ally of David and Solomon. Under Hiram's rule, Tyre became the leading city of Phoenicia. David made a treaty with Hiram against the Philistines, and Hiram provided materials to build the Temple in Jerusalem. He also provided ships for Solomon's trading interests.

HOSEA

8th-century prophet during the last years of the northern kingdom of Israel. Hosea's message is recorded in the Book of Hosea.

HOSHEA

Hoshea was the last king of Israel (732–22) and a comtemporary of Ahaz and Hezekiah. He usurped the throne and served as a vassal king to Tiglath-Pileser III and Shalmaneser V. He was later imprisoned, and Samaria was seized by the Assyrians.

HUR

Chief lieutenant of Moses who stood with Aaron during the battle against the Amalekites and held up Moses' arms to ensure victory for the Israelites.

ISAAC

Son of Abraham and Sarah. Isaac was the fulfilment of God's promise of a son by Sarah, with whom an eternal covenant would be established. God chose to test Abraham's faith by asking him to sacrifice Isaac. When he was about to kill the boy, God intervened and told Abraham to sacrifice a ram instead.

ISAIAH

8th-century prophet, counsellor, and traditional author of the Book of Isaiah. Isaiah was probably the son of Amoz, the brother of King Amaziah. He foretold the destruction of Israel by the Assyrians and warned against the sinfulness he saw among the people of Israel.

ISH-BOSHETH

Fourth son of Saul, who was made king of Israel by Saul's commander, Abner. He attempted to rule over all the tribes, but Judah refused to make an alliance. He was defeated by King David of Judah.

ISHMAEL

Son of Abraham and Hagar (an Egyptian concubine). Although Ishmael and Hagar were driven out by Sarah, Abraham's jealous wife, God promised that a great nation would descend from Ishmael.

ISRAEL

Name meaning "He strives with God" given to Jacob by God. Jacob became the ancestor of the Israelites.

ISSACHAR

Son of Jacob by Leah and ancestral head of the tribe of Issachar.

JABIN

Canaanite King of Hazor who led a coalition of Canaanite kings against the Israelites. He was defeated by Joshua. All the Canaanite kings were killed.

JACOB

Son of Isaac and Rebekah and younger twin brother of Esau. He bought Esau's birthright with a bowl of stew and later took Esau's blessing by deceiving their father. It was Jacob's twelve sons who became the ancestral heads of the tribes of Israel.

JAEL

Wife of Heber the Kenite who lived during the period of the Judges. She killed Sisera, commander of Jabin's army (Jabin was king of Hazor) by driving a tent peg through his head.

JAIR

Father of Mordecai and uncle of Esther.

JAPHET

Third son of Noah and brother of Shem and Ham.

JEHOAHAZ

1. Son of Jehu and king of Israel (814–798).
2. Son of Josiah and king of Judah (609–09) who reigned for three months before Pharaoh Neco deposed him.

JEHOASH

1. Son of Jehoahaz and king of Israel (798–82) who defeated the Syrian armies three times in accordance with the prophecy of Elisha.
2. Son of Ahaziah. He was saved from Athaliah's (daughter of Jezebel) murderous intentions by his aunt. He later revolted against the tyrannical rule of Athaliah and became king of Judah (835–796).

JEHOIACHIN

Son of Jehoiakim and king of Judah (598–97) who was taken into captivity by Nebuchadnezzar after only three months on the throne.

JEHOIAKIM

Son of Josiah and king of Judah (609–598). Pharaoh Neco made him king to replace Jehoahaz.

JEZEBEL AND AHAB

JEHORAM
1. Son of Jehoshaphat and king of Judah (848–41). When he became king, he murdered his six brothers and married Athaliah, the corrupt daughter of Ahab. During his reign, Judah and Israel had a closer alliance. He was later afflicted with an incurable disease and died without a royal burial.
2. Brother and successor of Ahaziah and king of Israel (852–41).

JEHOSHAPHAT
Son of Asa and king of Judah (872–48). He allied himself with the untrustworthy Ahab, king of Israel, and foolishly married his own son to Ahab's daughter. Despite his mistakes, he was a just and faithful king.

JOAB

JEHU
King of Israel, anointed by Elisha (841–14), Jehu killed King Joram and King Ahaziah and attempted to slaughter their families.

JEPHTHAH
Son of Gilead by a harlot who was driven out from his family. Jephthah was eventually asked to be a Judge (11th century). During his rule, he delivered Israel from the Ammonites.

JEREMIAH
7th-century prophet from a distinguished priestly family who lived during the last years of the kingdom of Judah. He predicted the fall of Jerusalem and the seventy years of exile in Babylon. Often persecuted, Jeremiah was driven to extreme despair, but he never gave up hope.

JEROBOAM I
Son of Nebat and the first king of Israel after the division of the kingdom (930–09). He set up golden idols, built shrines on the high places, and adopted the role of pagan priest.

JEROBOAM II
Son of Jehoash and king of Israel (793–53). During his rule, Assyrian domination decreased, and Jeroboam was able to expand the kingdom. However, he was criticized for the continuation of Baal-worship and the increasing number of people who were living in poverty.

JESSE
Father of David, descended from Adam and Seth through Shem and Boaz. He was a wealthy farmer from Bethlehem who became the ancestor of the royal and messianic line of David and, ultimately, Jesus.

JETHRO
Father-in-law of Moses and a Midianite priest. He looked after Moses' wife and sons during the Exodus.

JEZEBEL
Phoenician princess and wife of King Ahab who promoted Baal-worship in Israel. She gave great offence to many in Israel and was considered an idolatress and a harlot. She was eventually killed by being pushed out of a window and eaten by dogs. Her name is associated with female wickedness.

JOAB
Son of Zeruiah, David's sister, and commander of David's army. He was a ruthless leader who won many victories against Israel's enemies. He ended the rebellion against David by killing Absalom, David's son.

JOB
A native of Uz, whose unexplained suffering is the subject of the Book of Job. Job endured his afflictions by faith in God and this led to his eventual return to prosperity.

JOEL
1. Son of Samuel who became a Judge. His corruption led to the Israelite demand for a king.
2. Prophet whose words are recorded in the Book of Joel (date unknown). He interpreted a locust plague as a warning from God.

JONAH
8th-century prophet who tried to escape his calling from God to save the city of Nineveh. Jonah ran away from God by boarding a ship. When God sent a great storm, Jonah confessed his crime to the sailors, who threw him overboard. He miraculously survived inside the body of a great fish.

JONATHAN
Eldest son of King Saul and a close friend of David. Jonathan took David's side when Saul turned against him and warned David that his father wished him dead. Jonathan and all his brothers died in Saul's last battle against the Philistines.

JOSEPH
Favoured son of Jacob by Rachel. Joseph was sold as a slave to the Egyptians by his jealous brothers. Once in Egypt, he gained favour with the pharaoh by interpreting his dreams and rose to a powerful position. He protected Egypt from severe famine and also saved his own family. Later the tribe of Joseph was divided into Ephraim and Manasseh.

JOSHUA
Ephraimite son of Nun and successor of Moses, he led the second generation of the Exodus across the River Jordan into Canaan. He fought and won the battles of Jericho and Ai, which established the Israelites in the Promised Land.

JOSIAH
King of Judah (640–09) and son of Amon. Josiah ruled during the decline of the Assyrian empire. Josiah made many religious reforms. He rediscovered the Book of the Law and renewed the covenant with God. Against God's will, he attacked the Egyptians and was killed in the battle.

JOTHAM
Son of Uzziah and king of Judah (750–35). During his lengthy and just reign he strengthened Jerusalem's walls, built fortified cities, and defeated the Ammonites.

JUDAH
Son of Jacob and Leah and the forefather of the tribe of Judah.

KETURAH
Concubine of Abraham after the death of Sarah. She bore him six sons.

LABAN
Grandson of Nahor, brother of Rebekah, and father of Rachel and Leah. He tricked Jacob into marrying Leah even though he had promised Jacob that he could marry Rachel in return for seven years' work. He then made Jacob work for seven more years to marry Rachel.

LEAH
Daughter of Laban who became Jacob's first wife. Her father tricked Jacob into marrying her instead of Rachel, her younger sister.

LEVI
Son of Jacob and Leah and forefather of the Levite tribe.

LOT
Son of Haran and nephew of Abraham. Lot settled in the corrupt city of Sodom. When God decided to destroy the city, Lot and his family were allowed to escape. Lot went to live in a cave with his two daughters, who feared they would not get married and seduced him when he was drunk. They each bore a son, Moab and Ben-Ammi, who became the ancestors of the Moabites and the Ammonites.

MALACHI
5th-century prophet whose message is recorded in the Book of Malachi, which is the last book of prophecy in the Old Testament.

JOSEPH AND HIS BROTHERS

MANASSEH
1. Son of Hezekiah and king of Judah (697–42) who led Israel back into idolatry. After the exile in Babylon, he repented and became king again.
2. Son of Joseph who was adopted by Jacob and became one of the ancestral heads of the tribes of Israel.

MANOAH
Father of Samson. Manoah was told by an angel that his son would deliver Israel from the Philistines.

MENAHEM
Son of Gadi and king of Israel (752–42) who killed Shallum, the previous king of Israel. His rule was notable for its cruelty and idolatry.

MESHACH
Babylonian name given to Mishael, one of the friends of Daniel who refused to stop worshipping God.

MICAH
8th-century prophet whose message is recorded in the Book of Micah.

MICHAL
Younger daughter of Saul and first wife of David. She protected her husband when Saul plotted to kill him. She later criticized David for his behaviour in front of the crowds in Jerusalem, and for this she was condemned to die childless.

MIDIAN
Son of Abraham by Keturah (his concubine) and ancestral forefather of the Midianites.

MIRIAM
Sister of Moses and Aaron who rebelled against Moses' leadership in the desert, for which she was temporarily afflicted with leprosy.

MORDECAI
Cousin of Esther (who became the wife and queen of King Xerxes) during the exile in Babylon. Mordecai overheard a plot to kill the king and reported it to Esther. When Haman, the king's favourite official, plotted to destroy all the Jewish people, Esther told the king. Mordecai was promoted to high office, and Haman was hanged.

MOSES
Son of a Levite couple but brought up in the pharaoh's court in Egypt, he became Israel's greatest leader and prophet. With God's guidance, he brought the Israelites out of slavery in Egypt, received the Law from God on Mount Sinai, and finally led them to the Promised Land. The first five books of the Bible (the Pentateuch) are traditionally attributed to Moses.

NEBUCHADNEZZAR

NAAMAN
Commander of the Syrian army who was cured of leprosy by the prophet Elisha by washing seven times in the River Jordan.

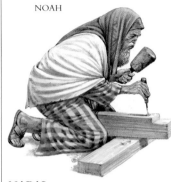

NOAH

NABAL
Wealthy Calebite and husband of Abigail who refused to give provisions to David and his army. His insulting behaviour angered David, who then decided to kill him. Nabal was spared death by Abigail, who appeased David.

NABOTH
Owner of a vineyard that King Ahab coveted. When Naboth refused to part with it, Jezebel, Ahab's wife, spread a rumour that he was guilty of blasphemy. As a result, Naboth was stoned to death.

NADAB
Son of Jeroboam I and king of Israel (909–08). He was killed in his second year as king by Baasha.

NAHOR
Son of Terah and brother of Abraham, he married his niece Milcah. Nahor's granddaughter was Rebekah, who married Isaac.

NAHUM
7th-century prophet born in south-western Judah whose message is recorded in the Book of Nahum.

NAOMI
Wife of Elimelech from Bethlehem and the mother-in-law of Ruth.

NAPHTALI
Second son of Jacob by Bilhah. He was the ancestor of the tribe of Naphtali.

NATHAN
10th-century prophet in King David's court who rebuked David for his adultery with Bathsheba. He prophesied that David would establish an everlasting dynasty.

NEBUCHADNEZZAR
King of Babylon (605–562) who captured Jerusalem and deported all the Israelite people to Babylon. He was a powerful and successful leader who embellished Babylon and made it into a magnificent city with palaces, temples, and the famous hanging gardens.

NEHEMIAH
Cup-bearer to King Cyrus and then governor of Jerusalem. After the return from exile, he initiated the rebuilding of the city walls. He also continued to re-establish God's Law in Jerusalem and to condemn any deviation from it. His words are recorded in the Book of Nehemiah.

NIMROD
Son of Cush and ancient Mesopotamian king who established a kingdom in Babylonia sometime before Abraham's day. He was a hunter and warrior and founded many ancient cities, including Babel.

NOAH
Son of Lamech and ninth descendant of Adam through Seth. God saved Noah and his family from the great flood by instructing them to build an ark.

RUTH

OBADIAH
6th-century prophet whose words are recorded in the Book of Obadiah. He prophesied against the Edomites, predicting that they would fall under the power of the Babylonians.

OMRI
Commander of the army of King Elah and later became the sixth king of Israel (885–74). He was known for establishing Samaria as the capital of the northern kingdom. This city was situated on trade routes and was easy to defend.

OTHNIEL
Brother of Caleb and 14th-century Judge. He recaptured the city of Debir, and, in doing so, he was given his niece Acsah for a wife.

PEKAH
Military officer who assassinated Pekahiah and became king of Israel (752–32). Although he was an ally of Rezin, King of Syria, he was defeated by the Assyrians and finally murdered by Hoshea.

PEKAHIAH
King of Israel (742–40) during the period before the destruction of its capital, Samaria. His brief reign ended when he was assassinated by Pekah, one of his military officers.

POTIPHAR
Egyptian officer in the pharaoh's guard who bought Joseph as a slave. Although he recognized Joseph's talent, he threw him into prison because his wife made a false accusation against him.

POTIPHERA
Father of Joseph's wife, Asenath, and an Egyptian priest.

RACHEL
Daughter of Laban, sister of Leah, and wife of Jacob. She had two sons, Joseph and Benjamin, and died giving birth to the latter.

RAHAB
Prostitute in Jericho who protected two Israelite spies by hiding them in bundles of flax on her roof. When Jericho was destroyed, she and her family were spared and they joined the Israelites.

REBEKAH
Daughter of Bethuel, wife of Isaac, and the mother of the twins Jacob and Esau. She helped Jacob, her favourite, obtain his father's blessing by tricking her husband, who was blind.

REHOBOAM
Son of Solomon and king of Judah (930–13). The kingdom divided under his rule when Israel rebelled against the heavy taxation that Solomon had imposed. The ten northern tribes formed the northern kingdom, ruled by Jeroboam. Rehoboam was left ruling the two southern tribes, Judah and Benjamin.

REUBEN
Eldest son of Jacob and Leah and the ancestral head of the tribe of Reuben. He persuaded his brothers not to kill Joseph and later suggested that the famine was a result of their mistreatment of him. However, he lost his birthright because he had an affair with Jacob's concubine.

RUTH

Moabite wife of Mahlon, the son of Elimelech, and daughter-in-law of Naomi. When her husband and sons died, she married Boaz, her kinsman.

SAMSON

11th-century Judge. He was a Nazirite, who possessed heroic strength because of his long hair. He fell in love with Delilah, who betrayed him. She cut Samson's hair and handed him over to the Philistines. He avenged himself by collapsing the pillars of a Philistine temple, which killed everyone inside, including Samson.

SAMUEL

Son of Elkanah and Hannah, 11th-century prophet, and the last Judge. Under his leadership, Israel recaptured the coastal cities from the Philistines. Samuel, despite warning the people of the dangers of a monarchy, anointed Saul – and later David – as kings of Israel.

SARAH

Wife and half-sister of Abraham. She was told by God that her son would be the forefather of a great nation. Barren for most of her life, she gave birth to a son, Isaac, in extreme old age.

SAUL

Benjamite son of Kish, Saul was chosen as the first king of Israel because of his strength as a military leader. Although he began his reign successfully, he disobeyed God and was eventually rejected as king. He died in battle against the Philistines.

SENNACHERIB

King of Assyria (705–681) who ruled during a period of great rebellion. He defeated Babylon, took over the cities of Judah, and attacked Jerusalem. He was later assassinated by two of his sons.

SETH

Third son of Adam and Eve and the father of Enosh.

SHADRACH

Babylonian name for Hananniah, Daniel's companion. He was thrown into a furnace because he refused to stop worshipping God.

SHALLUM

Son of Jabesh and king of Israel (753–52). He became king by assassinating Zechariah (the last of the Jehu dynasty). He was assassinated in the first year of his rule.

SHALMANESER

Son of Tiglath-Pileser III and king of Assyria (727–22). At first he enjoyed tribute from Hoshea, king of Israel, but then both Israel and Phoenicia rebelled. As a result he besieged Samaria but died before it had been conquered. Sargon II succeeded him and won the city.

SHAMGAR

Minor Judge (date unknown) who delivered the Israelites from the Philistines. He used an ox goad to kill 600 men in the Philistine army.

SHEM

Eldest son of Noah, he received Noah's blessing and became the ancestor of the Semitic race.

SIMEON

Second son of Jacob by Leah and ancestral head of the tribe of Simeon. He was kept in Egypt by Joseph to ensure that his brothers returned.

SISERA

Captain of the army of Jabin, king of Canaan. When his army was defeated by the Israelite army, led by Deborah and Barak, he took refuge in a nearby camp. He was killed by Jael, who had sided with the Israelites. Jael hammered a tent peg through Sisera's temple while he was asleep.

SAMSON

SOLOMON

Son of David and Bathsheba and third king of Israel. He led Israel into prosperity and built the Temple as a centre of worship. He was renowned for his wisdom. He is the accredited author of Proverbs, as well as the Book of Ecclesiastes and the Song of Songs. His many foreign wives led him into idolatry in later life.

TAMAR

Daughter of David who was raped by her half-brother Amnon. She was avenged by her brother Absalom, who killed Amnon.

TERAH

Father of Abraham and descendant of Shem. He possibly migrated from Ur because of foreign attacks on his tribe.

SAMUEL

SAUL

TIGLATH-PILESER

King of Assyria (745–27) who reorganized and reestablished the Assyrian empire. He conquered Babylon, expanded his territory, and gained control of Damascus as well as Galilee and Gilead. He also made the kings of Israel and Judah pay tribute to him.

TOLA

11th-century minor Judge from the tribe of Issachar.

URIAH

Husband of Bathsheba and Hittite officer who was killed under King David's orders because Bathsheba was pregnant with David's child.

UZZIAH

Son of Amaziah who is also referred to as Azariah and King of Judah (792–40). After a long and pious reign, he was afflicted by leprosy because he usurped priestly rights in the Temple.

XERXES

Son of Darius the Great and ruler of the Persian empire (486–65). He divorced his wife Vashti to marry Esther (the Jewish orphan). During his reign, he suffered many defeats against Greece, but the stability of his empire was unaffected.

ZADOK

High Priest whose family had controlled the priesthood from Solomon's time. He supported David during Absalom's revolt. After David's death, he helped secure the throne for Solomon.

ZEBULUN

Son of Jacob and Leah and ancestral head of the tribe of Zebulun.

ZECHARIAH

Late 6th-century prophet and priest whose visions and message are recorded in the Book of Zechariah. He tried to reawaken faith in the largely demoralized and apathetic Jewish people. He predicted a Messiah who would bring peace.

ZEDEKIAH

Son of Josiah and the last king of Judah (597–86). He was placed on the throne as a vassal king by Nebuchadnezzar after the conquest of Jerusalem in 597. Zedekiah later rebelled and Nebuchadnezzar sacked Jerusalem, taking the wounded king and the Jewish people to Babylon.

ZEPHANIAH

7th-century prophet during the reign of King Josiah of Judah whose words are recorded in the Book of Zephaniah. He believed that God's wrath was imminent but also that the house of David would survive.

ZERUBBABEL

Prince of Judah who was the spiritual and political leader when the Jewish people were in exile in Babylon. He led the first return to Judah and initiated the rebuilding of the Temple.

ZILPAH

Maidservant of Leah who was given to Jacob as a concubine. She had two children, Asher and Gad.

ZIPPORAH

Daughter of Jethro and wife of Moses. When God threatened to kill Moses because one of their sons had not been circumcised, Zipporah took out a stone and circumcised her son immediately.

SOLOMON

PEOPLE OF THE NEW TESTAMENT

The New Testament spans a period of about ninety years. It begins just before Jesus' birth and ends in the early years of the Christian Church.

ANANIAS
1. Husband of Sapphira. He tried to deceive the early Church.
2. A Christian in Damascus who cured Saul of his blindness.

ANDREW
Brother of Peter and one of the twelve disciples. He was first a disciple of John the Baptist and later joined Jesus' ministry.

ANNA
Prophetess who recognized the baby Jesus as the Messiah.

ANNAS
Former High Priest who questioned Jesus after his arrest.

AQUILA
Early Christian and husband of Priscilla. Aquila and his wife became loyal friends of Paul.

BARABBAS
Prisoner released from jail by Pontius Pilate at the crowd's request. Jesus was crucified in his place.

CAIAPHAS

BARTHOLOMEW
One of the twelve disciples. Church tradition claims he became a missionary in Armenia and India.

CAESAR AUGUSTUS
The first Roman emperor (31 BC–AD 14). Jesus was born during his reign.

CAIAPHAS
Son-in-law and successor of Annas. Caiaphas was High Priest at the time of Jesus' illegal trial in front of the Sanhedrin.

CLAUDIUS CAESAR
Roman emperor (AD 41–54) who was the successor to Gaius Caligula. He expelled many Jewish people from Rome because they were rioting.

CORNELIUS
Roman centurion in Caesarea who, together with his family, was converted to Christianity by Peter.

DEMETRIUS
Silversmith in Ephesus who started a riot against Paul. He claimed that Paul's gospel message would stop people from buying silver idols of the goddess Artemis.

ELIZABETH
Wife of Zechariah, mother of John the Baptist, and cousin of Mary, Elizabeth came from the priestly line of Aaron. Elizabeth was barren for many years until an angel announced that she would bear a son.

FELIX
Brutal and corrupt Roman governor (AD 52–60) who tried Paul in Caesarea and imprisoned him for two years. He was recalled to Rome because of his immorality.

FESTUS
Just Roman governor of Judea who replaced Felix and allowed Paul to be tried in Rome.

GABRIEL
One of the highest ranking angels. He appears four times in the Bible as a messenger from God; each appearance is connected with the coming of the Messiah.

GALLIO
Brother of the philosopher Seneca and Roman proconsul of Achaia. He refused to try Paul at a court in Corinth and had Sosthenes, Paul's enemy, publicly beaten.

HEROD AGRIPPA I
Grandson of Herod the Great. As king of Judah (AD 37–44), he persecuted the early Christians to gain favour with the influential Jews. He had Peter imprisoned and James, son of Zebedee, beheaded.

HEROD AGRIPPA II
Son of Agrippa I and king of Judah (AD 50–100). He was consulted by Festus during Paul's trial.

HEROD ANTIPAS
Son of Herod the Great, Antipas was Tetrarch of Galilee and Perea (4 BC–AD 39). He had John the Baptist arrested and beheaded on the request of his niece Salome, and later mocked Jesus before he returned him to Pilate.

HEROD ARCHELAUS
This son of Herod the Great was a violent and corrupt ruler (4 BC–AD 6). His brothers Antipas and Philip complained about his methods and he was banished to Rome.

HERODIAS
Granddaughter of Herod the Great and sister of Agrippa I. She is notable for arranging the execution of John the Baptist, who had proclaimed that her second marriage was immoral.

HEROD PHILIP
Son of Herod the Great and ruler of the northern part of his father's kingdom (4 BC–AD 34).

HEROD THE GREAT
King of Judah (37–4 BC) who ordered the massacre of all male infants in Bethlehem in an attempt to kill the Messiah he believed would rob him of his kingdom.

JAMES
1. Son of Zebedee, brother of John, and one of the twelve disciples. He was one of Jesus' closest companions.
2. Son of Alphaeus and one of the twelve disciples.
3. "Brother" of Jesus. He led the first Christian council.

JESUS
Son of God incarnate and the Messiah. His mother was the Virgin Mary. Jesus was born in Bethlehem in Judea and spent most of his life in Galilee. He died to take away the sins of the world.

JOHN THE BAPTIST

JOHN MARK (see MARK)

JOHN THE APOSTLE
Son of Zebedee, brother of James, and one of the twelve disciples. He was a close friend of Jesus and wrote the Gospel of John, the three epistles of John, and probably Revelation. He was present at the transfiguration and in the Garden of Gethsemane.

JOHN THE BAPTIST
Son of Zechariah and Elizabeth and the prophet who was sent by God to prepare the Israelites for the coming of the Messiah. Notable for his austere way of life, John urged the people to repent of their sins. He was beheaded by Herod Antipas.

JOSEPH
Carpenter husband of Mary, Jesus' mother. Joseph was told by an angel about the virgin birth.

LAZARUS

JOSEPH (BARSABBAS)
This disciple of Jesus was considered as a replacement for Judas Iscariot, but Matthias was chosen instead.

JOSEPH OF ARIMATHEA
Wealthy follower of Jesus and member of the Sanhedrin. He paid for the burial of Jesus.

JUDAS, SON OF JAMES
Son of James and one of the twelve disciples. He was probably also known as Thaddaeus.

JUDAS ISCARIOT
Son of Simon Iscariot and one of the twelve disciples. He was the treasurer of the twelve and betrayed Jesus for thirty pieces of silver. He later hanged himself.

LAZARUS
Brother of Martha and Mary from Bethany near Jerusalem. He died and was resurrected by Jesus.

PAUL

LUKE
Physician and author of Acts and the Gospel of Luke. Together with Mark, he accompanied Paul on his missionary journeys.

LYDIA
Business-woman who sold purple cloth. She was a Gentile who had been attracted to the Jewish way of life and was baptized by Paul in Philippi. She became Paul's first European convert.

MARK (JOHN)
Son of Mary of Jerusalem, he is the probable author of the Gospel of Mark. He accompanied Paul and Barnabas on the first missionary journey.

MARTHA
Elder sister of Mary and Lazarus (of Bethany) and friend of Jesus. She was loved by Jesus and acknowledged him as the Son of God.

MARY
Virgin mother of Jesus and wife of Joseph the carpenter. She was told that she would give birth to the Messiah, and she accepted her role as God's servant. She became a disciple of Jesus, and Luke records that she received the Holy Spirit at Pentecost.

MARY MAGDALENE
Disciple of Jesus, who served him throughout his ministry and was healed of demon possession. She was present at Jesus' death, at the empty tomb, and when Jesus' resurrection was announced. Jesus appeared to her first and told her of his coming ascension into heaven.

MARY OF BETHANY
Sister of Martha and Lazarus and friend of Jesus. She anointed Jesus' feet with perfume before his death.

MATTHEW
Also known as "Levi", Matthew was a tax collector from Capernaum and one of the twelve disciples. He wrote the Gospel of Matthew.

NICODEMUS
A Pharisee and member of the Sanhedrin who questioned Jesus' authority but later defended him. He helped prepare Jesus' body for burial.

PAUL
Pharisee, Roman citizen, and persecutor of the early Church, who converted to Christianity on the road to Damascus. He became the Church's first missionary and spread the Gospel throughout Asia Minor and Europe. He is believed to be the author of thirteen epistles written to the early Christian communities he established.

PETER
Brother of Andrew and Galilean fisherman, he was one of the twelve disciples. Although he was Jesus' chosen leader, he denied knowing him three times during Jesus' trial in Jerusalem. He later became head of the early Church. Tradition holds that he was crucified upside down during Nero's reign.

PHILIP
One of the twelve disciples. He came from the town of Bethsaida.

PONTIUS PILATE
Procurator (financial and military administrator) of Judea who condemned Jesus to death despite knowing that he was innocent.

PRISCILLA
Wealthy wife of Aquila and prominent member of the early Church, she helped Paul to establish the Church in Corinth and Ephesus.

PUBLIUS
Chief official on the island of Malta when Paul and his companions were shipwrecked. He offered hospitality to Paul and his companions.

PETER

SALOME
1. Daughter of Herodias who demanded the head of John the Baptist as a reward for pleasing her uncle Herod Antipas.
2. Disciple of Jesus from Galilee who was present at the crucifixion. Possibly the wife of Zebedee and the mother of James and John.

SAPPHIRA
Wife of Ananias who was struck dead after she tried to deceive the members of the early Church. Her husband suffered the same fate.

SAUL (see PAUL)
Hebrew name for Paul the apostle.

SILAS
Early Christian leader and Roman citizen who was chosen to accompany Paul on his second missionary journey. He also travelled with Paul throughout Asia Minor, Macedonia, and Achaia.

SIMEON
Also known as Niger, he was an early Christian who served the Church in Antioch before Paul started his first missionary journey. Simeon had prophetic powers.

SIMON MAGUS
Sorcerer in Samaria who tried to buy the power of the Holy Spirit from Peter and John.

SIMON OF CYRENE
Man from Cyrene who was made to carry Jesus' cross.

SIMON PETER (see PETER)
Peter the apostle's original name.

SIMON THE ZEALOT
One of the twelve disciples who was possibly a member of the fanatical political sect of the "Zealots".

STEPHEN
Hellenic Jew who became a deacon in the early Church. He was stoned to death by some Jews and became the first Christian martyr.

TABITHA
Early Christian who was known for her generosity. She died and was resurrected by Peter.

THOMAS
One of the twelve apostles, he refused to believe that Jesus had risen from the dead until he saw the wounds in his wrists and side.

TIBERIUS CAESAR
Roman emperor (AD 14–37) who reigned during Jesus' ministry.

TIMOTHY
Young companion of Paul during the missionary journeys who received two letters from Paul.

TITUS
Greek Christian who became a companion of Paul. He was sent to teach in Corinth and Crete.

ZACCHAEUS
Dishonest tax collector in Jericho who became Jesus' disciple.

ZECHARIAH
Priest and father of John the Baptist who doubted the angel's prophecy that he would have a son. As a result of his disbelief, he was struck dumb.

ZECHARIAH AND ELIZABETH

INDEX

ACKNOWLEDGEMENTS

Dorling Kindersley would like to thank the following people.
For additional editorial assistance: Hazel Egerton, Shirin Patel,
Selina Wood, Leo Vita-Finzi, Alastair Dougall
For additional design assistance: Martin Wilson, Janet Allis,
Sarah Crouch, Jacqui Burton, Clair Watson, Karen Nettelfield
Research assistance: Natasha Billing, Robert Graham

Map artworks: Sallie Alane Reason

Additional illustrations: Rodney Shackell

Index: Joanna Lane

DK Photography: Geoff Brightling, Peter Chadwick,
Andy Crawford, Philip Dowell, Nick Goodall, Steve Gorton,
Christi Graham, Frank Greenaway, Peter Hayman, Alan Hills,
Colin Keates, Dave King, David Murray, Nick Nicholls,
Gary Ombler, Tim Ridley, Karl Shone, Alan Williams

The publishers would also like to thank the following for their
permission to reproduce their photographs:

AKG Photos 11br, 98crb, 120bl, 142cl, 155cr, 176clb, 206bc,
209br, 288cla, 302clb, 314tr, 315tr, 338br, 345cra, 349br, 360br,
363tr; Eric Lessing 64tr, 64c, 104bl, 118cl, 127cra, 136bl, 154tr,
160bl, 166cl, 175br, 178bl, 183cr, 186cla, 204–205, 205c, 207tr,
211tl, 261cra, 262tr, 269br, 270tl, 285tr, 314cla, 351br, 355br, 360c,
361tc; Escorial Madrid 167br; **Ancient Art & Architecture
Collection** 17cl, 22br, 36tl, 84cra, bc, br, 90bl, 91cra, 98tr, 99cr,
107tr, 120cr, 122cl, 126cb, 137br, 148cla, 153br, 155bl, 163br, 174bl,
188cl, cr, 216tl, 231br, 232crb, 234cla, bl, 247br, 254bl, 256bl,
323br, 327tc, 342cl, 353tr, crb, 367cra; Chris Hellier 360cl; **Aquila**/
Mike Lane 78clb; **Artothek** 196clb; **ASAP** 252tl; Aliza Auerbach
310tl; Lev Borodulin 230cla; Mike Ganor 262cr; Douglas Guthrie
274bl; **Ashmolean Museum** 62cla; **Bijbels Museum, Amsterdam**
116bl; **The Bridgeman Art Library** 8tr, 9cb, 16br, 20cl, 210clb,
215cr, 218cla, 223br, 249cra, 268bl, 275br; Atkinson Art Gallery,
Southport 65tc; Birmingham City Museum & Art Gallery 211tr;
Brancacci Chapel, Santa Maria del Carmine, Florence 315ca; British
Library 196tr, 214bl, 224bl, 361cl; British Museum 150bl; Bonhams,
London 207cl; Courtauld Institute 10cl; Hotel Dieu, Beaune 361cra;
Palazzo Ducale, Mantua 314br; Giraudon 106tl, 197tr; Musée des
Beaux-Arts, Nantes 11ca; Musée Conde, Chantilly 197br, 284tr;
Louvre, Paris 83cra; Keble College, Oxford 330bl; Lambeth Palace
Library 15c; Santa Maria della Salute, Venice 89br; Santa Maria del
Popolo, Rome 326tr; National Gallery of Scotland 233br; Galleria
degli Uffizi, Florence 326cla; Museo dell'Opera del Duomo, Siena
296cl; Scrovegni (Arena) Chapel 29cra; V&A inside flap, 83br,
316bl, 327crb; Musée Departmental des Vosges, France 197tl;
Whitford & Hughes, London 61br; Winchester Cathedral,
Hampshire 196br; Wrightsman Collection, N.Y. 211clb; **The
British Library** 9cra; **The British Museum** 8cl, 9tc, 18cl, cr, br,
19cl, cr, br, 36crb, 37br, 40cl, 61cr, 64crb, 75br, 76cl, 95cra, 96bl,
99bl, 140bl, 143cr, 187crb, 208cb, 209clb, 235cra, 343tr; **The
Brooklyn Museum** 263br; **Cairo Museum** 66cl; **J Allan Cash**

43cra, 315c, 359cra; **Jean Loup-Charmet** 99tc, 208tr; **Lester
Cheeseman** 41br, 240bl, 292; **The Chester Beatty Library,
Dublin** 339cl; **The Christian Mission** 131r, 255tr; **Peter Clayton**
335crb; **Bruce Coleman Ltd**/ Atlantide 206cr; **C M Dixon** 60clb,
102cl; **ET Archive** 16bl, 99cl, 208br, 246tl, 284bc, 287tr; **Mary
Evans Picture Library** 110tr, 208cla, 245cra, 257br, 259cr;
Ffotograff/ Patricia Aithie 92clb, 143br; James Nash 327bl; **Werner
Forman Archive** 38cla; Metropolitan Museum of Art 272cl;
National Library, Athens 338tl; **Giraudon** 184clb, 185br; Louvre,
Paris 153tr, 172bl, 188bl, 345br; **Sonia Halliday Photographs**
94cla, 109crb, 113cr, 139cr, 154c, 182cla, 197cl, 213cr, 221crb,
222bl, 228cl, 232ca, 235br, 237crb, 260cl, 265br, 280clb, 287br,
288bl, 290cl, 291br, 295br, 312cl, 320cl, bl, 324bl, 335cra, 339bl,
340bl, 341br, 352clb, 361br, 365br; Laura Lushington 10bc, 206tr,
262tl, 326clb, 341tr, 350bl, 361bl; Jane Taylor 42bl, 68clb, 152cl,
311tr; James Wellard 48bl; **Robert Harding Picture Library** 20tr,
35cr, 49tr, 53tr, 54cl, 59cra, 103crb, 165br, 167tr; Philip Craven
87tr; Robert Francis 132cla; Photri 75cra; **David Harris, Jerusalem**
21cl; **Michael Holford** front cover, 11bl, 18tr, 36tr, 38bl, 64cl,
171tr, 195cra, 271tr, 327cl, 339cra; **The Hulton Getty Collection**
19tl, 300bl; **The Hutchison Picture Library** 35br, 241cr, 313tr;
Images Colour Library/ Charles Walker Collection 314bl; **Israel
Museum, Jerusalem** 115cr, 181crb, D Harris 120ca, 243crb; (The
Shrine of the Book, D Samuel and Jeane H Gottesman Centre
for Biblical Manuscripts) 8cl; **Jewish Museum** 117cr; **Life-File**/
David Heath 108cl; **Museum of London** 309br; **Magnum
Photos**/ Mayer 207br, 210cla, 263cra; **Manchester Museum** 70cla,
cra; **The Mansell Collection** 23r, 157br, 210tr, 315tl; **The
National Maritime Museum** 224tl, 338bl; **OSF**/ Robert Dowling
301br; **Panos Pictures**/ Sean Sprague 286bl; **Pictures Colour
Library** 271br; **Planet Earth Pictures**/ Alain Dragesco 158bl; **Zev
Radovan** 10cra, 16tl, 17tr, bl, br, 26tl, 27br, 37cla, 46clb, 47br,
51cra, 56cla, cra, 58bl, 63cra, br, 65cra, 66bl, 77tr, 84bl, 93br, 94bl,
97cr, 98cla, 99br, 100cl, 101cra, 105br, 110br, 115tr, 120bl, 125cr,
136cl, 145br, 146bl, 147cra, 154bl, 155ca, br, 156cla, 159br, 161tr,
163cra, 170cl, 177cr, 190tl, 191cra, 193cra, 208bl, 232bl, br, 262bl,
265cra, 263cl, bl, 264bl, 267cr, 308bl, 326crb, 327tr, 332cl, 336clb,
339tl, tr, 345cr, 350cl, 358bl; BLMJ Borowski Collection 11cr,
129cr, 151cra, 195br; **RMN**/H Lenandowski 41tr; **John Rylands
University Library** 9tl; **Peter Saunders Photography** 56bl; **Scala**
28bl, 69tr, 122bl, 130cl, 144bl, 328bl; **Tony Stone**/ Sarah J.
Frankling 21–22b; Richard Kaylin 21tr; Hugh Sitton 14–15; **Still
Pictures**/Christian Weiss 169cra; **Topham Picture Source** 357tr;
Viewfinder 306cl; **Victoria & Albert Museum, London** 214tl;
Lin White 209tl; **World Pictures** 360bl; **Zefa** 19tr, 25r, 33br,
164bl, 210br, 211br, 217br, 245crb, 317crb, 318clb, 319cra;
K.Goebel 180cla; Leidmann 20bl; Mueller 263tc; H Winter 141cra

c=centre, l=left, r=right, t=top, b=bottom, a=above

Every effort has been made to trace the copyright holders and we
apologize in advance for any unintentional omissions. We would be
pleased to insert the appropriate acknowledgement in any
subsequent edition of this publication.